Pattern of the past

Studies in honour of David Clarke

Pattern of the past

Studies in honour of
David Clarke

EDITED BY

IAN HODDER
Assistant Lecturer in Archaeology, University of Cambridge

GLYNN ISAAC
Professor of Anthropology, University of California at Berkeley

NORMAN HAMMOND
Professor of Archaeology, Rutgers University

CAMBRIDGE UNIVERSITY PRESS

CAMBRIDGE

LONDON   NEW YORK   NEW ROCHELLE

MELBOURNE   SYDNEY

Published by the Press Syndicate of the University of Cambridge
The Pitt Building, Trumpington Street, Cambridge CB2 1RP
32 East 57th Street, New York, NY 10022, USA
296 Beaconsfield Parade, Middle Park, Melbourne 3206, Australia

First published 1981

Printed in Great Britain
at the University Press, Cambridge

British Library Cataloguing in Publication Data

Pattern of the past.
1. Archaeology – Methodology – Addresses, essays,
lectures
I. Clarke, David Leonard
II. Hodder, Ian   III. Isaac, Glynn Llywelyn
IV. Hammond, Norman
930'.1'018   CC75   79-41379

ISBN 0 521 22763 1

Contents

Editors and contributors

ROBERT CHAPMAN   Department of Archaeology, Reading University

GEORGE DALTON   Department of Economics, Northwestern University, Illinois

ANN ELLISON   Wessex Archaeological Committee, Salisbury

ROLAND FLETCHER   Department of Anthropology, University of Sydney

ROBERT FOLEY   Department of Anthropology, Durham University

LES GROUBE   Department of Anthropology and Sociology, University of Papua–New Guinea

PAUL HALSTEAD   King's College, Cambridge

NORMAN HAMMOND   Department of Classics, Rutgers University

FRED HAMOND   Clare College, Cambridge

IAN HODDER   Department of Archaeology, University of Cambridge

GLYNN ISAAC   Department of Anthropology, University of California at Berkeley

WILLIAM LONGACRE   Department of Anthropology, University of Arizona

JOHN PARKINGTON   Department of Archaeology, University of Cape Town

ANDREW SHERRATT   Ashmolean Museum, Oxford

CHRISTOPHER TILLEY   Peterhouse, Cambridge

PAUL WILKINSON   Naskapi Band Council, Montreal

Preface

David Clarke was an archaeologist with extraordinary abilities. In particular he was a leader in the movement to establish the importance of explicit theory and logic in archaeological method. The originality and incisiveness of his own thinking on this matter inspired many to think more effectively in their own work. This was accomplished in part through his writings and also through the vigour of his interaction with colleagues and students. His untimely death left unfinished David Clarke's own potential contribution in this sphere. Those who recognised the impetus to thought given them by David determined to show some of the avenues of archaeological inquiry that David had inspired. This book is the outcome of that determination.

A plan for the tribute volume evolved in collective discussions and was submitted to Cambridge University Press, with Stella Clarke kindly agreeing to help. Contributors decided in advance to prepare essays that followed David Clarke's lead in searching for ways of discovering and interpreting pattern in the archaeological record of past human life. It is this theme that gives the book its title. The patterns explored include spatial, economic and social patterns. The editors and contributors trust that this collection is of value as a contribution to the evolution of archaeological logic. Because David Clarke provided major initiating stimuli to all of the contributors we also trust that the book serves as a fitting follow up on his leadership.

The editors and authors offer this volume in memory of and in tribute to a man we held in great respect and affection.

Norman Hammond
Ian Hodder
Glynn Isaac

Introduction

Towards a mature archaeology

IAN HODDER

David Clarke was

the acknowledged leader in this country of the 'new wave' of archaeological thinking. Possessed of a powerful intellect and a tirelessly inquiring mind, his short life was devoted to the task of trying to lighten our prehistoric darkness and to provide us with sharper tools. Opinion may still be divided over many aspects of his thinking, but there is no denying the enormous influence, which, in the course of a few short years, it has exerted on prehistorians, especially younger ones, in all parts of the world. (Evans 1977, p. 2)

Part of the reason for David Clarke's impact on archaeology was his broad encompassing vision of a mature and independent discipline. 'Archaeology, is archaeology, is archaeology...Archaeology is a discipline in its own right, concerned with archaeological data which it clusters in archaeological entities displaying certain archaeological processes and studied in terms of archaeological aims, concepts and procedures' (1968, p. 13). Such a statement opens the debate as to whether mature contributions can best be made by a separate discipline or by one fully integrated into the social sciences. This debate will be considered below. But, whatever the means considered appropriate for obtaining maturity, David Clarke's achievement was to outline, with greater clarity than anyone else, the full depth and potential of archaeology in the 1960s and 1970s. This was not to fossilise archaeology, but to start it on its adult course – the 'new wave'.

The archaeology that David Clarke outlined in *Analytical Archaeology* and in several articles (1972; 1973; 1977) was multistranded. It consisted of (1) types of theory used to study (2) types of system, working within (3) different paradigms. The vision of a unified discipline must depend on (1) and (2) since it is clear that the very different paradigms employed by archaeologists can lead to utter fragmentation. It is apparent from the papers in this volume that archaeologists still work with very different interests and assumptions. But the papers in the volume do illustrate the common use of the types of theory and types of system discussed by David Clarke and summarised in Fig. o.1. Each contribution concerns not one theory or subsystem, but examines the links and relationships between them. The three-dimensional matrix in Fig. o.1 provides the basis for the links generated in the articles in the book and

0.1. The interrelationships of the subsystems, subtheories and paradigms outlined by David Clarke.

for an understanding of the multivariate, multistranded relationships that are set up between the different types and levels of archaeological work. For example, a particular subsystem such as religion can be examined in relation to other subsystems using different levels of theory and within different paradigms (see Chapman, ch. 14 below).

1. TYPES OF ARCHAEOLOGICAL THEORY

In developing a 'comprehensive archaeological general theory' (1973, p. 16), the main operational subtheories are:

(i) Pre-depositional and depositional theory. The relationships between human behaviour and material culture.

(ii) Post-depositional and retrieval theory. Theories of survival and recovery of the evidence: disturbance, sampling, field strategies.

(iii) Analytical theory. The detection and analysis of pattern and structure in the surviving and recovered data.

(iv) Interpretive theory. The relationships between patterns in the data and interpretations of the patterns – the use of models.

Pre-depositional theory is examined especially in part I of this book. All the articles in this section are concerned with exposing or building models of the relationships between behaviour and material culture. In its emphasis on the relationship between people and things, pre-depositional theory necessitates work within living societies. The great expansion of ethnoarchaeology (some examples of which are given in part I) and the use of modern geographical models are part of this attempt to broaden our ideas about the way in which process in and amongst people can lead to pattern in things. But the clear behavioural emphasis in archaeology over the last decade has certainly limited the development of pre-depositional theory. In chapter 4, Fletcher continues the advances made in his previous work (1977), moving beneath the study of apparent and functionally related surface behaviours to the analysis of underlying structures and their transformations in material culture patterning.

Studies of modern societies have also led to major advances in *depositional theory* (part II in this book). Work from Kenya (Gifford 1978) and Australia (Gould 1971) to modern Tucson (Rathje 1974) has emphasised the indirect and complex relationships between refuse and behaviour (Schiffer 1976). Theories being developed in this sphere concern, for example, the relationship between the use life of an artifact and its frequency in refuse (David 1972), the effects of curation (Binford 1976) and the effects of the length and intensity of site use on artifact distributions (Gould 1978; Schiffer 1976). But, as with pre-depositional theory, a major constraint on this type of work has been the functionalist, behaviourist assumptions of recent archaeology. Gifford (1977) and Yellen (1977) note that there is cultural variation in the cutting up, distributing and discard of animal carcasses. But these cultural differences are simply seen as providing further traits with which to examine cultural affinity. There has been little or no attempt to examine the underlying logic and meaning of refuse deposits, despite indications (Douglas 1966) that attitudes to refuse are deeply enmeshed in conceptual schemes.

Post-depositional theory has long been a concern of archaeologists, as Atkinson's (1957) early consideration of worm disturbance demonstrates. Yet it is only recently that archaeologists have faced up to the need to develop models of the movement of artifacts within and between archaeological deposits, and models of survival and decay. The area of study termed taphonomy (p. 157) is an important new development, while artifact movement after deposition has been examined experimentally (Siiriäinen 1977), analytically (Limbrey 1975), ethnographically (Gifford 1978) and archaeologically. In the latter case, for example, the distribution of joining sherds, flakes and cores can lead to understanding of the processes involved in artifact disturbances (Hivernel 1978). The building of models about such processes (e.g. Siiriäinen 1977) must take into account the complex and specific factors affecting each archaeological deposit. Detailed and exhaustive work is necessary in particular contexts, as Foley (ch. 6) and Isaac (ch. 5) demonstrate for savanna areas in East Africa. Perhaps experimental work on post-depositional factors will become a common adjunct to archaeological excavation at each site – building specific theories at the micro scale.

As the full development of post-depositional theory began late, so *retrieval theory* has only recently been widely accepted as a central concern in archaeology. Problem-solving research strategies and rigorous sampling procedures are now fairly commonplace, in America if not in Britain. Zubrow and Harbaugh (1978) make a distinction between prospecting strategies – the initial search for sites – and sampling strategies – the systematic recovery of samples from 'populations' of material. Since archaeological populations are in fact only biassed samples, the significance of random sampling in archaeology will always be restricted (Cherry *et al.* 1978; Mueller 1975). Although rigorous sampling may reduce some of the archaeological bias (Foley, ch. 6), much of the data with which we have to work was collected very unsystematically. Chapman (ch. 14) emphasises the need to develop theories concerning the handling of such biassed and fragmentary information. Yet it remains difficult to see how biassed retrieval procedures can be modelled. Hamond (ch. 8) discusses both post-depositional factors (such as the sedimentary cover of sites) and retrieval bias (such as the localised activities and interests of museum and amateur archaeologists and the finding of early Neolithic sites in Germany largely as a by-product of commercial gravel extraction). While the process of settlement spread is modelled by Hamond, he does not model post-depositional and retrieval effects, and quite understandably. Most recovery biasses will have to be examined heuristically, although in rare cases the factors affecting retrieval may be considered so many and complex that stochastic modelling within stated constraints is realistic. There is certainly great potential for the development of theories concerning the robustness of pattern in the face of stochastic distortion and retrieval.

Pattern analysis, as part of *analytical theory* (parts II to IV in this book), has received a major boost in archaeology as a result of the injection of outside techniques. This is especially the case in taxonomy (Doran and Hodson 1975), and in the study of spatial structure (Hodder and Orton 1976; Smith 1976) and social organisation (e.g. Tainter 1977). However, much of this work has a heavy inductive, 'pattern playing', emphasis. The limitations of this approach, outlined by Hamond in chapter 8, include the lack of concern with the multiple processes which could have produced any single pattern. Analytical theory should be more concerned with process, and in this, computer simulation is a powerful tool. Experimentation with a range of competing hypotheses concerning, in Hamond's case, settlement spread becomes feasible. While simulation is an invaluable analytical tool, perhaps the major development that is needed in archaeological pattern analysis concerns methods for the recognition of pattern at different levels. For the moment, there has been little attempt to study organisational principles lying beneath surface patterns. Design analysis has begun to emphasise compositional principles such as symmetry (Washburn 1978), while the rules of generation of Palaeolithic art have been studied by Marshak (1977) and Conkey (1977) and of spatial structure by Hillier *et al.* (1976) and Fletcher (1977). Yet the full development of techniques for the identification of principles underlying a wide range of different types of archaeological material – from burial patterns to artifact and refuse distributions – remains a major challenge.

Most models for the *interpretation* of past patterns are derived directly from other social sciences. But over recent years, major differences have emerged in the way that these imported ideas are used in archaeology. For the 'law and order' archaeologists (Flannery 1973) argument is by correlation. It is assumed that law-like statements can be found of the form 'if I have design clusters I have matrilocal residence'. The general aim is to identify strong statistical correlations because there can be no logically necessary deductions from archaeological evidence to human behaviour. The main approach to interpretation cannot be through laws in any strict deductive–nomological sense. Rather, a more flexible approach, involving models and analogy and followed in practice by most archaeologists, must be allied to an emphasis on multiple working hypotheses as suggested by Stanislawski (1973) and Hamond (ch. 8) and to multivariate causality as examined by systems theorists (Flannery 1973). Any positivist approach has to contend with the criticisms of phenomenology and hermeneutics. While the debate is raging in related disciplines (Buttimer 1976; Entrekin 1976; King 1976; Relph 1970), archaeology stands by. Once again, full maturity will only be achieved by an involvement in these wider discussions concerning different interpretive procedures and epistemology.

All types of archaeological theory have made considerable advances in recent years. The different areas of the fledgling but fast-maturing science have been recognised, defined and filled out. A broad and rich body of theory is emerging. Yet, throughout the discussion presented above the major limits to growth have been where an inward-looking mentality has prevented debate of broader issues current within the social sciences. In particular, the debates concerning behaviourism, functionalism and structuralism, and concerning alternatives to the Hempelian philosophy, have often been disregarded. Similar limitations will be apparent in the discussions which follow.

2. TYPES OF SUBSYSTEM

The main emphasis of the systems theory approach is to focus attention on the networked nature of systems. The various components (subsystems) of a system are connected so that change in one leads to changes in another. 'The archaeologist must be aware of the complex connections between his subsystems input and output and that of the other interconnected subsystems networking the overall system. How else can the archaeologist hope to interpret the social, religious, economic and other kindred aspects of his material' (Clarke 1968, pp. 33–4). In practice, however, it is necessary to define social, religious, psychological, economic and material culture subsystems (*ibid.*, p. 83). There are links between the components of these subsystems, between the subsystems themselves, and with the environment system. The study of the Iron Age Glastonbury settlement (Clarke 1972) is a good example of an attempt to expose these links within one study.

The identification of different subsystems is based on the premise that different aspects of life can be separated and the links between them identified and examined. In particular, many archaeologists would accept that a distinct, *economic*, side of life could be distinguished and usefully studied in relative isolation. Despite the views of substantivists (see Dalton, ch. 1), palaeoecono-mists (Higgs 1975) seem little concerned with society and culture. A more integrated view is presented by Sherratt (ch. 10) and Halstead (ch. 11). Nevertheless, Sahlins' (1976) criticisms remain. Links are studied between subsystems, but the links and the subsystems are of the analyst's own making.

In discussions of *social* and *religious* subsystems, most archaeologists in recent decades have used various forms of ecological functionalism. This is seen clearly in the articles in this volume. For example, Chapman (ch. 14) suggests that unpredictable fluctuations in an arid climate in south-east Spain may have helped to stimulate nucleation and hierarchy in order to 'buffer' the effects of variation in the water supply. Sherratt (ch. 10) links a range of changes in the social subsystem to economic changes which themselves relate to population increase and innovation. In chapter 11, Halstead suggests that Cretan Bronze Age palaces and sanctuaries may have fulfilled an integrative role in a period of economic diversification. Hamond (ch. 8) suggests that social links are maintained between nearby Neolithic settlements in order to maximise the flow of information and exchange and provide surety in unfavourable conditions. Ellison (ch. 15) hints that widespread networks of pottery styles are related to a pastoral aspect of the economy in the Late Neolithic and Early Bronze Age in England, with arable farming in the Middle Bronze Age leading to local style clusters. In all these examples, the social and religious subsystems are explained by showing how they function in relation to the economy and environment.

Tilley, however, in the section of the book which concentrates on the social subsystem (ch. 13), examines some of the criticisms that have been made of the functionalist use of systems theory. He discusses alternative views which give greater independence and weight to social relations and which consider the conceptual constraints on socioeconomic change and variability. It is necessary to become involved in the debate in the social sciences concerning ecological functionalism.

The discussion by David Clarke (1968) of *psychological* and *material culture* subsystems adds important dimensions to the systemic approach favoured by many archaeologists. These subsystems do not appear, for example, in Renfrew's (1972, pp. 22–3) scheme since his technological and projective systems appear to have a different nature. While Renfrew stresses the limitations of a systems theory approach which does not consider individual perceptions (Tilley, ch. 13), Binford (1972) suggests that archaeologists are poorly equipped to be palaeopsychologists. For David Clarke, psychological and cultural patterns were more than mere reflections of other aspects of life. 'It would seem that cultures induce a broad psychological pattern on their generators, with considerable personal variation' (1968, p. 113). Subconscious concepts and values are seen as having an internal structure induced largely by language. The perception of an immature member of a society is organised and orientated by linguistic constructs and categories. Dislocation and disequilibrium in the relationship between the psychological sphere and the other subsystems lead to personal stress, strains and conflict. Fletcher (ch. 4) examines the way in which the limits to the densities at which people are willing to live are seen in individual stress as the frequency of interaction increases.

The very identification by David Clarke (1968, pp. 119–23) of a separate material culture subsystem in which information about the orientation of a culture's percepta was 'congealed', emphasises that mind and conceived pattern are more than mere epiphenomena of social and economic functioning and adaptation. Even if the encoded information in material culture was seen by David Clarke as being mainly survival information, the retention, in contrast to his American counterparts, of aspects of the normative view, means that the door is still open for us to consider the internal structure and logic of cultural pattern. The main challenge to systems theory in archaeology, met recently by Bennett and Chorley (1978) in geography, is to follow David Clarke in breaking out of a narrow ecological functionalism which over-emphasises equilibrium and adaptation. We need to accomodate the study of internal generative process and the structure of cultural meaning. These points will further be discussed in consideration of the morphological paradigm.

3. PARADIGMS

Tilley (ch. 13) suggests that the identification of four paradigms in archaeology (anthropology, geography, ecology and morphology) – three of which are clearly related to other sciences – argues against the idea of an independent and separate archaeology. But even if the call is for an archaeological discipline in its own right, all of David Clarke's work shows an awareness and willingness to consider the contribution that related disciplines could make. In each of the four paradigms (the term as used by David Clarke can best be seen as approaches, interests and assumptions), outside ideas and models are worked into the fabric of the emergent discipline.

The *anthropological paradigm* focusses on the relationships between patterning and variability in archaeological data and patterning and variability in the social structures behind that data. The use of ethnographic models to examine these relationships is discussed in part I of this book. The main problem posed within the paradigm is the proper use of analogy. If an aspect of societal organisation can be shown ethnographically to be related to an aspect of material culture patterning, to what extent are we justified in inferring from pattern back to social process? In a recent attempt to move 'beyond analogy', Gould (1978) suggests that the emphasis on similarities and analogies should be extended to contrasts. The archaeologist should identify ways in which his and the ethnographer's data differ because it is in the differences and 'surprises' that information on past non-material behaviour is contained. This suggestion leads to the further problem of how we explain pattern that is different from ethnographic experience. If social forms existed in the past which are now extinct, how are we to interpret them? Dalton (ch. 1) considers that extinct societies might be identifiable if they can be linked to polythetic genus-sets of societies. For example, acephalous stateless societies and tribal kingdoms form two different genus-sets. Having identified the constraints and constants associated with each set, it would be possible to look for or suggest the existence of many of the other traits associated with that set.

Dalton's societal types are built up by broad cross-cultural surveys and it is this type of broad study that is often considered of greatest value to archaeologists. For example, Sherratt (ch. 10) uses several correlations between economy and social behaviour derived from Murdock's *Ethnographic Atlas*, Chapman (ch. 14) uses Saxe's and Goldstein's ethnographic work on burial practices, and both Chapman and Ellison (ch. 15) base interpretations on the Peebles and Kus survey of characteristics of ranked societies. A distinctive aspect of this type of large-scale correlation is that the test of the analogy partly takes place outside archaeology. The larger the number of times that material and non-material behaviour traits co-occur in our present biassed set of surviving 'primitive' peoples, the more certain we feel that any particular application to archaeological data will be successful. The hypothesis is partially tested before it ever reaches the archaeological data. Since many of the hypotheses concern aspects of non-material behaviour such as patrilineal inheritance which cannot be tested independently in the archaeological record, great care is necessary in such applications.

Analogy derived from cross-cultural surveys is also limited by the tendency to relate superficial appearances of cultural patterning and behaviour. The nature and context of the links between people and things is often left unexamined. Thus, the amount of space in settlements has been shown empirically to be related to numbers of people inhabiting the settlements (e.g. Wiessner 1974). But the link itself has been assumed rather than examined. One aspect of Fletcher's contribution (ch. 4) demonstrates the 'cautionary tale' aspect of ethnoarchaeological work. He shows that correlations between spatial area and numbers of people cannot be supported by ethnographic data. But Fletcher also goes beyond the study of correlations to consider the underlying *way* in which people are related to and use space. The limiting constraint in the relationship between human densities and area concerns the spatial characteristics of communication and the finite frequency of interaction that human beings can tolerate and control.

The same emphasis on examining more closely the links between people and things is seen in the chapters by Longacre (ch. 2) and Hodder (ch. 3). Longacre's ethnographic work amongst the Kalinga resulted from dissatisfaction with an earlier model which suggested a relationship between matrilocal residence and localised design clusters. Ellison's (ch. 15) doubts about this hypothesis are further supported by ethnographic work in Zambia (ch. 3). Both the Stanislawskis (1978) and Longacre have shown how design clusters can be produced by a wide variety of factors and that design learning may cut across family and clan lines. Design distributions are not neutral referents for human activities. Rather, designs are used as expression within social strategies.

The studies in part I are concerned both with conducting broad but careful cross-cultural surveys and with examining at a smaller scale the detailed links between patterns in people and things. The links occur at different levels, at the level of material culture as expression (in the chapters by Hodder and Longacre) and at the deeper level of general and perhaps universal charac-teristics of human behaviour (as in Fletcher's article).

Part II is concerned largely with the *geographical paradigm*, which con-centrates on within-site and between-site activity patterns and the distribu-tions of features, structures and artifacts which are involved in them. David Clarke's (1977) introduction to *Spatial Archaeology* demonstrates the full richness and scope of this type of study. An important new development published since his introduction was written has been the attempt to define the syntax or grammar with which spatial patterns are built (Hillier *et al.* 1976). The possibility of identifying underlying structure in settlement patterns is, however, already present in David Clarke's (1972) analysis of the Iron Age Glastonbury settlement. Here, each of the modular units, composed of associations of a number of different house types within the settlement, is divided into a major familial section and a minor dependent sector. A similar bilateral symmetry is identified in the circle of houses in each compound. 'Perhaps the relationship between the dependent, low status half of the compound and the rich, high status half might represent a structural analogue of the relationship between the minor, female half of each unit area and the major, familial half' (1972, p. 837). The structural pattern of clusters of separate round houses with their various functions and arrangements in the Iron Age continues into the Romano-British arrangement of rooms within one rectilinear building – the latter case is a 'rectilinear transformation of the other' (p. 828). Ellison (ch. 15) identifies aspects of the same structure already emergent in the British Bronze Age.

The existence of a separate geographical paradigm in archaeology must be considered against criticisms that are being made of the very existence of geography as a definable area of study. Gregory (1978) notes the slender basis on which study of the spatial dimension is used to define a distinct discipline. Much geography, as in Thrift's (1977) work on time, is little concerned with spatial relationships, while many processes occurring over space are in fact studied as part of other disciplines (economics, transport studies, sociology, ecology). If it were not for the institutional emphasis in university organisation, geography would disappear within a wider social science. Similarly, in archaeology, while special statistics are needed to examine two-dimensional patterns, and while many social and economic models have an important distance component, it is not at all clear that we should separate geographical archaeology from other archaeological approaches. To do so would be to move against the trends visible in geography itself.

The *ecological paradigm*, represented by Parkington but also by Sherratt, Halstead and Wilkinson in part III in this book, is concerned with the adaptation of human systems within an environmental and ecological context. This has perhaps been one of the richest areas of recent research and development in archaeology. The criticisms which have been made of the approach concern, for example, the extent to which bone typology is any better or more interesting than pot typology, and the degree to which ecology is a sufficient explanation of human behaviour. The narrow emphasis on 'the economy for its own sake' is certainly avoided by the integrated accounts and studies of the chapters in part III. The ecological view tends to emphasise external causes of sociocultural change. This is one way in which this area of study may be considered to provide insufficient explanation. Tilley (ch. 13) follows structural-Marxists in suggesting that the environment constrains but does not determine. A full explanation must examine internal social processes (part IV). The economy is embedded in society so that the workings of the economy cannot be studied as a separate and independent sphere.

The usual rejoinder to such criticisms is that archaeologists study long-term change. Over the long term the social and conceptual are seen as necessarily fitting into and allowing whatever the ecological relationships demand. European prehistory abounds with 50 to 500 year sociocultural changes and there is considerable spatial variation in cultural form. While many of the temporal phases can be shown to have had an accumulative effect on the environment, very little of the cultural variation can be related closely to climatic alteration. Environmental change due to over-use by man is an effect of internal social process, not a cause. A depleted environment constrains social change, but it does not determine it. Some regional cultures, such as the early *Linearbandkeramik*, do seem to be adaptively related to particular environments, but, as Hamond shows (ch. 8), this relationship is often very complex. It is difficult to relate most of the groupings in later prehistory to distinct ecological zones. As with the geographical paradigm, perhaps more would now be gained by integration of the ecological approach into the study of social relations.

An apparently distinctive archaeological paradigm is the *morphological*. This involves the definition of regularities in the 'structural morphology of archaeological entities' and the exposition of 'the grammar of their developmental transformations' (Clarke 1972, p. 44; some aspects of taxonomic procedures are discussed in ch. 3 below). At several points in this introduction it has been suggested that a mature archaeology means an archaeology involved in, and contributing to, wider debate in the social sciences. One of the main restrictions on such debate is the maintenance of an ecological functionalist stance. But in David Clarke's definition of the morphological paradigm there are intimations of a debate with structuralism which might develop in the future. There is an emphasis (1972, pp. 44–5) on structural grammar and, as already noted, attempts were made to define underlying meaning in the Glastonbury study. In 1968 (p. 649) a differentiation was made between designata (the roles an artifact was intended for), percepta (the perceptions of an artifact) and concepta (the abstract idea of an object). Syntactics are then the relations between artifacts and attributes at every level of their organisation (designata, percepta, concepta), pragmatics are the relations between artifacts and their users and observers (percepta, concepta), and semantics the relations between artifacts and their roles in the physical world (designata). These three 'grammars', however, involve the typological relationships between traits, types and functions. They are limited, in David Clarke's sense, to the nature and relationships of different scales of entities. There is little concern with formal logic, structural meaning and levels of meaning. The 'calculus' of the manipulation and transformation of symbolic representations (1968, p. 651) seems, in practice, to involve similarities in the nature and classification of entities at the different scales of, for example, attribute, type, assemblage and culture. Yet it would be reasonable to suggest that David Clarke's view point opened the way into a wider and rather different arena, and so into a fuller and more productive debate within the social sciences.

There has been considerable work along all the dimensions of Fig. 0.1. This work, although stimulated by a concern with the special nature of archaeological data, has freely and fully incorporated ideas and models from other disciplines. A mature archaeology must be fully integrated into the social sciences. Indeed, the only areas where archaeology remains immature are exactly where it has stubbornly refused to keep in line with related disciplines. The emphases on positivism and functionalism are the main constraints preventing dialogue. David Clarke encouraged a spirit of movement and inquiry. His example pushes us to look outwards and forward, not inwards and back.

REFERENCES

Atkinson, R. J. (1957). 'Worms and weathering', *Antiquity* 31: 219–33
Bennett, R. J. and Chorley, R. J. (1978). *Environmental Systems: philosophy, analysis and control*, Methuen
Binford, L. (1972). *An Archaeological Perspective*, Academic Press
    (1976). 'Forty-seven trips' in E. S. Hall (ed.) *Contributions to Anthropology: the interior peoples of northern Alaska*, Ottawa National Museum of Man
Buttimer, A. (1976). 'Grasping the dynamism of lifeworld', *Annals of the Association of American Geographers* 66: 615–37
Cherry, J. F., Gamble, C. and Shennan, S. (1978). *Sampling in Contemporary British Archaeology* (British Archaeological Reports, British Series 50)
Clarke, D. L. (1968). *Analytical Archaeology*, Methuen

(ed.) (1972). *Models in Archaeology*, Methuen

(1973). 'Archaeology: the loss of innocence', *Antiquity* 47: 6–18

(ed.) (1977). *Spatial Archaeology*, Academic Press

Conkey, M. (1977). 'Context, structure and efficacy in Palaeolithic art and design', paper presented at the Burg Wartenstein Symposium, No. 74

David, N. (1972). 'On the life span of pottery, type frequencies, and archaeological inference', *American Antiquity* 37: 141–2

Doran, J. and Hodson, F. (1975). *Mathematics and Computers in Archaeology*, Edinburgh University Press

Douglas, M. (1966). *Purity and Danger*, Routledge and Kegan Paul

Entrekin, J. N. (1976). 'Contemporary humanism in geography', *Annals of the Association of American Geographers* 66: 615–37

Evans, J. (1977). 'Prehistory in the seventies, at home and abroad. Presidential address', *Proceedings of the Prehistoric Society* 43: 1–12

Flannery, K. V. (1973). 'Archaeology with a capital "S"' in C. Redman (ed.) *Research and Theory in Current Archaeology*, John Wiley

Fletcher, R. (1977). 'Settlement studies (micro and semi-micro)' in D. L. Clarke (ed.) *Spatial Archaeology*, Academic Press

Gifford, D. P. (1977). 'Observations of modern human settlements as an aid to archaeological interpretation', Ph.D. thesis, University of California, Berkeley

(1978). 'Ethnoarchaeological observations of natural processes affecting cultural materials' in R. A. Gould (ed.) *Explorations in Ethnoarchaeology*, University of New Mexico Press

Gould, R. A. (1971). 'The archaeologist as ethnographer: a case study from the Western Desert of Australia', *World Archaeology* 3: 143–77

(ed.) (1978). *Explorations in Ethnoarchaeology*, University of New Mexico Press

Gregory, D. (1978). *Ideology, Science and Human Geography*, Hutchinson

Higgs, E. S. (1975). *Palaeoeconomy*, Cambridge University Press

Hillier, B., Leaman, A., Stansall, P. and Bedford, M. (1976). 'Space syntax', *Environment and Planning B* 3: 147–85

Hivernel, F. (1978). 'An ethnoarchaeological study of environmental use in the Kenya Highlands', Ph.D. thesis, London University

Hodder, I. and Orton, C. (1976). *Spatial Analysis in Archaeology*, Cambridge University Press

King, L. J. (1976). 'Alternatives to a positive economic geography', *Annals of the Association of American Geographers* 66: 293–308

Limbrey, S. (1975). *Soil Science and Archaeology*, Academic Press

Marshak, A. (1977). 'The meander as a system: the analysis and recognition of iconographic units in Upper Palaeolithic compositions' in P. J. Ucko (ed.) *Form in Indigenous Art*, Duckworth

Mueller, J. W. (ed.) (1975). *Sampling in Archaeology*, University of Arizona Press

Rathje, W. L. (1974). 'The Garbage Project: a new way of looking at the problems of archaeology', *Archaeology* 27: 236–41

Relph, E. C. (1970). 'An inquiry into the relations between phenomenology and geography', *Canadian Geographer* 14: 193–201

Renfrew, C. (1972). *The Emergence of Civilisation*, Methuen

Sahlins, M. (1976). *Culture and Practical Reason*, University of Chicago Press

Schiffer, M. B. (1976). *Behavioural Archaeology*, Academic Press

Siiriäinen, A. (1977). 'Pieces in vertical movement – a model for rockshelter archaeology', *Proceedings of the Prehistoric Society* 43: 349–53

Smith, C. (ed.) (1976). *Regional Analysis*, Academic Press

Stanislawski, M. B. (1973). 'Review of *Archaeology as Anthropology : a case study*, by W. A. Longacre', *American Antiquity* 38: 117–22

Stanislawski, M. B. and B. B. (1978). 'Hopi and Hopi-Tewa ceramic tradition networks' in I. Hodder (ed.) *Spatial Organisation of Culture*, Duckworth

Tainter, J. A. (1977). 'Modelling change in prehistoric social systems' in L. Binford (ed.) *For Theory Building in Archaeology*, Academic Press

Thrift, N. (1977). 'Time and theory in human geography. Part 1', *Progress in Human Geography* 1: 65–101

Washburn, D. K. (1978). 'A symmetry classification of Pueblo ceramic designs' in P. Grebinger (ed.) *Discovering Past Behaviour*, Academic Press

Wiessner, P. (1974). 'A functional estimator of population from floor area', *American Antiquity* 39: 343–9

Yellen, J. E. (1977). *Archaeological Approaches to the Present*, Academic Press

Zubrow, E. B. W. and Harbaugh, J. W. (1978). 'Archaeological prospecting: Kriging and simulation' in I. Hodder (ed.) *Simulation Studies in Archaeology*. Cambridge University Press

PART I

Ethnographic models:
pre-depositional theory

I

Anthropological models in archaeological perspective

GEORGE DALTON

I was very fortunate to meet David Clarke and to talk to him a dozen times in the academic year 1973–4, when I was a visiting lecturer at the Department of Social Anthropology at Cambridge. I gave a paper, 'Aboriginal economies in stateless societies' (Dalton 1977a), to his seminar which touched on matters of interest to archaeologists. The seminar and the dozen informal chats were a delightful mixture of hilarity and serious talk.

The serious talk was very good indeed. After I spoke to his seminar, David put the following questions and points to me: How can I be sure that ethnographic analogues are not misleading to archaeologists? Why should the exchange transactions and networks I described for segmentary lineages in Highland New Guinea and the Northwest Coast of America also hold true for the much earlier economies studied by archaeologists? Archaeologists, after all, recover traces of extinct societies which may have employed exchange practices which now also are extinct and therefore possibly very different from the kinds of exchange practices social anthropologists know about from historical times. If, indeed, such were the case, then anthropological parallels would definitely mislead archaeological interpretation. (I mention in passing that the exact meaning of 'extinct societies' is very important here and will be brought up later in this paper.)

In his essay 'A provisional model of an Iron-Age society and its settlement system' David Clarke (1972b) had disparaging things to say about ethnographic parallels (p. 801) as well as approving statements (p. 827), which is in keeping with his general view that ethnographic models have the same potential for archaeologists as other sorts of models. All can be used and abused:

> we have stumbled into the morass of debate about the proper and improper use of historical and ethnographic 'parallels' in archaeological interpretation...it suddenly becomes clear that this ancient battleground is merely a particular setting of the universal debate about the proper and improper use of models in general...the dangers of historic-ethnographic analogues are simply those shared by all examples of model abuse, misuse and profanation...   (Clarke 1972a, p. 40)

(See also Clarke 1968, p. 33, ch. 9; 1970, p. 29)

But what then constitutes the proper use of ethnographic analogues? And if archaeologists are to use anthropological evidence and models, what exactly are the persuasive reasons for doing so? It seems we now have two problems: why may archaeologists use ethnographic parallels, and, if they may, how should they properly do so? I think that if the first can be answered satisfactorily, then the answer to the second follows.

I have had these problems in mind ever since we talked in 1974 and will explain how what seems to me a fairly persuasive case can be made in favour of archaeologists employing ethnographic analogues, what David Clarke described on p. 6 of *Models in Archaeology* (1972) as the second of the four paradigms of the New Archaeology: 'Anthropological paradigm – the study and identification of patterning and variability in archaeological data and its relationship to patterning and variability in the social structures with which it once formed an integral system; intimately linked with ethnographical control experiments...' My concern here is entirely with socioeconomic institutions, evidence, and models, those to be drawn from the literatures of economic anthropology and early economic history.

Visualise the problem of ethnographic parallels as a jigsaw puzzle, the solution to which requires fitting together pieces which are shaped differently. I first want to lay out the differently shaped pieces and then fit them together to see what picture emerges. The image of a jigsaw puzzle is quite appropriate for our problem because the pieces of evidence I want to assemble are of very different sorts. (Indeed, if an outsider like myself may be permitted to say so, archaeologists appear to be severely handicapped compared to their brethren in economics, anthropology, history, and sociology, doomed to try to reconstruct the jigsaw puzzles of prehistoric societies with less than one per cent of the pieces to work with, and very few of those present contiguous pieces.)

The most important section of the puzzle is the answer to the question, why did differently located clusters of societies studied by anthropologists and historians, clusters *not* in touch with one another, employ nearly identical socioeconomic institutions? I want to consider two cases, the social economies of stateless clan segments and those of early kingdoms. First, why did the lineages that comprised clan segments in Highland New Guinea before European incursion employ ceremonial exchange (*moka*) and primitive valuables (pearl shells) just as did the potlatching lineages that comprised clan segments on the Northwest Coast of America at the other side of the Pacific Ocean, e.g. the Kwakiutl (Strathern 1971; Rosman and Rubel 1971)?

To give a clear answer I must use several benign tricks, the first of which is to point out the identical constraints on their modes of material provisioning that follow from the clan segments not having the institutions and technology that provision modern industrial capitalist nations such as Britain, Japan and the U.S.A.: machine technology and applied science, national labour, resource and product market integration (part of which is the use of modern money),

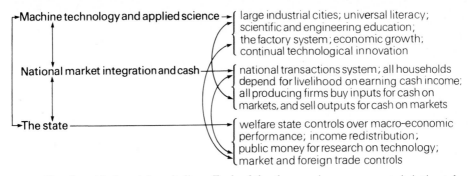

→Machine technology and applied science → large industrial cities; universal literacy; scientific and engineering education; the factory system; economic growth; continual technological innovation

National market integration and cash→ national transactions system; all households depend for livelihood on earning cash income; all producing firms buy inputs for cash on markets, and sell outputs for cash on markets

→The state— welfare state controls over macro-economic performance; income redistribution; public money for research on technology; market and foreign trade controls

1.1. Developed industrial capitalism. Each of the three major components is intimately linked to the other two and to the bracketed institutions, practices, and consequences directly associated with each, in mutually dependent ('feedback') fashion. See Myrdal (1957, chs. 1–3; Dalton 1974, ch. 1).

and the state. It is the absence of these which makes for close family resemblance in the institutions they do employ. More accurately, we shall see that there are several reasons why the clan segments employed nearly identical socioeconomic institutions (such as ceremonial exchange), one reason being that they were all similarly constrained in their modes of material provisioning.

It is also necessary to specify what all economies of time and place have in common; what is shared by prehistoric economies, those of the stateless clan segments in the anthropological record which I shall shortly return to, and our own radically different industrial capitalist and communist national economies of today. They all consist of human beings living in groups we loosely call communities or societies of some sort. Whether we consider a band of Stone Age hunters or the Soviet Union today, we know that we are considering persons who must be continually provisioned to survive physically (food), and societies that must be continually provisioned (bands, lineages, nations) to survive as corporate entities, that is, provisioned with whichever goods and services are necessary for the performance of whichever group needs and activities the culture of that society requires and the technology and resources of that society permit (weapons, marriage goods, fines in dispute settlement, material support for shamans, priests or members of the politburo). Wherever we find a human society which endures over time we can expect to find discernible principles, rules, and institutionalised procedures which explain its repetitive, continual material provisioning of persons and social group. Material provisioning is always structured, never left to chance, because material deprivation means death to persons and death to societies as corporate entities. What we mean by an 'economic system' is the organisational rules and institutions through which repetitive and continual material provisioning is arranged.

In their provisioning all societies make use of natural resources, human labour, technology (tools and knowledge) and, something for which there is no portmanteau word in English, institutionalised practices, devices and things such as external trade of some sort, monetary objects of some sort or market places of some sort. These are extremely important in economic anthropology and archaeology because they provide us with structural clues, but their workings are poorly understood outside of our own and the Soviet system. Markedly different economic systems (American capitalism and Soviet socialism) do in fact make use of some form of these practices, devices and things; for example, both systems employ external trade, monetary objects and market places of some sort (as well as trade unions and universities of some sort).

I want to place the greatest possible emphasis on the points that (i) some forms of external trade, monetary object or market place are widely used in utterly different economic systems – Roman Britain, Anglo-Saxon Britain, Norman Britain, Tudor Britain, industrial-welfare state-capitalist Britain today, the Soviet Union, Malinowski's Trobriand Islands; but that (ii) their organisation, functions and importance vary utterly in different economic systems; and (iii) their specific organisation, functions and importance in any single type of economy (such as capitalism or communism or stateless clan segments) are sensitive and revealing indicators of the basic principles of structured material provisioning in that specific type of economy. If ports of external trade in Anglo-Saxon England (Hodges 1978) and Ch'ing China (Mancall 1968) worked differently from British and Chinese foreign trade today, it is because the internal economic and political systems of Anglo-Saxon England and Ch'ing China differed from the economies and polities of Britain and China today. So too with monetary objects, as Grierson (1978) shows us, and also market places: 'markets differ as an African bush market does from the New York Stock Exchange' (Polanyi 1968, pp. 239–40).

The Northwest Coast social economies of the Kwakiutl and Nootka and those of Highland New Guinea and the Trobriand Islands that I now return to lacked all three major components of national industrial capitalism today. But they did employ some form of external trade, monetary object and market place whose organisation, functions and importance were all markedly different from their counterparts in capitalism today; the special form they did take in those small societies was a direct expression of their markedly different socioeconomic principles of material provisioning. In what follows I shall try to show that without the state, without dependence for livelihood on production for market sale and the use of modern money, and without machine technology and applied science, these differently located clan segments were similarly constrained in their modes of provisioning, also shared a number of features I shall call constants (particularly warfare, the threat of famine, similar religious beliefs, and smallness of scale), and were consequently forced by these constraints and constants to employ very similar socioeconomic institutions and techniques to provision themselves, not only the obvious ones of hunting, gathering and swidden agriculture, but also social and cultural contrivances utterly different from physical environment, such as ceremonial exchanges, primitive valuables and alliance networks. As one archaeologist puts it in a passage sympathetic to the use of ethnographic models, 'different degrees of [political] centralization have characteristic mechanisms of social integration, and...societies at similar levels have common needs which tend to be solved in similar ways' (Sherratt 1972, p. 508). Sherratt's article in this volume (ch. 10) makes similar assumptions in the use of ethnographic models.

The constraints on these societies were formidable. The most obvious was their inability to control or to compensate for the vagaries and nastinesses of nature, such as drought, flood, and disease afflicting plants, animals, and persons. These meant the occasional threat of famine and the more frequent threat of seasonal hunger. To be sure, the Kwakiutl and peoples in New Guinea did attempt to control and compensate for the destructive forces of nature that caused famine, but not with our techniques and institutions, as we shall see. Note that in our society the three core institutions plus technology work to prevent regional or national famine resulting from natural catastrophe. Machine technology and applied science mean not only high output per man hour or per acre, but also the ability to store abundance through freezing and canning food, to reduce crop and herd losses from pests and disease, to compensate for insufficient rain (dams, irrigation works), and to transport food quickly and massively to stricken regions of the country. Our international market and monetary systems mean that we have an ability to buy large quantities of food abroad. That we are organised into nation-states having central government means that a regional food shortage within the nation (which would be immediately known through modern communications) would be redressed either by food from governmental storehouses or food purchased by government and sent quickly to the stricken region.

In contrast, what were the devices employed by clan segments without states, (economy-wide) markets or machines to cope with the threat of hunger or with actual famine, when, as Hesiod put it, 'the gods have hidden the livelihood of man'? Here is a typical sample, easily compiled from anthropological writings: minute knowledge of everything edible in the physical environment; knowledge of the habits of game animals, birds and fish; storage through preserving meat, fish, grain and other foods (drying, smoking, making beer and cheese); domesticating animals; planting strips of land at different locations; planting famine insurance crops more resistant to drought (e.g. cassava) than the preferred staple, to be harvested only if the preferred staple fails; planting more than is normally required so that sufficient may be harvested if it is a bad but not disastrous growing season (Allan 1965); using magical incantation and sacrifice to propitiate the supernatural forces which control plant growth and control the appearance of game and fish (Malinowski 1935; Firth 1940); making use of the institutionalised social right to solicit gifts of food in emergency from marriage allies, military allies, ceremonial exchange allies, or trade allies; finally, what some of us have called 'emergency conversion' – in desperate extremity trading off women, children and valuables to strangers for food and seed, one step removed from infanticide, suicide of the old, and political emigration to become a client of an outside group in return for food and protection (Buxton 1958, pp. 85–8).

THE SOCIAL ECONOMIES OF STATELESS GROUPS

Lineages which cluster into small sets called sub-clans and larger sets called clans comprised the political, economic, social, and religious community. A lineage or cluster of related lineages was a political community in the sense that lethal fighting within the group was prohibited, the group carried out joint warfare, its adult male members had joint responsibility to pay compensation to outsiders hurt or killed by its members, to seek compensation or revenge for any of its own members hurt or killed by outsiders, and recognised internal leaders or big-men who initiated raids and warfare and peaceful activities and exchanges of several sorts with external groups (Middleton and Tait 1958, 'Introduction').

It was an economic community in the sense that specific natural resources used in hunting, fishing, gathering or horticulture – land, forests, waterways, metal-bearing ores, quarries – were recognised by both insiders and outsiders to be lineage property. Lineage members in good standing had an automatic right to use lineage property, outsiders did not without special permission (acquired typically through an alliance relationship of some sort).

It was a cohesive religious community because lineage members shared an idiosyncratic system of beliefs about their remote ancestors being their present guardian spirits with supernatural power over the forces of life and death, success and failure, victory and defeat, health and sickness, abundance and dearth. Lineage members had a common obligation to carry out religious rites and to give gifts to gods and spirits (first fruits, sacrifice before battle or journey) to ensure supernatural protection and benevolence.

It was a social and cultural community because of common local or regional residence and because of the rules lineages enforced on their members concerning permissible marriage-mates and residence choices, and because of the rights and obligations held in common to pay or receive bridewealth and bloodwealth. Lineage members shared common language, religious beliefs, and level of technology as well as a general outlook bred by proximity, frequent interaction, common lineage concerns, mutual dependence, the special group virtues attributed to their own common descent and the special defects and inferiorities they attributed to outsiders. All this was true for the differently located clusters of clan segments not in touch with one another.

In these stateless societies lineage groupings represented internal relations of dependence. Individual persons depended on their lineage membership, lineage-mates, lineage superiors and lineage ancestors for the natural resources which yielded ordinary material livelihood, for emergency material support in illness, accident, and old age, for bridewealth goods necessary to marry, for juridical and military protection against hostile outsiders, and for supernatural protection against hostile spirits, hostile persons, and the hostile forces of nature. Social cohesion and solidarity – which are not to be equated with bliss – were intensified, and lineage dependence reinforced, by the absence of alternative sources of material livelihood and security, and of political existence and protection outside the lineage community. The necessary and the good things of life and the avoidance of the bad were to be had only through lineage membership.

Lineage groupings ubiquitously formed networks or interaction spheres, external relations of hostility and alliance. They raided, wounded and killed to avenge, abduct women, capture weapons, slaves and land (Berndt 1964; Swadesh 1948; Chagnon 1968). Through marriage, ceremonial exchange, trade and military agreements, they formed relations of alliance with lineage segments of external clans to secure military aid, brides, trade goods, access to seasonal food resources or sources of obsidian and stone in possession of allies, emergency refuge and emergency food (Vayda 1967; Heider 1969; Strathern 1971).

There are several points to be emphasised. We are dealing here with *Gemeinschaften* in Tönnies' sense, with unusually integrated systems in which economy, polity, society, and culture are inextricably joined together because of the central importance of lineage membership, the core institution. The absence of our economic and political institutions and of our technology mean the presence of basic rules, principles, or institutions for material provisioning (and much else) utterly different from ours. Two of these are of particular interest: ceremonial exchange and primitive valuables (Dalton 1977a). It was characteristic of these closely integrated societies that the institutions they employed for wider social purposes (defence, dispute settlement) were also related to ordinary and emergency material provisioning.

Aboriginal *potlatch* and *moka* are to be understood only within the special configurations of internal relations of lineage dependence and external relations of alliance and hostility, which, in turn, are only to be understood as derivatives of the constraints and constants which shaped aboriginal economies in stateless societies. Ceremonial exchanges were transacted only between lineages in alliance. They were necessary to keep the peace of the alliance intact (and so permit other activities, such as trade, to be carried on securely). They were also used to celebrate important events and to transmit in public clan-leadership positions to rising men from eligible lineages. Primitive valuables were special goods – sea shells or jewellery made from sea shells, ornate stone axes, pigs – permissibly transacted only by eligible men in honorific social situations entailing obligatory payments to allies (and sometimes to enemies) for special services (sorcery, assassination, military aid), to make or keep intact lineage alliances (bridewealth, ceremonial exchange), to avoid or to end hostilities (bloodwealth, death compensation) and, in famine, to acquire emergency foodstuffs (Dalton 1971).

In such societies we cannot identify an 'economy' as a separate subsystem distinct from lineage, marriage and alliance. There is no name for the 'economic system' of these stateless clan segments because the agencies which arrange systematic material provisioning are themselves as much social and political as they are economic – lineage, marriage, military alliance, and such. Neither is there a standard conceptual vocabulary in English to describe many of these institutions, transactions, relationships and special goods that express the core attributes of these remarkably integrated societies so very different from our own. Occasionally we can use old words such as *corvée* and *prestation* (Mauss 1954). German words, except for *Gemeinschaft*, seem taboo, even when they are as vividly appropriate as Thurnwald's *Bittarbeit* for the invitation labour solicited to help with peak load work needs, such as planting, harvesting or house-building, to be followed by a feast or beer party by which the host thanks the invited workers (where labour markets do not exist and the labour of close kin is insufficient). Karl Polanyi and the several of us associated with him have contrived a conceptual vocabulary for socioeconomic institutions expressing the core attributes of non-market societies such as those we are dealing with here. I shall go into this matter later in the paper.

To return to the question posed earlier: why did these clusters of societies not in touch with one another employ nearly identical socioeconomic institutions, such as ceremonial exchanges and primitive valuables? The answer derives from the fact that the similarities between the New Guinea and North American clusters were greater than the differences between them (differences in language, climate, exact reckoning of descent, exact sources of subsistence, etc.), particularly their similarities in structured modes of individual and group provisioning and the prevailing situations of warfare and the threat of hunger. These similarities in constraints, constants and institutions – in small size and internal lineage organisation of social economy and polity, internal relations of lineage dependence, quality of technology, systems of religious belief, and similarities in the need for external relations of alliance for several purposes including trade, marriage and warfare – forced them to employ basically similar practices, such as ceremonial exchange and primitive valuables (and, indeed, propitiating rites, big-men, mortuary payments, bridewealth and much else). We recognise these widely dispersed lineage groupings as clearly belonging to the same cluster-set or genus, as my Oxford Universal Dictionary defines that term: 'A classificatory group comprehending one or a number of species possessing certain common structural characteristics distinct from those of any other group.'

'Basically similar' and 'nearly identical' do not mean 'identical'. Rosman and Rubel (1971) very clearly describe and explain the variations to be found among Northwest Coast potlatches, and in a recent paper (Dalton 1978a) I point out some reasons for the differences between the *kula* ceremonial exchange of the Trobriand Islands and the *moka* ceremonial exchange of Highland New Guinea. But these variations and differences are not as important as the basic similarities, the core attributes of the institutional and technological matrix of stateless clan segments. To indicate why, I shall use another benign trick, an analogy that is exactly appropriate to the point at issue, because what is at issue is the need to explain and justify the principles to be employed in grouping different societies within one named genus-cluster, as we do so easily for capitalism and communism, but not for the array of economies and societies studied by anthropologists and archaeologists.

If we were to compare the attributes of the universities of Oxford and Cambridge, and compare also the curious customs of their natives, we would come up with a listing of similarities and differences. Some obvious similarities are that both universities are made up of component colleges, their similar examination and tutorial systems, and their similar conscious preservation and nurturing of ancient custom – gowns, port, feasts, college offices and such. Some obvious differences would include the proportions of undergraduates reading science and engineering compared to religion and philosophy in each, that one has an All Souls and the other does not, and the larger number of women's colleges at Oxford. But if we were to compare Oxford and Cambridge on the one hand, with the University of Moscow and Texas Agricultural and Mining University on the other, Oxford and Cambridge would *now* look like twins – certainly genus-mates if not species-mates – the differences between them utterly trivial compared to their similarities, and, what is now more important, compared to their deep structural differences with the University of Moscow and Texas A. and M. Such, I believe, also to be the case when we compare the aboriginal economies in stateless societies in New Guinea (Oxford) and the Northwest Coast of America (Cambridge) with the politically centralised tribal kingdoms of Africa such as Lozi and Baganda (Texas A. and M.), and the still different peasantries in kingdom-states of Tokugawa Japan and Ch'ing China (University of Moscow).

The point, of course, is that no two societies or economies (or universities) are identical; but for an archaeologist to employ an anthropological parallel properly it is necessary for him to establish that the prehistoric society whose artifacts he recovers belongs to the same genus-cluster in the anthropological or historical record he is using as analogue. If we can identify the core attributes of several cohesive clusters of societies, such as the genus-cluster I here label 'aboriginal economies in stateless societies', we see that they are structured by practices, attributes and artifacts that necessarily are institutionalised together (because of their similar constraints and constants): small-scale, low density of population, lineages in clans, relations of hostility and alliance, primitive technology, ceremonial exchange, primitive valuables – are related or interdependent attributes and institutions. This is what matters. For example, we know that external trade *in such societies* is carried out in only a small number of characteristic ways, and further, that the anthropological literature may be expected to give information on which of these ways is practised under which circumstances. These matters have not been made abundantly clear to archaeologists because those of us who work in economic anthropology and early economic history have not yet created models to demonstrate persuasively the existence of the several clusterings – the genus-sets – and have not yet explained their systematic organisation; neither have we yet demonstrated that each clustering necessarily has characteristic institutions, characteristic modes of external trade and monetary usage, for example, which structure their material provisioning, and, at the same time, express their core attributes of political and social organisation. The creation of such analytical sets and the specification of their institutional correlates for the social economies of what are too loosely called bands, tribes and peasantries is, however, underway (Dalton 1972; 1977b).

THE STATE AND EARLY ECONOMIC INSTITUTIONS

To put the same question to a different cluster of societies: why do we find very similar socioeconomic institutions employed by early kingdom-states not in touch with one another, particularly institutional practices employed in their conduct of external trade (such as ports of trade and tributary relations of alliance)?

But first I must sketch in some background information about the enormous, complicated and controversial topic, 'the state and early economic institutions'. It is enormous because of the plethora of writing forthcoming in recent years on early kingdom-states in many parts of the world. Only North America, Australia, New Zealand, New Guinea and most of the islands of the Pacific Ocean seem not to have had kingdoms in historical times. The subject is complicated because there were so many different kingdoms in so many parts of the world over so many centuries of change and upheaval. The literature on Africa alone is now formidable as are the rapidly growing literatures on Japan and China. On kingdom-states in early Europe it is huge (reading the literature on Norman England alone could easily absorb a professional lifetime).

The state and early economic institutions is a controversial subject for several reasons. For some parts of the world and some time periods, Africa before the nineteenth century for example, factual information is seriously deficient (Vansina 1966). Where facts are missing interpretative guesses rush in and controversy ensues between persons guessing differently. Anthropologists, archaeologists and historians, moreover, interpret the structures of kingdom-states in markedly different ways because they *bring* to the factual data markedly different theoretical frameworks, preconceptions, models, and conceptual vocabularies, what David Clarke called controlling and conceptual models ('we observe what we believe and then believe in that which we have observed'), and what Thomas Kuhn has taught us to call paradigms. Here

I shall only mention three which are widely shared, and ignore the others, such as Wittfogel's (1957), White's (1949) and Hicks' (1969).

The first is what American anthropologists call the 'formalist' model, which is used by a number of British economic historians of Africa (Hopkins 1973; Gray and Birmingham 1970), some British and American economic anthropologists (Firth 1967; 1972; Ortiz 1967; Schneider 1974), some American economic historians of medieval Europe (North and Thomas 1973), and many British and American archaeologists (Adams 1974; Lamberg-Karlovsky 1975). The formalists employ formal economic theory, the conceptual terms, leading ideas and models of conventional price theory or micro-economics, the theory of market supply, demand and price determination for inputs and outputs bought and sold by households and firms, as these market models have been elaborated over nearly the century from Alfred Marshall (1890) to Paul Samuelson (1976, ch. 20–32). The formalist anthropologists and historians and the British archaeologists or 'palaeoeconomists' focus on cost-benefit decisions made by tribal and historical persons in pursuit of maximum material utility or profit, just as managers of households and business firms in modern America or Japan are presumed to act in their national market economies.

In short, formalists assume that early and primitive economies were merely pre-industrial variants of the market capitalism for which supply and demand analysis was invented. They assume that the similarities between modern market capitalism and the social economies of early kingdom-states (and of stateless clan segments) were more important than the differences between them; *they regard all economies of record as species variants of the genus capitalism.*

Marxians, of course, take a different view and therefore employ a different paradigm whose familiar conceptual vocabulary and leading ideas – surplus, exploitation, mode of production, relations of production, class, class conflict, economic determinism, the sequence of stages from primitive to industrial communism – attract a growing number of economic anthropologists and historians (see, e.g., Bloch 1975). I need not go into detail for an audience brought up on the writings of V. G. Childe, in which Marxian surplus, technological change and stages are pivotal.

The third paradigm was contrived by Karl Polanyi (1886–1964), although several of its ideas came from the much earlier writings of Bücher, Maine, Tönnies, Weber, Malinowski and Thurnwald (Polanyi 1968, ch. 5, 6; Köcke 1979). It seems to be stuck with the awkward name invented for it by its formalist critics, 'substantivism', or 'substantivist economics'. Briefly, Polanyi's work and its extensions and applications by others including myself consist of several basic propositions in support of which evidence is drawn from various socioeconomic systems: (1) that the market organisation which came to integrate nineteenth-century European industrial capitalism was historically and anthropologically unique, making such market-integrated societies significantly different in structure, performance, and consequences from those of any society that preceded them (Polanyi 1944; 1947); (2) that formal micro-economic theory, conventional supply and demand analysis invented to analyse capitalism, is extremely misleading, inappropriate and distorting when applied to non-market economies, such as the social economies studied by archaeologists and anthropologists (Polanyi 1971a; Dalton 1961); (3) that a special conceptual vocabulary coupled to a special set of leading ideas – in short, a separate and distinct paradigm, neither formalist nor Marxist – is necessary to understand the workings of non-market economies whose core attributes are systematically different from those of developed capitalism. The basic structural fact is that, in the absence of market integration, 'economy' is embedded in 'society' in the senses explained earlier in this paper for stateless clan segments: that the allocation of labour and natural resources to production activities (gathering, hunting, horticulture), the organisation of work, and the disposition of what is produced (or hunted, gathered, imported) are politically and socially controlled and directed. The conceptual vocabulary used to analyse such a non-Marshallian universe must be socioeconomic to express the paramount fact that no separate subsystem called 'economy' exists in such societies: redistribution, reciprocity, special-purpose money, ports of trade, administered trade, equivalencies, operational devices – these are the socioeconomic terms used (Polanyi 1957); (4) that this set of ideas, terms, and models, (1)–(3), be applied to actual social economies of time and place (e.g., Polanyi, Arensberg, and Pearson 1957; Dalton 1977a). I used some of these ideas in the earlier parts of this paper and will use others of them shortly, in considering the socioeconomic aspects of early kingdom-states, the second cluster.

The state and early economic institutions is a complicated and controversial subject for yet other reasons. An old topic, the origins of states (e.g., Oppenheimer 1914), is again current, and so we have recent assemblages of new and old theory and new and old evidence (Fried 1967; Service 1975). Finally, work of the highest importance has been forthcoming on the origins and usage of coined money in early states (Grierson 1959; 1978; Kraay 1964; Vidal-Naquet 1972), and on the socioeconomic structures of such important early states as those of Greece and Rome (Finley 1973), China (Fairbank 1968a; Elvin 1973), Asante (Wilks 1975) and Inca (Murra 1956), some of which at least is almost certainly too recent to have been absorbed by the several professional groups adhering to rival paradigms.

Fig. 1.2 was drawn solely with African kingdoms in mind. It is a model, ideal type, or conceptual framework meant to point out the structural features and their institutional correlates shared by many African kingdoms (before colonial rule). In what follows I shall describe what seem to be the constant African features, the variable African features, the similar features found

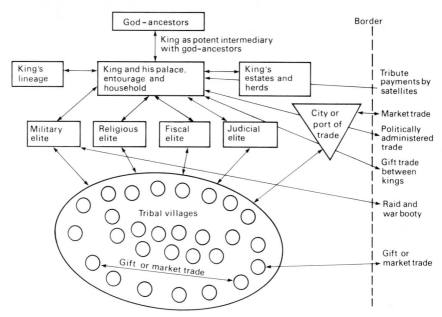

1.2.   Levels and sectors in an aboriginal (pre-colonial) African kingdom. Arrows indicate transactions.

widely in early kingdom-states in other parts of the world not in touch with Africa, and give particular attention to the characteristic forms of external trade in early kingdoms.

Scale. By the standard of today's nation-state, many pre-colonial African kingdoms were very small in population and territory, kingdoms containing 50,000–200,000 subjects being typical, very rarely approaching one million (Forde and Kaberry 1967; Mair 1962). Recall that prior to the period of the Danish invasions Anglo-Saxon England contained some seven or more kingdoms.

Levels and sectors. It is entirely realistic to portray early African kingdoms in terms of ranked levels (segments, groupings) of persons, and to emphasise the connective tissue of obligatory transactions between them; also to point out the existence of internal and external political-economic sectors. We invariably find at least three principal levels, the king, elite and commoners, with, of course, further gradations of status within elites (the king's ministers/petty chiefs) and among commoners (slaves/free people), as we also find in Anglo-Saxon and Norman England. These sociopolitical rankings have direct economic correlates: property rights and prerogatives, sources and amounts of income differ with rank. 'Sector' is a vague word signifying only part of the whole (in modern economies, the agricultural sector, foreign trade sector, etc.). The most important sectoral divisions that concern us are internal and external sectors, market and non-market sectors, and particularly the redistributive sector.

Sacred kings with many roles. The king is a religious, political, military, juridical and economic figure, acting towards constituencies above and below him and outside his kingdom. The king faces upward as potent intermediary with god-ancestors who decide victory or defeat, abundance or dearth.

In my view kingship everywhere and at all times has been in some degree a sacred office. *Rex est mixta persona cum sacerdote.* This is because a king symbolizes a whole society and must not be identified with any part of it. He must be in the society and yet stand outside it and this is only possible if his office is raised to a mystical plane. It is the kingship and not the king who is divine...

(Evans-Pritchard 1962, p. 84)

the [Chinese] emperor...was the mediator between heaven and earth...In the annual fertility rite he ploughed the sacred furrow not so that Chinese crops could grow but so that crops *per se* could grow. (Mancall 1968, pp. 63–4)

The king faces downward to his elite and commoners as governor, judge (it is he alone who decides capital punishment), wife-taker from constituent clans, taxing authority, punisher of disloyalty and sacrilege, rewarder of outstanding service, emergency provider, and spiritual embodiment of the kingdom's land and people, its present link with past and future.

Though a [Bantu] king may be spoken of as 'owning' his country, it is not simply inherited as a property. He inherits a total relationship with land and people (and cattle) for which only one of his line of descent is held to be fitted, and in virtue of this relationship he symbolizes the total polity so that its health reflects his health, and his least action may affect his whole kingdom. (Mair 1962, p. 217)

The king faces outward to his enemies as warrior and raider for slaves, cattle, and other booty, to his superior or overlord-allies as tribute-payer (and sometimes wife-giver), and to his inferior client-allies as tribute receiver (and sometimes wife-taker). He and his elite servants on his behalf control everything of importance in the kingdom because it is either valuable as a source of revenue (market places), or of foreign luxuries to be permissibly acquired only by king and elite (external trade), or because it is a political threat (guns, the presence of foreigners). What Finley says about classical antiquity is also true for early African kingdoms:

The authority of the state was total, of the city-states as of the autocracies, and it extended to everyone who resided within the territorial borders...There were no theoretical limits to the power of the state, no activity, no sphere of human behaviour, in which the state could not legitimately intervene provided the decision was properly taken for any reason that was held to be valid by a legitimate authority.

(Finley 1973, pp. 154–5)

(See also Sands 1908, p. 118; on methods used to limit and punish the abuse of power in African kingdoms, see Beattie 1959.)

The ideology of African kingship, which was expressed with particular force and clarity during installation ceremonies for a new king, was fertility, prosperity, abundance, protection, strength, victory, internal peace and justice (Fortes and Evans-Pritchard 1940, 'Introduction'; Mair 1977, ch. 3). Kings and elites always had a dual nature: they were public servants performing services, duties, functions and activities thought to be necessary and beneficial for their constituents, and they were public masters enjoying superior rights, goods, powers and privileges.

As with segmentary lineages in stateless clans described earlier, actual warfare (sometimes with annual regularity) or the ever-present threat of warfare – relations of hostility – was a prevailing condition, a constant in the kingdoms of pre-colonial Africa, as indeed, it was in early Europe and elsewhere. The king's military role as protector (and as raider for booty) was extremely important, and, as with the emergence of a united England under Alfred and his successors, was sometimes the origin of a kingdom. Just as the Anglo-Saxons said, 'Out of war is born the king', so too the Azande of East Africa, 'War begat the king.' So too a dozen other sayings and episodes elsewhere: 'The king is everywhere primarily a war lord, and kingship evolves from charismatic heroism' (Weber 1958, p. 251); 'Charles the Fat, unable to give protection and forced to pay tribute to the Vikings besieging Paris, was deposed in 887' (Barraclough 1957, p. 15). And John Bradshaw at the trial of Charles in 1649: 'the one tie, the one bond, is the bond of protection that is due from the sovereign; the other is the bond of subjection that is due from the subject. Sir, if this bond be once broken, farewell sovereignty!' (Wedgewood 1964, p. 161). One of the wisest of British social anthropologists introduced a book on African political systems by pointing out 'There are exceedingly few human societies known to us in which there is not some form of warfare, and at least a good half of the history of political development is in one way or another a history of wars' (Radcliffe-Brown 1940, p. xix). Some material culture correlates of strong centralised power and protection are discussed in chapter 3 below.

The redistributive sector. Polanyi used the term 'redistribution' to refer to the state sector of economy in what he called 'archaic' states (the meaning of 'archaic' will be explained shortly). Redistribution is meant to include the full set of economic activities undertaken by central government in early kingdoms: internal and external; receiving and paying out, in monetary objects, labour services, and in kind; fiscal and regulatory, scheduled, erratic, and contingent; royal estates; storehouses; gifts; tribute; taxation; war booty and ransom. As with modern dictatorships and democracies, so too with early kingdoms: wherever there is central government there is redistribution because a sizeable fraction of ordinary and special goods and labour services is acquired by the political/religious centre(s) for the material support of the ruler and his elite servants, and allocated by the centre for public services of defence, religious observance, roads, shrines, aid to the needy and suchlike. Disbursements from the centre are also used to reward outstanding service of prominent persons, and, very importantly, reflect the system of social stratification that prevails.

Polanyi used the term 'archaic' in a special technical sense to mean those socioeconomic institutions which are now defunct (such as ports of trade) found in early kingdom-states, institutions which did not survive into modern times of national market economy because the historical growth of markets either transformed them or created substitutes for them.

Material correlates of social stratification and political office; sumptuary rules, regalia of office, the king's goods and royal monopolies. The more pronounced the social and political stratification in any kingdom, the larger the number of ways it is expressed materially, to preserve, reinforce and legitimate the distance between upper and lower groups (caste in India being an extreme but not a unique example). All African kingdoms were socially stratified and most employed domestic slaves of some sort, usually war captives and criminals. Differences in rank were marked in many visible ways: permissible foods, modes of dress, number of wives, modes of punishment (the lash and impressment for commoners only, the equivalent of the silken rope for nobles), size or shape of houses, fences of distinct shape or materials, type of weapon, hairstyle, scarification, tattooing, and jewellery by social rank. In some kingdoms in Africa, as elsewhere, only the lowest social strata were obliged to pay ordinary taxes, exemption being a prerogative of upper groups, who, typically, performed military or religious services.

So too with insignia of political or religious office, such as metal collars, the carrying of batons, the wearing of official green or red, the king's messenger carrying a rooster or wearing a state sword with a golden hilt. The higher the office the more numerous and exclusive the material prerogatives and expressions of rank, with those reserved for the king alone to be found in every African kingdom. Royal goods, either very valuable (gold nuggets) or symbolically dangerous and powerful (lion skins), or both (elephants' tusks), were reserved for the king alone. These merge into royal 'monopolies', lines of production (gold mining) or sectors of external trade (slaves, ivory) reserved exclusively to the king or permitted to others only with his approval, the withholding of such goods being regarded as an act of political rebellion:

Ivory in the Bamenda Grassfields was a royal monopoly . . . Much of the ivory stored in the larger chiefdoms derived from the annual hunts on behalf of the king. The withholding of ivory from a king was a declaration of rebellion; a demand for it a demand for submission. Ivory transactions were therefore in the main gift-exchanges or royal favours, and a large store of ivory implied the ability to extend a ruler's area of influence.   (Chilver 1961, p. 253)

The symbol of royal power was the lion skin. Only the king could sit on one and then only on sacred days. If a lord refused to forward a skin to the king, it was an act of open rebellion.   (Vansina 1973, p. 378; see also p. 126)

The king [of Dahomey] possessed a number of economic monopolies...The king monopolized the trade in slaves, who were sold at the coast – mainly at Whydah – by royal traders [some trade in slaves was conducted by private African merchants, see Law 1977].   (Lombard 1967, pp. 89–90)

The chief had a right to the hindlegs of all the main animals killed, such as the hartebeest, waterbuck, kob, gazelle, duiker, buffalo, hippo, to the tusks of elephants and to the skins of lions and leopards.   (Southall 1953, p. 80)

Differences among pre-colonial African kingdoms. Here one must tread warily because the evidence is still pouring in, because there were so very many African kingdoms about which we have only scanty information, because there are complications due to the arrival just before A.D. 1500 of European traders bringing guns and luxury goods to exchange for slaves, gold and ivory, and because of Muslim political conquests. It is not that the differences among Africans kingdoms I shall immediately point out may prove to be wrong or trivial, but rather that there may still be other structural differences of an illuminating sort not yet discernible from the literature presently in being.

Briefly, the four clusterings for which good evidence is at hand separate themselves along the following lines.

(1) What I shall call feudal kingdoms, such as Nkole and Rwanda, in which a ruling elite of military-overlord-herdsmen so very sharply differentiate themselves from their physically different and more numerous agricultural client-servants that several anthropologists and historians describing the systems use words such as caste, feudalism, serfdom and conquest-states (Oberg 1940; Roscoe 1923; Maquet 1961; 1970; Mair 1962, pp. 125–247; Karugire 1971).

(2) Tribal kingdoms not engaged in European trade, like the Lozi (see ch. 3) and Baganda, tribal because their constituent units are clans and because neither in military nor food technology are they on a higher level than the stateless segmentary lineages in Africa (Gluckman 1943; 1961; Roscoe 1911).

(3) Tribal kingdoms heavily engaged in the European trade, such as Asante and Dahomey, which gave their kings and elites access to European guns and luxury goods, the guns being used for imperialist expansion to yield tribute and more slaves, the luxury goods to reward the expanding bureaucracy-elite (Wilks 1975; Polanyi 1966; Lombard 1967; Law 1977).

(4) Muslim kingdom-states resembled those of Europe, Japan and China containing peasantries much more closely than they resembled the other sorts of African kingdoms just described, in religion, a higher level of technology, military organisation, urbanisation, commercialisation and literacy. Islam meant a universal religion, literacy, full-time professional merchant traders, and continual religious, literary and commercial contact across the Sahara, north to the Mediterranean coast and northeast to Egypt. The Muslim kingdoms had cavalry as well as guilds of craftsmen (Nadel 1942; Smith 1967).

Tributary relations of alliance. Early kingdoms in Africa and elsewhere lacked two of the three major structures of industrial capitalism, machine technology and national market integration, and therefore lacked the multitude of features closely associated with them. In this sense they were constrained in their ways of arranging systematic provisioning. As with stateless clans, warfare was also ever-present and so African kingdoms also contracted external relations of alliance. But unlike the situation prevailing in stateless clans, warfare, alliance and external trade were the king's concern, matters arranged by central government. As the king of Asante told a visiting European in the early nineteenth century, 'Here only the king and great figures engage in trade, as I do' (Dupuis 1824, p. 167). And as a British archaeologist tells us, 'There is considerable evidence to suggest that all long-distance trading was controlled either by the Saxon kings or the church in Middle Saxon England' (Hodges 1978), which Polanyi generalises: 'In archaic society the chief or king and his immediate entourage are alone entitled to trade, that is to initiate the more or less warlike and diplomatic ventures which lead to the acquisition of goods from a distance' (Polanyi 1975, p. 138; see also, Dalton 1978b; 1978c).

These, then, are the typical features of tributary relations of alliance: weaker client-states make scheduled payments of tribute to stronger overlord states, payments which establish peace between them and allow the client-state to retain autonomy in its home rule but not in its foreign relations, which may not be conducted against the interests of the overlord king. Tribute payments may be made in ordinary goods (foodstuffs), luxury goods reserved for elite persons (swords, horses) or destined to be traded by the recipient king (slaves), treasure (gold, jewels), and coins. At the Hun and Viking end of the spectrum, tribute payments were extorted bribes under threat of violent raid; at the Chinese end they were a flexible instrument of diplomacy. To dangerous clients the Chinese paid bribes; with others it was more like gift exchange, most of the several sorts of grateful barbarians acknowledging the benefits they derived from the contact graciously permitted them with Chinese civilisation – literacy, coins, philosophy, religion – or from permission to trade in China. But in all cases (except, perhaps, Rome under the Republic) tribute represented political relations between unequal kingdoms. The trade of several sorts that accompanied it was closely controlled by government and contact with foreigners sharply circumscribed.

Contact with foreigners [in China] was restricted: most of it was limited to border areas, and all contact and trade were kept under close bureaucratic control... Boundary maintenance of this kind was important...[because] Foreigners very often did not understand the correct human relationships, and their influence must not be allowed to disturb those relations within China. They represented a general danger of cultural contamination. Also, there was no place in the Chinese ritual order for residents of the empire who were subjects of another prince.

(Wills 1968, pp. 252–3)

Other devices to reinforce alliance were also used, such as the overlord-king taking as wife the client-king's daughter or sister, or taking as guest-hostages the client-king's sons, or stationing one of his men in the client's court. Sometimes the client-king became military ally as well, obliged to send troops to join the overlord-king in warfare (Wills 1968; Sands 1908). Again, the overlord-king sometimes arbitrated disputes between his several client-kings. The frequency, amounts and kinds of tribute payments varied widely as did the return services received by client-kings. Typically, the obligations of client-kings were much more specific than those of the overlord-king toward his clients: 'Rome's duties to her clients for their services were never clearly defined' (Sands 1908, p. 110). Sands also tells us (pp. 127–39) that under the Emperors tribute changed from what it had been under the Republic. We are sometimes dealing in a grey area in which it is not always possible to distinguish between bribe, gift, tribute and tax.

What seems to be an important variant is described in detail for Imperial China (Fairbank 1968a; 1968b; Fairbank and Teng 1960; Wang 1953; Yu 1967). Here the tribute payments by client states were sometimes small (Korea was an exception), merely tokens of submission and clientage, but were necessary to elicit permission to conduct ordinary commercial trade with China.

EXTINCT SOCIETIES: SPECIES OR GENUS?

An oddly shaped piece of the jigsaw puzzle must be examined before we try to fit the several pieces together. David Clarke and other archaeologists expressed their qualms about ethnographic parallels by referring to 'extinct' societies. I discover that one of my former students, Frank Rackerby, put the point clearly in an unpublished paper in 1967:

Archaeologists sometimes operate as if the total range of human cultural variability exists in the ethnographic record. There is no valid argument that this is true. It is quite likely that cultural systems existed in the past which are today totally extinct and unrecorded. If the prehistoric economic data does not parsimoniously fit a model developed from the literature of economic anthropology the case may be that there is no analogous situation.

The force of this argument crucially depends on precisely what is meant by an extinct society. The treacherous analogy, of course, comes from the physical universe; the sabre-tooth tiger, the dodo and the passenger pigeon are now extinct. A pigeon is one thing, but what exactly do we mean by an extinct society or an extinct cultural system?

We know from the historical record that societies once existed (the Carib Indians, the Inca) whose populations were nearly extinguished by disease and warfare and whose political-economic-social structures were radically transformed by conquerors (the Spanish of 1500) who came permanently to settle from societies radically different from those of the conquered. In the ordinary meaning of words, Inca society – its political, economic, and social organisation and much of its cultural expression, such as religion – is now extinct. But in each of the historical cases what I think disappeared was a species, not a genus, because each had genus-mates somewhere in the historical record whose core attributes were sufficiently similar to permit us to cluster them together with the societies that disappeared or became radically transformed. Note that *all* early historical societies became extinct, even those which did not experience physical decimation of population but which nevertheless underwent radical transformation in the course of historical events. With regard to its political, economic and social structure, Anglo-Saxon England is now extinct, even though persons descending from Anglo-Saxon Englishmen now live. So too the France of Charlemagne and Tokugawa Japan.

For the argument doubting the legitimacy of ethnographic parallels in archaeological interpretation to have merit, it is not enough to say that prehistoric societies became extinct in the sense that the passenger pigeon became extinct, because other sorts of pigeons can still be examined, genus-mate pigeons whose basic structures are close enough to those of the passenger pigeon to allow us to reconstruct its core attributes from partial evidence – *if and only if we know that what we are attempting to reconstruct with partial evidence is a pigeon of some sort.* Here lies the necessity to identify core attributes and group societies into named genus-clusters.

For doubts about ethnographic parallels to have merit what would have to be extinct is an entire set of societies (not a species like the passenger pigeon, but a genus), the entire genus-set so structured in its core attributes as to be markedly different from any single society known to historians or anthropologists. This seems implausible to me for the following reasons. The ethnographic and historical records contain enormous diversity, from tiny hunting and gathering bands widely dispersed – some of which, like Australian aborigines, were not affected by Europeans until the nineteenth century, or clan groupings in the New Guinea Highlands until the 1930s – to large empire-states. Their main structural features of economy, polity and society do not vary randomly and do not combine in random fashion, but are related sets as shown for the state and stateless clusters described earlier.

The point can be explained by employing David Clarke's distinction between monothetic and polythetic groups (1968, pp. 35–42). If extinct prehistoric societies belonged to entire genus-sets consisting of unique configurations of core attributes having no close counterparts in historical societies, they would be monothetic groups or entities:

To the archaeologist the process of grouping objects into sensible groups, clusters or sequences has been a normal activity for decades. The nature of these groupings seemed quite clear; one made a list of attributes intuitively prejudging that it would give the 'best' grouping and then placed entities in the group if they possessed the attributes and outside if they did not. The intended nature of these groups was also

TABLE 1.1. *A model for archaeological entities, suggesting that these are structured as polythetic group populations and may not be treated as monothetic ones*

Attributes or artifacts	A	B	C	D	E	F	G	H	I	J	K	L	
1	×	×	×	×	×	×							
2	×	×	×	×	×	×							Monothetic group
3	×	×	×	×	×	×							
4	×	×	×	×	×	×							
5	×	×	×	×	×	×							
6							×	×	−	×	−	−	
7							−	×	×	−	−	×	Polythetic group
8							×	−	×	×	×	×	
9							−	×	−	×	×	−	
10							×	−	×	−	×	×	

× present   − absent
Source: Clarke 1968, p. 37.

transparently clear, they were solid and tangible defined entities like an artefact type or a cultural assemblage, each possessed a necessary list of qualifying attributes and they could be handled like discrete and solid bricks. This class of group is well known to taxonomists and is called a monothetic group – a group of entities so defined that the possession of a unique set of attributes is both sufficient and necessary for membership [Table 1.1] (Sokal and Sneath 1963, p. 13). The model for archaeological entities was a monothetic model. (1968, pp. 35, 37)

He goes on to argue that prehistoric societies (entities, groups, cultures) were polythetic, as he defines the term in words and portrays it in Table 1.1. So too are the attributes of the societies studied by historians and anthropologists polythetic, as he demonstrates in detail for American Indians and several other populations of historical record in chapter 9 of *Analytical Archaeology*.

The monothetic box of bricks model is still the prevailing concept tacitly underlying the definition of most archaeological entities. Prehistorians still seem to think that in order to define groups it is necessary that every member within the group must have all the qualifying attributes. In practice this ideal has never been demonstrated in archaeology; no group of cultural assemblages from a single culture ever contains, nor ever did contain, all of the cultural artefacts; no groups of artefacts within a single type population are ever identical in their lists of attributes. Instead, we are conscious that these groups are defined by a range of variation between defined limits, by populations of attributes or types of which a high proportion are variously shared between individual members of the group. This situation is not a monothetic grouping at all but belongs to the other great class of taxonomic groups – the polythetic groups [Table 1.1] (Sokal and Sneath 1963, pp. 13–15).

(Clarke 1968, p. 37)

He then defines a polythetic group and says that the model of polythetic groups will form the basis for much of the rest of his book, as, he believes, it should form the basis for all theorising in archaeology. To which I would add that the recognition of the polythetic nature of all human societies should be the basis for all analytical comparisons in anthropology and history as well. For our purposes, an 'entity' is a society and a 'group' is a genus-cluster.

A polythetic group is – a group of entities such that each entity possesses a large number of the attributes of the group, each attribute is shared by large numbers of entities and no single attribute is both sufficient and necessary to the group membership. Whereas there is only one form of monothetic group there are many varieties of polythetic grouping according to the number of shared attributes, the maximum and minimum number of attributes shared between any pair and the number of attributes possessed by each individual. One of the most important future tasks is going to be the definition of the precise nature of the polythetic groupings underlying archaeological taxonomy...this work will proceed on the assumption that the best model for most archaeological entities is a polythetic model of some kind. The later chapters will attempt to build up a soundly based hierarchy of defined entity concepts using this model and will pursue its far-reaching implications.

(Clarke 1968, pp. 37–8)

To apply this very useful distinction: every society or community of human beings conventionally is assigned to one or more loose classifications which puts it into a group category of some sort, so that every single society known to historians and anthropologists is a member of a set, group, or cluster containing other members, such as hunting band, lineage, clan, tribe, peasantry, kingdom, feudal society, nation. Whatever the group designation, every member society of every designated group has an economic system of some sort, as the term economic system was defined and illustrated earlier. In today's world of nation-states, we find it useful to employ three polythetic designations for grouping national economies: capitalism, communism, and underdeveloped, which are not mutually exclusive (China and Vietnam are both communist and underdeveloped). The designations are polythetic because no two nations bearing the same designation – capitalist Britain and Japan, communist Poland and the U.S.S.R., underdeveloped India and Nigeria – have identical economic attributes, although the members of each set have common core attributes which explain why we group them together. Another reason why the designations are polythetic is that a single attribute (e.g. industrialisation) is shared by nations we assign to different groups (capitalist Britain and communist Poland are both industrialised).

THE CASE FOR ETHNOGRAPHIC PARALLELS

We can now assemble the pieces of the puzzle to justify the use of anthropological evidence and models in archaeological interpretation.

Prehistoric societies were definitely like those studied by historians and anthropologists in that their modes of material provisioning were constrained by the absence of two or all three of the structures that provision capitalist nations today.

What seem to be constants in the historical and anthropological record, the threats of famine and warfare, very likely were constants for prehistoric societies also. If so, one can expect to find in the prehistoric record evidence for the institutionalisation of similar sorts of coping devices, including several sorts of alliance with outside societies, socially controlled long-distance trade, and religious beliefs centring on the supernatural determination of important worldly events and in the efficacy of influencing supernatural agencies by some combination of ritual, speech acts and sacrifice. There seem to be no atheists in burial mounds. But how the threats of famine and warfare are coped with and how the supernatural is beseeched and trade conducted will differ systematically in state and stateless societies.

If one means by extinct societies a species and not an entire genus, it seems quite likely to me that species-mates or genus-mates of the extinct species existed in historical times. If one means by an extinct genus one having no genus-mates surviving into historical times – a monothetic structure none of whose defining attributes existed in historical societies – it would have to be a genus whose component member-societies contained human beings whose biological needs for goods and services were markedly different from those of even the most primitive persons in hunting bands; or social groupings whose community needs (defence, religion, dispute settlement, marriage) were markedly different from those that appear to be constants in the historical and anthropological record; that is, social groups not having to cope with the threats of hunger and warfare, not believing in the supernatural determination of worldly events, not having to marry beyond a certain kin distance, not organised into groupings such as extended families, lineages, clans and kingdoms, and not making use of natural resources, technology and practices such as external trade. This may be plausible for groups of apes, but not, it seems to me, for societies of men and women.

Several times I have come across the phrase 'human behaviour' as that which some archaeologists hope to reconstruct persuasively by astute professional analysis of the artifacts they recover. I think this is an important conceptual error, and one that is related to the themes of this paper. The most they can hope to reconstruct is the type of culture group, the sort of gross economic-political-social structure of the group (the genus-set it belongs in), and its necessarily associated institutional correlates, such as the correlated forms of external trade and monetary usage; not anything as subtle and variable as human behaviour. It seems clear to me in reading, say, the surviving documents of Anglo-Saxon England (Whitelock 1955), or an analysis of the variable employment of tributary relations of alliance by the Ch'ing government (Fairbank 1968a), that archaeologists could not possibly reconstruct from artifacts the complicated rules for crime and punishment in Anglo-Saxon England, or detect the different tributary techniques the Chinese employed to control barbarians. I agree that 'it is impossible to infer social arrangements or institutions, attitudes or beliefs from material objects

TABLE 1.2. *Three polythetic genus-sets of early economies, polities and societies, and some component species*

1. Pre-colonial economies in stateless societies	2. Pre-colonial economies in tribal kingdoms	3. Pre-industrial economies in kingdom-states containing peasantries
Bands without property-owning lineage or clan groupings, social stratification, or known warfare (!Kung Bushmen) Lineages, clans and sections with ceremonial exchange (New Guinea, Trobriands, north-west coast of America, Australia – unusual regional cultural homogeneity; no states in region) Lineages and clans without ceremonial exchange (Nuer, Tallensi – less regional cultural homogeneity; states in region)	Autonomous chiefdoms (Mandari) Feudal kingdom variant, rare (Nkole, Rwanda) Ordinary tribal kingdoms (Lozi, Alur, Baganda) Imperialist kingdoms (Inca) Kingdoms engaged in extensive long-distance trade (Asante, Dahomey – imperialist, larger bureaucracy)	Muslim kingdoms in Africa Feudal kingdoms (Norman England, Tokugawa Japan) Paramount states (Roman Empire, Imperial China)
Core attributes: very small political-jural communities; band, lineage, or clan important units for all activities	*Core attributes*: sacred kings; lineage and clan effective units locally and represented in central government; idiosyncratic religion; primitive food and military technology	*Core attributes*: universal religion; some literacy; superior military technology; standing armies; sedentary agriculture; coined money; market sector and professional merchants; substantial cities; large bureaucracies; large populations and territory

Attributes and institutions shared by some or all member societies in different genus-sets: warfare, famine, territorial rights, belief in supernatural determination of worldly events, social stratification of some sort, relations of external alliance, absence of machine technology and of economy-wide market integration – sets 1, 2, 3. Hunting, gathering, swidden agriculture, bloodwealth, bridewealth, groom-service, primitive technology (absence of wheeled transport and plough) – sets 1, 2. Administered trade, ports of trade, ethnic enclaves of resident aliens engaged in trade, tributary relations of alliance, feudal variants, central government and therefore internal redistribution, *corvée* labour, master–client relationships of some sort – sets 2, 3.

alone' (Finley 1975, p. 93). But an archaeologist can, I believe, use ethnographic and historical parallels to identify the genus-set the society he excavates belonged to, if models of such genus-sets are persuasively shown to have explanatory power and convincing reasons are given to justify the employment of ethnographic and historical parallels.

Table 1.2 lists the three gross socioeconomic structures or polythetic genus-sets I find useful in economic anthropology (before the societies they refer to were made to change by European colonial rule or by industrialisation). They are models, that is conceptual inventions designed to explain something about the real world. The societies we variously call hunter–fisher–gatherer bands, segmentary lineages, or stateless clan segments, clearly belong in the same genus-set because their similarities are greater than their differences when we compare any society within this set to any society in either of the other two sets. How we differentiate the genus-group of pre-colonial economies in stateless societies into component species depends on which of the differences between the member societies in the same larger set we are analytically concerned to emphasise. Hunter–fisher–gatherer bands are usually clustered together and apart from other societies because of their smallness of scale, their seasonal movement to collect different foods and their very simple technology. But many such bands, Australian aborigines for example, do share alliance networks, warfare, ceremonial exchange, and, above all, statelessness, with the yam growers and pig breeders of Highland New Guinea, and the Australian aborigines also come together seasonally into larger encampments for ceremonial and alliance purposes, as do the Kwakiutl of the Northwest Coast. The !Kung Bushmen are a rare exception, who seem not to have lineage and clan organisation or warfare between bands (Marshall 1960). The further species differentiation I list emphasises the point that those employing ceremonial exchange are in those parts of the (pre-colonial) world that had no indigenous kingdoms; those not employing ceremonial exchange were in Africa where kingdoms did exist. What is being emphasised is the difference in relations of hostility and therefore in alliance formation and the political transaction of valuables between the two subgroups in the same larger cluster.

Pre-colonial economies in stateless societies differ less in their attributes and institutions than the members of the second genus-set, tribal kingdoms, all of whose member-societies have sacred kingship, an important redistributive sector, tributary relations of alliance, effective lineage or clan organisation at the local level and clan roles in central government (hence 'tribal' kingdoms).

I list four species variations, but again, the overriding justification for grouping within the same large cluster is that the similarities among the several species are greater than their differences *when we compare them to societies in the other large clusters*. There seem to be relatively few societies reported in the anthropological literature which are autonomous chiefdoms, that is chiefdoms without kingdoms, the Mandari of southern Sudan being the best case I could find (Buxton 1958). Upon examination, a number of chiefdoms without kingdoms turn out to be wrongly labelled so. Surely this is the case in Malinowski's Trobriands, where his 'paramount chief' is actually a big-man head of a sub-clan in a stateless society whose component sub-clans are stratified into dominant and subordinate groupings (Powell 1960). Southall's (1953) excellent account of the Alur (which he calls a 'segmentary state') convinces me it belongs in this large cluster of tribal kingdoms, along with Lozi and Baganda peoples. I agree with him, of course, that Alur lack the core attributes of the third set.

A few tribal kingdoms, like Asante and Dahomey, are hived off as a special subset because they were engaged in extensive trade with Europeans from which several important consequences ensued, such as having ports of trade and administered trade, using gold dust or cowrie within the kingdom in special ways, and having more elaborate social stratification (a result of having larger kingdoms with conquered and tribute-paying peoples on the periphery, more civil and military servants, and more foreign luxuries to distribute to them); indeed, the bureaucratic establishment of the king of Asante flourished to the extent that he hired Muslims and Europeans as scribes and ambassadors (Wilks 1966).

The third genus-set, kingdom-states containing peasantries, is of special interest because it has so many familiar members (kingdoms in early Europe, Japan, China), and refers to what archaeologists call civilisations. Most (perhaps all) the member societies have coined money, literacy, universal religion, substantial cities, formal bureaucracies, a distinctly higher level of military and food technology than tribal kingdoms, a standing army and professional soldiers, very pronounced social stratification, many craft specialists, sedentary agriculture, a market sector and professional merchants (Dalton 1972). In many of these kingdom-states containing peasantries, moreover, lineage and clan cease to be important units of property ownership, religious power, provincial government or central government representation, as they are in many tribal kingdoms.

It seems clear that the very polythetic designation, feudalism, should be regarded merely as a species variant within the larger cluster of kingdom-states containing peasantries. Polanyi (1971b) explains why we find feudal sorts in sets two and three. It seems likely to me that the six hundred years of Anglo-Saxon England began as autonomous chiefdoms and small tribal kingdoms (set two), but rather quickly acquired the core attributes of the third set. I hive off the Roman Empire and Imperial China as comprising a special species because they were paramount states, of unusual cultural and technological achievement, and because of their profound influence on the sizeable portions of the world within their tributary and cultural orbits. But they clearly belong within the genus-set of kingdom-states containing peasantries – Norman England, Charlemagne's France, Tokugawa Japan.

In my view, whatever (if anything) proves to be valuable in the distinctions emphasised by Marx in his 'Asiatic mode of production', or in Wittfogel's hydraulic despotisms, is best regarded as a species difference within this third large genus-set because neither the Asiatic mode nor hydraulic despotism could possibly be defined by monothetic attributes. These genus and species groupings are emphatically polythetic, not monothetic. Although core attributes for each genus-set can be identified, two or all three sets may have common attributes (such as warfare and similar supernatural beliefs in all three, or have the kingdom-state, which is present in the second and third groups alike). I am not at all wedded to the number of species in each set – this depends on the differences between the genus-mates that one is emphasising – or even to the number of sets or genuses, as I am to the underlying idea that employing polythetic groupings and subsets of this sort is necessary to reveal similarities and differences among early socioeconomic systems, and particularly to reveal the special organisation of external trade and usage of monetary objects characteristic of each set. These sets are constructed to serve my interests in economic anthropology. For example, there are structural reasons why we do not find ports of trade and coined money in stateless clan segments, and why we do find in them ceremonial exchange and the usage of primitive valuables in political transactions. It is these structural reasons I want to get at by employing genus-sets. One cannot do so without comparing societies *from all three sets* (for exactly the same reason that one cannot see what is structurally distinctive of Oxford unless one compares it to the University of Moscow and to Texas A. and M.).

Archaeologists, anthropologists, and historians are confronted with similarities and differences among many societies of time and place. One of our tasks, as David Clarke's entire body of work powerfully argues, is to invent conceptual models which enable us to extract what is important and not obvious from a welter of diversity, and to explain in persuasive fashion why what we have extracted is important by adducing evidence. There is no way to do this without constructing models. As David quite rightly said, 'Let a million models grow.' There are not, as Marxians quite wrongly believe, true and false models of the real world, such as the groupings in Table 1.2, but only revealing and misleading models we invent (not discover) in order to make specific analytical points about those aspects of the real world we are studying. Hence the importance I attribute to the principles of grouping to be employed. To group is to model for a specific purpose.

My own long involvement in paradigm disputes makes me doubt that archaeologists will be able to resolve theirs quickly. We in economic anthropology are lucky enough to have much more hard factual information than archaeologists have, but even so have not yet resolved the paradigm disputes among formalists, substantivists and Marxists in the more than twenty years since *Trade and Market in the Early Empires* was published (Polanyi *et al.* 1957). Having much less evidence and more paradigms in rivalry, resolution in archaeology will almost certainly take longer. The comparison is deliberately chosen and quite appropriate: the undetected semantic confusions, the unlovely nationalistic animosities, doctrinal incompatibilities and vociferous advocacy displayed in the Chang (1967) and Klejn (1973) fireworks are quite up to formalist-substantivist-Marxist standards (e.g., Cook 1966; Semenov 1974; Dalton 1969; 1976). All of us would benefit from following David Clarke's Wittgensteinian suggestion: 'the first task of the archaeologist interested in developing the power of his discipline is to concern himself with the careful definition of terms and the isolation of conceptual entities of value. ..only in such a way can order gradually be brought to a confused situation' (1968, p. 27). We would also benefit from following his Popperian suggestion: 'Archaeologists have concentrated far too much upon increasing the quantity of their data and far too little upon increasing the quality of their conceptual apparatus' (1968, p. 636).

ACKNOWLEDGEMENTS

I am grateful to Philip Grierson and Jasper Köcke for their critical comments.

REFERENCES

Adams, R. M. (1974), 'Anthropological perspectives on ancient trade', *Current Anthropology* 15: 239–58

Allan, W. (1965). *The African Husbandman*, Oliver and Boyd

Barraclough, G. (1957). *The Origins of Modern Germany*, Capricorn Books

Beattie, J. (1959). 'Checks on the abuse of political power in some African states', *Sociologus* 9: 97–115

Berndt, R. M. (1964). 'Warfare in the New Guinea Highlands', *American Anthropologist* 66: 183–203

Bloch, M. (1975). *Marxist Analyses and Social Anthropology*, Malaby Press

Buxton, J. (1958). 'The Mandari of the Southern Sudan' in J. Middleton and D. Tait (eds.) *Tribes without Rulers*, Routledge and Kegan Paul

Chagnon, N. A. (1968). 'Yanomamö social organization and warfare' in M. Fried, M. Harris, and R. Murphy (eds.) *War: The Anthropology of Armed Conflict and Aggression*, Natural History Press

Chang, K. C. (1967). 'Major aspects of the interrelationship of archaeology and ethnology', *Current Anthropology* 8: 227–42

Chilver, E. M. (1961). 'Nineteenth century trade in the Bamenda Grassfields, Southern Cameroons', *Afrika und Ubersee* 45: 233–58

Clarke, D. L. (1968). *Analytical Archaeology*, Methuen
(1970). 'Reply to comments on Analytical Archaeology', *Norwegian Archaeological Review* 3: 25–33
(1972a). 'Models and paradigms in contemporary archaeology' in D. L. Clarke (ed.) *Models in Archaeology*, Methuen
(1972b). 'A provisional model of an Iron-Age society and its settlement system' in D. L. Clarke (ed.) *Models in Archaeology*, Methuen

Cook, C. S. (1966). 'The obsolete anti-market mentality: a critique of the substantivist approach to economic anthropology', *American Anthropologist* 68: 323–45

Dalton, G. (1961). 'Economic theory and primitive society', *American Anthropologist* 63: 1–25

   (1969). 'Theoretical issues in economic anthropology', *Current Anthropology* 10: 63–102

   (1971). *Traditional Tribal and Peasant Economies: an Introductory Survey of Economic Anthropology*, Addison-Wesley Publishing Co.

   (1972). 'Peasantries in anthropology and history', *Current Anthropology* 13: 385–415

   (1974). *Economic Systems and Society*, Penguin.

   (1976). 'Review of A. G. Hopkins, an economic history of West Africa', *African Economic History* 1: 51–101

   (1977a). 'Aboriginal economies in stateless societies' in T. K. Earle and J. Ericson (eds.) *Exchange Systems in Prehistory*, Academic Press

   (1977b). 'Economic anthropology', *American Behavioral Scientist* 20: 635–56

   (1978a). 'The impact of colonization on aboriginal economies in stateless societies' in G. Dalton (ed.) *Research in Economic Anthropology*. vol. 1, JAI Press

   (1978b). 'Comment: what kinds of trade and market?', *African Economic History* 5: (in press)

   (1978c). 'Comment on ports of trade in early medieval Europe', *Norwegian Archaeological Review* 11: 102–8

Dupuis, J. (1824). *Journal of a Residence in Ashantee*, Cass (reprint)

Evans-Pritchard, E. E. (1962). 'The divine kingship of the Shilluk of the Nilotic Sudan' in *Essays in Social Anthropology*, Faber and Faber

Elvin, M. (1973). *The Pattern of the Chinese Past*, Stanford University Press

Fairbank, J. K. (1968a). *The Chinese World Order*, Harvard University Press

   (1968b). 'A preliminary framework' in J. K. Fairbank (ed.) *The Chinese World Order*, Harvard University Press

Fairbank, J. K. and Teng, S. Y. (1960). *Ch'ing Administration: Three Studies*, Harvard University Press

Finley, M .I. (1973). *The Ancient Economy*, Chatto and Windus

   (1975). 'Archaeology and history' in *The Use and Abuse of History*, Viking Press

Firth, R. (1940). *The Work of the Gods in Tikopia*, Percy Lund, Humphries

   (1967). *Themes in Economic Anthropology*, Tavistock

   (1972). 'Methodological issues in economic anthropology', *Man* 7: 467–75

Forde, D. and Kaberry, P. M. (1967). *West African Kingdoms in the Nineteenth Century*, Oxford University Press

Fortes, M. and Evans-Pritchard, E. E. (1940). *African Political Systems*, Oxford University Press

Fried, M. H. (1967). *The Evolution of Political Society*, Random House

Gluckman, M. (1943). *Essays on Lozi Land and Royal Property* (Rhodes-Livingstone Paper No. 10), Rhodes-Livingstone Institute

   (1961). 'The Lozi of Barotseland in northwestern Rhodesia' in E. Colson and M. Gluckman (eds.) *Seven Tribes of British Central Africa*, Manchester University Press

Gray, R. and Birmingham, D. (1970). *Precolonial African Trade*, Oxford University Press

Grierson, P. (1959). 'Commerce in the dark ages: a critique of the evidence', *Transactions of the Royal Historical Society, Fifth Series* 9: 123–40

   (1978). 'The origins of money' in G. Dalton (ed.) *Research in Economic Anthropology*, vol. 1, JAI Press

Heider, K. (1969). 'Visiting trade institutions', *American Anthropologist* 71: 462–71

Hicks, J. (1969). *A Theory of Economic History*, Oxford University Press

Hodges, R. (1978). 'Ports of trade in early medieval Europe', *Norwegian Archaeological Review* 11: 97–101

Hopkins, A. G. (1973). *An Economic History of West Africa*, Columbia University Press

Karugire, S. R. (1971). *A History of the Kingdom of Nkore in Western Uganda to 1896*, Clarendon Press

Klejn, L. S. (1973). 'On major aspects of the interrelationship of archaeology and ethnology', *Current Anthropology* 14: 311–20

Köcke, J. (1979). 'Some early German contributions to economic anthropology' in G. Dalton (ed.) *Research in Economic Anthropology*, vol. 2, JAI Press

Kraay, C. M. (1964). 'Hoards, small change and the origin of coinage', *Journal of Hellenic Studies* 84: 76–91

Lamberg-Karlovsky, C. C. (1975). 'The third millenium modes of exchange and modes of production' in J. A. Sabloff and C. C. Lamberg-Karlovsky (eds.) *Ancient Civilization and Trade*, University of New Mexico Press

Law, R. (1977). 'Royal monopoly and private enterprise in the Atlantic trade: the case of Dahomey', *Journal of African History* 18: 555–77

Lombard, J. (1967). 'The kingdom of Dahomey' in D. Forde and P. M. Kaberry (eds.) *West African Kingdoms in the Nineteenth Century*, Oxford University Press

Mair, L. (1962). *Primitive Government*, Penguin
    (1977). *African Kingdoms*, Oxford University Press

Malinowski, B. (1935). *Coral Gardens and their Magic*, American Book Company

Mancall, M. (1968). 'The Ch'ing tribute system: an interpretative essay' in J. K. Fairbank (ed.) *The Chinese World Order*, Harvard University Press

Maquet, J. (1961). *The Premise of Inequality in Ruanda*, Oxford University Press
    (1970). 'Rwanda castes' in A. Tuden and L. Plotnicov (eds.) *Social Stratification in Africa*, Free Press

Marshall, A. (1890). *Principles of Economics*, Macmillan

Marshall, L. (1960). '!Kung Bushman bands', *Africa* 30: 325–54

Mauss, M. (1954). *The Gift*, Free Press

Middleton, J. and Tait, D. (1958). *Tribes without Rulers*, Routledge

Murra, J. (1956). 'The economic organization of the Inca state', unpublished Ph.D. dissertation, University of Chicago

Myrdal, G. (1957). *Rich Lands and Poor*, Harper's

Nadel, S. F. (1942). *A Black Byzantium, the Kingdom of Nupe in Nigeria*, Oxford University Press

North, D. and Thomas, R. (1973). *The Rise of the Western World*, Cambridge University Press

Oberg, K. (1940). 'The kingdom of Ankole in Uganda' in M. Fortes and E. E. Evans-Pritchard (eds.) *African Political Systems*, Oxford University Press

Oppenheimer, F. (1914). *The State: Its History and Development Viewed Sociologically*, Vanguard Press

Ortiz, S. (1967). 'The structure of decision-making among Indians of Colombia' in R. Firth (ed.) *Themes in Economic Anthropology*, Tavistock

Polanyi, K. (1944). *The Great Transformation*, Rinehart
    (1947). 'Our obsolete market mentality', *Commentary* 3: 109–17
    (1957). 'The economy as instituted process' in K. Polanyi, C. M. Arensberg, and H. W. Pearson (eds.) *Trade and Market in the Early Empires*, Free Press

(1966). *Dahomey and the Slave Trade*, University of Washington Press

(1968). *Primitive, Archaic, and Modern Economies : Essays of Karl Polanyi*, Beacon Press

(1971a). 'Carl Menger's two meanings of economic' in G. Dalton (ed.) *Studies in Economic Anthropology*, American Anthropological Association

(1971b). 'Primitive feudalism and the feudalism of decay' in G. Dalton (ed.) *Economic Development and Social Change*, Natural History Press

(1975). 'Traders and trade' in J. A. Sabloff and C. C. Lamberg-Karlovsky (eds.) *Ancient Civilization and Trade*, University of New Mexico Press

Polanyi, K., Arensberg, C. M. and Pearson, H. W. (eds.) (1957). *Trade and Market in the Early Empires*, Free Press

Powell, H. A. (1960). 'Competitive leadership in Trobriand political organization', *Journal of the Royal Anthropological Institute* 90: 118–45

Radcliffe-Brown, A. R. (1940). 'Preface' in M. Fortes and E. E. Evans-Pritchard (eds.) *African Political Systems*, Oxford University Press

Roscoe, J. (1911). *The Baganda*, Macmillan

(1923). *The Banyankole*, Cambridge University Press

Rosman, A. and Rubel, P. (1971). *Feasting with Mine Enemy*, Columbia University Press

Samuelson, P. A. (1976). *Economics*, McGraw-Hill

Sands, P. C. (1908). *The Client Princes of the Roman Empire under the Republic*, Cambridge University Press

Schneider, H. K. (1974). *Economic Man, the Anthropology of Economics*, Free Press

Semenov, Y. I. (1974). 'Theoretical problems of economic anthropology', *Philosophy of the Social Sciences* 4: 201–31

Service, E. (1975). *Origins of the State and Civilization*, Norton

Sherratt, A. G. (1972). 'Socio-economic and demographic models for the Neolithic and Bronze Ages of Europe' in D. L. Clarke (ed.) *Models in Archaeology*, Methuen

Smith, M. G. (1967). 'A Hausa kingdom: Maradi under Dan Baskore, 1854–75' in D. Forde and P. M. Kaberry (eds.) *West African Kingdoms in the Nineteenth Century*, Oxford University Press

Sokal, R. R. and Sneath, P. H. A. (1963). *Principles of Numerical Taxonomy*, W. H. Freeman

Southall, A. W. (1953). *Alur Society*, Heffer

Strathern, A. (1971). *The Rope of Moka : Big-Men and Ceremonial Exchange in Mount Hagen, New Guinea*, Cambridge University Press

Swadesh, M. (1948). 'Motivations in Nootka warfare', *Southwestern Journal of Anthropology* 4: 76–93.

Vansina, J. (1966). *Kingdoms of the Savanna*, University of Wisconsin Press

(1973). *The Tio Kingdom of the Middle Congo, 1880–1892*, Oxford University Press

Vayda, A. P. (1967). 'Pomo trade feasts' in G. Dalton (ed.) *Tribal and Peasant Economies*, Natural History Press

Vidal-Naquet, P. (1972). 'The function of money in Archaic Greece' in W. I. Davison and J. E. Harper, *European Economic History*, vol. 1, *The Ancient World*, Appleton-Century-Crofts

Wang, Yi-T'ung (1953). *Official Relations between China and Japan 1368–1549*, Harvard University Press

Weber, Max (1958). *From Max Weber: Essays in Sociology*, ed. H. Gerth and C. W. Mills, Oxford University Press

Wedgewood, C. V. (1964). *The Trial of Charles I*, Collins

White, L. A. (1949). *The Science of Culture*, Grove Press

Whitelock, D. (1955). *English Historical Documents, c. 500–1042*, Eyre and Spottiswoode

Wilks, I. (1966). 'The position of Muslims in Metropolitan Asante' in I. M. Lewis (ed.) *Islam in Tropical Africa*, Oxford University Press

(1975). *Asante in the Nineteenth Century*, Cambridge University Press

Wills, J. E. (1968). 'Ch'ing relations with the Dutch' in J. K. Fairbank (ed.) *The Chinese World Order*, Harvard University Press

Wittfogel, K. A. (1957). *Oriental Despotism*, Yale University Press

Yu, Y. S. (1967). *Trade and Expansion in Han China*, University of California Press

2

Kalinga pottery: an ethnoarchaeological study

WILLIAM LONGACRE

There is long-standing concern among anthropological archaeologists with both the behaviour and the organisation of extinct societies. For example, anthropologists in the southwestern United States, working before the turn of the century, saw archaeology as the means for extending ethnology into antiquity. Some workers such as Fewkes and Cushing developed reputations for both their ethnological and archaeological contributions.

To solve questions about the nature of societies that existed in the past, some workers often made simplifying assumptions about the reflections of organisation and behaviour in cultural materials. Interest in the ways in which patterns in cultural materials reflect aspects of behaviour and organisation has continued in American anthropology to this day. Recent research has emphasised empirical approaches and ever more subtle relationships.

There appear to be two ways to refine the methods and theory to gain a more precise understanding about the ways in which organisational and behavioural aspects of societies are reflected in material culture. One involves the generation of models relating variables of behaviour to variability in the material domain and the testing of the model archaeologically. Such testing is difficult since archaeologists cannot examine behaviour independent of material culture. However, archaeologists interested in the possibility of demonstrating types of post-marital residence behaviour among extinct societies have adopted this approach.

Assuming female potters and that pottery making was learned and trans-mitted within the nuclear family, one would expect the development of micro-traditions of style through time. If residence tended to be uxorilocal, then these micro-traditions should appear spatially isomorphic with significant architectural units in a community. Stylistic variability of assumed male-produced items should not cluster spatially.

Archaeologists have tested this model initially in ethnohistorical contexts (Deetz 1965) and subsequently in prehistoric sites in Arizona (Hill 1970; Longacre 1970). The results of these tests have tended to be positive and have provided some confidence in our ability to ask questions about behavioural aspects of extinct peoples that are not conspicuously observable in the archaeological record (for a contrasting view see chapter 3).

The second approach involves the testing of such models among extant peoples where the investigator could control both the behaviour and the material variability at the same time. This form of investigation is becoming increasingly important among archaeologists (as ethnoarchaeology). But it is also an approach to research that is important among cultural anthropologists (e.g., Brown 1974) as well as to cultural geographers (e.g., Newton 1974). Fenton (1974) presents a review of material culture studies in anthropology and Oswalt (1974), Gould (1974) and Stanislawski (1974) present recent general discussions of ethnoarchaeology.

Ethnoarchaeology or archaeological ethnography or 'living archaeology' or 'action archaeology' is becoming an increasingly important source of information and method for archaeologists. The initial call to 'action archaeology' was made more than twenty years ago (Kleindienst and Watson 1956). Two years later the first monograph reporting the results of such a study was published (Thompson 1958).

Since that time a number of archaeologists have undertaken fieldwork in an ethnographic context to provide useful observations for archaeological inference. It is fair to say that many of these studies have been accomplished with hunter–gatherer populations throughout the world. For example, in 1968 an entire volume largely devoted to reports of such fieldwork and its integration with archaeological interpretation was published (Lee and DeVore 1968). Gould's work in Western Australia is well reported (1968a; 1968b; 1971; 1973) as is Yellen's work among the Bushmen (1977), and current fieldwork among hunters and gatherers is being undertaken by Binford, Griffin and Wilmsen among others.

Relatively less ethnoarchaeological research has been undertaken among 'tribal societies' to date. The work of David and Hennig (1972) among the Fulani, Longacre and Ayres (1968) with western Apache, Stanislawski (1969a, 1969b) among the Hopi and Hodder amongst the Lozi (ch. 3 below) are examples of such studies.

Our work with stylistic variability in ceramics in prehistoric sites in the southwest had suggested some potential for such analysis as a means for inferring aspects of behaviour and organisation of extinct societies. What seems to be called for is fieldwork in an appropriate ethnographic context where one could control variability in ceramics and other cultural materials as well as the aspects of behaviour and organisation that they might reflect. The ideal field situation would consist of a 'tribal society' with relatively small, permanent villages. Pottery production would be on a household basis for use within the household. And, ideally, the society should have been studied recently by a cultural anthropologist so the sociology of the group would be available.

I stress the fact that pottery and other cultural materials must be made by members of all households in the village for their own use. If pottery is being produced by specialists and distributed in the community, then the situation would be inappropriate for the focus of this study. If pottery is being produced for a market or for tourists, then selective pressures would be operative on potters to produce pots that would 'sell'. This would act to distort the more subtle effects that would tend to produce micro-traditions in a non-market economic system.

The late Edward P. Dozier alerted me to the possibility that an appropriate society for study may be found in the Philippines. He had undertaken fieldwork among the Kalinga, a tribal people living in the mountains of northern Luzon. He thought that pottery production and use on a household basis was probably still present among the more remote villages in the east Kalinga area. His work resulted in a monograph describing Kalinga society and culture (Dozier 1966), augmenting Barton's earlier work on Kalinga custom law (Barton 1949) and Scott's description of the Madukayan Kalinga (1958). Since then, Lawless (1977) has conducted a cultural ecological study in Pasil and Takaki (1977) has completed a study of exchange at Uma.

There is a long history of pottery making in the Philippines and various anthropologists have presented technical descriptions of various ceramic industries. An excellent example is the detailed description of Buhid pottery presented by Conklin (1953). Among others, Scheans and Solheim have produced a series of articles describing pottery making and drawing cultural historical inferences from ceramic styles and techniques (cf. Scheans 1965; 1966; Solheim 1952; 1954; 1959; 1964; 1965). But no comparable work on Kalinga pottery making was available.

The possibility that the Kalinga might indeed present an ideal field situation led me to undertake a field trip to the area to assess the situation. I spent a month in the Philippines in 1973 and visited several Kalinga villages along the Pasil River in northern Luzon. Pottery was being made on a household basis and the people told me I would be welcome to live among them for a long-term study. I returned to the area for twelve months of fieldwork during 1975–6.

The Kalinga are one of a cluster of interesting tribal peoples inhabiting the rugged central cordillera of northern Luzon. These tribes have long been of interest to anthropologists because of a number of features they share including bilateral descent, the presence of the blood feud with 'head hunting' and an impressive codified custom law and the institution of the peace-pact.

The Kalinga in Pasil live in small villages of from 200 to 500 people located on Pleistocene terraces overlooking the major rivers in the area. They are intensive rice agriculturalists raising two crops a year in irrigated terrace fields. In addition, they raise a variety of vegetable crops in swidden plots, a variety of tropical fruits as well as coffee, tobacco, and chili. They also raise water buffalo (carabao), pigs, dogs, and chickens – sources of meat protein on ritual occasions.

Most of my fieldwork was focussed upon the village of Dangtalan located

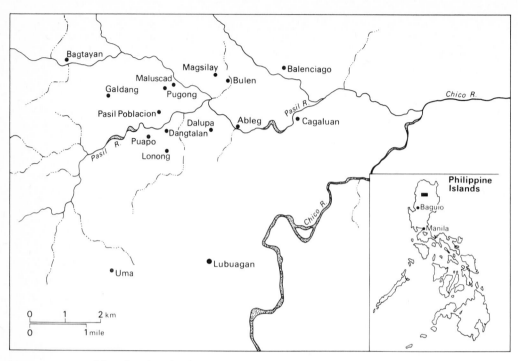

Map showing the field study area.

at an elevation of about 760 m on a Late Pleistocene terrace overlooking the Pasil River (Fig. 2.1). I also worked with potters from two small satellite communities, Puapo and Lonong, as well as with a small sample of potters from a second community, Dalupa.

Dangtalan consists of about 270 people distributed among some fifty-five households (Fig. 2.2). The town is arranged into three named, ward-like divisions (*Kigad*) which figure prominently in the defensive strategy of the community. These divisions are also used to schedule pan-community work groups as well as to organise various social and ritual events. The *Kigad* boundaries are marked by low stone walls in the Pasil communities although there is some distortion of the original spatial boundaries in Dangtalan. This was the result of the rebuilding of the community after a fire completely destroyed the village in 1955.

These ward-like divisions are important in understanding the defensive posture of Kalinga communities. Young men from about age fifteen until marriage sleep together in one house (*appon*) by division. In Dangtalan, this places three groups of young men together every night distributed across the village ready to respond as a unit to a raid. The *Kigad* are important in various aspects of Kalinga political and social life yet, as far as I can tell, they are unreported in the ethnographic accounts.

Pottery is made by virtually every household in Dangtalan and is in

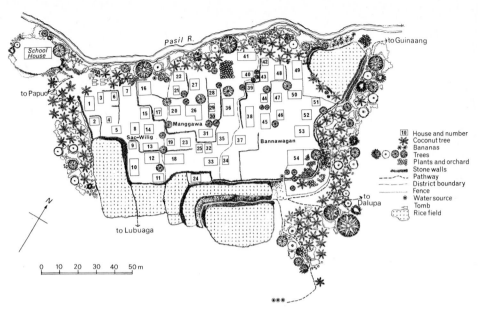

DANGTALAN BARRIO

2.2.   Plan of the Kalinga village (Barrio) of Dangtalan.

TABLE 2.1. *Kalinga pottery classification*

	Small size for one or two people	Regular size for four to six people	Large size for a number of people	Very large *c.* 140 l
Rice cooking	*Oggatit* *Ittoyom*	*Ittoyom*	*Lallangan* *Ittoyom*	
Vegetable/ meat cooking	*Oggatit* *Oppaya*	*Oppaya*	*Lallangan* (*oggan*) *Oppaya*	*Challay*
Water jar		*Immosso*		

Special categories:
  Im-immosso – a small version of the water jar used by young girls to learn to carry water jars balanced on their heads
  Amuto – wine jar, conical in shape, large
  Volnay – smaller wine jar, more globular in shape
  Pannogan – water basin
  Chong-chong – large size pot cover
  Su-kong – pot cover

widespread everyday use for cooking, water transport and storage, and the brewing and storage of *basi*, a sugarcane wine. The native system of classification focusses upon the projected use of the vessel. Thus, pots for rice cooking are differentiated from vessels for vegetable or meat cooking and water jars as well as wine jars. These classes are further segregated into named categories by size (Table 2.1).

The native system of classification is important because it provides insight into the ways in which this pottery-making and -using society thinks about pots. Many, if not most, such societies classify vessels in terms of functional categories and the Kalinga are no exception. Could a non-Kalinga 'discover' the native types? There are significant size and shape differences among the vessel types as well as other features that are related to functional differences. For example, rice cooking pots have a relatively restricted aperture compared to vegetable cooking pots. They also tend to be taller and narrower. *Ittoyom* (rice cooking pots) have a steeper rim angle as they are used with a cover.

Using a sample of 161 *oppaya* (vegetable/meat cooking pots) and 107 *ittoyom*, one can compare rim angles and aperture to height ratios for the two vessel types. The mean rim angle for *ittoyom* is 48.2° and for *oppaya* it is 44.0°. The aperture to height ratio for *ittoyom* is 0.78 and for *oppaya* it is 1.02. Using these metric data, one could indeed replicate the native system which would reveal functionally significant categories.

Kalinga pottery technology is interesting because the Kalinga potter employs hand modelling, coiling and scraping, and paddle and anvil techniques in building and shaping every pot she makes. Thus, every technique is used except the potter's wheel or the mould. All potters exploit the same clay source located just below the school. The clay contains an abundance of sand as a natural inclusion and no additional temper is added. The clay is mined using a tunnelling technique from the deposit about one metre below the surface. The clay requires no sifting or cleaning.

The clay (*soka*) is carried in a basket to the vicinity of the potter's house. There the clay is pounded with a pestle (*salsal*) on a flat rock (*salsallan*). Small amounts of water are added during this process until the desired consistency is obtained (*tiplyon*). The potter then shapes a lump of the plastic clay into a truncated cone-shaped slab (*pokol*). She places this onto a reused wooden serving plate (*chuyas*) which has been lined with leaves or a piece of plastic to avoid sticking.

The base of the pot is initially formed and the bottom portion of the vessel wall is shaped using a hand modelling technique. Using her fingers, the potter builds the vessel wall up to about one half the height of the vessel. She then adds short, thick coils of clay (*suyong*) to build the vessel to full height. The coils are pinched onto the vessel wall and smoothed with her fingers.

The exterior of the pot is then smoothed and the vessel wall shaped using her fingers and a split bamboo tool (*kilkil*). The *kilkil* has flattened sides and is about 20 cm long (Fig. 2.3). It is occasionally dipped in water and is always used with an upwards motion. The rim of the pot is then formed by adding coils and using the *kilkil*. The final shape and angle of the rim is produced using a cloth to which a little clay is added and dipped in water. The potter holds the cloth (*lapichas*) over the rim with her right hand and rotates the plate clockwise with her left hand until the rim is shaped and smoothed (*man-iisuwon*).

2.3. Kalinga potter using the *kilkil* to smooth a pot.

2.4. A Dangtalan potter using a *gili* to decorate her pots.

Then the pot is placed in the sun (*pakot-ongon*) for about one hour so the upper portion of the pot (*opson*) will dry. The final shaping and smoothing of the exterior wall of the upper portion of the pot is achieved using the *kilkil* and *lapichas* at this stage. The pot is returned to the sun for another hour for further drying. When the rim is fairly dry, it is polished using an opal polishing stone (*ichi-ed*).

After this, the potter adds a stamped and incised decoration just below the neck of the vessel (*bangang*). She uses a small, thin stylus of split bamboo (*gili*), the ends of which are pointed or notched, to impress the design (Fig. 2.4). The decorated zone consists of one or more bands of design (*gili*), although some potters sometimes omit this decoration altogether.

After the *gili* is completed, the pot is returned to the sun, and dried to the leather-hard stage. Then the upper portion of the vessel is thinned and shaped using a tool (*kaga-os*) fashioned from the upper 3 cm of an open tin can. This circular implement is used on the inside of the vessel only; excess clay is scraped away and allowed to accumulate in the bottom of the pot (*ovut*).

The clay in the bottom of the pot is pressed down using an anvil – a cobble sized stone (*vantuk*). This excess clay thickens the bottom of the pot. The vessel is then removed from the plate and the shaping and thinning of the base begins. To do this the potter employs the paddle and anvil technique. She holds the anvil (*vantuk*) against the inside of the base and strikes glancing blows with a small wooden paddle (*pyik-pyik*) (Fig. 2.5). Occasionally dipping the paddle in water, she thins and rounds the bottom of the pot. Smoothing is accomplished using the *kilkil* and *lapichas*.

After the base of the pot is smoothed, the vessel is placed in the sun upside down and dried for about two hours. Then, using the *kaga-os*, she further thins the vessel wall using her fingers to judge the desired thickness as well as the weight of the vessel. A thin wash of clay is applied to the interior of the vessel at this point using a cloth applicator (*usu-os*). A thin, wedge-shaped tool (*inanas*) made from coconut shell is used on the interior to even out the surface. Following this, the interior is finally smoothed using a wet cloth (*lapichas*).

The pot is then placed upside down in the shade to avoid too rapid drying and cracking. Depending on the weather, the pot dries for a half to a full day and then is ready for polishing. The pot is polished using the *ichi-ed* both outside and inside.

After polishing, a red paint (*pula*) is applied. It consists of pulverised red haematite mixed with water and is applied with a cloth. Generally, the paint is applied to the lip of the vessel and in a band or stripe near the zone of stamped decoration (*gili*). Water vessels (*immosso*) have the red paint applied over the entire exterior, providing a stylistic signal of the function of the *immosso*. The red paint is allowed to dry for about thirty minutes and then is polished over. When this is finished, the pot is completely dried in the sun for two to three days and is then ready to be fired.

2.5.   The paddle and anvil technique is used to shape and thin the bottom of the pot.

2.6. Adding split bamboo as fuel for the firing process.

The firing process (*gappya*) takes place in one of two designated places (*gagob*) away from the houses at either end of the village. If a potter has enough pots, she will fire them by herself. But usually three or four potters will fire their pots together. In that case, each potter stacks her own pots, arranges the fuel, lights her side of the fire and tends her pots during the firing.

Firing takes place in the open; no kiln is used. Small stones (*alligatong*) about 10 cm in diameter are arranged in groups of three on the ground. The largest pots are placed on the stones on their sides with the apertures facing out. Smaller pots are placed on these and gradually the stack is built. Dried, split bamboo (*al-al*) is placed in the spaces underneath and around the pots (Fig. 2.6), then dried kogon grass (*gulon*) and dried rice stalks (*iyot*) are added to cover the entire pile.

The fire is ignited from the bottom and after it is well under way the potter will open vents in the fuel using a long stick (*accuchak*). This serves to intensify the combustion of the bamboo fuel. The potter watches the colour of the firing vessels and when they glow red-hot, they are said to be 'cooked'. One or two *accuchak* are used to remove the pots from the stack and they are placed on the ground.

After cooling for a few minutes, the potter applies resin (*libo*) to the pots while they are still quite hot. The resin is applied to the interior of all pots and, for cooking vessels, to the exterior down from the rim to just below the zone of decoration. Resin is applied to the entire interior and exterior of water vessels.

The resin the Kalinga use is dammar collected from pine trees high up in the nearby mountains. The Kalinga term for the tree is *lita-o* and it is of the family Pinaceae, genus *Agathis Philippinensis warb*. The resin impregnates the vessel wall so that it is less porous.

Potters plan about two hours for the entire firing process but the actual firing time is very short, averaging only about twenty minutes. In spite of this, the fire reaches very high temperatures, and the ware produced is hard and well fired.

Mothers teach daughters the art of pottery making. Although the learning process is highly informal, girls from about age five are expected to watch their mothers making pots and gradually begin to practise. By late teens or early twenties most of the daughters are proficient potters, and thus most young women at the time of marriage are prepared to produce the pottery needed at the founding of a new household.

Once the household is established, women tend to produce pottery as members of a pottery-making work group. The work groups consist of from three to twelve women who are neighbours and there are seven such groups in Dangtalan. Although there is a stated preference for uxorilocal post-marital residence, in fact only about sixty per cent of the residence conforms to the rule. Thus, work groups may consist of related potters, but all of them also contain women who are not closely related.

Are there stylistic microtraditions that emerge as a result of the learning frameworks present in Kalinga culture? As mothers teach daughters who, in turn, teach their daughters, are there subtle stylistic correlates in the pottery produced by these related women that would allow us to identify microtraditions? Can individual potters be identified? What is the impact of participating in a pottery-making work group? Is there a village tradition? To answer these and other questions about the material correlates of organisation and behaviour among the Kalinga, I adopted two strategies.

On the one hand, I interviewed Kalinga potters at length to see what they thought the answers to these questions were and I designed some experiments to check the responses received. On the other hand, I selected a sample of potters including three sets of two and three generations to explore learning frameworks and kin groups, four pottery-making work groups and a control group of potters who are neither closely related nor who work together. From the thirty-three potters in my sample, I collected 284 vessels for analysis. Ideally, I wanted to obtain at least ten pots from each potter, but that proved impossible to do in each case. The average number of pots I collected from each potter was 8.6.

The entire sample of pots was ultimately transported to the National Museum of the Philippines in Manila where an intensive analysis was undertaken. This consisted of recording a number of attributes as well as producing detailed descriptions of each pot including drawings. Nearly 125 pots were sent to the University of Arizona at the end of the fieldwork where they are now housed as a part of the permanent collections of the Arizona State Museum. The larger share of the collection remains with the National Museum of the Philippines and both sets of pots are available for further study.

Obviously, for microtraditions to be discernable in the pots produced by Kalinga potters, there must be a one-to-one relationship between the pot and the potter. In other words, each pot must be produced by a single potter; there could not be several potters cooperating to make and decorate the vessels. Among the Kalinga, every pot is produced by a single potter with some rare exceptions.

Sometimes a young girl who has not mastered the complete process will not be able to finish a pot. In that case, the pot will be completed by another woman, almost always her mother. If extraordinary circumstances call a potter away before her pot is finished, she may give the unfinished pot to a member of her work group to complete. If the decoration is added by the second potter, then the pot is said to have been made by her. But the pot belongs to the first potter – the one 'who owns the clay'. If the pot is bartered or sold, it is she who gets the proceeds. The Kalinga I worked with could not remember an example of this occurring in the recent past, and no incident of a second potter completing a pot for another took place during the twelve months I was there.

The Kalinga potters claim that it is easy to identify the maker of a pot by observing a set of stylistic features on the vessel. They say that the most important features include the thickness of the rim, the vessel wall and the base; the length and angle of the lip; the form of the pot including the proportions of the body of the vessel and the length of the lip; and the decoration (*gili*). The Kalinga potters use these observations in identifying the person who made a particular vessel and they further say that the pots made by a mother and her daughters tend to be similar. When asked why, they explain that it results from the daughters watching and imitating their mothers over a period of years while they are learning to become 'expert' potters themselves.

There is a distinctive village style as well. Compared to other Kalinga villages, the pottery of Dangtalan is distinctive. The vessel wall and lip are relatively thicker, the lip is longer and thicker and tends to be less curved. The stamped decoration (*gili*) is relatively more complex. In contrast, the pottery of the nearby community of Dalupa is thinner, the bases of the pots are smoother and the lips tend to be more curved. The *gili* is relatively simple, often consisting of parallel lines. Although I never became proficient enough to be able to identity the maker of a particular pot by inspection, after I had been in the field for a considerable time I was able to identify the pottery from the various Kalinga communities. There are indeed distinctive village styles.

Are the Kalinga potters really able to identify individual potters through an examination of the pots? As I collected pots from my sample of potters, I catalogued them using a running log of vessel numbers and an assigned potter's number. They were stored in the house in which I lived in Dangtalan. After several months of collecting, I attempted an experiment. I took pots that I collected into the community and asked potters to identify the person who had made particular pots. I purposely selected pots that I had collected more than a month before so people would not remember them. Every potter I asked was able to identify the potter without difficulty. During the dry season (March–April), I had three Filipino graduate students in the field with me for six weeks. I had each of them repeat this experiment with pots I had collected six months earlier. Again, the Dangtalan potters had no difficulty in identifying the potters who had made the pots.

Are there discernable microtraditions that reflect the learning frameworks as the Kalinga say there are? An analysis of the nearly 300 vessels I collected from my sample of potters is still being carried out. But the results already obtained suggest that such is the case. An analysis of design elements has been carried out by Michael Graves (n.d.). He employed cross-classification of the design data followed by contingency table analysis in one series of tests and minimum logit chi-square regression in another.

Graves (n.d.) is able to suggest that the relationships between design elements and behaviour are far more complex than the models posited by archaeologists in the 1960s would suggest. He was able to demonstrate a relation between particular design elements and kin groups, but he was also able to identify work groups as well. He further isolated an age effect suggesting that design variability may change during a person's iifetime. He also demonstrated a relationship between the complexity of the *gili* and the season in which pots were produced. His study documents several sources of variability in design elements in addition to the learning framework. His results raise serious questions about the validity of attempting to infer post-marital residence from the distribution of design elements alone in prehistoric sites as we attempted in earlier studies (e.g. Longacre 1970). Analysis of more complex design features such as motifs, motif combinations, and symmetry seem to provide a stronger reflection of social relations and behaviour than design elements themselves.

Let us turn from this exploration of material correlates of behaviour to another important area of archaeological method and theory: understanding site formation processes. Space does not permit an extensive discussion of formation processes that I observed among the Kalinga, but certain observations are worth noting. In particular I was interested in the use life of various categories of pottery, the causes of pottery discard, and patterns of disposal.

The Kalinga say that pots do not break very often, but they do wear out. A pot is worn out when the resin dissipates and the interior begins to turn white. They say that rice begins to taste bad when a pot is worn out and they will no longer use it for cooking. Such a pot is then *chacha-an* and is generally reused for another purpose. A worn or even a cracked vessel may be used as a roasting pan for toasting coffee beans, for example. When that happens the pot is no longer an *oppaya* or *ittoyom* in the native system of classification; such a reused pot for toasting is labelled *linga*.

The Kalinga say that cooking pots, if they are careful, will last up to five years. Such a pot would be *loog*, 'very old'. Normally, they say, a cooking vessel in everyday use will last between two to three years. Water jars will last longer, up to ten or fifteen years. Wine jars 'will last forever if you are careful'. Thus, if the pot does not break, its use life should be measured in years rather than months. The people say that normally a family will break a pot only once every month or two. Breakage rates are highest during the wet season when the trails to the two village water sources are wet and slippery.

I adopted two approaches to monitor use life of Kalinga pottery. I made an inventory of all the pots in each house in Dangtalan and four other Kalinga villages, recording the potter, when each was made, and the *gili* of each. This resulted in a sample of nearly 1000 vessels. In addition, I monitored the breakage and wearing out of pots over the twelve months I conducted fieldwork in Dangtalan.

Rice cooking vessels tend to last slightly longer than vegetable cooking pots, but they both average about two years of use. Water jars tend to last three times as long and wine jars perhaps ten times as long. The larger rice and vegetable cooking pots last, on average, nine or ten years. As a general principle, the larger the pot the longer it lasts, and, as might be expected, use life is directly related to frequency of use.

Pottery breakage is about a monthly phenomenon as the Kalinga suggested. About ten per cent of the breakage in Dangtalan is caused by dogs. These animals are not pets and, except for special hunting dogs, are not fed or cared for by their owners. They scavenge for their food and, if a house is left unattended, they will enter and attempt to eat the contents of cooking pots left on the hearth. In the process, the pot is often knocked off the supports and breaks. Most commonly pots are broken by children, usually on the paths to or from the springs or at the spring as they are cleaning them.

If a pot breaks in the house, it is taken to the midden on the north side of the community and carefully placed under a tree or bush. They do so 'because a pot has a spirit too'. If a pot is broken in the village, the pieces are gathered and carried to the midden. The open areas among the houses have very few sherds in evidence as they are periodically swept. The densest sherd deposits are adjacent to the trails that lead to the water sources and at the springs themselves.

Thus we could expect to find very little sherd material associated with the habitation area in Dangtalan. But if the village had to be abandoned, the people say they would not take their pots. Rather they would carry seeds, food, weapons, items of wealth, and clothing. Since the majority of pots in the house are made by the woman who lives there, we would be able to use these pots to study aspects of behaviour and organisation by household.

The implications for archaeology resulting from this research are many. The findings bolster our suspicion that aspects of the behaviour and organisation of people are subtly encoded in stylistic correlates in the materials they make and use. Discovering these correlates gives us a powerful tool for studying patterns of behaviour and organisation in the prehistoric past. But quite clearly, much more attention must be paid to the cultural formation processes responsible for the formation of the archaeological record to make full use of the behavioural correlates and their spatial distributions in the archaeological record. It seems to me that these areas – discerning material correlates of patterns of human organisation and behaviour and assessing the cultural formation processes forming the archaeological record – are two of the most important research frontiers facing the archaeologist of today.

It is appropriate in a book designed to honour the contributions of David Clarke to report the results of this ethnoarchaeological project and to urge that more studies of this sort be undertaken. It is the type of study that he called for in print (e.g., 1972, pp. 23–4) and encouraged me to undertake in conversations and letters. He knew the great potential of such projects for the testing of models that we are interested in, and if this brief report stimulates continued interest in ethnoarchaeology, then its purpose is fulfilled.

ACKNOWLEDGEMENTS

My fieldwork during 1975–6 was supported by a National Science Foundation Grant no. SOC75–19006.

Obviously, none of the results reported here would have been forthcoming had it not been for the generous assistance of the Kalinga people. Their patience with me, their aid and their affection made my stay with them not only possible, but enjoyable. I thank the potters of Dangtalan, the family of Odis with whom I lived, and my two primary Kalinga assistants: Roberto Tima and Rosalina Bala-is. I am grateful to two students who are assisting with the analysis at the University of Arizona: Michael Graves who is undertaking various statistical analyses of decorative features and Mark Baumler for the rim angle measurements and height to width ratios reported here. I thank Brigid Sullivan for drafting Fig. 2.1 and Francisco Boado for Fig. 2.2. Photographs are by the author.

REFERENCES

Barton, R. F. (1949). *The Kalingas, their Institutions and Custom Law*, University of Chicago Press

Brown, Donald N. (1974). 'Social structure as reflected in architectural units at Picuris Pueblo' in M. Richardson (ed.) *The Human Mirror*, Louisiana State University Press

Clarke, David L. (1972). 'Models and paradigms in contemporary archaeology' in D. L. Clarke (ed.) *Models in Archaeology*, Methuen

Conklin, H. C. (1953). 'Buhid pottery', *Journal of East Asiatic Studies* (1): 1–12

David, N. and Henning, H. (1972). 'The ethnography of pottery: a Fulani case seen in archaeological perspective', *McCaleb Module*, 21

Deetz, James F. (1965). 'The dynamics of stylistic change in Arikara ceramics', *Illinois Studies in Anthropology* 4

Dozier, Edward P. (1966). *Mountain Arbiters, The Changing Life of a Philippine Hill People*, University of Arizona Press

Fenton, William N. (1974). 'The advancement of material culture studies in modern anthropological research' in M. Richardson (ed.) *The Human Mirror*, Louisiana State University Press

Gould, Richard A. (1968a). 'Chipping stones in the outback', *Natural History* 77 (1): 42–9

(1968b). 'Living archaeology: the Ngatatjara of Western Australia', *Southwestern Journal of Anthropology* 24: 101–2

(1971). 'The archaeologist as ethnographer: a case from the western desert of Australia', *World Archaeology* 3: 143–77

(1973). 'Australian archaeology in ecological and ethnographic perspective', *Warner Modular Publications* 7

(1974). 'Some current problems in ethnoarchaeology', in C. B. Donnan and C. W. Clewlow, Jr (eds.) *Ethnoarchaeology* Archaeological Survey, Monograph IV Institute of Archaeology, University of California

Graves, M. (n.d.). 'Ethnoarchaeological and archaeological approaches to ceramic design variability'. Preliminary Examination Paper, on file, Arizona State Museum Library, The University of Arizona

Hill, James N. (1970). 'Broken K Pueblo: prehistoric social organization in the American southwest', *Anthropological Papers of the University of Arizona* 18

Kleindienst, M. R. and Watson, P. J. (1956). '"Action archaeology": the archaeological inventory of a living community', *Anthropology Tomorrow* 5 (1): 75–8

Lawless, R. (1977). 'Societal ecology in Northern Luzon: Kalinga agriculture, organization, population, and change', *University of Oklahoma Papers in Anthropology* 18 (1)

Lee, Richard and DeVore, I. (eds.) (1968). *Man the Hunter*, Aldine

Longacre, William A. (1970). 'Archaeology as anthropology: a case study', *Anthropological Papers of the University of Arizona* 17

(1974). 'Kalinga pottery-making: the evolution of a research design', in M. J. Leaf (ed.) *Frontiers of Anthropology*, Van Nostrand

Longacre, W. A. and Ayres, J. E. (1968). 'Archaeological lessons from an Apache Wickiup', in S. Binford and L. Binford (eds.) *New Perspectives in Archeology*, Aldine

Newton, Milton B., Jr (1974). 'Settlement patterns as artifacts of social structure' in M. Richardson (ed.) *The Human Mirror*, Louisiana State University Press

Oswalt, Wendell H. (1974). 'Ethnoarchaeology' in C. B. Donnan and C. W. Clewlow, Jr (eds.) *Ethnoarchaeology* (Archaeological Survey, Monograph IV) Institute of Archaeology, University of California

Scheans, Daniel J. (1965). 'The pottery industry of San Nicholas, Ilocos Norte', *Journal of East Asiatic Studies* 9 (1): 1–28

(1966). 'A new view of Philippines pottery manufacture', *Southwestern Journal of Anthropology* 22 (2): 206–19

Scott, William H. (1958). 'Economic and material culture of the Kalingas of Madukayan', *Southwestern Journal of Anthropology* 14 (3): 318–37

Solheim, W. G. (1952). 'Pottery manufacturing in the islands of Masbate and Batan, Philippines', *Journal of East Asiatic Studies* 1 (1): 49–53

(1954). 'Ibang pottery manufacture in Isabela', *Journal of East Asiatic Studies* 3 (3): 305–7

(1959). 'Further notes on Philippines pottery manufacture: Mountain Province and Panay', *Journal of East Asiatic Studies* 8 (1/2): 1–10

(1964). 'Pottery and the Malayo-Polynesians', *Current Anthropology* 5 (5): 360, 376–84

(1965). 'The functions of pottery in Southeast Asia: from the present to the past', in F. R. Matson (ed.) *Ceramics and Man* (Viking Fund Publications in Anthropology, No. 41)

Stanislawski, Michael B. (1969a). 'What good is a broken pot? An experiment in Hopi-Tewa ethno-archaeology', *Southwestern Lore* 35 (1): 11–18

(1969b). 'The ethno-archaeology of Hopi pottery making', *Plateau* 42 (1): 27–33

(1974). 'The relationships of ethnoarchaeology, traditional, and systems archaeology', in C. B. Donnan and C. W. Clewlow, Jr (eds.) *Ethnoarchaeology* (Archaeological Survey, Monograph IV) Institute of Archaeology, University of California

Takaki, M. (1977). *Aspects of Exchange in a Kalinga Society, Northern Luzon*, University Microfilms International

Thompson, Raymond H. (1958). 'Modern Yucatan Maya pottery making', *Memoirs of the Society for American Archaeology* 15

Yellen, John E. (1977). *Archaeological Approaches to the Present, Models for Reconstructing the Past*, Academic Press

3

Society, economy and culture: an ethnographic case study amongst the Lozi

IAN HODDER

In chapter 9 of *Analytical Archaeology* David Clarke (1968) examined some ethnographic evidence for the structure and significance of material 'cultures'. The ethnographic examples available to him at that time were few in number and ethnoarchaeology had hardly begun. The recent fieldwork in Zambia which is described below and which was stimulated by David Clarke's discussion aims to provide more ethnographic information about cultural patterning at the regional scale. In particular, attention is focussed on the structures of cultural distributions, the human significance that can be attached to certain aspects of material culture patterning (pre-depositional theory), and the analytical techniques most suitable for recovering that significance.

The fieldwork amongst the Lozi in the western province of Zambia was initially concerned with pre-depositional theory – the relationship between human behaviour and material culture. The Lozi occupy the western part of Zambia, centring on the flood plain of the Zambezi. The rich peats of the seasonally flooded plain are largely treeless, while the sands of the surrounding areas (the bush) are lightly wooded. In the rainy season the royal centres and other settlements in the flood plain move to the higher edge of the plain. Many families thus have villages both on the plain's margin and on low mounds in the plain itself. The villages usually comprise the huts, kitchens and stores of an extended family group (Figs 3.1 and 3.2), although larger villages and conglomerations occur, for example at the royal centres of Lealui, Limulunga, Nalolo and Muoyo. Population density is generally low but settlement is clustered along the plain margin and around the edge of *damboe* marshes in the bush areas. The economy is based largely on arable farming, with cattle and fish important in the flood plain.

The villages studies (1977 dry season) occur in different environments in the heart of the Lozi area, Barotseland (Gluckman 1941). The Barotse kingdom was, in the middle of the reign of King Lewanika (1878–1916), approximately 400,000 sq. km in area. Within this kingdom lived about twenty-five Bantu-speaking tribes, many of whom had their main communities outside the realm. Many of these tribes spoke different languages, dialects, and had different social systems. For example, in contrast to the Lozi,

67

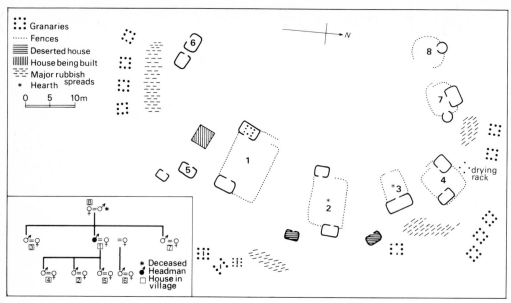

3.1. Plan of a Lozi village (19B) in the Zambezi flood plain. The numbers refer to the individuals in the inset diagram.

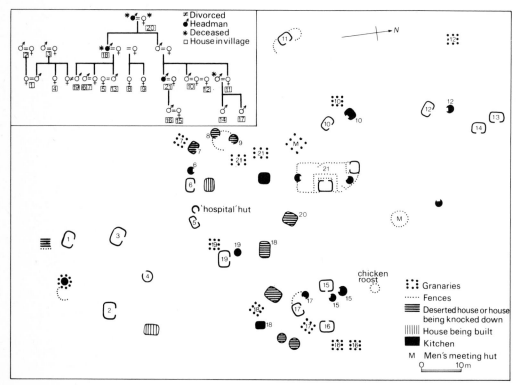

3.2. Plan of Mbunda village (17A). The numbers refer to the individuals in the inset diagram.

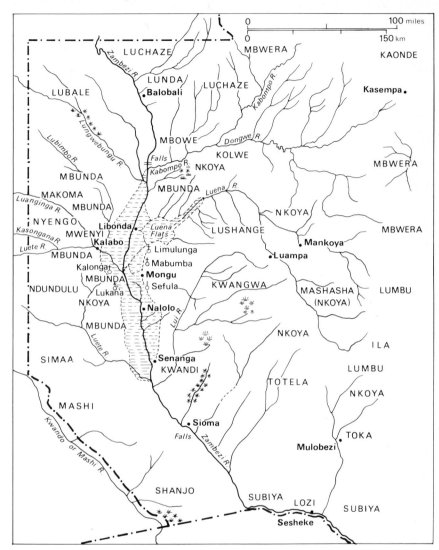

3.3. Turner's (1952) map of the Lozi peoples of western Zambia. The shaded area indicates the flood plain.

Mbunda place an emphasis on matrilineal descent and do not practise male circumcision.

Some attention will be paid here to the nature of 'tribe' in Barotseland. It is necessary to explain this term in the present-day context. The true Lozi are the Kwandi, Mbowe and Kwangwa. Closely allied and assimilated tribes who sometimes call themselves true Lozi are Nkoya, Nyengo and Shanjo, who, in the past, were not subject to raiding. Raiding of Ila and Toka was carried out in the past and these tribes form part of the Ila-Tonga group (including the Tonga, Totela and Subiya) who also sometimes call themselves Lozi. Old Mbunda who immigrated from the west in the earlier nineteenth century have become largely assimilated and may at one time have thought of themselves as Lozi, but newer Mbunda arrivals, together with Luvale, Luchaze, Lunda and Chokwe, would never describe themselves as Lozi, to whomever they were talking. All such immigrants (called *wiko* by the Lozi) are termed Mbunda here, with a subdivision made between Old Mbunda and recent Mbunda, the latter being those who moved into the area less than two generations ago. Problems in the identification of the 'tribes' will be discussed below.

By the end of the nineteenth century Barotseland presented an example of a highly developed 'tribal kingdom' or state (Caplan 1970; Gluckman 1941; Mainga 1973). Dalton on p. 33 of this volume classifies it as a distinctive form of tribal kingdom because of its clan system and its paucity of European trade. In the central area the king and his family held supreme power in military, judicial and administrative matters. District capitals held local power in surrounding areas, but remained subject to the king and forwarded tribute to him. Some foods and metal objects moved to the centre as tribute via district chiefs and non-territorial councillors, and were then redistributed. But most movement of products was by reciprocal gift exchange although long-distance trade items entered the kingdom mainly through the royal centres. There were no markets and there are few now. The Lozi raided peripheral tribes in order to make them pay tribute and in order to obtain servants and slaves.

However, when a British Protectorate was established, the king gave up his rights to try theft, murder, witchcraft and some other offences, and later serfdom (1906) and then tribute (1925) were abolished and royal officials were paid by the British authorities. A new centre, Mongu, developed as the commercial and administrative hub of the province and is now the provincial capital in western Zambia. Yet the royal centres remain, and remain important.

FIELD METHOD

Nowadays, those living near Mongu have jobs in the town and every effort was made to study areas which were not caught up in the wider Zambian economy to this extent. However, all villages in the area contain a considerable number of outside, imported goods while dress is European in style. The traditional manufacture and dispersal of material culture items is fast disappearing in the western province. In view of this it will be necessary to understand the way in which the present situation is affected by the modern world economy before attempting to extrapolate back into the past.

Visits were made to 107 villages (Fig. 3.4) and drawings and measurements taken of all items which occurred in sufficient quantity and which comprised sufficient traits to show stylistic variation. Interest in this study is centred on spatial variation and tribal differences and items were studied which would show the nature of this patterning. Thus complex, often decorated, items were

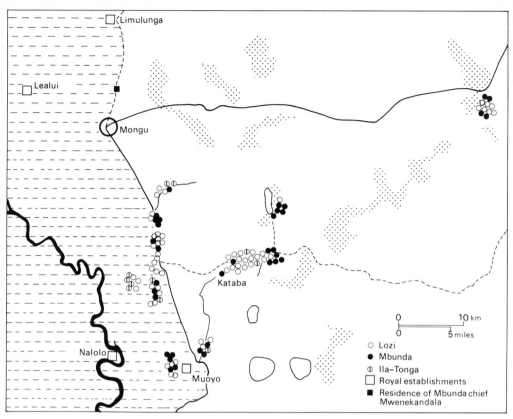

3.4.   The distribution of Lozi, Mbunda and Ila-Tonga villages visited in the Mongu district. The seasonally flooded plain and *damboes* are dotted.

studied in preference to simple undecorated items such as hoes and axes. Where, when and by whom each object was made or obtained were also ascertained. In each village, information was collected on the tribal affiliation of the inhabitants, the length of time the family had lived in the locality, the economic base of the village, and on marriage patterns. Plans were also made of selected villages.

The results obtained in this way, apart from those concerned with measurements of artifacts, suffer from the problems often associated with verbal information. Bad memory, a desire to exaggerate, misunderstanding in the process of translation, a wish to mislead and confuse, plus a host of other factors may have led to incorrect information being collected. Because of this, only the clearest and most unambiguous results will be discussed below.

Particular problems were associated with the assessment of the 'tribal' group to which each individual or village belonged. It will be shown below that cross-tribal marriages do occur and so some difficulty was encountered in assigning a village to a single tribe. This was especially difficult when trying

TABLE 3.1. *The numbers of artifacts (a) made in the village where found, (b) made in a near-by village in the same cluster of villages, (c) made in a village farther afield (more than two miles), and (d) obtained from travelling salesmen (hawkers)*

	a	b	c	d
Spoon	13	1	2	1
Tubana	2	0	8	3
D baskets	16	0	1	0
A, B, C pots	30	11	14	3
Mukeke wa kota	4	2	36	20
A stools	8	4	1	3
A baskets	7	12	11	24
Chika	28	31	33	25
D, F pots	2	0	22	6
Knives	11	29	25	14
Spatulae	43	7	17	17
B stools	2	5	18	17
E pots	3	4	9	1
B baskets	65	1	5	2
C baskets	11	0	3	1

to define subdivisions of the main groupings (for example, Kwandi, Kwangwa subdivisions of Lozi) since numerous different subgroupings were often represented in the same village. This problem was further aggravated by the inability of some people to give, for example, the tribal subgrouping (*mushobo*) of their spouses, and even by an inability or unwillingness to give their own tribe. This is partly because the subdivisions have little importance today and partly because the child of a mixed Lozi marriage, while usually taking the tribe of the father, will often use the mother's tribe, depending on circumstance. It is this very weakness and fluidity of the tribal concept in the Lozi area which is especially interesting and it will be discussed further below.

In view of the difficulties in assigning individuals to tribes, it is the major division between Lozi and non-Lozi (Mbunda) which is used here, with a subset of the Lozi, the Ila-Tonga group, considered for comparison. There was never any confusion or uncertainty about whether a person was Mbunda or not, and this is the one division on which one can rely. In the frequent cases where mixed villages occurred at this more general level, the tribe of the village headman was taken in assigning a tribal label to a village. This system provides the tribe of the central and main part of the village (e.g. see Fig. 3.2), and the tribe of the majority of the occupants.

PRESENT-DAY CULTURAL PATTERNING

In contrast to many areas in west and east Africa, the Lozi have a very weakly developed market system. Even the market at the provincial capital of Mongu is small in scale, while the markets at Sefula and Namushakende (the only

TABLE 3.2. *The percentages of the artifact types owned by the different tribal groups*

	Lozi	Ila-Tonga	Old Mbunda	Recent Mbunda	Total
Village percentages	*56.1*	*12.1*	*15.9*	*15.9*	*107*
Tubana	71.0	0.0	28.0	0.0	14
Spoons	68.0	21.0	5.0	5.0	19
D baskets	67.0	12.5	11.5	9.0	24
Mukeke wa kota	64.0	6.0	14.0	14.0	48
A stools	64.0	11.0	17.0	5.0	34
A, B, C pots	63.0	13.0	13.0	9.0	44
A baskets	62.0	10.0	12.0	15.0	58
Chika	57.0	10.0	13.0	18.0	134
E pots	57.0	0.0	14.0	28.0	14
D, F pots	52.0	9.0	28.0	9.0	21
Knives	45.0	19.0	15.0	19.0	86
B stools	44.0	9.0	18.0	27.0	43
Spatulae	43.0	12.0	16.0	27.0	96
B baskets	36.0	0.0	17.0	45.0	74
C baskets	5.0	0.0	5.0	88.0	17

TABLE 3.3. *The percentages of the artifact types made by the different tribal groups*

	Lozi	Mbunda	Ila-Tonga	Total
Village percentages	*56.1*	*33.3*	*10.5*	*106*
Mukeke wa kota	95.6	4.3	0.0	46
Tubana	91.6	8.3	0.0	12
D baskets	88.0	4.0	8.0	25
A, B, C pots	69.2	11.5	19.2	52
Spoons	70.6	17.7	11.8	17
A stools	52.9	29.4	17.6	17
Spatulae	31.6	64.5	3.9	76
D, F pots	29.1	66.7	4.2	24
Chika	18.3	80.8	0.8	120
B baskets	16.4	82.0	1.6	61
A baskets	8.7	91.3	0.0	46
B stools	6.2	93.7	0.0	32
Knives	2.7	95.9	1.3	74
E pots	0.0	93.7	6.2	16
C baskets	0.0	100.0	0.0	12

Note. The totals differ from those in Table 3.2 since it was not possible to obtain all the desired information for all the objects.

others in the area studied) are for small amounts of foodstuffs. Table 3.1 (p. 72) shows whether the objects studied had been made in the villages where used and found, had been obtained from nearby or farther villages, or had been obtained from travelling salesmen (hawkers). Foodstuffs are also largely obtained through local contacts.

Table 3.2 above shows the total numbers of the different artifact types

3.5.   Lozi and Mbunda artifacts: an A type pot, spoon, A type basket and two wooden eating bowls (*mukeke wa kota*). In the foreground is a spatula spoon and a knife.

studied. It also shows the percentages of these totals that were found owned by Lozi, Ila-Tonga and Mbunda (divided into Old and recent Mbunda) villages. If these artifacts were evenly dispersed throughout the villages studied, then the percentages of the different artifact types found belonging to each tribe should be similar to the percentages of the different village types. The percentages of Lozi, Ila-Tonga, Old and recent Mbunda villages are shown at the top of the table.

Thus, for example, 68 per cent of the wooden spoons (*lushwana lwa kota*) were found in Lozi villages and 5 per cent in Old Mbunda and recent Mbunda villages, while only 56 per cent of the villages visited were Lozi and 16 per cent Old and recent Mbunda. There is thus some preference shown by the Lozi for this artifact type, in contrast to the Mbunda. Table 3.3 (p. 73) shows the percentages of each artifact type that had been made by Lozi, Ila-Tonga and Mbunda (Old and recent). It is clear that the spoons are rarely made by Mbunda. Table 3.1 shows how the spoons were obtained. Most were made in the villages where used without further between-village exchange.

Like the spoons, the wooden bowls (*tubana*) and the D type of basket are found more commonly in Lozi villages and are made largely by Lozi. However, the exchange system differs in that the *tubana* are made by Lozi (mainly Kwangwa) carpenters to whom people are willing to travel considerable distances.

3.6.   Lozi and Mbunda artifacts: a D type pot (left), a *tubana* (centre), and a *chika* pounder (right).

3.7.   Lozi and Mbunda artifacts: a B type pot (left) and a wooden eating bowl (*mukeke wa kota*, right).

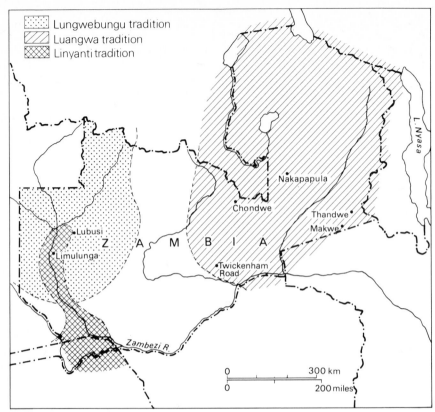

Lungwebungu tradition
Luangwa tradition
Linyanti tradition

Nakapapula

Chondwe

Thandwe
Makwe

•Lubusi

Z A M B I A

•Limulunga

•Twickenham
Road

Zambezi R.

L. Nyasa

0   300 km
0   200 miles

3.8.   Pottery traditions of the Zambian late Iron Age. Source: Phillipson 1974, p. 8.

The D type of basket is only one of four types which were identified. A and B are broad and shallow, B having markedly sloping sides. Both are used as containers for flour. C baskets, called *lingalo* by Mbunda and *chihele* by Luchaze, are small and deep and used as eating bowls. While A, B and C are mainly made by Mbunda women, D are mainly made by Lozi women. The D type is identical in form to the B type but is made in different material, being built up from bundles of grass only found on the plain itself. A baskets, on the other hand, are made from *manenga* which only grows on the plain edge where it is planted by Mbunda, Luchaze and Luvale, while B and C baskets are made from the roots of *mukenge* trees in the bush. But proximity to resources is not the only reason why different tribes make different baskets. Individuals distant from the grass or root they desire can obtain the raw materials from hawkers.

The B, C and D types are largely made for use in each village, but the A form, which probably does not have a long tradition in the area, is largely obtained from hawkers. It is of interest, therefore, that while the traditional forms (B, C and D) are mainly made within tribes and retained within them, one form (A) is specifically made for wider exchange so that, although this

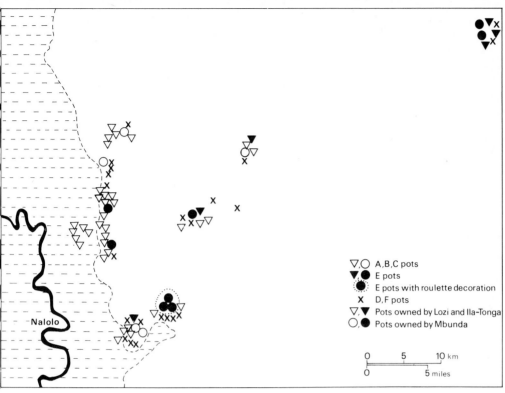

The distribution of pottery types.

form is mainly made by Mbunda, it is found frequently in Lozi villages. Further discussion of basket morphology will be provided below.

Large numbers of different pot forms and types of decoration could be identified. Individuals frequently make unique and novel forms, while special forms may be given by the royal court as gifts. For example, a Mbunda royal blacksmith was found with a remarkable 'two-level' painted pot in the form of a bowl with a bird above it. In general, however, pot forms can be grouped into a few major categories. A, B and C type pots – mainly tall-necked jars – are made on or near the Lozi plain. They are part of Phillipson's (1974) Linyanti tradition. Buff in fabric, they usually have geometric designs painted in red although there is great variability of design motifs, and flowers, for example, are sometimes found. Most Lozi and Ila-Tonga women make their own pots in their own villages. Because the best clays are on the plain, Lozi women living in the bush will travel up to 40 km to sources near the Zambezi in order to bring back suitable clays. A, B and C pots are more common on and near the plain, but are exchanged into the bush on a personal basis. Phillipson's map (Fig. 3.8) shows the distinction between A, B and C types near the plain and other types in the bush areas at a wider scale. But it is clear from the

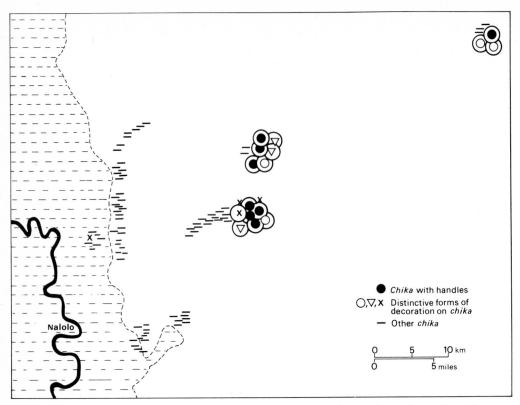

3.10.   The distribution of types of *chika*. Encircled symbols indicate distinctive *chika* types owned by Mbunda.

detailed map (Fig. 3.9) that there is no sharp delineation between the plain and bush pot distributions.

A typical form (E) made in the bush areas to the east of the plain is a round-based straight-sided bowl in a brown fabric. Unpainted but incised with geometric decoration near the rim, this type is typical of Phillipson's (1974) Lungwebungu tradition. The E form is made mainly by the Mbunda, and predominantly by male part-time potters who exchange their wares locally. Fig. 3.9 shows that localised traits such as roulette decoration occur.

A very different mechanism of pottery production and dispersal – resulting in very widespread distribution and uniformity of design – is found for D and F pots made mainly by Mbunda on the western edge of the plain at Lindjani (Liliachi). Large-scale production occurs here in wares which are taken in boats across the plain when it is flooded and exchanged locally by Mbunda and Lozi.

Apart from the latter, then, most pottery manufacture is a small-scale, part-time activity, occurring mainly in the dry season. Some comments on the differences between pots made by different women are provided on p. 94. Localised exchange between relatives and friends occurs and some localised

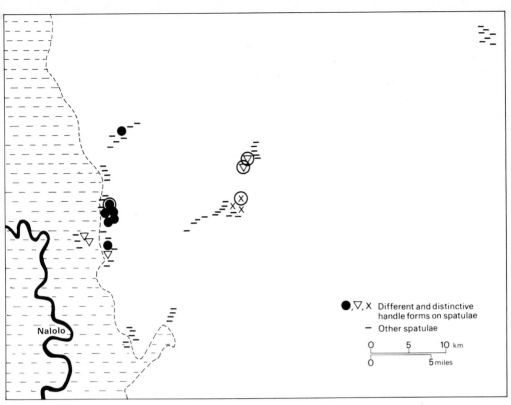

3.11.   The distribution of types of spatulae. Encircled symbols indicate types owned by
               Mbunda.

stylistic traits were found. Oral accounts indicate a similar situation in the
past. Most pottery was made outside the royal centres and was exchanged
locally. In the royal establishments such as Muoyo and Lealui there were a
few specialist potters, but most of the women potters there produced mainly
for consumers in and adjacent to the centres. Individuals sometimes came
to obtain pots from particular potters in the royal villages but, as already
noted, there was no market nor central place for the sale or exchange of
pottery.

   Wooden items are largely made by men. Eating bowls (*mukeke wa kota*)
used for meat and vegetable dishes are mainly made by Lozi (Kwangwa) in
the bush areas where, as opposed to the flood plain, wood is plentiful. *Mukeke
wa kota* are fairly widely exchanged, but other wooden objects such as spoons
(*lushwana lwa kota*), spatulae (*lusokwana*) and large wooden mortars (*chika*) for
pounding all sorts of agricultural produce are more often made in the village
where used. Related to this small-scale manufacture there is some evidence
for extremely localised styles of these items. The presence of handles on *chika*
and the types of decoration around the waist show confined distributions (Fig.
3.10), while the shapes of the handles of the spatulae (Fig. 3.11) and, to a lesser

TABLE 3.4. *Mean values (cm) for different traits on artifacts owned by the different tribal groups*

		Lozi	Ila-Tonga	Old Mbunda	Recent Mbunda
A baskets	width	41.9 (33)	41.5 (6)	39.7 (7)	41.6 (9)
B baskets	width	39.7 (25)	—	58.2 (11)	54.1 (34)
B baskets	height	13.2 (22)	—	14.5 (10)	12.8 (33)
spatulae	length	29.3 (39)	30.1 (11)	30.8 (14)	29.3 (26)
spatulae	width	8.7 (40)	8.5 (11)	9.1 (14)	8.9 (26)
chika	height	49.9 (74)	50.0 (13)	50.9 (18)	50.9 (25)
knives	handle length	8.6 (39)	8.7 (17)	8.2 (13)	7.7 (17)

Note. Numbers in parentheses indicate numbers in samples.

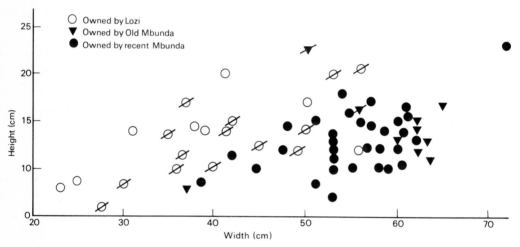

3.12.   The widths and heights of B baskets. Baskets made by Lozi are diagonally crossed.

extent, the decoration on the handles of the spoons indicate a similar structure. Localised traits of this form cut across tribal affiliations.

So far it has been clear that only a few items and types are especially common or scarce in different tribes. The overall cultural similarity between the tribes is also demonstrated by the dimensions of the different artifact types. Table 3.4 above provides some average size values for artifacts found in villages of the different tribal groups. It is clear that each tribal group tends to make and own artifacts very similar in size, the only clear anomalies being the widths of B baskets and, to a lesser extent, the lengths of the wooden handles of the small knives. Fig. 3.12 shows the widths and heights of the B baskets and there is some indication of a separation between Lozi baskets on the one hand, and Old and recent Mbunda baskets on the other. Even B baskets made by Mbunda *for* Lozi tend to be smaller than those they make for their own use.

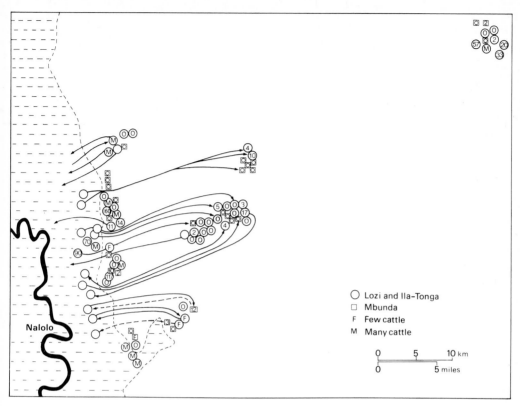

3.13.　The numbers of cattle said to be owned by the villages visited, and recorded instances of movements of Lozi (solid lines) and Mbunda (dotted lines) cattle between bush and plain. The lines do not indicate precise routes.

Despite a few such instances in which the Mbunda differ from the Lozi and Ila-Tonga, there is overall clear evidence of similarity in the cultural items owned by the different tribal groups. This is the first characteristic of which interpretation must be attempted.

DISCUSSION OF THE CULTURAL PATTERNING

In explaining the general cultural similarity between the tribes, it is considered of interest that there is a marked symbiotic economic relationship between different groups in the Lozi kingdom. Many of the tribes have craft and economic specialities and are dependent on each other.

This exchange and symbiosis especially exists between the flood plain and the bush. For example, cattle are moved from the plain in the wet season, and then down on to it again in the dry season (Fig. 3.13). In the dry season the cattle on the plain are looked after by friends and relatives of those who remain in the bush. In the wet season the cattle are taken back to their owners in the bush or to friends and relatives of those owners who remain on the plain margin. In return for being looked after, the cattle provide manure for the fields. Their milk, however, is the property of the owners. Thus, even people who do not own cattle can be involved in this cattle system.

Other specialities of the plain are maize and sweet potatoes and these move to the bush in exchange for cassava. Also, the plain produces good potting clays and the best pots, while the trees in the bush mean that the tribes there are the main producers of baskets and wooden containers. Gluckman (1941, p. 72) has catalogued the numerous specialities of the different tribes. For example, the Nkoya supplied beeswax for repairing wooden utensils, the Kwangwa provided hoes, fish spears, spears, axes, adzes, mats and baskets, the Lunda dugouts, and the Totela iron implements and honey. Generally there is little past or present evidence of conflict between the tribes within the kingdom, or of competition over resources. In the past, the presence of the king also helped to remove competition by providing an economic, administrative and juridical umbrella.

It is suggested here that, since each member of each tribe is involved in an inclusive symbiotic and non-competitive economic system, there is little need to express tribal differences symbolically. Rather, there is an advantage in demonstrating symbolic and cultural similarity with others in the same system. Thus the various Lozi and Ila-Tonga tribes are indistinguishable culturally and their tribal identities have become blurred. As already noted, many people were unsure of their tribal subdivision (Kwangwa, Kwandi, etc.) within the Lozi and Ila-Tonga groups. There is also complete spatial mixing of villages of different tribes, and families of different tribes may live in the same village. Thus, in general in the Lozi kingdom, a symbiotic interdependent economic relationship in which there is little conflict of interests has led to cultural blurring and similarity.

However, one group of tribes – the immigrant Mbunda – has been recognised as different. At present, the Mbunda *are* aware of their tribal affiliation, and they would never call themselves Lozi. Mbunda villages can be distinguished in that they more commonly have B and C baskets, and it has been suggested (Fig. 3.12) that B baskets which occur in Lozi villages are smaller, even when made for them by Mbunda. In addition, Mbunda rarely own the spoons. But such differences are not a result of a lack of awareness of each other's items. The symbiotic relationship results in intense interaction between Mbunda and Lozi. While Mbunda know of Lozi spoons, can describe them and could easily make them, 'they are Lozi objects and we do not have them'.

Why then, while most tribes have become culturally assimilated in the Lozi kingdom, have the Mbunda retained a certain distinctiveness? It is suggested here that the Mbunda are more 'visible' archaeologically because there *is* some degree of conflict of interests between Mbunda and Lozi. This competition within symbiosis has three main sources.

(1) Cattle. The numbers of cattle owned by each village were assessed in

the fieldwork. Although informants were hesitant about providing such information, it is quite clear (Fig. 3.13) that Lozi have large numbers of cattle compared to Mbunda. While Mbunda rarely own cattle, there is some evidence that they are sometimes involved in the cattle system so that they look after Lozi cattle and use them to manure their fields. The important distinction is that Mbunda rarely own cattle. Cattle are an important source of wealth and the Lozi have always had a cultural and economic concern with them (Prins, pers. comm.). The inability of Mbunda to obtain this cattle wealth is the first conflict of interests.

(2) One reason why the Mbunda do not have access to cattle is that they are not allowed to own the rich grazing lands on the plain. The Lozi on the plain can control the number of Mbunda cattle allowed to graze on the plain and they can thus determine how many cattle are owned by Mbunda. In more general terms, the plain provides a more productive, although riskier, soil than the bush. Thus the second source of competition between the Mbunda and the Lozi and Ila-Tonga is that access to this land is restricted to the latter two groups.

(3) A third conflict of interests concerns iron. The areas with iron ore are all in the bush. Iron is essential for working the matted peat in the plain (Prins, pers. comm.) and so was essential for the Lozi. Also, the restricted distribution of this resource gave the Lozi elite an opportunity for centralised control. The ore mining and iron production (for example, at Kataba) was controlled by the king. Individuals obtained metal by working for it in the iron production centres or by the exchange of goods at the centres. Mbunda were often involved in this work as skilled smiths, but the resource remained under the control of the Lozi elite.

It is as a result of this present conflict of interests over cattle and land, and in the past over iron, that Lozi and Mbunda have retained a cultural distinctiveness more than other tribal divisions. The structure of the cultural differences between the tribes relates, not to the intensity of interaction between them, but to the nature of that interaction and to the degree of economic competition. The competition and strain between the Lozi and Mbunda *wiko* (a perjorative term used by Lozi to describe Mbunda) is especially marked nowadays because of the relative weakness of the royal elite. As the modern Zambian administration gradually replaces the royal power, the subject tribes have tended to assert themselves against the Lozi for political ends. Tribal identities are more strongly felt (Turner 1952, p. 39). The Lunda and Luvale (both 'Mbunda' tribes) have been granted independence, and the Nkoya have made similar demands.

The distinctiveness of the Mbunda is also seen in the marriage pattern that was recorded during the fieldwork (Tables 3.5–3.7, see over). Table 3.6 shows the percentages of men marrying women in their own and other tribes. The preference for within-tribe marriage by Lozi and Mbunda men is clear, whereas Ila-Tonga men often marry Lozi but not Mbunda women (although

TABLE 3.5. *The numbers of marriages of individuals under 60 years old, their parents and grandparents*

Female	Male			
	Lozi	Ila-Tonga	Mbunda	TOTAL
Lozi				
grandparents	3	0	0	
parents	41	7	4	
individuals	54	6	6	
Total	98	13	10	121
Ila-Tonga				
grandparents	0	1	0	
parents	5	4	1	
individuals	19	5	5	
Total	24	10	6	40
Mbunda				
grandparents	0	0	0	
parents	0	0	25	
individuals	3	1	39	
Total	3	1	64	68
TOTAL	125	24	80	229

TABLE 3.6. *The percentages of men marrying their own and other tribes*

Women	Men		
	Lozi	Ila-Tonga	Mbunda
Lozi	78.4	54.1	12.5
Ila-Tonga	19.2	41.7	7.5
Mbunda	2.4	4.2	80.0

TABLE 3.7. *The percentages of women marrying their own and other tribes*

Men	Women		
	Lozi	Ila-Tonga	Mbunda
Lozi	81.0	60.0	4.4
Ila-Tonga	10.7	25.0	1.5
Mbunda	8.3	15.0	94.1

only a small sample of twenty-four Ila-Tonga men was obtained). Lozi men also rarely marry Mbunda. This table therefore suggests a link between Lozi and Ila-Tonga, with Mbunda being rather outside this network. The pattern is even more clear when the marriages of the women interviewed are examined (Table 3.7). Of Mbunda women 94 per cent said they were married to Mbunda men, while the Lozi–Ila–Tonga tie is clear with 60 per cent of

Ila-Tonga women married to Lozi men. The distinction between the Mbunda on the one hand and the Lozi, including the Ila-Tonga, on the other, is maintained even amongst sixth generation Old Mbunda immigrants who often still show clear preferences for Mbunda marriages. It is difficult to see these marriage patterns as the *cause* of the cultural patterning. Individuals *can* marry across tribes, and one Lozi man may marry both Lozi and Mbunda women. The marriage pattern is seen here as reflecting and relating to the same competition and conflict of interests as the cultural distributions.

Up to this point, the discussion has emphasised present-day social, economic and cultural patterning in Barotseland. One form of cultural patterning not mentioned above allows a certain amount of extrapolation into the past. A few people were found with various forms of facial cuts, and in the past a considerable amount of opinion was collected on these face marks. These opinions could often be checked by interviewing very old individuals, still with the cuts which are normally made before the age of fifteen. The main types of Lozi marks are a vertical line down the centre of the forehead and onto the nose, circles around the eyes and a reversed 'V' cut out of the upper front teeth.

The Mbunda, on the other hand, have a distinctive hairstyle but had no tribal face marks in the Mbunda (as opposed to Luvale) areas of origin in Angola. Those Mbunda (in the strict sense) who arrived in the nineteenth century adopted the Lozi face marks. More recent arrivals, however, have adopted the Luvale, Luchaze and Chokwe cheek and temple marks and sharpened teeth. Thus the period since the early twentieth century has seen a decline in the copying of Lozi face marks and the growth of a clearer dichotomy between Lozi and the Mbunda-*wiko* group as a whole.

Some evidence was found for a similar sequence in reference to artifact types. The C type of basket was mainly found in Mbunda villages. These were largely villages of Mbunda who had arrived in the area within the last two generations, and tribal distinctions are maintained nowadays in respect to this object. But Old Mbunda families who had arrived in the nineteenth century had gradually allowed the manufacture of this artifact type to lapse in parallel with the assimilation and adoption of Lozi traits. The earlier situation again seems to have involved less sharp distinctions.

The *tubana* is mainly owned and made by Lozi. However, three examples were found in Mbunda villages. In all three cases these were Old Mbunda villages. The greater assimilation of Old as opposed to recent Mbunda is seen in table 3.2, where there is some indication that Old Mbunda are more like Lozi than recent Mbunda (this pattern is also seen in an average link cluster analysis to be described below).

Why should there have been more cultural absorption of Mbunda in the past than now? It is suggested here that the main distinction between the past and present situations is the importance of the umbrella of the central elite. In the past, the centre controlled much of the competition between tribal groups. Individuals were ultimately dependent on the king rather than on the internal cohesion of their own tribal group. There is some evidence that in the past Mbunda were allowed land on the plain (Gluckman 1941). Mbunda were given important positions as royal hunters, smiths and so on, and the Mbunda elite was given some status and independence. The Mbunda chiefs (e.g. Mwenekandala) had their own palaces in the bush areas and participated in royal privileges. Thus dependence on other members of the same tribe was partly replaced by dependence on the elite. The Lozi king assured access to resources, and much of the reason for between-tribe conflict was removed. There was little need for cultural differences between tribes to be maintained. These have been reasserted more recently with the decline of the monarchy.

Thus a highly centralised political system may remove some of the sources of competition between tribal groups. However, unequal access to resources in a kingdom or state may be between levels or classes. Certainly the Barotse elite maintained control of a range of basic resources. For example, in the past they controlled iron deposits, had legal control of all land, controlled large herds of cattle, and controlled much of the long-distance trade. This is an example of elitism rather than ethnicity (Cohen 1974), and the elite's unequal access to limited resources was symbolised and reinforced by a series of distinctive cultural traits. For example, double clapperless bells (*ngongi*) are awarded by the king and queen of the Lozi to Lozi and Mbunda statesmen, royal hunters, blacksmiths and so on. These objects are handed down within families long after the death of the individual to whom they were awarded. They are most frequent in villages near the royal centres.

Other artifacts such as feather crowns, eland tail fly-switches with specially carved ivory handles, and in the past ivory wrist bangles, were also the property of particular sets of high-status or wealthy individuals in the kingdom. In addition, special gifts such as elaborate painted pots (see above p. 77) were given by the king and queen to specially honoured subjects.

Although no information could be collected on variations in the cultural distinctiveness of the Barotse elite over time, it is possible that the structure of differences between hierarchical levels will relate to the degree of conflict of interests between them as much as it does between ethnic groups.

SOME IMPLICATIONS FOR ANALYTICAL AND INTERPRETIVE THEORY
IN ARCHAEOLOGY

Analytical theory

The data described above can be used as a testing ground for some of the analytical methods traditionally popular in archaeology. For example, a common approach to the study of a collection of cultural information from 107 different sites would be to carry out some form of cluster analysis. An average link cluster analysis has been applied to the Lozi information, using

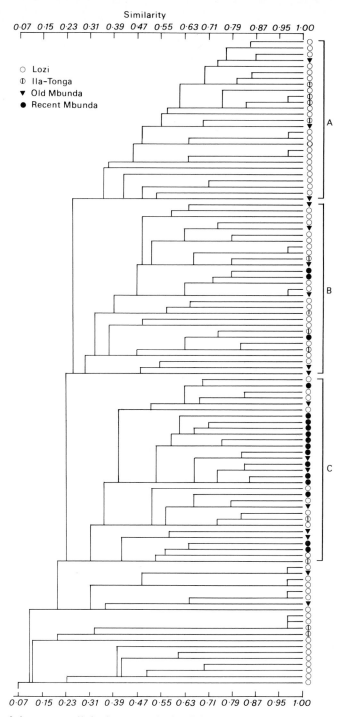

Similarity

O Lozi
Ⓘ Ila-Tonga
▼ Old Mbunda
● Recent Mbunda

.14. Results of the average link cluster analysis of the villages studied.

TABLE 3.8. *Values of the V coefficient for different pairs of artifact types (values significant at P = 0.01 are in italics)*

	(2)	(3)	(4)	(5)	(6)	(7)	(8)	(9)	(10)	(11)	(12)	(13)	(14)
Chika (1)	−0.11	−0.02	−0.04	0.16	−0.05	−0.05	−0.11	−0.07	0.02	−0.12	0.00	0.03	−0.03
A baskets (2)		−0.04	0.15	*0.30*	0.25	0.22	0.01	0.01	*0.20*	*0.27*	0.08	0.16	−0.09
B baskets (3)			*0.40*	0.17	0.35	−0.08	*0.18*	−0.01	−0.08	0.13	−0.15	0.00	*0.18*
C baskets (4)				*0.025*	0.19	0.03	0.32	0.06	0.00	*0.19*	−0.16	0.16	−0.04
Spatulae (5)					0.23	*0.30*	0.05	*0.21*	*0.19*	0.15	0.08	*0.25*	−0.00
Knives (6)						−0.10	0.01	−0.00	0.10	0.11	−0.17	−0.07	0.01
A, B, C pots (7)							−0.09	0.01	0.25	0.16	*0.20*	0.16	−0.04
E pots (8)								0.08	0.18	0.09	−0.08	−0.03	0.17
D, F pots (9)									0.07	0.07	−0.08	0.07	0.08
Spoons (10)										0.02	0.05	−0.03	*0.18*
Mukeke wa kota (11)											−0.05	0.14	0.04
A stools (12)												0.05	−0.02
B stools (13)													−0.09
Tubana (14)													

Gower's (1971) general coefficient to assess similarity between the villages based on the presence and absence of fourteen cultural traits. In carrying out this procedure it is assumed that depositional and post-depositional factors, while seriously affecting within-site patterns, will not have caused movement of items between villages after use.

The resulting dendrogram is shown in Fig. 3.14. As might have been expected from the discussion so far in this paper, there is no clear evidence of distinct clusters. However, the archaeologist searching for patterning within his data might feel he could distinguish three broad groups (A, B, C). While group C perhaps contains a higher number of Mbunda (especially recent Mbunda) than the other groups, there is absolutely no tribal nor other social, political, economic or activity difference between groups A and B. It is clear, then, that such forms of cluster analysis can produce 'archaeological' groupings which have no other significance. As Hodson *et al.* (1966, p. 321) note, average link cluster analysis 'will tend to find clusters even when the data do not lend themselves ideally to division into discrete groups'.

Another and more direct method of determining whether any traits are being used to define interest groups is to consider whether the traits show any non-random spatial associations. In many cases, the traits which are used to symbolise clearly distinct identities will stand out because of their high degree of association or clear segregation. The results of the V coefficient of association (Hodder and Orton 1976, p. 203) for fourteen artifact types are shown in Table 3.8 (p. 88). This coefficient varies from -1 (segregation) to $+1$ (association). The lack of significant segregation between artifact traits corresponds with the first general conclusion made above that there are few clear cultural distinctions between the tribes. However, the most significant degree of association ($P < 0.01$) is between B and C baskets which have already been identified as specially Mbunda traits. Of the ten villages with both these items, nine are Mbunda. There is also a high degree of association ($P < 0.01$) between B baskets and knives. Of the thirty-two villages with both these items, nineteen are Mbunda. Of the thirty-one villages in group C of the average link cluster analysis, twenty are Mbunda. Thus the V coefficient is as capable at identifying the tribal groups as the cluster analysis. In addition it does not produce 'spurious' groupings but allows a direct assessment of the non-random structure of the associations and segregations between traits.

This last point is of importance. It is the *structure* of associations and relationships that should be considered, not the overall *degree* of difference. Two social groups with a long history of contact, or a common origin, may have broadly similar cultural contents. But as competition between the groups develops, only very few items may be pulled out of the generally available pool and become significant as identity markers. Conversely, two groups may have had different histories and be generally very different in material culture but yet might have a non-competitive relationship when they finally come into contact. In the latter case, cultural traits may not have significance as identity

TABLE 3.9. *Values of spatial autocorrelation* (*I*) *for different artifact variables at different spatial lags* (*values significant at* $P = 0.01$ *are in bold italics, and those significant at* $P = 0.05$ *are in italics*)

		Spatial lags (km)						
	Expected	0– 2.5	2.5– 5.0	5.0– 7.5	7.5– 10.0	10.0– 12.5	12.5– 15.0	15.0– 17.5
Knife handle length	−0.01	**0.27**	**0.25**	**0.20**	**0.11**	**0.08**	*0.07*	*0.06*
B basket width	−0.01	**0.28**	**0.19**	0.04	*0.05*	0.01	0.02	0.01
B basket height	−0.01	*0.11*	0.07	0.01	0.01	0.01	0.01	0.01
A basket width	−0.01	*0.12*	0.05	0.00	0.01	0.01	0.00	0.00
Spatulae length	−0.01	0.03	0.03	0.02	0.02	*0.02*	*0.02*	—
Chika height	−0.01	0.03	0.00	0.00	—	—	—	—

markers and will blur across social boundaries. Thus the degree of cultural difference might be great but the structure of the difference may be a smooth cline in all traits rather than a sudden break in some. The archaeologist wishing to locate cultural patterning which has a social significance must thus use analytical techniques (study of fall-off curves, associations and group structures) which are sensitive to such patterning.

Interpretive theory

A number of archaeologists (e.g. Phillips 1975; Whitehouse 1969) including myself (Hodder 1978) have assumed that the nature and localisation of the production and dispersal of cultural items are related to stylistic variation. Thus it is often supposed that greater stylistic variation over space reflects dispersed small-scale production and dispersal, and widespread conformity indicates specialised and centralised production. The data collected from the Lozi area allow the relationship between stylistic patterning and the scale of production and dispersal to be examined in detail.

This relationship was first examined by assessing the degree of spatial autocorrelation in different traits. If nearby values of some variable are more highly correlated than distant values, there is said to be spatial autocorrelation. The I coefficient (Hodder and Orton 1976, p. 178) was used to assess autocorrelation for the variables shown in Table 3.9, above, at different spatial lags. At lag 1, the degree of autocorrelation between values 0 and 2.5 km apart was assessed, at lag 2 between values 2.5 and 5 km apart, and so on. As is shown in the table, spatial autocorrelation normally falls off with increasing distance between values.

The most significant results (under the null hypothesis of randomisation) are for the lengths of knife handles and the widths of B baskets (see also above p.80). However, the fall-off in spatial autocorrelation with increasing lags is more gradual (and bell-shaped, see Fig. 3.15) for the knives than for the

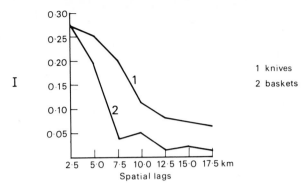

1 knives

2 baskets

3.15. Values of spatial autocorrelation (I) at different spatial lags for (1) lengths of knife handles, (2) widths of B baskets.

baskets. It is of interest, therefore, that Table 3.1 shows that, while many knives are made and obtained from outside the village of use, nearly all B baskets are made in and remain in the same village. However, this clear relationship between the scale of production and dispersal and stylistic variability is disturbed by the A baskets. These exhibit significant evidence of spatial autocorrelation at lag 1 ($P = 0.05$) and yet they are mainly obtained from travelling hawkers and from outside the village of use.

Spoons and spatulae are usually made and used in the same village and their distributions indicate localisation of traits on these items (Fig. 3.11). *Chika* are both made for village use and are widely exchanged and they show localised styles (Fig. 3.10). *Mukeke wa kota* are widely traded and show widespread similarities. However, the E type of pot which is frequently exchanged between villages also shows style localisations (Fig. 3.9).

The Zambian evidence thus supports results obtained from Kenya (Hodder 1977) that preferential movements of traders and localised consumer demands *can* lead to localised stylistic traits on widely traded items. Equally, in certain social contexts, localised village-based manufacture and on-site use can produce widespread conformity in styles. In the Lozi context it has been suggested that there is generally little competition between most tribes. As a result, the styles of most items do reflect the nature of their production and dispersal. Few constraints are in operation which might disturb this relationship. In a more highly constrained and competitive context in Kenya (Hodder 1977) the relationship is clearly broken. Locally produced items show great conformity over wide areas. It thus becomes very important for the archaeologist, working back from the cultural evidence to the behaviour which produced it, to compare the structure of stylistic variability of items with independent evidence for the scale of their production and dispersal. If the archaeologist wishes to examine social and economic constraints on individuals and groups, he cannot assume that stylistic patterning reflects either the nature of production or of interaction in any simple way.

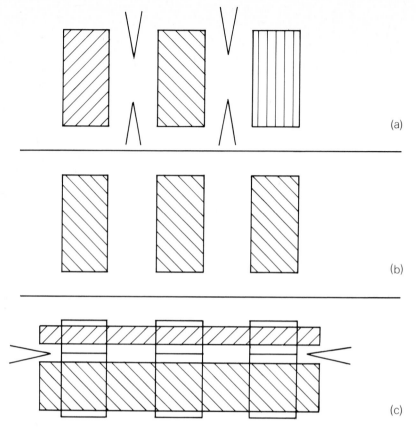

3.16.   Schematic representation of three types (a, b, c) of relationships between different groups. Very marked cultural distinctions are shown by different types of shading. Arrows indicate major loci of competition.

It is suggested, then, as a result of the work described above and in Kenya, and as a result of publications by social anthropologists such as Cohen (1974) and Barth (1969), that many aspects of cultural patterning can only be understood in terms of contemporary social and economic relations. In particular, it is suggested that competition for scarce resources is often related to the use of material culture to support within-group cohesion, coordination and self interest and to justify between-group rivalries. The structure of cultural differences and similarities thus depends less on the intensity of interaction than on its nature. Two groups such as the Mbunda and Lozi tribes may have a high intensity of contact, but the *nature* of that contact may be competitive, leading to the use of certain cultural items to support identity differences. In Fig. 3.16a are schematically depicted three social groups in competition for scarce resources, with distinct cultural differences and within-group conformity.

It should be emphasised that such an approach is not deterministic. The archaeologist does not have to assume that social and economic strains and competition *do* always lead to clearly structured cultural patterning. He often has abundant economic evidence of stress on the environment and in the economy (Cohen 1977), and he can relate this directly to his often abundant evidence of cultural distributions. Certain social and economic systems may be able to adapt without stress to severe degradation of the environment and pressure on population numbers. Others may not, and the archaeologist has the ability to monitor the way in which societies react to stress and to identify which parts of social systems are most susceptible to it.

Thus, while the growth of a highly centralised political system may lead to a decrease in competition and cultural distinctiveness between groups (Fig. 3.16b), this need not always be the case. The complexity of the Lozi example has shown that while some groups having different names and different social systems lose their cultural differences, others emphasise theirs. Once again, culture is not a neutral referent of social organisation and intensity of interaction but is used as part of economic and political strategies.

If economic and political tensions do arise in a highly centralised political system they may often involve a shift from conflict between 'tribal' groups (ethnicity) to conflict between levels (elitism) (Fig. 3.16c). But, once again, the jostling for power and for the control of restricted resources may occur in numerous ways. For example, one territorial ethnic group may come to dominate another hierarchically (Cohen 1974). The approach being suggested here does not need to suppose that all states or societies develop in comparable ways. Rather it focusses on the different ways individuals and groups relate to each other in economic and political strategies. The archaeologist has a unique ability to study the way in which individuals and groups manipulate or take advantage of restricted access to resources, because it is in such areas of tension that culture is used as a mechanism for supporting and justifying economic and political structures. In addition, we can examine whether major changes in the overall form of society – such as the collapse or rise of highly centralised political systems – follows on from the build up of tensions and contradictions in the immediately preceding system.

The same general hypothesis is also relevant for within-site patterning. The Longacre–Deetz–Hill hypothesis that matrilocal residence of female potters leads to localised pottery designs within sites has been widely questioned (e.g., Allen and Richardson 1971; Longacre, ch. 2 above). Certainly, in a Lozi village the continual reuse of huts and the changing occupants would blur any original pattern. But how is learning carried out, and if localisations within villages occur at any one time, are they the result of residence rules and learning networks?

Only one village could be examined in sufficient detail and had sufficient pots to allow such patterning to be studied. In the village in Fig. 3.1 three women who make pots for their own use were interviewed. The Subiya wife of the Nkoya headman living in compound 1 had been taught by her mother

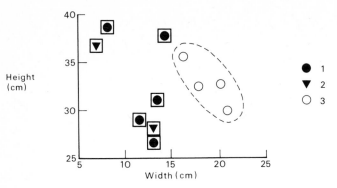

Widths and heights of pots from village 19B. Numbers refer to houses in Fig. 3.1. Symbols in squares represent painted pots.

before moving to the village. She made several pot forms including wide-mouthed (B) jars, all painted, and with width and height measurements shown in Fig. 3.17. Her daughter-in-law living in compound 2 (Fig. 3.1) made distinctively similar jars. They were of similar dimensions (Fig. 3.17), were also painted, and used the same distinctive and rather unique motif of scatters of isolated red-painted triangles. However, she had *not* learnt from her mother-in-law. She had learnt to pot before coming to the village, but had obviously copied, or been copied by, her mother-in-law.

A reverse pattern is found for the woman living in compound 3. Married to the brother of the headman, she *had* learnt to make pots in the village by watching the other two. Yet her pots were different – unpainted and varying slightly in dimensions (Fig. 3.17).

Thus, at the time the village was visited, two different style groupings occurred. These groupings are not the result of matrilocal residence (residence here is virilocal) nor are they the result of the learning network used. So why did the woman who had learnt from others in the village make different pots, while the women who had learnt potting in different outside villages made similar pots? In the village studied there was a noticeable degree of antagonism between the oldest man – the headman – and his brother (the husband of the woman who made unpainted pots in compound 3). This antagonism was reflected in bad relations between his wife and the two other women. Indeed, north of the headman's house (1) and that of one of his favourite sons (2) we always met considerable resistance so that it was never possible to visit houses 4, 7 and 8. This situation had occurred because our initial contact had been made with the other, southern, half of the village. Related to this antagonism within the village, the woman in house 3, although she had learnt to make pots by watching women in the southern half of the village, made them differently. The friendship and common feeling between the women in the southern half of the village was reflected in the similar pots they made even though they had learnt their craft in widely separate villages. Thus, even at the local within-village scale, it is not possible to discuss stylistic variability without taking into account social relations and tensions and the symbolic nature of material culture. Styles will only reflect learning networks and interaction patterns in certain forms of unconstrained social contexts, and in the particular instance described here styles contradict the learning networks.

ACKNOWLEDGEMENTS

The work in Zambia was funded by the British Academy and the University of Leeds. My debt of gratitude to Gwyn Prins, Emmanuel College, Cambridge for making the work in Zambia at all possible is incalculable. The report above would not have appeared but for his kindness and that of his wife, Miriam. Lindsey and Austin Sedgeley also played an important part in providing a friendly haven and in organising transport for us. I am most grateful to my guide Francis Lisulo and to the Permanent Secretary, Western Province for his cordial reception and aid.

REFERENCES

Allen, W. and Richardson, J. (1971). 'The reconstruction of kinship from archaeological data: the concepts, the methods and the feasibility', *American Antiquity* 36: 41–53
Barth, F. (1969). *Ethnic Groups and Boundaries*, Little, Brown
Caplan, G. L. (1970). *The Elites of Barotseland, 1878–1969*, Hurst
Clarke, D. L. (1968). *Analytical Archaeology*, Methuen
Cohen, A. (1974). *Two-Dimensional Man*, Routledge and Kegan Paul
Cohen, M. (1977). *The Food Crisis in Prehistory*, Yale University Press
Gluckman, M. (1941). *Economy of the Central Barotse Plain* (Rhodes-Livingstone Paper No. 7), Rhodes-Livingstone Institute
Gower, J. C. (1971). 'A general coefficient of similarity and some of its properties', *Biometrics* 27: 857–74
Hodder, I. (1977). 'The distribution of material culture items in the Baringo district, W. Kenya', *Man* 12: 239–69
(ed.) (1978). *The Spatial Organisation of Culture*, Duckworth
Hodder, I. and Orton, C. (1976). *Spatial Analysis in Archaeology*, Cambridge University Press
Hodson, F. R., Sneath, P. H. and Doran, J. E. (1966). 'Some experiments in the numerical analysis of archaeological data', *Biometrica* 53: 311–24
Malinga, M. (1973). *Bulozi under the Luyana Kings: political evolution and state formation in pre-colonial Zambia*, Longman
Phillips, P. (1975). *Early Farmers in West Mediterranean Europe*, Hutchinson
Phillipson, D. W. (1974). 'Iron Age history and archaeology in Zambia', *Journal of African History* 15: 1–25
Turner, V. W. (1952). *The Lozi Peoples of North-Western Rhodesia*, Ethnographic Survey of Africa
Whitehouse, R. (1969). 'The neolithic pottery sequence in southern Italy', *Proceedings of the Prehistoric Society* 35: 267–310

4

People and space: a case study on material behaviour

ROLAND FLETCHER

Space in settlements, and the number of people occupying that space, has become a topic of considerable concern and interest for a wide variety of reasons. Concern has stemmed from the impression that high residential densities have adverse effects on human behaviour. Interest has been stimulated by indications that human spatial activity within settlements displays various kinds of metrical order. Why such order should occur and the consequences of that order are being studied both in contemporary and archaeological contexts. There have been expectations that the layout of a settlement may reflect patterns of social organisation. Archaeologists have hoped that settlement size (the area of a settlement) might indicate community size (the number of people occupying the settlement).

The aim of this paper is to argue that the concern needs to be redirected, that an interest in spatial arrangements, even the simplest case of 'how many people on what area', can lead to useful information about community behaviour, and that this approach indicates that the wish to estimate community size from settlement area is a forlorn hope which has obscured the relationship between people and space in settlements.

Research on other animal species such as rats (Calhoun 1962) and deer (Christian et al. 1960) has suggested that crowding may generate adverse behavioural effects. The expectation was that for human communities various physical and social pathologies should be associated with high residential densities (Esser 1971).

Galle et al. (1972) studied such conditions in Chicago and decided that there was some support for the expectation. But Draper (1973) in a brief paper on the !Kung of the Kalahari, showed that residential density cannot in itself be the crucial variable. In their camps, the !Kung live at some of the highest known residential densities on this world, but they do not appear to display either physical or social pathologies. Draper argued that it is the frequency and nature of interaction between people that is crucial. In a !Kung camp the frequency with which one sees, hears and touches other people, and has to interact with the assorted debris of their daily lives, is mediated by the ease with which people can get away from each other. It is easy to leave a camp, either temporarily or to shift to a new camping place. And one camp site is not usually occupied for very long, though a dry season camp may be used for about six months (Yellen 1977).

Freedman, in 1975, made a more radical suggestion. He argued that a high frequency of interaction, associated with high residential density, does not in itself have adverse effects. Rather it will promote any trend whether toward viable or pathological conditions in a community. This conclusion is derived from studies of active behaviour: from analysing the attitudes, emotions, gestures, reactions, irritations and maladies of human beings in varied residential contexts.

There is, however, a problem with his idea. While he points out that a high frequency of interaction can be mitigated by structural design and social conventions, he does not expand upon the issue of the cost involved. But the implications are considerable. We cannot assume that a community will always be able to meet such costs. Even if at any one time the behaviour of the individuals in a community is viable, this does not mean that in the long term the community will thrive. It may be unable to sustain the expenditure of energy and effort that is temporarily making a high residential density workable. Looking at active behaviour in single communities in the short term is not therefore an adequate way of assessing whether or not particular spatial arrangements have deleterious effects on community life.

What seems to follow from both Draper's and Freedman's work is that high residential densities, unless they are associated with the expenditure of energy on structures and regulations of behaviour, will tend to produce high frequencies of interaction which may adversely affect the lives of individuals. Since the energy output of a community cannot be presumed infinite it also follows that even the remedy for immediate situations may in the long run have adverse effects on the community. High residential densities, by way of high frequencies of interaction, may then have the same kind of effect on human groups as they do on other animal species. The implication is that there will be residential density limits to the size of settlements and communities.

This can be examined by looking at a material component of human behaviour – the space in settlements – in relation to the number of people occupying that area. The relationship can be studied in a wide variety of settlements, over varied ranges of time.

By using this approach, it has been possible to identify an overall ceiling to general residential densities: a limit beyond which human beings cannot apparently be crowded together and sustain a viable community. There also appear to be *areal* constraints on community growth. These I refer to as major area fronts. They are not merely reflections of a limit to the number of people who can live in an operable community on a given economic basis. At a major area front, settlement areas remain relatively constant for a wide range of community sizes. The key point of the analysis is that the economic base of a community operates through the *relationship* between settlement area and community size. Area cannot be taken as a neutral referent for numbers of people because the two variables of community size and settlement size *interact* with each other. A community may be adversely affected by an excess of people per unit area, creating interaction difficulties whose solution lies beyond the energy capacity of the community.

A succinct description of the proposed model is that the overall density ceiling and the major area fronts reflect constraints generated by the need for effective transmission of information across a settlement if the occupant community is going to be viable.

METHODOLOGY

The topic being investigated is whether or not there are constraints on residential density and settlement area in the development of human communities. This study is a pilot project to see if further intensive research will be worthwhile. Assessment of the issue has been carried out by searching for regularities in disparate classes of data. Rigorous sampling procedures and precise statistical statements of association are not used, nor are they necessary or appropriate at this stage of analysis.

The analysis proceeds from an initial arbitrary collection of data (Fig. 4.1). The lack of a rigorous sampling procedure means that patterns observed in these data could be spurious. Thus, the patterns of other specific classes of data are also analysed (Figs 4.5–4.8) to see whether or not the indicated regularities occur repeatedly.

Two basic assumptions are involved in the study. First, that it is a two-way relationship between the material and the active components of human behaviour which is of interest. The former cannot merely be seen as an expression of or as a neutral referent or frame for the latter, but the latter may be severely constrained by the inertia of material behaviour.

The second viewpoint is a corollary of the first: that dissonance between settlement area and numbers of people *can* occur and should have an expression in active behaviour. There can be no assumption that settlement area will always conform to the requirements of viable active behaviour. Adaptation must be viewed as a process involving maladaptive as well as adaptive incidents. The emphasis of this paper is on the limits of operable community life and what happens at or beyond those limits.

Data collection

Area and community size estimates for a wide variety of settlements, scattered through time and space, have been collected. The settlements vary in form and area, economic basis, materials used, resource transportation methods, communications, social organisation and community size. Neither the original presentation of the data nor my retrieval of it had systematic characteristics which could have led to the order described in this paper.

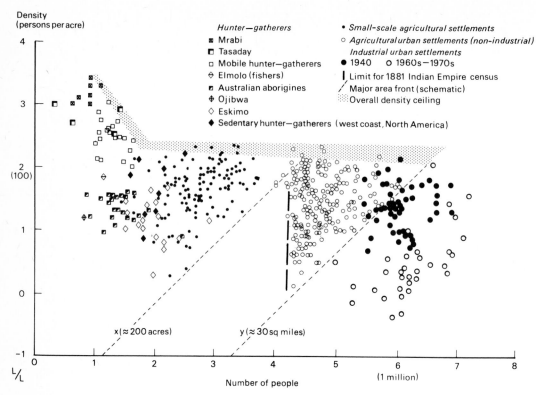

4.1. General area densities for human communities 700 B.C.–1970s A.D.

Data presentation

To make reference to the data easy in this pilot study, I have chosen to use the conventional classification of communities by settlement type and supporting economy (Fig. 4.1). I do not intend, in any way, to imply that this is either a necessary or correct classification. It just happens to be convenient and familiar. But it involves serious terminological problems which suggest that it ought to be replaced in discussions of settlement area and community size. Should we distinguish between the Haida as sedentary hunter–gatherers (Drucker 1963) and the Yanamamo (Chagnon 1974) as sedentary hunter–horticulturalists? Though I initially present the data in terms of the familiar settlement–economic categories, I do not intend to argue in favour of these terms as I am doubtful about the implicit assumptions of such labelling.

The data are presented using a Log–Log format. This is standard practice in the analysis of population and density data (Best *et al.* 1974). First of all, it allows an immense range of values to be plotted on one manageable diagram. By reducing exponential growth to a straight line, observation and description of regularities in the data are made much easier. Second, it helps comparisons of growth by presenting proportionate rather than absolute change. Increase

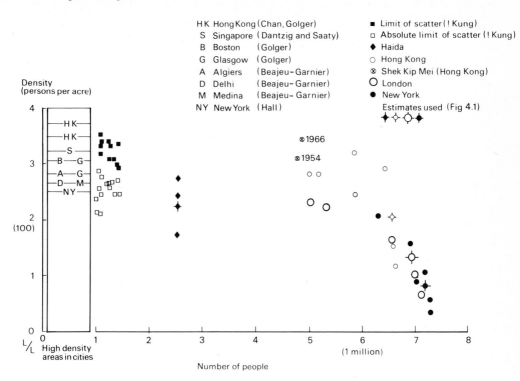

4.2.   Ranges of density descriptions.

can be perceived relative to the number of people or the area of settlement from which growth was initiated. By reducing the scale of the presentation of large values relative to small values, visual swamping of regularities in the small values is avoided.

CHARACTERISTICS OF THE DATA

Studying residential density demands a statement about the data which are being investigated. There are a myriad possible density–number of people–area descriptions of a settlement, each appropriate to different assessments of group behaviour. The descriptions cover an immense range, from individuals in relation to personal space to the numerous descriptions of the density characteristics of a settlement, ranging from maximum known local area densities within the settlement to the average density for the entire settlement area, however defined (Fig. 4.2).

I have chosen to concentrate on community size in relation to total designated settlement area, for three reasons. First, it involves the least dispute about the comparability of examples; second, it leads to a view of the overall workings of a community rather than to emphasis on one component of the community or one part of the settlement; third, and not least, choosing the overall view allows a large amount of data to be used which was never originally collected for this purpose. Also the low level of detail required is generous to the low standard of recording of some of the available data.

Area and population definition

The critical feature of the area and community size estimates for a settlement is that both variables have a characteristic indeterminacy. Defining the *exact* edge of a settlement and specifying *precisely* how many people live in that area cannot be done. An area *can* be designed and a census of population *can* be taken. But the area is designated according to its relevance to the researcher, and the census figure is only an index for how many people occupy that area. This is a feature which applies to any concentration of people, whether around the hearth of a hunter–gatherer camp for one night, or within the administrative bounds of an industrialised urban area over several decades.

Area and population estimates are not truths, merely devices to aid the comparison that a researcher wishes to assess. One can, of course, specify that every aggregate of people is unique, as in some ways they surely are, and cannot therefore be compared to each other. But my interest is comparison and I will accordingly designate areas and related populations in such a way that comparison may be made within those terms. For some purposes we may wish to compare residential densities and behaviour in the camps of mobile hunter–gatherers with densities and behaviour within the residence units of an agricultural village or an industrial town. If our concern is the behaviour of aggregates of not more than ten to fifteen persons, this is a reasonable exercise. But it does not mean that for other purposes the overall density in such a camp cannot be compared with the overall density for an entire industrial city. All that is required is that the terms of comparison be specified.

The data to be used come from nucleated occupation sites which have concentrations of buildings and people, since these are the settlements of direct relevance for a study of high residential densities. Some types of community are excluded, for example, dispersed agricultural settlements. What I wish to find out is whether or not there are or have been any limits to residential density and settlement area, constraining the concentration of people and structures.

My sources for the estimates of numbers of people are state census reports, which are primarily concerned with overnight residents; estimates by anthropologists of the number of people who live in a settlement; and reports by educated travellers who possessed some basis for comparing the numbers of people in a variety of settlements. There is, I think, some tendency towards underestimation. People do not seem to like census procedures and to the more casual observer, children and women may be almost invisible. But it would be absurd to argue that we are dealing with a conveniently consistent set of data. Some casual estimates are gross exaggerations whether deliberate or inadvertent. Mistakes may result from conflating regional or tribal populations on to specific settlements (Chandler and Fox 1974, pp. 3–4). But downright lies are another possible explanation.

In this pilot project the definition of general settlement area is crude. Best and Rogers (1973, p. 28) have remarked with honesty that defining a settlement area is 'essentially a subjective judgement'. Though there are as yet no rigorous procedures for defining the edge of a settlement, the Best and Rogers view is somewhat pessimistic. It is possible to state the kind of boundaries to settlement space which can be used. Some have 'bounded' areas – delimited by a wall or ditch, or by the edge of the space cleared from forest, bush or cropland. Other settlements are 'open'. Hunter–gatherer camps in semi-arid and arid lands are an example; as are industrial towns and cities which have extended out along their main roads.

Since my concern is interaction within settlements, I have to designate edges of settlements which are consequential to that topic. Activities which supply basic resources to the community whether those activities are carried out by people from the settlement, or by outsiders, are not my concern. The relevant overall boundary to a settlement is some kind of visual interface between settlement space and resource supply area. With bounded settlements this is not difficult to define. But designating the 'edge' of an open settlement is not so easy. There are, however, criteria which allow decisions to be made. For hunter–gatherers I have used Yellen's (1977) notion of an Absolute Limit of Scatter covering the debris and the activity areas around the shelters and cleared space of a camp. Some vegetable resources may be obtained within this area but most of the collecting goes on beyond that edge. People return to work and sleep at the camp.

For walled settlements with extra-mural suburbs, the researcher has to choose where the concentration of structures ends. Facilities such as hunting parks and shrine groves, if they are immediately adjacent to the built area, are to be included. They constitute, whether directly or indirectly, a 'lung' for the community.

For industrial cities the problem is serious. In part this is because of a transformation of scale whereby most of the people who live within the bounds of the settlement also work there all day. But it is still the case that the bulk of the primary resources originates elsewhere. There is no simple solution to the problem, so I have chosen to define the size of industrial towns and cities by recognised major administrative boundaries. This at least assists in clarity about the data. As with other settlements the area of an industrial city can include more than just the built-up area. At this stage I have chosen to make one restriction on how much 'rural' land is included. I do not use designations such as the Paris Region (Hall 1971, p. 66) which include large amounts of open country. The designations I shall use include the built area and immediately adjacent open land, for example, the Greater London Conurbation rather than the Greater London Region (Hall 1971, p. 35).

INTERPRETATION PROCEDURES

Maladaptive states

If there are density and area limits, we cannot presume that they are absolute and immutable. Pragmatically we must expect that at any one instant in time a community may exceed such limits. The critical point, however, is that the community should not persist in this tendency for very long. The duration of communities in a residential state inimical to coherent social life should, by definition, be short in comparison to the duration of a community within the parameters of operable group behaviour. At any one instant in time 'pathological cases' *should* be rare. Large numbers of settlement examples, even at one instant in time, should, with a few exceptions, display density–area limits. Also, an arbitrarily collected sample from widely dispersed geographical regions should be usable, since the likelihood of choosing mainly pathological cases is relatively low. Due to their scarcity through time, there are not likely to be very many cases of communities that are just about to disintegrate in the total of 'single instant' residential density descriptions of settlements. Likewise samples taken over long ranges of time, unless specifically terminal cases, should also display such limits. Long-term trends are then required for specific settlements to see how the limits affect communities.

Time regularities

There can be no assumption that evidence of density–area limits found within a given time span at or near the present can legitimately be extrapolated back to earlier periods. It may be that the identified limits are a product of selection through time, both by community behaviour and by the external circumstances of human groups. The research obligation is to find out whether or not the past resembled the present. If the maximum tolerated residential density for human communities has progressively declined over the past 40 000 years, then obviously our expectations about the future should at least anticipate a continuing decline. By contrast, evidence that maximum residential density has remained constant would lead to very different expectations. Information from the past and opinions about the data from the past are not neutral. They are tangled up both with the way we perceive the present and how we anticipate the future. If we wish to avoid, to some degree at least, the dangers of seeing *only* what we want to see, then our attitude to data from the past must become less cavalier. The current practice of social reconstruction by analogy to present patterns of behaviour is not helpful (Fletcher 1977a, pp. 49–68).

Explanations of cause

The use of area–population examples from diverse environmental and economic contexts acts as a control on particularistic local explanations, especially for any evidence of a density ceiling. A limit which applies whether the settlements are agricultural or industrial, built of timber, mud, fired brick or concrete, whether they operate as garrisons, trade centres or religious establishments and contain ethnically uniform or diverse populations, cannot be ascribed to any particular variable of raw materials, economy or social organisation.

Very different configurations of structures and clear space end up as the same area–people relationship in this study. Two cleared areas of equal size, carrying the same number of people, one evenly covered by buildings, the other with an extensive open space around a single multi-storey building, are the same as far as this study is concerned. From such generality one cannot therefore extrapolate to why people sleep on the roof. But conversely, if a density or area limit is evident, it represents a phenomenon that is independent of the way a building technology might be used to organise numbers of people on a given area. Nor can limiting values such as a density ceiling be explained away in terms of particular technological factors. For instance, any claim that transport technology in industrial societies requires more space than in agricultural settlements must be tempered by the countervailing condition that in industrial societies building technologies are available which can house many more people at high densities than in any agricultural or hunter–gatherer settlement.

The occurrence of regularities at this scale of order has to be understood in terms of general behavioural parameters such as the rate and capacity of information transfer, or the input–output relationships of resource supply. Such an analysis may *then* lead to specific implications about the behaviour of a particular human group and suggest whether some kinds of behavioural change will allow communities to make effective moves to new residential density arrangements.

DENSITY CEILING AND AREA FRONT

Density values can be plotted for a wide variety of different settlement types, based on different economies with community sizes ranging from two persons to twelve million (Fig. 4.1). We find that there appears to be a density ceiling which is not usually exceeded by the general residential densities for human communities. This ceiling drops steeply from about 2000 persons per acre for communities of five to ten people and then levels off with a slight but persistent tendency to a continuing decline with the increase in community size.

There is also some indication that the two settlement–economic classes of agricultural small-scale settlements and agricultural urban settlements (non-industrial towns and cities) are each delimited by a sloping 'front' (Fig. 4.1, x, y). The 'front' for any one settlement–economic class is a maximum area limit at which community size may vary, but general settlement area remains roughly constant.

The difficulty with the 'front' phenomenon is that the classificatory choices of the researcher might be creating an artifact of data presentation. Because of such difficulties I would not wish, at this stage of analysis, to claim that a 'front' at about 100–300 acres has been demonstrated. But the 'front' at 30–45 sq. miles which bounds agricultural urban settlements can be investigated in greater detail.

In order to discuss further the relationship between the density ceiling and the area 'front' pattern, I will first present the characteristics of each and then suggest a model which can provide an integrated view of these limits on community and settlement size.

The density ceiling

Various descriptions of the slope of the density ceiling are possible, ranging from a straight line (Slope I), to a broken slope (Slope II), and elaborations of the latter (Fig. 4.3).

Slope I has the poorest visual fit to the presented data. This slope would allow that many communities of 20–10000 people could have, or may have had in the past, much higher general residential densities (Fig. 4.3a). While I have as yet been unable to find such cases, we should beware of rejecting this description out of hand. All the hunter–gatherer estimates come, inevitably, from post-European contact, in most cases at least a hundred years after the initial regional contacts. A drop in residential densities may have been a reaction to the arrival of European diseases, weapons and other gear. This is something we have to find out about, not assume one way or the other.

Slope II is as far as I would care to push the detail of a description at the moment, though it may be that the shape of the slope is much more complex.

Slope II does help to indicate several features of the data. It suggests that there may be an important transformation in human group behaviour for communities of about fifty people. If the slope of the density ceiling for communities of ten to fifty people is extended from the break in Slope II it appears to be a ceiling for almost all the hunter–gatherer cases (Fig. 4.4). A notable exception is the Haida settlement of Ninstints with an estimated community size of 308 persons in A.D. 1853–41, on an occupied area of 1–2 acres. The diagram appears to indicate that the operable maximum residential densities of temporary hunter–gatherer camps decrease very markedly with an increase in community size. But in those settlements containing 100–1000 people, which are occupied for large parts of the year (e.g. agricultural small-scale settlements), the maximum density which can be carried seems

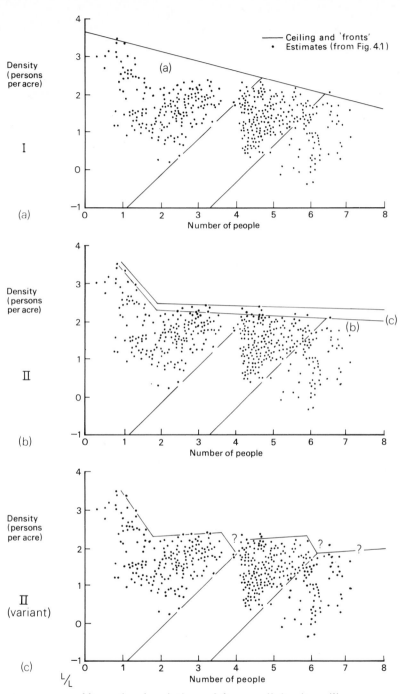

4.3. Alternative descriptions of the overall density ceiling.

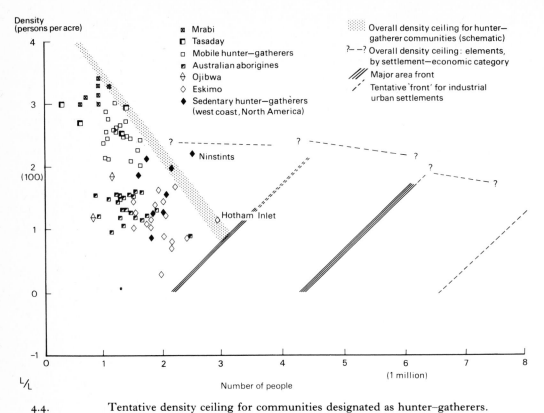

Density
(persons per acre)

⊠ Mrabi
▫ Tasaday
□ Mobile hunter—gatherers
◪ Australian aborigines
⬦ Ojibwa
◇ Eskimo
◆ Sedentary hunter—gatherers
(west coast, North America)

⠿ Overall density ceiling for hunter—gatherer communities (schematic)
?— —? Overall density ceiling: elements, by settlement—economic category
⫽⫽ Major area front
⟋ Tentative 'front' for industrial urban settlements

◆ Ninstints

Hotham Inlet

L/L

Number of people

(1 million)

4.4.   Tentative density ceiling for communities designated as hunter–gatherers.

to rise. A crucial variable which will require further investigation is the role that enclosed, permanent and sub-surface structures may play in controlling interaction frequencies, by acting as barriers to audibility and intervisibility.

At the other end of the density ceiling, Slope II suggests that the great industrial cities of the world have yet to mass in large numbers along the density ceiling (Fig. 4.3b). A few are certainly on or near it; Hong Kong is one example (Figs. 4.1, 4.2). In part, the scarcity of very high general residential densities for industrial sustained cities is probably just a consequence of the short absolute period of time over which this class of settlement has developed. The data given in Fig. 4.2 should not be taken to show that the ceiling necessarily drops markedly for communities in excess of a million people. The overall density ceiling allows that the existing 772 sq. miles of the Greater London Conurbation, which in the early 1960s held over eight million people, could contain about eighty million human beings! (Fig. 4.3c).

The density ceiling tends to decline as community size increases. This tendency is evident for a range of values, in data from Japan in 1970, the U.S.A. in 1940, and India in 1961 (Fig. 4.5a, b, c). But the presented data do suggest that there may also be local density ceilings below the overall density ceiling and that in any one region, for example India, there can always

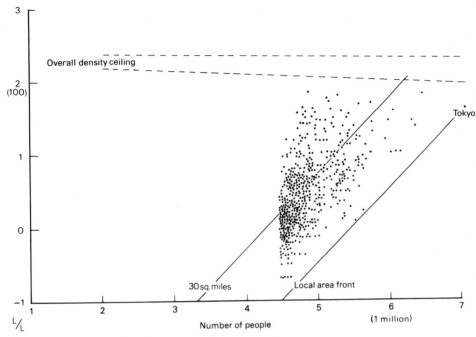

4.5a.   Towns and cities, of 30 000 people or more, Japan 1970.

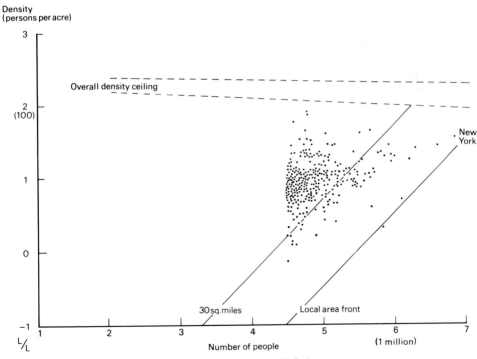

4.5b.   Towns and cities, of 30 000 people or more, U.S.A. 1940.

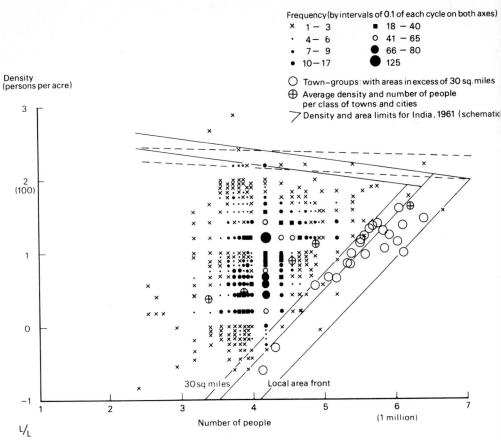

Frequency (by intervals of 0.1 of each cycle on both axes)

×	1 – 3	■	18 – 40
·	4 – 6	○	41 – 65
•	7 – 9	●	66 – 80
●	10 – 17	⬤	125

○ Town-groups: with areas in excess of 30 sq. miles
⊕ Average density and number of people per class of towns and cities
⟋ Density and area limits for India, 1961 (schematic

Density (persons per acre)

Number of people

4.5c. Towns and cities in India 1961. In the Indian census (1961) the towns and cities are classed by numbers of people. The divides between the groups of frequency values are made on values represented by relatively few or no examples.

be some anomalous values much higher than the local and the overall density ceiling.

An overall density ceiling thus seems to occur across the entire range of settlement type and community size as a regular feature independent of environment, economic base, social organisation or construction technology. An explanation needs to be sought in the general characteristics of human behaviour. In very broad terms, the amount of time people spend inside settlements and the length of time that a community is continuously occupied both increase as community size increases. The trend for Slope II is therefore towards a reduction in maximum residential density as the duration of settlement occupation increases. People seem to need more space for two reasons: as they spend more and more time in close proximity to each other, and as the size of settlements makes getting away from people more difficult. The suggestion made by Draper (1973) and the evidence supplied by

Freedman (1975) that the constraining factor is the frequency and manner of interaction among the people in a settlement would seem to be supported. What appears to be adversely affecting human communities is high frequencies of interaction whose effects may be expressed in varying combinations of capital cost and behavioural difficulties. The kinds of problems involved range from the irritations caused by other people's children or radios (Golger 1972) and the difficulties of dealing with people you meet (Mitchell 1971) to the noise and other pollutants from entertainment, public transport and industry. We should not, therefore, regard the ceiling phenomenon as evidence that it is residential density *per se* which limits the community. Rather the density values at the overall ceiling can more usefully be taken as an index for a multitude of situations generating the frequency of interaction that a community cannot sustain.

The area fronts

As well as the density ceiling, there is some indication of another parameter to group behaviour, which is displayed as an area limitation specific to a particular settlement set. Along an area front, community size can vary but settlement area remains approximately the same.

The problem with the evidence in Fig. 4.1 is the choices involved in a settlement–economic classification. This is particularly serious for the class of agricultural small-scale settlement since the category results from *excluding* those settlements which are called urban in their local region. But the ascription is in dispute. Claims are made for the 'urban' character of the *oppida* in Europe in the four hundred years before the Roman occupation (Alexander 1972, pp. 843–50). The site at Manching, for example (Kraemer and Schubert 1970; Collis 1975), with an area of about 1000 acres, is well in excess of the convention of 125 acres for the area of an 'urban' settlement (Pfeiffer 1977, p. 157).

However, the classification used has, by chance, revealed a characteristic of settlement development which can be identified in other sets of data. The census reports summarised in Fig. 4.5 display an area front feature. It would appear that, at any one time, the larger communities in a cultural region will tend toward higher general residential densities with a density ceiling as the upper limit on size. The area front tendency is not an exclusive characteristic generated by a settlement–economic classification. It is rather a regularity which manifests itself in large collections of settlements. There appear to be local area fronts as well as the possible major area fronts.

The next stage of inquiry is to find out whether the possible major area fronts can be considered to be of particular significance in settlement mechanics. In the various industrialised countries the position and slope of the local area front phenomenon can vary (Fig. 4.5a, b, c). The 'front' for town-groups in India in 1961 (Fig. 4.5c) is not the same as the area front for

Japanese cities in the 1970s (Fig. 4.5a). Plainly there are local area fronts composed of the large community sizes and the largest settlement size in existence at any one time in a given region. While it seems likely from the known examples that some kind of front will occur, the specific values of a local area front could change year by year as the communities and settlements of these industrial states become larger and larger. But it may also be that some area front values represent long-term constraints on settlement growth, beyond which an increase in size is not viable unless a transformation in the behaviour of the community also occurs. Substantial constraint at a major area front is implicit in the settlement–economic fronts, which are derived from diverse examples of settlements from a wide variety of circumstances.

Major area fronts. The area and density characteristics of non-industrial and industrial urban settlements can be studied to see if there was a major area limit on settlement size prior to the development of mechanised transport and communications.

This is a convenient issue to study because of the large supply of information. Also, the advent of mechanised industrialisation in large urban centres is historically well defined so that it is relatively easy to specify the class of agricultural urban centre, especially prior to A.D. 1800–50. What I want to illustrate is that area values of 30–45 sq. miles apparently constituted a barrier which resisted settlement and community growth until major changes in communication patterns occurred. These changes then allowed sustained shifts across this major area front to proceed.

The 1961 Indian census divides towns and cities into two categories; the majority, of individual settlements, and a few town groups resulting from the aggregation of several towns, cities and other residential and administrative facilities. An area front can be identified for both these major classes of settlement. Over the period from 1881 to 1961 (Figs 4.5c and 4.6) there was no major change in the position of the 'front' defining the maximum area of individual towns and cities, though more settlements have moved up to and just across that 'front'. The large shifts across the 'front' have been made by industrialised cities in India, and by the redefinition and amalgamation of adjacent urban areas as the industrialisation of India has developed. Even in 1961, most individual towns and cities lay well behind their 'front'. Areas of 30–45 sq. miles seem to have constituted a stabilising barrier to the growth of settlements for at least seventy years. There is some indication that particular area fronts may persist for long periods.

This can be assessed by checking these limits against the data on agricultural urban settlements between 700 B.C. and A.D. 1850 from Fig. 4.1 (Fig. 4.7a) and against a specific class of data – the terminal sizes of the largest cities on this planet, prior to the Industrial Revolution (Fig. 4.7b). The former broadly correspond to the limits indicated in the Indian data, while the latter lie

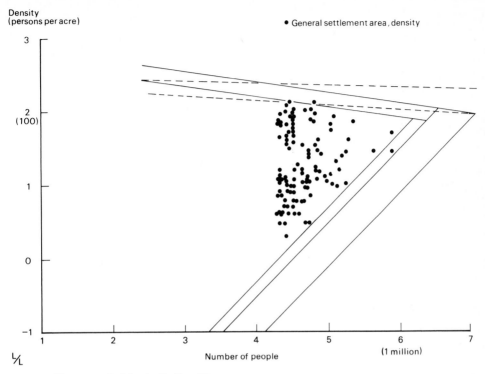

Density
(persons per acre)

● General settlement area, density

4.6.   Towns and cities in India 1881.

against the area front and on or just over the density ceiling, packed into the wedge between these two limits.

That the area front of 30–45 sq. miles has acted as a major barrier to growth follows from the range of time over which cities of half a million to a million people have been occurring. For at least a thousand years cities have existed, like Changan and Baghdad, containing a million people or more. Communities of half a million people have been in existence since the first centuries A.D., for example Rome and Loyang. But the population and area growth of these cities were constrained. They were the giants of their time, jammed between the density ceiling and what now appears as a major area front. Their huge populations neither produced nor aided further growth. They did not develop either mechanised communications or mechanised transport of resources. Instead the communities either stabilised or, more often, slid to disaster.

What happened in cities where industrial technology was eventually integrated into urban life is indicated by the growth of Paris and London (Fig. 4.8a, b). Both were already at or over the overall density ceiling by the mid seventeenth century. The general density for both cities had begun to move down, away from the ceiling in the eighteenth century, prior to the use of mechanised communication systems. Industrial technology then offered a solution to whatever problems had halted other cities with the same numbers

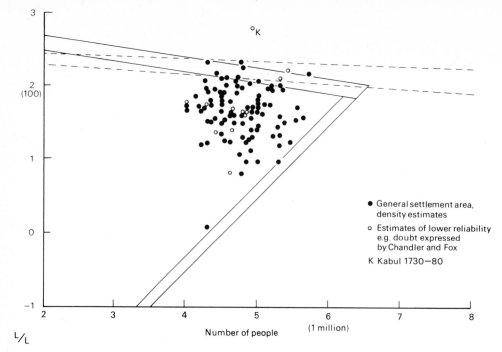

Density
(persons per acre)

General settlement area, density estimates

Estimates of lower reliability e.g. doubt expressed by Chandler and Fox

K Kabul 1730–80

L/L   Number of people   (1 million)

4.7a.   Agricultural urban settlements 700 B.C.–1850 A.D. Kabul 1730–80 is another example where the estimates of settlement size and community size can only be broadly related in time. Note the lack of examples in the point of the wedge between the density ceiling and the area front (see Fig. 4.7b).

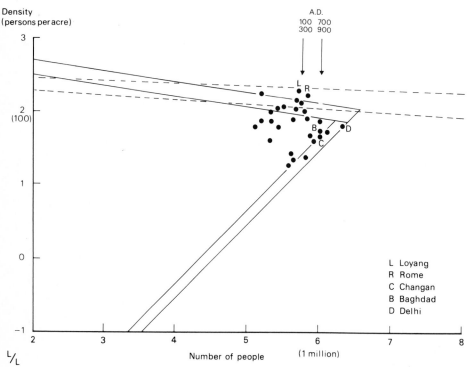

Density
(persons per acre)

A.D.
100 700
300 900

L Loyang
R Rome
C Changan
B Baghdad
D Delhi

L/L   Number of people   (1 million)

4.7b.   Capital cities 700 B.C.–1850 A.D. The estimate for Greater Delhi is in the time of Aurungzeb, covering all the towns which form Delhi. Note that though the wedge between the ceiling and the 'front' is in part occupied by estimates for various communities, there seems to be a tendency for some communities to avoid this zone.

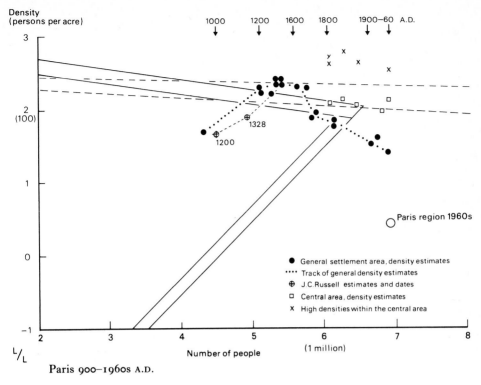

Paris 900–1960s A.D.

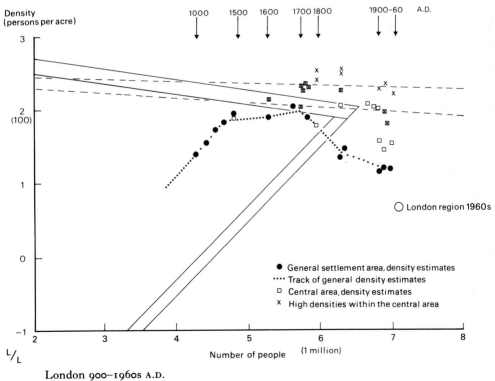

London 900–1960s A.D.

of people at the major area front. In the period 1800–50, they began to move across this barrier as mechanised communications allowed the daily movements of large numbers of people to and from suburban areas (Clark 1958). London and Paris thrived because they happened to coincide with technological developments which they then promoted while in turn being sustained by them.

Why then do local and major area fronts tend to occur? A minimal hypothesis is that the area limit is a function of communication costs, whether those costs come from moving messages or people. What the fronts specify is that as communities increase in size, the average amount of ground space per person will be reduced, *as if* a preferential selection for closer proximity rather than continued settlement growth is occurring. This is a surprising inverse to the constraints of the overall density ceiling pattern. In very simplistic terms, communication depends for its effectiveness on minimising the decay of signals over distance and time and on controlling the amount of 'noise' in the system (Cherry 1966). These criteria apply whether coded statements or people are being moved. An increase in residential density for a given settlement area reduces overall the distances across which statements or people must travel. But a situation can emerge where the signals from each communication event begin to interfere with each other.

In the great agricultural urban centres, having people close together as an aid to communication seems to have been more important than opening up space to enable bulk resources to come into the city. If the latter were the priority demand as community size increased there would be major fronts with a tendency towards a drop in residential density, necessary to supply the vital route space. Apparently, the communication system upon which the organisation of the community depends takes priority over the way in which the necessary resources can be supplied! This suggests that the appearance of a new communication system either using a new kind of signal, or speeding the movements of people, is the necessary precondition for a shift across a major area front. If the early stages of the communication change aid the organising of people as a labour resource to supply the energy to sustain further economic and communication changes, then the new economic–communications assemblage will allow, not merely larger communities, but also much lower residential densities for given community sizes than had previously been possible.

This interpretation suggests that a new method of resource transportation would *not* be sufficient in itself to enable a community to shift across a major area front and remain viable. All that increased resource movement might achieve would be to produce even more people at even higher residential densities or to increase settlement size beyond the communication capacity of the community. Only if the transport change also solved the communications problem, as happened in the Industrial Revolution, could communities make a sustained transition. Any device which will clarify signals, or will increase the duration or power of a signal, or will allow human beings in large numbers to get together and disperse more rapidly, should aid such a transition. Changes in the way material resources are transported are apparently secondary to communication changes, since they do not appear initially to be critical to transformation across a major area front.

The pattern of relationships between the density ceiling and the area fronts can be described in a general 'communications' model. Along the area front, the overall separations between people are reduced as community size increases. This should function to keep down the 'cost' of communication by reducing the overall transmission distance and time as much as possible. But this trend will ultimately reach a state where the communicators are so close together that the signals begin to interfere with each other. This 'noise' in the system will swamp effective communication. Such a state is indicated by the junction between an area front and the density ceiling. The density ceiling specifies that the frequency of interaction had reached a limit beyond which the community cannot operate. In other words, for a given community size, people are so close together that the coherence of their behaviour is swamped by the number of signals with which they are being bombarded and they cannot afford the energy needed to control the situation.

The area and density limits of a human community's behaviour are defined in this model by the spatial characteristics of communication and a finite frequency of interaction that human beings can tolerate or control.

CONSEQUENCES

We cannot assume that the identified overall density ceiling has been a constant in hominid behaviour. If we are to find out whether or not it has shifted, we will have to develop credible ways of getting community size estimates. Extrapolation from settlement area is not a legitimate procedure. This is no cautionary tale, advising that care must be exercised. Rather, the indication is that such reconstruction procedures by analogy are logically in error because material patterning cannot be regarded as merely a reflection of, or a neutral referent for, other phenomena, such as numbers of people or their social organisation. The relationship between settlement area and community size is one of the dynamic factors involved in the development and disintegration of a community. We cannot assume that the relationship is constant. This applies for all the settlements in a region over time and also during the existence of any one settlement. Severe miscalculations of community size would follow from extrapolating back from current residential densities for London. Furthermore, a major phenomenon in the process of that settlement's growth would have been obscured. The same may well apply to estimates of the community size for Uruk from 3500 B.C. to 2800 B.C. (Adams 1972, p. 87) or Teotihuacan from A.D. 100 to 500 (Millon 1974, pp. 44–5).

An investigation of the relationship between active and material behaviour, rather than a quick search for a handy ethnographic analogy, has shown that density states in settlements cannot be ignored even in writing a culture history, let alone in analyses of the long-term processes of community life. Bluntly, what we have failed to face is that we must continue to try and develop ways of estimating numbers of people from their mechanical derivatives – the garbage and the skeletal debris they leave behind (Cook 1972). Until we do so our investigations of community size, however achieved, will be fatuous, depending upon meaningless analogy by association to contemporary communities. The dynamic relationship between viable group behaviour, community size and residential area should apply across the entire range of spatial designations from settlement area to roofed living space and even to personal space. We cannot safely presume that human beings always manage to obtain the amount of personal space they would prefer (Martelli 1960, p. 259). That problem may be crucial to the prospects of a group of people (Presser 1965). Assuming constant ratios between people and areal features is of little, if any, analytic or interpretive value.

The occurrence of an overall density ceiling suggests that there may be other kinds of density ceilings, for numbers of people in relation to central area and other areal subdivisions of settlements (Fletcher 1977a, pp. 56–67). There may be a great deal of fruitful research to be done on planet-wide distributions of the maximum tolerable residential densities for differing designations of settlement area (Doxiadis 1968, p. 101). We need not waste our time trying to use such data to reconstruct the past. Our time would be more fruitfully taken up with attempts to describe and analyse oscillating densities of occupation as people move in and out of a settlement.

The other major implication of the overall density ceiling is that the way in which human groups control frequency of interaction is a crucial issue. Human groups create orderly patterns of space and structures. We might fruitfully begin to ask how such patterns aid or control intervisibility and interaudibility in community behaviour (Fletcher 1976, pp. 294–304; Fletcher 1977b, pp. 97–100).

A major area front was noted above which delimited the growth of agricultural urban settlements. What is now needed is an investigation to find out whether or not there have been other major area fronts. One of the primary requirements in future work will be much closer definition of what is meant by the edge of a settlement. The definition must be applicable to archaeological sites, because they constitute an essential source of data. Instead of amassing ethnographic detail, we need to look at archaeological data to see if there have been long periods when maximum settlement size did not increase. An orientation towards reconstructing past community size has unfortunately obscured the key point that it appears to be settlement area and communications within the settlement, rather than community size determined by food supply, which are the corollary of a transforming economic system. There may be a maximum community size which an economy can support. *But*, for that same economic base, it is the maximum settlement area which is the more general characteristic, since it can occur in association with a wide variety of community sizes. The constraints of economics seem to operate through the costs of the communication system and the control of interaction – not directly through the numbers of people who can be fed, watered and housed.

We need to find out whether or not other earlier major area fronts are only specific to local regions of the planet. If, however, we find that there are other major area fronts which occur in several continents, then we shall have to consider seriously that the area limits are a function not merely of local economic effects but of the general behavioural characteristics of our species. We might suspect this for urban settlements behind the 30–45 sq. mile area front. The specific economic systems which supported them were very varied, including different crops, diverse utilisation of animals and drastically different modes of transport. While a particular economic transformation, the Industrial Revolution, allowed the European towns and cities of the nineteenth century to cross that area front we cannot presume that only one solution is ever possible at a major area front. We have not had the chance to see if any others could have occurred, because the Industrial Revolution contained within it the need to, and the means to, achieve a rapid expansion over the planet. It may be, however, that the earlier great economic transitions, about which there is so much dispute, may be amenable to analysis as a range of economic changes several of which could facilitate transitions across one major area front.

The issue to be considered is: what economic systems could support a new mode of communication and enable a transition to occur across a major area front? Arguments about whether or not we are discussing hunter–gatherers or agriculturalists may then become obsolete (cf. Higgs 1975). No simple economy–settlement size relationship can be used. The size of the largest hunter–gatherer concentration I have found so far exceeds the area of many designated agricultural small-scale settlements. The site (Fig. 4.4) is located on Hotham Inlet in Alaska. It was used as a trading place for a week each summer. In the summer of 1881 there were 600–800 people in the camp, which extended for more than a mile along the shoreline. The nature of communication costs and the energy demands involved in spatial organisation need to be investigated further. If we can clarify these problems, then we might begin to assess whether a major area front is ahead of us and, if so, for what settlement size?

The phenomena described in this study have no simple correspondence either with our habitual view of day-to-day life or with a historical approach. The density ceiling and the major area fronts do not cause or correlate with any *particular* socially or historically familiar phenomena. They seem only to specify that the behaviour of a group will tend to move it away from those limits or the community will remain severely constrained until other forces external to the community come into action. For short-term situations Freedman is correct. High density conditions do not cause *specific* phenomena like pogroms, revolutions or emigration. These are merely some of the possible ways a community can behave as it moves into the density ceiling or a major area front. There are other, and diverse, possible patterns of behaviour. In the ninth and tenth centuries A.D. large numbers of people from Baghdad were moved to Samarra and then back again on several occasions (Adams 1965, p. 90; Le Strange 1924, p. xix). The way each community behaves will depend upon details of its internal operations, its social organisation, economic practices and other specific factors. Conversely, it cannot then be argued that these specifics cause or define the parameters to group behaviour: rather they constitute a finer grain of behavioural detail which operates within the more general communication-interaction parameters. That finer grain of detail is a legitimate topic of research but is in no sense the essential data for studying man. An approach to the material behaviour of man, which may use data from contemporary and historical contexts, is just as necessary.

The proposed communications model specifies that any settlement jammed into a density wedge between the overall ceiling and a major area front will tend towards persistent events which either stabilise or reduce the number of people it contains. Those events *need not* be disastrous, since a community might start a birth control programme or encourage peaceful emigration; but the events could be catastrophic, ranging through internecine conflict to betrayal during a seige, then destruction and massacre, as in Baghdad in the thirteenth century A.D. (Le Strange 1924, pp. 340–3). For each particular successive event, a social and historical explanation can be offered. But the repetition of problem after problem resembles the condition of a body undergoing stress and, in consequence, liable to a succession of specific maladies none of which is itself the primary cause. The model proposed here suggests the cause of that overall condition of stress.

CONCLUSIONS

It appears that we may be able to describe succinctly the long-term spatial behaviour of human communities in terms of a model of communication-interaction parameters. These parameters are expressed as a density ceiling and an area front phenomenon.

The identified regularities suggest that reconstructing past community sizes by analogy to contemporary residential densities obscures the topic it purports to investigate, and is logically inconsistent with trying to find out what the past was like. Area is not a neutral referent for numbers of people. We need a method of estimating community size from domestic rubbish and skeletal remains if we are to find out what has happened to the overall density ceiling in the past. We must also devise a more sophisticated way of describing the number of people who use a settlement.

Several features of the model, such as the possible occurrence of other major area fronts, rapid settlement area expansion for the initial moves across such a 'front' and the primary importance of communication innovations, can in the long term only be investigated directly in the archaeological record. The time depth and the basic pieces of information, such as settlement area, that are already accessible to standard archaeological procedures are essential to our understanding of settlement mechanics. To use this material a method for defining settlement area will be needed.

This pilot study of the relationship between people and space has suggested that a mundane material component of community behaviour, the internal patterning of space in settlements, may be of some consequence for the persistence of a human community. How people spatially arrange themselves and the structural baffles of walls, courtyards and residence units will affect the frequency and intensity of interaction in a settlement. We should then be able to see in the archaeological record how other communities have behaved when they approached a major area front or the overall density ceiling. We have the opportunity to see what such a situation looks like and also to assess whether or not a major area front lies ahead of our own great cities.

ACKNOWLEDGEMENTS

To David Clarke: his achievement was to encourage a wide variety of interests and methods. David sustained the feeling that there are many new questions to be asked, within and beyond the bounds of archaeology as we now recognise it. For his encouragement and his wish for a discipline of archaeology I am deeply grateful. For the loss of his skill and conversation – to do what one can is to respect and thank.

This paper is a descendant of David's interest and my own in the relationship between human beings and the material context of community life. While the emphasis differs from David's earlier attitudes in print, my own concern with the material components of human behaviour developed during discussions and disagreements with David in 1974–5. That the dialogue cannot continue saddens me.

My thanks to Peter White, Ian Hodder, Shelly Davis-King and Geoff Bailey for comments on this paper and its ancestors. I am grateful to Ian, to Mira Crouch and Raoul Pertierra for the opportunity to give seminars on the topic. My thanks also to the staff and students of the Department of Anthropology, Sydney University for their reactions and opinions – especially Tigger Wise for generally being difficult.

To Jim O'Connell, Doug Yen and Tia Negerevich my thanks for information and advice on hunter–gatherer communities.

I am indebted to Jennifer van Proctor for essential help in the preparation of this paper.

The errors of this paper are my responsibility.

SOURCES FOR THE FIGURES

Fig. 4.1

Hunter–gatherers. Cook 1956; Draper 1973; Fernandez and Lynch 1972, pp. 286, 289; Fraser 1968, pp. 25, 65, 115; Gubser 1965, pp. 346–52; McClellan 1975, pp. 236, 238; Murdoch 1887–8, p. 79; Nelson 1896–7, pp. 261, 262; J. O'Connell 1977 (pers. comm.); Rogers 1962, pp. 75, 76; Rohner 1967, pp. 18–23; Sen and Sen 1955, pp. 169–75; Tindale 1972, p. 243; Vagnby and Jacobs 1974, p. 242; Vanstone 1971; Vanstone and Townsend 1970, pp. 22, 27; Velder 1963; Waterman 1920; Woodburn 1972, p. 195; Yellen 1977, Maps and Tables.

Note:

(1) Cook (1956) and Waterman (1920) for information on Californian Indian settlements of Meta, Pekwan, Rekwoi and Woxtek.

(2) O'Connell (pers. comm.) information on aboriginal settlements in Central Australia.

(3) Velder (1963) gives plans of seven resting places spread along a ridge. I have treated each one as a separate 'persons per unit area' estimate.

Small-scale agricultural settlements. Chagnon 1974, pp. 130, 259; Clark 1967, p. 340; Dozier 1954, pp. 285–7; Dozier 1970, p. 122; Epstein 1962, pp. 21, 27, 197, 213; Fewkes 1895–6, p. 578; Fraser 1968, pp. 9, 10, 53; Hodge 1907, pp. 142, 143, 325; Indian Census (1961), vol. I.VI, Three Mysore Villages, and no. 3; then, Part VI for each state: vol. II, nos. 6, 16, 35, 38–42, 45, 46; vol. III, nos. 1–6; vol. IV, nos. 2, 3, 5; vol. V, nos. 2, 8–11; vol. VI, no. 20; vol. VIII, nos. 2–6, 8, 9; vol. IX, no. 7; vol. XI, nos. 1–8, 10, 12, 13, 16–21, 37, 38; vol. XII, nos. 2, 3, 5, 6; vol. XV, nos. 1, 9, 12, 14, 16, 22, 24; Delhi, vol. XIX, nos. 1–3, 6, 8, 11, 13, 14; Kathmandu Report 1969, pp. 64–70, 81; Kennedy 1967, p. 10; Kroeber 1919, Maps 1, 6; Lange 1959, p. 426, Pocket Map 2; Lockwood 1971, pp. 17, 86, 93, 125, 156, 161; Maybury-Lewis 1967, pp. 326, 329; Métraux 1935, pp. 115–17, Carte 2; Mindeleff 1886–7, p. 18, Pl. IV; Parsons 1962, p. 1; Rivière 1969, pp. 130–5; Schwimmer 1973, p. 41; Scully 1975; Titiev 1944, p. 50; White 1962, pp. 36, 48; Wright 1969, p. 23; Wyon and Gordon 1971, pp. 28, 52; Yde 1965, pp. 6, 7, 18; Young 1971, pp. 21, 25.

Note: Scully (1975) for plans of Pueblos.

Agricultural urban settlements (non-industrial). Chandler and Fox 1974; Indian Empire Census 1881, vol. I, p. 276 and vol. II, pp. 232–7; Ojo 1966, p. 27; Talbot 1926, p. 13.

Note: Chandler and Fox (1974) values used, when independent estimates for community size and settlement area are supplied.

Industrial urban settlements. Chan 1970, p. 12; Fooks 1946, pp. 49–50; Gruen 1965, p. 279; Hall 1971, pp. 30, 69, 182; Japan Statistical Year Book 1970, p. 19; Nordic Statistics 1968, p. 23; Turner 1976, p. 956.

Fig. 4.2

Beajeu-Garnier 1967a, pp. 264, 271, 276; Chan 1970, pp. 9, 12, 97; Dantzig and Saaty 1973, pp. 140, 141; Firth 1962, p. 49; Fraser 1968, pp. 25, 65, 115; Golger 1972, p. 58; Hall 1971, pp. 30, 31, 182; Hoover and Vernon 1959, p. 224; London Census 1971, pp. 44–62; *The Region's Growth* 1967, pp. 81, 82; U.S. Census Bureau 1960, p. 72; Yellen 1977, Maps and Tables.

Note:

(1) For !Kung: LS values only from camps with single occupations. ALS values for final occupations.

(2) For Hong Kong only highest densities given for subdivisions of the city, such as estates. See also London, wards and constituencies.

(3) Golger (1972, p. 58) records densities on corner lots in Sai Ying Pung at 10,000 P/A.

Fig. 4.4
Sources as Fig. 4.1 for hunter–gatherers.
  Note:
  (1) Hotham Inlet – E. W. Nelson (1896–7, pp. 261, 262)
  (2) Ninstints – D. Fraser (1968, pp. 25, 65, 115)

Fig. 4.5a
Japan Statistical Year Book 1970, pp. 18–23.

Fig. 4.5b
Municipal Year Book 1940, pp. 28–34.

Fig. 4.5c
Indian Census 1961, *Indian Towns and Cities. Vol. 1. Part II-A(i)*, pp. 363–633.

Fig. 4.6
Indian Empire Census 1881, vol. I, p. 276, vol. II, pp. 232–7.

Fig. 4.7a
Chandler and Fox 1974.
  Note:
  (1) Chandler and Fox values used, when independent estimates for community size and settlement area are supplied.
  (2) In Fletcher (1977, p. 66) I noted that Lanchow in A.D. 1870 and Tientsin in A.D. 1865 had general densities greatly in excess of the overall density ceiling. I suspect that these estimates result from conflating the numbers of people in the *hsien* on to the urban area: see Chandler and Fox (1974, pp. 286, 294).

Fig. 4.7b
Abu-Lughod 1969, p. 175; Adams 1965, p. 89; Aldridge 1969, pp. 19, 99; Andréadès 1920, pp. 73, 84, 89, 90, 95, 106: Bielenstein 1976, pp. 12, 16, 21; Chandler and Fox 1974; Encyclopaedia of Islam 1913, vol. I, pp. 815–26; Gamble and Burgess 1921, pp. 56, 94; Harcourt 1866, pp. 1–9; Heinrich 1976, pp. 168, 174; Herrmann 1966, p. 13; Hu Chia 1956, pp. 36–8; Le Strange 1924, pp. 325–6; Le Tourneau 1961, p. 4; Maclagan 1968, pp. 24–5; Moholy-Nagy 1968, p. 125; New Encyclopaedia Britannica 1974, pp. 1066–71; Rao and Desai 1965, p. 27; Rice 1967, p. 144; Rogers 1976, p. 20; Rozman 1973, pp. 288, 295, 296; Russell 1962, pp. 13, 35–42.
  Note: J. C. Russell (1958; 1972) generally inclines toward *much* lower estimates of the numbers of people in these large urban centres.

Fig. 4.8a
Barroux 1951, p. 205; Beajeu-Garnier 1967b, pp. 41, 42; Chevalier 1949, pp. 157–64, 287; Clark 1951, p. 496; Clout 1972, pp. 73–5; Couperie 1970; Dickinson 1951, p. 233; Doxiadis 1968, p. 101; Hall 1971, pp. 59, 61, 62, 69; Lucien 1923; Mumford 1966, p. 407; Rudé 1970, p. 35; Russell 1958, p. 119; Russell 1972, pp. 148–52; Sutcliffe 1970, pp. 1, 3, 27; Vizetelley 1971, pp. 4–6; Weber 1899, p. 463.
  Note: Smaller estimates of number of people by J. C. Russell suggest a more rapid increase in community size than the Chandler and Fox or Couperie estimates.

Fig. 4.8b

Brett-James 1935, pp. 321, 322, 495–515; Clark 1951, pp. 493, 496; Clark 1967, p. 340; Clayton 1964, pp. 13, 15, 16, 22, 47; Doxiadis 1968, p. 101; Hall 1963, pp. 19, 20; Hall 1971, pp. 30, 31, 62; Jacobs 1961, pp. 368, 380; Jenkins 1973, p. 29; London Census 1911–12, pp. 34–49; Norrie 1961, p. 3; Rudé 1970, pp. 36–9; Rudé 1971, pp. 4–5; Russell 1958, p. 69; Russell 1972, pp. 121–5; Stewart and Warntz 1958, p. 103; Trent 1965, pp. 252–3; Weber 1899, p. 463; Williams 1964, p. 18; Wrigley 1967.

Note:

(1) There are discrepancies in estimates of numbers of people e.g. A.D. 1700, Wrigley gives 575000; Dr George gives 674350 (see Rudé (1971, pp. 4–5)).

(2) From A.D. 1800. Central London encompasses the city and areas to the west.

REFERENCES

Abu-Lughod, J. (1969). 'Varieties of urban experience. Contrast, coexistence and coalescence in Cairo' in I. M. Lapidus (ed.) *Middle Eastern Cities*, California University Press

Adams, R. McC. (1965). *Land Behind Baghdad : a history of settlement on the Diyala Plains*, Chicago University Press

(1972). *The Uruk Countryside : the natural settling of urban societies*, Chicago University Press

Aldridge, J. (1969). *Cairo*, Macmillan

Alexander, J. (1972). 'The beginnings of urban life in Europe' in P. J. Ucko, R. Tringham and G. W. Dimblebey (eds.) *Man, Settlement and Urbanism*, Duckworth

Andréadès, A. (1920). 'De la population de Constantinople sous les Empereurs Byzantins', *Métron* 1(2): 68–119

Barroux, R. (1951). *Paris des Origines à nos Jours et son Rôle dans L'histoire de la Civilisation*, Payot

Beajeu-Garnier, J. J. (1967a). *Urban Geography*, Longmans

(1967b). *Atlas de Paris et de la région Parisieene*, Berger-Levrault

Best, R. H., Jones, A. R. and Rogers, A. W. (1974). 'The density-size rule', *Urban Studies* 2: 201–8

Best, R. H., Rogers, A. W. (1973). *The Urban Countryside*, Faber and Faber

Bielenstein, H. (1976). 'Lo-Yang in Later Han Times', *Museum of Far Eastern Antiquities Bulletin* 48: 1–142

Brett-James, N. G. (1935). *The Growth of Stuart London*, Allen and Unwin

Calhoun, J. B. (1962). 'Population density and social pathology', *Scientific American* 220: 139–48

Chagnon, N. A. (1974). *Studying the Yanamamo*, Holt, Rinhart and Winston

Chan, H. K. (1970). 'The provision of public housing in Hong Kong', unpublished M.A. thesis, Sydney University

Chandler, T. and Fox, G. (1974). *3000 Years of Urban Growth*, Academic Press

Cherry, C. (1966). *On Human Communication : a review, a survey, a criticism* (2nd edn), Massachusetts Institute of Technology Press

Chevalier, L. (1949). *La Formation de la Population Parisienne au XIXe Siècle*, Presses Universitaires

Christian, J. J., Lloyd, J. A. and David, D. E. (1960). 'Factors of mass mortality in a herd of Sika deer. *Cervus nippon*', *Chesapeake Science* 1: 79–95

Clark, C. (1951). 'Urban population densities', *Journal of the Royal Statistical Society, Series A* 114: 490–6

(1958). 'Transport-maker and breaker of cities', *Town Planning Review* 28: 237–50

(1967). *Population Growth and Land Use*, Macmillan

Clayton, R. (1964). *The Geography of Greater London*, Philip and Son

Clout, H. D. (1972). *The Geography of Post-War France: a social and economic approach*, Pergamon Press

Collis, J. (1975). *Defended Sites of the Late La Tène* (Supplementary Series, No. 2), British Archaeological Reports

Cook, S. F. (1956). 'The aboriginal population of the north coast of California', *University of California Archaeological Records* 16(3)

(1972). *Prehistoric Demography* (Current Topics in Anthropology, Vol. 3, Module 16), Addison-Wellesley

Couperie, P. (1970). *Paris through the Ages: an illustrated historical atlas of urbanism and architecture*, Barrie and Jenkins

Dantzig, G. G. and Saaty, T. L. (1973). *Compact City: a plan for a liveable urban environment*, Freeman and Company

Dickinson, R. E. (1951). *The West European City: a geographical interpretation*, Routledge and Kegan Paul

Doxiadis, C. A. (1968). *Ekistics: an introduction to the science of human settlements*, Hutchinson

Dozier, E. P. (1954). 'The Hopi-Tewa of Arizona', University of California, Publications in *American Archaeology and Ethnology* 44(3)

(1970). *Pueblo Indians of North America* (Case Studies in Cultural Anthropology), Holt, Rinehart and Winston

Draper, P. (1973). 'Crowding among hunter–gatherers. The !Kung Bushmen', *Science* 182: 301–3

Drucker, P. (1963). *Indians of the North-West Coast*, Natural History Press

Encyclopaedia of Islam (1913). Vol. I, Luzac and Company

Epstein, T. S. (1962). *Economic Development and Social Change in South India*, Manchester University Press

Esser, A. H. (1971). *Behaviour and Environment: the use of space by animals and men*, Plenum Press

Fernandez II, C. A. and Lynch, F. (1972). 'The Tasaday: cave-dwelling food gatherers of South Cotabato, Mindanao', *Phillipine Sociological Review* 20(3), 279–330

Fewkes, J. W. (1895–6). 'Archaeological expedition to Arizona in 1895', *Bureau of American Ethnology 17th Annual Report* 527–721

Firth, J. R. (1962). 'Housing in Hong Kong', *Architectural Association Journal* 78 (June-July): 46–52

Fletcher, R. (1976). 'Space in settlements: a mechanism of adaptation', Unpublished Ph.D. thesis, Cambridge University

(1977a). *Alternatives and Differences* (Supplementary Series, No. 19), British Archaeological Reports

(1977b). 'Settlement studies (micro and semi-micro)', in D. L. Clarke (ed.) *Spatial Archaeology*, Academic Press

Fooks, E. L. (1946). *X-Ray the City; the density diagram: basis for urban planning*, Ruskin Press

Fraser, D. (1968). *Village Planning in the Primitive World*, Studio Vista

Freedman, J. L. (1975). *Crowding and Behaviour*, Freeman and Company

Galle, O. R., Grove, W. R. and McPherson, J. M. (1972). 'Population density and pathology: what are the relations for Man?', *Science* 176: 23–30

Gamble, S. D. and Burgess, J. S. (1921). *Peking : a social survey*, Oxford University Press

Golger, O. J. (1972). *Squatters and Resettlement: symptoms of an urban crisis. Environmental conditions of low standard public housing in Hong Kong*, Harrassowitz

Gruen, V. (1965). *The Heart of Our Cities. The urban crisis: diagnosis and cure*, Thames and Hudson

Gubser, N. J. (1965). *The Nunamuit Eskimo : hunters of caribou*, Yale University Press

Hall, P. (1963). *London 2000*, Faber and Faber
    (1971). *The World Cities*, McGraw-Hill

Harcourt, A. (1866). *The New Guide to Delhi*, Savielle

Heinrich, E. (1976). 'Der Sturz Assurs und Baukunst der Chaldäerkonige in Babylon', *Archäologischer Anzeiger* 2: 166–80

Herrmann, A. (1966). *An Historical Atlas of China*, Djambatan

Higgs, E. S. (ed.) (1975). *Palaeoeconomy*, Cambridge University Press

Hodge, F. W. (ed.) (1907). 'Handbook of Indians north of Mexico', *Bureau of American Ethnology Bulletin* 30

Hoover, E. G. and Vernon, R. (1959). *Anatomy of a Metropolis. The changing distribution of people and jobs within the New York Metropolitan Region*, Doubleday and Company

Hu Chia. (1956). *Peking Today and Yesterday*, Foreign Language Press

Indian Census (1961). *Village Surveys, Vol. I. VI and Part VI for each State*, Census Commission
    Indian Towns and Cities, Vol. I. Part II-A (i), Census Commission

Indian Empire Census. (1881). *Statistics of Population Vols. I, II*, Census Commission

Jacob, E. F. (1961). *The Fifteenth Century 1399–1485* (The Oxford History of England, 6), Oxford University Press

Japan Statistical Year Book (1970). Bureau of Statistics

Jenkins, A. (1973). *London's City*. Heinemann

Kathmandu Report (1969). *The Physical Development Plan for the Kathmandu Valley*, His Majesty's Government of Nepal

Kennedy, T. F. (1967). *Afghanistan Village* (The World's Villages), Longmans

Kraemer, W. and Schubert, F. (1970). *Die Ausgrabungen in Manching 1955–61 Einfuhrung und Fundstellenübersicht* (Ausgrabungen in Manching I), Steiner

Kroeber, A. L. (1919). 'Zuni kin and clan', *Kroeber Anthropological Papers of the American Museum of Natural History* 18: 39–205

Lange, C. H. (1959). *Cochiti: A New Mexico Pueblo, past and present*, Texas University Press

Le Strange, G. (1924). *Baghdad during the Abbasid Caliphate from Contemporary Arabic and Persian Sources* (reissue), Oxford University Press

Le Tourneau, R. (1961). *Fez in the Age of the Marinides*, Oklahoma University Press

Lockwood, B. (1971). *Samoan Village Economy*, Melbourne University Press

London Census (1911–12). *London Statistics Vol. XXII*, London County Council
    (1971). *Census Data for London*, Greater London Council

Lucien, G. (1923). 'Origin and growth of Paris', *Geographical Review* 13: 345–67

Maclagan, M. (1968). *The City of Constantinople* (Ancient Peoples and Places), Thames and Hudson

Martelli, G. (1960). *Agent Extraordinary: the story of Michel Hollard*, Collins

Maybury-Lewis, D. (1967). *Akwẽ-Shavante Society*, Clarendon

McClellan, C. (1975). 'My old people say. An ethnographic survey of Southern Yukon Territory', *National Museum of Man Publications in Ethnology* 6(1)

Métraux, A. (1935). 'Les Indiens Uro-Čipaya de Carangas', *Journal de la Société des Américanistes*, New Series, 27: 75–128

Mindeleff, V. (1886–7). 'A study of Pueblo architecture, Tusayan and Cibola', *Bureau of American Ethnology 8th Annual Report* 13–235

Millon, R. (ed.) (1974). *Urbanisation at Teotihuacán, Mexico*, vol. 1, *Text*, vol. 2, *Maps*, Texas University Press

Mitchell, R. E. (1971). 'Some social implications of high-density housing', *American Sociological Review* 36: 18–29

Moholy-Nagy, S. (1968). *Matrix of Man. An illustrated history of urban environment*, Pall Mall Press

Mumford, L. (1966). *The City in History*, Penguin Books

Municipal Year Book (1940). The International City Manager's Association

Murdoch, J. (1887–8). 'Ethnological results of the Point Barrow Expedition', *Bureau of American Ethnology 9th Annual Report* 19–451

Nelson, E. W. (1896–7). 'The Eskimo about Bering Strait', *Bureau of American Ethnology 18th Annual Report* 3–518

New Encyclopaedia Britannica (1974) *Macropaedia*, vol. 15, Benton

Nordic Statistics, Yearbook of (1968), The Nordic Council

Norrie, I., (ed.) (1961). *The Book of the City*, High Hill Books

Ojo, G. J. A. (1966). *Yoruba Palaces: a study of Afins of Yorubaland*, London University Press

Parsons, E. C. (1962). 'Isleta paintings', *Bureau of American Ethnology Bulletin* 181

Pfeiffer, J. E. (1977). *The Emergence of Society: a prehistory of the Establishment*, McGraw-Hill

Presser, J. (1965). *Ashes in the Wind: the destruction of Dutch Jewry*, Souvenir Press

Rao, V. K. R. V. and Desai, P. B. (1965). *Greater Delhi: a study in urbanisation, 1940–1957*, Asia Publications

The Region's Growth (May 1967). New York Regional Planning Association

Rice, T.T. (1967). *Everyday Life in Byzantium*, Batsford

Rivière, P. (1969). *Marriage among the Trio: a principle in social organisation*, Clarendon

Rogers, E. S. (1962). 'The Round Lake Objibwa', *Royal Ontario Museum, University of Toronto, Art and Archaeology Division Occasional Paper* 5

Rogers, M. (1976). *The Spread of Islam* (Making of the Past), Elsevier-Phaidon

Rohner, R. D. (1967). 'The people of Gilford: a contemporary Kwakiutl village', *National Museums of Canada Bulletin* 225

Rozman, G. (1973). *Urban Networks in Ch'ing China and Togugawa Japan* Princeton University Press

Rudé, G. (1970). *Paris and London in the Eighteenth Century*, Fontana
  (1971). *Hanoverian London. 1714–1808*, Secker and Warburg

Russell, D. (1962). *Medieval Cairo and the Monasteries of Wādi Natrūn*, Wiedenfeld and Nicholson

Russell, J. C. (1958). 'Late ancient and medieval population', *Transactions of the American Philosophical Society* 43(3)
  (1972). *Medieval Regions and their Cities*, David and Charles

Schwimmer, E. G. (1973). *Exchange in the Social Structure of Orokaiva; traditional and emergent ideologies in the northern district of Papua*, Hurst

Scully, V. (1975). *Pueblo. Mountain, Village, Dance*, Thames and Hudson

Sen, B. K. and Sen, J. (1955). 'Notes on the Birhors', *Man in India* 35(3): 110–18

Stewart, J. Q. and Warntz, W. (1958). 'Physics of population distribution', *Journal of Regional Science* 1: 99–123

Sutcliffe, A. (1970). *The Autumn of Central Paris. The defeat of town planning. 1850–1970*, Arnold

Talbot, P. A. (1926). *The Peoples of Southern Nigeria: a sketch of their history, ethnology and languages with an abstract of the 1921 Census. Vol. IV*, Mitford

Tindale, N. B. (1972). 'The Pitjandjara', in M. G. Bicchieri (ed.) *Hunters and Gatherers Today: a socioeconomic study of eleven such cultures in the Twentieth century*, Holt, Rinehart and Winston

Titiev, M. (1944). 'Old Oraibi: a study of the Hopi Indians of Third Mesa', *Peabody Museum Papers* 22(1)

Trent, C. (1965). *Greater London; its growth and development through two thousand years*, Phoenix House

Turner, F. C. (1976). 'The rush to the cities in Latin America', *Science* 192: 955–62

U.S. Census of Population (1960). *10076, PC(1)-B series*, N.Y. No. *34B*, The Bureau of the Census

Vagnby, B. and Jacobs, A. H. (1974). 'Kenya: traditional housing of the Elmolo', *Ekistics* 227: 240–3

Vanstone, J. W. (1971). 'Historic settlement patterns in the Nushagak River region, Alaska', *Fieldiana. Anthropology* 61

Vanstone, J. W. and Townsend, J. B. (1970). Kijik: 'An historic Tanaina Indian Settlement', *Fieldiana. Anthropology* 59

Velder, C. M. (1963). 'A description of the Mrabi camp', *Journal of the Siam Society* 51: 185–8

Vizetelly, E. A. (1971). *Paris and her People: under the Third Republic*, Kraus Reprint

Waterman, T. T. (1920). 'Yurok geography', *University of California. Publications in American Archaeology and Ethnology* 16

Weber, A. F. (1899). *The Growth of Cities in the Nineteenth Century: a study in statistics*, Columbia University Press

White, L. A. (1962). 'The Pueblo of Sia, New Mexico', *Bureau of American Ethnology Bulletin* 184

Williams, P. (1964). *Life in Tudor England* (English Life Series), Batsford

Woodburn, J. C. (1972). 'Ecology, nomadic movement and the composition of the local group among hunters and gatherers: an East African example and its implications', in P. J. Ucko, R. Tringham and G. W. Dimblebey (eds.) *Man, Settlement and Urbanism*, Duckworth

Wright, H. T. (1969). 'The administration of rural production in an early Mesopotamian town', *University of Michigan. Museum of Anthropology Publication* 38

Wrigley, E. A. (1967). 'A simple model of London's importance in changing English society and economy. 1650–1750', *Past and Present* 37: 44–77

Wyon, J. B. and Gordon, J. E. (1971). *The Khanna Society: population problems in the rural Punjab*, Harvard University Press

Yde, J. (1965). 'Material Culture of the Wai-Wai', *Nationalmuseets Skrifter* 10

Yellen, J. E. (1977). *Archaeological Approaches to the Present* (Studies in Archaeology), Academic Press.

Young, M. W. (1971). *Fighting with Food: leadership, values and social control in a Massim society*, Cambridge University Press

PART II

Settlement pattern:
depositional, post-depositional and analytical theory

5

Stone Age visiting cards: approaches to the study of early land use patterns

GLYNN ISAAC

Human or animal land use can be considered as comprising a web of pathways over a piece of terrain. The concept can be made more explicit if one imagines fixing a transmitter onto each individual of any species for which a land use pattern is to be determined. Then, if a remote sensor high above continuously plotted the position of the transmitters, a map would form with lines marking the movements of the members of the species. For modern humans one would expect an image which was formed over several days to show criss-crossing networks of lines with clearly defined nodes at places to which people repeatedly returned. One set of nodes would involve the presence of groups of individuals at particular locales for many hours, especially their presence at certain nodes each night. These overnight nodes would mainly be what archaeologists term 'settlements'. Many of the plotted movement trajectories would prove to be irregular loops extending radially from the settlement nodes (Fig. 5.1a).

If this hypothetical movement recording were carried out for the species which is the closest living evolutionary relative of mankind, a very different pattern could be expected (Fig. 5.1b, c). Nodes would be far less conspicuous features, and those which were represented would be found not to involve repeated overnight groupings of individuals, but only temporary aggregations at attractions such as groves of fruit trees in season. There would be no points in space that could be called 'settlements'.

Different human societies would imprint traces that would differ greatly in scale, density and detailed configuration, but all would be compounded of repeating modules rather like that shown in Fig. 5.1. If available, knowledge of movement patterns such as is envisaged here could be used to discern important intra-specific differences in human social and economic systems, and, as already indicated, differences in movement patterns are also indicative of major differences between species in their social organisation and ecological relations.

Now, while we do not have movement and land use plans compiled in the way just imagined, ethnographic and zoologic data often allow one to envisage at least the approximate character of the trace which would be obtained for living human societies and for living animal species. But what of the past?

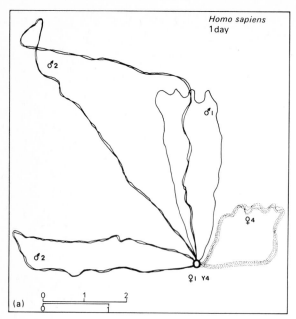
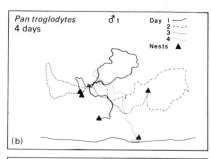
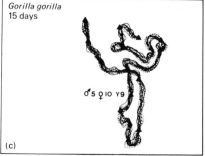

5.1.   A human pattern of movement in landscape compared with patterns recorded for
the closest living non-human relatives of mankind. (a) Zum/wasi (!Kung) hunter–
gatherers over one day. (b) A chimpanzee over four days. (c) A gorilla troop over
fifteen days. All are drawn to the same scale. Notice the relatively great area spanned
by the human 'radial' pattern.

What can be done if one's interest is in the evolutionary development of the
distinctive human pattern and in the prehistoric land use patterns of early
humans and protohumans? Our records of the past are meagre, but evidence
does exist.

    First, all animals possessing bodies which include hard, relatively imperi-
shable parts leave a potential record of their trajectory at one point in their
network of movements – the terminal point! At the moment of death, unless
the carcass is transported, the position reached by the organism is marked
by the presence of bones or a shell. Of these at least some may become fossils
more or less at the point of death, thereby creating a partial record of points
in the web of movement.

    For a piece of terrain where conditions of fossil preservation without
displacement are widespread, the aggregate of loci of the fossils may provide
statistical indicators of the segments of the sedimentary basin which were
most frequented by various fossil-forming organisms. Of course it must be
borne in mind that if individuals tended to die more frequently in some
portions of their range, or if the preservation rate was higher in some portions,
then the fossil record of land use (habitat preference) would be correspondingly
biassed (see the taphonomic studies of Behrensmeyer 1975, 1976 and in press;
Hill 1975 and in press).

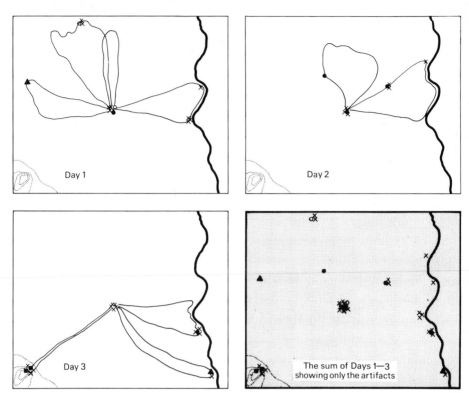

5.2.   The formation of scatters of different artifact forms over a landscape through daily movements from a single home base. A dense cluster of artifacts marks the home base node in movements – other minor scatters mark activity loci or transient camps.

Within this general framework the human species and its evolutionary antecedents constitute a special case. As with other vertebrates, humans may deposit their skeletal remains as markers at points scattered about the web of their movements, but they also mark their trajectories in other ways. At intervals throughout the life of each individual, distinctive objects, 'artifacts', may be discarded. As in the case of skeletal parts, if these discards are not secondarily transported, they serve to mark points in the web of movements of the population that formed and abandoned them. Fig. 5.2 provides graphic representation of the way in which these familiar processes operate to produce the potential for an archaeological 'image' of human and protohuman land use.

We have already seen that for the human species a cumulative map of the lines of movement of individuals shows the existence of conspicuous nodes in which the pathways of many movement episodes tend to begin and end. As Foley shows in chapter 6, the archaeological image provided by the location of artifacts exhibits analogous patterning: there are concentrated, localised accumulations of refuse which represent acts of discard repeated by numbers of individuals over a span of time. Common knowledge of contemporary human behaviour leads us to expect that many of these concentrated patches of material relicts are associated with 'settlement' nodes, but nodes which can be termed quarries, 'factories', butchery locales, etc. may also produce distinctive accumulations.

In idealised terms I have summarised the familiar processes whereby archaeological configurations may be indicative of past human use patterns. There are, of course, factors which complicate behavioural interpretation of the overall spatial patterns found in the real world:

1. Only those portions of human lines of movement along which durable artifacts are discarded will be represented in the imprint.

2. If the objects are transported after discard by natural agencies, they do not directly document points in the ancient web of movements.

3. Humans may deliberately transport discarded material away from its original place of discard. This process leads to the formation of 'secondary refuse' deposits (Schiffer 1976) which, though part of the articulated set of evidence, have to be recognised and suitably interpreted.

4. Archaeologists have access only to a miniscule sample of the total number of artifact discard acts which originally formed the entirety of the potential record for the area and time period in question. Bias due to differential preservation, to differential re-exposure and due to imperfect recovery, all have to be assessed and allowed for.

It should then be very clear that the archaeological record as it comes down to us is in no sense a simple 'map' of where humans discarded things, much less a map of where they used things or of where they went. However, it is a partial image, albeit distorted and blurred, and with care and caution inferences can be drawn about the spatial configuration of daily life and about aspects of the use of the landscape.

This introduction has been concerned with generalities about the way in which human behaviour generates a record of aspects of spatial organisation. The record for the last few thousand years is known in many areas to be rich and complex with intricate variations and permutations on the simplified themes indicated. However, in this essay I want to turn to the remote past and examine whether interpretational principles such as those outlined can help in the study of early stages of human life; stages in excess of half a million years; stages which might be termed 'protohuman'. More recent material is discussed by Foley in the chapter which follows.

My sense of the problems explored here has been greatly influenced by the work of David Clarke and he in fact read and commented on a draft of this paper a month before his death. I gratefully acknowledge this influence.

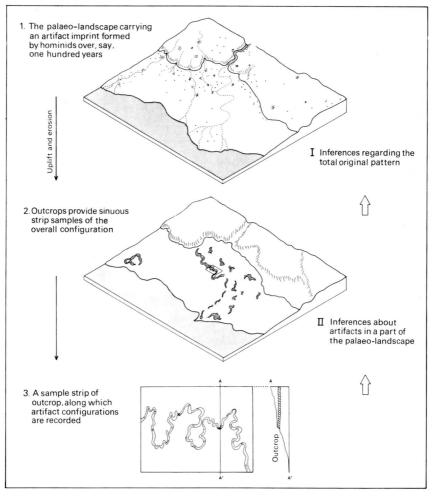

1. The palaeo-landscape carrying an artifact imprint formed by hominids over, say, one hundred years

Uplift and erosion

I Inferences regarding the total original pattern

2. Outcrops provide sinuous strip samples of the overall configuration

II Inferences about artifacts in a part of the palaeo-landscape

3. A sample strip of outcrop, along which artifact configurations are recorded

Outcrop

5.3. The processes which form the archaeological record of early hominid land use in sedimentary basins such as those of the East African Rift Valley. Reading the sequence from top to bottom shows the steps by which our sample of information becomes available to us. Reading from bottom to top, the sequence represents a chain of inferences. The diagram is based on Koobi Fora (Isaac and Harris 1978).

EMPIRICAL OBSERVATIONS

Fig. 5.3 illustrates the kind of configuration which confronts archaeologists who study early human life using the record preserved in a large-scale sedimentary formation – such as that of Olduvai (Leakey 1971; Hay 1976), the Omo (Coppens *et al.* 1976) or Koobi Fora (Leakey and Leakey 1978), etc. The record available for a given interval of past time represents a complex aggregate of samples. Each 'sample' is provided by the sinuous outcrop strip of one of a series of beds which can be determined to have been deposited within the time interval under study. By assembling the available data stepwise as shown in the figure, it may be possible to make an assessment of the characteristics of what was once the overall pattern.

The diagrams represent the sort of pattern which has been perceived in various early-man bearing formations in East Africa, and notwithstanding the fact that methods for surveying, recording and measuring are still in very early stages of development, it is possible to report on the general characteristics. Over some parts of the floors of the sedimentary basins there existed, and was preserved, a low density *scatter* of discarded artifacts – isolated flakes or cores or small groupings of a few items. Very rough guesses of the minimum density of objects per unit area would be less than one piece per 10000 m² and superimposed on this background scatter it is common to find some patches where objects occur in much higher densities (e.g. 1–100 per m²). It is these patches or concentrations of materials that are commonly called 'sites' and archaeological attention has been focussed almost exclusively upon them. Although the densities of the scatters between patches are often extremely low, the areas are very large and it is probable that for the early prehistoric period many more artifacts lie outside 'sites' than are contained within them.

There are two other aspects of the observed pattern to which attention should be drawn. First, both discarded artifacts and hominid skeletal remains constitute fossilised visiting cards. Their distributions are not necessarily the same and the two kinds of records need to be considered and interpreted jointly (Isaac and Harris 1978, Fig. 4.2). Second, animal bones, like artifacts, were scattered over the palaeo-landscape and they, like 'artifacts', show a patchy distribution. The coincidence or non-coincidence of relatively dense patches of bone with relatively dense patches of discarded artifacts has given rise to an empirical classification of 'site' types (Isaac 1978; Isaac and Harris 1978; Isaac and Crader in press):

Type A concentrated patch of artifacts only.
Type B a concentration of artifacts coincident with numerous bones from the carcass of a single large animal.
Type C coincident concentrations of artifacts and the bones of many different species of animal.
Type O concentrated patch of bones only.

The recognition of the existence of a background scatter of artifacts, with superimposed concentrations and the recognition of variable patterns of association between clusters of bones and clusters of stone artifacts, are based on empirical observations; however, they have great potential importance in the interpretation of patterns of early protohuman life.

THE STRUCTURE OF THE SPATIAL ARRAY: AN HIERARCHIC MODEL

In the foregoing section and in Fig. 5.3 I have treated the archaeological record as a patterned array of points in space. If one is to build a theory or model that will allow the array to be interpreted one should perhaps start by asking what are these points? What are the irreducible units of spatial analysis? What is the archaeological equivalent of a fundamental particle? For present purposes in palaeo-anthropological archaeology the fundamental particle should probably be taken as any individual discrete item that provides evidence of protohuman presence. Normally these will be individual artifacts however small and trivial, but they could include such items as a distinctively broken bone, a scooped out pit, or whatever. The location of each of these irreducible items would constitute the points on the base plot of a comprehensive spatial analysis.

From our knowledge of the human way of life and from our acquaintance with the empirical features of the record, we would expect to find a hierarchy of linked sets, incorporating the 'fundamental points'. Pursuing the physics analogy, one can perhaps recognise the equivalent of an atomic particle. Perhaps in archaeology this is the set of objects representing a behavioural event which is in a sense indivisible. A set of conjoinable pieces from a single knapping episode might be one example. Others would be the job lot of bones from a single meal; a unified configuration of post holes and so forth.

The next level in the hierarchy, the equivalent of a molecule or compound, can, like molecules, be of very variable scale, but it would always be a complex cluster of archaeological datum points representing a number of episodes or a number of different actions. Most archaeological sites are entities at this level. Whether or not we can resolve the components, they are in fact clusters of clusters.

At still higher levels, 'sites' form a patterned set across the face of a region with their location determined by factors such as the distribution of resources, the density and organisation of population and the network of communication and trade. This level is what is commonly referred to as a 'settlement pattern', a 'regional system', or a 'between-site system'. In a general way the hierarchy just outlined parallels that set up by David Clarke (1977) but for the purposes of analysis of patterns of very early land use a variant along the lines indicated is needed (Fig. 5.4).

It should be noted that instances of levels one and two can either be independent entities or can exist as components of the next one or two hierarchical levels. Level 4 is that total array of all locations of hominid relicts in a region. A level 4 array could in theory be made up entirely of unclustered fundamental datum points (level 1) without the existence in the particular case of any second or third order groupings.

It should also be noted that the single action-episode cluster is incorporated into the system because common experience of the organisation of human

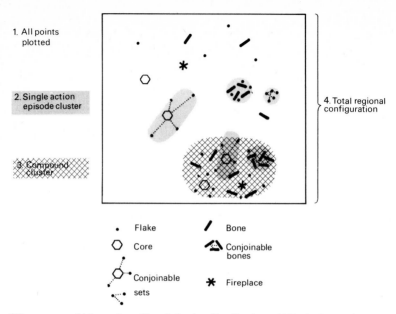

1. All points plotted

2. Single action episode cluster

3. Compound cluster

4. Total regional configuration

· Flake

◇ Core

⬡ Conjoinable sets

∕ Bone

◭ Conjoinable bones

✳ Fireplace

5.4. The proposed hierarchy of levels in the distributions of Early Stone Age relics. This is a variant on the system of Clarke (1977) that allows for the fact that houses and 'structures' are virtually absent from the early record. Each plotted item in the diagram is a fundamental datum point (level 1). Some but not all of these are grouped into level 2 clusters. Compound cluster (level 3) may involve both groupings of individual datum points and internally recognisable action-episode clusters (level 2). The totality of the distribution of points over a given area, regardless of intermediate clustering, is level 4.

behaviour establishes the fact of its existence. Manifestations of this level are sometimes recognisable as such in the archaeological record, but very often the distinction between sets of items comprising several individual action-episode clusters becomes blurred or totally obscured when they are grouped in a compound cluster (level 3).

Perhaps the foregoing account of a model and the hierarchic framework used to describe it can be made more explicit by reference to an actual example. While in Australia in 1976, I was privileged to be given a brief tour of the Lake Mungo area by Wilfred Shawcross and John Mulvaney. The configuration of archaeological relicts that was shown to me there exemplified very clearly the structure we were groping to discern in our studies of much older, but apparently analogous materials in East Africa.

During part of the Upper Pleistocene the 'Lake' Mungo depression, which is now a dry, saline playa, contained an extensive, shallow body of fresh water which was part of a whole system of lakes in the Willandra region (Bowler 1971). From the downwind shore of the lake sand, silt and clay were continually blown so as to form a large crescent-shaped dune field of very low relief. Stone-using human inhabitants of the region came at intervals and used the dune area in various ways and left their marks on it. As time passed both the deposition of sand and human usage of the area continued so that the leavings of successive episodes tend to be separated from previous ones by small thicknesses of sand. Eventually the deposition of the Mungo Formation ceased. After a period of soil formation other deposits covered it; but in recent times the process has gone into reverse. Perhaps because of over-grazing, the ancient dune ('lunette') is being eroded by wind and rain and from wide relatively flat expanses the deposits are being stripped by the removal of successive thin 'skins' of sediment. As this natural excavation proceeds, relics of past human usage emerge at the surface. Initially the original configuration is preserved, but as time goes on material is let down and a lag concentrate forms, which is superimposed on the material *in situ*. Even so, walking about, it is possible to form an impression of the structure of the original arrays re-exposed.

The primary data points that are unequivocal human visiting cards consist of such traces as individual stone artifacts ('tools', cores and flakes), or the remains of a fireplace. These may occur as isolated items remote from any other visible human relict or they may occur as parts of clusters representative of a level 2 or 3 entity.

Clusters indicative of a single indivisible action episode are also visible – for instance, small clusters of flakes from a common core, burials or cremations and clumps of mussel shells, each apparently indicative of a single 'meal'. (An individual isolated mussel shell cannot readily be treated as a primary archaeological datum point, because it might just as well have been deposited by a bird or mammalian carnivore.)

Compound clusters of varying character also occur. They range from small-scale occurrences consisting of a fireplace and a clump of mussel shells, to scatters of stone artifacts, some broken bones and/or shells extending over many tens of square metres. The internal structure of these clusters could not be perceived in a brief tour such as I was given. Parts of some examples of such compound occurrences have been excavated by Shawcross (1975); by McBryde (n.d.); by Bowler *et al.* (1970) and elsewhere in the area by McIntyre (n.d.).

Clearly the interpretation of the configuration of the Lake Mungo archaeo- logical array must be made by Shawcross and the others who are engaged in detailed, systematic studies, but this simple description of the configuration has perhaps indicated the potential of the framework set out in Fig. 5.4.

Nowhere in the world has the total array of relics from any ancient non-agricultural society been preserved and then rendered available in its entirety through gentle erosion. What is available varies greatly between areas and between spans of time within an area.

The following are examples of low energy sedimentation mechanisms, which can cover extensive portions of a landscape preserving intact broadcast arrays of relics with all four levels observable and analysable: (1) aeolian sedimentation as in a dune field (e.g. Lake Mungo) or a loess mantle; (2) flood plain sedimentation on the valley floor of a big river (e.g. the Nile (Wendorf and Schild 1976; Wendorf and Marks 1975)); (3) volcanic ash falls in the vicinity of volcanic vents (e.g. Eburru in Kenya (Isaac 1972), or Laetolil, Tanzania (Leakey and Hay 1979)); (4) alluvial and lake margin sedimentation in a lake basin (e.g. the Rift Valley study areas of Olduvai (Leakey 1971; Hay 1976) or Koobi Fora (Leakey and Leakey 1978)).

At another extreme, only isolated nodes in the former array may be preserved – as for instance in the case of many cave sites or the Terra Amata open-air Acheulian site (de Lumley 1969).

The manner in which nature has selectively preserved part of a once widespread configuration and then selectively, by erosion, made available a part of the past, has to be considered in designing research and interpreting results.

POSSIBILITIES FOR RESEARCH DESIGNS

In relation to varying objectives and in response to differences in the preservation or recoverability of the array of relicts, several different approaches have emerged in attempting land usage inferences from the configuration of 'stone-age' archaeological remains.

(1) The first might be designated as the 'classic' *distribution map* study, as in Groube's contribution to this volume (ch. 7). After a region has been explored extensively, the locations of all 'sites' are plotted on a map. In almost all cases 'site' refers to a 'compound cluster' in the terminology developed earlier in this essay. Another class of distribution map which plots find-spots of distinctive artifact forms or constituent materials (e.g. hand-axes or bell beakers, obsidian, etc.) generally covers a far wider area than that envisaged here and has usually been used in studies of cultural geography or of trade networks rather than in studies of land use economies (cf. Hodder and Orton 1976, ch. 5).

Given a reasonably comprehensive plot of the locations of sites pertaining to a particular phase in land use patterning, it is conventional to look for regular 'repeated' relationships between site loci and other geographic factors, for example, topography, water bodies, soil zones, vegetation zones, and specific localised resources. Sites with different characteristics may show different associations. Relationships may be assessed by 'inspection' (e.g. Fox 1932) or may involve systematic quantitative measures of associations (cf. Hodder and Orton 1976 for general treatment of such methods). Comprehensive distribution maps can also be analysed for information about the spacing of sites and about the geometry of differentiation amongst them (cf. Hodder and Orton 1976 ch. 4).

(2) A second contrasting approach has achieved prominence under the designation *site catchment analysis* (Vita-Finzi and Higgs 1970; Jarman 1972),

used by Parkington in this volume (ch. 12). Instead of looking at a map in search of repeated relationships between a series of sites and some geographical factors such as was discussed above, this method takes a single site and maps or inventories the 'resources' accessible from that site. In the pioneer works of the Higgs school, 'accessible' was taken to refer to terrain lying within 5 km (for farmers) or within two hours' walking time for hunter–gatherers. More sophisticated work with site catchment techniques together with a critique of the whole approach is contained in Flannery (1976, ch. 4). In that work Zarky's study makes comparisons between the incidence of certain resources within each catchment and averages for the area as a whole. Flannery's own study attempts an empirical estimation of what the catchment area for various commodities actually was and shows that it may be best to think in terms of a nested series of enveloping catchments. Both these studies make explicit an aspect of site catchment analysis that has been too seldom stated. When applied to a single site the technique is simply a useful descriptive device. It is only when the catchment characteristics of a series of sites are examined statistically in search of one or more repetitive patterns that the technique serves to define systems of land use.

An important advantage of site catchment analysis stems from the fact that it does not demand the preservation and discovery of substantial parts of an articulated set of sites, as does distribution map analysis. Data for a series of 'isolated sites' that are believed to have been formed as nodes within the same or similar land use systems can be compiled and the sample of catchment characteristics analysed for regularities.

(3) Another approach is to model the economic and social factors which might be expected to determine the placement of sites within a particular region and then either to do a graphic *simulation* of the distribution which could be expected or to predict in quantitative terms the character and placement of sites (Hodder 1978). The goodness of fit between simulated or predicted patterns and the observed patterns is then taken as a measure of the closeness with which the socioeconomic model does approximate the system which created the observed sites. Examples of this approach are the work of Thomas (1973; 1974) and that of Jochim (1976), while Hamond (ch. 8 below) introduces one of the most advanced examples of this type of work. If this method is applied, alternative input configurations need to be tried, since similar resultant site location patterns may result from more than one combination of input variables.

(4) The fourth approach to be discussed might be seen as a special, intensive version of the distribution map method. It involves collecting information not simply about site distribution, but about the overall distri-bution patterns of fundamental datum points. Sites emerge in the analysis as compound clusters and inferences can be attempted regarding the behavioural and ecological meaning of scatters between sites as well as that of the sites themselves.

Clearly spatial analyses that deal with the distribution of compound clusters (sites) alone are treating only a part of the total configuration. Often this is because only major nodes (sites) within the original system are preserved and detectable. However, where sediment blankets have preserved comprehensive articulated broadcast sets of remains it behoves us at least to try to find out whether studies of the overall pattern do add anything to conventional site location studies. Clearly it is seldom feasible to comb the whole of a large area in search of individual isolated discards so that this approach will have to use sampling techniques.

Robert Foley has independently been pursuing this line of research as reported in his contribution to this volume (ch. 6). He has termed the approach 'off-site archaeology'. I would prefer a designation that makes it clear that sites are concentrations of special interest within a broad-cast array. Following the title of a paper that I and John W. K. Harris wrote in 1975 ('The scatter between the patches'), I would suggest the interim rubric *scatters and patches analysis*.

For those segments of prehistory where the archaeological record consists mainly of small discarded artifacts and food bones, this fourth approach may prove a particularly important additional method and it is at problems in the Palaeolithic that this essay is directed. We are fortunate that many of the localities which preserve very early archaeological evidence do so under circumstances where 'scatters and patches' analysis is possible. The concluding portion of this essay provides examples of three of the four approaches as applied in investigating early hominid patterns of life and land use in East Africa. I have not yet been involved in simulation work. The figures and the discussion provide indications of the applicability of three of the approaches just discussed without attempting definitive interpretation.

EXAMPLES

The *site distribution* approach is illustrated in Fig. 5.5. This shows the known sites from Bed I at Olduvai Gorge (Leakey 1971; Hay 1976) plotted in relation to the detailed palaeo-geographic reconstruction achieved through the meticulous work of Hay. Also shown are the outlines of the margins of the main and side gorges. Inspection of Fig. 5.5 reveals a marked clustering of sites in the area between the margins of the perennial lake and the toe of an alluvial fan. Those reported were all on the lake margin flood plain with two lying to the east of the lake and the other nine (some of which are multi-level sites) to the east. How is such a map to be interpreted? The first point to recognise is that our information on the distribution of the sites does not cover the whole rectangular field represented in Fig. 5.5. Consequently point pattern analysis techniques, such as those treated by Hodder and Orton (1976), are not applicable without modifications. Site locations can only be determined along the outcrops of the relevant sedimentary layers. Fig. 5.5

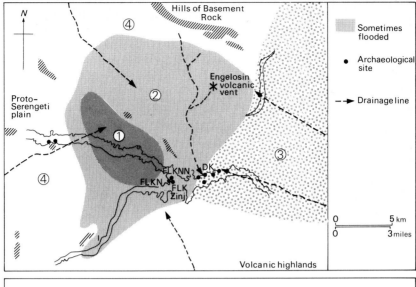

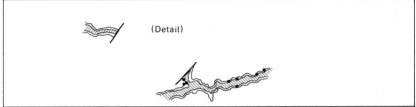

5.5. An example of the 'distribution map' approach applied to studies of early land usage – the location of sites in Bed I Olduvai Gorge (after Leakey 1971, Hay 1976). The sites are shown in relation to environmental zones (as indicated by sedimentary facies). (1) Lake (permanently flooded). (2) Flood plain surrounds of the lake that was swampy and sometimes inundated. (3) An alluvial fan at the foot of the nearby volcanic highland. (4) The blank areas to the west and north were dry plains; those to the south are left blank for lack of information. The margins of the eroded gorge are shown superimposed on the reconstructed palaeogeography. The detail below serves to emphasise that the recorded distribution is only known from outcrop strips along the slopes of the erosion cuts.

makes it explicit that what is available is in fact two irregular transects which sample the geography of the floor of a lake basin. The location of sites along the transect is determinable through systematic survey. Once understood in this light, various questions can be asked about the configuration of sites in this sample. First, is there a demonstrable tendency for the sites to be associated with some of the distinctive palaeo-environmental sectors of the transect rather than others? An observed number of sites per length of outcrop can be compared with an expected number, given a null hypothesis of no preferred location for sites in any of the terrestrial environments. The permanently submerged lake floor needs to be excluded from this comparison since our expectation for number of sites there is zero! This is the classic formulation for a chi-square test of association, though the numbers involved are marginally adequate for such a formal test. The chi-square values, for what they are worth, do not run counter to the inferences drawn by Leakey (1971) and Hay (1976) that the Bed I sites are preferentially associated with the lake margin zone on the eastern shores of the palaeo-lake. They also indicate that the positive association may only be with some sectors of the lake margin zone, since the western sample sector has sites effectively at the expected incidence, and the sector in the side gorge has no observed sites against an expectation of about 4. Hay has suggested that the portion of the transect where the sites cluster was differentiated from the remainder of the lake margin zone by having a greater influx of water which formed relatively fresh pools and swamps around this edge of what was otherwise a saline lake (Leakey 1971; Hay 1976, p. 48).

A second series of questions that one might seek to ask relates to the spacing amongst sites considered as a system and without regard to habitat differences. Within a zone where sites occur, were they clustered or were they randomly spaced? How far apart were those nodes in the artifact-discarding activities of early hominids? Unfortunately the answers to these questions only have full meaning if the nodes under consideration are contemporary, and contemporaneity at the required level of resolution is hard to establish. However, interspersed in these beds are volcanic ash-fall layers which mark out time lines. These can be used to show which sites are *not* contemporary and from this it emerges that almost every one of the nine sites in the approximately 4 km long southeast lake margin sector of the transect can be excluded from being contemporaneous with any other. This negative finding is potentially interesting and suggests that at any given time the locales to which artifacts were transported and discarded were reasonably well spaced out. Archaeologists will need to work with mathematical geographers to learn how to model probable two-dimensional spacing from data collected along linear outcrops.

The foregoing analysis of spatial data for Olduvai Bed I is presented to exemplify the problems of applying the classic distribution map approach to 'buried' landscapes such as are partially preserved in sedimentary basins. Other related approaches are possible; Hay tackled the problem of the association of archaeological sites with particular environments of deposition by analysing his field section logs to determine the average number of vertical metres of section surveyed in each facies for each site encountered (Hay 1976, Table 32). For Bed I in the main gorge the results are shown in Table 5.1.

Clearly since the facies were differentially distributed in the palaeo-landscape, this analysis is a form of spatial analysis and it is a method which deserves to be applied elsewhere. It facilitates incorporating the separate occupation levels of a multi-component site as distinct analytical entities. The section logs relate to a series of sample transects across the outcrop strips and further inferences about the spacing and associations of sites might well be obtainable through more extensive analysis of such data sets.

TABLE 5.1. *Relationship between section thickness and site frequency*

Facies	Total thickness measured	No. of sites (or levels) encountered	Metres of section per site
Lake	133	0	—
Lake margin (eastern)	139	18	7.7
Lake margin (western)	123	2	61.5
Alluvial fan	316	0	—
Alluvial plain (eastern)	97	0	—

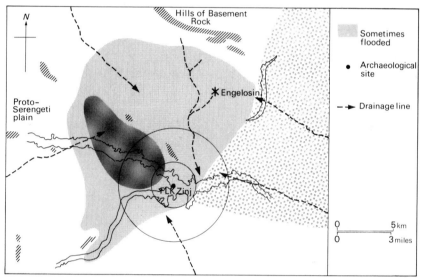

5.6.

An example of the site catchment approach applied to the study of early hominid land use. Two kilometre and five kilometre catchment circles drawn around the Bed I FLK Zinjanthropus site at Olduvai showing the palaeo-geographic zones which were readily accessible from the site.

R. L. Hay's and M. D. Leakey's monographs make it clear that in addition to the concentrations called 'sites' or 'occupation floors' there are stray artifacts scattered through the sediments with the frequency being highly variable between layers and between areas. Measurements of this variability are not yet available so that the relations between the classic site distribution pattern and the 'scatters and patches' pattern are not yet determinable.

The Olduvai example has been chosen for presentation because the data are published and because of the unprecedented thoroughness of the geological and palaeo-geographic information available. Related kinds of data are being assembled in other areas of eastern Africa, for instance at the Omo (Chavaillon 1976; Merrick *et al.* 1976; Merrick 1976) and at Koobi Fora where J. W. K. Harris is pursuing palaeo-geographic studies in conjunction with the

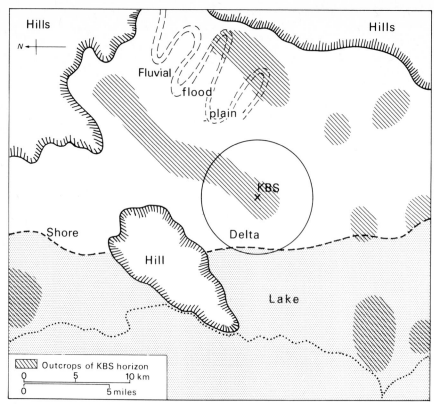

A five kilometre site catchment circle drawn around the KBS site in the Koobi Fora area. The catchment area consisted predominantly of delta flood plain (presumably grassland and swamp traversed by ribbons of riverine bush) but also including lake shore environments and edge of better drained river flood plain environments. The hatched areas show schematically the areas of outcrop from which information on the KBS horizon derives (based on Behrensmeyer 1975; 1976).

geologist I. C. Findlater (Harris 1978; Harris and Herbich 1978; Isaac and Harris 1978; Harris and Isaac in press).

The *site catchment* approach is exemplified in Fig. 5.6 and 5.7. Clearly there are severe problems in doing such an analysis for very ancient sites where the environs of the site today are profoundly different in topography and biota from the environs that existed at the time the site was formed. The problem can be seen to be further complicated when one takes into account that our information about the surroundings of the site is based on an outcrop strip. In some cases (e.g. Fig. 5.7) this strip is sinuous and recurved so that it 'samples' terrain on every side of the site under study. In other cases the outcrops can form essentially a linear transect and the configuration of habitats and resources on both sides of the transect must be based on extrapolations.

These difficulties are formidable, but given that fairly detailed and reasonably reliable environmental reconstructions can be assembled in some cases, it does seem worth while to make tentative exploratory use of the approach and to test its utility.

As already explained, when site catchment analysis is applied to individual sites, it is simply a descriptive device but, as Flannery (1976) has shown, if quantitative data be compiled from catchment data for a series of sites, then the method acquires potential as an analytical tool. Two types of quantification are readily envisaged; (1) the estimated percentage of certain habitat zones within 5 km of the site and (2) the minimum distance from the site to certain key resources or resource clusters. If such data are compiled for a large series of sites, then quantitative analyses would become feasible. The analysis should range from univariate summarising statistics (frequency distribution, means and deviations), through bivariate correlations to multivariate approaches such as principal components analyses (cf. Wood 1976).

The *scatters and patches* approach is one which has been relatively little developed – as yet. Examples known to me of work tending in the direction of treating the distribution of 'sites' and of isolated artifacts as parts of a single system include David Thomas (1973; 1974), Bettinger (1977) and Robert Foley (ch. 6 below). Since 1974 we have been attempting to incorporate this approach into the research of the archaeological segment of Koobi Fora Research Project (Isaac and Harris 1975; in press). In order to provide an example, I will briefly summarise the procedures and the character of the results. Analysis is still proceeding and a full report by J. W. K. Harris and myself will be published elsewhere.

The bottom diagram in Fig. 5.3 presents a plan of an erosion front cutting back through a stratified sequence of sediments such as characterise East African archaeological locales like Olduvai, Omo, Koobi Fora, Melka Kunturé etc. The erosion front is sampling parts of a sequence of superimposed palaeo-landscapes such as the one represented in the top diagram. Artifacts distributed at each 'horizon' are first exposed by the moving erosion front along a sinuous outcrop. Subsequently, gravity and erosional processes may move the pieces down slope where they may become mixed with other artifacts from other outcrops. Ultimately they will either disintegrate as a result of weathering or find their way into the deposits of the present-day rivers and streams. Clearly the series of freshly exposed objects along an outcrop is a sample of the contents of the layer taken along a sinuous transect that traverses a small part of the palaeo-landscape with which the layer was associated during the time of its formation. Equally, all post exposure processes distort and bias this initial sample.

Given an interest in the overall distribution of artifacts on the palaeo-landscapes over which early hominids roamed, how is information to be collected? Sampling by excavation over tens of square kilometres of exposure is obviously impracticable. The question then becomes can we use samples derived by the 'excavation' being done by 'mother nature'? Is the blurring and distorting process, the noise, strong enough to obliterate the signal? The only way to find out was to try! The results so far suggest that the signal can be discerned.

In our work we are mainly concerned with two kinds of archaeological variables: (1) the *density* of artifacts per unit area (or per unit volume of sediment); (2) the *composition* of artifact sets from different sectors of the palaeo-landscape (percentage of type, technique or raw material categories).

The investigation is predicated on the view that these archaeological variables are very possibly 'dependent' variables, the values of which will show predictable relationships to a series of 'independent' palaeo-geographic variables. The two initially considered are: (1) distance of the sample point from the rocky hills of the basin margin; (2) topographic situation as reflected by lithologies indicative of different modes of deposition, e.g. conglomerate and sands indicate portions of stream channels, clays and silts indicate flood plains. For the area under initial investigation, the Karari escarpment, some other potential variables such as distance from the lake shore are effectively constant and consequently did not enter into this particular inquiry. Other potentially significant independant variables may be added when more detailed geological work has been done. These would include distance between the sample point and a large perennial river or distance from the nearest conglomerate suitable as a source of raw material and so forth.

Since the horizons sampled are of progressively younger age as one ascends the series of outcrops, it is necessary to attempt to control for time in the analysis and the outcrops were divided into a series of stratigraphic levels.

The first requirement was to secure a broad and reasonably representative coverage of information which could serve as a background for more refined and focussed investigations. We attempted to acquire this by classifying and counting artifacts on each outcrop within a series of transect strips taken across the erosion front at stratified random intervals (Fig. 5.8) (see Isaac and Harris in press). There is great variation in both the density and the percentage data for the series of sample points. Given the complex interaction of variables, patterns of relationship will have to be worked out with caution, but there is every reason to expect that the spatial pattern being sampled will provide more balanced information of early land use than does site distribution analysis by itself.

The second step in developing this approach has been to take samples at intervals along the outcrop of a particular layer. In the first instance outcrops which contain an important excavated site (a concentrated patch) have been chosen. Fig. 5.9 illustrates this procedure, which is still in an early stage of application. Ultimately some way of acquiring a random sample of outcrops should be devised, since it is as important to know where material is not to be found as it is to know where it is found.

Both these methods should allow us to address questions such as, was the

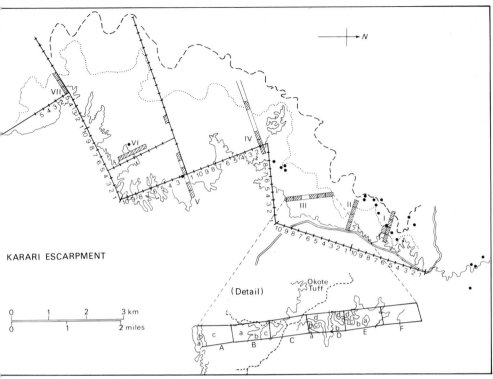

KARARI ESCARPMENT

(Detail)

.8.　An example of the scatters and patches approach: overall distribution patterns sampled by means of transects across the outcrops of a stratified sequence of layers each representing a palaeo-landscape. (From the work of Isaac and Harris (in press) on part of the Upper Member of the Koobi Fora Formation.) The layout with transects placed by a stratified, random procedure is shown. Dots indicate dense patches of artifacts classifiable as sites. The detail shows the recording units used in one transect. Each unit is the outcrop of a distinctive lithology.

morphology of the artifact sets in areas of high density (sites) the same as that of the set discarded as a dispersed scatter over the terrain?

The only explicit data known to me, relating to differences in stone discards between sites and non-site scatters, is that furnished by Gould (1977) on the basis of ethnographic observations in Australia. Here he did observe important differences. We became aware of his observations after embarking on our study and it reinforced our sense of the potential interest of the inquiry. During the course of the fieldwork, examples of all of the first three levels of the hierarchy set out in this essay were encountered; isolated artifacts, small clusters which range in scale from mini-sites with a few tens of pieces to mega-sites with thousands of artifacts.

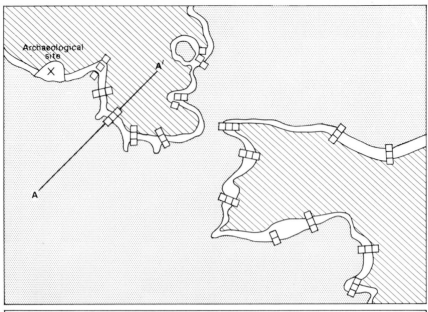

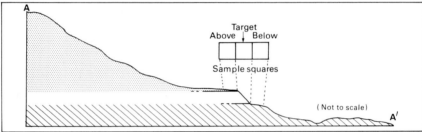

5.9. The scatters and patches approach: the overall distribution pattern of stones and bones in a particular horizon is sampled by means of a series of squares placed at randomised intervals between 10 and 50 paces apart along the outcrop. The profile is a diagrammatic representation of the topographic configuration involved in one application of this method. At each sample point a central square measures the composition and density of items on the target outcrop. Control data are gathered from squares above and below.

PATTERNS WITHIN CLUSTERS

Detailed treatment of intra-site spatial pattern analysis is beyond the scope of this essay. Another member of the Koobi Fora Research Project, Ellen Kroll, is currently engaged in a careful investigation involving a variety of methodological experiments which she will report in due course. However, there are some general points which need to be made about logical relations between intra-site analysis and the comprehensive study of the overall spatial configuration.

The point has already been made that sites are commonly 'clusters of clusters'. Even for the earliest known sites we modern humans tend tacitly

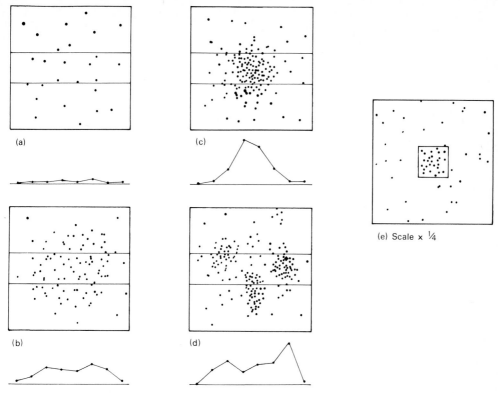

5.10.   A–D show diagrams of point pattern configurations which have already been recorded through the plotting of stones and bones at excavated early archaeological sites in East Africa. All are compound clusters but the hominid behaviours that formed each of them may have differed considerably as regards the number of site usage episodes, the duration of each episode, the number of individuals and the number of social 'modules' participating in any given episode. The nature of the economic and/or social usage pattern involved in each episode may also have differed. Frame E shows the relatively diffuse frame A superimposed on a background one-tenth as dense; this illustrates that all of the compound clusters need to be considered in relation to their 'background' scatter configurations.

to assume that many of these are fossilised camping places, 'home-bases', if you will, and all that that implies (Isaac 1976; 1978). This is a proposition that needs to be tested rather than assumed, hence intra-site analyses need to start at a fundamental level without taking for granted the basic behavioural meaning of the cluster and without plunging directly into the exegesis of detail such as the recognition of 'activity areas' and so forth (cf. Whallon 1973; 1974). This is why it is so important that intra-site spatial analysis be conducted along with studies concerned with the overall array. It is especially important to know about the density of the background of discarded material, within which the concentrations are conspicuous anomalies.

Fig. 5.10 offers a simple classification of point pattern configurations which have already appeared in published plans of early sites. Clearly, it is entirely possible that the series represents accumulations which formed as results of quite different behavioural modes. Some sites may simply represent places in the landscape where actions that were commonly dispersed over the landscape recurred often enough to generate a concentrated patch of refuse. An example of this might be repeated individual feeding, with tool use, under a long-lived shade tree. Other patches may well represent special foci in hominid life that involved enactment of particular parts of the behavioural repertoire that were much less commonly performed outside of these special foci. (Modern human home-bases are foci of this second kind.) In the former instance the material present and its arrangement might be expected to resemble simply a concentrated, mechanical aggregate of the low density background materials. Examples of the second type might well differ from the background both in the composition of the leavings and in its arrangement. These are some of the problems to be dealt with in a comprehensive study. We need to work with the testing of as large a series of alternative hypotheses as our ingenuity allows.

CONCLUSION

Clearly all three approaches, which have been exemplified, hold promise of helping us to infer and understand early hominid ways of life. Surely the fourth, involving simulation, will also become important as more is known and as more relevant contemporary ecological data are collected. Research should proceed by trying out different variants of all of these and comparing the results, searching for convergences.

For at least two reasons the scatters and patches approach may turn out to have particular importance in the study of the spatial configurations of the very early archaeological record. First, once recognised, the peculiar but inevitable 'outcrops-strip' character of the record places severe limits on the application both of normal site distribution map analysis and of site catchment analysis. Second, as we explore back into the remote past, it becomes more and more dangerous to assume that the basic organisation of socioeconomic behaviour was structured according to principles that are universal among humans today. If we wish to determine at what stages home-base nodes, food sharing and division of labour became established, we need to scrutinise with a minimum of prior assumptions the total arrangement of early archaeological datum points. We are fortunate that in addition to contributing their bones as markers, and sometimes footprints, early protohumans dropped bits and pieces of modified materials in many places. The spatial configuration of all of these 'visiting cards' constitutes the most powerful clue we have to the beginnings of the human condition.

ACKNOWLEDGEMENTS

The ideas presented in this essay have been formed in the course of working with a team of colleagues and students in the archaeological segment of the Koobi Fora Research project – especially John W. K. Harris, Henry Bunn, Yusuf Juwayeyi, Zefe Kaufulu, Ellen Kroll, Nicholas Toth and Kathy Schick. Many of the ideas were clarified during a seminar series at Berkeley dealing with prehistoric land use patterns. The seminar was taught jointly with J. Desmond Clark, to whom I owe much. While a visiting fellow in Peterhouse Cambridge in 1976, I discussed land use patterns with David Clarke, just before his untimely death, and with Rob Foley, with whom the dialogue continues. As a visitor to the School of General Studies at the Australian National University, Canberra, I was privileged to participate in seminars and field visits that helped me formulate the ideas in this paper. Participants to whom I am especially grateful include John Mulvaney, James O'Connell, Nic Peterson, Isabel McBryde and Wilfrid Shawcross. Besides drafting the figures, Barbara Isaac constantly makes suggestions and valid objections.

REFERENCES

Behrensmeyer, A. K. (1975). 'The taphonomy and paleoecology of Plio-Pleistocene vertebrate assemblages east of Lake Rudolf, Kenya, *Bulletin of the Museum of Comparative Zoology* 146 (10)
    (1976). 'Taphonomy and paleoecology in the hominid fossil record', *Yearbook of Physical Anthropology 1975* 19: 36–50
    (in press). 'The recent bone of Amboseli Park, Kenya in relation to East African paleoecology' in Burg Wartenstein Symposium *Taphonomy and Vertebrate Palaeoecology: with special reference to the late Cenozoic of sub-Saharan Africa*, Wenner-Gren Foundation for Anthropological Research
Bettinger, R. L. (1977). 'Aboriginal human ecology in Owens Valley: prehistoric change in the Great Basin', *American Anthropology* 42 (1): 3–17
Bowler, J. M. (1971). 'Pleistocene salinities and climatic change: evidence from lakes and lunettes in Southeastern Australia' in D. J. Mulvaney and J. Golson (eds.) *Aboriginal Man and Environment in Australia*, Australian National University Press
Bowler, J. M., Jones, R., Allen, H. and Thorne, A. G. (1970). 'Pleistocene human remains from Australia: a living site and human civilisation from Lake Mungo, Western New South Wales, *World Archaeology* 2: 39–60
Chavaillon, J. (1976). 'Evidence for the technical practices of Early Pleistocene Hominids: Shungura Formation, Lower Valley of the Omo, Ethiopia' in Y. Coppens, F. C. Howell, G. Ll. Isaac, and R. E. F. Leakey (eds.) *Earliest Man and Environments in the Lake Rudolf Basin*, Chicago University Press
Clarke, D. L. (1977). *Spatial Archaeology*, Academic Press
Coppens, Y., Howell, F. C., Isaac, G. Ll. and Leakey, R. E. F. (eds.) (1976). *Earliest Man and Environments in the Lake Rudolf Basin: Stratigraphy, Paleoecology and Evolution*, University of Chicago Press
Flannery, K. V. (1976). *The Early Mesoamerican Village*, Academic Press
Fox, C. (1932). *The Personality of Britain: its influence on inhabitant and invader in prehistoric and early historic times*, National Museum of Wales
Gould, R. A. (1977). 'Ethno-archaeology; or, where do models come from? a closer

look at Australian aboriginal lithic technology' in R. V. S. Wright (ed.) *Stone tools as Cultural Markers*, Australian Institute of Aboriginal Studies

Harris, J. W. K. (1978). 'The Karari industry, its place in East African prehistory', Unpublished Ph.D. thesis, University of California, Berkeley

Harris, J. W. K. and Herbich, I. (1978). 'Aspects of Early Pleistocene hominid behaviour east of Lake Turkana, Kenya' in W. W. Bishop (ed.) *Geological Background to Fossil Man*, Scottish Academic Press

Harris, J. W. K. and Isaac, G. Ll. (in press). 'Early Pleistocene site locations at Koobi Fora, Kenya', in *Proceedings of the VIII Pan African Congress on Prehistory*, Nairobi

Hay, R. L. (1976). *Geology of the Olduvai Gorge: a study of sedimentation in a semi-arid basin*, University of California Press

Hill, A. (1975). 'Taphonomy of contemporary and late Cenozoic East African Vertebrates', unpublished Ph.D. thesis, University of London

  (in press). 'Early post-mortem damage to the remains of some East African mammals' in Burg Wartenstein Symposium *Taphonomy and Vertebrate Palaeoecology: with special reference to the late Cenozoic of Sub-Saharan Africa*, Wenner-Gren Foundation for Anthropological Research

Hodder, I. (ed.) (1978). *Simulation Studies in Archaeology*, Cambridge University Press

Hodder, I. and Orton, C. (1976). *Spatial Analysis in Archaeology*, Cambridge University Press

Isaac, G. Ll. (1972). 'Comparative studies of Pleistocene site locations in East Africa' in P. J. Ucko, R. Tringham and G. W. Dimbleby (eds.) *Man, Settlement and Urbanism*, Duckworth

  (1976). 'The activities of Early African Hominids: a review of archaeological evidence from the time span two and a half to one million years ago' in G. Ll. Isaac and E. R. McCown (eds.) *Human Origins: Louis Leakey and the East African evidence*, W. A. Benjamin

  (1978). 'The food-sharing behavior of protohuman hominids', *Scientific American* 238 (4) 90–107

Isaac, G. Ll. and Crader, D. (in press). 'Can we determine the degree to which early hominids were carnivorous?' in R. S. O. Harding and G. Teleki (eds.) *Omnivorous Primates: Gathering and Hunting in Human Evolution*, Columbia University Press

Isaac, G. Ll. and Harris, J. W. K. (1975). 'The scatter between the patches', paper presented to the Kroeber Society, University of California, Berkeley

  (1978). 'Archaeology' in M. G. and R. E. Leakey (eds.) *Koobi Fora Research Project*, vol. 1, Clarendon

  (in press). 'A method for determining the characteristics of artifacts between sites in the Upper Member of the Koobi Fora formation, East Lake Turkana', in *Proceedings of the VIII Pan African Congress on Prehistory*, Nairobi

Jarman, M. R. (1972). 'A territorial model for archaeology: a behavioural and geographical approach' in D. L. Clarke (ed.) *Models in Archaeology*, Methuen

Jochim, M. A. (1976). *Hunter-Gatherer Subsistence and Settlement: a predictive model*, Academic Press

Leakey, M. D. (1971). *Olduvai Gorge*, vol. 3, *Excavation in Beds I and II*, Cambridge University Press

Leakey, M. D. and Hay, R. L. (1979). 'Fossil footprints in the Pliocene deposits of Laetolil, Tanzania', *Nature* 278: 317–23

Leakey, M. G. and Leakey, R. E., eds., (1978). *Koobi Fora Research Project*, vol. 1, *The Fossil Hominids and an Introduction to their Context 1968–1974*, Clarendon

Lumley, H. de (1969). 'A Paleolithic camp at Nice', *Scientific American* 220: 50–2

McBryde, I. (n.d.). 'Archaeological investigation in the Lake Mungo area', paper presented at a symposium, Australian National University, July 1976

McIntyre, (n.d.). 'Archaeological investigations in the Willandra Lake area', paper presented at a symposium, Australian National University, July 1976

Merrick, H. V. (1976). 'Recent archaeological research in the Plio-Pleistocene deposits of the Lower Omo, southwestern Ethiopia' in G. Ll. Isaac and E. R. McCown (eds.) *Human Origins: Louis Leakey and the East African evidence*, W. A. Benjamin

Merrick, H. V., de Heinzelin, J., Haesaerts, P. and Howell, F. C. (1976). 'Archaeological occurrences of Early Pleistocene age from the Shungura Formation, Lower Omo Valley, Ethiopia', *Nature* 242: 572–5

Schiffer, M. (1976). *Behavioural Archaeology*, Academic Press

Shawcross, W. F. (1975). 'Thirty thousand years and more', *Hemisphere* 19: 26–31

Thomas, D. (1973). 'An empirical test of Steward's model of Great Basin settlement patterns,' *American Antiquity*, 38: 155–76

Thomas, D. H. (1974). *Predicting the Past: an introduction to anthropological archaeology*, Holt, Rhinehart and Winston

Vita-Finzi, C. and Higgs, E. S. (1970). 'Prehistoric economy in the Mount Carmel area of Palestine: site catchment analysis', *Proceedings of the Prehistoric Society* 36: 1–37

Wendorf, F. and Marks, A., eds. (1975). *Problems in Prehistory: North Africa and the Levant*, Southern Methodist University Press

Wendorf, F. and Schild, R. (1976). *Prehistory of the Nile Valley*, Academic Press

Whallon, R. (1973). 'Spatial analysis of occupation floors: the application of dimensional analysis of variance' in C. Renfrew (ed.) *The Explanation of Culture Change: models in prehistory*, Duckworth

(1974). 'Spatial analysis of occupation floors II: the application of nearest neighbour analysis,' *American Antiquity* 39: 16–34

Wood, B. (1976). *The Evolution of Early Man*, Peter Lowe

6

Off-site archaeology: an alternative approach for the short-sited

ROBERT FOLEY

In this paper I shall examine the processes underlying the formation of the archaeological record. The nature of these processes suggests that archaeological material is spatially continuous, and that the site may not form the most suitable framework for analysis. The formation processes described here are behavioural and post-depositional, two major levels of theory recognised by David Clarke (1973).

In *Analytical Archaeology* David Clarke explicitly stated that the context of an archaeological system is vital, but that it lay outside the specifically behavioural analysis examined in that book (1968, p. 14). However, even in passing over the subject, there is something of value. Data recovery and data collection are explicitly put within an experimental framework (Clarke 1968, p. 14 and Fig. 2). In other words, the archaeological record does not simply 'exist', but should be viewed as sets of phenomena available for experiment at all levels. It is this experimental approach that I wish to stress in this paper. The archaeological record is not a fixed and immutable entity but a product of our own perception. Hitherto this perception has been limited, and we have been afraid to experiment with our data source, its origins and character, and equally reluctant to probe its complexity.

Clarke's most explicit statement on post-depositional factors comes in 'Loss of innocence' (1973). Although there is no analysis of the nature of these processes, he rightly stresses that depositional, post-depositional, and retrieval theory are all integral parts of archaeological theory, and that these aspects of theorising and experimentation must be done before any attempt at data analysis or interpretation of behaviour (1968, p. 16). His model is essentially a hierarchical one. At its base lies the range of behaviour and background information that existed prior to discard or death. This was then sampled by depositional processes (what was discarded), which in turn was sampled by post-depositional processes. This again was sampled by our recovery procedures. His model is pyramidical, analogous to the energy pyramid used in ecology. Moving up the steps of the pyramid one is gradually faced with loss and transformation of information, similar to the loss and transformation of energy (Elton 1927; Whittaker 1970).

There has developed, in association with palaeontology, a new research direction – 'taphonomy' – that studies the processes whereby the fossil record is formed, and the biasses inherent in these processes (Behrensmeyer, 1975; Hill 1975; Brain 1967a; 1967b; 1969). For the archaeologist a corresponding concern is the transformation of human behaviour into a recoverable archaeological record (Schiffer 1976; Gifford 1977). Human behaviour is filtered by geomorphological processes; the archaeologist must attempt to reconstruct the original transforms.

The other aspect of Clarke's work to which this paper relates is his concern with units and entities (1968). He discusses extensively the logical way of constructing higher-order units of artifact assemblages. It was assumed that artifacts would occur primarily in a site context, and that entity hierarchies, especially the assemblage, would be constructed from this basis. This paper suggests that under some circumstances the site is not the best unit of analysis, and what Clarke called the fundamental unit of archaeology, the artifact, can be used in other than a strictly morphological context.

Post-depositional theory is an essential element of archaeological theory. The key relationships in this field of study are those between spatially non-discrete archaeological material and geomorphology on the one hand, and behaviour on the other. The theory presented here has been developed in response to the Holocene archaeological record in the savanna regions of East Africa. Permutations of this approach may almost certainly be extended, both to hunter–gatherer archaeology in other regions, and the remains of simple agricultural societies. One instance of a research problem for which this approach can be suggested as a solution is the study of the Neolithic in Britain. As MacInnes (1971) has stated, there is a paucity of recognisable settlement sites in this period, and yet the scatter of characteristic lithic forms is widespread.

RATES AND NATURE OF SETTLEMENT INCREMENT AND SITE
FORMATION

The human species' use of material culture, and the fact that items are made, used, and discarded led to the formation of the archaeological record. The opportunity to study human behaviour through archaeology must be considered to start with the development of tool making. However, access to human behaviour is possible through the process of artifact discard, which is a function of the rate of use and the distribution of human activity. This can be further refined by noting that access to prehistoric behaviour is further influenced by the fact that human activity is preferentially concentrated at spatial foci.

However, not all debris-producing activity conforms to this spatially centralised pattern. Some material is discarded away from the settlement, and thus the simplest model of initial artifact distribution may be described as a series of concentrations grading out to a dispersed artifact scatter (Fig. 6.1).

This pattern is simple enough taken in its static form – as a section through

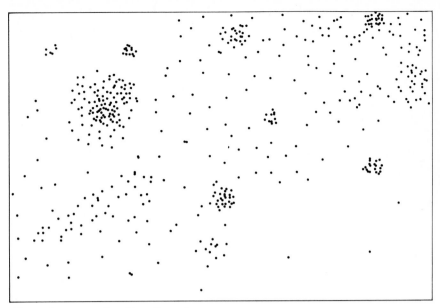

6.1.   General pattern of artifact discard.

time. However, archaeological discard is a continuous process through time, and thus for the archaeologist studying the accumulated effects of thousands (if not millions) of years of discard, further complexity must be incorporated into the model.

Continued occupancy in an area will increase the absolute density of artifacts. A blurring of the pattern can also occur. Site locational systems usually operate on an areal or regional scale – i.e. it is less the exact location of a settlement that is the determining factor, but its habitat context. If the locational determinants of settlements are maintained through time then the result will be greatly increased debris formation in the preferred habitats as a whole, with the loci of the individual settlements becoming less distinct. In contrast to this, habitats unsuitable for settlement will remain free of any significant artifactual accumulations. In this simplified model patterns of positive and negative habitat preference will be discernable through differences in densities of discarded artifacts.

Such a pattern can be intensified by specific settlement location practices. For example, in systems where re-occupation of old settlements is prohibited or avoided for a certain period, as is sometimes the case with the Maasai and other groups (Western, pers. comm.; Yellen 1967, pp. 58–9), then the rate at which the whole of the habitat is littered with occupational debris will be increased. This pattern contrasts markedly with that found in the later stages of prehistory in the Middle East and Eastern Europe (see Sherratt, ch. 10 below), where tell formation indicates a very different social structure and attitude towards settlement location (e.g. Adams 1968), and also with regions

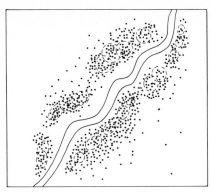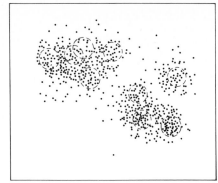

6.2. Settlement development and resulting artifact distribution: (a) ribbon (fluviatile) pattern; (b) radial (or concentric) pattern.

where rock-shelters and caves were available for continuous resettlement (an appropriate example is provided by Parkington, ch. 12 below).

Furthermore, in response to natural features, the pattern of resettlement can itself take on particular configurations. Observations in the Suguta valley of northern Kenya, a fluviatile system, showed that dry season Turkana settlement development was linear, following the course of the rivers, and therefore material debris formation took on a blurred ribbon pattern (see also Clarke 1972, Fig. 1.7). This may be contrasted with the non-linear constraints of the Ilkisongo Maasai in the Amboseli Basin (Fig. 6.2).

This pattern of accumulated settlement formation, and its consequences for the archaeological record, can be taken further by describing the processes which govern the development of a distribution pattern through time. Initially resource distribution will determine the habitats occupied, but within a particular habitat small-scale factors will operate to select a particular dwelling place. For example, given that a group of hunter-gatherers must locate themselves in the proximity of a lake, both for their own water requirements and because of plant and animal resources seasonally clustered in that vicinity, they should still have a choice of whether to camp on the lake edge or some distance away. In many cases they will opt for the latter, thus minimising the effect of insect pests, flooding, and causing least disturbance to their potential prey. Analogous 'real' situations are to be found among the Hadza who will occupy a sandy ridge away from the lake edge (Lars Smith, pers. comm; Woodburn 1968, p. 50), and the Nuer, who are forced within their general locational requirements to select high ground for their settlement because of seasonal flooding (Evans-Pritchard 1940).

For the sake of example, let us construct a model where the preferred settlement habitat for a group is restricted to a ridge of land away from the lake, about 1 km by 5 km in size. Assuming that this ridge is uniform in its suitability for settlement throughout, and that each settlement or camp site occupies and has an impact on an area 100 by 100 metres in size, then, allowing for no overlap, there are 500 potential settlement cells. From this point we can experiment with the way in which the area can gradually be covered with archaeological material over time. The simplest of these would be a situation which involved one settlement per year with no relocation within a given seasonal occupation possible throughout that time. This would obviously result in a totally uniform cover within 500 years. We can refine this model, which is obviously oversimplified, in various ways – for example, by varying the rate of site formation and abandonment, by increasing the number of groups exploiting the area, allowing relocation after a certain period of time, and demanding certain distances between sequential settlements. These would vary the period before uniform occupancy had occurred, and probably in most practical situations total uniformity would never occur. In all cases, however, the result would be that over a number of years occupation of an area following an open settlement system would result in a fairly continuous spatiual pattern of archaeological debris. In attempting to refine this model to approximate reality more closely it would be necessary to formulate and weight the factors leading to both clustering (habit, utilisation of old settlement material, suitability) and dispersal (e.g. firewood availability).

On behavioural grounds, therefore, we would expect to find in regions that meet the expectations outlined above, such as the savanna areas of East Africa, a pattern tending towards continuous rather than discrete artifact distribution in preferred settlement habitats. We may further develop this idea in relation to site density data of a different kind. Strauss (1977) discusses the density of sites in the Cantabrian region of Spain during various periods of the Palaeolithic. His paper is one of the few examples where quantitative data on site densities is available. Strauss' argument is that the varying number of sites in the region through the Palaeolithic reflects the importance of the resources of the region and the strategies of hunting employed. The point of this discussion is somewhat different, and in no ways undermines the argument of relative values made by Strauss. Instead I want to look at the number of sites in relation to the expected number of settlements.

Taking the Upper Magdalenian, the period with the most numerous sites (thirty-four) as the example, we may analyse this number in terms of settlement. The area under study is approximately 114 300 km² (Strauss 1977, Fig. 2.1). Estimating the carrying capacity of this area for a hunter–gatherer economy is clearly hazardous, but general values quoted include 1 person per 100 square miles for Australia (Radcliffe Brown 1930), three per 100 square miles for North America (Kroeber 1939), and forty-one per 100 square miles for the Kalahari Bushmen of Botswana (Lee 1968). These regions are unlikely to have as abundant resources as Cantabria, and we could expect a higher population density (Birdsell 1953). However, in order not to exaggerate the argument I shall take the very low value of one person per 100 km² – that is a total population for the region of approximately 1143 at any one time. Using the classic figure of an average group size of twenty-five (Lee and DeVore

1968; Marshall 1960), this would mean approximately forty-five groups exploiting Cantabria. We are now faced with the problem of how many settlements would accrue over time. Using the one settlement per year value mentioned in the previous exercise, this would mean 45 000 settlements per millennium. Strauss (1977, p. 69) discusses seasonality, and suggests that groups would have been to some extent seasonal in their occupation of zones within the region. This would have the effect of increasing the number. Even allowing for resettlement on a 50 per cent scale, the total figure is still in excess of 20 000 per millennium. Following this ecological line of argument, we would predict for the period of the Upper Magdalenian more than 50 000 settlements. What this means in terms of sites is unclear, but more than thirty-four would be expected. Of course there are many assumptions here, but I have been at pains to minimise the predicted number of settlements. Cantabrian hunter–gatherers were probably less constrained by environment than extant Australian aborigines of the Central Desert Region or Kalahari bushman. However, the point is still valid that a percentage 'perception' rate of less than 0.001 is hardly ideal, and that alternative sources of information should perhaps be utilised. It is unlikely that this area is atypical of the archaeological record, but, rather than abandoning the archaeological record in despair, we might well ask what happened to all the other material, and what other routes of information recovery exist.

Thus far I have discussed three aspects of formation processes. Firstly, that of artifact discard involving both clustering and dispersing tendencies; secondly, the cumulative nature of these processes through time; and thirdly, that the structure of these processes is that of numerous and repetitive small-scale events.

This model has so far ignored an important component of the archaeological record, namely the structures associated with settlements that so occupy the archaeologist. It would be expected that these would preserve the underlying particulate structure of the settlements. I would suggest that for nomadic peoples this is seldom the case, and that the normal sequence of destruction of settlement patterns would be as follows:

Stage 1   Destruction of associated structural features.
Stage 2   Destruction (albeit differentially) of organic remains.
Stage 3   Destruction of the artifact distribution pattern.

This is expressed in Fig. 6.3. Evidence in support of these overlapping stages is not easy to obtain, as it involves monitoring of sites over long periods of time, and nowhere has this been attempted. Some supportive evidence lies in the fact that most tropical hunter–gatherer and pastoral camps use only the most ephemeral of structural equipment, selected for its ease of transport or ease of procurement from the environment, and indeed much is taken away with the occupants or swiftly disintegrates after abandonment (Robbins 1973, p. 212). Further work obviously has to be done on this aspect of the

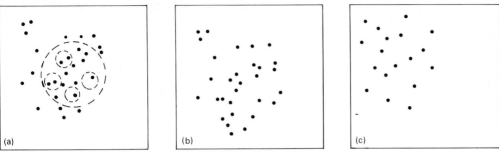

6.3.   Sequence of destruction of settlement: (a) situation at discard; (b) loss of associated structures; (c) loss of distributional information.

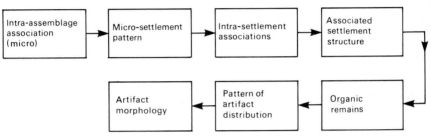

6.4.   'Typical' process of information loss in the archaeological record.

taphonomical processes operating on hunter–gatherer sites, but there seems reason to think that the sequence suggested above may not be too far from the truth. Fig. 6.4 schematically outlines the information loss associated with the stages of destruction described above. This pattern is again neither comprehensive nor universal, but it does suggest that we can, by recognising common post-depositional processes, obtain greater and more systematic access to some aspects of prehistoric human behaviour than was previously considered possible.

In the light of the foregoing the following generalisations may be presented regarding the distribution of artifactual materials. Firstly, the archaeological record of mobile peoples should be viewed not as a system of structured sites, but as a pattern of continuous artifact distribution and density. And secondly, information on land use patterns may in some cases be better obtained through the study of non-discrete artifact distributions in specific zones than from orthodox site distributions.

BEHAVIOUR, DISCARD, AND THE ARCHAEOLOGICAL RECORD

Table 6.1 attempts in a very simplistic manner to express the degree to which certain basic human technological activities may be independent of home bases.

Assigning spatial loci to these activities, general as they are, has been

TABLE 6.1. *Settlement specificity of basic human activities*

Basic human activities	Settlement specific code
Food aquisition	
animal	C
vegetable	C
Food preparation and consumption	
Artifactual	B
manufacture	B
aquisition	C
repair	B
use	B
Settlement/house	
material aquisition	C
construction	A
Materials: clothes pots, containers, etc.	
aquisition	B
manufacture	B
use	B
Ceremonial activities	?

A = settlement specific; B = liable to occur both on and off settlement; C = liable to occur away from the settlement.

difficult within such a broad framework, and is clearly susceptible to further refinement. In particular, different social, economic and environmental situations will alter some of the spatial relationships, which are suggested only as gross approximations. It does, however, become clear that few human activities are totally confined to the settlement and, equally, few occur solely away from the settlement. A more accurate view is perhaps that for simple economies, debris-producing activities are home range specific, with clustering in parts of that range. Obviously the densest cluster of activities and debris will normally occur on the settlement itself. The settlement will not, however, be the only cluster within the home range. Centres for other activities will occur: hunting blinds; artifact preparation sites; tree-felling areas; water-holes; ceremonial locales; shade areas; and raw material sources.

There is much evidence for these patterns in both the ethnographic and the archaeological literature. Among the Maasai the *moran* (warriors) never eat cattle within the settlement, and consequently they select shady areas for their meat-eating activities. These may often be reused (V. Morse, pers. comm.). In the same way, the Hadza will often choose shady areas away from the settlement to sit and talk and play their games (Woodburn and Hudson 1966). Another Maasai example would be the use of rock-shelters for ceremonial activities. This has been demonstrated both for ethnographic and archaeological contexts (Gramley 1971; 1975). Hole *et al.* (1969) in their study of the Deh Luran plain suggested that many localities were places where hunting parties rested or prepared their artifacts. Butchery sites are also well documented in the archaeological record, from the Hippo site (FxJj³) from Koobi Fora (Isaac *et al.* 1976) to the large-scale elephant butchery shown at Torralba and Ambrona (Howell 1966) and, most dramatically, some of the bison kills in America (e.g. Wheat 1972).

Loci related to gathering are less conspicuous in the archaeological record, and have seldom caught the ethnographer's eye. Generally eating food away from the settlement is common among non-Western societies (Woodburn and Hudson 1966; Marshall 1956) and similar patterns are likely to have occurred in prehistory. A further example of off-settlement activity is provided by Gould (1968), who has shown that tree-felling activities among Australian aborigines often leave specialised stone tool assemblages and debris – e.g. heavy duty tools and resharpening flakes.

Another focal, although off-settlement, activity would be the extraction of lithic materials from their sources. Factory sites of this nature are well documented in the literature, especially for the English Neolithic (Smith 1974, pp. 105–6). Recognition of less concentrated non-settlement activity areas might be more problematic, but would be expected to exist.

Thus far in describing the role of artifacts in various activities and their spatial configurations it has been implicitly assumed that there is a direct relationship between artifact use and artifact discard. This major assumption underlies much archaeological work, but requires further examination. Recent work by Binford (1973) has taken up some of these themes, suggesting that the relationship between artifact use and discard is complex. His work among the Nunamuit Eskimos suggests that artifact discard is not a random process, either spatially or qualitatively. There appear to be two variables involved: potential use left in the artifact, and the amount of effort involved in replacement – which can be alternatively described as the amount of effort that went into the making of the artifact to be discarded. Binford (1973) further suggests that this affects the locale of discard – for example, an artifact is thrown away when a place on the landscape is reached where the artifact will be of no value.

The location of discarded material thus provides a potentially biassed record of the overall distribution of usage. Consideration of the dynamics of manufacture, transport, use and discard is clearly important. For the study of activities this is beyond doubt, and Ammerman and Feldman (1974) offer a refined attempt at solving this problem. Another important contribution towards a more sophisticated understanding of archaeological formation processes and prehistoric human behaviour is that of Isaac and Harris (1976) and Isaac (1971). While still subject to this bias, the broader approach described here, with its emphasis on gross artifact density differentials, may be less sensitive to these discard factors.

For hunter–gatherer and other nomadic societies the attention conventionally paid by archaeologists to evidence preserved on sites omits an important component of archaeological data. Sites, in the sense of dense localised concentrations of artifacts and structures, represent only a small fraction of the potential archaeological record. For descriptive purposes the term *off-site archaeology* may be used for studies concerned with the total population of artifacts rather than just the discrete clusters within it (on-site archaeology). Off-site seems a preferable term to *non-site*, recently proposed by Thomas (1975); the latter does not seem to express the complementary nature of the approaches. A third term, 'scatters and patches' analysis, is introduced by Isaac in ch. 5 above.

In constructing a model to demonstrate the existence and nature of an archaeological record away from the site it has been necessary to present on-site and off-site processes as in some way contrasting. The behavioural basis of the archaeological record described above, however, shows that a continuum model for both behaviour and archaeological formation would be appropriate. The differences between the site and the off-site material are the result of differences in frequency of activity rather than qualitative differences. Neither on-site nor off-site theory alone can account for the extent and nature of archaeological variability (Gifford, pers. comm.). Developing an integrated continuum model of behaviour and archaeological formation will be essential to further work.

POST-DEPOSITIONAL CONSIDERATIONS

Consideration of the mechanisms of formation of the archaeological record leads to the conclusion that artifact distribution with the artifacts themselves as the units contains much spatial and behavioural information. The approach requires development of relevant sampling and investigation techniques, and consideration of the variables that govern the observable data set of continuously distributed artifacts. These variables include in the first place the behaviour determining discard, but subsequently the post-depositional factors that control distribution, preservation and visibility. Information on prehistoric populations flows through these variables, from the stage of raw material extraction for artifact manufacture to observation of artifacts by the archaeologist (Fig. 6.5).

This discussion focusses on the information retrievable from the observation of surface artifact densities – the number of observable artifacts per unit area on or in a landscape or sediment. A secondary factor in evaluating densities is the degree of dispersion, such as that demonstrated by Thomas (1972) for projectile points and winter encampments in the Reese River Project. Density and dispersal require specific (and separate) sampling strategies, although these are common to other disciplines (Mueller-Dombois and Ellenberg 1975; Gerard and Berthet 1971). For the archaeologist, however, visibility must also be considered. Exposure of the sedimentological matrix is the prerequisite of archaeological observation, filtering all information retrieval. The operation of post-depositional factors on density dispersal and visibility

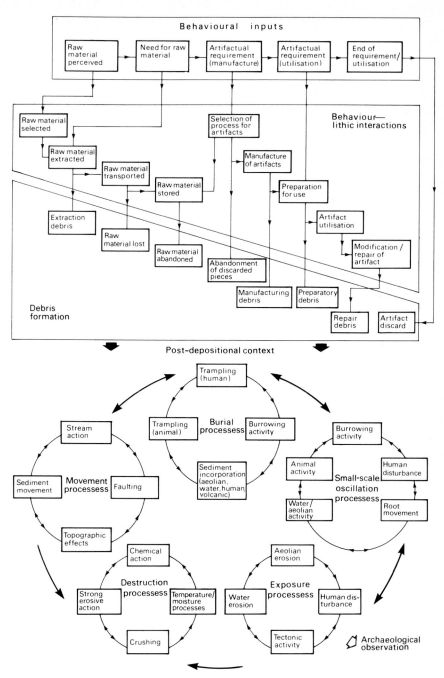

6.5.   Flow chart of artifact dynamics.

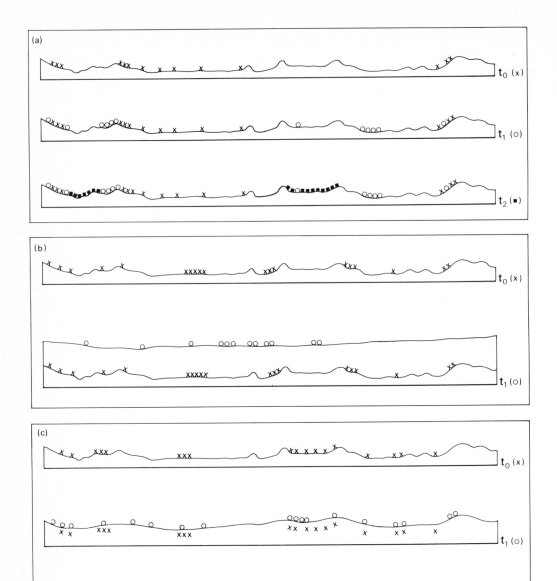

6.6.   (a) Cumulative effect of simple artifact discard. (b) Cumulative artifact discard on a landscape suddenly buried. (c) Cumulative artifact discard on a gradually aggrading landscape.

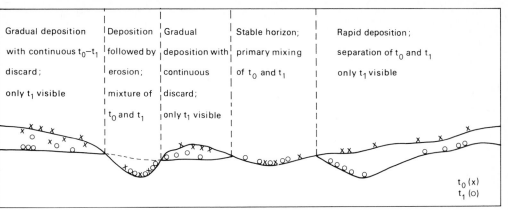

6.7. Cumulative discard effects on a complex landscape.

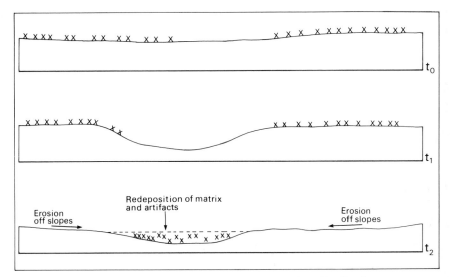

6.8. Effects of lateral movement in burial processes on artifact distribution.

is an inherent aspect of off-site studies. What follows is an attempt to describe how these factors operate.

Artifact discard

An archaeological record begins when artifacts cease to be used and are discarded onto the landscape. Initially artifact densities are a function of the rate of discard. Distribution will reflect activity, although it has been shown (Binford 1973; Gould 1968; Schiffer 1976) that the relationship may not be simple or direct. Fig. 6.5 illustrates the point that not all discard occurs at the same point in the artifacts dynamics. Whatever the rate or nature of discard, however, the effect is cumulative (Fig. 6.6a).

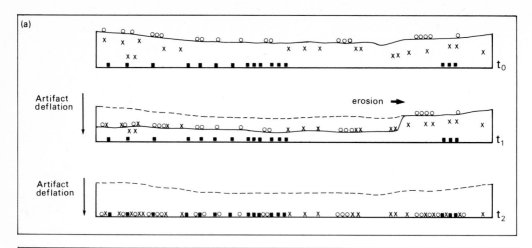

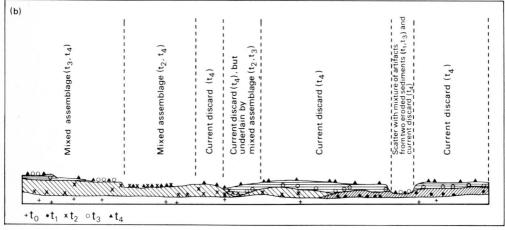

6.9.   (a) Effect of gradual exposure on artifact distribution. (b) Effect of patchy nature of sedimentation, erosion and exposure on artifact distribution.

Artifact burial

Subsequent to discard three things can occur to an artifact. It may be buried suddenly and completely (Fig. 6.6b); it may be gradually buried while discard is continuing (Fig. 6.6c); it may be left exposed (Fig. 6.6a). Several points may be noted here. Firstly, the burial processes tend to be local; palaeolandscapes were as diverse as contemporary ones, being dissected by channels, moulded by drainage, and subject to localised erosion. Consequently combinations of all these processes may occur within a restricted area (Fig. 6.7). Secondly, deposition is seldom simply gravitational, sediments are usually deposited with at least some lateral vector, and thus the distribution of artifacts may be altered (Fig. 6.8). And thirdly, there may be a considerable interval between discard and burial when other factors (see below) are operating; it cannot be assumed that buried means *in situ*.

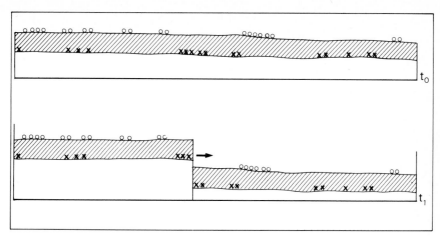

6.10.   Effect of geological faulting on artifact exposure.

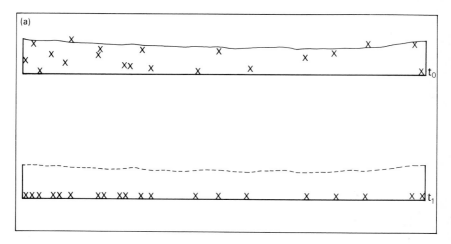

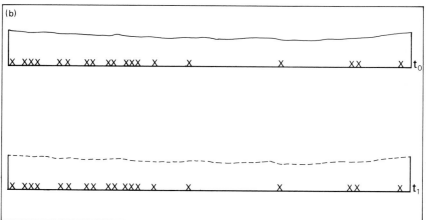

6.11.   Effect on artifact densities of erosion of sediments: (a) where previous burial had
been gradual; (b) where previous burial had been sudden.

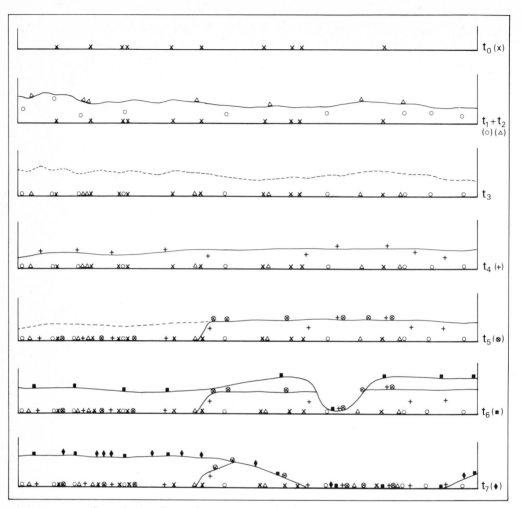

6.12.   Cumulative effects of recurrence of burial and erosion processes.

Artifact exposure

Artifacts may be continually exposed from discard, or else be buried and then subsequently exposed. Archaeological visibility is dependent upon exposure. Exposure will normally be gradual (Fig. 6.9a), and also patchy in distribution (Fig. 6.9b). Erosion is the usual mechanism of exposure, but faulting (Fig. 6.10), such as that seen in the Shungura formation of the Omo Valley (Coppens *et al.* 1976), may be responsible. Exposure processes are crucial to artifact density studies. Firstly, the effect of erosion will depend on the nature of the original burial. If gradual, then the subsequent erosion surface will represent a palimpsest of a long-term span, and the density would be increased (Fig. 6.11a). If sudden, then the original density would be maintained (Fig. 6.11b). Secondly, with deposition there may be considerable

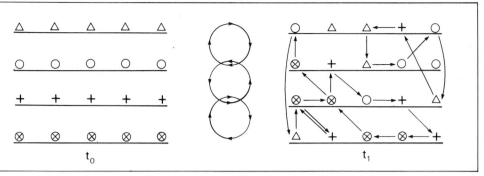

6.13. Model of small-scale artifact movement and exchange; see Cahen and Moeyersons (1977) for an archaeological example of this.

lateral movement. This is often observed in relation to scarp features, and account must be taken of this movement, especially with regard to dispersal. Thirdly, although erosion will usually result in the formation of palimpsests, it should be remembered that all archaeological situations are palimpsest (hourly, daily, seasonal, annual etc.), and it is only the scale that varies. Time averaging is essential to the discipline. Fourthly, the burial–exposure cycle can occur more than once (Fig. 6.12). And fifthly, all these processes are cumulative.

Artifact exchange and oscillation

Aside from these large-scale mechanisms, localised and small-scale processes may operate on artifacts, the cumulative effect of which is significant. These may operate vertically:
>   Burrowing animals
>   Root action
>   Trampling – human (especially on settlements)
>   – animal
>   Freeze/thaw processes
>   Wetting/drying processes
>   Soil formation processes (e.g. decaying vegetation)

or, horizontally:
>   Kicking/scuffing of artifacts
>   Wind processes – prevailing direction
>   – dust devils
>   Burrowing animals

These processes, about which little is known (but see Cahen and Moeyersons 1977; Siiriäinen 1977), may either have a predominant vector (e.g. wind direction) or else a more balanced exchange may occur (Fig. 6.13).

Against these variables two considerations should always be borne in mind. The first is that the more movement of artifacts both laterally and vertically, the greater the loss of information. And secondly, with time all artifacts will be destroyed; organic material will decay, and inorganic material will be physically and chemically weathered to the point where their attributes as humanly modified objects will be lost. The extent to which these two trends will have occurred must be taken into account in any off-site study.

AMBOSELI: AN EXAMPLE OF OFF-SITE ARCHAEOLOGY

Building on the principles of the foregoing discussion we may now look at the problem of measuring and evaluating artifact distributions. Before examining the major aspects involved in this it may be useful to look briefly at some details of an artifact density survey carried out by the author in the Amboseli Basin, southern Kenya during 1976 and 1977. Previous experience in surveys for archaeological material in East Africa had suggested to me many of the ideas discussed in this paper. From these I decided to initiate a project that was specifically designed to test off-site concepts and to develop suitable field methodologies. Analysis of the results is still underway, and only a brief outline can be given here.

The Amboseli was selected as the fieldwork area for several reasons. Firstly, the region was archaeologically unexplored, but as a lake basin it could be expected to have a similar type of archaeological record as other lakes in East Africa. As a relatively flat and open ecosystem it would offer a high degree of archaeological, especially artifactual, visibility. Furthermore, as a Game Park it had been subject to intensive ecological monitoring and study, thus providing a useful amount of background information about the ecological dynamics (Western 1973; 1975; Western and van Praet 1972; Altmann and Altmann 1970; Behrensmeyer and Storsell n.d.; Williams 1972). I hoped to investigate by this method the development of pastoralism as an alternative adaptation to hunting–gathering in East Africa, and, as the Amboseli is in Maasailand, the interaction of wild ungulates and the Maasai herds could be used as an analogue to the prehistoric relationships (Foley 1977a). The aims of the project were to examine the man–land relationships and distribution of archaeological remains in relation to resources along the lines suggested by the author elsewhere (Foley 1977b).

A preliminary report and brief description of the first stage of fieldwork has been presented elsewhere (Foley, in press). Throughout the programme, stress was placed on efficient sampling, following the sort of procedures used by the vegetation ecologists (Mueller-Dombois and Ellenberg 1975). Artifacts share many properties with plants, in having a small unit size in relation to a very large spatial context, and also by having a patchy distribution. Throughout the programme the artifact was used as the unit of collection. The sampling consisted of an initial stage of stratified random collection and analysis across 600 km² of the Amboseli, to provide a basic topography of artifact density. Apart from the artifact numbers and their attributes, background information was also collected. This was followed by a second stage of selective sampling to test for the effects of particular environment variables such as soil compaction, erosion rates, soil type, vegetation cover, etc. This second stage was designed to suggest correction factors for some post-depositional processes that could be expected to operate. Other experiments were attempted using plotted artifacts actually to measure their movement over the short term.

Certain aspects of the study are of general theoretical and methodological interest. The quantity of material that was observed in the Amboseli justified the principle of off-site archaeology. There is a mean of more than 40000 artifacts per square kilometre on the surface. That this reflects a diffuse and scattered pattern is supported by the fact that out of 257 transects only 14 per cent failed to produce any artifacts. It is unlikely that such a high density would be maintained on a large scale throughout East Africa owing to the particular ecological and geological context of the Amboseli, but it supports the idea that much archaeological material is preserved away from orthodox sites.

While this figure appears large it should be put into the context of the time covered, in the same way as was suggested earlier for the Cantabrian sites. Given a period of deposition of approximately 5000 years, the figure would mean a discard rate of eight artifacts per cent square kilometre – i.e. in the Amboseli as a whole the number of artifacts discarded on average per year was only 4800. When it is remembered that this number includes a vast amount of small debitage, not very much is present for a society dependent upon lithic technology. This seems to expose an area of profound ignorance in prehistoric studies – what are the rates of use and discard of lithic artifacts? It is difficult to suggest ways in which this lack of data can be rectified (Schiffer 1976, pp. 30–1).

CALIBRATION OF FORMATION PROCESSES

As well as knowing the processes at work on artifacts it is equally essential to be able to measure them. Actual definition of measurement techniques will require considerable experimental observation, but set out below are some of the parameters that should be considered.

Artifact discard

This is activity and culture dependent, and presumably very variable. It is likely that rates of discard and the pattern they reflect will only be accessible through the ethnographic record. A few extremely well calibrated archaeological sites might provide auxiliary information. However, site calibrations are not likely to be very helpful for disparate artifact scatters which reflect a different activity. Small seasonal or special activity sites will be more useful in this respect (for example, some of the British mesolithic sites, where length of occupation can be assessed (Clark 1972)). Essentially discard is a time parameter that will take on different values for different areas and activities. Density is the most accessible measurement. Absolute discard rate (D) would be measured by

$$D = \frac{\text{No. of artifacts per unit area}}{\text{Length of time during which discard occurred}}$$

This will be difficult to assess accurately for large areas, and relative discard rate will have to be used – i.e. simply the number of artifacts per unit area. Artifact densities over large areas represent this value once corrections have been made for post-depositional factors. Ethnography can perhaps then supply models for calibration of the relative rates.

Burial rate

As this is a geomorphological rather than archaeological rate it is geomorphological techniques that should be used, such as attempts to correlate sediment thickness with time (cf. McBurney 1967). In most open areas such correlations are not likely to be significant on a broad scale. The processes of burial, and the opposite process, erosion, will seriously affect density values if they are computed on the basis of number of artifacts per unit area on the surface. Deeply buried topographies will have a low two-dimensional density, in contrast to eroded surfaces. Corrections for this must be made in the context of the time period during which the artifacts were laid down. This, then, is the crux of an artifact density study, and must be accounted for by sampling more than just surface occurrences.

Artifact exposure

All observable archaeological phenomena are a measure of exposure (except perhaps caves). Archaeological research may be correlated with erosion systems at various scales. Given, therefore, the importance of erosion processes to archaeology it is regrettable that they should be so notoriously difficult to calibrate. The archaeological consequences are usually palimpsest formation, which may be difficult to calibrate. Conversion to three-dimensional density values will even up the opposite processes of burial and erosion. The dilemma is that the situation which produces the most archaeological information – erosion – will be the most difficult to calibrate.

Artifact exchange–oscillation

As was discussed earlier, this small-scale factor will vary according to whether one vector is predominant. Access to this set of processes will be through an experimental approach. In the context of archaeological burial it should be remembered that burial beyond a certain point will bring the exchange to a halt. Both vertically and laterally this may be a concentrating factor. Small-scale cumulative movement may be capable of moving artifacts to the 'edge' of a system, but not out of it. For example, the lateral movement caused by dust devils will work as long as the topography is flat enough. When the artifacts are brought to the edge of the flat area, the process will stop, and artifacts will concentrate. The vertical equivalent would be downward movement until a layer of harder, artifactually impervious sediment is reached (caliche layers, welded tuff etc.) when the process is stopped.

Artifact movement

Artifact movement, both rate and direction, will normally be in the context of matrix movement. Rates of lateral movement are generally easier to assess than burial or erosion rates because the determining factors of topography, drainage, water movement are more easily measured. An important component in lateral movement is sorting of particle size as a function of force of flow. Size frequencies along a transect will give a good indication of the direction and movement rate of artifacts. Both density (especially the scale at which density is being assessed) and distribution will be affected by movement, and corrections through size frequency transects and correlations of topography and density will be necessary.

Artifact destruction

The local nature of destruction patterns render them difficult to measure. For the sake of consistency it is probably best to treat inorganic artifacts separately from organic. However, the unsystematic nature of destruction leaves this variable unrefined. Some information may be derived from measuring the proportion of broken pieces, as this may be the first stage of destruction.

Visibility

Visibility falls into a somewhat different category, primarily concerned with assessing the type of sample presented to the archaeologist by the other processes described. It may be measured by the proportion of visible sediment to total sediment, both overall and adjusted for different time periods. In this context the effects of vegetation cover need also to be considered. Uninhabitable sediments (e.g. deep water sediments) should be excluded from the ratio (Fig. 6.14). Correlations of the visible sediment ratio with the artifact densities will be useful for correcting density values to allow for partial access.

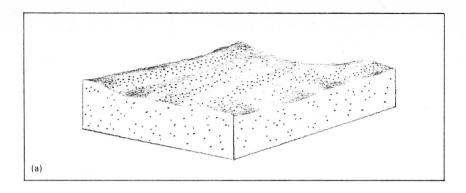

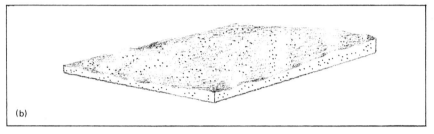

6.14. Archaeological visibility: (a) a landscape with high surface area:sediment volume ratio, and thus low archaeological visibility; (b) a landscape with low surface area:sediment volume ratio, and thus high archaeological visibility.

DISCUSSION AND CONCLUSIONS

Archaeological remains form and are preserved through a diverse set of processes, both behavioural and geomorphological. The result is a variety of spatial patterns. This paper has pointed to the value of the distribution and density of artifacts away from orthodox sites. The initial basis for this approach are the processes of artifact discard, particularly the non-discrete nature of human debris formation. The effect of this through continual occupation of an area is intensified by the cumulative characteristics of discard. Following discard, artifact distributions are subject to further dynamics, no longer behavioural, but geomorphological. These processes manipulate the distributions prior to access by the archaeologist, and careful separation of the disparate strands of post-depositional forces is required prior to prehistoric synthesis. The potential of off-site archaeology can be realised only through the careful and explicit analysis of post-depositional processes, and a recognition of the independent nature of spatial information.

The model described presents various problems which will require further attention (see also Isaac, ch. 5 above). These include the question of how much temporal resolution may acceptably be lost to obtain increased spatial information, determining the scale at which artifact density variation is operating, and thus the most appropriate sampling strategies; the measurement

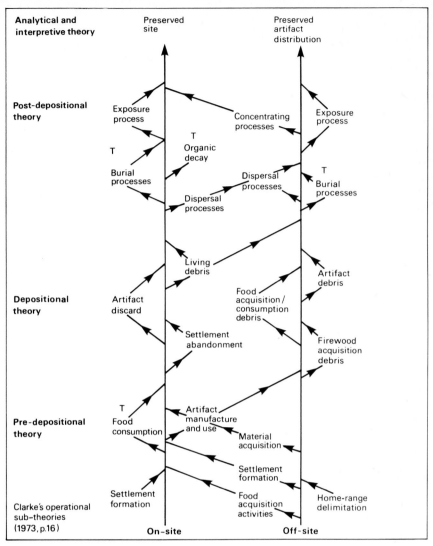

6.15.   Flow of on-site and off-site information through Clarke's operational subtheories (1973, p. 16).

of patchy but continuous distributions; and the extent to which the model applies to other geomorphological and behavioural contexts. Further research into the nature of the archaeological record will, it is hoped, suggest ways in which these present limitations may be minimised.

The work described here may be seen as a reflection of two developing areas of archaeological concern – taphonomy and spatial analysis. Taphonomy reflects an increasing concern with the state of the data when it reaches the archaeologist. While this is leading to a serious revision of many of our previously held beliefs (e.g. Hill 1975; Brain 1976) it is also opening up new areas of research. Many of these relate to an increasing use of ethnographic data for testing the procedures of archaeological analysis (Hodder 1977). Others suggest that there is information preserved that has previously been ignored or under-valued (Klein 1977; Shipman 1975). In other words, increasing rigour will not only modify our previously oversimplified understanding of the nature of archaeological inferences, but also show lines of reasoning that have previously been unrecognised. This positive attribution can be seen in Hill's (1975) model for disarticulation of mammals under 'natural' processes as opposed to butchery processes.

Another overall trend within archaeology has been an increased interest in spatial patterns. Partly a reflection of the increased influence of geographical techniques following the 'geographical revolution' of the 1960s (Goudie 1976; Hodder and Orton 1977; Clarke 1972; 1977b), it is also related to the increased importance of spatial models in the behavioural sciences as a whole (e.g., MacArthur and Wilson 1967). Off-site archaeology is an archaeological response to this, attempting to gain better access to spatial rather than chronological information pertaining to the behaviour of prehistoric man. In particular, the information being sought is ecological and economic (see Clarke's (1972) 'ecological paradigm') for, while seasonality and annual fluctuations are temporal dimensions of resource distribution, the main component is spatial. Above all else it is this information that off-site archaeology is attempting to improve. Prehistoric man operated over a landscape, and his survival depended on his ability to organise his activities over this landscape. His immediate dimension is also the one on which we should map our understanding of his behaviour.

This paper has attempted to develop an operational theory that incorporates both a better understanding of the taphonomical basis of the archaeological record and the recognition of the spatial dimension of human behaviour. It might thus be considered a response to David Clarke's (1977a, p. 28) challenge for archaeology to

develop its own related range of spatial theory, capable of simulating extinct situations, suitable for dealing with the difficult but not impossible spatial characteristics of archaeological samples and, in its various branches, able to embrace non-settlement site data from linear, sectored, spiral, multiple nucleii cemetry spatial patterns to three-dimensional stratigraphical clusters. We are only just beginning to explore the possibilities of archaeological spatial theory...

ACKNOWLEDGEMENTS

Financial support for the field aspects of the work presented here came from the Swan Fund (Pitt-Rivers Museum, University of Oxford) and the Emslie Horniman Fund (Royal Anthropological Institute). The work was carried out under the auspices of the National Museums of Kenya and the Department of Archaeology, Cambridge. I thank them all for their support. Professor Glynn Isaac provided much encouragement in both field and theoretical aspects. Vicki Morse was a constant source of helpful ideas and practical assistance throughout the project. Dr Andrew Hill provided not only generous hospitality in Kenya, but also a high level of taphonomical skepticism. Dr Diane Gifford read an earlier draft of this paper and provided many helpful comments that I have now incorporated. Responsibility for the views presented, however, must rest entirely with the author. Should there be anything of value here, then it is through the help, influence, and encouragement of the late David Clarke. It is my hope that this contribution in some small way reflects my debt to him as a friend and teacher.

REFERENCES

Adams, W. Y. (1968). 'Settlement patterns in microcosm: the changing aspect of a Nubian village during twelve centuries' in K. C. Chang (ed.) *Settlement Archaeology*, National Press Books

Altmann, S. A. and Altmann, J. (1970). *Baboon Ecology: African field research*, S. Karger

Ammerman, A. J. and Feldman, M. W. (1974). 'On the "making" of an assemblage of stone tools', *American Antiquity* 39: 610–16

Behrensmeyer, A. K. (1975). 'The taphonomy and palaeoecology of Plio-Pleistocene vertebrate assemblages east of Lake Rudolf, Kenya', *Bulletin of the Museum of Comparative Zoology* 146 (10): 473–578

Behrensmeyer, A. K. and Storsell, D. (n.d.). 'Report on geological investigations, Amboseli National Park', 1975 (mimeo)

Binford, L. R. (1973). 'Inter-assemblage variability – the Mousterian and the "functional" argument' in C. Renfrew (ed.) *The Explanation of Culture Change: models in prehistory*, Duckworth

Birdsell, J. B. (1953). 'Some environmental and cultural factors influencing the structure of Australian aboriginal populations', *American Naturalist* 87 (834): 171–207

Brain, C. K. (1967a). 'Hottentot food remains and their bearing on the interpretation of fossil bone assemblages', *Scientific Papers of the Namib Desert Research Station* 32: 1–11

(1967b). 'Bone weathering and the problem of bone pseudo-tools', *South African Journal of Science* 63: 97–9

(1969). 'The contribution of Namib Desert Hottentots to and understanding of Australopithecine bone accumulations', *Scientific Papers of the Namib Desert Research Station* 39: 13–22

(1976). 'Some principles in the interpretation of bone accumulations associated with man' in G. Ll. Isaac and E. McCown (eds.) *Human Origins: Louis Leakey and the East African evidence*, W. J. Benjamin

Cahen, D. and Moeyersons, J. (1977). 'Sub-surface movement of stone artifacts and their implications for the prehistory of Central Africa', *Nature* 266: 812–14

Clark, J. G. D. (1972). *Star Carr: a case study in bioarchaeology*, Addison-Wellesley

Clarke, D. L. (1968). *Analytical Archaeology*, Methuen

(1972). 'Models and paradigms in contemporary archaeology' in D. L. Clarke (ed.) *Models in Archaeology*, Methuen

(1973). 'Archaeology: loss of innocence', *Antiquity* 47: 7–18

(1977a). 'Spatial information in archaeology' in D. L. Clarke (ed.) *Spatial Archaeology*, Academic Press

(ed.) (1977b). *Spatial Archaeology*, Academic Press

Coppens, Y., Howell, F. C., Isaac, G. L. and Leakey, R. E. (1976). *Earliest Man and Environments in the Lake Rudolf Basin*, University of Chicago Press

Elton, C. (1927). *Animal Ecology*, Sidgwick and Jackson

Evans-Pritchard, E. E. (1940). *The Nuer*, Oxford University Press

Foley, R. A. (1977a). 'Prehistoric pastoralism and palaeoenvironments', paper presented to the Seminar on African Pastoral Society, Institute of African Studies, Nairobi, March 1977

 (1977b). 'Space and energy: a method for analysing habitat value and utilization in relation to archaeological sites' in D. L. Clarke (ed.) *Spatial Archaeology*, Academic Press

 (in press). 'The spatial component of archaeological data: off-site methods and some preliminary results from the Amboseli Basin, Southern Kenya', *Proceedings of the VIIIth Pan-African Congress in Prehistory and Quarternary studies*

Gerard and Berthet (1971). 'Sampling patchy distributions' in Pielou *et al.* (eds.) *Statistical Ecology*, vol. 1

Gifford, D. P. (1977). 'Observations of modern human settlements as an aid to archaeological interpretation', Ph.D. thesis, University of California, Berkeley

Goudie, A. (1976). 'Geography and prehistory', *Journal of Historical Geography* 2(3): 197–205

Gould, R. A. (1968). 'Living archaeology: the Ngatatjara of Western Australia', *Southwestern Journal of Anthropology* 24: 101–22

Gramley, R. (1971). 'Archaeological survey and excavations at Lukenya Hill, Kenya', unpublished report, Institute of African Studies, Nairobi

 (1975). 'Hunters and pastoralist in East Africa', Ph.D. thesis, Harvard University

Hill, A. P. (1975). 'Taphonomy of contemporary and Late Cenozoic East African vertebrates', Ph.D. thesis, University of London

Hodder, I. (1977). 'The distribution of material cultural items in the Baringo district, Western Kenya', *Man*, New series, 12(2): 239–69

Hodder, I. and Orton, C. (1976). *Spatial Analysis in Archaeology*, Cambridge University Press

Hole, F., Flannery, K. V. and Neeley, J. A. (1969). 'Prehistory and human ecology of the Deh Luran plain, an early village sequence from Kuzistan, Iran', *Memoirs of the Museum of Anthropology, University of Michegan* 1

Howell, F. C. (1966). 'Observations on the earlier phases of the European Lower Palaeolithic' in J. D. Clark and F. C. Howell (eds.) *Recent Studies in Palaeoanthropology*, American Anthropology Special Publications 68(2): 88–201

Isaac, G. L. (1971). 'Comparative studies of Pleistocene, site locations in East Africa' in P. Ucko *et al.* (eds.) *Man, Settlement and Urbanism*, Duckworth

Isaac, G. L. and Harris, J. (1976). 'The scatter between the patches', paper presented to the Kroeber Anthropological Society

Isaac, G. L., Harris, J. and Crader, D. (1976). 'Archaeological evidence from the Koobi Fora Formation' in Y. Coppens *et al.* (eds.) *Earliest Man and Environments in the Lake Rudolf Basin* (Prehistoric Archaeology and Ecology Series), University of Chicago Press

Klein, R. G. (1977). 'The ecology of man in South Africa', *Science* 197: 115–26

Kroeber, A. L. (1939). *Cultural and Natural Areas of Native North America* (Publications in American Archaeology and Ethnology), University of California Press

Lee, R. B. (1968). 'What hunters do for a living? or how to make out on scarce resources' in R. B. Lee and I. DeVore (eds.) *Man the Hunter*, Aldine

Lee, R. B. and DeVore, I. (1968). *Man the Hunter*, Aldine

MacArthur, R. H. and Wilson, E. O. (1967). *Theory of Island Biogeography*, Princeton University Press

McBurney, C. B. M. (1967). *The Haua Fteah*, Cambridge University Press

McInnes, I. J. (1971). 'Settlement in Later Neolithic Britain' in D. D. A. Simpson (ed.) *Economy and Settlement in Neolithic and Early Bronze Age Britain and Europe*, Leicester University Press

Marshall, J. (1956). *The Hunters* (16 mm film), Film Study Centre of the Peabody Museum, Harvard University

Marshall, L. K. (1960). '!Kung Bushman bands', *Africa* 30: 325–55

Mueller-Dombois, D. and Ellenberg, H. (1975). *Aims and Methods of Vegetation Ecology*, Wiley

Radcliffe-Brown, A. R. (1930). 'Former numbers and distribution of the Australian Aborigines', *Official Yearbook of the Commonwealth of Australia* 23: 671–96

Robbins, L. H. (1973). 'Turkana material culture viewed from an archaeological perspective', *World Archaeology* 5 (2): 208–14

Schiffer, M. B. (1976). *Behavioural Archaeology* (Studies in Archaeology), Academic Press

Shipman, P. (1975). 'Implications of drought for vertebrate fossil assemblages', *Nature* 257: 667–8

Siiriäinen, A. (1977). 'Pieces in vertical movement: a model for rock-shelter archaeology', *Proceedings of the Prehistoric Society* 43: 349–51

Smith, I. (1974). 'The Neolithic' in C. Renfrew (ed.) *British Prehistory*, Duckworth

Strauss, L. G. (1977). 'Of deerslayer and mountain men: palaeolithic faunal exploitation in Cantabrean Spain' in L. R. Binford (ed.) *Theory Building in Archaeology* (Studies in Archaeology), Academic Press

Thomas, D. H. (1972). 'A computer simulation model of Great Basin Shoshonean subsistence and settlement patterns' in D. L. Clarke (ed.) *Models in Archaeology*, Methuen

    (1975). 'Non-site sampling in archaeology: up the creek without a site?' in J. W. Mueller (ed.) *Sampling in Archaeology*, University of Arizona Press

Western, D. (1973). 'The structure, changes and dynamics of the Amboseli ecosystem', Ph.D. thesis, University of Nairobi

    (1975). 'Water availability and its influence on the structure and dynamics of a large mammal ecosystem', *East African Wildlife Journal* 13: 365–80

Western, D. and van Praet, C. (1972). 'Cyclical changes in the habitat and climate of an East African ecosystem', *Nature* 241: 104–6

Wheat, J. B. (1972). 'The Olsen-Chubbuck site, a Paleo-Indian bison kill', *American Antiquity* 37 (1): memoir 26

Whittaker, R. H. (1970). *Communities and Ecosystems*, Macmillan

Williams, L. A. J. (1972). 'Geology of the Amboseli area', *Geological Survey of Kenya Report* 90

Woodburn, J. (1968). 'An introduction to Hadza ecology' in R. B. Lee and I. DeVore (eds.) *Man the Hunter*, Aldine

Woodburn, J. and Hudson, S. (1966). 'The Hadza: the food quest of a hunting and gathering tribe of Tanzania' (16 mm film), London School of Economics

Yellen, J. E. (1976). 'Settlement patterns of the !Kung' in R. B. Lee and I. DeVore (eds.) *Kalahari Hunter–Gatherers*, Harvard University Press

7

Black holes in British prehistory: the analysis of settlement distributions

LES GROUBE

To David Clarke, archaeological models were primarily devices for separating 'noise' from information, a method of simplifying complex observation 'whilst offering a largely accurate predictive framework structuring these observations' (1968, p. 32). Unfortunately this operational definition has become muted over the years; the word 'model', overused, has become a fashionable synonym for 'hypothesis', 'theory' or 'explanation'. Many modern models are noisier and more complex than the original information, denying the essential requirement of simplification. Indeed 'pollution' by noisy models is now a major menace to archaeology, reducing much useful information to mere verbiage.

This paper is an attempt to re-assert Clark's operational definition of an archaeological model by examining the noisiest but most basic of all archaeological data-records, the *distribution map*. Despite the recent upsurge in studies of spatial analysis – fundamentally, a noise-reduction strategy – 'static' and 'interference' still disrupt the 'message' contained in distributional data. The normal methods of spatial analysis concentrate on translating and refining the dimly perceived message; the strategy of this paper is to examine the nature and sources of noise in archaeological distribution maps and, wherever possible, to reduce their impact upon information flow.

ARCHAEOLOGICAL 'NOISE'

Noise is essentially irrelevant information which disturbs or obscures the transcription and translation of a 'message'. The message, of course, is the interpretation, the 'meaning' of the patterns in any body of data. The word 'noise', long established in computer-talk, is ultimately derived from physics, particularly radio and astrophysics when random wave transmissions or, more frequently, different patterned transmissions cause interference. In computer-talk, 'noise' refers to the irrelevant information which confuses and obscures underlying tendencies in complex data analysis. The control and reduction of such 'noise' is often the sole purpose of ponderous computer calculations. Noise invariably obscures and sometimes irretrievably garbles the messages contained in the information: its control and reduction are essential requirements of archaeological analysis.

There are two main sources of noise in archaeological maps: interference between simultaneous 'positive' messages within and around the archaeological information set and noise derived from the absence of information: missing elements, disrupted connections between positive information (general data discontinuity) – paradoxically the noise of silence.

The standard procedure for controlling interference between 'positive' messages is by filtration: excluding all information which does not belong to a specified data set. The most obvious and frequent filtration is 'synchronic control' – restricting map information to contemporary or near contemporary elements. An alternative (diachronic) strategy is to include only elements inside a defined site category regardless of chronology or cultural affiliations (e.g., settlement or burial sites) in order to emphasise interconnections with other diachronic factors (e.g., with natural resources, trade routes, soil types, etc.). Geographical filtration is also frequent, restricting 'correlative data' to defined features (e.g., rivers, soils, height above sea level). Whatever the strategy the method is similar: filtering out or suppressing noise irrelevant to the task in hand – model building in Clarke's sense. It is not surprising that Clarke includes archaeological maps in his category of Iconic models (1968, p. 445–63).

Unfortunately, archaeological messages are seldom coherent; they are discontinuous and interrupted; elements and interconnections are invariably missing. The task, indeed, is to re-establish connections and discover, if possible, faint traces of the missing elements. Because the information system – the elements and interconnections – changes with evolving land usage, different cultural, technological or political emphases throughout different histories of decay and destruction, the resultant messages are extraordinarily confused. The strategy of filtration, therefore, often fails to achieve results with such incoherent information. Only with certain site types (e.g., earthwork fortifications) where the survival characteristics are good (i.e. few elements are missing) is the noise from data disruption at an acceptably low level.

More deceptive, however, is the fact that much correlative information, particularly of geography, is more coherent than surviving archaeological data and tends to monopolise archaeological maps. The nature of any physical landscape, although manipulated by man, changed and changing over time, nevertheless powerfully influences human activity and thus the location of survivals of that activity. Topography, pedology, climate and so on dominate archaeological maps because the landscape is a variable constraint system to all forms of life and settlement history must reflect the impact of these restraints. Thus quite critical facts, such as the spacing of major settlements, their location in relation to natural resources or their density, can be so affected by geographical factors as to obscure other more important patterns.

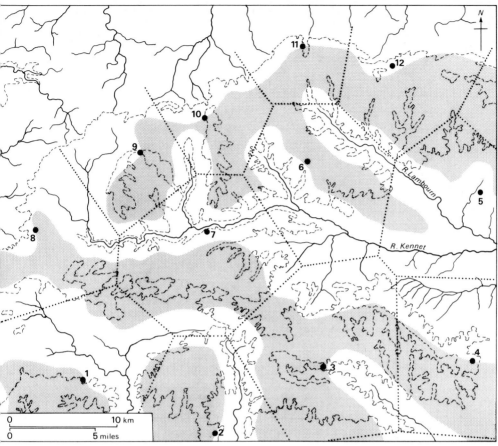

Hillforts on the North Wessex Downs *c.* 200 B.C. The shaded area shows land more than one mile from the nearest permanent water supply. 1. Broadbury Banks; 2. Sidbury; 3. Bevisbury; 4. Beacon Hill; 5. Bussocks; 6. Membury; 7. Forest Hill; 8. Oldbury; 9. Barbury; 10. Liddington Castle; 11. Uffington Castle; 12. Segsbury (Cunliffe 1976).

This problem is most economically illustrated by example. A recent map of the North Wessex Downs (Cunliffe 1976, Fig. 2) has been chosen, because it is an exemplary demonstration of the use of a map model to reinforce an argument derived from independent observations, that is the differing water requirements of sheep and cattle (Fig. 7.1).

This map incorporates the main features of a model: 'simplification', 'noise separation' and a 'predictive framework structuring the observations'.

Simplification and noise separation have been achieved initially by filtering out certain topographical information. The area chosen (apart from a small area in the Vale of the White Horse) is geologically and pedologically uniform – rolling chalkland landscape intersected by typical downland valleys.

Only two contour lines and the rivers indicate general topography. Archaeological noise has been removed by 'synchronic control', restricting the input to hillforts *c.* 200 B.C.

The predictive framework is supplied by plotting the land (shaded) more than one mile from a 'permanent water supply'.

From this 'structuring of observations', that is the close correlation of fort locations with the boundary of the shaded zone, Cunliffe cautiously argues that 'developed hillforts were optimally sited to exploit the two resource potentials (land suitable for sheep and land suitable for cattle)' (1976, p. 138). Unfortunately, the landscape constraint, the topographical noise, interferes with this apparently commonsense correlation.

Hillforts, by definition, will only be located in certain slope-enhanced environments. The geomorphology of a chalk landscape limits the occurrence of steep slopes which are found predominantly along the chalk escarpment or along the 'bluff-edges' of some river valleys, precisely where the forts tend to be located. An apparent exception (Fig. 7.1, site no. 5, Bussocks) is actually on the edge of a local 'hill' which escaped the selected contour filter.

As the natural environments in which 'hills' occur (bluff-edges or the escarpment) are systematically related to the drainage pattern, the location of the hillforts must also be systematically related to rivers and water proximity. Thus the authority of the map in Fig. 7.1 is only a second-level correlation, the first level being topographical. It will be immediately obvious, however, that there are some parts of the region with desirable topographical advantages which were apparently not fortified in this period (although they were at other periods), e.g. Walbury Hill (where there is a fort) or along the upland to the immediate north of the headwaters of the River Avon. This important observation is discussed at greater length in a later section.

ARCHAEOLOGICAL 'BLANKS'

The noise of silence, the 'blanks' in archaeological maps, are the second major source of message disruption for archaeologists. The existence of blanks, of course, is a logical necessity of the existence of sites. Archaeological data are, at their simplest, merely a patterned presence–absence information set and the negative absences are by definition a necessity of, and as important as, the positive presences. Blanks, however, vary in noise level and significance for the archaeologist.

The least important 'blank' is the background, the 'vacuum' of archaeological space – the informationless backdrop upon which positive and negative patterns can be detected.

Patterned blanks vary in their information content and significance to archaeologists: *craters* are holes in distribution maps created by subsequent natural or human destructive agencies. A prominent but seldom appreciated natural crater is the chalkland itself, where relatively rapid chemical dissolution removes much structural evidence. Floods, landslips, coastal degradation, earthquakes, etc. can destroy or disrupt archaeological distributions leaving 'craters' among the remnants.

An unfortunate and deceptive characteristic of much human destruction is that it is often *patterned*, leaving spurious 'negative shapes' in the positive data. An example of this is the role of Iron Age, Roman or medieval agricultural episodes on the survival of Bronze Age barrows. In areas of intensive arable activities, barrow distribution, in the absence of a prehistoric Ancient Monuments Act, should be severely cratered. Although there is evidence that barrows were often respected by later farmers – or used as boundary markers – many barrows, boundary ditches and other surface features of the Bronze Age must have been destroyed by unknown later arable episodes. Where such episodes are relatively unsystematic (that is random), the disruption to an underlying systematic pattern will not be fatal: where the obliteration is patterned (e.g. as field systems), then spurious distribution boundaries will be imposed upon the earlier remains.

Certain regions will be more susceptible to cratering than others because of a continued preference for certain types of soil, crops or economic strategies. These preferential regions will generate more incoherent 'silent noise' than less-favoured areas. Thus peripheral areas (e.g. moorland) often yield more coherent (although chronologically or functionally restricted) evidence than 'heartland' areas (e.g. the southern chalklands) where land, and therefore destruction, is at a premium.

A *bias hole* refers to that sinister source of noise in distribution maps – inadequate or biassed data. Areas where inadequate or differential prospecting creates spurious boundaries in positive information are frequent in archaeological distribution maps. Fieldwork standards vary considerably and the authority of negative (and positive) information varies with them. Archaeologists are particularly sensitive to this problem (see, for example, Cherry *et al.* 1978) and it is generally easy to identify and remedy.

Although sampling bias is being slowly eliminated by the systematic surveys of the Royal Commission on Historical Monuments and local archaeological units in Britain, it has tended to delay recognition of genuine 'holes' in distribution maps and to act as an excuse for postponing investigation of the causes and significance of such holes.

The most important negative evidence in distribution maps are *black holes*, which, like those of the astrophysicist, are areas of dense (energy) information. The discovery and delineation of black holes must yield powerful insights into the significance of positive evidence. *A black hole in archaeology is a significant absence of specific data in a synchronic landscape*: they can be discovered only after other types of holes (crater or bias) have been reduced or eliminated. Black holes are as important – or more so – than the positive evidence which gives them existence. They have many different origins, the most important being as follows.

Demographic black holes

The absence of archaeological remains (assuming other types of blanks have been eliminated) can often have the simplest of explanations; that the contemporary population could not occupy the entire landscape. Obviously the technological 'level' of any population is critical – higher densities can be expected of agriculturalists than of hunters, although the former may have fewer visible remains and the latter may well be less particular in the regions selected for exploitation. Within any techno-ecological level, however, the critical factor is the demographic status of the population, whether it is an initial colonising population (i.e. expanding), a mature (climax) population or, rarely, in decline. Thus the relatively discrete concentrations of Neolithic evidence in Britain (with many black holes) reflects as much the initial colonising status of the population as land preferences by early farmers. The significance of any data absence must be assessed against the demographic status of the population.

Ecological black holes

Within a generalised hunter–gatherer society most of the landscape is potentially usable (see Parkington, ch. 12 and Foley, ch. 6, this volume), but with more specialised agriculturalists factors such as soil fertility, ground drainage, aspect, availability of water, the nature and density of forest cover (for clearance) and so on, become increasingly important (see Halstead, ch. 11 this volume). Forest clearance of the rapidly podsolising soils and inadequate drainage of most of the sand and gravel areas of southern Britain eventually created heathlands which became major (post-Bronze Age) ecological black holes. The equally poorly drained claylands, supporting heavy wet-oak forests, were inhibitive of rapid colonisation and were avoided for millennia, an ecological black hole persisting from the Neolithic to perhaps as late as the Iron Age. The ruggedness and steeper slopes of the western hill country also restricted arable expansion even where good soil existed. Such black holes, part of the variable constraint system of the landscape, obviously change in significance and boundaries over time and are determined not only by underlying topographic characteristics and the economy practised, but also by human modifications. Thus ecological black holes (such as the heathland) can be created; others are part of the topographic–pedological structure inherited from the geological past.

Sociopolitical black holes

The most elusive black holes have their origin in the prevailing sociopolitical conditions. Sometimes ephemeral but often surviving anachronistically beyond the life span of the communities which gave rise to them, culturally derived black holes result from some form of avoidance or restraint system adopted by the community.

The most important black holes of political origin are territorial boundaries which, particularly when there is no physical marker such as a ditch or fence, may be evident only from the absence of contemporary remains on or near them. Territorial boundaries tend to be areas of mutual avoidance not merely or even necessarily to minimise border disputes. They mark the outer limits (parameters) of a closed system unified by ideological commonalties such as descent, language or authority structure. The identity and integrity of the unifying system within a territory is reinforced not only by the existence of the boundary but also by limiting or avoiding many activities on or close to the boundary (e.g., settlement foundation, farming, etc.) thus creating a black hole in the contemporary cultural landscape. Boundaries *within* a unified system, such as tenurial holdings (in contrast to territorial boundaries), will not necessarily be characterised by avoidance of activities (e.g., boundaries between farms) and thus have to be reinforced by some sort of markers (e.g., ditches). Boundary markers in the middle of contemporary black holes are likely to identify territories whereas boundaries with uninterrupted contemporary remains are more likely to be internal (tenurial) subdivisions of a territory.

A consequence of avoidance of territorial boundaries (i.e. those around the parameters of a system) is that black holes may well be the only way of identifying them and that boundary markers such as ditches are more likely to be demarcatory divisions within a single territory than between territories. To minimise the burden of reduced economic activities close to territorial boundaries they are often located along ecological black holes (e.g., rivers, ridges, cliff edges) and thus are difficult to identify. 'No man's land' (i.e. a political black hole) is often placed where man seldom requires land, along natural interruptions in the landscape.

Within any territory there are many other black holes originating from the sociocultural system. In respect of houses and buildings, for examples, the village green (or indeed Hyde Park) is a cultural black hole where specialised usage limits or defines activities and therefore restricts physical remains. Maintained woodland or forest is an economic black hole in an agricultural landscape. Restraints upon usage (planning) which result in social or economic black holes are not restricted to complex or centralised societies: the New Zealand Maori, for example, used *tapu* to control access to forests and fishing grounds (Firth 1959, p. 254).

The sites of ritual activities, particularly those associated with death, can also result in black holes in the archaeological landscape. Normal activities could be restricted or prohibited in or close to cemeteries or burial grounds. Incidents such as battles or disasters might result in temporary abandonment or avoidance. Superstitions about certain areas (e.g., bogs or heavy forest) could also create black holes in the distribution of archaeological remains.

Widespread myths about were-wolves or other fearsome monsters must have generated some avoidance patterns in prehistoric Europe.

Many black holes of social and/or political origin will never be amenable to archaeological interpretation, but it would be a foolish archaeologist who sought explanation for absence of evidence only in ecological or demographic terms. Most societies maintain complex systems of age, sex, rank or kinship avoidance: some of these will have a distorting effect upon the distribution of archaeological evidence.

Residual black holes

An important type of black hole is the residual or anachronistic black hole, an area of restricted activity inherited from an earlier period. An obvious example of this today is the New Forest, originally created to protect and maintain hunting rights, now an anachronistic black hole in the agricultural landscape of southern England. Although the original boundaries of the forest have been somewhat trimmed it survives today in a new role, as a recreation area, a fine example of a residual black hole. Although the longevity of the New Forest, formally protected by parliament, may be exceptional, inherited black holes will be increasingly frequent in a fully used landscape. One of the most obvious reasons for this is that continuing *ad hoc* exploitation can result in loss or diminution of some resources, particularly woodland or agricultural land, and despite changed circumstances it is often more economic to maintain what has survived than to create new areas (e.g., the New Forest). In an economy which depends for fuel and building materials upon trees, surviving stocks will be maintained, thus increasingly becoming areas of restricted activity with specified rights of collection or cultural black holes. In their original context, however, they were merely the unused parts of the landscape (i.e. demographic black holes). Thus an important characteristic of residual black holes is change of function; from an ecological or demographic blank to a culturally maintained blank.

An important inherited black hole is, therefore, the heathland. Originally wooded with reasonable agricultural potential, the rapid podsolisation of the sand and gravel soils with poor drainage and continued firing and mismanagement created an ecological black hole. As the advantages of heathland furze and peat for household fuel were rapidly appreciated, the heathlands may have been deliberately maintained, thus becoming economic black holes in relation to many site types. It is interesting that the Forestry Commission still uses fire to maintain the diminishing heathland environment.

Although any residual black hole which is accepted and maintained by a later generation is in its new role a cultural black hole, it is important to distinguish such inherited forms from those created by the contemporary community. They will often appear out of conformity with the later overall synchronic pattern (i.e. anachronistic) or otherwise remain inexplicable. A territorial boundary, for example, although originally sited along what was an ecological black hole (e.g., in forest) might, in a following period, after forest clearance, divide unconformably a single valuable ecological zone. Boundary avoidance would thus be a considerable burden and the exact boundary would probably require reinforcement by a ditch or fence.

A subtle but very important type of residual black hole is that derived, like the heathland, from land mismanagement or outmoded economic strategies in the past. Failure to understand the rapid fertility loss of chalkland, for example (an ignorance still prevalent today), must have resulted at various times in such poor arable returns that parts of the chalkland were converted to pastoral or abandoned to second growth. Such black holes, the result of succeeding agricultural strategies inherited by later generations, are transitory but nevertheless must affect the distribution of certain synchronic evidence (e.g., field systems).

THE DISCOVERY OF BLACK HOLES

Black holes cannot be distinguished from more mundane types of blank merely by inspection. The great majority of holes in distribution maps will prove to have a simple origin: weak fieldwork (bias holes), destruction (craters) and most often topographic and ecological restrictions. The physical landscape must be looked upon as a flexible but powerful constraint system quite unlike the uniform flat sheet of paper upon which maps are printed. The landscape is like an extremely variable, rubbery manuscript paper with deep ruts, areas of roughness and many tears which interfere with and structure the marks upon it. The archaeologist must, initially, reduce the noise disturbance from this variation before seeking significant blanks in site distributions.

The isolation of black holes must proceed from the systematic elimination of the more obvious but irrelevant sources. The first and easiest reduction is from inspection for fieldwork weaknesses: the elimination of bias holes. No distribution map has any worth if there is wide variability in fieldwork standards.

The control of topographic-ecological variability, which has such an influence on human exploitation, is a major objective of all archaeological analysis. In the interpretation of distribution maps it is of critical importance.

The most daunting problem of discovery of black holes is in a rich archaeological landscape. Although large areas of missing evidence are easy to define, smaller holes are often lost in a crowded site distribution particularly where, as is common, inter-site distance is variable. The noise of distance variation determined by topographic, ecological or other constraints often obscures genuine pattern disruptions of greater interpretative significance.

Sites which are either transitory (a camp site) or accidental (a stray find site) dominate archaeological distribution maps, tending to have high densities in favourable areas. In the absence of fine chronological filters, inter-site distance has little relevance for short-term sites, for it is the random result of accumulated long-term usage, a palimpsest of patterns which are often impossible to separate. The most the archaeologist can do is to demonstrate that some areas are more favourable than others for the location of such sites.

The more permament is a site type, however, the more likely is the pattern of presence and absence to have significance. Thus, settlements and fortifications are obvious candidates for the discovery of 'significant absences in a synchronic landscape' (black holes), whereas find sites tend to exaggerate (by accumulation) landscape constraints. Burial mounds, although transitory in initial usage, remain permanent features of the landscape and thus influence the location of further barrows. They are, therefore, more useful than find sites in locating significant blanks, but with so few barrows absolutely contemporary in formation (unless following a calamity), a true synchronic pattern is difficult to demonstrate. The discovery of black holes must, initially at least, be confined to synchronic settlements or fortifications.

It is generally assumed with such sites that location is not random but rather a balanced compromise between topographical and ecological conditions, sociopolitical forces *and* the presence of other sites. In addition, it is highly probable that despite landscape variability, inter-settlement distance conforms to a characteristic range, with a minimum distance controlled by resource competition and a maximum distance determined by the threshold for the weakening of social, political and/or linguistic links with neighbouring sites. Obviously means of transport, extent of trade, the nature of the terrain, soil fertility and so on affect this inter-settlement distance. In a relatively homogeneous territory, the location of contemporary settlements should conform to a consistent overall distance range, a norm for that region at that time. Unfortunately settlement nodes are seldom stable for long (particularly if the population is expanding) so that any synchronic pattern can have conflicting inter-settlement norms during stages of transition. An obvious example of this is *infilling*, when new settlements are founded between existing settlements, halving the older inter-site norm. This is a frequent phenomenon in Roman Britain, with new settlements founded close to the mid-point between older towns. Thus, in addition to the variability imposed by the landscape constraints, the vicissitudes of dynamic settlement changes obviously add to the archaeologists' burden. Thus simple techniques such as establishing average inter-site or maximum and minimum nearest neighbour distances can have considerable difficulties, compounding the problem of identification of distributional abnormalities.

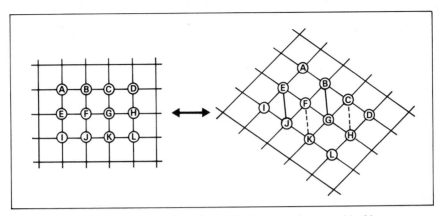

7.2.   An example of the transformation of a grid of squares into a grid of hexagons.

THE GEOMETRY OF MISSING EVIDENCE

Despite the fact that regularity or symmetry in settlement distribution is rare, a *tendency* towards regular spacing is often apparent. Iron Age fortifications in Britain, for example, show a remarkable overall spacing regularity which has been exploited in recent years in the construction, by Thiessen polygons, of theoretical territories around contemporary forts. David Clarke, among others, has demonstrated this regularity by showing that major forts can be located within a grid of hexagons (1968, p. 509). The hexagon, of course, is the *only* geometric figure with six equal nearest neighbour distances. One of the important building blocks of nature, as argued below, it offers a powerful instrument to discover archaeological blanks in any settlement pattern with a relatively regular inter-site spacing. Logically, *but without deliberate design*, such a site pattern must fall into a series of overlapping, usually distorted, hexagons with sides of nearest neighbour links. The degree of distortion is determined by the variability in inter-site distances.

Any site distribution must be divisible also into contiguous and overlapping triangles, quadrilaterals, pentagons, septagons, etc., but it is only the equilateral triangle and hexagons which have the admirable characteristic of equal distances between *nearest* neighbours. The regular hexagon, of course, is composed of six equilateral triangles, and it is this *ideal* geometric 'model', in the strict sense of David Clarke's definition, which underlies any synchronic pattern of settlements where the inter-site spacing tends to be regular. *If all landscape, social and economic constraints are relaxed, settlements would strive to fall into a pattern of regular hexagons except at the periphery of the system, the boundary, where the regularity must accommodate to the territorial limits.* This statement offers a powerful mode of site location analysis.

Before exploring the utility of the hexagon in the discovery of distribution gaps, it is necessary to reinforce this argument about hexagonal site patterns. An alternative geometric spacing system is a grid of squares, but from the

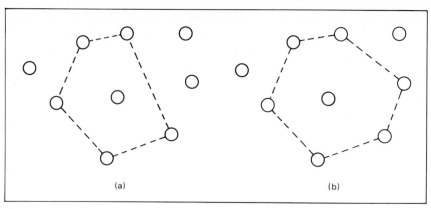

7.3.

A pentagon (a) and hexagon (b) drawn through the same distribution of sites (points).

geometry of the square it must be accepted that nearest neighbour distance cannot be equal as the diagonal link is always longer than the sides of the square. In practice, however, the distance difference is small and in addition a grid of squares can easily be transformed into a grid of hexagons (Fig. 7.2).

It must be immediately noted that the regular hexagon A–B–G–K–J–E in Fig. 7.2 encloses a seventh point (F), so that any hexagon of points (if the nearest neighbour distances are to approach equality) involves *seven*, not six, points. The seventh, of course, is also the node of another six hexagons. Many combinations of six points can be joined together to enclose a polygon (e.g., in Fig. 7.2 A–B–F–J–I–E or A–B–C–G–F–E) but these are not of concern if they are not part of an overlapping hexagonal system. It is the presence of the enclosed point which is of concern in finding gaps in network distributions.

Thus it is easy to define initially an n-sided *polygon of sites (or points) as being any site enclosed by its n nearest neighbours in any direction* (Fig. 7.3).

The advantage of a hexagon of sites in preference to any other polygon lies in the fact that

(1) it is an ideal equal-distance solution to spacing of points, and (in contrast, for example, to equilateral triangles, an alternative equal-distance figure) any site is simultaneously involved with seven hexagons (another eighteen sites), whereas a site within a network of equilateral triangles is involved in six triangles but only six other sites (i.e. a hexagon);

(2) it is possible to find the *geometric centre* for any n-sided figure; for the hexagon this is relatively simple. Before discussing the theoretical significance of the *centre* of a polygon it is necessary briefly to outline the simple geometry involved:

(a) The centre of any triangle is defind by the intersection of the bisectors of the angles.

(b) The centre of any quadrilateral can be defined as the interaction of the diagonals.

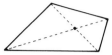

(c) The centre of a pentagon is defined by the centre of the triangle subscribed by joining the centres of three contiguous (but not overlapping) triangles connecting the five points.

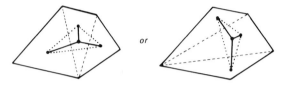

(d) The centre of a hexagon is defined by the centre of a triangle formed by the intersection of the lines joining the opposite angles. (The more regular the hexagon, of course, the smaller this triangle.)

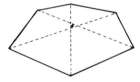

What is the archaeological significance of the geometric centre of a polygon of sites? It is remarkable that even when the links are variable the enclosed site within the polygon is often on or close to the geometric centre. Fig. 7.4 gives a number of examples drawn from various distribution maps.

The centre of any regular or irregular polygon is the point of 'least resistance' to all the enclosing points (or sites), in that the *sum* of the distances to all enclosing sites is the smallest possible. The geometric centre is the 'best fit' in any regular or irregular enclosure of sites. This should not be interpreted to mean that site location has been determined by drawing straight lines and bisecting the angles of triangles but that, in an effort to achieve relatively even spacing in relation to neighbouring sites, ecological resources, etc. (an even subdivision of an uneven landscape), sites *tend* to fall into a regular structure and, as the only figure where nearest neighbour links are always equal, normally into a hexagonal structure. *Thus the hexagon is the ideal geometric model for any site array where inter-site distances (particularly with neighbours) are relatively regular.* The centre of any hexagon – particularly if the sides are not wildly variable – is a likely location for the seventh (enclosed) site.

In any regular hexagon, the centre is equidistant from all the neighbouring points, but as the inter-point distance varies, so must the centre shift and

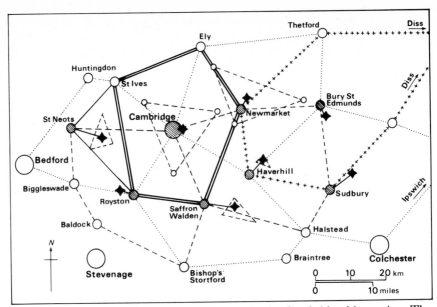

7.4a.   Site pentagons and hexagons for major towns in the Cambridgeshire region. The geometric centres of the polygons are close to the central sites.

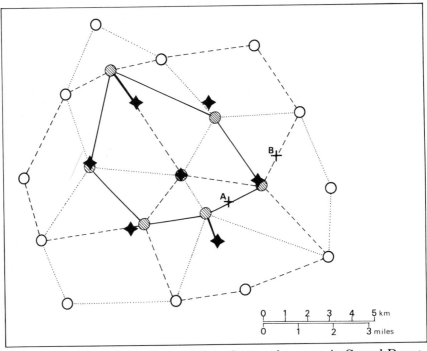

7.4b.   Site hexagons for major settlements of the fourteenth century in Central Dorset. Two major settlements (A and B) on this map are interpreted as infill sites (i.e. halving the average inter-site distance) and can be shown to be the geometric centres of their own site hexagons, as can be anticipated from the formal hexagonal structure.

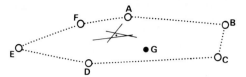

7.5.

Example of a very distorted hexagon in which the geometric centre is close to one of the other sites (A).

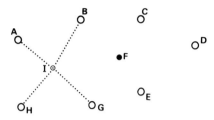

7.6.

The prediction of a site (I) within a quadrilateral.

distances from that centre become increasingly variable. In a very distorted hexagon (where the sides have wide range of distance variation) the geometric centre will fall close to one of the other sites and thus offend minimal distance constraints (as in the example for seven sites A–G in Fig. 7.5). It is still, however, the smallest sum distance to the six enclosing points. In this figure the long link C–D, over three times that of the shortest link C–B, has so distorted the hexagon that there is really no satisfactory predictable location within the enclosure for the seventh site. Such an extreme situation, however, could not exist if there were a *tendency* towards regular spacing. In addition, and this is crucial in assessing the significance of this form of analysis, there are too few sites to make satisfactory geometric prediction.

As any site to a hexagonal system is by definition systematically related to eighteen other sites, it necessarily requires at least twelve or more sites to make satisfactory geometric predictions. If there were another five sites with equilateral nearest neighbour links, quite satisfactory pentagons could be established. The number of sites in the pattern is obviously critical.

Another important limitation on this form of investigation is that the *site population must be approaching maturity or saturation within the prevailing space concepts*. This, of course, is usually an assumption and limits the persuasion of such geometric arguments, but it is a common assumption in many archaeological contexts. It is only with a mature site population that regularity can be expected, otherwise 'demographic holes' will disrupt the pattern.

Because hexagons are systematically related to quadrilaterals, the inter-section of the *quadrilateral of sites* (i.e. the central site with its four nearest neighbour sites) will *also* locate the centre, but less efficiently as only four instead of six sites are used. Nevertheless it is a reasonable indicator. Thus by extrapolation, the diagonals connecting any four sites can locate a potential

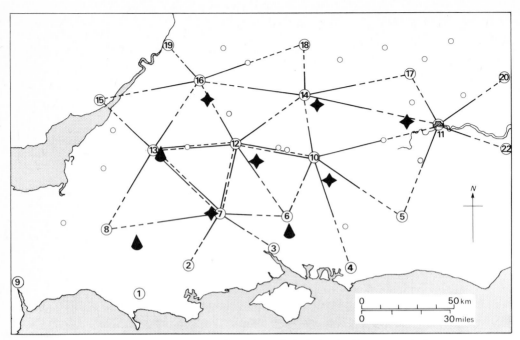

7.7.   Major and minor towns of southern Britain in the Roman period.

missing site but *only if*, in line with the previous argument, it can be demonstrated that such a new site is also part of a hexagon. In Fig. 7.6 the intersection of lines HB and GA locate another possible site location (I) which obviously forms the node of the hexagon I–B–C–D–E–G such that the intersection of ID, CG and BE relocates site F. Without this final test of I, the use of intersecting diagonals alone to discover a potential missing site is too weak. The method is important in discovering missing elements, but only if the hexagonal pattern is sufficiently intact elsewhere for coherence.

The persuasion of the hexagonal structure is apparent in Fig. 7.7 which includes all the minor and major towns of southern Britain in the Roman period plus a few extra sites, for example Badbury, Alfodean, which apparently never achieved the importance their foundation suggested. The efficiency with which site hexagons subdivide Roman southern England and predict the *approximate* locations of the enclosed (seventh) site (star) or confirm the existence of a central site in relation to a sixth node (triangle) is apparent from Fig. 7.7, and is stated formally in Fig. 7.8, where the major road links are also plotted. The conformity between the minimal distance road links and the minimal distance hexagon links is close: if the order across all six intersecting lines at any one point was not close to that on the ground, some roads on the hexagonal diagram would have to bypass towns or towns would have to be in two nodal positions simultaneously. There is *no* conflict between the hexagonal model and the road system.

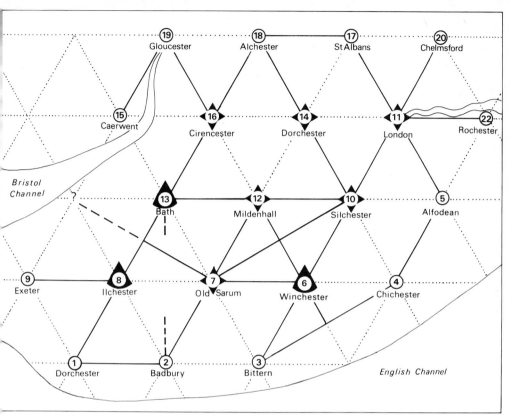

7.8.   Major road links in the idealised pattern of towns of southern Britain in the Roman period.

One further issue must be raised before using this geometric device to discover the 'existence' of black holes in a crowded archaeological landscape. The preceding argument about the inevitability of settlements in an archaeological landscape conforming to a hexagonal network arrangement implies, as a *geometric necessity*, that many settlements will be on or close to straight lines. A quick glance at Fig. 7.2 or 7.8 will show that any site in a regular hexagonal structure is on the intersection of six (or twelve) straight lines connecting points in the system, and thus any site pattern approaching saturation must produce many accidental 'ley lines', not by coincidence, but by the very geometry of even spacing. Ley lines are not so much planned as the innocent by-product (but no less valid for that reason) of *even spacing of settlements or sites on a two-dimensional landscape*. Indeed, there is no way, if even spacing between settlements is to be approximated, that some near straight lines (i.e. ley lines) will not be discoverable between sites. It is simply a geometric necessity of regular spacing.

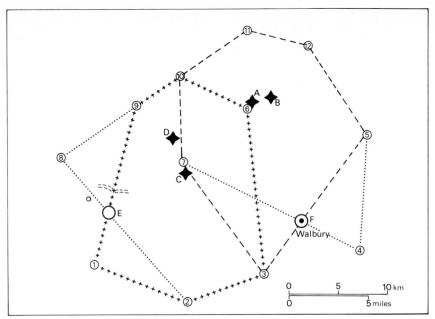

Fortifications on the north Wessex Downs (see Fig. 7.1.) used for testing by hexagons the position of forts *c.* 200 B.C.

BLACK HOLES ON THE NORTH WESSEX DOWNS

The preceding section, dull as it may appear to the average archaeologist, is a theoretical introduction to the discovery of black holes in the pattern of synchronic fortifications on the north Wessex Downs shown in Fig. 7.1. It is a preface to the geometry of spacing; the more sophisticated studies of modern geographers (Haggett 1965) review the immense problems of spatial distribution in wider contexts. The concern here is only with a crowded landscape where the sites tend to be regularly spaced, conforming to a mutual repulsion model where, using the nearest neighbour statistic (R), high values (e.g. > 2.0) can be anticipated (Haggett 1965, p. 232). Much more complicated procedures are needed where the population of sites is still expanding or is incomplete (i.e. when there are many demographic black holes).

Nevertheless, the simple procedure of locating the missing geometric centres or nodes of site hexagons gives a crude but effective method of discovering blanks in distribution patterns. It only remains to use this method on an appropriate synchronic landscape in an effort to recover potential 'black holes'. The fortifications on the north Wessex Downs mapped by Cunliffe (Fig. 7.1) give an excellent area to test the preceding methods: the site hexagons for forts of *c.* 200 B.C. are given in Fig. 7.9. Because the nearest neighbour links are almost identical between sites 7–1, 7–2, 6–3, and 6–5, site hexagons with alternative nodes and centres have been constructed: 1–2–3–6–10–9 (enclosing 7, centre C), 8–2–3–6–10–9 (enclosing 7, centre D);

7–4–5–12–11–10 (enclosing 6, centre B); 7–3–5–12–11–10 (enclosing 6, centre A). The geometric centres are, as predicted, close to actual sites, with the hexagons with the centres A and C having a slight preference (geometrically) over the alternatives. As the number of sites included in this exercise is at the minimum, such ambiguity is inevitable.

In addition to confirming the evidence of sites close to the hexagon centres, it is possible to investigate the possibility of *missing* nodes. The intersections of the diagonals 3–5, 4–7 (F) is thus a potential missing node and, almost unerringly, Walbury, a large and impressive fortification apparently not in use in *c.* 200 B.C., occupies the location. In contrast, E, the intersection of the diagonals 1–9, 2–8, also a potential missing node, has no fortifications on or near to the point, although 3 km to the north there is the large ditch, Wansdyke, and 3 km to the west the small fortification of All Cannings Cross. The interpretation of the failure to locate the anticipated nodal site at point E is discussed after the final attempt to remove, if possible, some of the noise of irrelevant distance variation.

MAP DISTORTION

A crude but effective method of eliminating or reducing irrelevant noise is by topological distortion: by allowing the map scale to accommodate some of the unwanted variability.

In an effort, perhaps, to become more respectable to scientists, archaeologists have tended to treat absolute distance (measured in metres, miles, etc.) with greater respect than is appropriate with human behaviour. In almost all societies, regardless of complexity or technological level, distance and the concept of distance is *relative*. Thus if settlements are separated by one day's journey, actual inter-site distance (in miles) will vary widely according to the topography of the route, the presence of obstacles, the means of transport available and so on. With jet travel, Spain has become the new Blackpool of the Midlands, with absolute distance less relevant than cost and availability.

Absolute distance may well be the prerogative of navigators and geographers but social–political distance (Evans-Pritchard 1940, ch. 3) is a more relevant scale for human affairs, as anyone living in Berlin can appreciate. The archaeologist's task in mapping is to *transform* the prosaic metres of his base map into social–political–economic scales which will differ considerably from absolute distance. Thus archaeologists should feel no obligation to conform exactly to metric equivalents nor to assume that a distance scale in human terms is arithmetical. Absolute distance, however, is not discardable; but it can be transformed or manipulated. Thus it is the effect of absolute distance upon cost which determines that it is Spain and not the Bahamas which is the new Blackpool of the Midlands. Absolute distance is a constraint in its own right but particularly in shorter distances is seldom as important as archaeologists, bound to Ordnance Survey standards, assume.

```
  10 km
 1  0  0  1  0  1  1  0  0  0  0  0  1  1  0  0  0  0  0  0
 0  0  1  1  0  0  0  0  0  0  2  2  3  2  2  2  2  2  2  1
 0  0  1  1  0  1  1  0  2  2  2  1  1  1  1  1  1  1  1  1
 1  1  0  0  1  1  1  1  3  2  1  1  1  1  1  1  1  1  1  1
 1  1  1  2  2  1  1  1  2  2  1  1  1  2  2  2  1  1  1  1
 1  0  2  2  1  2  2  1  2  2  1  1  1  2  2  2  0  0  1  0
 0  1  1  1  2  2  2  1  1  1  1  2  1  1  1  1  1  1  1  1
 0  1  0  0  1  2  1  1  1  1  2  1  1  1  1  1  1  1  1  1
 1  2  2  1  1  1  1  1  1  1  0  1  1  1  1  1  1  1  1  1
 2  1  1  2  2  1  1  1  1  1  0  1  1  1  1  1  1  1  1  1
 2  1  1  2  2  2  2  2  1  1  1  1  0  0  1  0  1  1  1  0
 1  1  1  1  1  1  1  1  0  0  0  1  1  2  2  2  3  1  1  1
 1  0  0  1  1  1  1  1  1  0  1  2  1  1  1  2  2  2  3  1
 1  2  2  2  2  1  1  1  1  1  1  1  2  1  2  2  1  2  2  1
 2  2  1  2  2  1  1  0  0  1  1  1  1  1  2  1  1  1  1  1
 1  1  0  0  1  1  1  1  1  2  1  1  1  1  1  1  1  1  1  1
```

7.10.   Number of contour lines (of different value) in each 2.5 km² of the map (Fig. 7.9).

Map distortion obviously alters the *shape* of the constructed hexagons, but should not fundamentally alter the relationships established on the ground. After map distortion, for example, the missing nodal site, Walbury, should still be located by the intersection of the diagonals 3–5, 4–7, although the precision of fit may be altered. It follows, therefore, that if the criteria chosen for the map distortion have no correlation with the existing inter-site distance variability, there will be *no* improvement in fit (probably the reverse), but if a more regular geometric shape emerges, a correlation between site distance variability and the chosen distortion criteria is likely. Thus a final test of the hexagonal structure of the site locations on the north Wessex Downs, and a confirmation of the existence of 'black holes' at points E and F in the 200 B.C. landscape, is the attempt to eliminate, by map distortion, the 'noise' of irrelevant inter-site distance variation.

As argued above, earthwork fortifications must be located where suitable hill (enhanced slope) environments exist. It is interesting that the topography in the region of E and F is very suitable for fort building (exploited, of course, by Walbury at F), emphasising the significance of these theoretically missing

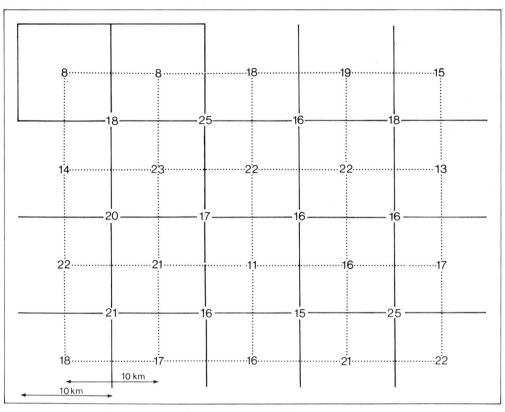

7.11.   Number of contour lines in each 10 km² of the map (Fig. 7.9). Areas with large numbers of contours are obviously very hilly.

nodes. A valuable initial distortion device, therefore, is to remove or lessen the significance of the flat regions, river valleys, etc. where hillforts could not be built; that is, to distribute the topographic features favourable to fort location more evenly over the map area.

This was achieved by the relatively crude method of counting the number of contour lines within each 2.5 km² area of the map, and altering the map shape to equalise some of this variation (Figs. 7.10 and 7.11).

The critical problem, obviously, is how to convert these raw figures into a new organisation of the map space, so that slope enhanced environments suitable for fort construction are more evenly available in the landscape. The method used here, although not the only method, is relatively simple, requiring the conversion of the sum scores in Fig. 7.11 into radii of circles. A difficulty instantly emerges in establishing a scale for this conversion, and there appears to be no readily apparent rule except that an excessive scale will disrupt already existent patterns (distort rather than improve geometric regularity) and, in addition, make it impossible to fit the circles together, which is the next operation. A simple procedural point therefore is to keep

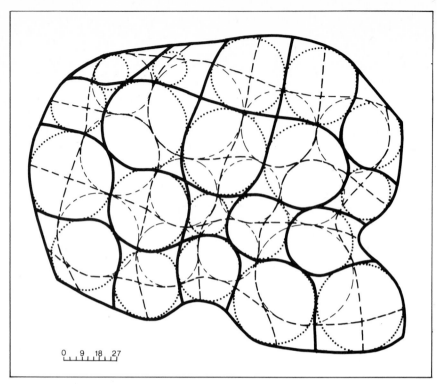

7.12.   Circles and redrawn grid lines derived from Fig. 7.11.

the scale conversion as small as possible to keep the rows and columns of the original grid system intact when the circles of varying sizes are 'pushed' together. This procedure is relatively easy. The circles should be fitted together so that they touch adjoining circles whilst maintaining as far as possible their true grid relationships. Obviously, overlap and some gaps are inevitable. Thus from Fig. 7.11 the first series of sum scores (those in circles) define circles within the original 10 km grid. The overlapping sum scores identify the mid-points of the grid, at 5 km intervals. Although, obviously, some variation in shape is possible in fitting the circles together, the overlapping scores offer constraints upon this variation. The overlapping procedure, of course, could be continued, thus further subdividing the area.

The points of contact between each circle and its nearest neighbours mark the positions through which the new grid lines (N–S and E–W) must be drawn. Fig. 7.12 shows the fitted circles and redrawn grid lines derived from Fig. 7.11 by the arbitrary scale shown on the figure.

The method, although crude, is a useful first approximation to redistributing 'enhanced slope environments' on the north Wessex Downs and, as seen below, was sufficient to improve the regularity of the site hexagons (or reduce inter-site distance variation).

The twelve fortifications identified by Cunliffe are now replotted on the

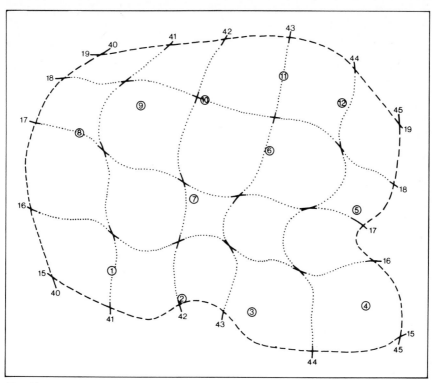

Fortifications on the north Wessex Downs replotted on the distorted grid of Fig. 7.12.

distorted grid by their grid references (Fig. 7.13). With these altered locations the new geometric centres and missing nodes of the site hexagons are constructed (Fig. 7.14). A remarkable, almost exact hexagonal pattern emerges for the more easterly sites, with the hypothesised 'black hole' of Walbury still precisely located, but now part of a very clear hexagonal system. Site 3, Bevisbury, however, is no longer a convincing fit, and it is therefore interesting that another fortification, Balksbury, outside the area included in this map, is a better nodal fit if these procedures are extended southwards.

The observation that on or near Walbury is indeed a 'black hole' in the 200 B.C. pattern is strengthened by this distortion procedure, for it is very obvious that a site is 'missing' in that area which is, as the presence of Walbury and the distorted map emphasise, topographically suitable for defensive works.

The gradual divergence of the continuous sides of the two easterly hexagons suggests that the arbitrary scale adopted for Fig. 7.12 may be slightly too large.

If Walbury is included in the site network, a new site hexagon, 1–2–Walbury–6–10–9, can be constructed around site 7. It is immediately obvious that this hexagon is not as regular as the more easterly, suggesting that either the distortion criteria are unsuitable in this region or additional

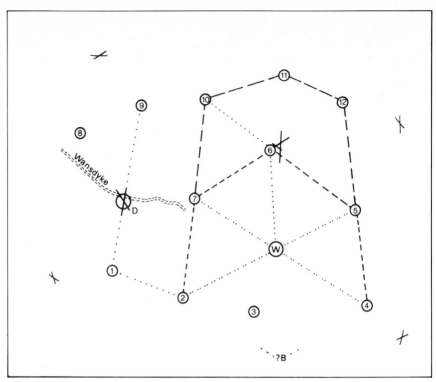

7.14.   Constructions of the new geometric centres and missing nodes based on the altered map (Fig. 7.13).

factors are present. It is, therefore, of considerable significance that after topographic noise reduction, the predicted nodal location D now falls upon Wansdyke, a possible ancient boundary system. Thus the stretching of link 1–9 may be due to *avoidance* of this boundary if Wansdyke or a related feature was in use in 200 B.C. The effect of this type of avoidance upon our distortion criteria (if it could be included) would be to reduce the impact of favourable topography in that region and would thus shorten the link 1–9 and restore a more regular hexagonal structure.

This level of interpretation, however, particularly including other fortifications in the region, cannot be pursued in this paper. It is sufficient to establish the existence of two possible black holes in the 200 B.C. landscape by this geometric device. Several important observations do, however, emerge.

1. As is generally claimed for Iron Age forts, the site distribution appears to be approaching saturation – a capacity site population – or the hexagonal structure would not be so readily detectable.

2. The availability of suitable topographic environments can be seen as an important (but not the only) factor in inter-site distance variability, or the

distortion exercise would not have produced such an improvement in geometric regularity.

3. As was anticipated, hexagonal structures cannot be perfect towards the edge of a system so that the more westerly site pattern, which can be variously interpreted as an imperfect hexagon with residual sites or a nearly perfect septagon etc., may merely reflect the powerful constraint of the chalk escarpment and the territorial limit of the downland.

The remaining fortifications within the mapped area have very interesting relationships to the 200 B.C. site pattern, but an examination of this must await the investigation of a much broader landscape with many more synchronically filtered sites as well as an independent test of the topographic noise-reduction techniques employed here. Despite the tenuous 'predictive framework structuring the observations', it is hoped that this paper is a useful demonstration of Clarke's operational definition of an archaeological model.

REFERENCES

Cherry, J. F., Gamble, C. and Shennan, S. (eds.) (1978). *Sampling in Contemporary British Archaeology* (British Archaeological Reports, British Series, 50), Oxford B.A.R. publications
Clarke, D. L. (1968). *Analytical Archaeology* Methuen
Cunliffe, B. W. (1971). 'Some aspects of hillforts and their cultural environments' in M. Jesson and D. Hill (eds.) *The Iron Age and its Hillforts*, Southampton University Press
  (1976). 'The origins of urbanisation in Britain' in B. W. Cunliffe and T. Rowley (eds.) *Oppida: the Beginnings of Urbanisation in Barbarian Europe* (British Archaeological Reports, British Series, 11), Oxford B.A.R. publications
Evans-Pritchard, E. E. (1940). *The Nuer*, Oxford University Press
Firth, R. (1959). *Economics of the New Zealand Maori*, Wellington
Haggett, P. (1965). *Locational Analysis in Human Geography*, Aldine

8

The colonisation of Europe: the analysis of settlement processes

FRED HAMOND

The discipline of archaeology has undergone a number of significant changes over the last decade, particularly in the expansion of its content. This has occurred in two respects. First, there has been an increasing awareness of the information contained in archaeological data. Such data encompass three types of information: *formal, spatial,* and *temporal.* The first consists of those physical and chemical properties of artifacts and structures which make up our data. The second comprises those recurrent spatial relationships, or *patterns,* which are often associated with such artifacts and structures. Their elucidation and interpretation is a central theme of the recently emerged subdiscipline of spatial archaeology (Clarke 1977; Hodder and Orton 1976). The third aspect concerns the sequential development of such patterns over time; the elucidation and explanation of such *processes* (Harvey 1969, p. 419) forms the subject matter of processual archaeology (e.g., Plog 1974; Zubrow 1975).

The second component of this expansion has been in the consideration of an increasing range of data thought to be of archaeological relevance. One aspect of such data which has received considerable attention, particularly in America, has been the *settlement.* This comprises the localised residential and occupational activities engaged in by a group of people. Settlements in particular, and sites in general, provide a suitable unit of data for the study of the relationships of human groups with one another, and with the landscape which they inhabit (Carlton 1966; Chang 1968; 1972; Clarke 1972a; 1972b; 1977; Gumerman 1971; Parsons 1972; Struever 1968; Trigger 1967; Ucko *et al.* 1972). Considerable attention has been focussed on sites' locational attributes and how these change over time. Given that such patterns and processes reflect regularities and changes in human behaviour, albeit indirectly (Binford 1972; Clarke 1972a; Schiffer 1976), archaeologists are in the unique position of being able to elucidate, and possibly explain, aspects of hominid behaviour over many thousands of years. Although many theories and methods developed in other disciplines, particularly geography, anthropology and economics, have been usefully utilised in the investigation of these phenomena, they are but partial and short-term in relation to the complex long-term problems under analysis (Clarke 1972a, p. 26; 1977, p. 1). Indeed

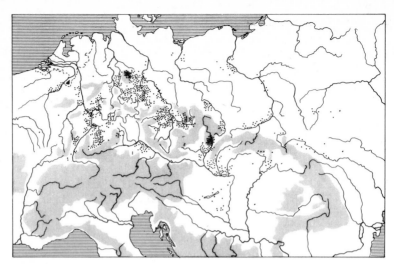

8.1.   The Linearbandkeramik culture (from P. J. R. Modderman, 'Die geographische Lage der bandkeramischen Siedlungen in den Niederlanden', *Palaeohistoria* 6/7 (1958–9), 1–6).

their use has perhaps obscured the real problem, often emphasised by Clarke, of developing theories of long-term hominid behaviour on the basis of indirect traces in bad samples (Clarke 1973, p. 17).

It is the purpose of this essay to summarise a recent exploration of this problem as related to the initial agrarian colonisation of Europe in the sixth and fifth millennia B.C. (Hamond 1978a). The first section summarises what is known of the Linearbandkeramik culture (LBK) which is associated with these early Neolithic communities. This is followed by a more detailed outline of LBK settlement in the Lower Rhine Basin. Models of settlement colonisation applicable to this area are then developed, and tested against the observed data. Finally the implications of this essay for the study of the LBK in particular, and long-term archaeological processes in general, are discussed.

THE LINEARBANDKERAMIK CULTURE

The LBK culture, found throughout central and northern Europe in the sixth and fifth millennia B.C. (Fig. 8.1), is characterised by a distinctive cultural assemblage of pottery types, stone implements and settlements, and an economy based primarily on domesticated plants and animals, particularly wheat, cattle, pigs and sheep (Müller-Karpe 1968; Murray 1970; Tringham 1971; Whittle 1977; Quitta 1960; Milisauskas 1977). The general lack of cultural continuity with preceding Mesolithic cultures (Tringham 1968), coupled with its remarkable uniformity and close affinities with Balkan Neolithic groups, suggest that the LBK culture reflects an actual movement of people from the southeast, rather than an indigenous Mesolithic development, or a diffusion of cultural traits. It thus represents the first agrarian colonisation of Europe. Excavations of a number of sites, especially Elsloo, Geleen, Sittard and Stein (Bohmers *et al.* 1958–9; Modderman 1970; 1972; 1975), Langweiler 2 (Farruggia *et al.* 1973), Langweiler 9 (Kuper *et al.* 1977), Köln-Lindenthal (Buttler and Haberey 1936), Müddersheim (Schietzel 1965), Hienheim (Modderman 1971a), Bylany (Soudsky 1966; Soudsky and Pavlú 1972), and Olszanica (Milisauskas 1976), and regional syntheses of LBK settlement patterns, in particular in the Rhineland, Middle Danube, and Elbe-Saale (Sielmann 1971, 1972), Lower Rhineland (Dohrn-Ihmig 1973a; 1974; SAP 1971 to 1977), and Little Poland (Kruk 1973), enable the nature of LBK settlements to be reconstructed in detail, and the spatial patterning of LBK sites to be elucidated. On this basis, there have been a number of attempts to explain the process of LBK colonisation. In this section, I shall first outline the nature of LBK settlement, then summarise and evaluate current explanations of their development.

The nature of LBK settlements

LBK settlements are characterised by houses of distinctive construction, the plans of which allow three discrete longhouse types to be recognised (Modderman 1970, Fig. 12). Though there may be differences in the construction, internal use and social significance of such buildings, the consensus is that each contains at least a dwelling unit, sufficient to house an extended family of six to ten people (Modderman 1970, p. 109; 1975, p. 268; Soudsky and Pavlú 1972, p. 317). Invariably adjacent to these longhouses are pits, primarily used as earth quarries and grain silos, and secondarily for rubbish; they often contain substantial amounts of pottery, assumed to have been in use during the life of their respective longhouses. Typological and stratigraphic analyses of such data have permitted these longhouses to be dated within a century, thus enabling the layout and development of LBK settlements to be reconstructed in detail.

At first sight, an LBK settlement appears to have a high density of housing. However, on assigning each house to its respective ceramic phase, the village becomes a hamlet comprising farmsteads separated by distances in the order of 100 m (Soudsky and Pavlú 1972, Fig. 2; Modderman 1970, pls. 175–6; Farruggia *et al.* 1973, pls. 58–63; Kuper *et al.* 1977). Though of low density (about one household per hectare within the settled area), such hamlets are of considerable extent, often exceeding 30000 m². The complete excavation of a 1.3 km stretch of the Merzbach valley on the Aldenhovener Platte indicates that such hamlets are but part of much larger settlements, extending linearly over several kilometres (Fig. 8.2). The distribution of surface find-spots elsewhere in the Lower Rhineland also supports this finding (Hamond 1978a, Fig. 3.10). The recognition of hamlets is probably thus a consequence of the partitioning of such continuous settlement by numerous watercourses, rather than of any social groupings. As will be seen in the next

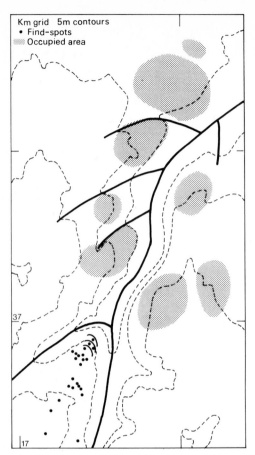

8.2.   LBK settlement on the Aldenhovener Platte (from SAP 1974).

section, the vast extent of such sites poses problems in their delineation, and in the quantification of their spatial patterning.

There are two schools of thought regarding the temporal development of LBK settlements. The first is that they were discontinuously occupied, their periodic abandonment being the result of short-term resource shortages (because of soil exhaustion through over-exploitation), thus causing an imbalance between population and subsistence resources (Buttler and Haberey 1936, p. 161; Sangmeister 1943–50, p. 98; Soudsky and Pavlú 1972, p. 325). The second view is that they were continuously occupied over many centuries (Modderman 1970, p. 210); their spatial development may be modelled in terms of a short-term spatial drift, the result of house renewal, and a longer-term expansion and contraction, due to a fluctuating population (Fig. 8.3).

It can be shown, however, that the apparent evidence for short and discontinuous occupation could be accounted for by the collection of too small an artifact sample from too few find-spots within settlements of long and

Site section over four phases

8.3.   The changing size and location of LBK settlement through site drift, growth and contraction.

continuous duration (Hamond 1978a, p. 86). Not only does the evidence not conclusively support the first viewpoint, but the reason given as its cause – short-term soil exhaustion – is unlikely. Given the low overall population density, the method of cultivation – probably a permanent rotation of cereals with legumes – and the extremely high fertility of loess-based soils on which most LBK sites are situated, it is unlikely that there was any over-exploitation of the soil (cf. Modderman 1971b).

To summarise, LBK settlements appear to consist of farmsteads linearly dispersed along watercourses, for distances upwards of several kilometres. Moreover, they appear to have been occupied continuously over many centuries.

LBK patterns and processes

In this section, I shall outline current analyses of LBK settlement develop-ment. First, the reasons postulated for the spread of LBK settlements are considered. It is generally accepted, for the reasons stated in the introduction to this section, that this phenomenon reflects a colonisation of Europe by agriculturalists. Given the evidence both for a high degree of settlement continuity, and for the creation of new sites, one cannot explain this colonisation in terms of a constant population periodically relocating their sites. A more obvious reason for it, and one that is now generally accepted, is population growth, perhaps of the order of 3 ± 1 per cent per annum (Ammerman and Cavalli-Sforza 1973a, p. 349).

How might such settlement development have occurred, and in particular why did sites locate where they did? First, let us consider the observed spatial patterning of LBK sites. At a pan-European scale, the distribution of LBK sites shows areas of relatively dense clustering, separated by areas of little or no settlement (cf. Fig. 8.1); these clusterings correspond to *Siedlungskammern* – habitable geographical areas of low altitude. Within such settlement cells, most sites are found on loess-based soils. The apparent consistency of this pattern throughout Europe has, though, tended to obscure regularities which exist with other features of loess landscapes, and with environmental factors besides soil. The availability of water, in particular, seems to have been an important consideration within areas of loess-based soil, few sites being found at a distance from it. The quality of the soil may also have been of relevance, with degraded, stony and heavy loess-loams being avoided (Dohrn-Ihmig 1974, p. 52). Moreover, in the Rhineland, site densities were highest under specific combinations of rainfall, temperature, aridity and soil type that were most favourable for agriculture. Within these areas of settlement, LBK sites sometimes exhibit clustering. Hodder (1977, p. 270) notes that in the Untermaingebiet, phase 2 sites are significantly nearer to phase 1 sites than are later sites. These observations suggest that social factors, reflected in parent–daughter site distances, besides environmental factors, may have been considered in choosing a site's location.

There is thus evidence that a deliberate settlement location strategy was followed. Clarke (1972a, p. 24) and Ammerman and Cavalli-Sforza (1973b, p. 13) suggest that, all else being equal, a site was located as near to its parent as was feasible. Such movement was not, however, completely deterministic, there also being a semi-random component (Clarke 1972a, p. 20; Ammerman and Cavalli-Sforza 1973a). Sielmann (1972, p. 46) has also suggested that those areas whose environmental characteristics were most similar to those from which migration occurred were occupied before more dissimilar areas, and that the best agricultural areas were settled before less favourable areas. Such strategies would, on the one hand, minimise the cost of movement to a new site and, on the other, maximise the certainty of the behaviour of a relatively unknown environment, and also the resource return for a given labour input.

An evaluation of current explanations

How far has the above work on the analysis of settlement patterns succeeded in explaining why and how LBK settlement developed in the way it did? Let us first evaluate the suggested cause of settlement spread, namely population growth. There are a number of alternative ways in which increasing populations may be absorbed within settlements. If accommodated within existing settlements, they may be confined within the site's existing spatial boundaries, through increasing the occupancy of each house (by extending their floor areas), and/or increasing the density of housing; alternatively the settled area may be expanded. The other major option is to create new settlements. The observed data shows no significant progressive increase in floor areas, or in house densities; nor are sites expanded indefinitely (see Fletcher, ch. 4 this volume). There is, however, much evidence for the creation of new settlements. We must therefore ask why this last option seems to have been chosen in preference to the others as the mechanism of population absorption. This question will be reconsidered later.

Let us now consider the suggested locational strategies behind the observed settlement patterns, and the reasons postulated for the pursuit of those strategies. First the data from which the settlement patterns have been elucidated will be considered, then the logical routes by which the suggested locational strategies have been formulated will be considered.

The reality of observed settlement patterns is highly dependent upon the spatial and temporal quality of the settlement evidence. As will be demonstrated, the distribution of such data, either in space or time, may not be entirely representative of their actual prehistoric distribution. The nature of LBK settlements – comprising large quantities of durable artifacts and structures distributed over a wide area – makes it unlikely that they will have been totally destroyed by subsequent occupation, land use and soil erosion; this last factor is an especially severe weathering process in loess landscapes. Deposition of soil, rather than its removal, may however have considerably altered the once extant site distribution. Of 129 LBK find-spots in the Lower Rhine Basin whose circumstances of recovery are recorded, sixty have been found through earth-moving activities, in which they have been cut through or their soil overburden removed. It is impossible to gauge, except by the most detailed of soil surveys, how many sites may have been so obscured.

The archaeological techniques employed to recover the data may also bias the prehistoric map. A detailed analysis of archaeological activity in the western Jülicher Börde, and its relation to the known distribution of Neolithic sites (Hamond 1980), shows an archaeological distribution map to be potentially influenced by at least four factors:

1. The location of archaeologists, mostly amateurs, active in the area: to a large extent the location of their home-base determines their activity spheres.

2. The extent of archaeological fieldwork: this attenuates considerably with increasing distance from each centre of archaeological investigation.

3. The nature of archaeological fieldwork: systematic fieldwalking is more efficient and effective in discovering new sites than unsystematic and extensive activity.

4. The rate of progress of archaeological fieldwork in different areas: a differential rate of development will be reflected in a relatively complete knowledge for some areas, and a very incomplete picture of other areas.

Such factors should therefore be borne in mind when interpreting site distributions, and in assessing the reality of an *absence* of sites.

The temporal interpretation of distribution maps may also be suspect, especially when sites are relatively dated using some supposed time-fossil. Dohrn-Ihmig (1974, p. 58), for example, notes that many of the supposedly older LBK sites in the Lower Rhineland might in fact be younger. Moreover, our knowledge of sites' continuity and duration of occupation may also be biassed because of the unsystematic ways in which they are sampled for material.

How are locational explanations formulated on the basis of these data? Two logical pathways, one deductive, the other inductive, are apparent. Following the deductive approach,

the...researcher *begins* his research work with an idea or hypothesis about how to interpret or explain his data; he then deduces from the hypothesis (or set of them) the kinds of evidence he would *expect* to find in his materials if his hypothesis is correct (or not correct). Then, by gathering and examining the *relevant* data, he is able to evaluate the degree to which the facts actually conform to what he expected if his proposition were correct (i.e. goodness of fit). (Hill 1972, p. 69)

Such an approach characterises the work of Ammerman and Cavalli-Sforza (1973a; 1973b), Clarke (1972a), and Hodder (1977). By contrast, the inductive approach *begins* with an examination, supposedly objective, of the data, from which explanatory generalisations are inferred. Sielmann's work (1971; 1972) typifies this latter approach by first elucidating settlement patterns from the data, then inferring explanations therefrom.

Though each approach places a different emphasis on the order of research, they share a number of similarities. Both observe, collect and record data within some subjective framework, whether this be operational or controlling (Clarke 1972; Hill 1972, p. 70). Moreover, neither approach logically 'proves' any hypothesis (Watson *et al.* 1971, p. 8); logically, hypotheses may only be disproved (falsified; cf. Popper 1972). The value of the deductive approach lies in providing a framework for the generating of hypotheses which cannot be readily induced from an examination of the data alone (Clarke 1972a, p. 41). Moreover, it permits the testing of both these, and the already inferred hypotheses, against the data, whilst taking into account its spatial and temporal limitations.

The link between explanatory hypotheses and data is provided by *models* and their *predictions*. A model is a conceptual tool for the better understanding of hypotheses. Essentially it acts as a simplifying device, containing certain properties whose behaviour is analogous to those of reality. It is thus not totally equivalent to reality, but a 'subset' of it (Clarke 1972a). Predictions of how the data ought to behave, should the model be correct, may then be made, and compared with the observed data. A non-correspondence between the expected and observed data indicates the original hypothesis to be incorrect, assuming the data is of adequate quality for a fair test to be made. The hypothesis may then be reformulated and retested. A correspondence does not necessarily imply, though, that it is the only explanation of the data. Through formulating multiple working hypotheses (Chamberlin 1890), those that receive more support from the data than others may be delineated. Even these may not be the best explanations, but must be regarded as such until replaced with better alternatives. In short, the formulation of explanation

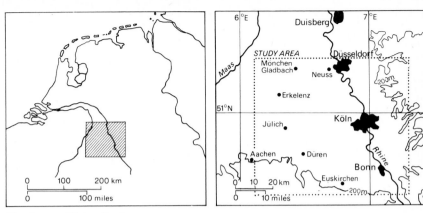

8.4.   The Lower Rhine Basin.

requires the testing of a number of alternative hypotheses against the data, encompassing 'social' and 'economic' variables.

LBK SETTLEMENT IN THE LOWER RHINE BASIN

The Lower Rhine Basin (Fig. 8.4) has been chosen as the area within which to explore models of LBK settlement for three reasons. First, it encompasses a considerable number of LBK find-spots, 143 in all. Our knowledge of them is the product of over fifty years' archaeological research in the area, notably at Köln-Lindenthal (Buttler and Haberey 1936), Müddersheim (Schietzel 1965), on the Aldenhovener Platte by the project team Siedlungsarchäologie des Neolithikums auf der Aldenhovener Platte (SAP) (Farruggia *et al.* 1973; Kuper *et al.* 1977; SAP 1971 to 1977), through *Landesaufnahme* of six *Kreise* (Janssen 1976), and by Dohrn-Ihmig (1973a; 1974). Second, it is a well-defined geographical region, with gentle relief and predominant loess cover, bordered on the south and east by the Central German Highlands, and on the north and west by sands and gravels of the Rhine and Maas. Finally, it encompasses a reasonable range of environmental variability which has been mapped in great detail.

The many excavations of LBK occupation areas show them to be charac-terised by a range of structures – pits, post holes, burnt loam, and sometimes hearths and ditches – and considerable quantities of ceramic and stone artifacts. The character of this material permits the easy recognition of LBK settlement on the basis of surface artifact scatters alone. In some instances only stone artifacts are found, in particular isolated *Schuhleistenkeile* (shoe-last celts). As there is a possibility of these belonging to the succeeding Rössen culture, such sites have not been selected for analysis: only sites containing unquestionably LBK pottery are considered below.

The dispersed nature of LBK settlements has already been noted. A consequence of this is that find-spots in close proximity, even up to several

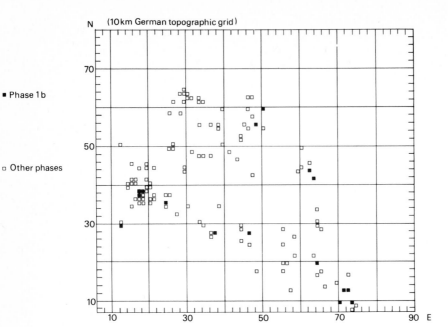

N (10 km German topographic grid)

- ■ Phase 1 b
- □ Other phases

8.5.   Phase 1b and other LBK settlement zones in the Lower Rhine Basin.

hundred metres apart and separated by watercourses, may belong to the *same* settlement, rather than to separate settlement units. This probability is particularly high in those numerous cases where the published find-spot locations represent the central point of much larger artifact scatters. Unfortunately there is insufficient information on the spatial extent of these find-spots to enable discrete settlement units to be discerned. However, in order to proceed with an investigation of their development, it is obviously necessary to have a uniformly defined unit of analysis. Accordingly, the study area was divided into 6132 one kilometre squares, *settlement zones* being defined as those squares containing LBK occupation. In all, 124 zones were thus defined (Fig. 8.5); these are the basic unit of analysis for the succeeding investigation.

Five carbon-fourteen dates are available for the study area, and a further fourteen from Dutch Limburg. The standardisation and calibration of these dates shows them to have an imprecision of *c.* 200 years at the 95 per cent confidence level. Such imprecision is of a similar order of magnitude as the duration and rate of settlement development which is being investigated. Such absolute dates are therefore of little value in the determination of individual site chronologies. Nevertheless, considered as a whole, they indicate that the LBK Culture existed for upwards of a millennium in the Lower Rhineland, from 56/5500 to 46/4500 B.C. (calibrated).

The distribution of the earliest settlement zones (phase 1b) shows no concentration of zones in a particular area which might suggest the direction from which these colonists came (Fig. 8.5). Rather, the map shows these zones

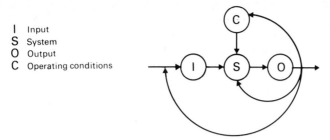

I Input
S System
O Output
C Operating conditions

8.6.   The components of a processual model.

to be distributed reasonably uniformly throughout the area of subsequent settlement. Thus to gauge the direction from which the initial colonisation took place, we must turn to adjacent areas.

Dohrn-Ihmig's analysis (1973a) of LBK developments in the Lower and Middle Rhine has shown that the earliest pottery in the Neuwieder Becken dates from phase 1c, that is, after the initial colonisation of the Lower Rhineland. However, phase 1b material has been found in the Middle Weser (Linke 1976), suggesting an initial colonisation possibly from the northeast, rather than from the southeast as is often supposed (e.g., Sielmann 1972, p. 58). This suggestion is also supported by the similarity of Lower Rhineland pottery to that of the Aćkovy phase in Central Germany (Dohrn-Ihmig 1973a, p. 139). Nonetheless, given the poor survival of early material, and the difficulty of discovering it, it is not impossible that phase 1b material awaits discovery in the Middle Rhineland. We shall return to this point later.

The problem is thus to explain the mechanism by which the area was initially colonised and subsequently infilled.

MODELS OF LBK SETTLEMENT DEVELOPMENT IN THE LOWER RHINE BASIN

To explain a process it is here considered necessary to develop a model based on a hypothesis of why and how the process might have occurred; the modelling of such a process is known as *simulation* (Schultz and Sullivan 1972, p. 7). A processual model may be conceptualised as having the following components: an *outcome*, O, of a *system*, S, subjected to certain *inputs*, I, and operating under certain *conditions*, C, through time. The whole operates within a specified space and time dimension, being regulated through a series of *feedback loops*. These act in such a way that the output from the system may affect its input, the conditions under which it operates, or the system itself (Fig. 8.6).

In the present context, population excess may be regarded as the temporal input to a locational system, which is governed by a locational strategy, the spatial and temporal output of which is settlement spread. Each of these components will now be considered in turn.

Excess population. The variety of ways in which increasing populations could be absorbed within settlements has already been outlined. The evidence suggests that the creation of new settlements was the main response to such increases. Why should this have been so? To sustain a growing population, additional subsistence resources must obviously be created. If the population is to be contained within an existing site, that site's exploitation areas must be increased, and/or the resource output per unit of already exploited land increased. Under the first option, there is, however, an upper limit to the area which can be economically exploited. more distant areas are increasingly uneconomic to utilise as the energy expended in reaching them, especially on foot, increasingly outweights the returns from their exploitation (Found 1971, p. 70; Kunstadter 1972, p. 322). Given this upper limit on the settlement's expansive capacity, such strategy would not be viable in the long term without other developments, for example in improved transportation. The second option may be implemented by raising the energy input per unit of land (intensification), and/or improving the exploitation system's extractive efficiency for the same energy input, for instance by more efficient crop rotation. However, this option necessitates technological and/or social adjustments, which may require a great deal of effort, and introduce an element of uncertainty into future cultivation practice. A third alternative is to expand the settlement. Again this would not have been a long-term solution, as there are topographic limitations to their indefinite expansion. The creation of new settlements, where this is possible, thus represents the most optimal long-term solution to the problem of absorbing increasing populations, though, in the short term, the other solutions described above may also have been invoked.

Let us now formulate a model of population growth in the Lower Rhine Basin. Population changes within a region are the net outcome of changes in the amount of in-migration to the region, its indigenous population growth, and out-migration to other areas. In-migration plays a significant role in increasing a region's population at the commencement of its colonisation, and out-migration becomes increasingly significant as the infilling of the area progresses. It will be assumed that indigenous population growth predominates in the colonisation and infilling of the region after its initial penetration. In the analysis of the region therefore, both in- and out-migration will be regarded as insignificant in comparison to indigenous growth. It will also be assumed that any pre-existing Mesolithic population made no significant contribution to population growth in the area.

Population growth may be modelled by a mathematical curve of logistic growth form in which the key variables are the initial population level, its initial growth rate, and its upper limit, this being dependent on the carrying capacity of the site's surrounding area. How is such growth reflected in settlement spread?

The energy requirements of, for example, forest clearance, house construction and agricultural activity would have necessitated the existence of a small labour force from the very start of a settlement. There is thus a threshold population below which a settlement zone could neither be established nor viably maintained. In an LBK context, this may have been of the order of one or several family groups, comprising 20 ± 10 people (cf. Birdsell 1957, p. 55). It follows that an existing settlement zone's population would have to attain at least twice this level before a new settlement zone could be created, and the parent zone maintained in operation. Thus settlement fission would be unlikely before a zone's population had reached 40 ± 20 people (for other estimates of population densities, see Fletcher, ch. 4 this volume).

Birdsell (1957) has shown that initial net population growth rates of various societies in virgin landscapes were remarkably similar, at around 3 per cent per annum, despite differences in their social composition, technology, economy and environment. The initial net growth rate of LBK populations will accordingly be modelled at 3 ± 1 per cent per annum (cf. Ammerman and Cavalli-Sforza 1973a, p. 349).

There are considerable theoretical and practical difficulties in modelling maximum population levels in LBK settlement zones (e.g., Hayden 1975, p. 12). Moreover, one can only guess at what level populations stabilised below their theoretical maximum. We shall therefore model fission as taking place as soon as it is possible to do so., i.e. when a zone's population reaches 40 ± 20 people. With an initial population level of 20 ± 10 people, and growth rate of 3 ± 1 per cent per annum, this upper level would have been achieved some twenty to fifty years after the zone's establishment. Such a model is not entirely unrealistic, population levels of a similar order of magnitude being suggested by the evidence from the Aldenhovener Platte.

Finally, we shall assume, for the reasons discussed earlier, that all settlements were successfully founded, without subsequent abandonment.

Settlement location. The choice of an area in which to locate a settlement is the outcome of a complex decision-making process, involving at least three interacting factors: the locational strategy pursued, the decision environment within which the choice of location is made, and past experience (Fig. 8.7). Each of these factors will now be discussed.

We may suppose that *locational strategies* which sought to ensure the long-term survival of settlements were pursued. Given the largely self-sufficient nature of these communities, the mode of exploitation of their surrounds would have heavily influenced the strategies pursued. Moreover, given the settlers' imprecise knowledge of their environment, an element of uncertainty would have been attached to its exploitation. Hence the concept of risk would have figured in the locational strategies pursued.

There are a number of modes of resource exploitation, ranging from minimising, through satisficing and optimising to maximising. In an LBK context a satisficing strategy is most likely to have been pursued (Simon 1957; Wolpert 1964). By such a strategy, only the resource output necessary to satisfy the needs of a reasonable existence is achieved.

As a consequence of an incomplete knowledge of an environment's

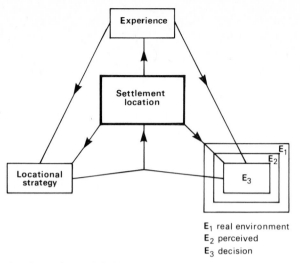

E₁ real environment
E₂ perceived
E₃ decision

8.7.   A schematic model of settlement relocation.

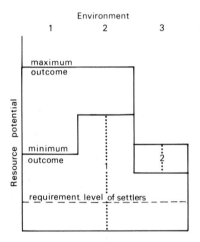

1 maximum minimum outcome
2 minimum maximum loss

8.8.   'Minimax' and 'maximin' strategies in relation to environments under varying conditions.

behaviour, there will be a degree of risk attached to its exploitation; the more incomplete this knowledge, and the more restricted a society's technological and economic base, the higher the ensuing risk would have appeared. How would such imputed risk have been dealt with?

An area's productivity may be viewed under both favourable and unfavourable conditions. In underdeveloped societies of low adaptive potential, such as the LBK, there is probably more concern to minimise losses under unfavourable conditions than to maximise gains under favourable conditions (Savage 1951). Risk will therefore be minimised rather than gains maximised.

This end may be achieved by following a *maximin* strategy, which aims to maximise the minimum outcome under unfavourable conditions should they arise (Fig. 8.8; Found 1971, p. 114). In contrast to a 'minimax' strategy which seeks to minimise the maximum loss, a 'maximin' strategy ensures the maximum difference between the environment's resource output under periodically unfavourable conditions and that output actually required; most insurance is thus provided against disastrous conditions should they arise, and the risk in moving to a relatively unknown environment minimised.

A 'maximin' strategy may be pursued by settling those environments which, even under atypically bad conditions, have the highest resource potential, and by maintaining potential channels of resource exchange through maximising the potential incidence of social interaction, in particular between the newly founded site and its parent (cf. Paget 1960, p. 326). Only a few locations are likely to permit both aims to be pursued simultaneously. Elsewhere the best strategy would therefore be to pursue either, or a combination of, these strategies, which may be described as resource oriented and socially oriented respectively.

To summarise, a successful locational strategy enables a settlement to be located such that two requirements are satisfied. First, that sufficient resources are obtainable from its surrounding area (under a satisficing mode of exploitation) to ensure its long-term survival. Second, that risk inherent in the exploitation of this area is, where necessary, minimised.

The *decision environment* comprises the available information which is of relevance to the locational strategy (Found 1971, p. 131), and through it the locational strategy is implemented. This environment is a subset of the perceived environment which comprises those aspects of the real natural and social environments which are consciously acknowledged.

What information is of relevance to the decision environment? Contemporary geographical evidence (Downs 1968, p. 10), the accounts of early explorers (e.g., in Canada: Mackintosh 1934), and ethnographic literature (e.g., the Chimbus of New Guinea: Brookfield and Brown 1963, p. 33) all suggest that those factors which affect the success of the locational strategy pursued will figure prominently in the decision environment. First, those features of the natural environment which affect an area's resource exploitation, and second, those features which impinge upon social interaction between settlements will be considered.

Those resources necessary to sustain an agricultural community include water, woodland, arable and grazing land (Everson and Fitzgerald 1969, p. 9). In a virgin landscape, some of these resources may not have been immediately available; nevertheless, they could have been inferred by considering those features of the natural environment which directly influenced their extent and quality. As it is impossible to reconstruct these colonists' decision environment, we are restricted to a consideration of those features of the natural environment which ultimately would have influenced their

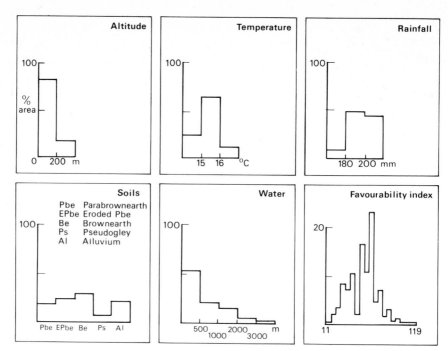

The environment of the Lower Rhine Basin: a summary.

decision environment. Five major factors govern the agricultural potential of an area: altitude, temperature and rainfall during the main growing season (May–July), soil type, and distance to water (cf. Park and Eddowes 1975, p. 13). Each kilometre square of the Lower Rhine Basin has been characterised by the predominant value of each of these features therein (distance to water has been calculated as the average minimum distance of 100 regularly distributed points within each square to water). Fig. 8.9 summarises the environmental characteristics of the study area.

How might such features have been evaluated? Although there are a number of geographical studies of environmental evaluation, they are limited to assessments of particular aspects of it, for example residential desirability. Gould's work (1969) suggests that such aspects are evaluated on an ordinal scale, ranging from 'good', through 'indifferent' to 'bad', rather than on an interval scale by which they are absolutely rated. However, because of the highly interdependent nature of environmental features, they are likely to have been evaluated as a whole, rather than individually. Consequently, it is necessary to combine the above factors within a single environmental index of agricultural favourability. One method of doing this is to rank the values of each environmental factor on an interval scale ranging from 1, denoting the most favourable values, to 25, denoting the worst values; indifferent values would thus score 13 on this scale. A favourability index of their combined effect may then be derived by adding the scores for each area together. The

TABLE 8.1. *Environmental evaluation: an example*

	Element A		
Favourability index	1	13	25
Element B			
1	2	14	26
25	26	38	50

Index: 1 = good, 13 = indifferent, 25 = bad.

TABLE 8.2. *Environmental evaluation: a model*

Environment		Index	Environment	Index
Altitude (m)			*Soil*	
0–200		1	parabrownearth	1
200+		25	eroded pbe	7
Temperature (°C)			brownearth	13
−15		25	pseudogley	19
15–16		13	alluvium	25
16+		1	*Water* (m)	
Rainfall (mm)			−500	1
−180	+pseudogley or alluvium	1	500+	25
−180	+pbe or eroded pbe or brownearth	25		
180–200		13		
200+	+pseudogley or alluvium	25		
200+	+pbe or eroded pbe or brownearth	1		

Index: 1 = good, 13 = indifferent, 25 = bad.

relative ordering of this index thus denotes the relative agricultural favourability of each area (Table 8.1).

Lower altitudes are obviously more favourable to agriculture than higher ground. Warmer conditions also promote cereal growth. However, growth is also conditioned by available soil moisture, which is dependent upon rainfall and soil texture. Fine textured soils have a relatively high water content and often become waterlogged under relatively high rainfall conditions. Likewise, medium-textured soils are also unsuitable for cereal cultivation under relatively low rainfall conditions. Most favourable is either a combination of low rainfall and fine-textured soils, or high rainfall and medium-textured soils. As regards soils, the best are those of high inherent fertility when the realisation of this is unimpeded by other natural factors. Finally, those areas having a high density of watercourses, reflected in a low average distance to water, are obviously more favourable for settlement, all else being equal. The evaluation scheme adopted for the Lower Rhine Basin is set out in Table 8.2 (cf. Fig. 8.9). In applying these data to an LBK context, we may assume, for a number of reasons (Hamond 1978a, p. 95), that contemporary relief patterns, and watercourses, as well as relative differences in climate and soil, may be transferred directly to the Bandkeramik period.

Areas regarded as unsatisfactory for settlement are those which contain an environmental factor whose value does not permit even a satisficing mode of resource exploitation. In this study, areas above 200 m, or having non-loess-based soils, will be regarded as unsuitable. Moreover, a resource oriented 'maximin' strategy could best be pursued in those areas having the most favourable environmental index. The purpose of locating in such environments, it should be remembered, is not to maximise productivity, but rather to minimise risk.

Finally, for reasons discussed elsewhere (Hamond 1978a, p. 239), the decision environment of any area will be modelled as if the colonists had a complete knowledge of it, irrespective of their distance from it.

Having considered the environmental features of the decision environment, we may now consider its social aspects. Some of the social implications of LBK settlement are examined by Tilley in chapter 13 below. Numerous studies (e.g., Morrill and Pitts 1967) have shown that interaction between settlements attenuates rapidly with increasing distance of separation. Under a socially oriented 'maximin' strategy, we would therefore expect a daughter site to be located at the minimum possible distance from its parent, in order to maximise the potential of social interaction and exchange. Such movement in a homogeneous environment gives rise to clone colonisation (Bylund 1960, p. 226). Of course, an unsettled area must be preserved around each site, to allow sufficient space for exploitation. In the case of LBK settlement in the Lower Rhine Basin, the population of each settlement zone would exploit its respective kilometre square; adjacent unoccupied squares may thus be settled.

Migration not only has a distance, but also a directional component. Thus areas of relatively easy access are likely to attract more migration than those of difficult access. Because of the considerable environmental uniformity of the study area, it is assumed that all areas within it had equal access. Thus the probability of migration will be assumed to be the same in all directions, all else being equal.

Both the decision environment and locational strategy would have been influenced by *past experience*. Colonists new to an area will probably have had relatively little knowledge of its environment, and their locational strategy will have been developed for situations elsewhere. Consequently, the decision environment may be a highly inaccurate view of reality. Thus, having chosen a settlement area, it is likely to be found unsatisfactory, even if a 'maximin' strategy was pursued. Despite locating unsuccessfully, the colonists' experience of the region's environment, and knowledge of the outcomes of

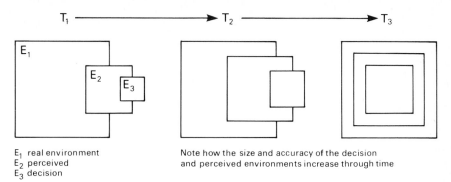

E₁ real environment
E₂ perceived
E₃ decision

Note how the size and accuracy of the decision
and perceived environments increase through time

8.10.   The changing decision environment brought about by increasing experience.

particular locational strategies, will have been increased. Their decision environment is thus enlarged and made more accurate, whilst their locational strategy will adapt to meet the new situation (Fig. 8.10; cf. Pred 1967; 1969). Through time locational requirements become increasingly met as more accurate decision environments are created and locational strategies similar to past successful ones adopted.

As infilling of the region progresses, so the constraints of its *boundaries* become increasingly apparent. Only in part do the boundaries of the study region follow the natural topographic boundaries of the Eifel and Süderberg-land mountains. Thus the region most certainly cannot be regarded as a closed system from which there is no out-migration. For present purposes, however, the region may be modelled as if it was completely bounded. It is thus necessary to ensure that the number of zones generated by the model does not approach saturation conditions such that these artificial boundaries would affect significantly the spatial development of the simulated settlements.

Initial conditions. In order to start the simulation model running, its initial state must be specified. Thus the direction, location and magnitude of the earliest settlement must all be defined.

We have already seen that the Lower Rhineland was most probably colonised from the Münster Bay area, adjacent to the northeast corner of the study area. Accordingly, in-migration will be modelled from the northeast, though in-migration from the southeast will also be investigated to see whether colonisation from this direction is also possible given the available settlement evidence.

Moreover, in order to simplify the model, it will be assumed that all LBK sites in the Lower Rhine Basin had one common ancestral settlement, the excess population of which penetrated the region from the above directions.

4. Resource–distance optimisation	3. Distance minimisation	2. Resource maximisation	1. Resource maximisation Distance minimisation

<table>
<tr><td>3</td><td>1</td><td>①</td><td>2</td><td>2</td></tr>
<tr><td>3</td><td>2</td><td>3</td><td>3</td><td>3</td></tr>
<tr><td>①</td><td>②</td><td>●</td><td>4</td><td>3</td></tr>
<tr><td>4</td><td>3</td><td>3</td><td>4</td><td>1</td></tr>
<tr><td>3</td><td>2</td><td>2</td><td>1</td><td>1</td></tr>
</table>

<table>
<tr><td>3</td><td>1</td><td>1</td><td>2</td><td>2</td></tr>
<tr><td>3</td><td>2</td><td>3</td><td>3</td><td>3</td></tr>
<tr><td>1</td><td>②</td><td>●</td><td>4</td><td>3</td></tr>
<tr><td>4</td><td>3</td><td>3</td><td>4</td><td>1</td></tr>
<tr><td>3</td><td>2</td><td>2</td><td>1</td><td>1</td></tr>
</table>

<table>
<tr><td>3</td><td>1</td><td>①</td><td>2</td><td>2</td></tr>
<tr><td>3</td><td>2</td><td>3</td><td>3</td><td>3</td></tr>
<tr><td>①</td><td>2</td><td>●</td><td>4</td><td>3</td></tr>
<tr><td>4</td><td>3</td><td>3</td><td>4</td><td>1</td></tr>
<tr><td>3</td><td>2</td><td>2</td><td>1</td><td>1</td></tr>
</table>

<table>
<tr><td>3</td><td>1</td><td>1</td><td>2</td><td>3</td></tr>
<tr><td>3</td><td>2</td><td>3</td><td>2</td><td>3</td></tr>
<tr><td>1</td><td>①</td><td>●</td><td>4</td><td>5</td></tr>
<tr><td>3</td><td>2</td><td>①</td><td>3</td><td>4</td></tr>
<tr><td>3</td><td>4</td><td>2</td><td>3</td><td>3</td></tr>
</table>

● Parent settlement   ○ Squares which may be occupied
1–5 Environmental rating of adjacent km squares

8.11.   'Maximin' strategies.

Models of settlement development

From the above discussion, it is clear that a number of factors may be encompassed within a model of settlement spread. This section outlines those models to be examined through simulation, then discusses the reasons behind their choice.

Model 1 regards all kilometre squares as being equally suitable for settlement; neither environmental variability nor differences in degree of social contact are regarded as important, all areas having an equal risk of settlement failure. Further settlement of already settled zones is also permitted. Movement into the region will be regarded as having been from the northeast.

Model 2 is similar to model 1, save that no further settlement is permitted in squares already settled.

Model 3 is similar to 2, save that settlement is only permitted in those squares which can provide a satisfactory level of resources. Each unoccupied square having a satisfactory environment has thus an equal chance of being settled, irrespective of its actual environmental properties or distance from the parent site. Each of these squares has thus an equal risk attached to it. In this model, squares which lie above 200 m, or have non-loess-based soils, will be regarded as unsuitable for settlement.

Model 4 is similar to model 3, save that areas having a rainfall below 180 mm are also considered unsuitable.

Model 5 marks a further refinement, in that risk is also considered. It is reduced through pursuing a resource oriented strategy, such that, of the available unoccupied squares having satisfactory environments, the nearest best one is chosen for settlement (Fig. 8.11 (1,2)).

Model 6 is the same as model 5, except that entry to the region is from the southeast.

Model 7 is, in all respects, similar to model 5, save that risk is reduced through adopting a socially oriented strategy. Here the best nearest square is chosen for settlement (Fig. 8.11 (1,3)).

Model 8 is the same, except that entry is from the southeast.

Though the first model is quite unrealistic, it is nevertheless a useful yard-stick against which the other models' outcomes may be compared. The effect of disallowing settlement in already settled squares may be gauged through comparison with model 2. Model 3 is more realistic in that unsuitable environments cannot be settled. Within these constraints, locational behaviour is considered to be random. Such a model might be applicable to the early stages of the region's colonisation, within a problem oriented strategy. Given the slender basis on which those environments unsuitable for settlement have been chosen, it would be wise to examine the sensitivity of the model to variations in its operating conditions. Accordingly model 4 has been devised, the effect of introducing a rainfall condition being gauged through a comparison of its outcome with model 3. Models 5 to 8 are more sophisticated in that risk is also considered. The relative importance of economic and social factors to settlement location may be gauged by comparing their extreme cases, models 5 and 7, and 6 and 8. It would also be interesting to see whether the entry point of the original colonists to the region could be detected from the resultant spatial distribution of settlement zones. Although the archaeological evidence suggests colonisation was from the northeast, it is not inconceivable that it was from the southeast; models 5–6 and 7–8 examine the effects of varying the location of the entry point.

Here then is a selection of models, through the simulation of which some of the factors important for settlement development may be investigated. Common to them all are the following assumptions:

1. A site will be created, with equal likelihood, within twenty to fifty years of the founding of its parent.

2. All sites successfully locate elsewhere, with no subsequent abandonment. The locational strategy will thus be assumed to be constant over time, previous experience having demonstrated its success.

3. The natural environment remains unchanged throughout the course of the simulation.

4. Migration is assumed to be equally probable in all directions, all else being equal.

5. Where several kilometre squares are equally available for settlement, the one actually settled will be determined by random selection.

6. The region is regarded as being geographically closed to in- or out-migration after its initial settlement.

Model behaviour

In order to establish the behaviour of each model, a number of their overall spatial characteristics were measured over successive fifty year intervals of their operation. Their *specific* locations are not considered. As the models are stochastic, there is a low probability of each kilometre square being occupied. Thus, each model would need to be run hundreds of times in order to ascertain the probability of settlement of each kilometre square. Given the time required for each stimulation run (*c.* 45–60 seconds), this is impractical at this stage in the models' exploration.

A fundamental difference between deterministic and stochastic models is that, whereas the former have unique outcomes, the latter have a number of outcomes, each having a varying probability of occurrence. Hence no two runs of a stochastic simulation model necessarily arrive at the same outcome, nor indeed need they agree with the model's most probable state, this being the most probable regional behaviour of a large number of settlements over a long time period. In some cases the parameters of the model's range of outcomes are mathematically determinable. For example, on tossing two coins, the probability of obtaining two heads or two tails is one in four, whereas the probability of obtaining a head and a tail is one in two. In many cases, however, as with the models outlined above, such computation is impractical. In order to calculate their theoretical outcomes, in particular their means, one must therefore rely on calculations based on their observed outcomes over a number of runs.

The repeated running of a stochastic model is equivalent to drawing a simple random sample of all its outcome states; in simulation literature this procedure is often known as Monte-Carlo sampling. Though the cumulative average outcome of a series of such outcomes converges towards its theoretical mean as the number of runs increases, such a value is never attained (Shannon 1975, p. 183).

Fortunately, the utilisation of such a probablistic sampling procedure permits the parameters of the model's theoretical outcomes to be mathematically derived on the basis of the mean and variance of the samples drawn from it. In doing so, we may reasonably assume the sampled outcomes to be normally distributed around the mean of the population being sampled. Such an assumption can be made if it is known that the theoretical population is itself normally distributed about its mean. In the present context, we can reasonably assume this to be the case (Shannon 1975, p. 187).

MODEL PREDICTION AND TESTING

In order to test the above models, it is necessary to compare their predictions, resulting from the repeated simulation of their behaviour, against the data. A use of a computer is essential if these procedures are to be quickly and accurately carried out. Accordingly, these models were translated in FORTRAN IV, and implemented on an IBM 370/165 computer; central processing time was in the order of 45–60 seconds, and storage approximately 300 K. The behaviour of these eight models was simulated over a total of eight-eight runs, resulting in the production of over 8000 bits of information on sixteen aspects of these models' temporal and spatial consequences. Each aspect was then summarised by a respective mean value and variance. In order to minimise

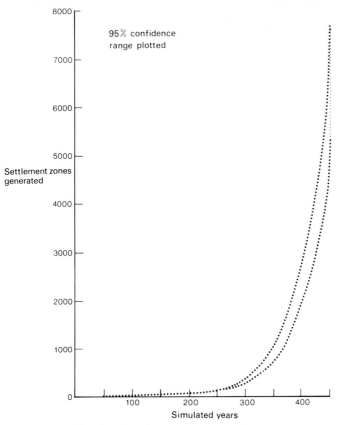

8.12a.   Simulated settlement zone growth.

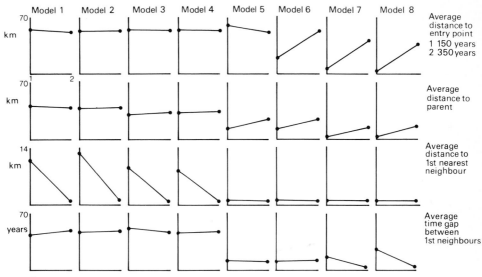

8.12b.   Outcomes of simulation models: temporal and spatial properties.

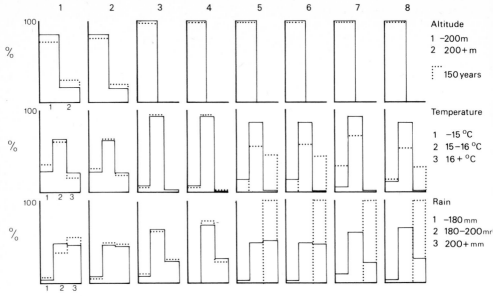

8.12c.   Outcomes of simulation models: altitude, temperature and rainfall.

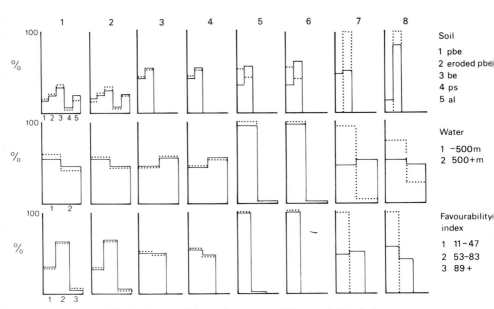

8.12d.   Outcomes of simulation models: soil, water and favourability index.

the effects of the models' starting conditions, which may be atypical, no record of the models' behaviour was made during the early stages of the operation of each model. Moreover, the operation of the models was terminated after 350 years in order to minimise boundary effects which would otherwise have been apparent. The mean outcomes of each model's properties are presented in Fig. 8.12.

Model comparison

Because of the inherent temporal and spatial limitations of the archaeological record, it was considered inappropriate in such exploratory analyses to compare in detail the predicted and observed data. Rather, only their initial and final states will be considered. How should the properties of these models be compared? To recap, each measured property comprises a mean value and variance about this. A comparison of means alone is insufficient to establish whether two parameters differ to an extent greater than could be expected by chance. For example, if such means have a large variance, then a large difference between them might be encompassed within their sampling distribution. Conversely, even a small difference might be statistically significant were the variances sufficiently small. Given that such models are ultimately to be compared with the archaeological data, however, their statistical properties are perhaps of less importance than their archaeological implications. Fortunately it can be shown that archaeologically perceptible differences are certainly of statistical significance (Hamond 1978a, p. 266).

Model behaviour

Rather than exhaustively discuss the behaviour of each model (see Hamond 1978a, p. 268), I shall outline some of the conclusions that may be drawn.

1. A growth rate of 0.03 persons per annum results in a phenomenal increase in site numbers. By 200 years after the initial penetration of the region, approximately forty settlements are found to have been created. By 400 years, over 2500 settlement zones have been founded, and by 450 years, well over 6000. Even with a relatively slow rate of population increase, the Lower Rhine Basin would thus have become saturated with settlement after approximately four centuries, though, as has been shown, the LBK probably lasted nearer a millennium in this area.

In reality, of course, settlement would have expanded into adjacent areas of Dutch Limburg before such saturation conditions were achieved. Moreover, it is likely that such a growth rate will only have been maintained in the area of frontier settlement, being slower within already settled areas. It is clear, therefore, that some form of logistic model of *regional* population growth would be a more appropriate description of regional settlement expansion than the exponential model used here (cf. Ammerman and Cavalli-Sforza 1973b). Under such growth, a site's population would have been regulated, not only internally as has been modelled here, but also by the density of settlement in its locality. Nevertheless, by expanding our time scale for the later periods of the models' simulation, we may approximate to such logistic growth conditions. Thus the models' final outcomes should not be regarded as having arisen by 350 years, as simulated, but at a much later date, nearer to a millennium after the initial colonisation of the area.

2. The comparisons of the models' behaviours have demonstrated the need to take into account a range of factors in the explanation of settlement patterns and processes. The interaction of locational strategy with the decision environment, modified by the location of the entry point to the region and by boundary conditions, has a considerable influence upon the course of colonisation. The distributions of sites located according to strategies which are basically resource oriented (models 5, 6) are, as expected, found to be influenced primarily by the spatial arrangement of the region's environmental characteristics. In contrast, the course of colonisation under socially oriented strategies (models 7, 8), even though they have an economic component, are influenced primarily by the direction from which initial colonisation of the region took place.

3. No one variable uniquely characterises the behaviour of any of these processual models. Only by considering the initial state, temporal trends in, and final outcomes of, a variety of variables, can such models be broadly distinguished.

4. The effect of changes in some of the variables upon the models' outcomes is largely determined by the nature of the other variables. Thus, a slight increase in the population growth rate, or in the numbers of settlements initially locating in the study area, would greatly increase the number of sites in existence after only several centuries. Small changes in the decision environment are found to have little effect upon any model's outcome. This is demonstrated by models 3 and 4 which are indistinguishable, even though the latter model permits no settlement in the driest areas; such areas comprise only a small proportion of the region which may be settled. The actual location of the entry point to the region has little effect on any model's outcome, with the exception of socially oriented models. These are highly sensitive to all but the smallest changes in the location of this point.

5. Some models may only be distinguished on the basis of intra-zonal, as opposed to inter-zonal, evidence. Thus, models 1 and 2 could not be distinguished on the basis of their respective regional site patterns, but only by examining the change and stability of house numbers within settlement zones.

6. The final outcomes of all models suggest that adjacent settlement zones do not necessarily have any ancestral relationship to each other. Although the observed linear arrangement of LBK settlements suggests a process of outward expansion, such an arrangement could also have arisen from settlement fission and location from elsewhere.

7. Because only relatively imprecise dating methods are available to us, sites may appear to be contemporary, even though they may have been founded at different times.

8. Processual models which are essentially random in their locational behaviour (models 1–4) converge rapidly to their final forms. No significant trends would therefore be detectable through time. Conversely, most para-

meters of models 5–8 do change through time, particularly as regards their patterning with respect to the natural environment. It is thus unrealistic to attempt to explain settlement patterns over a particular time period in isolation from their preceding development. Moreover, changes in settlement patterning do not necessarily imply that different locational strategies were being pursued. Rather, it is the decision environment which is changing.

Model validation

In order to compare the models' predictions with the archaeologically observed data, it is first necessary to deduce the archaeological consequences of the models, and then to decide on an acceptable level of fit between them and the data.

First, let us consider the archaeological manifestations of the modelled behaviour. Certainly, some aspects such as site-environment patterns and trends can be measured directly in an archaeological context. Other aspects may not, however, be so apparent. Given the spatial incompleteness of the data, observed nearest neighbour trends are unlikely to represent the situation as it once existed. Moreover, it is doubtful whether settlement zones can ever be connected with their ancestral settlements. However, such site–site relationships may be reflected in other aspects of the data which are more readily apparent, and which do not suffer sample bias to the same degree. Notable in this respect are pottery styles and traditions. Several hypotheses might be developed regarding the ceramic manifestations of the spatial relationships of daughter and parent sites within a region as a whole, and between sites of different ancestry in close proximity. It might be argued, for instance, that the further the daughter sites located from their parents, the greater would be the diffusion of ceramic styles through the region (Fig. 8.13 (1, 2)). However, where groups of different ancestry are near to each other, one might expect a considerable amount of cross-fertilisation, as well as the emergence of more local traditions (Fig. 8.13 (3)). Hence we might expect that where daughter sites are located far from their parents, but near to other sites, not only would regional ceramic homogeneity be apparent, but also a number of local styles.

The next problem is to decide what represents a close fit between theoretical and observed data. Given the many biasses inherent in the observed data, an *exact* comparison of the predicted and observed data would be unwise. A possible solution is to simulate the effects of these biasses upon the predicted archaeological map, then compare the resultant map with the observed one (cf. Clarke 1972a, p. 26). In the Lower Rhine Basin at least, the difficulty in quantifing archaeological fieldwork precludes the ready adoption of this method. For the moment, therefore, it will be assumed that gross differences between theoretical and observed patterns are likely to have been preserved despite these biasses. Moreover, the more similarities between

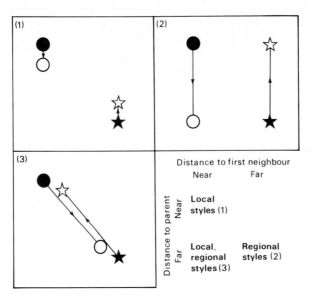

8.13.   Pottery styles: their relationship to inter-site distance.

model prediction and data, the more likely it is that the observed data have been created by similar processes (cf. Shannon 1975, p. 208).

Table 8.3 sets out the archaeological predictions of the eight models simulated, and Table 8.4 the corresponding observed patterns. Let us now consider the degree of agreement between them.

1. Fig. 8.5 shows there to be no clustering of early LBK sites about any one point. Rather, early sites are to be found throughout the region, as far as its westernmost extremities. Such behaviour is predicted by models 1–5.

2. Dohrn-Ihmig's (1973a; 1973b) analyses of LBK pottery development in the Lower Rhine Basin indicate that earlier pottery was relatively uniform in style throughout the area. However, by the younger LBK, a number of more local variations had developed concurrently with more regional traditions (e.g., the Rhine-Maas group). Models 1–4 predict such developments to have occurred.

3. No time difference can be detected between observed LBK sites which are in close proximity. Such contemporaneity is predicted by all models.

4. In relation to altitude, all known settlement zones lie below 200 m. This pattern is predicted, broadly, by all models.

5. With respect to temperature, 95 per cent of all known settlement zones are within the regime 15–16 °C; only 5 per cent are to be found below 15 °C, and none in the warmest areas. Again, all models predict such behaviour.

6. Approximately 60 per cent of observed settlement zones lie within the rainfall regime 180–200 mm. A further 32 per cent lie in wetter areas, whilst only 7 per cent lie in the driest areas. Models 3–4 and 7–8 predict such patterns. Given the trends inherent in models 5–6, they too may predict such behaviour.

TABLE 8.3. *Archaeological outcomes of simulation models*

	Model							
	1	2	3	4	5	6	7	8
Entry point	Sites throughout region in early stages of colonisation					Earliest sites around entry points		
Pottery styles	Regional homogeneity + local variation					Regional heterogeneity		
First neighbours	All sites archaeologically contemporary							
Altitude (m)				−200				
Temperature (°C)				15–16				
Rainfall (mm)	180–200+		180–200		180–200; 200+(?)		180–200	
Soil	pbe, eroded pbe, be, al		pbe, eroded pbe		eroded pbe		pbe; eroded pbe(?)	eroded pbe
Water (m)	−500, 500+				−500		−500, 500+(?)	
Favourability	medium		high, medium		high		high(?); medium	

TABLE 8.4. *The observed environmental distribution of LBK settlement zones*

Environment	Percentage of settlement zones
Altitude (m)	
− 200	100
200 +	0
Temperature (°C)	
− 15	5
15–16	95
16 +	0
Rainfall (mm)	
− 180	7
180–200	60
200 +	32
Soil	
pbe	61
eroded pbe	19
be	3
ps	6
al	10
Water (m)	
− 500	60
500 +	40
Favourability index	
11–47	58
53–83	42
89 +	0

7. In relation to soil, 80 per cent of all zones are on loess-based soils, the major of these being on parabrown earth (pbe). Model 7 possibly predicts this relationship if we take into account its inherent temporal trends.

8. With respect to water availability, 60 per cent of zones are found in those areas whose average minimum distance from water is less than 500 m. This pattern is predicted by models 1–4, and possibly models 7–8.

9. Considering agricultural favourability in general, 58 per cent of settlement zones lie in areas of the highest favourability, the remainder lying in areas of medium favourability. Such a distribution is predicted by models 3–4, and possibly models 7–8.

Table 8.5 summarises the degree of correspondence between each model's prediction and the known distribution of LBK settlement zones. Given the coarse level at which comparison is being made, it is hardly surprising to find that some aspects of the data are predicted by a large proportion, if not all, of the investigated models. Most agreement between predicted and observed distributions is found in models 3 and 4; these predict all but one aspect of the observed data's characteristics. To recap, these models permit random location in any part of the region, provided it is not already occupied, and has a satisfactory level of exploitable resources. Under model 3, areas which contain non-loess-based soils and which are above 200 m in altitude are

TABLE 8.5. *A comparison of predicted and observed data*

	Model							
	1	2	3	4	5	6	7	8
Entry point	+	+	+	+	+	−	−	−
Pottery	+	+	+	+	−	−	−	−
First neighbours	+	+	+	+	+	+	+	+
Altitude	+	+	+	+	+	+	+	+
Temperature	+	+	+	+	+	+	+	+
Rainfall	−	−	+	+	?	?	+	+
Soil	−	−	−	−	−	−	?	−
Water	+	+	+	+	−	−	?	?
Favourability index	−	−	+	+	−	−	?	?

+ correspondence between model and observed data
? possible correspondence
− no correspondence

deemed unsuitable for settlement; model 4 stipulates that areas having less than 180 mm of rainfall during the growing season are also unsuitable.

Interestingly, all models are unsuccessful at predicting the patterning of sites in relation to soils. Nevertheless, in relation to the environment as a whole, there is good correspondence between the predictions of models 3 and 4 and what is observed. Given the many simplifying assumptions inherent in our models, it would indeed be surprising if there was exact agreement between all the predicted and observed data.

Discussion of results

A comparison of the theoretical outcomes and archaeological predictions of a number of settlement process models has indicated that only by considering both a large number of hypotheses, and examining the observed archaeological data in a variety of ways, can we hope to formulate explanations of LBK settlement development. Within the terms of the limited number of simulation models and their properties that have been considered, it would appear that satisficing locational strategies best account for the observed data as it is known at the moment.

Four aspects of the results are of particular interest. First, site patterning with respect to soil was poorly predicted by all models, with the possible exception of model 7. Clearly this feature merits further investigation. Three avenues of research are suggested. The first is to explore the behaviour of models in which more importance is attached to soil than to other factors. The second is to examine the development of loess-based soils during and after the Neolithic period, and in particular the degree of differentiation between pbe and eroded pbe which was then apparent. The third avenue of research is to conduct detailed fieldwork in selected areas of eroded pbe in order to see whether the relative absence of sites thereon could be accounted for by their destruction through soil erosion.

The second point of interest is that the element of risk does not appear to have been of significance in the location strategies. This implies that the incoming colonists had a reasonable knowledge of both the environment of the Lower Rhine Basin and of the outcome of their locational strategies when pursued in such an environment. At first sight such an observation is rather surprising, considering that the colonists were new to the area. However, if we remember that adjacent *Siedlungskammern* have very similar natural environments, then it would have been reasonable to assume that the environment of regions in the process of being colonised were broadly similar to the colonists' home environments. Hence there would be little risk attached to the founding of a daughter settlement.

Third, it would appear that economic rather than social factors were of importance to LBK colonists. Such a conclusion is not unexpected, given that they were probably to a very large degree self-sufficient in terms of agricultural resources.

Finally, given this basically constrained random location, the direction from which settlement took place cannot be inferred from the initial site distribution, or its trend in spatial development.

CONCLUSIONS

To the extent that the above models combined both social and environmental factors in the elucidation and explanation of the mechanism of LBK settlement spread, they may be said to be an improvement on past methodologies. Moreover, contrary to the implications of an analysis of the observed settlement pattern, satisficing, rather than maximising, resource exploitation strategies would appear to have been pursued. Nevertheless, this study is but the first step in the exploration of the complex problem of long-term settlement development. It is evident that theories of such development are as yet little advanced and deal largely with only specific aspects of the data. Of necessity, therefore, much of the discussion has been exploratory and doubtless simplistic. Such an approach is justified, however, if we accept that it is only through such explorations that both theory and data can be better understood.

The conclusions of the last section should not be regarded as the end point in the sequence of hypothesis generation–prediction–validation, but merely the beginning of the development of realistic processual hypotheses. Having delineated the broad nature of the model which best accounts for the data, we may begin to examine some aspects of its behaviour not previously investigated. In particular, much information may be gained by examining the model's spatial consequences in addition to the generalised aspatial statistics which have been considered above. Such modelling is of course expensive in terms of computer time, because of the large number of model runs that would be required in order to generate a meaningful probabilistic site distribution map. The spatial predictions of such models may then be tested against the distribution of known data. If they should find support, then fieldwork may be centred upon those areas where sites are predicted but not as yet observed. This procedure thus directs fieldwork to those areas where a limited amount of fieldwork can most profitably be carried out (Hamond 1978b).

It would also be profitable to consider some of the assumptions underlying the model's operation in a more realistic fashion. We might begin, for example, to experiment with logistic models of regional settlement growth. This would have the effect of extending the time span within which a daughter site must locate. Moreover, we might locate a proportion of a fissioning population in other sites, as well as in newly founded settlements. In short, there are a multitude of ways in which such models may be explored, once their basic structure has been established.

Indeed, the discovery of one model which broadly accounts for the data should not preclude the further search for alternative models. Thus, we might consider the effects of combining different aspects of the above models. This might be attempted, for instance, for a model having a random and, on average, long-distance parent–daughter migration component during the region's initial colonisation, and a shorter-distance clone type of infilling later.

Such models might usefully be applied in areas having less homogeneous environments than the Lower Rhine Basin. Both the Elbe-Saale and Unter-main areas have enough data of sufficient quality to merit such an exercise. More interesting, though, would be to consider locational strategies in the regions lying at the boundary of two major ecological regions, where we might expect a high degree of risk to be connected with settlement location. We might expect, for instance, that a high degree of economic, and perhaps social, readjustment occurred in such areas. Indeed, this is suggested by the emergence of the Alföld LBK in the Great Hungarian Plain which lies at the transition between major climatic zonations of Europe. This culture is found to be intermediate in character between the markedly different Körös culture of the Balkans, and the LBK culture of Central Europe (Krudy 1977). In such cases one might expect 'maximum' locational strategies to be more appropriate than those which regard uncertainty and risk as relatively insignificant.

As regards the implications of this study for our knowledge of the LBK culture, we might note the rapidity with which settlement may spread across a region, even during its initial penetration. If settlement is already distributed across an area in the early stages of its colonisation, it is just as likely to expand into adjacent *Siedlungskammern* than remain within that region (as would be the case under a slower rate of spread into the region). Access between such regions is thus likely to have been a major determinant of the direction which this spread takes. Indeed the construction of a processual model encompassing intra-regional environmental homogeneity and inter-regional heterogeneity would be an interesting and worthwhile exercise.

Another major implication of the above models is that, sooner or later, the pursuit of a particular locational strategy is no longer possible. When such conditions arise, major adjustments may be necessary; certainly the emergence of the Rössen culture, characterised by nucleated as opposed to dispersed settlement, suggests that significant adjustments were indeed made.

The development of the above models has also highlighted the need for a thorough analysis of LBK settlements' spatial and temporal boundaries. It is obviously more realistic to consider such models in relation to settlements as a whole, rather than in terms of artificially created settlement zones. This requires the systematic and intensive surveying of a considerable area of land in order to delineate the settlement's boundaries. Moreover, a thorough reappraisal of pottery typologies is required in order to distinguish their social and chronological information content. To this end, spatial and temporal variations of pottery styles within a small region might be analysed. Indeed the Aldenhovener Platte would be an extremely suitable area in which such research might be fruitfully carried out.

Finally, we may consider the implications of the above analyses for the study of archaeological processes in general. Certainly, it has been productive to explore, at a general level, various hypotheses of settlement development, if only to highlight the extremely complex, but as yet largely unexplored, nature of this problem. However, it should be evident that the full value of such conceptual hypotheses can only be realised if operational models are derived from them and, furthermore, that their predictions are compared with the observed data. In this way can those particular aspects of the data most useful in the formulation of broader generalisations be identified, and the potential and limitations of both theory and data gauged.

ACKNOWLEDGEMENTS

I gratefully acknowledge the stimulus of the late David Clarke in the instigation of this work, and the assistance of Dr J. Brandt, Dr M. Dohrn, Dr I. Hodder, Prof. J. Lüning *et al.*, Dr W. Piepers, Dr S. Shennan, J. A. Sheridan, Dr A. G. Sherratt and the Department of Education and Science (N.I.) in its preparation.

REFERENCES

Ammerman, A. J. and Cavalli-Sforza, L. L. (1973a). 'A population model for the diffusion of early farming in Europe' in C. Renfrew (ed.) *The Explanation of Culture Change: models in prehistory*, Duckworth

(1973b). 'Bandkeramik simulation models: a preliminary report', unpublished MS., circulated privately

Binford, L. R. (1972). *An Archaeological Perspective*, Seminar Press

Birdsell, J. B. (1957). 'Some population problems involving pleistocene man' in

'Population studies: animal ecology and demography', *Cold Spring Harbour Symposium on Quantitative Biology* 22: 47–69

Bohmers, A., Bruijn, A., Modderman, P. J. R. and Waterbolk, H. T. (1958–9). 'Zusammenfassende Betrachtungen über die Bandkeramik in den Niederlanden', *Palaeohistoria* 6/7: 225–30

Brookfield, H. C. and Brown, P. (1963). *Struggle for Land: agriculture and group territories among Chimbu of New Guinea Highlands*, Oxford University Press

Buttler, W. and Haberey, W. (1936). *Die bandkeramische Ansiedlung bei Köln-Lindenthal* (Römisch-Germanische Forschung, 11), De Gruyter

Bylund, E. (1960). 'Theoretical considerations regarding the distribution of settlement in inner north Sweden', *Geografiska Annaler* 42: 225–31

Carlton, T. H. (1966). 'Archaeological settlement patterns: an interpretation', Ph.D. thesis, Tulane University

Chamberlin, T. C. (1890). 'The method of multiple working hypotheses', *Science* 15: 92 (reprinted in *Science* 148: 754–61)

Chang, K. C. (ed.) (1968). *Settlement Archaeology*, National Press Books
  (1972). *Settlement Patterns in Archaeology* (Addison-Wesley Module in Anthropology, 24: 1–26), Addison-Wesley

Clarke, D. L. (1972a). 'Models and paradigms in contemporary archaeology' in Clarke, D. L. (ed.) *Models in Archaeology*, Methuen
  (1972b). 'A provisional model of an iron age society' in Clarke, D. L. (ed.) *Models in Archaeology*, Methuen
  (1973). 'Archaeology: the loss of innocence', *Antiquity* 47: 6–18
  (ed.) (1977). *Spatial Archaeology*, Academic Press

Dohrn-Ihmig, M. (1973a). 'Untersuchungen zur Bandkeramik im Rheinland', Ph.D. thesis, Cologne University
  (1973b). 'Gruppen in der jüngeren nordwestlichen Linienbandkeramik', *Archäologisches Korrespondenzblatt* 3: 279–87
  (1974). 'Untersuchungen zur Bandkeramik im Rheinland', *Rheinische Ausgrabungen* 15: 51–142

Downs, R. M. (1968). *The Role of Perspective in Modern Geography* (Bristol University Department of Geography Seminar Papers, series A, 11), University of Bristol, Department of Geography

Everson, J. A. and Fitzgerald, B. P. (1969). *Settlement Patterns* (Concepts in Geography, 1), Longman

Farruggia, J. P., Kuper, R., Lüning, J. and Stehli, P. (1973). 'Die Bandkeramische Siedlungsplatz Langweiler 2', *Rheinische Ausgrabungen*, 13

Found, W. C. (1971). *A Theoretical Approach to Rural Land-Use Patterns*, Arnold

Gould, P. R. (1969). 'Problems of space preference measures and relationships', *Geographical Analysis* 1: 31–44

Gumerman, G. J. (ed.) (1971). *The Distribution of Prehistoric Population Aggregates* (Proceedings of the Southwestern Anthropological Research Group, Prescott College Anthropological Reports, no. 1), Prescott College Press

Hamond, F. W. (1978a). 'The simulation of early Neolithic settlement development in the Lower Rhine Basin', Ph.D. thesis, Cambridge University
  (1978b). 'Regional survey strategies: a simulation approach' in J. F. Cherry, C. F. Gamble and S. J. Shennan (eds.) *Sampling in Contemporary British Archaeology* (British Archaeological Reports, British Series, 50), B.A.R. publications
  (1980). 'Biases inherent in archaeological fieldwork', *Archaeo-Physika* 7: 193–216

Harvey, D. (1969). *Explanation in Geography*, Duckworth

Hayden, B. (1975). 'The carrying capacity dilemma: an alternative approach' in A. C. Swedlung (ed.) *Population Studies in Archaeology and Biological Anthropology : a symposium* (Memoirs of the Society of American Archaeology, 30), Society of American Archaeology

Hill, J. N. (1972). 'The methodological debate in contemporary archaeology: a model' in D. L. Clarke (ed.) *Models in Archaeology*, Methuen

Hodder, I. (1977). 'Some new directions in spatial analysis', in D. L. Clarke (ed.) *Spatial Archaeology*, Academic Press

Hodder, I. and Orton, C. (1976). *Spatial Analysis in Archaeology* (New Studies in Archaeology, 1), Cambridge University Press

Janssen, W. (1976). 'Die archäologische Landesaufnahme in Rheinland', *Rheinische Ausgrabungen, sonderheft* 1: 11–13

Krudy, K. M. (1977). 'Settlement ecology of the Körös and Linear pottery cultures in Hungary', Ph.D. thesis, Institute of Archaeology, London University

Kruk, J. (1973). *Studia osadnicze nad neolitem wyzyn lessowych*, Polska Akademia Nauk, Institut Historii Kultury Materialnej

Kunstadter, P. (1972). 'Demography, ecology, social structure and settlement patterns' in G. A. Harrison and A. J. Boyle (eds.) *The Structure of Human Populations*, Clarendon Press

Kuper, R., Löhr, H., Lüning, J., Stehli, P. and Zimmerman, A. (1977). 'Die bandkeramische Siedlungsplatz Langweiler 9', *Rheinische Ausgrabungen* 18

Linke, W. (1976). *Frühestes Bautertum und geographisches Umwelt* (Bochumer Geographische Arbeiten, 28), Scöningh

Mackintosh, W. A. (1934). *Prairie Settlement : the geographical setting* (Canadian Frontiers of Settlement, 1), Macmillan

Milisauskas, S. R. (1976). *Archaeological Investigations on the Linear Culture Village of Olszanica*, Polska Akademia Nauk, Institut Historii Kultury Materialnej

(1977). 'Adaptations of the early Neolithic farmers in central Europe' in C. E. Cleland (ed.) *For the Director : research essays in honor of James B. Griffith* (Anthropological Papers, Museum of Anthropology, University of Michigan, 61), University of Michigan

Modderman, P. J. R. (1970). 'Linearbandkeramik aus Elsloo und Stein', *Analecta Praehistorica Leidensia* 3

(1971a). 'Hienheim', *Analecta Praehistorica Leidensia* 4: 1–25

(1971b). 'Bandkeramiker und Wanderbauerntum', *Archäeologische Korrespondenzblatt* 1: 7–9

(1972). 'Die Hausbauten und Siedlung der Linienbandkeramik in ihrem westlichen Bereich' in J. Lüning (ed.) *Die Anfänge des Neolithikums vom Orient bis Nord Europa* (Fundamenta, series A, 3 part Va), Böhlau

(1975). 'Elsloo, a neolithic farming community in the Netherlands' in P. Bruce-Mitford (ed.) *Recent Archaeological Excavations in Europe*, Routledge and Kegan Paul

Morrill, R. L. and Pitts, F. R. (1967). 'Marriage, migration and the mean information field: a study of uniqueness and generality', *Annals of the Association of American Geographers* 57: 401–22

Müller-Karpe, H. (1968). *Handbuch der Vorgeschichte, 2 : Jungsteinzeit*, Beck'sche

Murray, J. (1970). *The First European Agriculture*, Edinburgh University Press

Paget, E. (1960). 'Comments on the adjustment of settlements in marginal areas', *Geografiska Annaler* 42: 324–6

Park, R. D. and Eddowes, M. (1975). *Crop Husbandry*, Oxford University Press

Parsons, J. R. (1972). 'Archaeological settlement patterns', *Annual Review of Anthropology* 1: 127–50

Plog, F. T. (1974). *The Study of Prehistoric Change*, Academic Press

Popper, K. (1972). *The Logic of Scientific Discovery*, Hutchinson

Pred, A. (1967). 'Behaviour and location; foundations for a geographical and dynamic location theory: part 1', *Lund Studies in Geography* (series B) 27

    (1969). 'Behaviour and location; foundations for a geographical and dynamic location theory: part 2', *Lund Studies in Geography* (series B) 28

Quitta, H. (1960). 'Zur frage der ältesten Bandkeramik in Mitteleuropa', *Praehistorische Zeitschrift* 38: 1–38, 153–88

Sangmeister, E. (1943–50). 'Zum Charakter der bandkeramischen Siedlung', *Bericht der Römisch-Germanischen Kommission* 33: 89–109

SAP (1971) [Eckert, J., Jürgens, A., Kuper, R., Löhr, H. and Schröter, I.]. 'Untersuchungen zur neolithischen Besiedlung der Aldenhovener Platte, I', *Bonner Jahrbücher* 171: 558–664

    (1972) [Eckert, J., Ihmig, M., Kuper, R., Löhr, H. and Lüning, J.]. 'Untersuchungen zur neolithischen Besiedlung der Aldenhovener Platte, II', *Bonner Jahrbücher* 172: 344–94

    (1973) [Farruggia, J. P., Kuper, R., Lüning, J. and Stehli, P.]. 'Untersuchungen zur neolithischen Besiedlung der Aldenhovener Platte, III', *Bonner Jahrbücher* 173: 226–56

    (1974) [Kuper, R., Löhr, H., Lüning, J. and Stehli, P.]. 'Untersuchungen zur neolithischen Besiedlung der Aldenhovener Platte, IV', *Bonner Jahrbücher* 174: 424–508

    (1975) [Kuper, R., Löhr, H., Lüning, J., Schwellnus, W., Stehli, P. and Zimmerman, A.]. 'Untersuchungen zur neolithischen Besiedlung der Aldenhovener Platte, V', *Bonner Jahrbücher* 175: 191–229

    (1976) [Boelicke, U., Kuper, R., Löhr, H., Lüning, J., Schwellnus, W., Stehli, P. and Zimmerman, A.]. 'Untersuchungen zur neolithischen Besiedlung der Aldenhovener Platte, VI', *Bonner Jahrbücher* 176: 209–317

    (1977) [Boelicke, U., Koller, E., Kuper, R., Löhr, H., Lüning, J., Schwellnus, W., Stehli, P., Wolters, M., Zimmerman, A.]. 'Untersuchungen zur neolithischen Besiedlung der Aldenhovener Platte, VII', *Bonner Jahrbücher* 177: 481–559

Savage, L. J. (1951). 'The theory of statistical decisions', *Journal of the American Statistical Association* 46: 55–67

Schietzel, K. (1965). *Müddersheim. Eine Ansiedlung der jüngeren Bandkeramik im Rheinland* (Fundamenta, series A, 1), Böhlau

Schiffer, M. B. (1976). *Behavioural Archaeology*, Academic Press

Schultz, R. L. and Sullivan E. M. (1972). 'Developments in simulation in social and administrative science' in H. Guetzkow, P. Kotler and R. L. Schultz (eds.) *Simulation in Social and Administrative Science*, Prentice-Hall

Shannon, R. E. (1975). *Systems Simulation: the art and the science*, Prentice-Hall

Sielmann, B. (1971). 'Der Einfluss der Umwelt auf die neolithische Besiedlung Südwestdeutschlands unter besonderer Brücksichtigung der Verhältnisse am nördlichen Oberrhein', *Acta Praehistorica et Archaeologica* 2: 65–197

    (1972). 'Die frühneolithische Besiedlung Mitteleuropa' in J. Lüning (ed.) *Die Anfänge des Neolithikums vom Orient bis Nordeuropa* (Fundamenta, series A, 3 part Va), Böhlau

Simon, H. A. (1957). *Models of Man*, Wiley

Soudsky, B. (1966). *Bylany : Osada nejstaršich Zemĕdeicu z mladšĕ doby Kamennĕ* (Pamatniky naši minulosti, 4), Ceskoslovenska Akademie Vĕd.

Soudsky, B. and Pavlů, I. (1972). 'The linear pottery culture settlement patterns of central Europe' in P. J. Ucko, R. Tringham and G. W. Dimbleby (eds.) *Man, Settlement and Urbanism*, Duckworth

Struever, S. (1968). 'Problems, methods and organisation: a disparity in the growth of archaeology' in B. Meggers (ed.) *Anthropological Archaeology in the Americas*, Anthropological Society of Washington

Trigger, B. (1967). 'Settlement archaeology: its goals and promise', *American Antiquity* 32: 149–60

Tringham, R. (1968). 'A preliminary study of the early neolithic and latest mesolithic blade industries in southeast and central Europe' in J. Coles and D. Simpson (eds.) *Studies in Ancient Europe : essays presented to Stuart Piggott* Leicester University Press

(1971). *Hunters, Fishers and Farmers of Eastern Europe 6000–3000 B.C.*, Hutchinson

Ucko, P. J., Tringham, R. and Dimbleby, G. W. (1972). *Man, Settlement and Urbanism*, Duckworth

Watson, P. J., LeBlanc, S. A. and Redman, C. L. (1971). *Explanation in Archaeology : an explicitly scientific approach*, Columbia University Press

Whittle, A. W. R. (1977). *The Earlier Neolithic of S. England and its Continental Background* (British Archaeological Reports, International Series (supplementary), 35), B.A.R. Publications

Wolpert, J. (1964). 'The decision process in a spatial context', *Annals of the Association of American Geographers* 54: 537–58

Zubrow, E. B. W. (1975). *Prehistoric Carrying Capacity : a model* (Cummings Studies in Archaeology), Cummings

PART III

Subsistence pattern:
analytical and interpretive theory

9

Population, resources and explanation in prehistory

PAUL WILKINSON

The term 'population pressure' is rarely defined by prehistorians, perhaps because it seems to be self-explanatory, but it and related terms are used increasingly as explanatory devices for prehistoric change and are usually held to imply an imbalance between people and resources. Smith (1972, p. 6), for example, contended that population pressure could be defined usefully only 'by reference to...settlement pressing against clearly defined ecological limits'; and Harner (1970, p. 68) proposed that population pressure existed 'when the demand for subsistence resources exceeds the supply'. In contrast, 'equilibrium' is held to exist when populations regulate themselves homeo-statically at or below the carrying capacity of their territories (Binford 1968, p. 327; Smith 1972, p. 7). For brevity, I use the word 'territory' to mean the area regularly exploited by a group in the course of its seasonal sub-sistence cycle.

Several ethnographic studies (see references below) have described groups of hunter–gatherers that were apparently below the carrying capacity of their territories in the sense that they were held not to have consumed all the food resources in their territories. Some prehistorians have extended these observations into a general statement describing a supposedly normal situation for modern and prehistoric hunter–gatherers and have supported their views with the ethological observations and theories of Wynne-Edwards (1962). One common expression of such a view (Lee and DeVore 1968, p. 11; Casteel 1972, p. 36) is that hunter–gatherer populations tend to regulate their numbers at 20 to 30 per cent or less of the carrying capacity of their territories.

The belief that hunter–gatherers usually regulate their numbers below carrying capacity has influenced studies of the origins of food production and other prehistoric changes. Binford (1968, p. 327) formulated a viewpoint with respect to the origins of food production that has been accepted widely and that has its counterpart in archaeological explanations for the appearance of virtually all major innovations in the prehistoric record: 'if we recognize that an equilibrium can be established so that populations are homeostatically regulated below the carrying capacity of the local food supply, it follows that there is no necessary adaptive pressure favoring means of increasing the food supply'. Smith (1972, p. 11), Polgar (1972, p. 206), and Harris (1973a, pp.

251

2–3) adopted a similar view, which has led prehistorians investigating the origins of food production to concentrate their attention on situations of observed or suspected imbalance between populations and their food supplies, notably the Late Pleistocene and Early Holocene.

I wish to review briefly some of the evidence cited to support the claim that hunter–gatherers tend to regulate their populations below carrying capacity, with the following questions in mind. Do the data cited demonstrate convincingly that hunter–gatherers regulate their populations relative to food supply? It is legitimate to extrapolate from a small sample of recent or contemporary hunter–gatherers to prehistoric groups? Does 'equilibrium' in the sense in which it is commonly used imply the absence of adaptive pressure favouring economic, social, technological and other forms of change?

For convenience, I distinguish here between factors that regulate and limit respectively the size and density of populations (Eltringham 1971, p. 95). *Regulatory* factors may be defined as those that determine the size and density of populations without destroying them, whereas *limiting* factors are those that render impossible their survival.

THE ETHNOGRAPHIC EVIDENCE

The ethnographic studies most often cited by prehistorians to support their claim for equilibrium among hunter–gatherers include Clark (1951) on the Hukwe Bushman, several studies of Australian aborigines (e.g. Birdsell 1953; McCarthy 1957), Huntingford (1955) on the Dorobo, Bose (1964) on the Onge, Woodburn (1968) on the Hadza, and Lee (1968, 1969) on the !Kung. Some of these studies apparently demonstrated that the populations investigated were below the carrying capacity of their territories in the sense that they did not consume the entire standing crop of edible resources, but others, although cited as having done so (e.g., in Binford 1968), do not refer explicitly to carrying capacity and even seem to indicate the contrary (e.g., Clark 1951).

Several comments are germane. First, the field studies cited were brief, one (Bose 1964, p. 302) as short as thirty days, none of them exceeding a few years. The favourable balance between people and resources that was recorded may have resulted from a recent historical 'accident' that had depressed population or because the people were studied in a period when resources were unusually abundant; indeed, reductions in population size seem to be almost the rule in early post-contact times. Second, demonstrating that a population does not consume the total standing crop of resources in a particular area does not prove that the population in question regulates itself relative to food supply or that it is below carrying capacity.

The size and density of human populations can be regulated by factors other than food. In the cases of the !Kung, Hadza, Hudwe and some Australian groups, the authors commented on the seasonal scarcity of water. If, as seems possible, water in the dry season is an important regulatory factor for these groups (see Lee 1969; p. 78 on the !Kung), they may have been at or even above carrying capacity, even though they did not use all the food supplies. Lee (1968, p. 33) provided some support for this belief in the case of the !Kung:

For the greater part of the year, food is locally abundant and easily collected. It is only during the end of the dry season..., *when desirable foods have been eaten out in the immediate vicinity of the water holes* [my italics] that the people have to plan longer hikes...and carry their own water to those areas where the mongongo nut is still available.

If the !Kung are sufficiently numerous to exhaust all the easily accessible nuts, they may be at or close to carrying capacity. If their numbers were greater, presumably the easily accessible foods would be exhausted earlier in the dry season, longer marches would have to be undertaken sooner, and a point would be reached at which food resources became exhausted in all areas accessible from waterholes.

Clark (1951, p. 60) noted the existence of a 'starvation dance' among the Hukwe bushman and commented (p. 62) that 'obviously...these people lived in a perpetual state of semi-hunger interspersed and relieved by periodic orgies of eating'.

The !Kung bushmen illustrate well some of the difficulties of calculating carrying capacity, difficulties that beset range biologists and ecologists as much as ethnographers. Carrying capacity cannot be calculated simply by dividing the calorific value of standing crop of edible resources by the food requirements of the study population but must allow for such factors as the accessibility of the resources, the ease with which their exploitation can be integrated into a viable round of subsistence activities providing adequate supplies of all essential resources at every season, and the technological competence of the human populations to exploit the resources available to them. In chapter 12 below Parkington applies such a model to a prehistoric coastal site in South Africa. Carrying capacity must be calculated from the 'accessible biomass', with appropriate allowance for such regulatory or limiting factors as blizzards, the timing of freeze-up and thaw, the ice conditions in the Arctic (Damas 1968), prolonged winds and rough seas among coastal fishermen (McCarthy 1957), and droughts or floods among inland hunter–gatherers (McCarthy 1957; White and Peterson 1969, p. 49).

As Hammond stresses in chapter 8 above, particular attention must be paid to Liebig's so-called 'law of the minimum', which emphasises the important limiting or regulatory effect of the scarcest indispensable, irreplaceable resource at its period of greatest rarity or inaccessibility, *regardless of the amount in which it is required*. Casteel (1972), for example, found a marked discrepancy between the observed numbers of some North American groups and the carrying capacity of their territories as calculated from the standing crop of edible resources. A closer correspondence was obtained in some cases by recalculating carrying capacity from winter supplies of fish, which were probably the scarcest indispensable resource in the annual subsistence cycle. Interestingly, Casteel's results tended to refute the belief cited earlier that hunter–gatherers may regulate their numbers at 20 or 30 per cent of carrying capacity. According to Gross (1975), the numbers of the Kuikuru horticulturist–hunters of South America may also have been limited in recent times by the amount of protein that they could obtain.

Even brief field studies of modern hunter–gatherers may, if they are fortunate, reveal seasonal fluctuations of essential resources, but the law of the minimum may be expected to operate also over longer periods (Boserup 1965, p. 49; Helm 1968, p. 84). McCarthy (1957, p. 91) cited Spencer and Gillen that 'there are times when even the Aborigine with all his bushcraft ...is unable to contend against the fierce heat and drought of the centre and perishes miserably'. Sporadic crises and catastrophes are known to have affected adversely Eskimo hunters (Balikci 1968, p. 82), primitive farmers in Thailand and Micronesia (C. F. W. Higham, pers. comm.), as well as many modern, highly industrialised societies.

To answer my first question: ethnographic studies do not seem to me to have demonstrated convincingly that hunter–gatherers tend to regulate their numbers at or below the carrying capacity of their territories. Some of the groups studied may have been at or near carrying capacity in the short or long term, others were at least intermittently above carrying capacity, while others were probably regulated by factors other than food. Whilst it is true that 'equilibrium' implies only a central tendency about which major and minor, short- and long-term deviations inevitably exist, the available evidence seems to me to be inconclusive as to what is the central tendency – if there is one – and what the deviations. In fairness, none of the ethnographic studies cited by prehistorians was designed originally to answer precisely the types of question posed subsequently of them or to serve as a basis for generalisations about prehistoric man. None of them measured carrying capacity, but relied instead on subjective evaluations of the relationship between food supplies and people. It is not surprising, therefore, that they are unable to support the inferences subsequently made from them by prehistorians.

THE ETHOLOGICAL EVIDENCE

The ethological evidence adduced to support the theory of socially maintained equilibrium is usually that collated by Wynne-Edwards (1962). Wynne-Edwards contended that many animals regulate their populations below the size at which they would threaten their food supplies by means of social, behavioural mechanisms.

Leaving aside for the moment the obvious comment that it is presumptuous to discuss the mechanisms used by human populations to regulate their numbers below carrying capacity before it has been demonstrated unambiguously that they do in fact so regulate their numbers, and disregarding temporarily disputes about Wynne-Edwards' interpretation of the evidence (e.g. Gibb 1968; Klopfer 1969, pp. 99–102), two comments must be made.

First, prehistorians invoking Wynne-Edwards have omitted his important qualifying observation that social mechanisms come into play when no other regulatory factors set a lower limit to population density: 'towards the fringe of its range the existence and population density of any particular species of animal is often overwhelmingly dictated by the physical conditions of its environment – heat, cold, drought, shelter' (Wynne-Edwards 1962, p. 11). Given that many or all contemporary and recent hunter–gatherers occupy areas that are 'marginal' in the sense that they are climatically extreme, have been disturbed by adjacent agricultural and/or technologically developed societies, or have been impoverished biotically since the Pleistocene, Wynne-Edwards' hypothesis makes it unlikely that social mechanisms would be required to regulate populations in such areas, and the ethnographic data discussed are at least as consistent with such a belief as with any other.

Second, Chitty (1960, p. 111) has pointed out that the assumption that populations of animals are capable of self-regulation does not imply that all populations always do regulate themselves. Indeed, it is perhaps more likely that they do not, since the fact that 'a self-regulatory mechanism has been evolved by natural selection implies that it has been adapted in relation to a more or less limited range of environmental conditions. In unnatural or atypical situations, therefore, the mechanism will not necessarily prevent abnormal rates of increase or recurrent food crises'. Populations of hunter–gatherers in different types of habitats may be regulated, therefore, by different mechanisms, and populations in the often richer and more diversified habitats of the Pleistocene may not have been regulated in the same manner as modern hunter–gatherers.

In answer to my second question, therefore, I suggest that, even if they were known, it would be dangerous to extrapolate the regulatory mechanisms observed in modern, 'marginal' hunter–gatherers to the presumed hunter–gatherers of the Palaeolithic. The archaeological record itself is scanty and equivocal on the relationship between Palaeolithic populations and their resources. If, on the one hand, claims that early colonists in North America (Martin 1967) and Australia (Jones 1968, pp. 202–5), for example, exterminated many species and genera of large game animals through over-exploitation are validated, the case for socially maintained equilibria in all optimal situations will be weakened. On the other hand, the persistence of recognisable archaeological 'cultures' and economies for millennia argues for the maintenance of some sort of equilibrium in other circumstances.

POPULATION PRESSURE

We now face the question of whether population equilibrium as defined above connotes an absence of pressure in the sense of Binford (1968, p. 327). In other words, do situations of equilibrium not encourage adaptive pressure favouring means of increasing the food supply or other innovations? If pressure is defined narrowly as an excess or threatened excess of people over resources, equilibrium clearly implies an absence of pressure, although even this does not necessarily militate against the development and spread of innovations. On the other hand, population pressure and the potential development and spread of economic and other innovations may be said to exist if the number of surviving offspring produced by an organism or population (its fecundity, in the genetical sense) is lower than that organisms's biological capacity for reproduction (its fertility). This is more than a semantic quibble, since prehistorians are guided by their definition of pressure to specify particular areas and periods on which to concentrate the search for traces of early food production or other innovations, and they interpret the evidence from excavations along lines suggested by their definitions. My definition of pressure, however, leads to a very different orientation of research and interpretation.

Hunter–gatherer populations today are capable of doubling or tripling their numbers per generation, depending upon the interval between generations (Birdsel 1957; 1068, p. 230), yet in practice they do not often do so. Binford (1968, p. 326) cited ethnographic documentation that modern hunter–gatherers regulate the potential excess of fertility over mortality by such cultural mechanisms as infanticide, abortion, and proscriptions on intercourse. But this is not to say that they experience no population pressure, only that they avoid an imbalance between people and resources, which is not the same thing. The very necessity for cultural means of regulating fertility and mortality argues as much for as against the existence of population pressure.

It follows, therefore, that economic, demographic or other benefits will accrue, at least in the short term, to populations that develop techniques of overcoming the factors that inhibit their growth, *even though there was no initial imbalance between these populations and their resources.* The innovations in question need not only concern food, but may include methods of overcoming any limiting or regulatory factor: for example, trade, water and food storage, transportation, increased technological efficiency, or the effects of sedentism on birth-spacing, as well as cultural and social innovations.

It is a corollary of my argument that techniques for overcoming regulatory or limiting factors, such as increased food production or trade, will have been universally advantageous throughout prehistory.

I do not intend to pursue deeply the implications of this observation, save to note that in the case of explaining the origins of food production it resolves 'commonsense' objections (e.g., Sauer 1952, pp. 20–1; Caldwell

1973, p. 3) to current theories that food production could not have developed in contexts of population pressure because of the need to eat domesticable grain or stock, or from lack of time and manpower. Population pressure as a 'cause' of food production in my sense does not connote actual or imminent hunger (though it includes it). Equally, my view escapes two flaws of recent, demographic 'environmental crises' explanations of the origins of food production (e.g., Binford 1968). First, if it is true, as proponents of such explanations of food production suggest, that hunter–gatherers regulate their populations as much as 80 per cent below carrying capacity, one must posit a massive and sudden reduction of accessible biomass, which reduction must be without replacement of other viable resources, before population stress favouring food production could develop. The development of food production to counteract environmentally induced shortages of food is more consistent with the view that populations do not regulate themselves homeostatically below carrying capacity than with the converse. Second, Harris (1973a, p. 13) has indicated the apparent inconsistency in a theory such as Binford's (1968) of homeostatically self-regulated populations being induced into food production to counteract environmental perturbations, that it 'still begs the question of how the process of population increase gets started...in the first place'. Given my view of population pressure, population increase is neither necessary nor particularly probable.

In answer to my third question, therefore, I do not believe that population equilibrium necessarily implies an absence of adaptive pressure favouring economic, social, technological and other forms of change.

CONCLUSIONS

Much of prehistory, much of this book, and much of the work of David Clarke have been concerned with recognising and explaining change. Whether such change has been explained in sociocultural, economic, demographic or other terms, as Tilley shows in chapter 13 below, there has been a tendency to view change, at least implicitly, as almost invariably resulting from the disintegration, insufficiency or loss of adaptive value of the culture, system, economy or whatever that preceded it.

The purpose of this brief essay has been to show two things: first, the extent to which the orientation and interpretation of archaeological research may be guided by unquestioned assumptions about the most basic concepts; and, second, to show that some of the changes observed in the archaeological record may be without discernable 'causes' or 'stimuli' and are as likely to reflect the 'success' as the 'failure' of that which preceded them and that which they replaced.

ACKNOWLEDGEMENTS

I am grateful to my former colleagues in the Anthropology Department, University of Otago, Dunedin, New Zealand, and to Dr C. Hickey of the University of Alberta for advice and criticism.

REFERENCES

Balikci, A. (1968). 'The Netsilik Eskimos: adaptive processes' in R. B. Lee and I. DeVore (eds.) *Man the Hunter*, Aldine.

Binford, L. R. (1968). 'Post-Pleistocene adaptations' in S. R. and L. R. Binford (eds.) *New Perspectives in Archaeology*, Aldine

Birdsell, J. B. (1953). 'Some environmental and cultural factors influencing the structuring of Australian aboriginal populations', *American Naturalist* 87: 171–207

(1957). 'Some population problems involving Pleistocene man', *Cold Spring Harbor Symposia in Quantitative Biology* 22: 47–69

(1968). 'Some predictions for the Pleistocene based on equilibrium systems among recent hunter–gatherers' in R. B. Lee and I. DeVore (eds.) *Man the Hunter*, Aldine

Bose, S. (1964). 'Economy of the Onge of Little Andaman', *Man in India* 44: 298–310

Boserup, E. (1965). *The Conditions of Agricultural Growth. The economics of agrarian change under population pressure*, Allen and Unwin

Caldwell, J. R. (1973). 'Cultural evolution in the Old World and the New, leading to the beginnings and spread of agriculture', Paper presented to the 9th International Congress of Anthropological and Ethnological Sciences, Chicago, Ill., U.S.A.

Casteel, R. W. (1972). 'Two static maximum population-density models for hunter–gatherers: a first approximation', *World Archaeology* 4: 19–40

Chitty, D. (1960). 'Population processes in the vole and their relevance to general theory', *Canadian Journal of Zoology* 38: 99–113

Clark, J. D. (1951). 'Bushmen hunters of the Barotse forests', *The Northern Rhodesia Journal* 1: 56–65

Damas, D. A. (1968). 'The Density of Eskimo societies' in R. B. Lee and I. DeVore (eds) *Man the Hunter*, Aldine

Eltringham, S. K. (1971). *Life in Mud and Sand*, English Universities Press

Gibb, J. A. (1968). 'The evolution of reproductive rates: are there no rules?', *Proceedings of the New Zealand Ecological Society* 15: 1–6

Gross, D. R. (1975). 'Protein capture and cultural development in the Amazon Basin', *American Anthropologist* 77 (3): 526–49

Harner, M. (1970). 'Population pressure and the social evolution of agriculturalists', *Southwestern Journal of Anthropology* 26: 67–86

Harris, D. R. (1973a). 'Alternative pathways towards agriculture', Paper presented to the 9th International Congress of Anthropological and Ethnological Sciences, Chicago, Ill., U.S.A.

Harris, D. R. (1973b). 'The prehistory of tropical agriculture: an ethnoecological model' in C. Renfrew (ed.) *The Explanation of Culture Change: models in prehistory*, Duckworth

Helm, J. (1968). 'The nature of Dogrib socioterritorial groups' in R. B. Lee and I. DeVore (eds.)' *Man the Hunter*, Aldine

Huntingford, G. W. B. (1955). 'The economic life of the Dorobo', *Anthropos* 50: 605–84

Jones, R. (1968). 'The geographical background to the arrival of man in Australia and Tasmania', *Archaeology and Physical Anthropology in Oceania* 3: 186–215

Klopfer, P. H. (1969). *Habitats and Territories. A study of the use of space by animals*, Basic Books

Lee, R. B. (1968). 'What hunters do for a living, or, how to make out on scarce resources' in R. B. Lee and I. DeVore (eds.) *Man the Hunter*, Aldine

(1969). '!Kung Bushman subsistence: An input–output analysis' in D. Damas (ed.) *Contributions to Anthropology: ecological essays* (Bulletin 230), National Museums of Canada

Lee, R. B. and DeVore, I. (1968). 'Problems in the study of hunters and gatherers' in R. B. Lee and I. DeVore (eds.) *Man the Hunter*, Aldine

McCarthy, F. D. (1957). 'Habitat, economy, and equipment of the Australian Aborigines', *Report of the 32nd Congress of the Australian and New Zealand Association for the Advancement of Science* 32F: 88–97

Martiln, P. S. (1967). 'Prehistoric overkill' in P. S. Martin and H. E. Wright, Jr (eds.) *Pleistocene Extinctions: the search for a cause*, Yale University Press

Polgar, S. (1972). 'Population history and population policies from an anthropological perspective', *Current Anthropology* 13: 203–1

Sauer, C. O. (1952). *Agricultural Origins and Dispersals*, American Geographical Society

Smith, P. E. L. (1972). 'Changes in population pressure in archaeological explanation', *World Archaeology* 4: 5–18

White, C. and Peterson, N. (1969). 'Ethnographic interpretations of the prehistory of Western Arnhem Land', *Southwestern Journal of Anthropology* 25: 45–67

Woodburn, J. (1968). 'An introduction to Hadza ecology' in R. B. Lee and I. DeVore (eds.) *Man the Hunter*, Aldine

Wynne-Edwards, V. C. (1962). *Animal Dispersion in Relation to Social Behaviour*, Oliver and Boyd

10

Plough and pastoralism: aspects of the secondary products revolution

ANDREW SHERRATT

Als man Milch trank und den Ochsen an den Pflug spannte, waren wesentlich alle Bedingungen für unsere asiatisch-europäische Kultur vorhanden.[1]

Eduard Hahn, 1896

The contrast between the development of agriculture in the Old and New Worlds is an instructive one. In both, the domestication of a cereal crop allowed a massive increase in population, first in village communities and later in towns and cities. The major difference lay in the role of animal domesticates. In the New World there were few counterparts to the range of domesticated animals which were an integral part of Old World systems; in North America only the turkey, and in South America the guinea-pig and the Andean camelids, played a comparable role to the sheep, cattle and equids of Eurasia.

The first implication of this contrast is the primary role in the 'Neolithic revolution' which was played in both hemispheres by the domestication of plants, and especially cereals. Cultivation alone, without the extensive use of domestic animals, was able to sustain even complex urban societies. But it is not without significance that the next threshold, that of industrialisation, was attained only in the Old World; for the employment of animal-power as the first stage in the successive harnessing of increasingly powerful sources of energy beyond that of human muscle was only possible where these animals were domestic, not wild. The critical differences between the utilisation of animals in the Old and New World lay less in their uses as a source of meat than in their emergent properties when other applications were explored – their 'secondary products'.

The distinguishing feature of agrarian development in the Old World, therefore, is the interaction between plant and animal domesticates. Of major importance in this process is the plough – the first application of animal-power to the mechanisation of agriculture. Closely connected with this is the use of the cart, with its contribution not only to more intensive farming but to the transportation of its products. These two innovations resulted from a new application of domesticated cattle. Comparable advances in transport resulted from the domestication of the equids and their use as draught- and pack-animals. Also, secondary features of domesticated ovicaprids – notably the development of wool in sheep – allowed a new range of uses for these animals in providing fibres suitable for textiles. Finally, the regular milking of domesticated animals provided a variety of storable products and made possible a continuous flow of food without slaughtering the stock.

These features were not part of the original complex of plant and animal domestication in the Old World. Archaeological evidence for this range of secondary uses and products of domesticated animals is naturally very varied and of uneven value. Nevertheless, where these features can be dated, it is apparent that they only appear five millennia or so after the beginnings of agriculture in the Near East, and some three or four millennia after its introduction to Europe. There was thus a long primary phase of agricultural development before the secondary uses of domesticated animals were discovered and applied. Moreover, many of these features appeared within a similar span of time, some four to five thousand years ago. While they are by no means exactly contemporary, their appearance together at approximately the halfway point in the development of agriculture in the Old World, marking the beginnings of a phase of interaction between the plant and animal components and the earliest non-human sources of energy, perhaps deserves some explicit recognition: and it is in this spirit that I venture to burden an already over-taxed archaeological vocabulary with yet another revolution – the Secondary Products Revolution of the Old World.

These secondary products had important applications both in the intensification of agricultural production and in the sphere of transport, trade, and personal mobility. The plough increased production and made economic the cultivation of a range of poorer-quality soils; it thus resulted in the colonisation of a wider area than had been possible under previous systems of cultivation. Both the ox-cart and the horse, as well as the pack-donkey, opened up new possibilities for bulk transport and reduced the friction of distance. They made economic a range of locations and settlement types, including systems with cities, which would otherwise have involved huge amounts of effort. The development of textiles made from animal fibres gave for the first time a commodity which could be produced for exchange in areas where arable production was not the optimal form of land use. The use of milk made much larger herds economical, making use of exhausted and otherwise marginal land and encouraging the development of the pastoral sector with transhumance or even nomadism.

This bundle of innovations produced two types of society and subsistence systems which were unknown in pre-contact aboriginal America: plough-using agriculturalists, and pastoralists. The two were frequently in geographical proximity and interaction and their relations – both of conflict and symbiosis – are a recurring theme in the history of the Old World. Anthropologists have long recognised (and are increasingly emphasising; Goody 1976) the importance of plough agriculture as a predictor of social systems involving new mechanisms of inheritance as a result of the importance which the transmission of land acquires in such economies. Groups with a major pastoral component, too, have characteristic social features, such as strongly patrilineal descent groups, which are unlikely to have been associated with earlier hoe cultivators. The revolution was thus not simply a matter of subsistence and economics: it was a threshold of social development as well.

It would be surprising if so radical a set of changes were without evident traces in the archaeological record. While the secondary utilisation of animals can be shown from representations, or occasionally glimpsed directly where the evidence is favourably preserved, the striking changes in the distribution and character of settlement in Europe in the third millennium B.C. are eloquent testimony to a major alteration in the condition of life. Coming at a time when settlement in many of the older-settled areas had expanded to its limits, and long-term soil deterioration had begun to set in, these changes define a 'second generation' of agrarian economies in Europe, and the beginnings of a new cycle of expansion in the Bronze Age.

The 'secondary products revolution' thus separates two stages in the development of Old World agriculture: an initial stage of hoe cultivation, whose technology and transportation systems were based upon human muscle-power, and in which animals were kept purely for meat; and a second stage in which both plough agriculture and pastoralism can be recognised, with a technology using animal sources of energy. The former mode of life is now extinct in the temperate and sub-tropical parts of the Old World, though it may have important analogies with agriculture or semi-agriculture as practised in aboriginal temperate North America. The secondary products revolution marked the birth of the kinds of society characteristic of modern Eurasia.

DATING EVIDENCE

The use of animal traction

Although cattle were fully domesticated at least by the sixth millennium B.C., they were not systematically used as traction animals until the later fourth millennium, when a specific technology was developed to make use of this. The most important applications were to the plough and the cart. The evidence will be reviewed separately here, but it is clear that the two spread as a closely related complex.

The cart. Earliest unambiguous indications of the use of the cart (Figs 10.1, 10.2) come from archaic Sumerian pictograms from Uruk in southern Mesopotamia (Falkenstein 1936, signs 742–5). These date to the first half of the fourth millennium B.C. (3200–2800 b.c.).[2] From the succeeding Early Dynastic period there is a wealth of evidence from representations and actual cart burials. Clay models of vehicles with two or four solid wheels occur at

10.1.   Clay tablets from Uruk with symbols in pictographic script, including sign for 'cart'. Uruk period, late fourth millennium B.C. (after Falkenstein 1936).

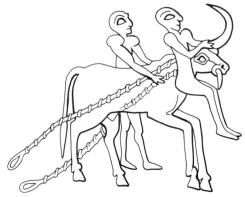

10.2.   Impression of cylinder seal of the Uruk period, showing two men harnessing an ox (British Museum) (drawn by Ann Searight).

this time over a wide area including northern Syria, northern Iraq, eastern Turkey, northern Iran and Transcaucasia. Mesopotamian examples are mostly vehicles for use in war, but the ones from further north include 'covered wagon' forms well suited for use in regions at the junction of steppe and forest (Piggott 1968).

Comparable vehicles are known to have been used at least during the third millennium B.C. on the steppe-lands north of the Caucasus and the Black Sea. Several groups of barrows near Elista on the Kalmuk steppe between the Caucasus and the Volga have produced evidence of carts. The most famous example, Tri Brata, contained both wooden wheels and a model of a two-wheeled cart. A somewhat later example from Kudinov on the lower Don contained a complete four-wheeled wagon. Similar finds occur on the lower Dniepr.

In Eastern Europe the most striking evidence is the handled drinking-cup in the form of a four-wheeled wagon from Budakalász near Budapest in Hungary, now with another example (Fig. 10.3a) from Szigetszentmárton (Kalicz 1976). These belong to the Baden culture, as does the cemetery of Alsónémedi with its double ox burial indicative of paired draught (see below p. 282; Korek 1951; Behrens 1964). A somewhat larger vessel in the form of a cart, without wheels but with two animal (ox?) protomes protruding from

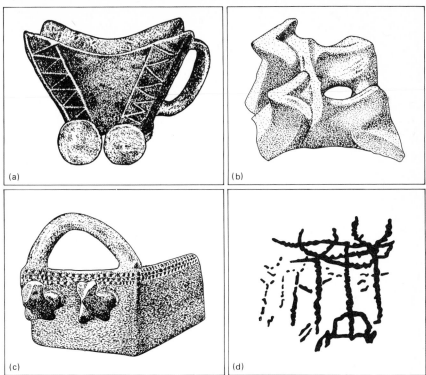

10.3. Early evidence of ox-traction in Europe: (a) cup in the form of a wagon from a Baden culture grave at Szigetszentmárton, Hungary; (b) handle in the form of two yoked oxen, TRB culture, Krężnica Jara, Poland; (c) pottery 'cart' with two protomes, Baden culture, Radošina, Slovakia; (d) pecked scene of oxen drawing cart, from a megalithic cist at Züschen, Germany (after Kalicz 1976, Němejcová-Pavúková 1973 and Uenze 1958).

the front, comes from Radošina in Slovakia (Fig. 10.3c), from an early Baden (Boleraz) context (Němejcová-Pavúková 1973, Fig. 3). Radiocarbon dates for this culture indicate a date of 3400–3100 B.C. (2700–2400 b.c.). Double ox burials appear at the same time in over a dozen examples in the Globular Amphora culture in Poland and central Germany (and may be present in Middle Neolithic Denmark, though bone is less well preserved). Evidence from representations is also available in the form of a pottery handle showing a pair of yoked oxen from Krężnica Jara, Lublin (Fig. 10.3b), in the context of the southeast TRB group, datable to the later fourth millennium B.C. (mid third millennium b.c.), and also from a stone with a pecked schematic scene (Fig. 10.3d) in a Hesse collective-burial cist at Lohne (Züschen) with a similar dating (Uenze 1958). The scene is a vertical view of pairs of oxen yoked to what are probably carts. A similar view of a four-wheeled vehicle has recently been found in a TRB context at Bronocice in southeast Poland (Milisauskas and Kruk 1978).

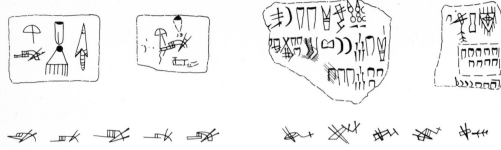

10.4.   Clay tablets with symbols in pictographic script including the sign for 'plough':
left from Uruk, Mesopotamia (Uruk period); right from Susa, Khuzestan (proto
Elamite period) late fourth millennium B.C. (after Falkenstein 1936 and Scheil 1923).

Finds of actual cart components have been made in Europe only in
waterlogged contexts. Wheels from the Netherlands and Denmark have been
dated by pollen analysis and radiocarbon dating to the third millennium B.C.
Corded-ware period (van der Waals 1964). Two yokes, one from Switzerland
and one from Lower Saxony, may also be of third millennium date (Gandert
1964).

Turning east, there are many examples of models showing solid-wheeled
carts from the Harrapan culture of the mid third millennium B.C. in northeast
India. In China, however (as also apparently in Egypt), the wheel only arrived
in its spoked form in the second millennium. This spread across central Asia
was associated with the use of the horse, and is considered below.

The evidence thus suggests that wheeled vehicles were first produced in
the Near East in the fourth millennium B.C., and that they rapidly spread from
there both to Europe and India during the course of the third millennium,
and across the central Asian steppes in the second. The occurrence of model
wheels in New World contexts, indicating that the principle was known even
though wheeled vehicles were not used in transport, shows that the availability
of draught animals was the critical factor in this technology.

The plough. Again, earliest indications are in pictograms (Fig. 10.4) (Falkenstein 1936, sign 214; Scheil 1923, signs 668–77). The basic model seems to
be the same in both cases, with two stilts (handles) and a composite
draught-pole. Representations of such ploughs (or, more accurately, ards) are
plentiful as ritual scenes on cylinder-seals in the Akkadian period around 2300
B.C., both in Mesopotamia and Assyria. These sometimes show a developed
form with a sowing funnel (Fig. 10.5), a device for sowing in regular lines
which was especially useful with irrigation and generally in semi-arid
conditions because of the deep implantation of the seed (Christiansen-Weniger
1967).

The plough, also in a two-handled version, is first evidenced in Egypt in

10.5.   Impression of cylinder-seal showing two-handled plough (ard) with sowing funnel.
Akkadian period (late third millennium B.C.) (Ashmolean Museum).

the mid third millennium, in a third-dynasty representation (Hartmann 1923). The construction of the Egyptian plough owed features of design like the rope binding to earlier hoe types.

In contrast to these Near Eastern forms, the earliest European ones are simpler and have only a single handle (Figs 10.6, 10.7). In the Mediterranean region it consisted of a flat sole into which were inserted both the stilt and the draught-pole. Further north, the even simpler design of the crook-shaft was used – a branch with a recurving projection, carved from the trunk itself, into which was set the stilt. As in Egypt, this resembled local hoe types, and was indeed the basic form of hafting in use at the time.

Ploughs of the sole-ard type are demonstrated from Early Bronze Age Cyprus from small terracotta models, and the signs of the Cretan pictographic and Linear A scripts make it clear that this design was also in use there in the Bronze Age. It is not known what form was in use in Anatolia, but it was probably also a one-handled type. The crook-ard is known to have been in use in the second millennium north of the Black Sea in the area around Kiev, as shown by finds from Polessje, Tokari and Sergeiev, the first radiocarbon dated to the early second millennium B.C. (Šramko 1971). There is no reason to suppose that it was not in contemporary use in the better-watered parts of the true steppes further south.

The use of the plough in the later third millennium in Harrapan India has recently been demonstrated by finds of plough-marks at Kalibangan in the Punjab (Steensberg 1971). Its arrival in China, however, seems even later than that of wheeled vehicles, and occurred only in the first millennium B.C.

In southern Europe, finds of ploughs and plough-like objects are known

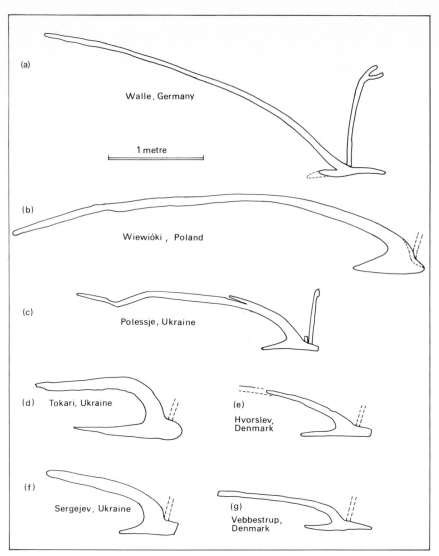

Finds of ards of crook-ard type from northern Europe and the Ukraine: (a) Walle, Germany; (b) Wiewióki, Poland; (c) Polessje, Ukraine; (d) Tokari, Ukraine; (e) Hvorslev, Denmark; (f) Sergejev, Ukraine; (g) Vebbestrup, Denmark. (After Glob 1951 and Šramko 1971.)

from second and third millennium circum-Alpine lakeside-village sites such as the Lago di Ledro near Trento and Seeberg-Burgäschisee Süd near Berne. The former yielded a crook-ard, the latter a rather similar 'hand-ard' or *Furchenstock* (Battaglia 1943; Müller-Beck 1965). The most extensive series of early plough finds, however, comes from the North European Plain (Glob 1951). Four crook-ards are known from Jutland, of which two are dated to the second millennium. Another, three metres in length, came from Walle

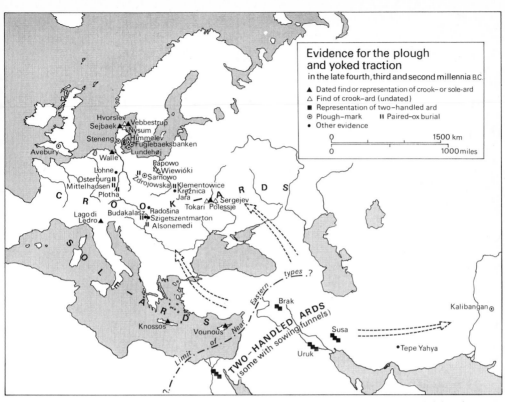

10.7.   Map of plough-marks, ard finds and representations, showing division between two-handled Near Eastern forms and European sole- and crook-ards.

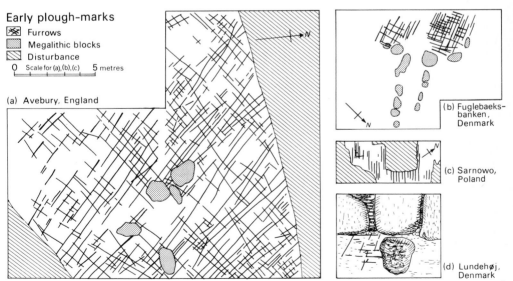

10.8.   Plough-marks preserved under north European long-barrows: (a) Avebury, England; (b) Fuglebaeksbanken, Denmark; (c) Sarnowo, Poland; (d) Lundehøj, Denmark. (After Evans 1967; Ebbesen and Brinch-Peterson 1973; Ørsnes 1956; Dąbrowski).

Plough-marks	Paired-ox burials	Yoke model	Cart drawing	Cart models	Plough finds	Wheels	Date B.C.

10.9.   Summary of evidence on the date of early ox traction in Europe (scale in hundreds of dendro-calibrated carbon-fourteen years).

in East Friesland, Germany. Two more examples are known from the bend of the Vistula in Poland.

These finds of actual ploughs do not date the introduction of the implement. It has long been known that traces of criss-cross plough-marks are preserved under third millennium round-barrows in northwest Europe; but now six examples preserved under late fourth millennium long-barrows are known, from Britain to Poland (Fig. 10.8). At Sarnowo in Kujavia a trapezoid barrow of the Wiórek phase of TRB overlay parallel plough-furrows. A radiocarbon date for a pit beneath the barrow gave a *terminus post quem* in the early fourth millennium (Bakker *et al.* 1969, p. 7; Wiślański 1970) and a more direct date is suggested from a nearby Wiórek site at Zarębowo dated to 3400 B.C. (2674±40 b.c.). In Denmark four examples are known, dating to the Middle

TABLE 10.1. *The earliest cultural contexts of features of the secondary products complex in Europe*

B.C.	North-central Europe	Carpathian Basin	Western steppes	
4000	Roessen	Tiszapolgár	Tripole BII	
3500	Early TRB	Bodrogkeresztúr	Tripole CI	
	Middle Neolithic	Baden	Tripole CII (Usatovo)	⇐ Plough Cart (Milk?)
3000				
	Corded-ware/ Beaker	Vučedol	Pit-graves	⇐ Wool Horse Tumuli Alloying
2500	Early Unětice	Nagyrev	Catacomb- graves	
	Late Unětice	Otomani	Timber-graves	⇐ Chariot
2000				

Neolithic, around 3400–3200 B.C. (2600–2500 b.c.). They are Lundehøj on Møn (MN II–IV: Ørsnes 1956), Fuglebaeksbanken on Stevns in west Zealand (MN Ib: Ebbesen and Petersen 1973), Himmelev 53 in central Zealand (MN Ib) and Steneng in south Jutland (Skaarup 1975, note 239). Finally, in southern England a long-barrow at Avebury, Wiltshire covered an area of plough-marks some fifteen metres square. It was radiocarbon dated by material from underneath and within it to 3500–3200 B.C. (2800–2500 b.c.: Fowler and Evans 1967). The coincidence of these dates is remarkable.

There is also a striking similarity between the dates for the appearance of the plough and the cart, and when the evidence is plotted in conjunction (Fig. 10.9) it forms a consistent pattern. The plough and cart seem to have been developed somewhere in northern Mesopotamia by the early fourth millennium B.C., and to have spread in not much more than 500 years as far as northwest Europe (Table 10.1), where it arrived around 3300 B.C. (2600 b.c.). Assuming a similar rate of spread to other parts of Europe, it would have reached the Aegean by around 3400 B.C. (2700 b.c.), and Iberia by 3200 B.C. (2500 b.c.).

This horizon has long been recognised as marking a major change in culture and settlement patterns. It marks the beginning of the Early Bronze Age in Transcaucasia, Anatolia, the Aegean and the Balkans; the Tripole–Usatovo transition in the Ukraine; the Baden culture in central Europe; the Middle Neolithic (Passage-grave) period in northwest Europe, and the Chalcolithic

Tripole

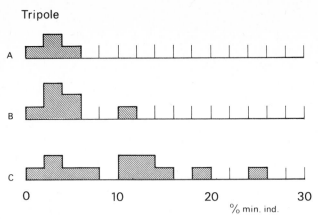

Percentages of horse (minimum numbers of individuals) in faunal assemblages of the three phases of the Tripole culture (data from Murray 1970).

of southwest Europe. There is thus reason to believe that the introduction of this traction complex, and perhaps other features, was of major importance in European culture-history; and that its spread to other areas may have been equally significant.

Animals for riding and transport

The fourth millennium also saw the domestication of four or five species of animals which, although hunted in earlier periods, had not been economical to domesticate. These, however, were animals which could be ridden, or used as pack- or draught-animals, and included equids and camels. Their suitability as transport animals helps to explain their independent but near-contemporary domestication from Egypt and Arabia to the Ukraine and Turkmenia.

The equids. The genus *Equus* entered the Old World in the Late Pliocene, and the modern distribution of species is the result of geographical speciation during the Pleistocene. This produced four main groups within the desert–steppe belt: zebras in sub-Saharan Africa, asses in north Africa, half asses (hemiones) or onagers in the Near East, and true horses in Eurasia.

The horse (*Equus caballus*) was widespread in the steppe-tundras of the last glaciation, and survived in small numbers in forested areas in the Holocene; but its main habitat was the steppe belt from the Ukraine to Mongolia. The contexts of the earliest horse domestication were the sedentary cattle-keeping but non-agricultural communities of the middle Dniepr, neighbours of agricultural Tripole groups in the parallel river valleys further west in the late fifth and fourth millennia B.C. These sites of the Sredni Stog group of the Dniepr–Donets culture contain Tripole B imports. At one of these, Dereivka, south of Kiev, a large number of bones of a small variety of horse have been recovered, and dated by radiocarbon to around 4400 B.C. (Telegin 1971). These have been widely accepted as indicative of an early stage of domestication, and features of material culture interpreted as riding equipment. The keeping of horses spread from this area only in the mid fourth millennium, at around the time when the traction complex was becoming widespread. The percentage of horses in Tripole C assemblages shows a leap from 5 per cent to 15 per cent over the previous period (Fig. 10.10), at the same time that sheep became more common than cattle both among Tripole groups and the successors of the Sredni Stog group. This coincided with a widespread colonisation of the true steppe area in the interfluves between the major river valleys, and formed part of the radical economic changes behind the emergence of the Pit-grave culture in this area.

Horses spread more slowly into forested Europe than did the traction complex, but became widespread in the later third millennium. They are evidenced in large numbers on the Island of Csepel below Budapest, and at Roucadour (Lot) in southern France in the Beaker period, when they also seem to have reached Ireland (Nobis 1971; Wijngaarden-Bakker 1975). At the same time they spread down into the Near East through the Caucasus and eastern Anatolia, down to the Levant and Mesopotamia. Riders on horseback are shown on terracotta plaques of the Old Babylonian period, and though difficult to distinguish from the native onagers, horses are well documented by the later third millennium, though the expense of keeping them in a sub-tropical environment restricted their ownership.

The onager (*Equus hemionus*) was a widely hunted species in the Near East during the early Neolithic. Lightly built and fast-moving, it is not easy to domesticate and is often shown muzzled in Mesopotamian representations. It was probably first used in the steppes of Assyria or Khuzestan in the later fourth millennium B.C., before the spread of the caballine horse, and is most probably the equid shown on proto-Elamite tablets (Scheil 1923). In Early Dynastic times during the third millennium they were applied as draught animals to the solid-wheeled battle-cars with two or four wheels of the kind shown in the Agrab model or on the Standard of Ur. They were harnessed in the same way as cattle, and controlled by means of a nose ring: but it took four animals to pull even the two-wheeled cars. Terracotta plaques show that onagers were ridden at least by the later third millennium, but they were never used as pack-animals.

The southwards spread of the horse displaced the onager from most of its uses, including that of traction animal. The vehicles with which it was used, however, underwent a more rapid development to make them more suitable for equids. This probably took place in northern Mesopotamia, Anatolia and northern Iran: an early stage is shown by the use of the cross-bar wheel with a central splat and two struts on a seal from Tepe Hissar, and true spoked wheels are known from Cappadocia from the end of the third millennium (Moorey 1968). In Mesopotamia in the early second millennium, traction equids were still controlled by a nose ring: but on the Eurasian steppes the new light vehicles were joined to more sophisticated traditions of horsemanship using the bit. Horse bits and spoked wheels are together evidenced in eastern Europe shortly after 2000 B.C. in sites of the Madarovce and Otomani

10.11.   Pottery model of donkey with panniers, broken from the rim of a vessel. From Cyprus, EB III (late third millennium B.C.) (Ashmolean Museum).

cultures, where bone cheek-pieces and clay models of four-spoke wheels have been found in Hungary, Slovakia and Moravia (Tihelka 1954; Bona 1960; Vizdal 1972). The spoke-wheeled cart spread equally rapidly eastwards across the steppes, and it is represented in a drawing on a pot of the Timber-grave culture, and on rock engravings in Kirgizia and Kazakhstan (Cherednichenko 1976). It was probably by this route that spoke-wheeled vehicles reached China.

The third equid to be domesticated at this time was the ass or donkey (*Equus asinus*). Its natural distribution is from Algeria to Sinai and possibly into the Levant. The advantage of the species is its docility and low dietary needs, making it a most economical animal especially in the Near East and Mediterranean. It thus provided a natural complement to the horse in this region. It was known as a domesticated animal for pack use in the EBA of Palestine around 3000 B.C. and in Egypt from the early third millennium B.C. onward. It was used in Cyprus in the later third millennium as a pack animal, as shown in EB III figurines (Fig. 10.11). Especially when crossed with the horse to produce the mule, the vigorous but infertile inter-specific hybrid, it was perhaps the most important form of bulk, long-distance transport, and must have formed the basis for the expanding overland trade networks of the later third and second millennia, such as the well-documented route linking Assur with the *Karum* of Kanish. In this role, it was of even greater economic importance than the horse itself.

The camels. Like the equids, camels also spread through the Old World in the Pleistocene, though they did not penetrate so far or split into geographical species to the same extent. While all belong to the species *Camelus dromedarius*, they fall into two regional populations which were probably independently domesticated. The more primitive woolly, two-humped or 'Bactrian' camel is adapted to the cooler steppe and mountain fringe of Eurasia, and the more advanced, single-humped dromedary or 'Arabian' camel to the more arid areas of Arabia and north Africa. The advantage of the camel as a transport animal is that it can carry twice as much as a donkey, faster, for less frequent feeding and watering (Bulliet 1975).

The one-hump camel was probably domesticated from at least the early third millennium, and is possibly shown loaded on a pot from the cemetery of Abusir-el-Melek in lower Egypt; while the two-humped form is shown on a contemporary bronze pick from Khurab in southern Iran (Zeuner 1963). The two-hump form seems to have been part of the traction complex, being controlled by a nose ring and shown pulling vehicles in central Asia, for instance on third millennium cart models with solid wheels and a camel's head from Turkmenia, or on rock drawings showing camels pulling spoke-wheeled carts from the region of Minusinsk (Bulliet 1975, pp. 153, 185). Camel bones are known from the Andronovo and Timber-grave cultures, and camel-hair was claimed at Maikop. The one-hump form, traditionally controlled by a noseband, became more common in the first millennium as Arab groups opened up the desert trade routes.

With the equids and the camels, five independent but parallel episodes of domestication took place during the fourth millennium, partly in direct association with the traction complex, and partly in adjoining parts of the semi-arid zone. Asses and camels in north Africa, onagers in the Near East itself, and horses and camels in the Eurasian steppe and semi-desert zone, all contributed to a more general transportation complex able to deal with a wide range of conditions. Within this area, individual animals spread and replaced or complemented the others, as well as expanding beyond this nuclear area into many parts of the Old World. Together they produced a revolutionary increase in transport potential.

Milk and wool

Milk. Basic to the economics of keeping animals for exploitation in the ways discussed earlier in this article is the use of milk. If animals are being used for purposes other than meat, they are too valuable a resource to slaughter simply when required for food. While surplus males may be eaten, larger numbers of females are needed for breeding stock. To carry the numbers of beasts required for a working population and a breeding population, some continuously usable food-product is really necessary – milk or in some cases blood.

Milk has several advantages. From a dietary point of view, it supplies the amino-acid lysine which is missing in cereal-based food. It contains fat, protein and sugar in a balanced form, and is a useful source of calcium. Being liquid, it is easily handled, and can be converted into a variety of storable products. These qualities, together with its almost universal association with domesticated livestock at the present time, have led many writers to assume that milking was practised from the earliest Neolithic onwards.

But the matter is not so simple. In the first place, animals which are not specially bred for the purpose do not produce large quantities of surplus milk; and moreover may not readily surrender it to the herdsman. Nor are human populations physiologically well adapted to use, as adults, the specific form of sugar which milk contains. Indeed, most adults suffer an unpleasant, even dangerous, reaction to drinking milk – 'a bloated feeling, flatulence, belching, cramps and a watery, explosive diarrhoea' (Kretchmer 1972, p. 72). Realisation that Euroamerican populations are unusual in their tolerance to milk as adults has come only recently. Tests with American negroes first showed that the adult ability to digest milk is not present in mankind as a whole (Bayless and Rosenzweig 1966), and tests of populations around the world showed how restricted that ability is (McCracken 1971). This realisation made sense of the evidence being assembled on the distribution of the milking habit itself (Simoons 1969, 1970). It was so long in being recognised because of the concentration of research and medical skills among the populations most tolerant of milk – European and American whites. In the present context, it is of fundamental importance.

Milk has three components: fat, protein, and milk-sugar, known as lactose. This last is a disaccharide, composed of glucose and galactose, and is synthesised only in the mammary gland. It is broken down in the small intestine by the enzyme lactase, which splits the disaccharide into glucose – which is used directly – and galactose, which is metabolised by the liver. In the absence of lactase, the lactose remains undigested and is fermented by the bacteria of the colon. It is this which causes the explosive diarrhoea. The cause of lactose intolerance is thus lactase deficiency (Kretchmer 1972).

In all mammals except human lactose-tolerant populations, the production of lactase is at a maximum shortly after birth and ceases after infancy – in man, from two to four years of age. This represents the normal situation, and fits the pattern of other temporarily produced enzymes. Lactase production is not stimulated to any extent by the continued ingestion of lactose. Lactose-tolerance is transmitted genetically, and indeed is a dominant trait, although incompletely so. American black populations are approximately 70 per cent intolerant in comparison with ancestral west African populations, who at the present time are 98 per cent intolerant. Lactose-intolerance is particularly high among Chinese, Thais, agricultural West Africans (though not nomadic groups like the Fulani), South Americans and New Guineans, of those tested. In short, lactose-tolerance is the result of a relatively recent evolutionary episode, and adult milk-drinking a late and restricted feature of human diet (Kretchmer 1972; Simoons 1969).

The elaborate preparation of milk products may have been necessary because of a limited tolerance of lactose. Fermented products such as yogurt and cheese have a lower lactose content than fresh milk (McCracken 1971), and it is a general pattern in the Mediterranean that most of the milk is processed in this way. Low levels of tolerance are common today in Greece and south Italy, and such processing is analogous to the preparation of bitter manioc for consumption in South America.

The well-known Chinese aversion to milk, often cited as an example of an irrational food preference, is part of a more widespread phenomenon with a basic biological explanation. The geographical distribution of the practice of milking (Simoons 1970, p. 702) shows a continuous area from Morocco to eastern India (with non-milking enclaves there suggesting a recent expansion of the practice), extending southwards in east Africa but not penetrating into southeast Asia and Oceania. It comprises those areas connected via the steppe corridor and the Sahara, the arid belt across Africa and Eurasia. In the centre of this area are the mountains of the Near East and surrounding steppes. The distribution suggests a mid Holocene origin for the practice, somewhere in this central area, and it seems likely that milking and milk-consumption form another aspect of the complex of secondary uses and products which has been outlined above; indeed, it was probably a precondition for these developments.

The limited tolerance of human populations to milk is only one side of the problem: the reluctance or inability of the cow to provide it is the other. For a modern perspective on this we may turn to the pastoral groups studied by ethnographers (Cranstone 1969). These illustrate the difficulties faced by people who do not have the highly bred milch animals of northwest Europe. The problem is to allow the animals to accumulate their milk, and to persuade them to let it down to a human milker. Cows are often separated from their calves during the day, to prevent their taking milk. However, they or some surrogate need to be present at the milking, to stimulate lactation and to activate the milk ejection reflex (Amoroso and Jewell 1963). The action of letting down the milk is a true reflex, involving the release by the pituitary gland of the hormone oxytocin which stimulates contraction of the muscles which press on the milk storage sacs. This reflex may be activated by stimulation either of the teat and mammary gland, or (because of the role of oxytocin in initiating uterine contractions) the vagina and cervix. It is thus a common custom among present and ancient pastoralists to blow, often using a special tube, into the rectum or vagina of the animal during milking. The milker is thus positioned behind the animal, rather than at the side as is otherwise more convenient. Instruments for this purpose have been identified archaeologically, for instance in the Baden culture (Banner 1956) and in south Russia (Galkin 1975).

10.12.   Cylinder-seal and drawing of its impression, showing reed-built byres with calves
and milk jugs, with frieze of adult animals above. The seal itself is surmounted by
a silver ram. From Iraq, Uruk period (late fourth millennium B.C.) (Ashmolean
Museum).

10.13.   Inlaid scene of milking, forming part of the frieze of the temple to Nin-Hursag built
by A-an-ni-pad-da at El Ubeid, Iraq. Early Dynastic (mid third millennium B.C.)
(British Museum).

These features were once widespread, not only among specialised pastoralists
but in all the groups which practised milking. Uruk period seals show the
adult cattle returning to huts where the young have been stalled during the
day (Fig. 10.12). From the Early Dynastic III period comes the famous relief
from the temple of Nin-Hursag at El Ubeid, built by A-an-ni-pad-da, second
king of the first dynasty of Ur. This shows in great detail the actual
milking – from the back, with the aid of an insufflator – and the processing
of the milk (Fig. 10.13). The small udders on these early cows suggest that
they were not highly bred for milk, and such stimulation would be essential.
The milking position behind the animal is also shown in an Early Dynastic
inlay from Kish; and it was still in use in Minoan times, as shown by a sealing
(Fig. 10.14) from the Archives Deposit at Knossos (Evans 1935). Goats are
also shown being milked on Early Dynastic cylinder-seals. In Egypt a hobbled
cow is shown being milked in the presence of a calf in the tomb of Ti in the

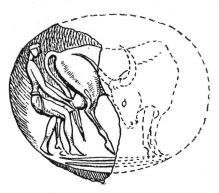

10.14.   Sealing from Late Bronze Age Knossos showing milking from behind (after Evans 1935 (4), Fig. 534).

Old Kingdom (Klebs 1915, p. 63). Milking is apparently shown on some central Saharan rock drawings from Tassili and the Fezzan, but their date is difficult to determine and there is no evidence that they are earlier than the third millennium B.C. (Simoons 1971; Clark 1976).

The biochemical and iconographic evidence thus suggests that although milking was known by the time of the first representations in early urban contexts in the Near East, it was not of much greater antiquity. Is there any other evidence which would date the adoption and spread of the practice? One suggestion comes from pottery. It has long been noted that the Bronze Age sees a radical change in the kinds of vessels which constitute typical assemblages. Specifically, the open bowls which dominated Neolithic assemblages were supplemented by a range of drinking and pouring vessels, and a variety of pails (Fig. 10.15). In the Mediterranean, the jugs and cups have been attributed to the discovery of wine (Renfrew 1971, p. 282), and this may be the case, but the changes affect a much wider area than that feature could explain. They clearly reflect some dietary innovation occurring in southern, central and northern Europe within a similar time range. Some types of Bronze Age pottery, like the Appenine 'milk boilers' or the Cypriot 'milk bowls' have already been characterised as being for such use. It seems likely that the widespread adoption of shapes appropriate for the manipulation of liquids is connected with the spread of the milking habit and the use of milk products. This would explain the often uncanny resemblances between distant areas, which have usually been used to argue for major migrations. The massive array of parallels assembled by Kalicz between the Baden culture and Anatolian Early Bronze Age cultures, for instance, finds an acceptable explanation here. Parallels between EBA Bulgaria and Cyprus become comprehensible. The universal appearance of strapwork-ornamented bucket-shaped pots, from one end of Europe to the other, becomes less surprising; while the *Fischbuttengefäss* which appears in central Europe with the Baden culture has long been explained in Ghassulian contexts in Palestine as a churn.

Central Europe   Balkans   Cyprus

NW Europe   Balkans   Italy

10.15.   Pottery forms concerned with the manipulation of liquids and associated with the spread of the secondary products complex. It seems likely that they were primarily for milk and milk-products.

Such lactic products, if such they were, probably had initially some ritual and social significance, especially if they included the intoxicating products of fermentation such as kumish. Precisely such an association is demonstrated in the Baden culture cemeteries of Hungary, where the two cart burials at Alsónémedi were accompanied by identical assemblages consisting of a finely made pottery jug, cup, dipper and bipartite bowl. From the grave which produced the Szigetszentmárton cart model came a precisely similar combination; and that model was itself a cup! The association of drinking and driving evidently began at an early stage in their history. These coincidences strengthen the view that we are dealing with an interdependent complex of features, which spread to a large extent in association.

Wool. The textile-fibre which became most important in the Old World, wool, was not present in the first four to five millennia after the initial domestication of the sheep. Vegetable fibres formed the basis of the earliest textiles, as in the New World, where cotton (*Gossypium*) fibre was developed by agricultural groups to supplement the older tradition of skin and leather clothing. Flax (*Linum usitatissimum*) was the most common Old World vegetable fibre, and already woven into elaborately patterned linen textiles before the emergence of wool. This persisted in some hot countries even after wool became common elsewhere: Egyptian Old Kingdom sheep were commonly of non-woolly types. Wool sheep were not introduced into Egypt until the Middle Kingdom.

The date at which wool sheep developed is being made more precise by microscopic examination of prehistoric fibres (Ryder 1969). These have already suggested that claims of an early date for woollen fibres (as at Çatal Hüyük) are mistaken. As with milking and paired-draught traction, the earliest evidence comes with the beginning of a literary and pictorial record during urbanisation in Mesopotamia. While such evidence gives only a *terminus ante quem,* the replacement of linen by woollen textiles can be traced in some detail from waterlogged contexts in Europe, and these show that the transition had not occurred there before the mid third millennium B.C. It seems most likely, therefore, that it had developed not long before the first indications in the Near East. Examination of further samples will make this more precise.

The wild sheep has a brown, hairy coat with short, woolly underhair. It was the development of underhair at the expense of the coarser outer hairs or kemps which produced the wool sheep. This was probably deliberately selected, in cold environments where the tendency was already present in wild populations. Lighter colours of fleece were also sought, though early sheep were probably more pigmented than today's breeds.

By the time of the Uruk pictographs (Falkenstein 1936) there were over thirty signs representing sheep. Pictorial evidence from the Proto-literate period indicates that both hairy and woolly sheep were known, as well as the fat-tailed breed. Sheep which are shown as being milked belong to the spiral-horned variant of the wool sheep (Zeuner 1963, p. 173; Amoroso and Jewell 1963). Early Dynastic sculptures and cylinder-seals not infrequently show woolly sheep alongside hairy ones, while Old Babylonian shearing lists indicate the organisation of wool collection (Kraus 1966, p. 47) and the importance of the spring shearing in the agricultural calendar. The wool would at this stage have been plucked, as it was naturally moulted, and somewhat finer wool obtained as many of the coarser hairs were left behind.

Marked changes in the exploitation of sheep appear in Europe in the third millennium. In Hungary, sheep increase as a percentage of bones on sites to 40 per cent or more, in comparison to figures of around 10 per cent in the preceding period (Bökönyi 1974, Figs 1 and 2). A similar change occurs in the Early Bronze Age in the Alpine region and in Greece (Halstead, chapter 11 below). In addition, the withers height increases dramatically, and there are higher percentages of mature and old animals. Horns also increase in size, though individuals without horns are common. These Bronze Age sheep must have resembled the still-surviving Soay breed.

These changes become comprehensible when attention is paid to the textiles preserved in the Swiss lake villages (Vogt 1937). Of the fourth- and early-third-millennium examples, all are linen, with leather being used for garments requiring greater robustness. Wool appears in the late third millennium. The proliferation of Early Bronze Age pin types represents the adoption of fastenings suitable to the loose woollen weaves which were introduced in this period, replacing the buttoned leather clothing of the Neolithic. The extensively preserved Bronze Age costumes from Danish coffin burials (Hald 1950) indicate the types of garment produced.

One factor which favoured the expansion of textile production was the change to a predominant male role in agriculture, leaving the women free to spin and weave (see below). As medieval economic historians have long been aware, woollen commodities are among the most basic items of inter-regional trade, and are usually the first manufactured goods to be traded on a large scale. Exports in developing areas shift from basic subsistence items like grain to manufactured products. This process can be observed in Mesopotamia during the course of the third millennium, and the development of such trade may have had an important role in extending the urban network. The role which wool and textiles played in the economies of the second millennium is clear from the textual evidence, both in Mesopotamia, Anatolia, and in Crete (Killen 1964).

The economics of secondary products exploitation

When animals are raised purely for meat it is economic to slaughter them while they are relatively young. For instance, the same amount of fodder (33 000 kg of hay-equivalent) would raise seven calves to two years as would be needed to take three of them to three and a half years; and the former strategy yields 40 per cent more meat (Lotka 1956, p. 120). The increase in live weight for the first two years is roughly proportional to the amount of feed consumed, but after that age the live weight increases more slowly while the feed consumption stays constant (*ibid.*, p. 133). It is therefore advantageous to crop the population at this point (or even earlier, when there are seasonal fodder shortages), leaving only breeding stock, mostly females. Even the breeding stock, however, would not be kept beyond the age of reproduction.

Milking is a highly efficient mode of exploitation, giving four or five times the amount of protein and energy from the same amount of feed as would exploitation for meat. The use of cattle for beef recovers about 3.5 per cent of the energy which they have consumed in feed: with modern breeds the use for milk recovers 18 per cent (*ibid.*, p. 136). Vitamins and salts (like calcium compounds) which are present only in small quantities in muscular tissue are abundant in milk. The kill-off strategy must be thus adjusted to maximise the number of lactating animals, by increasing the proportion of mature females. Male animals may either be mostly slaughtered very early (even at birth in a documented example from medieval Ireland: Amoroso and Jewell 1963, p. 135), or else kept for a longer period as an insured meat supply in extreme environments. Thus the Karimojong of Uganda, although dependent largely on milk (Dyson-Hudson and Dyson-Hudson 1969), may have only 12 per cent of lactating animals in their herds because of the high proportion of males (40 per cent), the long maturation period for cattle (three and a half to four years), the long period between calves (fourteen months), and the short lactation period (eight months or less). Female animals kept for milk are usually retained for long periods: an Estonian herd recorded in 1651 had half its cows over seven years and a third over ten years old (van Bath 1963, p. 287).

Animals used for traction are usually castrated males which at the age of three to four years are almost fully-grown, and have been trained as draught-animals since the age of two or three. The numbers of animals which must be maintained depends on the total amount of work during the year, and the extent to which it has to be done simultaneously. In India (especially the Central region), a short wet-season makes it imperative that each peasant should have a pair of bullocks to get his cultivation completed in time, since it must be done at once when the rains come (Clark and Haswell 1964, p. 55): this need underlies the maintenance of large numbers of scavenging cows as breeding stock, even though their milk yields are poor (Harris 1966). In medieval Europe there was increasing pressure on working livestock because of the expanding arable, even though plough teams were shared by the community (Warriner 1939).

The interpretation of kill-off patterns in a prehistoric European cattle population has been considered by Higham and Message for the TRB Middle Neolithic settlement of Troldebjerg in Langeland, Denmark (1969). On the basis of metacarpals, radii and mandibles, they reconstructed a pattern with low mortality in animals of both sexes up to two or three years of age, differential slaughter of castrated males from that age up to four years, with about a sixth of all animals surviving beyond that point. This argues against a pure meat economy, but does not suggest very highly developed exploitation of secondary products. It suggests small numbers of milch cows, and the possibility of a few traction-animals. The pattern conforms to Boessneck's observations (1956, p. 34) from Bavarian Neolithic settlements, that half the animals slaughtered were young to subadult. The handful of systematic investigations which have so far been made on this material, however, needs to be multiplied many times before comparative patterns can be defined.

For sheep, Payne (1973) has reported early results from his continuing investigation into comparative patterns of mortality. He has suggested model life-tables for differing types of exploitation (*ibid.*, Figs 1–3). For meat. similar considerations apply as to cattle: the optimum period for cropping surplus stock is between one and a half and two and a half years, with males preferentially slaughtered at this point. Milk production makes it advantageous to keep at least half of the female animals beyond five years, and some even up to ten. With wool production, males become equally valuable at these ages also, so that there is a roughly symmetrical distribution with a high proportion of both sexes being kept up to six years and beyond. Historical samples studied by Payne show animals being carried up to eight years, as does a Bronze Age sample from the west Anatolian site of Beycesultan: by contrast, the sheep from the Early Neolithic site of Nea Nikomedia in north Greece were all killed before four years of age, many in their first year (Payne, pers. comm.). Ducos has suggested that kill-off patterns characteristic of secondary products utilisation began in Palestine with the Ghassulian (1973, p. 84). Halstead (chapter 11 below) has investigated these suggestions in Neolithic Greece and concludes that secondary products were not a feature of early stock economies there. The evidence from osteological studies thus supports the contention that domestic animals before the fourth and third millennia B.C. were exploited only for their meat, and that the spread of secondary products utilisation brought about major changes in animal husbandry.

INTERACTIONS AND EFFECTS

A general model

The evidence reviewed above suggests that a number of major innovations occurred in the Near East and adjacent areas in the middle or later fourth millennium B.C.; and that these innovations spread and interacted with each other so as to cause major economic changes during the course of the third millennium. This revolution in animal husbandry involved using old domesticates in new ways, and in domesticating a new range of species. It

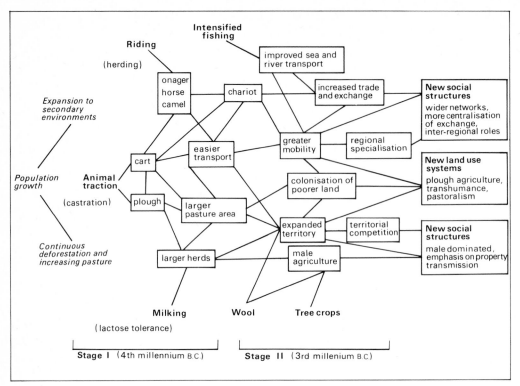

10.16   Interaction of the components of the secondary products complex through time.

resembled the previous phase of Near Eastern domestication in the eighth and seventh millennia in that different parts of the area, evolving in parallel with local resources, each contributed to a package of compatible elements with widespread application. A general explanation may therefore be suggested.

These developments were not accidentally coincident. They represented a variety of similar responses to a common problem, the pattern of population growth and territorial expansion which had been initiated by the beginnings of animal and plant domestication in that area some four thousand years before. Such problems became especially acute with the need to penetrate increasingly marginal environments in a landscape containing sharp contrasts in climate and terrain within short distances. They were partly dependent on biological changes both in man, in the case of tolerance to lactose, and his stock, for instance with wool. They involved an increased scale of investment in animal husbandry, and together they produced a new phase of man–animal relationships (Fig. 10.16).

An increase in the scale of animal keeping was the basic feature. The population of domestic animals had to contain both breeding stock and working or production stock, as well as any beasts kept solely for meat. The maintenance of such an increased population was greatly facilitated by the practice of milking. It was this which made other uses possible, by allowing the continuous cropping of a subsistence product from a standing herd.

As agricultural communities expanded to the edges of the Fertile Crescent, they encountered extensive semi-arid areas which supported large mobile animal populations. Because of the uncertainty it involved, in areas without alternative resources, hunting was not a viable economy. With a product like milk which could be continuously obtained, and especially with the added mobility given by draught- and riding-animals, such areas could be exploited by pastoralism. Because of the easier alternative methods of increasing subsistence, especially by small-scale irrigation, this pattern was slow to evolve. The evolution of lactose-tolerant populations removed an important brake on the development of such systems, which could themselves develop techniques of milk processing (initially for storage) which rendered it usable by non-tolerant populations. The adaptation could thus spread more rapidly than its genetic basis.

Where did this process of adaptation take place? It is probably misleading to look for any closely defined region of origin, but it would appear that the process was occurring during the late Ubaid period in the second half of the fifth millennium B.C. and first half of the fourth, in northern Iraq, Syria and Palestine. The Ghassulian culture in Palestine shows a ceramic inventory including vessels for pouring and manipulating liquids, including the famous 'butter churn', and the suggestion of a mortality pattern among its livestock of the kind indicating secondary products has already been noted. Equally suggestive are the large numbers of sites which appear at this period in the arid areas of south Palestine and Sinai (Rothenberg 1970), indicative of methods of coping with such dry environments, and important also in the acquisition of raw materials like copper. Indeed, the formation of populations in the dryer interstices would have had an important effect on patterns of trade and contact (Sherratt 1976).

The application of certain features of this system was not restricted, however, to semi-arid areas. The use of draught-animals, especially, had revolutionary implications for cultivation in better-watered areas. Not only did the cart improve transport on the farm, but the innovation of a 'mechanical hoe', the plough, increased the farmer's ability to prepare his land by a factor of up to four or more. (For the economics of this, see Clark and Haswell 1964, p. 55.) This both increased the productivity of good land, and made economical the preparation of land from which a poorer yield might be expected. It seems likely that the plough played a critical role in the cultivation of tree crops which began at this period (Zohary and Spiegel-Roy 1975). An intensification of agricultural production was thus a parallel development to the expansion of pastoral populations. Furthermore, the large-scale production of wool, an animal product suitable for manufactures, provided a greatly increased potential for trade. It was the juxtaposition of contrasting environmental zones which produced in the Near East such innovating co-action (Fig. 10.17; cf. Clarke 1968, p. 355).

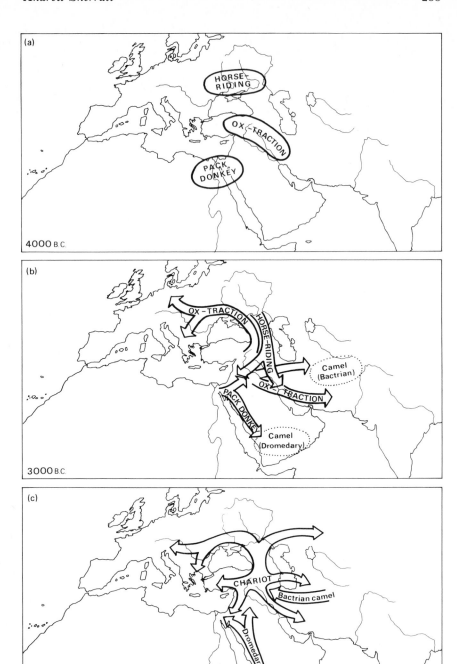

10.17. Origins and interaction of the main elements of the secondary products complex:
(a) 4000 B.C., primary developments; (b) 3000 B.C., inter-regional exchange and
spread; (c) 2000 B.C., continuing exchange and interaction.

This agricultural revolution was well under way by the later fourth millennium in Mesopotamia and Khuzestan where the massive increase in population on the alluvium created an extensive demand for raw materials. Ramifying trade links spread advanced techniques into the hinterlands, while the increasingly urbanised populations of the lowlands began the manufacture of woollen textiles. At the same time, semi-dependent pastoral populations continued to grow in the areas where grain-growing was unprofitable.

The links between these differentiating subsistence specialisations, intensive cultivation and mobile pastoralism, were probably deeper than simple trading relationships. Such diversity opens up the possibility of polyethnic and symbiotic social systems (Barth 1969), with a fluctuating balance between sedentarisation and nomadisation, or long-term flows of population between economies with different patterns of fertility and mortality – notably across ethnic boundaries (Barth 1964, ch. 9). Such a complex system, despite its inbuilt homeostatic features, has the potential for violent change when there are rapid shifts in the balance of power: the relationship between villager or town-dweller and nomad was always ambivalent. The degree of interdependence involved in a closely adjusted timetable for stubble grazing and use of winter pastures always contained the potential for conflict.

The dual economy of plough and pastoralism was characteristic of areas of ecological diversity. Thus in mountain areas the pastoral sector was occupied by transhumant groups which were directly analogous to the nomads of the arid plains. This pattern became characteristic not only of the Zagros and the Taurus but also of the Tertiary fold mountains of southern Europe, where it was also a creation of the third millennium.

In more arid areas, pastoralism spread without the plough. While plough cultivation spread along with the rest of the secondary products complex both to Europe and to India, it did not reach into Africa further than the upper Nile. Pastoralism, involving milking, was common in the Sahara probably by the later fourth and almost certainly by the third millennium B.C., and with the third-millennium desiccation some of these populations were forced southwards (Clark 1976). The continuing penetration into east Africa took a ploughless and cartless pastoralism down the tropical grassland corridor, as cattle replaced the native wild ungulates. Cattle were much less efficient than these animals, some of which (like the eland) were potentially herdable; and indeed it was their plentiful provision of milk, urine and dung – which in the native antelopes were sparse and concentrated – that made the introduced animals so valuable a resource (Kyle 1972).

On the Eurasian steppes, pastoralism did not become divorced from traction and the plough was used in oasis situations. On the other hand, the well-known Chinese intolerance to lactose inhibited the development of a pastoral sector and thus a ready supply of draught-animals, which may explain the occurrence of draw-spades and plough-like instruments pulled by human traction (Leser 1931). In India, Harris (1966) has argued that the very large numbers of animals needed for ploughing with the sharp onset of the monsoon necessitates a large population of generally poorly nourished cattle. He has also suggested that the prohibition on pork in large parts of the Near East stems from the need to devote resources to animals giving secondary benefits of milk or traction.

The spread of the secondary products complex, then, offered new opportunities to populations in many areas of the Old World. Many of the characteristic features of the present-day ethnographic pattern can be traced back to this dispersal.

Changes in agricultural systems and settlement patterns

The changes which the secondary products revolution brought to prehistoric Europe and the Near East are best demonstrated by the major changes in settlement pattern which are characteristic of the fourth and third millennia B.C. Before looking at the archaeological evidence, however, a brief comment on models of early agricultural economies is needed.

It has often been assumed that the earliest agriculture was some form of shifting cultivation, involving a 'slash and burn' system of temporary clearings which were allowed to revert to woodland after a few years of cropping. Such systems are widely known from agriculturally less developed areas in the tropics and in peripheral parts of Europe. Ester Boserup (1965) has suggested a general model of agricultural change in which the fallowing cycle is progressively reduced as population pressure forces intensification of production. Plough agriculture would thus be a threshold of development separating temporary from permanent cultivation.

The archaeological evidence from Europe and the Near East, however, does not support such a scheme, and suggests that it may be misleading to apply directly a model based largely on cultivation in the tropics to the situation in temperate and sub-tropical regions. In these areas, cultivation began by being concentrated in small areas of high-yielding land which did not require a long fallowing cycle. Only later did cultivation spread to poorer soils where longer fallows were required. In temperate Europe, slash and burn systems are characteristic of the poor soils under coniferous forest in Finland and the Carpathians (Balassa 1972) which were among the last to be settled agriculturally. The introduction of the scratch-plough to Europe made it economical to cultivate a wider range of soils than before, and thus to extend the area of cultivation.

In the Near East and Europe, present evidence suggests an early stage of spatially restricted, fairly intensive cultivation of areas of high productivity (Allan 1972), followed by an expansion of the cultivated area either through irrigation or by tackling more extensive areas of less-productive land. The earliest cultivation systems in the Near East seem to have resembled the floodwater-farming of the American southwest (Bryan 1929), and to have concentrated on naturally watered mudflats by lakes, rivers and springs.

Expansion in the sixth millennium took place by small-scale irrigation by water-spreading on alluvial fans, marking the beginning of the Early Chalcolithic pattern (Oates and Oates 1976). Forms of settlement reflect a continuing interest in localised resources, with substantial and long-lived settlements like Jericho and Çatal Hüyük existing at an early stage and tell sites continuing to be characteristic. Despite this stability, however, many of these early agricultural sites continued to obtain their animal protein by hunting or loose herding. Gazelle were still the animal staple at Jericho, while frescoes of cattle at Çatal Hüyük and onagers at Umm Dabagiyeh show that there was little incentive to full domestication in open areas supporting large herds.

In central Europe, it has been usual to see the first Neolithic communities as slash and burn agriculturalists with shifting cultivation and settlement (*Wanderbauerntum*). This idea was supported by tropical and boreal-forest analogies, by the existence of temporary clearance phases in pollen diagrams, and by inference from the fact that the settlements did not form tells. This would conform with expectations on the Boserup (1965) model. However, close study of Early Neolithic settlement, especially in Poland and in the Netherlands and adjacent parts of Germany (Kruk 1973; Modderman 1970), has demonstrated the stability and longevity of such sites. The absence of tell formation relates more to differences in building material than to the character of agriculture, and individual locations were continuously occupied for comparable spans of time, up to 1000 years in some cases.

Moreover, the locations chosen for such sites show a marked preference for high-quality loessic soils, and within these for waterside positions. In Little Poland, where the topography has sufficient relief to show locational preferences with particular clarity, it is clear that these valley-bottom locations offered access only to a relatively narrow area of land along the rivers. The distribution of such sites is conspicuously linear throughout central Europe, and the exploited zone was spatially very restricted although of maximum productivity. Such limited clearances in the primary forest would have offered very limited grazing. Cattle must have been kept only in small numbers and probably partly stall-fed in the characteristic longhouses.

The economy would thus have resembled a garden system not unlike the horticulture or semi-agriculture of the southeastern parts of pre-contact North America. While some comparison may be made with hoe cultivation in the tropics, this temperate hoe cultivation has no true analogy in the Old World, where it represents an extinct economic type which has everywhere been replaced by plough cultivation.

These early agricultural systems were characterised by a highly selective pattern of land use, in which population was concentrated in a few zones of high productivity, and relatively small areas of land were intensively cultivated. (For a detailed case study of the Greek Neolithic see chapter 11 below.) The system allowed the maintenance of large herds only where there were significant tracts of naturally open countryside accessible from the 'oases'

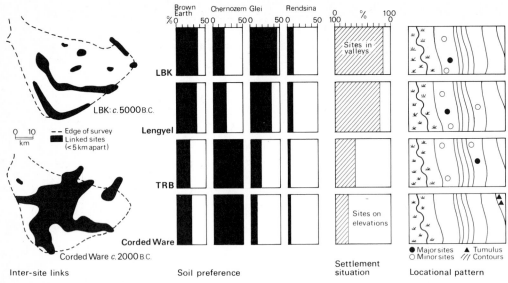

10.18.   The development of settlement in the loess uplands of Little Poland from 5000 to 2000 B.C.: locational preferences and resulting contact networks. Note the similarities between the first and last pairs, and the shift between Lengyel and TRB, with the introduction of the plough (data from Kruk 1973).

of settlement. Grazing was increasingly problematic as such systems penetrated into European forest environments. The lack of large-scale forest clearance is reflected in a toolkit lacking large, wide-bladed axe forms.

The effect of the spread of plough cultivation was to produce major alterations in the structure and distribution of settlement. By contrast to the limited areas along rivers which the earliest settlers opened up in the forest, the wider areas opened up by third-millennium groups would have provided the necessary grazing for the animals needed to till them, and the new system operated on an extensive rather than a localised, intensive basis. The sites chosen for settlement were less long lived, and more rapid turnover of cultivated area would have left sufficient fallow for a more balanced form of mixed agriculture in which the pastoral component was able to grow continuously with the progress of deforestation. The appearance at a similar date from England to Russia of mines and quarries to produce material for effective flint and stone axes for forest clearance is eloquent testimony to this new scale of attack on the woodland (Sherratt 1976).

An increase in the animal component of agriculture which was thus made possible would have introduced for the first time problems of over-wintering numbers of stock, but would also have provided manure in useful quantities. For the first time a balanced crop–livestock husbandry came into being, with different requirements and patterns of land use.

In central and northern Europe, on the loess lands and the North European Plain, functionally undifferentiated villages of longhouses were replaced by the variety of sites which are characteristic of the TRB and related cultures.

These included hamlets, nucleated villages or small ceremonial centres, hill-top sites (*Höhensiedlungen*) and monumental mortuary shrines, often made of the large stones cleared by ox-traction to allow ploughing. Settlement broke out of the tight constraints which had previously produced a highly linear pattern of the type dealt with by Hammond (ch. 8 above), immediately related to watercourses, and spread to a wider range of often dryer and less fertile soils, sometimes abandoning formerly cultivated areas of loess (Fig. 10.18).

The main expansion of hoe agriculture had taken place on medium (silt-grade) soils like loess. The main expansion of agriculture based on the scratch-plough in the later third and second millennia took place on lighter land, especially on sandy soils which were less able to withstand prolonged cultivation. The vast numbers of round-barrows in areas like central Jutland, for instance, bear tribute to the speed with which Late Neolithic and Early Bronze Age farmers effectively reduced large areas of precariously wooded glacial outwash-sands to infertile heathland. The occurrence of Bronze Age tumuli under forest in many parts of Europe show that, once exhausted, such land was often never re-colonised. This cycle of expansion reached its limits in the later second millennium, when heavier types of ard capable of turning a sod were developed as settlement spread to the still little-used heavy clay and alluvial soils (Table 10.2).

The move from a pattern of concentrated and localised agricultural exploitation to a wider use of the terrain for light plough cultivation and extensive grazing had a marked effect on settlement patterns further south. It is a notable feature of the later fourth millennium B.C. that the pattern of tell sites established over the previous two millennia underwent substantial modifications over a wide area, from Transcaucasia to the Balkans. Instead of long-lived tell sites in the valleys near to water, valley-edge or spur sites appear and settlements are found in upland locations. The tell sites which do continue are usually larger, frequently fortified, and with greater intervening distances (Sherratt 1972). The disappearance of large, nucleated Neolithic sites is also evidenced from the Tavoliere of Apulia, where the large ditched settlements have been documented by aerial photography. The shift of population to the plain edge and surrounding mountains in the Bronze Age indicates the relative advantage of a milk-based pastoral economy over intensive low-land cereal cultivation. The model has a wide predictive value throughout the Mediterranean, especially where extensive upland areas suitable for transhumance surround lowland plains.

In the Near East, these processes lay behind the increasingly urbanised character of settlement. Population expanded in the fourth millennium B.C. in areas like the terraces of the Konya Plain or the alluvium of lowland Mesopotamia. In the latter case, the use of the plough was part of the irrigation-based system which made possible a fivefold increase in the number of sites during the Uruk period. Subsequent development involved an increasing concentration of population in a few defended centres. Whether

TABLE 10.2. *Summary of the main phases of economic and social development in Europe north of the Mediterranean, from 6000 B.C. to A.D. 1500*

Period of colonisation	Technology	Animal husbandry	Main soil type occupied (and reasons for relative abandonment)	Settlement type	Social context
Neolithic 6000–3000 B.C.	Hoe cultivation	Exploitation for meat	Intermediate Silt-grade, especially loess (*lessivation –* *formation of* *clay pans*)	Undifferentiated village/hamlet lattice	Egalitarian
Late Neolithic and Bronze Age 3000–1000 B.C.	Light ard cultivation Solid-wheeled cart	Meat, milk, wool and traction	Light Sandy soils (*Podsolisation –* *loss of nutrients* *and formation of* *iron pans*)	Village/hamlet/ funerary monument plus regional centre	Big-man
Late Bronze Age and Iron Age 1000 B.C.–A.D. 1000	Heavy ard cultivation (sometimes with turned sod) Spoke-wheeled cart and chariot Rotary quern	Wool, meat, milk and traction	Heavy Clay soils	Proto-urban/ palace centre/ urban	Chiefdom and state
Medieval A.D. 1000–A.D. 1500	Heavy plough Horse traces and stirrup Wind- and watermills Pivoted axle	Wool, meat, milk and traction	Marginal Clay soils and marginal lands	Urban	State

such defences were erected against potentially hostile pastoralist populations in the drier areas between the irrigated farming areas, or against the other cities of the region, such concentrations of agrarian population were made possible by use of the ox-drawn cart for local transport.

Longer-distance transport links were also made possible by the domestication of equids as transport-animals. The fertile but stoneless and metal-less alluvial basin of the Euphrates and Tigris generated an enormous demand for raw materials. The size of the hinterland over which effective trade links existed has been demonstrated to extend for up to 1000 km in each direction. To the southeast, the discovery of Proto-Elamite tablets at Tepe Yahya demonstrates links from Khuzestan to Kirman as early as the later fourth millennium; while at the same time the site of Habuba el-Kabireh in northern Syria indicates links along the Euphrates to southern Iraq (Lamberg-Karlovsky and Lamberg-Karlovsky 1971; Strommenger 1976). In the third millennium the importance of east-central Anatolia to Mesopotamia is shown both by the military expeditions of Sargon and the Anatolian origin of gold from the royal graves at Ur (Maxwell-Hyslop 1977). By the second millennium the overland trade routes northwards from Assur and westwards from Mari were major distribution lines for bulk supplies both of raw materials like metals and manufactured products like textiles. These would have been impossible without the use of transport-animals.

While the Mesoamerican evidence shows that animal-traction is not a necessary precondition for the development of urban communities, the rarity and much later appearance of towns in the New World suggests that while a variety of settlement systems may eventually reach an urban form, the higher energy of Old World systems greatly accelerated movement along this trajectory.

Pastoralism and linguistic change

The secondary products revolution had large-scale effects in the semi-arid areas of the Old World. The Eurasian steppes in particular saw important changes in the distribution and density of population.

Previously, in the fifth and early fourth millennia, population had been largely concentrated in the valleys of the major rivers flowing into the Black Sea. Agricultural settlements of the Tripole culture were confined to the forest steppe parts, with cattle-keeping, fishing and collecting groups of the Dniepr–Donets culture along the rivers in the true steppes.

With the arrival of the cart and traction complex and the spread of the horse, both groups began to make a greater use of the drier interfluves; and sheep became the predominant domestic animal. The effect of new transport possibilities and probably also milking was to create on the steppes an economy with sufficient mobility to be able to exploit effectively the previously neglected zone stretching eastwards into central Asia; though at this stage such pastoralism was probably 'transhumant' rather than 'nomadic'.

This set of economic changes precipitated the formation of a new cultural group on the basis of the previous riverine groups and under strong technological influence from the Caucasus. A characteristic of this group was the erection of burial mounds covering graves in increasingly elaborate pits and wood-lined chambers – the Pit-grave, Catacomb-grave and Timber-grave phases of expanding steppe culture. These herding and farming groups penetrated eastwards along the Eurasian steppe belt as far as the Volga–Ural interfluve in the early third millennium, and (using spoke-wheeled vehicles) as far as the Altai in the early second.

Some backwash of this expansion was also felt in Europe. Wool sheep and the horse, along with tumuli and alloy metallurgy, spread westwards from 3000 onwards and spoke-wheeled vehicles followed at the end of the third millennium. The opening up of the European forests, and especially the creation of large areas of heathland on sandy soils, allowed a wider network of contacts and facilitated the penetration of steppe elements into the temperate forest area.

It is instructive to compare the effects of horses and wheeled vehicles to the spread of imported Spanish horses among the tribes in the Plains area of north America (Roe 1955). As well as tempting a variety of formerly settled riverine groups to colonise the prairies and create the classic Plains Indian cultures of popular image, it also gave the opportunity for mounted Athebascan sheep-herders – like the Navajo – to spread over a thousand kilometres from the home area of their language group.

The spread of settlement in the semi-arid corridors of the Old World had important implications for linguistic distribution there. The expansion of population in east Europe and central Asia provided the opportunity for the spread and differentiation of a previously localised language group which now occupies a major area of Eurasia. The dispersal of these Indo-European languages was paralleled by the similar expansion and differentiation of the Semito-Hamitic group in the Near East and north Africa.

Philologists have long contended that the extensive resemblances in form and vocabulary between geographically removed languages like Latin and Sanskrit imply a common ancestral *Ursprache* which differentiated after dispersal: and that moreover since such resemblances rapidly decay, it must have taken place relatively recently. An often quoted estimate for such a dispersal (Robins 1964) is 3000 B.C. – to some extent a circular argument from the archaeology, but consistent with observed rates of change (Swadesh 1968). The eastward movements of populations onto the steppes in the third millennium B.C. linked east Europe with the Pontic and Trans-Caspian regions as far as the Tarim Basin and the Iranian Plateau, and there seems no doubt that it was such relatively rapid movements in the semi-arid zone which gave Indo-European its geographical range. This is also consistent with the first appearance of specifically Indo-Iranian names in northern Syria and Mesopotamia in the second millennium B.C.

The extent to which Indo-European languages were already present in the forested parts of Europe is uncertain. Nevertheless there are good philological grounds for inferring some westwards spread of Indo-European languages in the second millennium B.C., and this could well have taken place in the context of the changes in settlement and economy documented in a previous section.

Social structure

Besides the large-scale effects of the secondary products revolution in creating new forms of subsistence economy, its effects on the texture of social relations was equally important. By its major alterations in the allocation of subsistence roles between the sexes it created new social structures and patterns of organisation, and by giving a new importance to the transmission of land it necessitated new mechanisms of inheritance.

The arguments for associations of this kind are inevitably based on cross-cultural surveys, and especially the *Area Files* of the Institute of Human Relations and the *Ethnographic Atlas* (Murdock 1967) abstracted from them. Interpretations of such material in historical terms is especially dangerous: but the archaeological perspective given above on the spread of features such as the plough allows a time dimension to be fitted to the recurrent patterns of association which have become clear from statistical analysis of this data. Such considerations allow a sketch of the kinds of society which may have been characteristic of temperate hoe-based horticulture.

In common with some of the systems based on the intensive collecting of localised subsistence products on a sedentary basis, agriculture involved the transmission of property consisting of facilities such as fields and houses. It is therefore usually associated with continuing kin-based corporations such as lineages, often with a specifically unilineal mode of inheritance (Harner 1970). The mode of inheritance is strongly influenced by patterns of residence: in an uxorilocal system, where the husband joins the wife's community on marriage, transmission in likely to follow the female line. Residence systems, in turn, reflect the relative importance of the sexes in subsistence pursuits. In simple hoe agriculture, the major subsistence contribution comes from female labour in sowing, weeding and harvesting. There have been some suggestions that a clear worldwide association occurs between simple hoe-based agricultural economies and matrilineal inheritance, and that this asociation would be even stronger were it not for the effect of recent influences (Keesing 1975). Societies based on matrilineal lineages are thus likely to have been typical of early agricultural communities in the Old World. This pattern is characteristic of aboriginal societies in the woodlands of the American southeast which have been identified as the closest parallels to pre-plough agriculturalists in Europe (Driver 1961).

Both plough agriculture and pastoralism, by contrast, show a strong association with male dominance in subsistence activities, virilocal residence, and patrilineal descent. This pattern is often reinforced by the kinds of warfare which are common when large quantities of livestock are present. On a world sample, two-thirds of plough agriculturalists and two-thirds of pastoralists have purely patrilineal inheritance. Moreover such societies are likely to evolve beyond the lineage mode of production, to be composed of larger non-localised clans or to become stratified as scarcity of land becomes increasingly important.

Changes in the sexual allocation of tasks affected non-agricultural production. The decline of the female role in agriculture released labour from the fields to the home, making possible an expansion in spinning, weaving and textile production. This increase in scale made economical the use of more elaborate forms of loom. Archaeologically, traces of weaving equipment become much more prominent in the third millennium (e.g., Trump 1960).

Besides reallocating productive roles between the sexes, plough agriculture introduced new principles to the transmission of property. Greater flexibility of land use and the ability to use wider holdings gave a new importance to the acquisition and devolution of land. The advantages of 'marrying out' came to be balanced by the advantages of keeping land within the descent group, retaining resources within the productive unit. Marriage would thus tend to become an important move in the determination of patterns of land-holding, and a focus of interest to the descent group as a whole (Goody 1969). Such a concern leads to arranged marriages in which women, as carriers of property, have to be appropriately matched to maintain the status of the family. These features are likely to be more pronounced the greater the scarcity of land and the more intensive its use.

Goody (1976) has recently contrasted the kinds of property transmission characteristic of plough-less Africa with those commonly found among the plough-based agriculturalists of Eurasia. He characterises the contrast as the difference between homogeneous devolution, where property is transmitted between members of the same sex and there is no community of property on marriage, and diverging devolution, where children of both sexes inherit and marriage establishes a joint fund. In the former case, typical of African hoe cultivators, property reverts to the lineage of a deceased person, and is not passed to his or her offspring: in the latter, typical of Eurasian plough cultivation, marriage produces successive recombinations of holdings in each generation. Diverging devolution is characteristic of societies where land forms a major heritable commodity, and is associated with a particular emphasis on marriage and control over the choice of mate.

In examining a worldwide sample from the *Ethnographic Atlas* (Murdock 1967), Goody found diverging devolution to be characteristic of over half of the societies of Eurasia, including the most populous, but to occur in only a twentieth of the African examples; and moreover that the earliest Eurasian law codes show this contrast to reach back to the second millennium B.C. Features which showed a high correlation with diverging devolution were advanced and plough agriculture, male farming, in-marriage, monogamy, prohibited pre-marital sex, and kinship terminologies separating siblings from cousins. Such features are often associated with stratified and state societies. Goody (1976, p. 25) suggests that the increase in production made possible by the plough had major implications for interpersonal relations: 'For differentiation arose even at village level and the scene was set for the development of relationships such as lord and serf, landlord and tenant, which exist in Eurasia but not in Africa.'

In so far as forms of society are determined by the organisation required for work and the types of property which are passed between generations, we may apply these insights to the historic situation in Eurasia. The secondary products revolution produced an economy dominated by men, who played a dominant role in handling large livestock either as herds or in ploughing. Women became increasingly relegated to the domestic sphere. Where the absolute amount of cultivable land was relatively restricted, as in the Near East and the Mediterranean, ownership of land became increasingly subject to competition. Differences in access to land became the basis of growing inequalities, while the transmission and coalition of property became a major preoccupation of the landed classes.

In inland Europe, the archaeological evidence indicates that land was still relatively plentiful as the Bronze Age farmers continued to clear primary forest on somewhat less fertile soils. These features were probably not precipitated, therefore, until the end of the second millennium when organised field systems were laid out, heavier forms of plough were developed, and extensive indications of status differences appeared. Second-millennium Europe may thus have exemplified a second extinct economy of the temperate zone – an extensive light-plough cultivation with a predominantly male role in agriculture but without the highly differentiated social order where groups struggled to maintain their status by the vertical transmission of property. The 'rich' graves with prestige items at this time probably represent a 'big-man' system rather than true chiefdoms (Sahlins 1963). Essentially a transient type, such societies have not survived to reach the pages of the *Ethnographic Atlas* (Murdock 1967); only the extreme contrast between tropical matrilineal shifting hoe cultivators with homogeneous devolution, and the more northerly patrilineal intensive plough cultivators with stratified societies and diverging devolution, suggests the possibility of structurally intermediate ancestral forms.

CONCLUSION

Eduard Hahn's perceptive remarks quoted at the beginning of this paper still stand as a fundamental observation about the origins of western society. The progress of archaeological research, however, has provided a time-depth which allows a further definition of the processes involved. As the beginnings of agriculture and domestication have been traced further back into the post-glacial period, so the major developments of the fourth and third millennia B.C. have emerged as a second burst of economic innovation with far-reaching consequences.

The spread of the plough was arguably the most important development in Old World prehistory after the adoption of cereal cultivation itself. It firmly tied together the arable and pastoral sectors of husbandry in an interdependent system, and it fundamentally affected the character of settlement and the structure of society. Use of the plough was only part of a wider set of changes, however, which marked a new phase in man–animal relationships, involving larger numbers of domestic animals, the domestication of new species, and new uses for long-domesticated ones.

The use of animals for traction purposes seems to have begun in Mesopotamia, and involved first the familiar ox and then the onager, spreading to include the Bactrian camel in the lands east of the Zagros. Riding was developed on the steppe-plains north of the Caucasus and the Black Sea, as the horse was domesticated. Pack-transport began in the lands around the head of the Red Sea with the domestication of the ass, and then of the dromedary. The production of wool was probably a development in the sheep populations of the Taurus–Zagros arc. These innovations spread and interacted, some animals changing role or adding new ones. Basic to all of them was probably the beginning of milking, giving a continuously available form of animal food and making economical the keeping of large numbers of animals which could be put to a variety of uses.

The focus of all these developments was the Near East, in different parts of which the various elements emerged and spread. The key to this productivity lay in large part in the diversity of adjacent environments which this area offers. The arid belt of the Old World crosses north Africa and swings northeast into central Asia: but it is interrupted in its course by the great chain of Tertiary fold-mountains running from the Alps to the Himalayas, which catch the rain-bearing winds of winter. This intersection of desert, mountain and sea provides an intimate mixture of zones with different stresses and opportunities, maximising the possibilities of innovation and providing a theatre in which interaction and cross-fertilisation can take place.

The impact of the secondary products revolution was felt principally in that part of the agricultural zone of the Old World characterised by cereal crops, rather than the tropical part where root-crops were cultivated. Its innovations spread rapidly along the arid corridors and penetrated into more temperate regions. The axis of Old World development from Europe to India came into being as a result. These influences penetrated only slowly and incompletely into east Asia. There an alternative system of protein capture based on fish (especially in rice-paddies) and on the pig was already supporting a relatively dense population, and the expanded pastoral sector which the secondary products revolution required could not easily be brought about. For this reason, the civilisation of China was in many respects comparable to those civilisations of the New World, where domestic animals played a minor role.

Beyond the zone of cultivation, the practice of milking allowed the infilling of arid areas by animal-based groups, and produced a secondary impact on the hunting peoples of the northern forests. The milking of reindeer by Lapp populations is a notable example. In Africa, milking may have spread relatively early from its southwest Asian focus, but pastoralism was imposed on existing systems of tropical hoe cultivation. It did not achieve the organic linkage with cultivation that was characteristic of Eurasia, and animals were not used as sources of energy.

The effects of the secondary products revolution thus spread widely both to north and south of the main axis, affecting much of the Old World. Many of the cultures recorded ethnographically therefore were, like the historical societies of Eurasia, products of the second half of the post-glacial period.

As David Clarke showed in 'Mesolithic Europe: the economic basis' (1976), archaeological data are most effectively used in the context of wider ethnographic comparison; not by taking recent groups as direct analogies of prehistoric ones, but by analysing both in the perspective of evolutionary change. The societies which flourished in temperate and sub-tropical Eurasia in the Early Holocene form an important extinct phylum of human culture, which cannot be directly compared to any surviving groups. Their character was completely altered by the secondary products revolution, which created many of the basic features of the modern world.

ACKNOWLEDGEMENTS

This paper would not have been possible without the pervasive influence of David Clarke. Many of its ideas have their roots in his suggestions and remarks. His enthusiasm and criticism have been sadly missed in writing it.

NOTES

1 'When milk was drunk and the ox yoked to the plough, all the essential conditions were present for our Asiatic–European culture' (Hahn 1896, p. 75).
2 All dates quoted as B.C. are dendrologically calibrated radiocarbon dates, calculated from the MASCA scale. Dates quoted as b.c. (usually in brackets after each B.C. date) represent the original radiocarbon determinations.

REFERENCES

Allan, W. (1972). 'Ecology, techniques and settlement patterns' in P. J. Ucko and G. W. Dimbleby (eds.) *Man, Settlement and Urbanism*, Duckworth

Amoroso, E. C. and Jewell, P. A. (1963). 'The exploitation of the milk-ejection reflex by primitive peoples' in A. E. Mourant and F. E. Zeuner *Man and Cattle* (Royal Anthropological Institute Occasional Paper No. 18), R.A.I.

Bakker, J. A., Vogel, J. C. and Wiślański, T. (1969). 'TRB and other C14 dates from Poland (Part A)', *Helinium* 9: 3–27

Balassa, I., ed. (1972). *Getreidebau in Ost- und Mitteleuropa*, Akademiai Kiado

Banner, J. (1956). *Die Peceler Kultur*, Akademiai Kiado

Barth, F. (1964). *Nomads of South Persia*, Allen and Unwin

(ed.) (1969). *Ethnic Groups and Boundaries*, Allen and Unwin

van Bath, B. H. S. (1963). *The Agrarian History of Western Europe AD 500–1850*, Arnold

Battaglia, R. (1943). 'La palafitta del Lago di Ledro nel Trentino', *Memorie del Museo Civico di Storia Naturale della Venezia Tridentina* 7

Bayless, T. M. and Rosenzweig, N. S. (1966). 'A radical difference in incidence of lactase deficiency', *Journal of the American Medical Association* 197: 968–72

Behrens, H. (1964). *Die neolithisch-frühmetallzeitlichen Tierskelettfunde der Alten Welt*, Veröffentlichungen des Landesmuseums für Vorgeschichte in Halle

Bibikova, V. I. (1969). 'Do istorii domesticatsii konya na pivdennomu skhodi Evropi', *Arkheologiya* (Kiev) 22: 55–67

Bökönyi, S. (1974). *History of Domestic Mammals in Central and Eastern Europe*, Akademiai Kiado

Boessneck, J. (1956). 'Tierknochen aus spätneolithischen Siedlungen Bayerns', *Studien an vor- und frühgeschichtlichen Tierresten Bayerns* 1

Bona, I. (1960). 'Clay models of Bronze Age wagons and wheels in the Middle Danube Basin', *Acta Archaeologica Hungarica* 12: 83–111

Boserup, E. (1965). *The Conditions of Agricultural Growth*, Allen and Unwin

Bryan, K. (1929). 'Floodwater farming', *Geographical Review* 19: 444–56

Bulliet, R. W. (1975). *The Camel and the Wheel*, Harvard University Press

Cherednichenko, N. N. (1976). 'Kolesnitsi Evrasii epokhi pozdnei bronzi' in *Eneolit i Bronzovi Vek Ukraini*, Institute of Archaeology, Kiev

Christiansen-Weniger, F. (1967). 'Die anatolischen Säpflüge und ihre Vorgänger im Zweistromland', *Archaeologischer Anzeiger* 2: 151–62

Clark, C. and Haswell, M. (1964). *The Economics of Subsistence Agriculture*, Macmillan

Clark, J. D. (1976). 'The domestication process in sub-Saharan Africa with special reference to Ethiopia', paper presented to the IXth U.I.S.P.P. Congress, Nice

Clarke, D. L. (1968). *Analytical Archaeology*, Methuen

(1976). 'Mesolithic Europe: the economic basis' in G. Sieveking, I. Longworth and K. Wilson (eds.) *Problems in Economic and Social Archaeology*, Duckworth

Cranstone, B. (1969). 'Animal husbandry: the evidence from ethnography' in P. J. Ucko and G. W. Dimbleby (eds.) *The Domestication and Exploitation of Plants and Animals*, Duckworth

Driver, H. E. (1961). *Indians of North America*, Chicago University Press

Ducos, P. (1969). 'Methodology and results of the study of the earliest domesticated animals in the Near East (Palestine)' in P. J. Ucko and G. W. Dimbleby (eds.) *The Domestication and Exploitation of Plants and Animals*, Duckworth

(1973). 'Sur quelques problèmes posés par l'étude des premiers élevages en Asia du sud-ouest' in J. Matolcsi (ed.) *Domestikationsforschung und Geschichte der Haustiere*, Akademiai Kiado

Dyson-Hudson, R. and Dyson-Hudson, N. (1969). 'Subsistence herding in Uganda', *Scientific American* 220: 76–89

Ebbesen, K. and Brinch-Petersen, E. (1973). 'Fuglebaeksbanken: en jaettestue paa Stevns', *Aarbøger for Nordisk Oldkyndighed og Historie* 1973: 73–106

Evans, A. (1935). *The Palace of Minos at Knossos*, Macmillan

Falkenstein, A. (1936). *Archaische Texte aus Uruk*, Ausgrabungen der Deutschen Forschungsgemeinschaft in Uruk-Warka

Fowler, P. and Evans, J. (1967). 'Plough-marks, lynchets and early fields', *Antiquity* 41: 289–94

Galkin, L. L. (1975). 'Odnoiz drevneishikh prakticheskikh prisposoblenii skoto-vodov', *Sovietskaya Arkheologiya* 1975 (3): 186–92

Gandert, O-F. (1964). 'Zur Frage der Rinderanschirrung im Neolithikum', *Jahrbuch des Römisch-Germanischen Zentralmuseums* 11: 34–56

Glob, P. V. (1951). *Ard og Plov i Nordens Oldtid*, Jysk Arkaeologisk Selskab

Goody, J. (1969). 'Inheritance, property and marriage in Africa and Eurasia', *Sociology* 3, 55–76

(1976). *Production and Reproduction*, Cambridge University Press

Hahn, E. (1896). *Die Haustiere und ihre Beziehungen zur Wirtschaft des Menschen*, Duncker and Humblot

Hald, M. (1950). *Olddanske Tekstiler*, Kongelige Nordiske-Oldskriftselskab

Harner, M. (1970). 'Population pressure and the social evolution of agriculturalists', *Southwestern Journal of Anthropology* 26: 67–86

Harris, M. (1966). 'The cultural ecology of India's sacred cattle', *Current Anthropology* 7: 51–9

Hartmann, F. (1923). *L'Agriculture dans l'ancienne Egypte*, Libraries-Imprimeries Réunies

Higham, C. and Message, M. A. (1969). 'An assessment of a prehistoric technique of bovine husbandry' in D. Brothwell and E. S. Higgs *Science in Archaeology*, Thomas and Hudson

Kalicz, N. (1963). *Die Badener (Peceler) Kultur und Anatolien*, Akademiai Kiado

(1976). 'Ein neues kupferzeitliches Wagenmodell aus der Umgebung von Budapest', *Festschrift für Richard Pittioni zum siebzigen Geburtstag*, Deuticke

Keesing, R. M. (1975). *Kin Groups and Social Structure*, Holt Reinhart Winston

Killen, J. T. (1964). 'The wool industry of Crete in the Late Bronze Age', *Annual of the British School of Archaeology at Athens* 59: 1–15

Kisban, E. (1969). 'Die historische Bedeutung des Joghurts in den Milchverarbeitungssystemen Südosteuropas' in L. Földes (ed.) *Viehwirtschaft und Hirtenkultur*, Akademiai Kiado

Klebs, L. (1915). *Die Reliefs des alten Reiches*, Abhandlungen der Heidelberger Akademie der Wissenschaften

Korek, J. (1951). 'Ein Gräberfeld der Badener Kultur bei Alsónémedi', *Acta Archaeologica Hungarica* 1: 35–91

Kothe, H. (1953). 'Völkerkundliches zur Frage der Neolithischen Anbauformen', *Archaeologisch-Ethnographische Forschungen* 1: 28–73

Kraus, F. R. (1966). *Staatliche Viehhaltung im altbabylonischen Lande Larsa*, Mededelingen der Koninklijke Nederlandse Akademie van Wetenschappen

Kretchmer, N. (1972). 'Lactose and lactase', *Scientific American* 227: 70–9

Kruk, J. (1973). *Studia Osadnicze nad Neolitem Wyżyn Lessowych*, Ossolineum

Kuzmina, E. E. (1974). 'Kolesnii transport i problema etnicheskoi i sotsialnoi istorii drevnego naseleniya Juzhnorusskikh Stepei', *Vestnik Drevnei Istorii* 4: 68–87

Kyle, R. (1972). 'Will the antelope recapture Africa?', *New Scientist* 23 March 1972

Lamberg-Karlovsky, C. and Lamberg-Karlovsky, M. (1971). 'An early city in Iran', *Scientific American* June 1971

Leser, P. (1931). *Entstehung und Verbreitung des Pfluges*, Aschendorff

Lotka, A. J. (1956). *Elements of Mathematical Biology*, Dover

Maxwell-Hyslop, R. (1977). 'Sources of Sumerian gold', *Iraq* 39: 83–6

McCracken, R. D. (1971). 'Lactase deficiency: an example of dietary evolution', *Current Anthropology* 12: 479–517

Milisauskas, S. and Kruk, J. (1978). 'Bronocice: a Neolithic settlement in southeastern Poland', *Archaeology* 31: 44–52

Modderman, P. J. R. (1970). *Linearbandkeramik aus Elsloo und Stein*, Nederlandse Oudheden

Moorey, P. R. S. (1968). 'The earliest Near Eastern spoked wheels and their chronology', *Proceedings of the Prehistoric Society* 34: 430–2

(1970). 'Pictorial evidence for the history of horse-riding in Iraq before the Kassite period', *Iraq* 32: 36–50

Müller-Beck, H. (1965). *Burgäschisee-Süd Teil 5, Holzgeräte und Holzbearbeitung*, Acta Bernesia

Müller-Wille, M. (1965). *Eisenzeitliche Fluren in den festländischen Nordseegebieten*, Landeskundliche Karten und Hefte der Geographischen Kommission für Westfalen

Murdock, G. P. (1967). *Ethnographic Atlas*, Pittsburgh University Press

Murray, J. (1970). *The First European Agriculture*, Edinburgh University Press

Narr, K. J. (1962). 'Frühe Pflüge', *Mitteilungen der Anthropologischen Gesellschaft in Wien* 92: 221

Němejcová-Pavúková, V. (1973). 'Zu Ursprung und Chronologie der Boleraz-Gruppe' in B. Chrpovsky (ed.) *Symposium über die Entstehung der Badener Kultur*, Slovak Academy of Sciences Press

Nobis, G. (1971). *Vom Wildpferd zum Hauspferd*, Fundamenta

Oates, D. and Oates, J. (1976). 'Early irrigation agriculture in Mesopotamia' in G. Sieveking, I. Longworth and K. Wilson (eds.) *Problems in Economic and Social Archaeology*, Duckworth

Ørsnes, M. (1956). 'Om en Jaettestues konstruktion og bruk', *Aarbøger for Nordisk Oldkyndighed og Historie* 221–34

Payne, S. (1973). 'Kill-off patterns in sheep and goats: the mandibles from Aşvan Kale', *Anatolian Studies* 23: 281–303

Piggott, S. (1968). 'The earliest wheeled vehicles and the Caucasian evidence', *Proceedings of the Prehistoric Society* 34: 266–318

Renfrew, C. (1972). *The Emergence of Civilization*, Methuen

Robins, R. H. (1964). *General Linguistics: an introductory survey*, Longmans

Roe, F. G. (1955). *The Indian and the Horse*, University of Oklahoma Press

Rothenberg, B. (1970). 'An archaeological survey of south Sinai', *Palestine Exploration Quarterly* 4–29

Ryder, M. L. (1969). 'Changes in the fleece of sheep following domestication' in P. J. Ucko and G. W. Dimbleby (eds.) *The Domestication and Exploitation of Plants and Animals*, Duckworth

Sahlins, M. D. (1963). 'Poor man, rich man, big man, chief: political types in Melanesia and Polynesia', *Comparative Studies in Society and History* 5: 285–303

Salonen, A. (1968). 'Agricultura Mesopotamica', *Annales Academiae Scientiarum Fennicae*, Series B, 149

Scheil, V. (1923). 'Textes de compatabilité proto-Elamites', *Memoires de la Delegation en Perse* 17

Sherratt, A. G. (1972). 'Socio-economic and demographic models' in D. L. Clarke (ed.) *Models in Archaeology*, Methuen

(1973). 'The explanation of change in European prehistory' in A. C. Renfrew (ed.) *The Explanation of Cultural Change*, Duckworth

(1976). 'Resources, technology and trade' in G. Sieveking, I. Longworth and K. Wilson (eds.) *Problems in Economic and Social Archaeology*, Duckworth

Simoons, F. J. (1969). 'Primary adult lactose intolerance and the milking habit: a problem in biological and cultural interrelations (1)', *American Journal of Digestive Diseases* 14: 819–36

(1970). 'Primary adult lactose intolerance and the milking habit: a problem in biological and cultural relations (2)', *American Journal of Digestive Diseases* 15: 695–710

(1971). 'The antiquity of dairying in Asia and Africa', *Geographical Review* 61: 431–9

Skaarup, J. (1975). *Stengade : ein langeländischer Wohnplatz mit Hausresten aus der frühneolithischen Zeit*, Meddelelser fra Langelands Museum

Smith, P. E. L. and Young, T. C. (1972). 'The evolution of early agriculture and culture in Greater Mesopotamia: a trial model' in B. Spooner (ed.) *Population Growth : Anthropological Implications*, M.I.T. Press

Šramko, B. A. (1971). 'Der Hakenpflug der Bronzezeit in der Ukraine', *Tools and Tillage I* 4: 223–4

Steensberg, A. (1971). 'Drill-sowing and threshing in southern India', *Tools and Tillage I* 1: 241–56

Strommenger, E. (1976). 'Habuba Kabira-Süd: Erforschung einer Stadt am Syrischen Euphrat', *Archaeologisches Korrespondenzblatt* 6: 97–102

Swadesh, M. (1968). 'Glotto-chronology' in M. Fried (ed.) *Readings in Anthropology*, Crowell

Telegin D. I. (1971). 'Über einen der ältesten Pferdezuchtherde in Europa', *Rapports et Communications de l'URSS VIII Congres Internat. Sci. Prehist. et Protohist*, Moscow

Tihelka, K. (1954). 'Nejstarší hliněně napodobeniny čtyřramenných kol na území ČSR', *Památky Archeologické* 45: 219–24

Trump, D. (1960). 'Pottery anchors', *Antiquity* 34: 295

Uenze, O. (1958). 'Neue Zeichensteine aus dem Kammergrab von Züschen' in W. Krämer (ed.) *Neue Ausgrabungen in Deutschland*, Römisch-Germanische Kommission des Deutschen Archaeologischen Instituts

Vizdal, I. (1972). 'Erste bildliche Darstellung eines zweirädigen Wagens vom Ende der mittleren Bronzezeit in der Slowakei', *Slovenska Archaeologia* 20: 233

Vogt, E. (1937). *Geflechte und Gewebe der Steinzeit*, Monographien zur Ur- und Frühgeschichte der Schweiz

van der Waals, J. D. (1964). *Prehistoric Disc-Wheels in the Netherlands*, Wolters

Warriner, D. (1939). *Economics of Peasant Farming*, Oxford University Press

van Wijngaarden-Bakker, L. H. (1975). 'Horses in the Dutch Neolithic' in A. Clason (ed.) *Archaeozoological Studies*, Elsevier/North-Holland

Wiślanski, T. (1970). *The Neolithic in Poland*, Ossolineum

Zeuner, F. E. (1963). *History of Domesticated Animals*, Hutchinson

Zohary, D. and Spiegel-Roy, P. (1975). 'Beginnings of fruit-growing in the Old World', *Science* 187: 319–27

11

Counting sheep in Neolithic and Bronze Age Greece

PAUL HALSTEAD

By the seventh millennium B.C.,[1] small farming communities were established in the lowlands of mainland Greece and on the large island of Crete. These early farmers cultivated cereals and pulses and kept cows, pigs, sheep and goats. Exchange between communities was sufficiently developed for obsidian from the island of Melos to be widely distributed, but the volume of goods circulating was probably very small, given the low level of transport technology and socioeconomic organisation of the time. As yet there is no evidence that social status and authority were determined by anything other than age, sex and personal qualities. During the succeeding 6000 years of the Neolithic and Bronze Age, there was a substantial rise in population, settlement spread to areas which were not initially favoured (e.g., the Cyclades and the hills of Crete, Fig. 11.1) and, in many areas, larger concentrations of population emerged. Increasing social differentiation and proliferation of the range and quantity of goods circulating within and between communities culminated in the development of the Minoan and Mycenaean civilisations. For these complex societies we have documentary as well as archaeological evidence of an institutionalised palatial elite, which organised the redistribution of agricultural produce, raw materials and manufactured goods around fairly sizeable territories and which engaged in some long-distance trade.

The decipherment of the Linear B script of the Mycenaean palace archives has naturally stimulated interest in the economic base of these palatial civilisations (Finley 1957), while archaeologists have suggested that economic developments over the preceding five millennia may have contributed to their emergence. For example, Renfrew (1972) has stressed the role of trade in this emergence. He also argued that, during the later Neolithic, increasing diversification in subsistence economy (especially the addition of the olive and vine to the Neolithic combination of cereals and pulses) encouraged exchange between individuals and communities with particular access to different resources. A broader subsistence base will also have allowed a larger population to be supported (*ibid.*). Sherratt (1973) sees the limited extent of good arable land in the southern Aegean as one reason for the development of both olive cultivation and the seasonal exploitation of sea-fishing and upland grazing areas. As well as creating further economic diversity, these

307

11.1. Map of Greece and the Aegean, showing regions mentioned in the text. Land above 300 m is shaded.

seasonal activities will have promoted contact between the many scattered communities which were eventually integrated within the Bronze Age civilisations (Sherratt 1976; Bintliff 1977a).

Evaluation of these hypotheses, however, is hindered by the paucity and poor quality of the available data, and recent discussion of recovery techniques and sampling procedures (Payne 1972; Cherry 1977, p. 60) recognises this problem. Perhaps a more fundamental difficulty, which no amount of sieving or surveying can rectify, is the fact that every one of the relevant classes of evidence offers only a partial record, and we do not know what fraction of the original whole we are seeing. For instance, fish bones are much less likely to survive in the ground than mammal bones, while some plant species are far more likely than others to be found carbonised on a settlement or to be represented in a pollen core. Likewise, the Mycenaean archives never tell us if they were recording virtually all economic activity in each 'kingdom' or whether only a small fraction of all production and transactions came under the scrutiny of the palaces. As a result, we do not know the relative importance of field crops and tree crops, of plant foods and animal foods or of durable and perishable exchange items. As for assessing the relationship between subsistence and exchange economy, we are largely reduced to guesswork in deciding whether Bronze Age redistribution, manufacturing and trade just provided a small elite with the luxuries which served as their badge of office or whether essential items were in regular circulation on a significant scale.

Any attempt to reconstruct economy and, even more so, any study of the interaction between economy and environment (see Parkington, ch. 12 below), demography or social organisation requires the interplay of many different classes of evidence which must, where possible, be quantified in order to be comparable. Renfrew (1972, 1977) adopted this approach in assessing the likely population size and territorial extent of Minoan and Mycenaean states and then considering the level of social, political and economic organisation appropriate in that context. In Messenia (McDonald and Rapp 1972) and Crete (Dewolf *et al.* 1963; Bintliff 1977a), comparisons have been made between archaeological estimates of the size of Bronze Age population in particular areas and the potential carrying capacity of those areas under traditional or historical systems of land use.

This essay attempts to contribute to the study of economy in Neolithic and Bronze Age Greece in two different ways. It is assumed that Neolithic communities were virtually self-sufficient in procuring the largest and most regular of their subsistence requirements – food. For the Bronze Age, by contrast, where we are often dealing with levels of organisation and technology quite capable of moving large amounts of subsistence or luxury goods, assessment of the relative levels of self-sufficiency and exchange is taken to be one of the major problems confronting us.

Accordingly, our first objective is to throw some light on the nature and scale of land use around a 'typical' Neolithic community, and so to provide a framework within which the diverse sources of information on Neolithic subsistence can be integrated. Available evidence for the size of Neolithic communities is used to estimate the scale on which foodstuffs had to be produced. Next, the likely importance in this respect of different animal and plant species is assessed in the light of the limitations placed upon their exploitation by their own physiology and ethology and by their environment.

In this context, the fragmentary and biassed record of bone and seed samples is finally used to formulate a model of Neolithic subsistence.

Clearly there are grave dangers in generalising about land use and subsistence economy in a country of such environmental heterogeneity as Greece and, partly for this reason, the scope of this study has deliberately been restricted. Thus the term 'land use' is taken literally and consideration is not given to aquatic resources, the potential of which obviously depends not only on regional variations in marine and freshwater ecology but also on the distance of each settlement from the nearest stretch of water.[2] Furthermore, discussion of the exploitation of terrestrial resources concentrates, though not exclusively, on the lowland arable areas where population was densest and settlement most stable and where, in the southern Aegean, the Bronze Age palace centres arose.

Similar generalisations about land use during the Bronze Age face some additional problems. Bronze Age settlements often display far greater variability of internal organisation, which obscures the status of bone and seed samples (cf. Halstead, Hodder and Jones 1978). Moreover, the Bronze Age probably saw greater diversity of economy, both between regions and, within any one region, between settlements of different size and rank. Finally, we return to the problem of the growth of exchange and the breakdown of local self-sufficiency. The last part of this essay addresses itself, therefore, rather tentatively, to the likely effects on Bronze Age land use of factors such as human alteration of the environment, the availability of new domesticates and the emergence of larger aggregates of population. Some suggestions are then made about ways in which we might investigate the relationship between exchange and self-sufficiency in the Late Bronze Age with the sort of data available to us.

ENVIRONMENT

Greece is a mountainous country with fairly limited expanses of lowland. By and large, the lowlands enjoy a mild, wet winter climate and a hot, dry summer. Plant growth tends, therefore, to be restricted more by summer aridity than by winter cold. In the uplands, by contrast, harsh winters and cool summers encourage plant growth in the summer months and, traditionally, the seasonally complementary nature of these two altitude zones has led to large flocks of sheep and goats migrating between winter grazing areas in the lowlands and summer pasture in the uplands. Overall, rainfall decreases from west to east and temperature from south to north, so that climate is most favourable for plant growth all the year round in western Greece, while the southeast experiences the driest summers and the northeast the coldest winters.

The climate of Greece has never been static but, as yet, there is no convincing evidence for any major changes in the period under review (cf.

Bintliff 1977a, p. 51). Geomorphological change is more apparent and Bintliff has shown that most of the heavy valley alluvium now used for irrigation agriculture was not available until recently. On the other hand, the lighter arable soils which were available must have been considerably better, both in structure and in mineral and organic content, at the start of the seventh millennium B.C. than after 9000 years of tillage and cropping.

The aspect of environment which has, perhaps, been subject to the greatest change is vegetation. Recent palynological research (summarised in Bintliff 1977a, pp. 66–83) has shown that most of the country was fairly well wooded at the start of the Neolithic. In the southeast mainland, southern Aegean islands and eastern Crete, vegetation was probably more open, but still considerably more wooded than today (Turrill 1929, p. 192; Payne 1975, p. 122; Bintliff 1977a, pp. 72–83). The process of lowland deforestation is obscured by the absence of polynological evidence from the most arid areas and by the difficulty of distinguishing between local and regional factors in pollen cores. However, lowland clearance was evidently well advanced by the third millennium B.C. in south Greece while, in the north, open country may still have been patchy in the Late Bronze Age. Extensive upland clearance seems to have been a feature of the fairly recent past.

Although the total plant biomass of Greece will have been far greater prior to deforestation, the proportion effectively available to man as food will have been considerably smaller. It will be argued below that the more useful nut and fruit trees did not initially form a major part of the lowland arboreal community, while the ground flora species whose seeds, bulbs, shoots or leaves can be eaten by man would have occurred in largest numbers in places where thin soils, steep topography or aridity conspired to prevent tree growth. Afforestation will also have hindered man's indirect exploitation of the plant community through the ruminants attested on excavated settlements (cow, sheep, goat and deer). To these animals the trunks and branches of trees are inedible and the leaves largely inaccessible. As a result, the herbivore population of wooded areas will have been so scattered as to make hunting very difficult and herding impossible. Again, the optimal areas will have been those unsuitable for trees and, although considerable expanses of open vegetation doubtless existed in many parts of the uplands, their exploitation will often have been prevented by the lack of a complementary, lowland source of winter grazing. The well-wooded, richer soils of the lowlands could only be favoured for human settlement, as they clearly were in the Neolithic and Bronze Age, when man modified the environment by opening up the woodlands for cultivation or to improve grazing conditions.

POPULATION–SIZE AND DISTRIBUTION

Problems, both of locating settlements and of assessing their extent, density of occupation and degree of contemporaneity, invest archaeological estimates of regional population size (Renfrew 1972, pp. 249–55) with a high level of inaccuracy. Nonetheless, a substantial increase in population between the Early Neolithic and Late Bronze Age does seem highly probable for most regions (Bintliff 1977b, p. 7).

Of more particular concern here is the size of population at individual settlements and, during the course of the later Neolithic and the Bronze Age, there is a marked increase in the variability of settlement size. Larger centres emerge in the main, lowland arable areas (Renfrew 1972), while smaller sites proliferate, especially in the uplands and in parts of the lowlands more marginal for early agriculture (e.g., Warren 1972, p. 272; Halstead 1977, p. 24). An extreme example of the growth of a large centre is provided by Knossos in Crete, which grew from 0.25 hectares in the pre-pottery Neolithic to 5 hectares in the Late Neolithic (Evans 1971), while a Late Bronze Age extent of some 50 hectares is implied by Hood's (1958, p. 5) survey map. By contrast, an Early Bronze Age foundation at Debla in the hills of western Crete covered less than 0.1 hectare (Warren and Tzedhakis 1974). In spite of differences of occupation density, it can safely be assumed that this considerable divergence in the extent of settlements reflects substantial differences in numbers of inhabitants. The contemporaneous existence of large communities, with potential for specialisation of occupation, and of smaller communities, in marginal or specialised locations, will obviously have offered some stimulus to the development of exchange between communities. However, Gamble (forthcoming) has recently stressed a more direct implication of community size for economy. For a given system of land use, the larger a community is, the larger the area needed to support it. The resulting increase in distances to fields, pasture lands and so on entails a rise in labour costs and so may constitute a powerful stimulus to economic change.

Turning, then, in more detail to the size of these communities, some useful order-of-magnitude estimates are possible for the Neolithic. Renfrew (1972, p. 238) has suggested that Neolithic settlements (in lowland arable areas at least) are 'typically' 0.4–0.8 hectares in extent, and a very similar range is implied by a far larger sample in French's survey of Thessaly (Halstead 1977). Renfrew proposes an occupation density of 200 inhabitants per hectare for these settlements and I have calculated comparable figures by the following method. In Neolithic levels with well-established house plans (Sinos 1971), the percentage of the excavated (and undisturbed) area taken up by house floors ranges between *c.* 25–35 per cent for the dispersed occupation at Early Neolithic Nea Nikomedia (Macedonia), and *c.* 50 per cent for the most densely occupied exposures at Middle Neolithic Otzaki (Thessaly) and Late Neolithic Knossos (Crete). An idea of how many of these structures were occupied simultaneously would require extensive excavation with that question in mind, but some allowance is made here for this factor in assuming, arbitrarily, that 10–30 per cent of the extent of a Neolithic settlement normally consisted of house floors in contemporaneous use. Using Narroll's (1962) figure of 10 m² of floor area per person for simple houses such as those usually found for the Greek Neolithic, we arrive at an estimate of 100 to 300 persons per hectare of settlement. If the lower figure is adopted, the number of inhabitants of a lowland settlement will normally have been between forty and eighty, while the upper figure gives a range of 120 to 240 persons. Encouragingly, this range of 40 to 240 inhabitants is not unlike that suggested by Forge (1972) as normative for sedentary, egalitarian communities. In his review of 'Neolithic' cultivators in New Guinea, he found that the maintenance of internal order and coherence was only compatible with a basically egalitarian social structure for groups of about 70 to 350 people (see, however, Fletcher's discussion, ch. 4 above). In Thessaly, Renfrew's typical Neolithic settlement size was maintained through the three millennia of the Early, Middle and Late Neolithic, and it was only from the Final Neolithic onwards that settlements of one hectare or more became the norm (Halstead 1977). It may be significant that, precisely from the end of the Late Neolithic, two of these sites have revealed large, central 'megaron' buildings, isolated from the rest of the settlement by a series of concentric walls (Theocharis 1973, p. 101). If this means that a hierarchically differentiated community first appeared at this stage, then we may have independent evidence that our estimate of 40 to 240 inhabitants at earlier Neolithic settlements is realistic.

The norm of one hectare for Final Neolithic and Early Bronze Age settlements in Thessaly is also that adopted for the Early Bronze Age of the Aegean generally by Renfrew (1972, p. 244), who also notes that some sites are now more densely occupied than was usual in the Neolithic. Communities of 300 or more are, then, quite possible, which again accords well with our application of Forge's model.

For the Late Bronze Age, Renfrew suggested that major settlements usually covered between one and four hectares, while the maximum extent of sites such as Gla (in Boeotia) or Knossos may reach 50 hectares or more. On the other hand, the internal organisation of these largest settlements is very heterogeneous and little is known of the use of space outside the limited area of the palaces themselves. At this juncture, we content ourselves with the observation that Aegean Bronze Age centres are tiny by comparison with ancient Mesopotamian cities (Renfrew 1972, p. 242).

NEOLITHIC SUBSISTENCE ECONOMY

Nutrition and the exploitation of plants

David Clarke (1976) stressed that the relative importance of the various animal and plant species exploited by man for food can be measured in many different ways. Here we concentrate initially on the provision of calories, because energy is the largest of man's nutritional requirements. We then consider the acquisition of protein and vitamins which, though needed in smaller amounts, could still have been critical factors if in short supply.

Among some human groups animal foods are the basic source of energy but, in most parts of the world, plant foods can support a larger population. In Greece, the concentration of Early Neolithic population in the well-wooded lowlands makes an animal-based economy quite unlikely for most of these early groups, as a few calculations will highlight. Dahl and Hjort (1976, p. 220) estimate that a family of six must kill about 120 sheep per year, if mutton is their main source of calories. Given what is known of the age structure of Greek Neolithic flocks, this strategy would require a *live* flock of something like 300 to 400 sheep, say sixty per person. A lower ratio, of twenty-five sheep per person, was recorded recently for the Sarakatsani, a group of nomadic pastoralists in northern Greece (Campbell 1964, p. 7). The Sarakatsani, however, exploited their sheep for secondary products as well as meat, and the proceeds of selling surplus milk and wool could pay for a far larger quantity (in calorific terms) of flour and olive oil (*ibid.*, pp. 363–4). A Neolithic community of somewhere between 40 and 240 inhabitants might, therefore, need something like 1000 to 6000 sheep, if it derived most of its calories from ewe's milk and mutton. However, if meat alone was the staple (cf. Sherratt, ch. 10 above), the number of sheep required might be between 2400 and 14 400. Prior to deforestation, the herding of such large numbers of sheep would have been quite impracticable in most parts of lowland Greece and, indeed, it will be argued below that the number of stock kept was normally quite small (cf. Fleming 1972). Even lower densities of wild ruminants could have been maintained in this environment, and the hunting of smaller mammals or birds does not offer a viable alternative for communities of the size envisaged. Davidson (1976) has demonstrated the impracticability, even in favourable circumstances, of supporting a group of only twenty persons by hunting one of the more prolific of the smaller mammals, the rabbit, while the larger and more gregarious species of birds are mostly restricted in Greece to the environs of lakes and marshes.

For the provision of the bulk of man's energy requirements in the Greek Neolithic, therefore, we turn to plant foods and, as the human digestive system cannot effectively break down cellulose, we are looking specifically for plant foods in which calories are stored in a concentrated and accessible form – seeds, nuts and fruits (Table 11.1). For instance, whereas a daily intake

TABLE 11.1. *The calorific value of selected plant foods in kcal per 100 g edible portion*

Olive oil	900
Cereals	350–60
Dried pulses	350–75
Green pulses	50–100
Dried fruits	280–300
(fig, apple, plum, grape)	
Fresh fruit	65–90
(fig, apple, cherry, berries)	
Nuts	
walnut	700
pistacchio	640
acorn	270
chestnut	200
Bulbs	40–50
Roots	30–50
Greens	20–50
(leaves, stalks, shoots)	
Mushrooms	25

Source After Pellet and Shadarevian 1970 and Diem 1962.

of 2000 calories could be met by about 600–700 g of bread, lentils or dried figs, and by little more than 200 g of olive oil, the amount of mushrooms needed would be a prodigious 8 kg.

Seeds (cereals and pulses), nuts (*Pistacia atlantica* and acorns) and fruits (fig, grape, olive and *Cornus mas*) are all attested among carbonised plant remains from Greek Neolithic settlements (J. M. Renfrew 1973a), but it is unlikely that any of these species occurred naturally in large stands in the wooded lowland areas. For some of the cereals and pulses there is more or less convincing botanical evidence that substantial stands were maintained artificially by cultivation (*ibid.*), but in the case of nuts and fruits there is no such indication. Indeed, the sporadic Neolithic finds of pips from grapes, olives and pears are morphologically reminiscent of modern wild varieties. As well as the obvious examples of such species whose fruit has been improved in size and taste by domestication, villagers often draw a distinction today, for certain species of nut tree, between 'wild' trees growing on bare hillsides or mountain slopes, which bear few nuts, and high-yielding 'domestic' ones which flourish in more favoured spots. The enormous yields quoted by Clarke (1976) for Mediterranean nut trees are, in many cases, probably as much the result of human interference as are the cereal yields obtained in the Mediterranean lowlands with traditional methods of agriculture. Higher yields of fruits and nuts probably resulted initially from the selective removal of competing vegetation by farmers or herdsmen, and the process will have been accelerated on occasion by the planting of these species in more favourable locations. However, the development and diffusion of higher-yielding varieties will in most cases have been retarded, partly because the wild species were generally distributed in barren or high areas away from the

TABLE 11.2. *The relative importance of cereals and pulses in carbonised seed samples from Neolithic and Bronze Age Greece**

| Period | No. of samples in which one species of cereal or pulse is present at: | | | | Sites |
| | (a) 75% + | | (b) 10% + | | |
	Cereals	Pulses	Cereals	Pulses	
Early Neolithic	4	2	12	12	Achilleion, Gediki, Soufli (Thessaly); Knossos (Crete); Nea Nikomedeia (Macedonia)
Late and Final Neolithic	3	1	1	0	Sesklo, Pyrasos (Thessaly); Kephala (Cyclades)
Early Bronze	3	4	0	5	Lerna (Argolid)
Middle Bronze	1	4	5	2	Lerna (Argolid)
Late Bronze	2	3	1	1	Iolkos (Thessaly)
TOTAL	13	14	18	20	

Sources
Achilleion, Gediki, Soufli, Sesklo, Pyrasos, Iolkos: J. M. Renfrew 1973a
Knossos: Evans 1968
Nea Nikomedeia: van Zeist and Bottema 1971
Kephala: J. M. Renfrew 1977
Lerna: Hopf 1962
* Samples of less than 25 seeds omitted.

concentrations of Neolithic population, but particularly because of the long growth cycle involved. For three of these species, the olive, chestnut and walnut, we have palynological evidence for the date at which they first became major components of lowland vegetation. Olive cultivation is indicated from the later third millennium B.C. at least in Messenia (Wright 1972), and perhaps from as early as the fourth millennium B.C. in Boeotia (Greig and Turner 1974). In Macedonia (Bottema 1974; Greig and Turner 1974) and Acarnania (Wright 1972), the olive, walnut and chestnut all become widespread for the first time during the second millennium B.C. Fruits and nuts were evidently eaten during the Neolithic, but the available evidence suggests that they were too limited and too scattered a resource to make a significant contribution to the calorie intake of most lowland communities.

Cereals and pulses remain as the most plausible staple in the Greek Neolithic, but archaeological evidence for their relative importance is hard to evaluate. Carbonised plant remains are, as yet, our best source of information, but seeds are preserved in this way under a variety of very different circumstances (Dennell 1972). Material carbonised in a parching or cooking accident, or when a storage area catches fire, may be found as a sample in which one species of cereal or pulse is heavily predominant (say 75 per cent or more). In such cases it is fairly certain that the dominant species was harvested for consumption (or sowing), but there is an inherent bias towards the preservation of cereals: emmer, for example, one of the cereals most commonly attested in prehistoric Greece, is usually parched before it is threshed, whereas pulses are not. Nevertheless, the handful of such samples available (Table 11.2, column a) does suggest that pulses were at least as important as cereals. The number of samples can be increased by using the more heterogeneous samples, which probably derive from burnt floor or midden deposits. Such deposits may contain the detritus from a wider range of processing activities and, on the whole, plants which are not very prone to carbonisation are more likely to be represented in them. On the other hand, these deposits often contains 'weeds' discarded in the cleaning of seed corn. In an attempt to exclude seeds not meant for consumption, column b of Table 11.2 only records a species of cereal or pulse as present when it makes up an arbitrary 10 per cent (or more) of a sample. Again, the implication is that pulses were not less important than cereals in Neolithic or Bronze Age Greece.

Some pulses were doubtless eaten green in season, but during most of the year dried pulses only will have been available, and these have the same calorific value as cereals. Thus, the combined annual consumption of cereals and pulses may have been something like 200 kg per head (Clark and Haswell 1970), or between 8000 and 48 000 kg per village (for Neolithic communities of between 40 and 240 persons).

So far we have only considered the provision of energy, but the combination of cereals and pulses has major implications for another aspect of nutrition. Pulses are a very rich source of protein and, together, cereals and pulses provide all the amino-acids required by man. Such a diet would not supply all the vitamins needed, but the small amounts required would have been found in the variety of shoots, nuts, fruits, bulbs and greens which were doubtless gathered as relishes. Today, these relishes are largely found in scrub or ruderal habitats and are mostly unavailable in summer (Clark-Forbes 1976, p. 130). In the more wooded environment of the Neolithic, such plants may have been available in smaller numbers, but still in sufficient quantity for the small communities of the time. Moreover, even at the height of summer, edible greens will have been growing in some of the more shady spots.

Early Neolithic agriculture

Present knowledge of the environmental, demographic and technological background to Neolithic cultivation, though limited, is sufficient for it to be clear that yield figures for plough agriculture in medieval northern Europe or early-twentieth-century Greece are quite inappropriate. It is particularly significant that the ox-drawn plough can cultivate large areas and so make agriculture viable with low average yields which would not be acceptable to a Neolithic farmer armed with only a hoe, mattock or digging-stick (Boserup

1965). Moreover, although only primitive varieties of cultigens were available in the Neolithic, there are a number of reasons for thinking that yields may have been rather higher than those obtained in the 1920s with traditional Mediterranean plough agriculture.

Firstly, the wheat yields of 550–650 kg per hectare quoted for Greece and Cyprus (Admiralty 1944, vol. 2, p. 55; Reifenberg 1938) and of 400–500 kg per hectare quoted for North Africa and Palestine (Reifenberg 1938) are averages which include figures from extensive areas of low productivity. By contrast, Neolithic cultivation in Greece was concentrated on a restricted range of fertile soils (Bintliff 1977a). Furthermore, the structure and nutrient status of these soils must have been considerably better, at least for the first few years of cultivation, than at present. If yields of 500–800 kg per hectare are possible in Galilee in good years from wild stands of einkorn and barley (Zohary 1969, p. 56), then initial cereal yields of, say, 800–1000 kg per hectare do not seem improbable for the Greek Neolithic. Similarly high yields may have been obtained from pulses, judging by the general comparability of pulse and cereal yields under a traditional dry-farming regime in the arid east of Turkey (Hillman 1973, p. 237).

Dennell and Webley have suggested (1975), for the Neolithic of southern Bulgaria, that as much as a third or a quarter of the crop will have been needed for sowing the next year, but such pessimism seems unwarranted for Neolithic Greece. Such low seed–yield ratios are indeed known from medieval England (van Bath 1963), where cold, heavy soils inhibit germination (Gill and Vear 1966) but, on the warm, light soils of the Mediterranean, each seed may produce several tillers. Thus even in the arid conditions of eastern Turkey (Hillman 1973, p. 237), recent yields for both pulses and cereals were between six- and tenfold, while in Roman Italy cereal yields may customarily have been between ten- and fifteenfold (White 1963). Moreover, these figures are for seed sown by broadcasting, which uses up about twice as much seed as drilling methods (McConnell 1883). Under a presumed Neolithic system of hoe or digging-stick cultivation, seed could have been planted rather than broadcast and this would have enhanced seed–yield ratios considerably. It is suggested, therefore, that Early Neolithic farmers did not normally have to lay aside as seed corn a significant proportion of the cereal or pulse crop.

If the high yields proposed here for early agriculture are accepted, the area in cultivation in any one year will have been very small: the suggested range for the amount of grain and pulses consumed in a year by a Neolithic village (*c.* 8000 to 48 000 kg) could have been harvested from as little as 10 to 50 hectares. Small-scale forest agriculture systems are well known in the tropics, where high initial yields decline rapidly because the high rainfall and poor soils lead to rapid leaching of nutrients and crops compete unfavourably with the lush regrowth of natural vegetation (Boserup 1965). As a result, fields are only cultivated briefly between long periods of fallow. In the Mediterranean, however, leaching is a very slow process while, because of the marked summer

TABLE 11.3. *The average distance to fields from a lowland Neolithic village*

	A village in the middle of arable land (100% of its catchment is arable)	A village on the edge of arable land (50% of its catchment is arable)
Area cultivated in one year (ha)	10–50	10–50
Total area cultivated assuming alternate year fallow (ha)	20–100	20–100
Minimum distance to furthest field (metres)	250–570	360–800
Average distance to fields (metres)	180–400	260–560
Average walking time to fields (assuming 10 min for 1 km)	1.8–4.0	2.6–5.6

Source: Cf. Chisholm 1968, p. 112.

drought, annual crops compete well on cultivated ground with the regenerating natural vegetation. The decline in yields will, therefore, have been gradual and a long-fallow system of 'shifting cultivation' may not have been the most attractive strategy. If a short-fallow system prevailed, the total area of land used for cultivation will have been very small – only 20 to 100 hectares even with alternate year fallowing – and the average time taken to walk from a Neolithic village to the fields will have been between about two and five minutes (Table 11.3). At one Early Neolithic settlement, Servia in Macedonia, the incidence of shade-loving species among the land snails (Hubbard 1979, p. 228) certainly favours the existence of only limited areas of cleared ground around the site.

The preceding discussion has argued the case for highly productive, small-scale agriculture in the first few years of cultivation at a settlement (see also Sherratt, ch. 10 above), but there are implications of farming small clearings in a wooded environment which may have made such a regime viable in the long term too. Firstly, with such a small area under cultivation, a fairly high proportion of the fields will have been near enough to the settlement to be fertilised by human manure and household refuse. The application of animal manure, too, will have been far more regular than under the traditional system whereby animals spend much of the year grazing far away from the arable area. In a wooded environment where so much of the vegetation is out of reach for domestic animals, fallow weeds and the stubble from crops will have been valuable grazing resources. Even animals feeding in the woods by day will have been penned at night, because of predators, on fields near the settlement, thus ensuring a net in-flow of nutrients from the enormous reservoir stored in the trees around the cultivated area. Thirdly, if pulses and cereals were being grown in similar quantities, as the archaeological evidence suggests, they may well have been grown in rotation. Admittedly this has not been standard practice in traditional Mediterranean agriculture, and Bintliff

(1977a, p. 105) has suggested that the growing of pulses may have been inhibited by dry soils. Experiments in Cyprus have certainly shown that the water consumption of pulses is high enough for a subsequent cereal crop to yield less than it would after bare fallow (James and Frangopoulos 1939, p. 11) but, of course, a field sown with cereals and pulses in rotation can produce more food than one in which a cereal crop alternates with bare fallow. The crucial problem with pulses is that they are a far more labour-intensive crop than cereals (White 1970, p. 191; Gamble forthcoming). Today, as a result, when intended for human consumption, they are generally grown intensively in small, productive garden-plots, while pulses grown extensively in rotation with cereals are used as animal fodder or green manure. In the Neolithic, however, before the introduction of the ox-drawn ard (see below, p. 330), the frequent tilling of the fields needed to maintain bare fallow will have made this method of preserving soil moisture considerably less attractive while, on the other hand, the labour costs of the extra weeding, hoeing and so on required by pulse crops will have been less of a problem, given the proximity of the fields to the settlement. In these circumstances, the rotation of cereals and pulses may well have been the most attractive option and some evidence that crop rotation was practised comes from the observation that early seed samples regularly contain an admixture of other crop species (J. M. Renfrew 1966). Dennell has noted the same phenomenon in early samples from southern Bulgaria (1978, pp. 91–3), where he suggested that the high level of crop admixture resulted from the residuals of previous crops grown on the same plots. As well as increasing the amount of food produced per unit of land, rotation has the advantage that pulse crops enhance the nitrogen status of the soil, while the part of the plant left after the harvest may also have made an important contribution to animal fodder, and so to manuring: if some pulses were picked green, as a fresh vegetable, and others perhaps picked a little early, before the pods dehisced, the resulting 'hay' may have been considerably more nutritious than the dessicated straw from the cereal crops.

With cereals and pulses grown in rotation on well fertilised fields, Early Neolithic agriculture may well have operated with quite rare fallowing, to check weed growth, and our estimate of the area required for cultivation may be pessimistic. Moreover, with such a balanced system of farming, any decline in soil fertility may have been both slight and very gradual. To find out how Neolithic land use actually *did* develop we must examine the evidence of animal husbandry.

The development of land use through the Neolithic: the evidence of changing patterns of animal husbandry

Even if the average Neolithic farmer did not derive much of his diet from domestic animals, he may still have attached considerable importance to them. Enjoyment of meat is common in man (Isaac 1978, p. 92), while in many

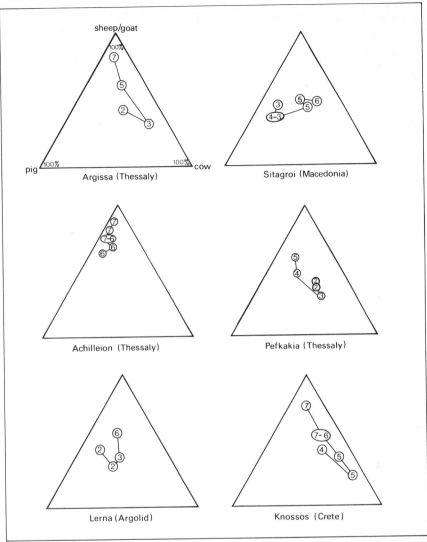

Changes in the relative frequency of sheep/goat, cow and pig at sites with faunal material from several successive phases (the numbers – 7, 6, 4–3, 2 etc. – indicate the date of each phase in millennia B.C.; successive phases are linked by straight lines). Sources: Argissa – Boessneck 1962; Sitagroi – Bökönyi 1973; Achilleion – Bököny, quoted by Gimbutas 1974, p. 286; Pefkakia – Jordan 1975; Lerna – Gejvall 1969; Knossos – M. R. Jarman pers. comm. (preliminary data only).

societies domestic stock serve as symbols of wealth or prestige, as well as being a reserve of food for emergencies (Dahl and Hjort 1976). Early farmers may also have been well aware of the advantages of keeping animals for maintaining the fertility of their fields. Certainly, the manner in which cereals, pulses, the domestic ruminants and pigs normally appear together on Early Neolithic settlements across most of Europe suggests the diffusion of an integrated system of food production rather than of a loose array of domesticates.

The particular range of animals kept at any time reflects a balance between, on the one hand, the availability of different types of fodder (stubble graze, woodland browse, kitchen waste etc.) and, on the other hand, certain specific requirements such as of oxen for ploughing, calves for sacrifice or adult sheep for wool. A study of the proportions in which the various species were kept, therefore, and of the age and sex composition of the herds, is an important source of information, both on overall patterns of land use and on more detailed aspects of farming strategy.

Fig. 11.2 sets out the evidence for changes in the relative numerical importance of the main domestic animals during the Neolithic and Bronze Age. It appears that sheep/goat dominated initially and then over the succeeding 3000–5000 years gradually gave way to cattle and, to a lesser extent, pigs. At some time between the fourth and second millennium B.C., sheep/goat once more became the dominant animal. (Related changes in other parts of Europe are discussed by Sherratt, ch. 10 above.) Sheep and goat are grouped together because their bones can only be distinguished in a minority of cases. The evidence from Argissa, Ayia Sofia, Pefkakia and Prodromos in Thessaly, from Lerna in the Argolid and Knossos in Crete, however, consistently suggests that sheep outnumbered goats very heavily in the Early Neolithic and that subsequently the ratio of goats rose steadily and then fell again, much in parallel with the increase and then decline in the proportion of cattle.

The likelihood of a bone being preserved, recovered and identified varies markedly both between animals, because of differences of species, age and sex, and between archaeological sites, because of differences of bone preservation, recovery techniques and analytical methods. As a result, the data on which Fig. 11.2 is based are very coarse, but they are unlikely to have created the long-term trend which has been observed at all open settlements with faunal evidence from a long period of time. The trend recorded here is one of change in the proportions in which the domestic animals were killed and, unfortunately, the available information on the age at death of these animals is not sufficient to reconstruct the proportions of the different species in the living herds. There is some indication from Pefkakia (Thessaly) and Sitagroi (Macedonia), at least, that both cattle and sheep/goat were being killed a little later in the Bronze Age than in the Neolithic but, again, there is no evidence that the apparent trend in livestock proportions is an artifact of inter-specific differences in the age at which animals were killed.

As has already been said, the proportions in which the different species were kept represents a compromise between man's changing needs and the suitability of each species to a changing environment. There is no indication, from material such as figurines, for an ideological emphasis on any one species during the Neolithic. Moreover, all the species display the heavy immature death-rate characteristic of animals exploited primarily for their meat. There is, therefore, no evidence that the use of secondary products, such as milk, wool or traction, had assumed sufficient importance to make any one species particularly valuable. Bökönyi (1973, pp. 167–8) has suggested that the composition of these Neolithic faunas does not reflect human selection but simply the relative availability of each species. However, such is the fecundity of these animals that their relative proportions could have been adjusted very rapidly, and any initial incompatibility with their natural environment could have been rectified too quickly for it to be registered by archaeology, given the coarseness of available dating techniques. On the contrary, the very gradual nature of the increase in cattle and goats suggests the influence of long-term environmental realities rather than ephemeral shifts in the value man placed on different animals. It seems worthwhile, therefore, to look at the ecological preferences of each species.

The pig is an excellent forager in woods (Freeman 1973, pp. 12–13) but, where woodland is the dominant form of vegetation, the foraging is difficult to supervise. At Argissa, Knossos, Lerna and Pefkakia the percentage of pigs in the fauna remains fairly stable through time. This may mean that, while the proportions of the three ruminants were fluctuating in response to human alteration of the local environment, pigs were largely being fed on a less changeable resource – kitchen waste. They would still have foraged around the settlement for roots, tubers and grubs and, if restricted to a small enough area, they could have dug over the fallow plots (Seymour and Seymour 1973, p. 173) and so, to some extent, have served the hoe agriculturalist as a plough (cf. Boserup 1965). Some support for this idea comes from the suggestion (von den Driesch and Enderle 1976) that the injuries observed on many of the pig skulls at Late Neolithic Ayia Sofia resulted from fighting among animals penned together in crowded conditions. The pigs could most profitably be taken into the woods in autumn, when the seasonal glut of fungi, acorns and so on could fatten them up before the cold of winter when pig's fat would be most useful in the human diet.

The feeding preferences of the ruminants overlap, but some generalisations are possible because of broad physiological and ethological differences. Cattle, because of their greater body size, need considerably less fodder per unit of body weight (cf. Clutton-Brock and Harvey 1978) and can tolerate a poorer quality diet (Bell 1971, p. 91) than the smaller sheep and goats. In consequence, if man was making more of the natural vegetation available to animals by breaking down branches from trees, cattle would be easier to feed than sheep or goats. On the other hand, the labour involved in providing leafy fodder literally by the ton (Whitehead 1948, p. 53; Clark 1952, pp. 124–5) would be considerable and the low percentage of cattle in Early Neolithic Greek faunas suggests that this resource was only used as a supplement when other types of browse or graze were scarce. Cattle, because of their stature, and goats, because of their agility, are able to reach leaves of trees and shrubs which are inaccessible to sheep, but initially such browse will have been too sparse for either species to be easily *herded* in woodland. However, cattle and goats would flourish if 'bush' vegetation developed on abandoned fields. Both crop stubble and fallow weeds are most effectively exploited if grazed first by cattle and then by sheep. Cattle cannot graze close to the ground, but they can make use of the taller, coarser material and in the process open up the vegetation (cf. Bell 1971) so that the smaller ruminants can reach fallen grains and low weeds. Sheep can exploit such concentrated areas of grazing more efficiently than goats, because they move and feed in fairly tight groups. Goats roam more widely and are thus better equipped for using more dispersed resources (Williamson and Payne 1965, pp. 284–5).

The modest percentage of cattle and predominance of sheep over goats in the Early Neolithic suggests that the main grazing resource in use was a combination of stubble in the summer and autumn and fallow fields in the winter and spring. It seems, then, that Early Neolithic farmers were indeed able to keep fields in cultivation on a long-term basis and that, in consequence, very little cleared land was abandoned and allowed to revert to browse for goats and cattle.

In the millennia succeeding the Early Neolithic, however, the proportion of cattle and goats did increase and this does presumably reflect the progressive disturbance of the vegetation and the development of lower, more accessible browse at the expense of mature woodland. The very gradual nature of the process is consonant with the long-term effects of human and animal depredations for firewood and fodder, and need not imply that a serious decline in soil fertility was causing the regular abandonment of cultivated land or the development of bush-fallow agriculture. However, over the course of the four millennia of the Neolithic, the net effect of such alteration of the environment may have been considerable and an increasing divergence seems likely between the vegetation of the arid southeast Aegean and the wetter north and west of the country.

In the southeast vegetation is always likely to have been more open than elsewhere and, because aridity inhibits the establishment of young trees (Bintliff 1977a, p. 72), the regeneration of cleared woodland is slower. In consequence, the progress of lowland deforestation may have been relatively rapid and man may, at an early stage, have favoured the growth and proliferation of selected nut or fruit trees to the point where they became a very attractive resource. Of these trees, the olive is of outstanding importance because its oil is exceptionally rich in calories and keeps very well. Olives now grow in the coastal regions of virtually the whole of Greece and the earliest archaeological find of an olive stone is from as far north as Thessaly (J. M. Renfrew 1973b, p. 161), but there are good reasons why olive cultivation may first have flourished in the southeast. In this, the driest area of the Aegean, annual fluctuations in the quantity and seasonal distribution of rainfall may often have a critical effect on cereal or pulse yields. The olive is also affected,

But it needs rain in different seasons (Forbes 1976). As a result, the olive may often have provided a viable alternative to a failed field crop, initially as a gathered wild resource and later as a cultivated one. To the palynological evidence for earlier cultivation of the olive in southern Greece than in northern Greece can be added the predominance of olive *prunings* among the charcoal from Myrtos, an Early Bronze Age settlement on the southeast coast of Crete (Rackham 1972, p. 303). Indeed the apparent spread of open settlements, akin to Myrtos, in eastern Crete during the Early Bronze Age (Warren 1972, p. 272) may well have been made possible by the addition of the olive to existing cultivars.

Deforestation will also have increased the numbers of livestock which could be maintained and, in particularly favourable locations, domestic animals may have begun to make a major contribution to human subsistence. The best documented example of this is west Thessaly where, in addition to the great expanse of arable land on which Early Neolithic settlements abound, the wide flood plain of the river Peneios provides an extensive source of summer grazing. As deforestation by early farmers gradually created a complementary source of winter grazing, the exploitation of this rich resource will have become increasingly attractive. It is tempting, therefore, to see the progressive abandonment of the early settlements through the Middle, Late and Final Neolithic (unpublished survey data of Dr D. French) as the result, not of the depopulation of this fertile area, but of the development of a pastoral economy practised by mobile and, perhaps, small groups whose settlement traces are too ephemeral to be recognised in the current archaeological record. Evidence for the early stages of this development comes from the group of Early Neolithic settlements located on low rises above the flood plain at Prodromos. The sites have produced plentiful evidence of crop processing and the excavator has suggested that cultivation took place on these rises, in between the scattered settlement areas (Hourmouziadis 1972). This implies summer occupation for harvesting, but the slaughter of livestock was, it seems, concentrated in winter – perhaps in response to the restricted availability of grazing at this time of year. Moreover, in the earliest phases of occupation, prime meat cuts were apparently being removed from Prodromos. These joints were perhaps smoked or dried and taken as rations by herdsmen moving out onto the flood plain in the summer months; this would enable them to spare the current crop of young animals until the onset of winter and so take full advantage of the plentiful summer grazing. The removal of these joints seems to have declined in the later occupation phases, perhaps as progressive clearance reduced the seasonal imbalance in grazing and so enabled larger herds to be kept (Halstead and Jones forthcoming). Examination of the later stages of this suggested trend towards pastoralism is, of course, hindered by the difficulty of finding occupation sites, but development of the ability to exploit the milk as well as the meat of domestic stock (Dahl and Hjort 1976) would have made an animal-based economy far more viable. A similar process may have occurred rather later in the Drama basin in Macedonia, where the margins of Lake Phillipi could have been a comparable source of summer pasture. Here, a fair scatter of sites is known from the Neolithic and Early Bronze Age, but only a handful of settlements are known from the later Bronze Age and these are at the far end of the basin from the lake (Davidson 1971).

Though such seasonally wet expanses adjacent to major arable areas are common in northern Greece, because of topography and rainfall, they are unusual in the south. One obvious exception is upland Arcadia, where the pasture afforded by the 'sink-hole' lakes was greatly prized in antiquity (Semple 1932, p. 322) and may conceivably hold the key to an apparent hiatus in settlement during the Late Neolithic (Howell 1970). In southern Greece generally, on the other hand, the faster pace of deforestation and the naturally more open vegetation will have made accessible grazing more ubiquitous, albeit more dispersed. The proliferation of cave occupation during the Late Neolithic in southern Greece (Theocharis 1973, p. 90) suggests increasing exploitation of areas of rugged relief or barren soil cover more suited to herding than to cultivation. It is often assumed that such 'marginal' locations were occupied by lowland farmers transhuming seasonally with their stock, but perennial occupation by *small* groups is in many cases equally plausible – especially if dairy products were now being used. For reasons of topography, the transhumant exploitation of such areas from lowland farming settlements could only really be achieved with sheep or goats – the dominant animals in the Neolithic levels at the caves of Franchthi in the Argolid (Payne 1975) and Kitsos in Attica (Jullien 1971) – and so might be expected to reveal itself in an increased representation of these smaller ruminants in the fauna from lowland arable sites. Unfortunately, the only relevant data come from Knossos, in Crete, where ovicaprids increase in the Late Neolithic, and Lerna, in the Argolid, where ovicaprids do not assume greater importance until the Late Bronze Age, and neither site can be taken as typical of Crete or southern Greece. However, given the difficulty of recognising archaeologically the presence of a few young males transhuming with the flocks of a lowland village, the possibility that many of these caves were occupied perennially by small groups must be entertained seriously.

There may, then, have been increasing diversity of subsistence economy during the later Neolithic – pastoral nomadism with cattle in the wetlands of Thessaly, the herding of sheep or goats in the less fertile parts of southern Greece, the cultivation of the olive perhaps initially in the dry southeast of the Aegean. On the other hand, the evidence of animal husbandry suggests that in those parts of the lowlands most suited to agriculture a stable pattern of small-scale cultivation prevailed. In this case, the later Neolithic explosion of settlement in the Cyclades and in the less fertile parts of Crete and southern Greece is perhaps less the result of population pressure on arable land forcing the colonisation of marginal areas than of developments such as olive cultivation or the milking of livestock making these areas more attractive for settlement. Renfrew (1972) suggested that such economic diversification was a stimulus to the integration of different communities, but a more crucial factor may have been social and ritual dependence on the older, larger settlements by the smaller communities which now proliferated in these marginal areas. Thus, in Crete, the period during which large palaces were first built coincides in a striking number of cases with the foundation date of the rural 'peak sanctuaries' (Cherry 1978, p. 430) which may have fulfilled this integrative role.

BRONZE AGE ECONOMY

Changes in community size and land use

Investigation of the economy is hampered for the Bronze Age by the greater variability now apparent among settlements in size, rank and internal organisation, but changes in community size have in themselves some major implications for patterns of land use and may allow some useful generalisations to be made.

Larger communities are a feature of the Final Neolithic and Early Bronze Age (Renfrew 1972; Halstead 1977) and may have had a radical effect in making less attractive the type of intensive 'gardening' envisaged for the Neolithic. With greater average distances to fields, the labour costs of weeding and so on would rise, while the further fields would not receive household refuse or human manure. As a result, there may well have been a tendency for the labour-intensive pulses to be grown in-field and for cereals to be grown out-field. Indeed, if the mixture of cereals and pulses in early seed samples did result from the contamination of crops by seeds from the previous harvest in either the same or an adjacent field (above, p. 320), then the greater purity of samples from later Greek prehistory (Renfrew 1966, p. 30) may, in part, reflect such a spatial segregation of cereal- and pulse-fields. In the out-field area, the lower yields and more frequent fallowing consequent upon disruption of the cereal–pulse rotation would have further increased both the area under cultivation and the average distance to fields, while, in-field, pulses would have been competing with cultivated herbs, spices and fibre plants.

There is little direct evidence for the materials used for clothing in Neolithic Greece, but it is clear that spun thread, whether flax or wool, was in use from the seventh millennium B.C. (C. Renfrew 1973, p. 188), while the cultivation of flax from the beginning of the Neolithic is now documented from Servia in Macedonia (Hubbard 1979, p. 227). Subsistence requirements are, of course, harder to assess for clothing than for food, but my own inquiries among modern Greek villagers suggest that a figure of 2–3 kg per person per year in southern Greece and of 5 kg per person per year in northern Greece may be a reasonable estimate. These figures tally well with Bronze

Age Mesopotamian clothing rations (Gelb 1965) and with the relative sizes of the sheep and human populations in nineteenth-century A.D. Crete (Raulin 1858), and they are probably comparable with Cato's recommended rations for Roman slaves (White 1970, p. 364). On this basis, a Neolithic village of 100 souls would need annually some 200–500 kg of wool to meet its clothing requirements.

A comparable weight of fibre could be obtained from a very small area of cultivated flax: even if twice as much flax were required and yields were only half those quoted for nineteenth-century Crete (Raulin 1858), the area needed would only be somewhere between 2 and 5 hectares. Thus flax would be an attractive source of fibre, where suitable land was not in short supply. With larger communities, however, the scarcity of both rich soil for growing the crop (J. M. Renfrew 1973a, p. 124) and of water for retting it will have made flax an increasingly unattractive material for clothing.

Alternatively, clothing could be made from wool: if Neolithic sheep produced the same amount of wool (0.2–0.7 kg each) as feral Soay sheep (Boyd *et al.* 1964), a target of 200–500 kg would require flocks totalling something like 400 to 1000 sheep. If the flocks were taken elsewhere in summer, this number of sheep might be maintained through the winter on as little as 40–100 hectares of lowland fallow grazing (Campbell 1964, p. 24) but, with the infrequent fallowing suggested above for the Neolithic, the amount of winter grazing for sheep available to a lowland community of 100 inhabitants may have been substantially less.

The breakdown of Neolithic garden cultivation may have made reliance on wool for clothing more feasible. In Greece, fallow weeds grow reasonably well through the winter and luxuriantly in spring, but die back in summer. If fallowing was infrequent in the Neolithic, the poorer but more abundant stubble from crops may well have ensured that there was no seasonal imbalance in the availability of grazing for sheep. With expansion of the area in cultivation and more frequent fallowing, available winter grazing will have greatly surpassed the carrying capacity of stubble fields during the dry summer months, and will thus have provided a strong incentive for sheep to be moved away from the agricultural settlements in summer. The renewed importance of the smaller domestic ruminants in the Late Neolithic (Knossos) or during the Bronze Age (Sitagroi, Argissa, Pefkakia and Lerna) may indeed indicate increased usage by lowland communities of upland graze and browse, and at Argissa and Lerna, at least, it is clear that this development represents an increase in the importance of sheep rather than of goats. Evidence for the sex ratio in flocks of sheep is also a useful index of the significance attached to wool production. Where meat or milk is the main objective of sheep husbandry, only a few males need be kept into adulthood for breeding. The remainder can be killed at a young age, as seems to have been the practice in Neolithic and Early Bronze Age Thessaly (Table 11.4). Male sheep, however, produce more wool than females (Killen 1964) and it may be

TABLE 11.4. *The ratio of male to female sheep among pelves with fused acetabulum (i.e. from animals more than one year old)*

Site	Date	No. of males	No. of females	Source
Prodromos	Early Neolithic	16	42	Halstead and Jones forthcoming
Agia Sofia	Late Neolithic	3	18	von den Driesch and Enderle 1976
Pefkakia	Final Neolithic	1	28	Jordan 1975
Pefkakia	Early Bronze	1	6	Jordan 1975
Pefkakia	Middle Bronze	7	7	Jordan 1975
Pefkakia	Late Bronze	2	0	Jordan 1975

significant that male and female sheep appear to have survived infancy in roughly equal numbers at Pefkakia during the second millennium B.C. There is, then, a certain amount of osteological evidence for a growing emphasis on wool production during the Bronze Age, as has been revealed more dramatically in the Alpine lake villages where the preservation of textiles indicates a switch from flax in the Neolithic to wool in the Bronze Age (Sherratt, ch. 10 above). The emergence of larger communities created both the need and the potential for wool production, and a third factor may have been the availability of a new breed of sheep. Boessneck (1962, p. 47) has attributed a marked increase in the size of sheep in the third millennium (at Argissa, Pefkakia and Sitagroi) to the diffusion of a more woolly variety of sheep, while for the Late Bronze Age Killen (1964) has suggested an average yield of 0.75 kg of wool per sheep from flocks of wethers and of 0.6 kg per sheep from flocks of ewes.

The cultivation of the olive also seems to have been spreading by the third millennium B.C. and, as with the use of sheep for their wool, one factor may have been the diffusion of a more productive variety, whether this had developed within the Aegean or outside it. The olive, too, may have counteracted the disadvantages of larger communities, firstly by yielding twice as many calories per hectare as cereals or pulses (Renfrew 1972, p. 301) and thus allowing a smaller area to be cultivated, and secondly by spreading the increased agricultural workload over a greater part of the year. Both the olive and woolly sheep may have had considerable influence on the further development of Aegean civilisation, because both can provide the raw material for low volume, high value exchange products (aromatic oils and ornate textiles) and because both can make extensive use of child labour (in harvesting and herding), which may have encouraged the raising of larger families and, in consequence, a rapid increase in population size.

A third possible response to the higher labour costs of working larger fields at an increased distance from the settlement is the use of animal power, either for tilling the fields or for transporting the harvested crop. The horse and the ass are first attested in Greece (osteologically) in the Early Bronze Age – the former at Servia in Macedonia (Watson 1979, p. 229) and the latter at Lerna in the Argolid (Gejvall 1969) – and both may have been used as pack animals. Cattle could presumably have been used in the same way, but they have more potential as draught animals pulling an ard or cart, and there is evidence for both functions from the third millennium B.C. or slightly earlier in areas to the north and east (Sherratt, ch. 10 above; Korfmann 1976). As yet the earliest evidence from Greece implying the use of cattle for draught purposes is a cart model from Crete from the end of the third millennium B.C., but perhaps more important than the date of the adoption of animal-traction, the ard and wheeled vehicles is the question of how widespread was their use. In the case of ox-traction, at least, some idea could be gained from changes in the age and sex structure of prehistoric herds of cattle, but the evidence available at present is negligible. Nevertheless, it may be worth drawing a broad distinction between north and south Greece in terms of the likely importance of ox-traction. In many parts of the north, harsh winters and the unavailability of, in particular, the olive may have made ox-traction particularly useful for preparing the ground for cereal and pulse crops in the brief periods in early winter and spring when both climate and ground conditions were suitable. This part of the country is also fairly favourable for raising cattle, and the adoption of animal-traction may have been a contributory factor in the widespread relocation of settlements visible in Thessaly in the third millennium B.C. (Halstead 1977). In south Greece, on the other hand, the maintenance of traction-animals is considerably more difficult, especially during the dry summers leading up to the autumn ploughing period. Thus, if olives (and perhaps other tree crops) were making a significant contribution to calorie-intake, the area tilled by the average farmer may not have justified the 'expense' of keeping oxen. Certainly, in Roman Italy it seems likely that the maintenance of traction-animals was not economical on family holdings unless they were engaged in cereal monocropping or were producing a sizeable surplus (White 1970, pp. 336–46). Some hint that oxen (as opposed to beef cattle, which are killed at about the age when oxen first start working) were being maintained in fairly small numbers in Bronze Age south Greece comes from the palace archives at Knossos, where each ox is recorded individually by name (Chadwick 1976, p. 127).

The use of animal-traction may also have stimulated further social and economic changes in the Bronze Age. The emergence of larger communities will have increased the scope for craft specialisation, and animals may have been used to transport raw materials from outlying areas or to move goods between different communities. Moreover, the use of animal-traction as a labour-saving device in agriculture may have been crucial to the maintenance of full-time specialists such as rulers, administrators, craftsmen and so on. Finally, it should be noted that traction-animals, because of the difficulties of raising and keeping them in southern Greece, may have contributed to the emergence and maintenance of the Bronze Age elites. Horses are clearly associated with chariots, in both the archives and the mural art of the palaces, and clearly any minority able to maintain them had access to a source of considerable prestige, if not to a real deterrent (Chadwick 1976, pp. 164–71). Equally, disparities of wealth may have been encouraged by restricted access to oxen (and so to large-scale agricultural production) – a point which will be returned to in the following section.

Clearly, any substantial increase in the size of communities should have had a disruptive effect on the integrated and small-scale gardening envisaged for the Neolithic, and there is some evidence for such a change taking place. The suggestion has been made that increased purity of archaeological seed samples may reflect the separation of pulse and cereal growing into in-field and out-field zones. The particular location of Middle and Late Bronze Age 'peak sanctuaries' in Crete (Rutkowski 1972, p. 184) may indicate extensive summer use of upland pastures and, as a complementary supply of winter grazing would not be available on land under a gardening regime, this may indicate the existence of fairly large areas in cultivation with frequent fallowing. The cultivation of considerable areas is also implied by the observation that, in parts of southern Greece, the larger Late Bronze Age centres usually occur only in locations with access to large and consolidated tracts of arable land (Bintliff 1977b, p. 11). On the other hand, these centres are generally surrounded by smaller villages and farms (*ibid.*, p. 10) and, especially if emphasis on olive cultivation may have allowed a reduction in the area farmed from each settlement, much of the landscape may still have been cultivated in a small-scale and intensive fashion. Certainly, the oxen tablets from Knossos argue against the general adoption of extensive plough agriculture in one part of the southern Aegean.

The evidence of the Late Bronze Age palace archives and questions of scale

By the Late Bronze Age, there is clear evidence from the southern Aegean of considerable economic activity above the level of local self-sufficiency. At the regional level, the Linear B archives give a tantalising glimpse of palace bureaucracies at Knossos and Pylos controlling the disposition of land, labour, food rations, raw materials and manufactured goods over much of Crete and Messenia respectively; Finley (1957, p. 135), and Renfrew (1972, p. 296) after him, saw these documents as evidence for a massive redistributive operation. At the inter-regional level, mainland fine pottery (in particular, containers suitable for aromatic oils) has been found in quantity in the east Mediterranean (Stubbings 1951) and elsewhere, while metals, ivory and various luxury items attested archaeologically and in the documents must have come from abroad; Chadwick (1976, p. 141) has gone so far as to write of an economy 'dependent on sea-borne trade'.

Chadwick (1976, pp. 67–8) and Renfrew (1972, pp. 254–5) have both attempted to quantify some of this evidence for Late Bronze Age economy by assessing the number of people in receipt of rations (i.e., the number of people not producing their own food), and then to place these figures in context by comparing them with archaeological estimates of the overall regional population. Present archaeological estimates of population size are, in all likelihood, wildly inaccurate, while interpretation of the Linear B tablets is hampered by our ignorance of how extensive was palace involvement in the economy (Finley 1957, pp. 134–5). However, there is every reason to expect that, with more rigorous methods of locating settlements and better information from excavations as to their internal structure, future estimates of population size will be more reliable. This essay restricts itself, therefore, to suggesting a few areas in which the interplay of archaeological and documentary evidence may give some indication of the extent of palatial involvement and of the relative importance of exchange and local production in the economy.

For instance, Killen has shown that the Knossos tablets record palace control over flocks of sheep totalling about 100 000 head and ranging over central Crete (1964 and pers. comm.). This number of sheep could produce somewhere in the region of 70 000 kg of wool. We know that some, at least, of this wool was converted into luxury textiles (Killen pers. comm.) and so, taking the figures for wool requirements suggested above, these flocks could not have clothed more than 20–30 000 people. If the Late Bronze Age population of central Crete was substantially in excess of this figure, as Renfrew has suggested (1972, p. 255), then it is clear that large numbers of sheep (or, perhaps, considerable areas of flax) existed outside the control of the palace.

A similar conclusion can be drawn from Chadwick's observation (1976, pp. 108–9) that the documents only record crops in which the palace is interested. Thus, although pulses have been found in storage jars in the Late Bronze Age palaces at Iolkos in Thessaly (Table 11.2), Mycenae in the Argolid (Wace 1921–3, p. 49) and Knossos in Crete (Evans 1899–1900, p. 21; Haussoullier 1880, p. 127), there is no mention of them in any of the surviving documents. It was suggested above that, whereas cereals and pulses may have been grown together under small-scale hoe cultivation, cereals alone would have been grown under extensive plough agriculture. If, as seems plausible, plough oxen were so rare that even the palaces only had a few of them, then these recorded cereals may come from major royal estates where plough oxen were in use, while the presence of pulses in the palace storerooms may mean that much of the food consumed in the palaces was produced locally without the interference of the bureaucracy. One such royal estate may have existed in the Mesara basin in south-central Crete at Dawo, against which toponym one document records a total of at least 775 tons of wheat (Chadwick 1976, pp. 117–18). If this grain had been drawn from the whole Mesara, or a large part of it, then it could represent a quite reasonable tithe. But with other commodities the Knossos tablets record production at a very local level, which is not consistent with the delegation to Dawo of all responsibility for collecting a wheat tithe from the Mesara. Alternatively, these 775 tons of wheat may have been produced just in the vicinity of Dawo, in which case we may be dealing not with a tithe but with the total production of an area of, perhaps, between 2000 and 6000 hectares – depending on yields, frequency of fallowing and the proportion of land given over to other crops. These suggestions could be tested archaeologically, firstly by looking for osteological evidence of the extent to which oxen were in use at settlements of different rank, and secondly by a study of the pattern of rural settlement in the Mesara.

Turning to evidence for the scale of craft production, an interesting group of documents from Pylos records the existence of 400 bronze-smiths scattered around Messenia. Chadwick (1976, p. 141) admits that they may have worked only part time, but prefers to see this number of smiths as evidence of an export trade in finished metal goods. In so doing he is forced to assume (*ibid.*) that the amount of bronze issued to each smith (about 4 kg) is so small because strict rationing was enforced in the last days of the palace. If, on the other hand, we assume that 4 kg was the normal yearly issue of bronze, we might think of these smiths not as producing finished goods for export but as repairing agricultural and other tools; most of their raw material would come from recycled metal and the palace issue might just balance the amount lost through normal wear and tear. Alternative interpretations of these bronze industry records must be considered in the light of archaeological evidence for the size of population served and for the extent to which metal was in everyday use. In this context, examination of animal bones from settlements of different rank could indicate how far metal cleavers were used for butchery. A study of this type at the Bronze Age settlement of Assiros Toumba in central Macedonia, where evidence for metal and for metal working is far less plentiful than in southern Greece, showed that bronze was in use for this task (Jones and Halstead forthcoming).

Finally, we might note that if these Pylos tablets do record a normal annual issue of bronze, then the total amount involved, about 1000 kg (Chadwick 1976, p. 140), could have been supplied by just one journey of a small boat such as that found at Cape Gelidonya (Bass 1967) – a view which puts Mycenaean 'external trade' in a more modest light than usual.

CONCLUSION

An essay of this nature inevitably ends on a defensive note: reliable and relevant data are clearly a scarce commodity. But if excavators are to spend substantially more time and money on the recovery of organic remains from settlements, then they must be persuaded that information of interest will be gained; palaeoeconomic research in Greece to date has not been reassuring on this point (Gamble forthcoming).

This essay takes archaeological evidence for the small size of Neolithic communities in Greece and offers one possible model of land use – that of small-scale, stable gardening with crop rotation and regular manuring. Pulses seem to be as important as cereals in the agriculture of prehistoric Greece and, arguably, this departure from the traditional picture is only practicable under a small-scale regime. Similarly, it is argued that archaeologically observed regularities in the proportions of different livestock species at Neolithic settlements reflect the integration of animal husbandry into just such a pattern of land use.

One important implication of an economy based on small-scale gardening is that pressure of numbers of people on available arable land is not likely to have been responsible for the colonisation of agriculturally marginal areas or the adoption of new economic strategies (cf. p. 307 and Wilkinson, ch. 9 above). The observed spacing between Neolithic settlements may rather reflect the need for access to wild foods in years with a bad harvest, while the broadening of the subsistence base to include, in particular, olive cultivation may have taken place for a similar reason. It is suggested that community size is of more direct relevance to patterns of land use and that the growth of larger communities in the later Neolithic and Early Bronze Age may have undermined the earlier gardening economy and so have favoured innovations such as the growing of olives (especially in southern Greece and Crete) and ploughing (perhaps particularly in northern Greece).

A further implication of this Neolithic gardening system is to remove the seasonal imbalance in the availability of grazing which nowadays is charac-teristic of arable lowlands in the Mediterranean: as a result, summer use of upland pastures cannot be assumed as the inevitable concomitant of animal husbandry in a country of marked altitudinal relief. Pastoral economies may have developed at an early date in particularly favourable circumstances, especially once the ability to exploit stock for their milk was acquired. However, widespread use of upland pastures is not likely to have occurred until the development of more extensive agriculture with more frequent fallowing created a surplus of lowland winter grazing. In much of southern Greece, the cultivation of the olive and the parallel development of small, dispersed settlements alongside the larger centres during the Bronze Age may have meant that large tracts of such fallow grazing were restricted to a few royal estates specialising in extensive plough agriculture. This may account for the prominence of sheep and wool records in the Late Bronze Age palace archives.

ACKNOWLEDGEMENTS

I am indebted to David and Lisa French for the Thessalian survey data; to George Hourmouziadis and Ken Wardle for the opportunity to study material from Prodromos and Assiros Toumba respectively; to Mike Jarman for preliminary results from his work at Knossos; to Clive Gamble for access, prior to publication, to 'Animal husbandry, population and urbanisation' and to Andrew Sherratt for access to an early draft of his contribution to this volume; to Mary Beard, Bill Cavanagh, Michael Jameson, Peter Jarman, Wim Jongman, Marsha Levine, Philip Lomas, Edward O'Donoghue, Bill Phelps, Paul Redhead, Peter Rowley-Conwy, Dan Rubenstein, Richard Saller, Anthony Snodgrass and Tony Spawforth for a variety of criticisms, suggestions and references. In particular, thanks to Andy Garrard, Glynis Jones, John Killen and John O'Shea for many invaluable discussions and for their generosity with information and ideas from unpublished work of their own.

NOTES

1 The chronology used here is based on calibrated carbon-fourteen dates. Roughly speaking, the Early, Middle, Late and Final Neolithic periods correspond to the seventh, sixth, fifth and fourth millennia B.C. respectively. The Early Bronze Age is roughly equivalent to the third millennium B.C., while the Middle Bronze Age belongs to the first and the Late Bronze Age to the second half of the second millennium B.C. The Minoan palaces flourished in Crete between *c*. 2000 and 1450 B.C., while their Mycenaean counterparts existed in Crete and southern Greece between that date and 1200 B.C.

2 Two of the sites discussed below, Lerna and Pefkakia, are coastal and so are likely to have made use of marine resources, but their coastal location does not demonstrate a heavy reliance on sea-foods. The fish, shellfish and crustaceans of the Mediterranean are neither very plentiful nor easily exploited (Houston 1964, p. 40), and coastal shallows, such as those accessible from Lerna and Pefkakia, are favoured by migratory fish which are only available seasonally. Thus, though highly prized, it is doubtful whether sea-foods can provide the economic base of a community of any size, except within a developed economy where they can be exchanged for large amounts of staple foodstuffs.

REFERENCES

Admiralty (1944). *Greece* (Geographical Handbook Series), Naval Intelligence Division
Bass, G. F. (1967). 'Cape Gelidonya: a Bronze Age shipwreck', *Transactions of the American Philosophical Society*, new series, 57:(8)
van Bath, B. H. S. (1963). *The Agrarian History of Western Europe, AD 500–1850*, Arnold
Bell, R. H. V. (1971). 'A grazing ecosystem in the Serengeti', *Scientific American* 225 (1): 86–93
Bintliff, J. L. (1977a). *Natural Environment and Human Settlement in Prehistoric Greece*, British Archaeological Reports
    (1977b). 'The history of archaeo-geographic studies of prehistoric Greece' in J. L. Bintliff (ed.) *Mycenaean Geography*, British Association for Mycenaean Studies
Boessneck, J. (1962). 'Die Tierreste aus der Argissa-Magula vom präkeramischen Neolithikum bis zur mittleren Bronzezeit' in V. Milojčić, J. Boessneck and M. Hopf *Die Deutschen Ausgrabungen auf der Argissa-Magula in Thessalien 1 : das präkeramische Neolithikum sowie die Tier- und Pflanzenreste*, Rudolf Habelt
Bökönyi, S. (1973). 'Stock breeding' in D. R. Theocharis *Neolithic Greece*, National Bank of Greece

Boserup, E. (1965). *The Conditions of Agricultural Growth*, Aldine

Bottema, S. (1974). *Late Quaternary Vegetation History of Northwestern Greece*, University of Groningen

Boyd, J. M., Doney, J. M., Gunn, R. G. and Jewell, P. A. (1964). 'The Soay sheep of the island of Hirta, St Kilda', *Proceedings of the Zoological Society of London* 142: 129–63

Campbell, J. K. (1964). *Honour, Family and Patronage*, Oxford University Press

Chadwick, J. (1976). *The Mycenaean World*, Cambridge University Press

Cherry, J. (1977). Discussion recorded in J. L. Bintliff (ed.) *Mycenaean Geography*, British Association for Mycenaean Studies

  (1978). 'Generalization and the archaeology of the state' in D. Green, C. Haselgrove and M. Spriggs (eds.) *Social Organisation and Settlement*, British Archaeological Reports

Chisholm, M. (1968). *Rural Settlement and Land Use* (2nd edn), Hutchinson

Clark, C. and Haswell, M. (1970). *The Economics of Subsistence Agriculture* (4th edn), Macmillan

Clark, J. G. D. (1952). *Prehistoric Europe: The Economic Basis*, Methuen

Clarke, D. L. (1976). 'Mesolithic Europe: the economic basis' in G. de G. Sieveking, I. H. Longworth and K. E. Wilson (eds.) *Problems in Economic and Social Archaeology*, Duckworth

Clark-Forbes, M. H. (1976). 'Farming and foraging in prehistoric Greece: a cultural ecological perspective' in M. Dimen and E. Friedl (eds.) *Regional Variation in Modern Greece and Cyprus: towards a perspective on the ethnography of Greece* (Annals of the New York Academy of Sciences 268), New York Academy of Sciences

Clutton-Brock, T. H. and Harvey, P. H. (1978). 'Mammals, resources and reproductive strategies', *Nature* 273: 191–5

Dahl, G. and Hjort, A. (1976). *Having Herds* (Stockholm Studies in Social Anthropology 2), University of Stockholm

Davidson, D. A. (1971). 'Geomorphology and prehistoric settlement of the plain of Drama', *Revue de Géomorphologie Dynamique* 20: 22–6

Davidson, I. (1976). 'Les Mallaetes and Mandúver' in G. de G. Sieveking, I. H. Longworth and K. E. Wilson (eds) *Problems in Economic and Social Archaeology*, Duckworth

Dennell, R. W. (1972). 'The interpretation of plant remains: Bulgaria' in E. S. Higgs (ed.) *Papers in Economic Prehistory*, Cambridge University Press

  (1978). *Early Farming in South Bulgaria from the VI to the III Millennia BC*, British Archaeological Reports

Dennell, R. W. and Webley, D. (1975). 'Prehistoric settlements and land use in southern Bulgaria' in E. S. Higgs (ed.) *Palaeoeconomy*, Cambridge University Press

Dewolf, Y., Postel, F. and van Effenterre, H. (1963). 'Géographie préhistorique de la région de Mallia' in H. and M. van Effenterre (eds.) *Mallia, Site et Nécropoles*, fascicle 2 (Études Crétoises 13), Paul Geuthner

Diem, K. (1962). *Documenta Geigy, Scientific Tables* (6th edn), Geigy (UK) Pharmaceuticals Division

von den Driesch, A. and Enderle, K. (1976). 'Die Tierreste aus der Agia Sofia-Magula in Thessalien' in V. Milojčić, A. von den Driesch, K. Enderle, J. Milojčić-v. Zumbusch and K. Kilian *Magulen um Larisa in Thessalien, 1966*, Rudolf Habelt

Evans, A. J. (1899–1900). 'Knossos, 1: the palace', *Annual of the British School at Athens* 6: 3–70

Evans, J. D. (1968). 'Knossos Neolithic Part 2: summary and conclusions', *Annual of the British School at Athens* 63: 267–76

   (1971). 'Neolithic Knossos – the growth of a settlement', *Proceedings of the Prehistoric Society* 37 (2): 95–117

Finley, M. I. (1957). 'The Mycenaean tablets and economic history', *Economic History Review* 10: 128–41

Fleming, A. (1972). 'The genesis of pastoralism in European prehistory', *World Archaeology* 4: 179–91

Forbes, H. A. (1976). 'We have a little of everything' in M. Dimen and E. Friedl (eds.) *Regional Variation in Modern Greece and Cyprus: towards a perspective on the ethnography of Greece* (Annals of the New York Academy of Sciences 268), New York Academy of Sciences

Forge, A. (1972). 'Normative factors in the settlement size of Neolithic cultivators (New Guinea)' in P. J. Ucko, R. Tringham and G. W. Dimbleby (eds.) *Man, Settlement and Urbanism*, Duckworth

Freeman, L. G. (1973). 'The significance of mammalian faunas from Palaeolithic occupation in Cantabrian Spain', *American Antiquity* 38 (1): 3–44

Gamble, C. S. (forthcoming). 'Animal husbandry, population and urbanisation' in C. Renfrew and J. M. Wagstaff (eds.) *An Island Polity: the archaeology of exploitation in Melos*, Cambridge University Press

Gejvall, N-G. (1969). *Lerna I: The Fauna*, American School of Classical Studies at Athens

Gelb, I. J. (1965). 'The Ancient Mesopotamian ration system', *Journal of Near Eastern Studies* 24: 230–43

Gill, N. T. and Vear, K. C. (1966). *Agricultural Botany* (2nd edn), Duckworth

Gimbutas, M. (1974). 'Achilleion: a Neolithic mound in Thessaly', *Journal of Field Archaeology* 1: 277–302

Greig, J. R. A. and Turner, J. (1974). 'Some pollen diagrams from Greece and their archaeological significance', *Journal of Archaeological Science* 1: 177–94

Halstead, P. (1977). 'Prehistoric Thessaly: the submergence of civilisation' in J. L. Bintliff (ed.) *Mycenaean Geography*, British Association for Mycenaean Studies

Halstead, P., Hodder, I. and Jones, G. (1978). 'Behavioural archaeology and refuse patterns: a case study', *Norwegian Archaeological Review* 11: 118–31

Halstead, P. and Jones, G. (forthcoming). 'Early Neolithic economy in Thessaly – some evidence from excavations at Prodromos', *Anthropologika* 1

Haussoullier, B. (1880). 'Vases peints archaiques découverts à Knossos', *Bulletin de Correspondance Hellénique* 4: 124–7

Hillman, G. (1973). 'Agricultural productivity and past population potential at Aşvan', *Anatolian Studies* 23: 225–40

Hood, M. S. F. (1958). *Archaeological Survey of the Knossos Area*, British School at Athens

Hopf, M. (1962). 'Nutzpflanzen vom Lernaïschen Golf', *Jahrbuch des Römisch-Germanischen ZentralMuseums, Mainz* 9: 1–19

Hourmouziadis, G. (1972). 'Excavations at Prodromos, Karditsa' (in Greek), *Arkhaiologikon Deltion* 27 (B2): 394–6

Houston, J. M. (1964). *The Western Mediterranean World*, Longmans

Howell, R. (1970). 'A survey of Eastern Arcadia in prehistory', *Annual of the British School at Athens* 65: 79–127

Hubbard, R. N. L. B. (1979). 'Ancient agriculture and ecology at Servia' in C. Ridley and K. A. Wardle 'Rescue excavations at Servia 1971–1973: a preliminary report', *Annual of the British School at Athens* 74: 226–8

Isaac, G. (1978). 'The food-sharing behavior of protohuman hominids', *Scientific American* 238 (4): 90–108

James, H. M. and Frangopoulos, A. M. (1939). 'Summary of work at the Central Experimental Farm', *Cyprus Agricultural Journal* 34 (1): 5–19

Jones, G. and Halstead, P. (forthcoming). 'The economy' in K. A. Wardle *Excavations at Assiros Toumba, Central Macedonia*

Jordan, B. (1975). *Tierknochenfunde aus der Magula Pevkakia in Thessalien*, Institut für Palaeoanatomie, Domestikationsforschung und Geschichte der Tiermedizin der Universität München

Jullien, R. (1971). 'La Faune: batraciens, reptiles et mammifères', *Bulletin de Correspondance Hellénique* 95: 726–30

Killen, J. T. (1964). 'The wool industry of Crete in the Late Bronze Age', *Annual of the British School at Athens* 59: 1–15

Korfmann, M. (1976). 'Demircihüyük, 1975', *Anatolian Studies* 26: 36–8

McConnell, P. (1883). *The Agricultural Notebook*, Crosby Lockwood

McDonald, W. A. and Rapp, G. R. (1972). 'Perspectives' in W. A. McDonald and G. R. Rapp (eds.) *The Minnesota Messenia Expedition*, University of Minnesota Press

Narroll, R. S. (1962). 'Floor area and settlement population', *American Antiquity* 27 (4): 587–9

Payne, S. (1972). 'Partial recovery and sample bias' in E. S. Higgs (ed.) *Papers in Economic Prehistory*, Cambridge University Press

(1975). 'Faunal change at Franchthi Cave from 20,000 BC to 3,000 BC' in A. T. Clason (ed.) *Archaeozoological Studies*, North-Holland and American Elsevier

Pellet, P. L. and Shadarevian, S. (1970). *Food Composition Tables for Use in the Near East*, American University at Beirut

Rackham, O. (1972). 'Charcoal and plaster impressions' (Appendix 3) in P. Warren *Myrtos*, Thames and Hudson

Raulin, M. V. (1858). 'Description physique de l'île de Crète', *Actes de la Societé Linnéenne de Bordeaux* 22: 9–204 and 307–434

Reifenberg, A. (1938). *The Soils of Palestine*, Thomas Murby

Renfrew, C. (1972). *The Emergence of Civilisation*, Methuen

(1973). 'Trade and craft specialisation' in D. R. Theocharis *Neolithic Greece*, National Bank of Greece

(1977). 'Retrospect and prospect' in J. L. Bintliff (ed.) *Mycenaean Geography*, British Association for Mycenaean Studies

Renfrew, J. M. (1966). 'A report on recent finds of carbonised cereal grains and seeds from prehistoric Thessaly', *Thessalika* 5: 21–36

(1973a). *Palaeoethnobotany*, Methuen

(1973b). 'Agriculture' in D. R. Theocharis *Neolithic Greece*, National Bank of Greece

(1977). 'Plant remains' (Appendix 3) in J. E. Coleman *Keos, 1, Kephala*, American School of Classical Studies at Athens

Rutkowski, B. (1972). *Cult Places in the Aegean World*, Polish Academy of Sciences

Semple, E. C. (1932). *The Geography of the Mediterranean Region*, Constable

Seymour, J. and Seymour, S. (1973). *Self-Sufficiency*, Faber and Faber

Sherratt, A. G. (1973). 'The interpretation of change in European prehistory' in
    C. Renfrew (ed.) *The explanation of culture change*, Duckworth
    (1976). 'Resources, technology and trade in early European metallurgy' in G. de
    G. Sieveking, I. H. Longworth and K. E. Wilson (eds.) *Problems in Economic
    and Social Archaeology*, Duckworth
Sinos, S. (1971). *Die Vorklassischen Hausformen in der Ägäis*, Philip von Zabern
Stubbings, F. H. (1951). *Mycenean Pottery from the Levant*, Cambridge University
    Press
Theocharis, D. R. (1973). *Neolithic Greece*, National Bank of Greece
Turrill, W. B. (1929). *The Plant-Life of the Balkan Peninsula*, Oxford University
    Press
Wace, A. J. B. (1921–3). 'Excavations at Mycenae: the granary', *Annual of the
    British School at Athens* 25: 38–61.
Warren, P. (1972). *Myrtos*, Thames and Hudson
Warren, P. and Tzedhakis, J. (1974). 'Debla, an Early Minoan settlement in
    Western Crete', *Annual of the British School at Athens* 69: 299–342
Watson, J. N. (1979). 'Faunal remains' in C. Ridley and K. A. Wardle
    'Rescue excavations at Servia, 1971–1973: a preliminary report', *Annual of the
    British School at Athens* 74: 228–9
White, K. D. (1963). 'Wheat-farming in Roman times', *Antiquity* 37: 207–12
    (1970). *Roman Farming*, Thames and Hudson
Whitehead, G. K. (1948). *The Ancient White Cattle of Britain and their Descendants*,
    Faber and Faber
Williamson, G. and Payne, W. J. A. (1965). *An Introduction to Animal Husbandry
    in the Tropics* (2nd edn), Longmans
Wright, H. E. (1972). 'Vegetation history' in W. A. McDonald and G. R. Rapp
    (eds.) *The Minnesota Messenia Expedition*, University of Minnesota Press
van Zeist, W. and Bottema, S. (1971). 'Plant husbandry in Early Neolithic Nea
    Nikomedeia, Greece', *Acta Botanica Neerlandica* 20: 524–38
Zohary, D. (1969). 'The progenitors of wheat and barley in relation to domestication
    and agricultural dispersal in the Old World' in P. J. Ucko and G. W. Dimbleby
    (eds.) *The Domestication and Exploitation of Plants and Animals*, Duckworth

12

The effects of environmental change on the scheduling of visits to the Elands Bay Cave, Cape Province, S.A.

JOHN PARKINGTON

Interpretations of faunal remains may be phrased in terms of either local environmental factors or human subsistence activities, as the fauna is a complex reflection of both local ecosystems and man's place within them. This essay attempts to bring the two aspects together by considering the effects of environmental change on one particular part of human settlement, the timing of visits to a site. A number of assumptions about settlement patterns amongst hunter–gatherers and about what faunal and artifactual assemblages represent in terms of settlement are made. It is assumed that hunter–gatherers led mobile existences and that the particular form and pattern of movement is determined in large part by the distribution and availability of resources, both food and raw materials (see also Foley, ch. 6 above). In particular it is assumed that sites are occupied because of the set of resources which are available within easy reach of them and that movement between sites is related to differences in resource availabilities from place to place and from time to time. The corollaries of these assumptions are that faunal and plant remains reflect the reasons for and timing of site occupation and that sites and their assemblages are but segments of an overall settlement pattern related to regional resource availabilities. A distinction is made here between faunal evidence from a single site, which has local significance, and faunal evidence from a set of interrelated assemblages, which has regional significance. One final assumption, which follows from those previously mentioned, is that if the set of local resources changes for some reason then this may lead to alterations in the timing or duration of occupation of particular sites and, by extension, to the regional settlement pattern.

Operating in this framework, this paper presents evidence from a single site (the Elands Bay Cave on the southwestern coast of the Cape Province) and attempts to relate local environmental circumstances to the timing of visits to the cave.

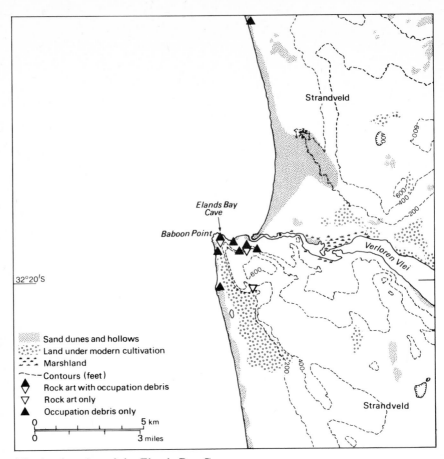

I2.I.   The local setting of the Elands Bay Cave.

ELANDS BAY CAVE

The present location of the Elands Bay Cave is shown in Fig. 12.1, whilst
its regional setting is presented in Fig. 12.2. Clearly the site occupies a very
favourable position, including in its catchment rocky and sandy shores, the
lower reaches of the Verlore Vlei estuary as well as the rocky cliff and sandy
plains to the east. A wide range of marine, estuarine and terrestrial foods can
be harvested within a few kilometres of the site, and these advantages are
reflected in the location of at least twenty archaeological occurrences near the
mouth of the estuary. The concentration of archaeological debris along rocky
shorelines, which in this part of the Atlantic coast constitute less than 10 per
cent of the total, has already been noted (Parkington 1976).

The hinterland of the site consists of a series of north–south orientated
zones of rather variable potential. These are, from west to east, the Sandveld,
the Cape Folded Belt (subdivided by the valley of the Olifants river) and the
Karoo basin. The area falls wholly within the winter rainfall zone of the

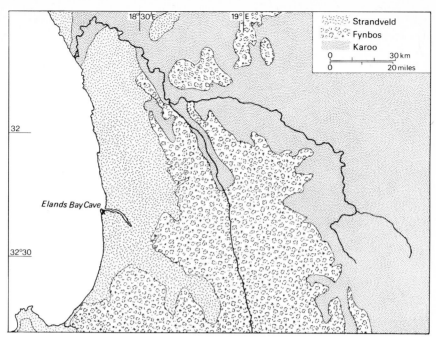

The regional setting of the Elands Bay Cave.

southwestern Cape, receiving more than 70 per cent of annual rainfall in the colder months of April to September. Rainfall is lowest on the coast and in the Karoo where annual amounts may be well below 100 mm, and highest in the Cape Folded Belt with some stations recording over 1000 m. The vegetation communities of both Sandveld and Karoo are adapted to low rainfall and porous soils whilst those of the Cape Folded Belt comprise the classic 'fynbos' forms (Acocks 1953). Surface water is permanently available in the valley of the Olifants river and the great variety of topography and habitat in the Cape Folded Belt generally means that there exists a varied set of plant and animal resources.

Using both archaeological and historic sources it has been argued (Parkington 1972; 1976; 1977) that hunter–gatherers of the Late Holocene exploited this set of resource zones by movements which took them into the Folded Belt in the dry months and into the Sandveld and Karoo regions in the wet months. In this way the more temporary potentials of these latter could have been tapped when the plant and animal foods of the Folded Belt were least available. More specifically the reliable shellfish resources of the coast could have replaced plant foods normally utilised but which are less abundant in the wet winter months. In this context the occupation of the Elands Bay Cave would have been scheduled for some part of the winter and would have been one segment in a settlement pattern including Sandveld, Cape Folded Belt and Olifants river valley sites.

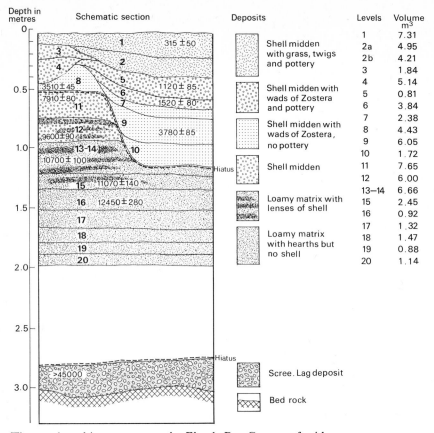

12.3.   The stratigraphic sequence at the Elands Bay Cave as of mid 1977.

However, occupation at the Elands Bay Cave is documented by faunal remains for at least 30 000 years, covering an important period of change at the end of the Pleistocene. So far about 17 000 years of occupation have been sampled, with the only major episode of non-deposition coming in the Early Holocene, between 8000 B.P. and 4000 B.P. (Fig. 12.3). Faunal identifications from the site are tabulated (Tables 12.1, 12.2, 12.3 and 12.4) and will be used as the basis for discussion of, first, changes in the local environment and, secondly, the reaction of human groups to those changes.

Changes in local environment

Changes in resource availabilities in the vicinity of the Elands Bay Cave at the end of the Pleistocene were brought about by two phenomena, both related to the melting of the major ice sheets and its effects. With the relaxation of the high pressure systems over the ice caps of both hemispheres at the end of the Pleistocene, climatic zones shifted polewards. In the Cape the most important manifestations of this were a general rise in temperatures

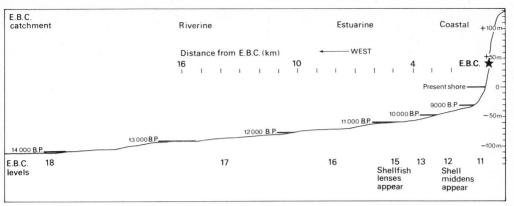

12.4.   Schematic cross-section of the off-shore contours at the Elands Bay Cave.

and a reduction in the area affected by the cyclonic rains of the westerly wind belt. Thus whereas in the Late Pleistocene cyclonic storms may have reached the Cape throughout the year, in the Holocene the whole system moved south and passed by the Cape in the summer, producing a winter rainfall regime. It is likely that the Holocene arid environments of the Karoo north of the winter rainfall area were well within that area during glacial periods of the Late Pleistocene (van Zinderen Bakker 1976) whilst the present winter rainfall area, including the Elands Bay Cave, received at least some rain in all seasons. The combination of altered rainfall distribution and lowered temperatures seems certain to have resulted in different animal and plant resource availabilities.

A second phenomenon of equal significance was the terminal Pleistocene rise in sea level which within six or seven thousand years transformed the Elands Bay Cave catchment from inland riverine to coastal estuarine. Although it is difficult to offer precise figures on coastline movement and sea level rise, a rough guide to the changes relevant to the Elands Bay Cave sequence is presented in Figs 12.4 and 12.5. The coastal resources of the southwestern Cape are extremely rich largely because of the very high primary productivity of the upwelling system known as the Benguela Current (Hart and Currie 1960). Changes in the location of the coastline in relation to the stable Cape Folded Belt must have prompted changes in exploitation systems designed to utilise one or other or both.

Although the sample sizes are as yet rather small, it is likely that levels 16 to 20 can be taken together as representing a relatively stable Late Pleistocene situation from about 17000 B.P. to about 12000 B.P. During this period when the coastline advanced from about 37 km to about 12 km west of the site and when temperatures rose presumably gradually, the local environment supported a number of large animals, many of them grazers. The faunal assemblage is dominated by rhino, equids, buffalo and eland, suggesting that there was a higher grass component than is normal in fynbos communities.

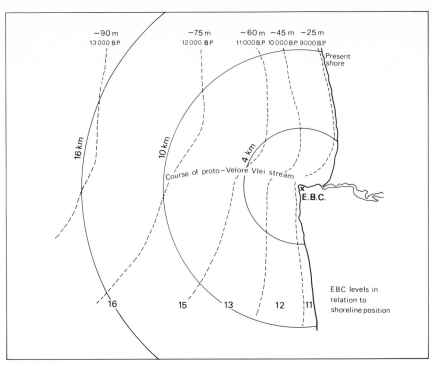

12.5.   Hypothesised shore lines and their relation to the location of the Elands Bay Cave.

However, the presence of *Raphicerus*, and in particular the grysbok, would probably point not to grassland but to a mosaic of fynbos and grassy swathes. The very low marine component presumably reflects the distance of the coastline, and the small number of ducks and cormorants is typically riverine. The higher numbers of gannets toward the end of this period has been linked to the rise of sea level and the formation of islands off the coast, as gannets and penguins, unlike cormorants, are unable to roost on the mainland (Avery and Siegfried pers. comm.). Thus during the Late Pleistocene the major influence on the local environment of the Elands Bay Cave was probably the changes in temperature and rainfall distribution which may have had the effect of lowering the carrying capacity by reducing habitats suited to large grazing forms. There is no way of demonstrating such changes as yet since it is difficult to measure the energy expenditure involved in catching the animals represented on a faunal list.

Between levels 15 and 11 at the site, dating from 11 000 B.P. to about 8000 B.P., a number of cumulative changes are visible which illustrate more rapid alterations of the local environment brought about by both climatic change and sea level rise. This is particularly interesting because Fig. 12.4 would suggest that it was precisely by level 15 that the coast approached within a 'Higgsian' distance of the site (that is, it moved from 12 km to about 5 km west of the cave: Higgs and Vita-Finzi 1972). Assuming that shellfish were

TABLE 12.1. *Elands Bay Cave: terrestrial mammal fauna*

	1	2	3	4	5	6	7	8	9	10	11	12	13/14	15	16	17	18	19	20
Erinaceus cf. *frontalis*, hedgehog	—	—	—	1	—	1	—	—	—	5	1	12	3	1	—	—	—	1	1
Leporidae gen. et sp. indet (2 spp.), hares	—	—	1	1	—	1	1	1	1	—	2	3	2	—	—	2	1	1	1
Bathyergus suillus, dune mole rat	1	1	2	1	—	1	1	1	5	26	2	30	14	3	2	2	2	4	4
Hystrix africae-australis, porcupine	1	1	1	1	—	1	?1	1	1	1	1	1	1	1	1	—	1	1	—
Papio ursinus, chacma baboon	1	1	1	1	—	—	1	—	—	?1	1	1	1	—	—	—	—	—	—
Canis cf. *mesomelas*, jackal	2	1	1	1	—	—	—	—	3	3	1	6	—	—	—	1	—	—	—
Vulpes chama, silver jackal	—	—	—	—	—	—	—	—	1	1	1	1	1	—	—	—	—	—	—
Lycaon pictus, hunting dog	—	—	—	—	—	—	—	—	—	?1	—	—	—	—	—	—	—	—	—
Ictonyx striatus, striped polecat	—	—	—	—	—	—	—	—	—	—	—	2	1	1	1	1	—	—	1
Mellivora capensis, honey badger	—	—	—	—	—	—	—	—	—	—	—	—	1	—	—	—	—	—	—
Herpestes ichneumon, Egyptian mongoose	1	1	1	1	—	1	1cf	—	1	1	1cf	—	—	1	1	—	—	?1	—
Herpestes pulverulentus, Cape grey mongoose	—	—	—	1	—	1	—	1	1	1	1	1	2	—	—	—	1	—	—
Felis libyca, wildcat	—	—	—	—	—	—	1cf	—	—	1cf	—	—	1	—	1	—	—	—	—
Felis cf. *caracal*, caracal	—	—	1	1	—	1	—	2	3	1	2	2	1	2	—	2	2	1	—
Panthera pardus, leopard	—	—	—	2	—	—	—	—	—	1	1	1	1	—	—	1	—	—	—
Orycteropus afer, aardvark	—	1	—	—	—	1	1	—	—	1	—	1	1	—	1	1	1	1	—
Procavia capensis, rock hyrax	2	2	2	2	—	1	—	2	3	4	2	8	7	2	—	2	2	—	—
Loxodonta africana, elephant	—	—	—	—	—	—	—	—	—	1	1	1	1	—	—	1	—	1	—
Equus capensis, 'giant Cape horse'	—	—	—	—	—	—	—	—	—	—	—	—	1	—	1	—	—	—	—
Equus sp. indet., indeterminate equid	—	—	—	1	—	—	—	—	—	—	1	1	1	1	1	1	1	1	1
Rhinocerotidae gen. et sp. indet., rhinoceros	—	—	—	—	—	—	—	—	—	—	—	1	1	—	—	—	—	—	—
Hippopotamus amphibius, hippo	—	1	1	1	—	—	—	1	—	—	—	—	—	—	—	—	—	—	—
Suidae gen. et sp. indet., pig	—	—	—	—	—	—	—	—	—	—	—	—	1	—	—	—	1	—	—
Taurotragus oryx, eland	—	—	—	—	—	—	—	—	—	1	1	3	6	1	1	—	1	1	—
Hippotragus cf. *leucophaeus*, blue antelope	—	—	—	—	—	—	—	—	—	—	—	—	1	—	—	1	1	—	—
Alcelaphus buselaphus/Connochaetes gnou, hartebeest/wildebeest	—	—	—	—	—	—	—	—	—	—	1	1	3	—	—	—	—	—	—
Sylvicapra grimmia, grey duiker	5	2	—	1	—	1	—	2	—	2	2	3	3	2	—	—	—	—	—
Oreotragus oreotragus, klipspringer	3	1	—	1	—	—	—	—	2	—	—	1	1	—	—	—	—	—	—
Raphicerus campestris, steenbok	3	1	—	1	—	2	—	—	2	1	2	10	3	—	—	1	1	—	—
Raphicerus melanotis, grysbok	1	1	1	—	—	—	—	—	—	—	2	8	5	2	2	—	—	—	—
Raphicerus spp., steenbok/grysbok	8	4	3	4	1	3	—	5	9	6	12	30	16	6	3	4	2	1	1
Ovis aries, sheep	1	2	—	1	1	1	1	—	—	1	—	—	—	1	1	—	1	—	—
Syncerus caffer, Cape buffalo	1	—	—	—	—	—	—	—	—	—	—	3	2	1	1	—	1	1	1
Pelorovis antiquus, giant buffalo	—	—	—	—	—	—	—	—	—	—	—	—	—	—	—	1cf	—	—	—
Bovidae – general																			
Small (Neotragini)	8	4	5	3	1	3	1	5	9	6	12	30	17	6	3	4	2	3	1
Small medium (*Sylvicapra*, *Ovis*, et al.)	7	4	2	2	2	2	1	3	3	2	3	3	4	2	1	1	2	3	1
Large medium (Alcelaphini and Hippotragini)	1	1	1	1	—	—	—	—	2	2	2	2	2	2	1	1	1	1	—
Large (*Taurotragus* and Bovini)	1	1	—	1	—	—	—	—	2	2	1	6	8	2	2	2	1	1	1

Counts by R. G. Klein

TABLE 12.1 *Elands Bay Cave : avifauna*

Birds	1	2	3	4	5	6	7	8	9	10	11	12	13	15	16	17	18	19	20
Phalocrocorax capensis, Cape cormorant	41	38	13	21	7	11	7	4	27		13	116	17	5	1	1	1	1	3
Phalocrocorax carbo, White-breasted cormorant	3	0	2	2	2	1	1	1	2		1	13	2	1	1	0	0	0	0
Phalocrocorax neglectus, Bank cormorant	2	1	1	1	0	0	0	0	1		0	1	0	0	0	0	0	0	0
Phalocrocorax africanus, Reed cormorant	0	0	0	1	0	0	0	0	0		1	2	0	0	0	0	0	0	0
Spheniscus demursus, Jackass penguin	8	11	4	8	1	5	1	1	4		3	13	6	8	0	0	0	0	0
Morus capensis, Cape gannet	1	1	1	1	0	1	1	0	1		1	11	8	6	2	3	1	1	0
Phoenicopteridae, Flamingoes	1	1	1	1	0	0	1	1	2		1	1	0	0	0	0	0	0	0
Pelecanidae, Pelicans	1	0	0	0	0	0	0	0	0		1	1	0	0	0	0	0	0	0

Counts by G. Avery

TABLE 12.3. *Elands Bay Cave : fish, rock lobster and seals*

	1	2	3	4	5	6	7	8	9	10	11	12	13	15	16	17	18	19	20
Fish																			
Lithognathus lithognathus, White Steenbras	6	19	4	29	6	37	9	16	54		42	540	14	2	0	0	0	0	0
Rhabdosargus globiceps, White Stumpnose	0	15	4	15	0	2	1	16	1		18	154	10	1	0	0	0	0	0
Mugilidae, Haarder	2	0	2	1	1	1	1	3	0		2	44	60	1	1	2	2	1	0
Lobster																			
Jasus lalandii, Cape Rock Lobster	400	223	49	268	82	57	27	72	49		129	496	14	1	0	0	0	0	0
Seals																			
Arctocephalus pusillus, Cape Fur Seal	6	5	2	5	2	4	1	2	3		4	39	3	1	1	0	0	0	0

Counts by C. Poggenpoel and J. E. Parkington

TABLE 12.4. *Elands Bay Cave: mass of tortoise bone and ostrich egg shell fragments*

	Tortoise bone mass (kg per m³)	Ostrich egg shell mass (kg per m³)
1	0.31	26.4
2	0.48	26.3
3	0.58	28.8
4	0.28	19.3
5	0.06	27.2
6	0.18	11.7
7	0.09	21.4
8	0.25	22.3
9	1.60	31.9
10		
11	3.01	52.10
12	12.6	259.66
13	24.43	833.68
15	12.6	264.28
16	12.9	743.69
17	3.73	259.37
18	8.21	348.40
19	10.05	353.97
20	4.40	185.52

gathered by women and that such activities are a better reflection of site catchment than the hunting of mobile game, it is interesting to note the first appearance of lenses of shellfish in level 15 dated to 11 000 B.P. with the sea apparently 5 km distant.

Between levels 15 and 11 the coastline advanced from 5 km to only a few hundred metres from the site and presumably the final effects of the rise in temperatures and changes in rainfall distribution were felt. Another related event was the drowning of more and more of the lower reaches of the Verlore Vlei valley, changing the cave catchment from riverine to upper estuarine to lower estuarine and finally to coastal.

Habitats suited to large grazers seem to have disappeared in this interval and at least two animals, a giant horse and a giant buffalo, became extinct as a result (Klein 1972; 1974). Other large animals such as rhino and the Cape buffalo are absent or notably rarer after 9000 B.P., and are replaced in the faunal assemblages by smaller forms more adapted to browsing than grazing. This phenomenon has been documented throughout the Cape Folded Belt and adjacent coasts and clearly results from the changes in temperature and rainfall mentioned earlier. Holocene forms include alcelaphine and neotragine bovids associated with the winter rainfall fynbos vegetation mosaic. It is noteworthy that amongst the browsing bovids the grysbok is recognised earliest in the cave sequence whilst steenbok and duiker appear later. Although samples are small this may reflect something of the character of the local environment and in particular a shift from 'typical fynbos' to the fynbos-related vegetation known as coastal strandveld, dominated by the family Restionaceae. Modern observations near to the Elands Bay Cave have shown that both duiker and steenbok prefer strandveld habitats whilst the grysbok prefers fynbos bush (Millar, pers. comm.).

The approach of the coast is of course much more clearly reflected in the rise to dominance of marine animals between 11000 and 9000 B.P. The order in which marine forms appear in the faunal sequence may have as much to do with subsistence strategies as with environmental conditions, as marine foods are not equally transportable nor equally attractive in competition with terrestrial resources of equivalent size. Most marine foods first appear in level 15 but dominate the faunal assemblages only from level 12, a change which in terms of depositional character is marked by a transition from brown loams with lenses of shells to true shell middens with little interstitial fine grained material other than ash. Very high frequencies of cormorants, marine fish, rock lobsters and seals relative to the frequencies of terrestrial animals in levels younger than 9500 B.P. reflects the fact that the coastline with its rich set of animal foods was by then located a kilometre or so from the cave (see Fig. 12.4). The dominance of cormorants amongst marine birds may well be a consequence of their less migratory habits and of their ability to roost on the mainland as well as on coastal islands.

Changes in that part of the Verlore Vlei which could be exploited from the cave are reflected in the mammal, bird and fish components of the fauna. Hippo remains, whilst never common at the site, are restricted to levels after 11000 B.P. at which time the frequencies of the bones of shallow water birds such as flamingos and pelicans also rise. It seems that by 11000 B.P. the drowned lower reaches of the river had penetrated to within exploitable distance of the site. Further confirmation is provided by the very dramatic rise in the numbers of fish of the Mugilidae family by about 10000 B.P. These fishes are known to penetrate further into estuarine waters than any other marine species. Mugilidae are still common in level 12 at about 9500 B.P. but thereafter decline in numbers and are overshadowed by fish of the Sparidae family which penetrate only into the lower reaches of estuarine environments.

The sizes of steenbras in terminal Pleistocene levels may also inform on changes in the local environment, particularly the relationship between the location of the cave and the estuary. In levels 12 and 11, between 9500 and 8000 B.P., during the final rise of sea level to its present position there are considerable numbers of very small steenbras in the faunal collections, whilst these are absent thereafter. Since soon after birth steenbras fry enter estuaries and remain there until they are ready to spawn, this may reflect a tendency to fish partly in the vlei in the earlier period, yet only in the marine environment later. This in turn may relate to the relative distances from cave to vlei and from cave to coast as the coast finally shifted to its present position within 200 metres of the site. Between 9500 B.P. and 8000 B.P. the estuary mouth may have been as close to the cave as the shore was, whereas now it is much further.

Some features of level 13, dated to about 10 500 B.P., require comment in relation to the changing local environment of the site. The density of ostrich egg shell fragments and tortoise bone is high in levels 15 to 20 but in both cases reaches a pronounced peak in level 13 before dropping consistently through levels 12 and 11 and reaching stable low levels in levels 8 to 1. In these cases it is difficult to distinguish availability (reflecting environmental circumstances) from selectivity (reflecting subsistence activities) but it is very likely that changes in availability are involved. Certainly the higher Pleistocene figures for ostrich egg shell fragments may be taken as reflecting an environment more suited to ostriches, but the figures for tortoise bone may mean that in the Holocene fewer tortoises were collected partly because of a loss of land to the sea and partly because a number of marine alternatives of equivalent size were available. However, the rise in both figures in level 13 probably has a different explanation. It is quite likely that by 10 500 B.P. the contribution of protein by large grazing animals was less certain and that it was not as yet possible to replace that contribution by one from marine foods from this site. Until the coastline came close enough to be exploited from the Elands Bay Cave, visits to the site may have involved a subsistence pattern which of necessity placed more reliance on gatherable protein such as tortoises and eggs. The peak in these items may thus reflect a temporary solution to the problems presented by the changing local environment particularly in protein intake. In this respect it is notable that tortoise numbers are often high in near-coastal habitats (Greig, pers. comm.).

Somewhere between 9000 B.P. and 8000 B.P. the coastline reached its present position but surprisingly this marks the beginning of a 4000 year interruption in the accumulation of sediments in the cave. Excavations are planned in some other sites near the mouth of the Verlore Vlei to discover whether this is a feature of the cave or whether it is a more general phenomenon related to changes in local environment. Until more information is available the coincidence of the appearance of fully modern conditions and the cessation of occupation remains suggestive but inexplicable.

Shortly after 4000 B.P. the cave was re-occupied by human groups, though there is good reason to suppose that a number of carnivores had used the site during the depositional hiatus, causing great disturbance to already existing levels. In most cases the disturbed areas are very easy to recognise as they are unstratified and homogenised by comparison with *in situ* deposits.

The deposits of the last 4000 years are lenses of shell midden dominated by marine fauna but with consistent numbers of steenbok, grysbok, hyrax, dune mole-rat and a range of small to large carnivores. The contrast with the larger fauna of the Late Pleistocene may be seen in the ratio of small and small-medium to large and large-medium bovids. Where as in the Late Pleistocene the ratio of minimum numbers of individuals is 15 to 12, in the Late Holocene it is 53 to 6. Fynbos faunal communities are characterised by large numbers of small browsing territorial bovids such as the grysbok and the duiker and by low numbers of grazing forms. The most important changes in local environment during the Late Holocene are changes in the human environment, marked by the appearance of domestic animals in the last 2000 years.

To sumarise, there is no doubt that the environmental changes associated with the Pleistocene to Holocene transition resulted in substantial change to the catchment of the Elands Bay Cave. This is manifested in the faunal sequence at the site not only among the mammalian remains but among birds, fish, reptiles and invertebrates. Studies of pollens and sediments now in progress may throw further light on the modification of the local environment. As a result it may be predicted that as change accelerated between 11 000 B.P. and 9000 B.P. the prehistoric populations would have continually re-assessed their attitude to the cave, its catchment and the role of its occupation in their annual settlement. In the next section some evidence is presented to show that such reassessment led to changes in the scheduling of visits to the cave.

The scheduling of visits to the Elands Bay Cave

Since Late Holocene observations are more numerous and widespread than those from the Pleistocene, it is convenient to consider that period first. The uppermost ten levels at the Elands Bay cave are dominated by shellfish remains and contain very little evidence for the exploitation of plant foods. There are plant remains but these are mostly bedding grasses, twigs and pieces of kelp. In this respect the cave is in marked contrast with inland sites in the same area, where the residues of plant foods, and in particular parts of underground tubers and corms, are abundant. This contrast has been taken as a reflection of the complementary occupation of inland and coastal sites and of the temporary replacement of plant foods by shellfish during coastal settlement. Moreover, since in the winter rainfall area both underground and above ground plant foods are more abundant in the dry summer months and much less so in the winter, it has been assumed that coastal settlement in the Late Holocene was scheduled for some part of the winter (Parkington 1972; 1976; 1977). Similar interpretations have been made for sites along the southern coast of South Africa (Deacon 1976; Klein 1974; 1977).

There is some evidence from the uppermost levels at the Elands Bay Cave to support this interpretation apart from the notable absence of plant food remains. Both tortoises and dassies are very prominent in inland faunas of the Late Holocene (Parkington and Poggenpoel 1971) but are infrequent at equivalent time periods at Elands Bay. Whilst this may reflect a preference for marine alternatives or the lowered terrestrial catchment of coastal sites, it is likely that tortoises are less active and thus less available in the colder months of the year. Perhaps more positive evidence comes from studies of marine molluscs and seal mandibles. In the Late Holocene levels at the site, the black mussel *Choromytilus* comprised between 40 per cent and 60 per cent of identifiable shellfish and in one case over 80 per cent. These animals may become toxic in the summer months when the increased upwelling occasionally stimulates a massive population explosion of poisonous dinoflagellates which accumulate in filter-feeding mussels. Not all such 'plankton blooms' include poisonous forms but sampling has shown that toxic levels have occurred almost annually, particularly in the sheltered bays of the Elands Bay area (Grindley and Nel 1968, 1970). It seems very unlikely that prehistoric populations would have consistently harvested potentially dangerous resources except in the safer winter period.

Measurement of the mandible sizes of seals from the Late Holocene levels shows a mean size very similar to that of recently culled seals from the late winter or early spring months (Table 12.6; Best pers. comm.; Parkington 1972; 1976). It would have been almost impossible for prehistoric groups to have taken such a range of yearling pups unless visits were scheduled for some time within the period July to October.

The most economic explanation of both the positive characteristics of the Elands Bay data and the complementarity of inland and coastal observations seems to be that coastal settlement in the Late Holocene was rather strictly scheduled. This is not surprising in an environment where there is a predictable and reliable seasonality in climatic factors and thus a regimentation in vegetative cycles and animal behaviours. In other regions of the Cape the constraints of environment in terms of resource distributions in space and time may have been considerably less, allowing more flexible settlement decisions to have been made.

It is unfortunate that the environments and economies of the Early Holocene observations cannot be determined at the Elands Bay Cave. However, prior to this hiatus in deposition there is evidence for consistent re-scheduling of occupation times in response to the rapidly changing local environment. The interpretation offered here is that during the Late Pleistocene visits were scheduled for the summer months, but that, largely because of the approach of the coastline, they shifted in the terminal Pleistocene to the spring months and in the Early Holocene to the later part of winter and early spring.

The density of tortoise bone by level (Table 12.4) provides one strand of the argument. Examining the record from the top level down, the figures rise to a peak through levels 11 and 12 to level 13 and then drop to a stable shelf in levels 15 to 20. The values for this early period are still considerably higher than in the Holocene. This is not an artifact of the changing depositional rate in these levels because the figures far exceed the fluctuations in all other faunal elements with the exception of ostrich egg shell fragments. It has been noted by both researchers and farmers that tortoises become highly active in the spring, slightly less so in the summer and are not often encountered in the winter. Thus one possible explanation of the figures is that the peak marks a shift in level 13 into occupation during the spring hyperactive time with

TABLE 12.5. *Elands Bay Cave : shellfish frequencies*

Per-centage	1	2	3	4	5	6	7	8	9	10	11	12	13	15
Limpets	30	47	40	44		40			4		85	58	98	99
Mussels	31	34	50	48		50			84		9	11	1	—
Whelks	26	11	8	5		6			10		1	29	1	—
Other	13	8	3	3		4			2		5	2	1	1

TABLE 12.6. *The mean sizes and standard deviations of monthly samples of seal mandibles of animals whose age at death was known (Rand 1967), compared with similar data from samples from the Elands Bay Cave*

	N	Mean	Standard deviation
November	13	99.5	6.74
EBC levels 12 + 13	37	97.0	5.70
October	28	95.0	3.50
September	30	92.7	4.0
August	23	93.0	3.5
EBC levels 1–10	27	91.0	7.94
July	11	87.9	2.3

the partial decline evident in lower levels implying summer occupation. It is of course possible that what is being documented here is simply the appearance of the shore, the loss of surrounding terrestrial habitat and the availability of marine alternatives in the Holocene.

A second strand in the argument relates to the frequencies of mussels and limpets in the terminal Pleistocene levels at the cave. It is noticeable (Table 12.5) that the earliest shell lenses at the site in levels 15 and 13 contain only limpets, whilst mussels appear in small numbers in level 12, increasing in level 11 to parity with limpets. If it is assumed that prehistoric groups were aware of the danger in eating filter-feeding mussels during the summer months, these figures could be taken as reflecting a shift from occupation during the dangerous season through to occupation at a safer season. Limpets never accumulate toxic substances and may be eaten throughout the year. It is certainly a fact that of all the middens known along this part of the Atlantic coast only the levels from the terminal Pleistocene at the Elands Bay Cave and one other midden are dominated by limpets. Although this interpretation is tempting it may be that the gradual appearance of mussels in these levels simply represents the colonisation of the coast by black mussels which had not found suitable habitats in the Late Pleistocene environment (Klein 1972).

There is a small but perceptible difference in the mean size of seal mandibles from the Late Holocene and those from the terminal Pleistocene (Table 12.6). Whilst those from levels 1 to 11 most resemble the modern

TABLE 12.7. *Elands Bay Cave: percentages of very young individuals of Raphicerus (steenbok or grysbok) as reflected in unworn deciduous premolars and unfused epiphyses*

Levels	N	Percentage d P4UW	N	Percentage unfused epiphyses
1–9	57	12.0	164	23.0
11	19	32.0	46	32.6
12	50	40.0	114	35.0
13	30	44.0	44	50.0
15–20	26	26.0	93	30.10

Counts and identification by R. G. Klein

TABLE 12.8. *Recorded births of Raphicerus by month*

Months	No. of recorded births	As percentage of total births
Jan.	0	
Feb.	3	
Mar.	3	32
Apr.	2	
May	1	
June	1	12
July	1	
Aug.	3	
Sep.	3	40
Oct.	4	
Nov.	2	16
Dec.	2	

Information supplied by Professor R. Bigalke

August or September means, those from levels 12 and 13 are almost the same as the modern October mean. It is difficult to assess the significance of this shift in view of the range of measurements from the two samples, but a re-scheduling of a month or two would make precisely such a difference to the mean size of seal available.

It was noticeable during excavation that there were above average numbers of very small grysbok or steenbok mandibles in level 13 and perhaps also in adjacent levels. The percentages of immature animals, measured either on tooth eruption data or the fusion of epiphyses (Table 12.7), shows clearly that in level 13 there is indeed a peak of individuals which were probably newborn. It should be noted that this represents a shift in the ages of *Raphicerus* killed and not in the density of animals per level, and is thus not subject to problems of changes in rates of deposition. The correspondence between these figures and the densities of tortoise and ostrich egg shell fragments is remarkable and surely not coincidental. From high values in Late Pleistocene levels the numbers of newborn animals reach a peak in level 13, then drop consistently in levels 12 and 11 and are very low in the Late Holocene levels. The question as to whether these data have seasonal implications is hampered by the great difficulties encountered in studying the habits of small shy animals such as the steenbok and grysbok. The result is that the most accurate data on birth peaks among these animals came from tame pairs (Table 12.8). Nevertheless the observations seem at present to show two birth bulges in the autumn and spring months, a bimodal distribution which may point to the role of photoperiodic changes in the timing of births (Bigalke pers. comm.). If these data are a true reflection of conditions in the wild, then the Elands Bay Cave fluctuations may imply a re-scheduling of visits and therefore a shift in prey ages. One interpretation would be that the rise to level 13 and subsequent drop to the Holocene low represents a shift through a pattern of occupation during the spring birth bulge. However, the autumn bulge is perhaps only slightly less likely.

There may be information on the scheduling of visits to be got from the bird remains, but the samples as yet are too small. For example it seems very likely that the gannets were obtained as corpses washed up by the sea since these birds are much less land-orientated than the cormorants. From some preliminary beach walks (Avery and Cooper, pers. comm.) it appears that gannets are washed up more frequently in the summer months whilst breeding than in the winter months when birds tend to disperse to the feeding grounds at sea. Thus the relatively high numbers of gannets in levels 17 to 13 may reflect summer orientated visits as much as the number of breeding islands, and the Holocene concentration on the less migratory cormorants may reflect the relative absence of gannets. However, these must be considered very tentative remarks.

To summarise, there are a number of sets of evidence which, although individually open to several interpretations, may be said to have cumulative significance. All are consistent with the hypothesis that during the terminal Pleistocene, faced with relatively rapid environmental change, prehistoric groups re-scheduled their visits to the Elands Bay Cave from summer to spring and ultimately to late winter. Other shifts are visible at this time, which may or may not be related to seasonality. Thus, at the very end of the Pleistocene, very large numbers of tortoises and ostrich egg shell fragments, as well as a rise in the numbers of eland remains, may reflect a short-term solution to subsistence problems at the site between longer-term patterns based on large migratory game in the Pleistocene and marine foods in the Holocene. Interestingly, this interpretation would fit the changes in artifact frequencies at the site (Pettigrew *et al.* forthcoming) in which the terminal Pleistocene pattern represents a drift away from the Late Pleistocene pattern but *not* in the direction of that of the Holocene. Once again the impression of a short-term solution to rapidly changing circumstances is gained.

The key to the interpretation of the sequence is the consistently transitional position of levels 12 and 11 between the patterned Holocene situation and the highly 'individual' level 13. It is in these levels that seal mandible sizes drop, that tortoise bone densities drop, that shell middens appear, that the percentages of newborn *Raphicerus* drop and that mussels appear. There are a number of artifacts such as fish gorges, ground stone discs and scrapers made from mussel shells which are virtually confined to this part of the sequence. It is difficult to avoid the conclusion that at this time new subsistence strategies were being evolved, and that this meant innovation in artifact manufacture and re-assessment of scheduling arrangements.

ELANDS BAY CAVE IN WIDER PERSPECTIVE

The Elands Bay Cave has presumably always been occupied briefly as one segment of a settlement system involving the occupation of many open and cave sites in a more or less seasonally orientated schedule. It is interesting to speculate on how the segmentation of this site into a regional system might have changed over the time scale for which evidence exists. There are two obvious possibilities. It may be that the systems did not change between Late Pleistocene and Holocene times but that different manifestations of the system are superimposed on one another at sites such as Elands Bay Cave as the local environments changed. In this interpretation the cave would have been at first an inland, then a near coastal and finally a coastal stop on an unchanging annual beat between mountains and sea. The second possibility is that the regional systems of which occupations of individual sites are but segments may have changed considerably at the end of the Pleistocene. This would mean that not only the timing of occupation but also the relationship between occupations at related sites would have changed.

Unfortunately very little data exists by which these alternatives can be tested. Hilary Deacon has suggested (1976, pp. 163–4) that there were in fact major differences between Late Pleistocene and Holocene subsistence systems. He argues that the former, orientated around big-name hunting, correlates with 'large local group organisation, low population density, large territorial range and the absence of fixed territorial boundaries', the latter, orientated around plant food gathering and the hunting of small non-migratory animals, with 'organisation into smaller foraging groups with a higher overall density on the landscape, with territorial range more restricted and territorial boundaries more fixed' (1976, p. 163). This model whilst attractive and feasible remains untested in the absence of sets of Late Pleistocene data from sites which could reasonably be thought of as segments of settlement systems as defined here. It is quite probable, however, that when such data are recovered the situation in at least some parts of southern Africa will be as Deacon has described. It may be anticipated that not all Late Pleistocene settlement systems will look alike.

In the absence of primary observations, some circumstantial evidence in support of the second possibility outlined earlier and the one suggested by Hilary Deacon may be mentioned. In the first place, the environmental changes of the terminal Pleistocene did not simply involve shifts in a standard set of zones, but saw the elimination of particular patterns of resource distributions and the creation of new ones. Both the rainfall distribution of the Late Pleistocene and the spatial configuration of coast, coastal plain and mountains were peculiar to that period and were no longer encountered in the Holocene. Holocene settlement must therefore have been radically re-organised to meet new circumstances. Following on from this is the observation that terminal Pleistocene assemblages of both animal remains and artifacts (those between about 12000 B.P. and 8000 B.P.) seem to differ from those of either the Holocene or Late Pleistocene (prior to 12000 B.P.) but are not transitional in the sense of illustrating the gradual transformation of the one into the other. Janette Deacon (1979) has suggested a threefold subdivision of the Late Stone Age of the southern Cape in which the Albany of the terminal Pleistocene is in fact less like the Wilton of the Holocene than is the Robberg of the Late Pleistocene. At the Elands Bay Cave in levels from about 12000 B.P. to 9000 B.P. there are artifactual changes which do not seem to lead in or into the artifactual patterns of the Holocene. Thus the percentage of shale artifacts increases in those levels but decreases again after 8000 B.P. and ground stone artifacts and bone fish gorges are more common between nine and ten thousand years ago than either before or since. Similarly in the case of faunal remains the terminal Pleistocene levels seem to be marked by concentrations and peaks quite peculiar to that period. This suggests, but in no way proves, that the prehistoric peoples of the terminal Pleistocene were improvising in the face of radically altering environmental circumstances and that this improvisation produced a set of visibly distinct material remains.

The difficulty in establishing the Late Pleistocene settlement arrangements, of which the occupation of the Elands Bay Cave forms a part, illustrated the great importance of the spatial dimension in archaeological research design. Holocene arrangements are fairly well known in this area (Parkington 1972; 1976; 1977) because of the spread of observations across the landscape. It will be some time before earlier periods are as well studied, providing materials to test the suggestions of Hilary and Janette Deacon that population density, social organisation and subsistence strategy were all radically altered during the terminal Pleistocene.

ACKNOWLEDGEMENTS

I would like to acknowledge the very substantial contribution of Richard Klein, Cedric Poggenpoel and Graham Avery in studying the mammals, fish and birds respectively not only from the Elands Bay Cave but also from numerous other Cape sites. Their primary observations have permitted most of the reconstructions of

Cape archaeologists. The idea of a 'flip-over' in scheduling at the end of the Pleistocene was conceived in discussion with David Clarke.

Figures 12.4 and 12.5 are based on offshore bathymetric data supplied by Dr W. G. Siesser of the Department of Marine Geoscience at the University of Cape Town and on estimates of the age of lower sea levels of southern Africa supplied by Dr A. J. Tankard of the South African Museum in Cape Town.

Financial assistance from the Human Sciences Research Council, the Swan Fund and the University of Cape Town is gratefully acknowledged.

REFERENCES

Acocks, J. P. H. (1953). *Vled Types of South Africa* (South African Botanical Survey Memoir 28), Government Printer

Deacon, H. J. (1976). *Where Hunters Gathered : a study of Holocene Stone Age people in the Eastern Cape* (S.A. Arch. Soc. Monograph Series No. 1)

Deacon, J. (1979). 'Changing patterns in the Late Pleistocene/Early Holocene Prehistory of Southern Africa as seen from the Nelson Bay Cave stone artefact sequence', *Quaternary Studies*

Grindley, J. R. and Nel, E. (1968). 'Mussel poisoning and shellfish mortality on the West Coast of South Africa', *South African Journal of Science* 64: 420–2

(1970). 'Red water and mussel poisoning at Elands Bay, December 1966', *Fisheries Bulletin*, South Africa 6: 36–55

Hart, T. J. and Currie, R. I. (1960). 'The Benguela current', *Discovery Reports* 31: 123–298

Higgs, E. S. and Vita-Finzi, C. (1972). 'Prehistoric economies: a territorial approach' in E. S. Higgs (ed.), *Papers in Economic Prehistory*, Cambridge University Press

Klein, R. G. (1972). 'The Late Quaternary mammalian fauna of Nelson Bay Cave (Cape Province, South Africa): its implications for megafaunal extinctions and for environmental and cultural change', *Quaternary Research* 2: 135–42

(1974), 'A provisional statement on terminal Pleistocene mammalian extinctions in the Cape Biotic Zone (southern Cape Province, South Africa)', *South African Archaeology Society, Goodwin Series* 2: 39–45

(1977). 'The ecology of Early Man in Southern Africa', *Science* 197: 115–26

Parkington, J. E. (1972). 'Seasonal mobility in the Later Stone Age', *African Studies* 31: 223–43

(1976). 'Coastal settlement between the mouths of the Berg and Olifants rivers, Cape Province', *South African Archaeological Bulletin* 31: 127–40

(1977). 'Soaqua: hunter–fisher–gatherers of the Olifants river, western Cape', *South African Archaeological Bulletin* 32

Parkington, J. E. and Poggenpoel, C. (1971). 'Excavations at De Hagen, 1968', *South African Archaeological Bulletin* 26: 3–36

Pettigrew, J., Sievers, C. and Parkington, J. E. (forthcoming). 'An interpretation of the artefacts from the Elands Bay Cave, western Cape'

Rand, R. W. (1967). 'The Cape Fur-Seal (*Arctocephalus pusillus*) 3. General Behaviour on Land and at Sea', *Investigational Report of the Division of Sea Fisheries*, Cape Town 60: 1–39

van Zinderen Bakker, E. M. (1976). 'The evolution of late Quaternary palaeo-climates of Southern Africa', *Palaeoecology of Africa, the Surrounding Islands and Antarctica* 9: 160–202

PART IV

Social pattern:
analytical and interpretive theory

13

Conceptual frameworks for the explanation of sociocultural change

CHRISTOPHER TILLEY

Any explanation of change inevitably depends upon the investigator's image of the interrelationship of man and nature. Alternative conceptual frameworks may differ so fundamentally in their basic assumptions and presuppositions that there may appear to be no adequate resolution. Broadly, these may be viewed as 'idealistic' and 'materialistic' perspectives, providing a classic arena for debate throughout the history of philosophical thought. How are archaeologists to account for, understand and explain the changes that may be perceived in material culture patterning? A number of crucial questions arise for consideration: is an adequate conception of archaeological thinking inevitably radically pluralistic or should our explanatory and conceptual frameworks approximate to a single fundamental form? Do different conceptual frameworks involve any common suppositions? Are all kinds of conceptual frameworks equally ultimate or do some, more than others, depend upon the context of questioning?

In *Analytical Archaeology* (1968, p. xiii) David Clarke described archaeology as an 'undisciplined empirical discipline', lacking a scheme of systematic and ordered study based upon declared and clearly defined models and rules of procedure. Over a decade later archaeology may have lost its 'innocence' but 'sophistication' seems to have produced too few significant advances in its ability to contribute towards an understanding of material culture patterning which, in part, constitutes the social world. The central difficulty is that archaeologists lack a common problematic determining the types of problems that are posed, the form in which these problems are tackled and what is seen as being sufficient and necessary for their solution. This paper considers two approaches orientated towards the study of sociocultural change; systems theory and structural-Marxism. An attempt is made to evaluate these conceptual frameworks in terms of their utility for an understanding and explanation of change.

Change is always predicated of some object or configuration of units and implies alteration, the substitution of one form for another. Novelty must, therefore, be considered an important element in non-cyclical change. A fundamental question is why new elements or configurations enter the system under consideration. In human systems both 'change' and 'stability' relate to processes. As such we should regard both in terms of a continuous trajectory without clearly defined beginnings or ends. Change is multidimensional and consequently entails a number of levels of analysis. We may consider two basic forms of the verb 'to change', the transitive and the intransitive. The former directs our attention to human action, intention and choice while the latter implies a macro-view of social life in which the goals and needs of individuals become largely irrelevant to the change process. The latter viewpoint is subscribed to by many archaeologists (cf. Hill 1977, pp. 292–7). The thesis is that change may be adequately conceived and explained at the level of population rather than the individual in terms of underlying socioeconomic directives which in some sense may be unintended.

SYSTEMS THEORY AS A FRAMEWORK FOR EXPLAINING AND UNDERSTANDING SOCIOCULTURAL CHANGE

Archaeologists concern themselves with the patterned remains of complex interaction patterns between actors in past sociocultural systems. We clearly need techniques and a terminology which will enable us to understand and explain such complexity and interaction. As a framework for analysis, systems theory would appear to have few current peers. The notion of 'systemness' would appear to be basic to any analysis. Harvey (1969, p. 475) notes that all explanation is contingent upon the definition of some closed system within which analysis can proceed. Systems theory permits closure while retaining much of the complexity of the real world. Clarke (1968, pp. 43–130) argued that systems theory provided a powerful analogue model by means of which we could approximate and simulate archaeological processes. Since then this position has become almost an orthodoxy. A certain measure of complacency may be discerned in much of the recent literature symptomatic of the neglect of many unresolved problems relating to the ontological, epistemological and theoretical issues arising from archaeological research. Systems theory provides neither a coherent philosophy nor methodology for the discipline and various aspects of the theory must be evaluated in terms of their utility for explaining sociocultural change.

Both Berlinski (1976) and Salmon (1978) have made the suggestion that much of the attention paid to systems theory has been a somewhat irrelevant distraction – a restatement in a new terminology of concepts available elsewhere, providing no unique general principles or laws. Much of the work appears to be little more than a restatement in systems terminology of the functionalist, organismic model used for so long in sociology and anthropology where a particular behavioural pattern or sociocultural institution is understood and 'explained' in terms of the role it plays in keeping a given system in proper working order and maintaining it as a going concern. Accounting for change has proved to be something of a problem when viewed within a systemic perspective as a result of the emphasis put upon homeostasis and pattern maintenance. The participants in the seminar on prehistoric change (Hill 1977) all insist that change can only be externally induced as a result of morphogenic positive feedback processes resulting from a change in the system's environment. The view is that the cumulative effect of regulatory mechanisms and deviation counteracting devices will offset and countermand change unless there is a particularly violent oscillation in the system's environment, which causes the normal operation of the homeostatic mechanisms to break down. Then positive feedback processes are set into operation until a new equilibrium state is reached. Unfortunately this type of approach all too often leads to the postulation of a few 'prime movers' such as trade (Renfrew 1969; 1972), population increase (Cohen 1977) or the environment (Binford 1964).

One aspect of archaeological systems theory is to put a great deal of stress upon the concept of adaptation. Dunnell (1978, p. 197) makes the suggestion that 'evolutionary archaeology should be understood as an explanatory framework that accounts for the structure and change evident in the archaeological record in terms of evolutionary processes (natural selection, flow, mutation, drift) either identical to or analogous with these processes as specified in neo-Darwinian theory'. This leads him to a distinction between style and function: 'Style denotes those forms that do not have detectable survival values. Function is manifest as those forms that directly affect the Darwinian fitness of the populations in which they occur.' If this is so it is remarkable how little function and how much style is evident in the social world and if the concept of cultural evolution has any validity it indicates that a progressively smaller percentage of human behaviour has any survival value at all (Burnham 1973).

Binford states that 'adaptation is always a local problem and selective pressures favouring new cultural forms result from non-equilibrium conditions in the local ecosystem' (1972, p. 431), and that 'changes in the ecological setting of any given system are the prime causative situations activating processes of cultural change' (1964, p. 440). The suggestion here is that it is possible to predict human behaviour from techno-environmental conditions and arrive deductively at explanatory deterministic models.

This raises the problem that there is no counterpart in social theory of Darwinian evolutionary theory. Societal adaptation always has to do double service as both consequence and cause of change. This can only lead to tautology when the concept of adaptation is used to explain the existence of particular traits. To say that adaptive traits are present in a system or that those traits present are adaptive adds nothing to our understanding of process. The concept of social adaptation is sterile because it lacks an independent measure apart from comparative demographic success which fails to account for the vast majority of the particular forms and configurations of material culture.

The loose use of the concept of adaptation by many archaeologists leads

to an extension of this concept to a whole variety of cultural forms. Rappaport
(1967, pp. 224–42; 1971a) proposes that ritual is an information exchange
device communicating cultural, ecological and demographic data across the
boundaries of social groups. Other rituals supposedly regulate the dispersal
of human populations, and preserve a balance between farmed and fallowed
land and keep domestic animal herds within an adaptive 'goal range'
(Rappaport 1971b). Thomas (1972) uses these ideas in an analysis of the
fandango ritual cycles of the Shoshone indians, while Flannery and Marcus
(1976) utilise them as part of an investigation of Formative Oaxaca and the
Zapotec cosmos. But, anything that does not subject the people or the social
system to material destruction may be called adaptive. Adaptation can tell us
little about the specific form a culture takes or why it changes in a particular
fashion. It can only determine limits of existence or non-existence.

The enormity of the degree of interaction involved in human systems, and
the fact that many of these social exchanges are mutually conflicting or
compensating, means that the behaviour of a large number of variables, when
considered together in multivariate analyses, may appear to be chaotic or
random with respect to a limited number of parameters. In geographical
research this resulted in concepts such as the 'random spatial economy'
(Curry 1964; 1967). Given the complexity of the real world situation it may
be of benefit to utilise only a few key variables in the analysis of change. Plog
(1974, p. 57) chooses energy, population, differentiation and integration. The
choice of the words 'differentiation' and 'integration' is unfortunate as these
are imprecise terms for a set of consequences of other changes and remain
inadequate for any *explanation* of change. The degree of integration or
differentiation is only useful as a description. Their position as conditions for
further change is vague and indeterminate in practice.

Most systems analyses, in stressing internal systemic incompatibility,
neglect internal conflicts, contradictions, competition and coercion between
the actors of a social system. Without these there can be little creativity,
innovation or other factors promoting internal change. Conservative values
of persistence are always stressed resulting in exogenous causality. This sharp
division between causality and external change and internal stability, in effect,
echoes the Comtean division of sociology into social statics and social
dynamics. The concern with the maintenance of internal systemic compatibility and the stabilising effect of norms and institutions presumes that there
are atomistic tendencies in all societies. The explanation of stability in terms
of the functional integration of entities and subsystems is a good argument
neither for cause nor necessity (Hempel 1959). In the case of biological
organisms, only one explanation of an organic analogy is possible. It is
explained when it can be shown that it has the effect of maintaining structure.
The activities of human beings, although they may be socially orientated, may
not have any role to play in the maintenance of social structure. The
explanation of social actions as performing functions carries no implication

that without them the society would not survive. All they imply is that without them certain goals would not be achieved.

Sociocultural change cannot be considered simply as a feedback process consisting of a system's trajectory being influenced by the consequences of its previous behaviour and its present state. We may be able to predict the possible behaviour of a system but this does not necessarily provide us with much understanding of why the system works in a particular fashion. Feedback is not merely reducible to a functional relationship between input and output variables, as many archaeologists have assumed, so that we may infer in a fairly straightforward manner the content of our 'black boxes' (Clarke 1968, pp. 59–62). Feeding back is a process dependent upon the structural properties of the system in question. The analogy regarding groups of individuals as a unitary system persisting over time and responding to ecological pressures in such a way as to create changes in output is inadequate. Just because a system maintains more internal variety does not necessarily mean that it will be able to respond more efficiently to changes in its environment as Plog (1974, p. 53; 1977, p. 48) suggests. It is possible to take the contrary position, based upon thermodynamic principles, that the more concentrated the energy in a specialised system, the greater ability the system has to work and produce a major change.

As societies are composed of individuals with different values and aspirations, internal conflicts and tensions would seem to be inevitable. There is always likely to be a lack of concensus with regard to prevailing norms of conduct or their interpretations. Buckley (1967, pp. 128–9, 159–63, 206–7) stresses internal changes within social systems. Tensions and conflicts lead to negotiated decisions, thus creating new systemic structure and organisation. The system, in effect, changes in order to remain stable and permit its own reproduction. Disfunction and a lack of concensus would seem to be vital for social evolution.

In general, we may propose that there are likely to be varying degrees of interdependence amongst the components of a human social system. At one extreme each element will be involved in mutual interchanges with all the others. At the other extreme mutual interchanges will only take place between one or a few components. The components of a system may have varying amounts of their functional requirements satisfied by, and thus have varying degrees of dependence upon, other elements making up a system. Subsystems can therefore be regarded as having varying degrees of *functional autonomy*. Mutual interaction need not be symmetrical. The functional autonomy of subsystems is of considerable significance for an analysis of the development of tensions and contradictions within a system, and hence for an analysis of social change. Gouldner (1959; 1975, pp. 210–15) regards tensions to be an inherent and immanent characteristic of human social systems as a result of the component parts of a system tending to try and maintain their functional autonomy in the face of pressures from the system trying to control and regulate its components. To the degree that a component possesses some measure of functional autonomy it should be expected to retain it and resist full integration. In 'tribal' systems there may be a considerable degree of conflict between local household production, usually with only a limited surplus (Sahlins 1972), and the requirement of local chiefs for growing amounts of surplus to engage in prestige goods accumulation and exchange. Friedman and Rowlands (1977) postulate alternative pathways for the development of such systems either towards Asiatic states or a breakdown of chiefly authority altogether as manifested in the gumsa–gumlao cycles in highland Burma. Techno-environmental conditions eventually constrain an inflationary spiral of prestige goods accumulation and the over-production of subsistence commodities at a local level, leading to political collapse and the gradual development of new hierarchies related to the exchange of women and local differences in domestic lineage production.

Bloch (1971, p. 216) notes the general problem of the establishment of identity in change on a societal basis, resting with the fact that the actors in a social system consider themselves to have a continuing identity irrespective of action, and yet at the same time are only what they appear to be to others at a particular time and place. In all societies, we may postulate, there is an inherent contradiction between the exigencies of the present, the goals of the individual, past conceptions and ideals of action, and the present needs of the social group. Societies can never be completely integrated wholes as some systems thinking would seem to require, but often have a tenuous and superficial unity with only temporary stable states of structural compatibility permitting social reproduction and replication. Threshold states are inevitably reached when the external and internal dynamics of the system prevent its basic entities from remaining in the same state. A society as a whole cannot directly be said to be either goal directed nor feedback controlled.

Sahlins (1976), from an idealist and structuralist standpoint, produces a powerful critique of the notion that sociocultural systems are formulated out of practical interest and utilitarian activity. The basis of his argument is that the distinctive quality of man is not that he must live in the material world, but that he does so according to a meaningful scheme of his own devising. Culture conforms to material constraints in the terms of a specific symbolic scheme which is only one of innumerable alternatives. Like Lévi-Strauss, Sahlins is arguing for a mediating level between praxis and practices in the form of a conceptual scheme. Neither matter nor form have any independent existence, but are realised as particular thought structures and patterns of meaning. Functional value and rationality are always relative to the given cultural scheme. The corollary to this is that no cultural form can ever be simply read off or reproduced from a given set of material forces as if culture were a dependent variable and techno-environmental conditions the independent variable. Material forces are significant but significance 'is a symbolic quality. At the same time this symbolic scheme is not itself the mode of expression of an instrumental logic, for in fact there is no other logic in the sense of a meaningful order, save that imposed by culture on the instrumental process' (1976, p. 206). The cultural scheme is, in effect, critical in determining the form and intensity of the effect which material forces will have upon the overall cultural system: 'For all their facticity and objectivity, the laws of nature stand to the order of culture as the abstract to the concrete, as the realm of possibility stands to the realm of necessity, as the given potentialities to the one realization, as survival is to the actual being' (1976, p. 209). Material culture does not consist merely of objects used by people as an 'extrasomatic means of adaptation for the human organism' (Binford 1962, p. 218). Far more important, perhaps, is the role of material culture as the representation of ideas, a projection and externalisation of the inner self. Material culture can be considered to incorporate coded information in patterned sets in a manner analogous to the sounds and words and sentences of a natural language (Leach 1976, p. 10; 1977, pp. 167–8). Men do not shape or grind stones as such. They always enter into relations with raw materials in a specific way governed by structures of meaning. Now, clearly, this position is at odds with the basic presuppositions of systems theorists and cultural materialists such as Harris, who asserts that 'everything that we experience or do is real. But everything we experience or do is not equally effective for explaining why we experience and do what we do' (1976, p. 331). To Harris this entails ruling out the primacy of mind and meaning from human affairs. The human beings within cultural systems are economically orientated, make least cost and rational decisions and it is not necessary that these be conscious. This is also the view of Hill (1977, p. 86), Jochim (1976, p. 25) and the palaeoeconomic school (Higgs 1972; 1975). It is assumed that as man experiences his environment, his behavioural system and consequently the material culture patterning will be shaped by that experience. Those behavioural patterns which best meet the constraints of an environmental niche will be rewarded and those that do not will in the long term be extinguished. Human consciousness and meaning have no utility in the explanation of sociocultural change. In fact, in cybernetic systems, the properties of meaning and order must ultimately be transferred from man to the ecosystem, conceived as a set of regulated thermodynamic relations:

We can assert that any ongoing ensemble of events and objects which has the appropriate complexity of causal circuits and the appropriate energy relations will show mental characteristics. It will compare, that is be responsive to difference ...it will 'process information' and will inevitably be self corrective either toward homeostatic optima or toward the maximization of certain variables...In no system which has mental characteristics can any part have unilateral control over the whole. In other words the mental characteristics are immanent, not in some part but in the system as a whole (Bateson 1972, pp. 315–16).

The contention in this paper is that any form of reductionism is unlikely to lead to any advance in our understanding of sociocultural change. An adequate conception must include a consideration of thought as well as bodily movement. Sahlins seems to go to an extreme in supposing that culture conforms to a logic of its own. The form of a culture is constrained by the social reality that it symbolically constructs. As Ingold (1979) points out, culture divorced from social rationality is practically inert. Culture serves to translate a social and conceptual rationality into practical effectiveness.

Renfrew (1972, p. 496) is clearly unhappy with the reductionism that cybernetics inevitably entails when he states:

> The interactions among the subsystems of the society take place chiefly at the level of the human individual, since the subsystems of a culture are defined ultimately by the activities of individuals. It is the individual who equates wealth with prestige or social rank, for instance, or who forms for himself a projection of the world where social roles and religious concepts both find a place. Here essential differences between human and animal behaviour, differences fundamental to the growth of human culture, deserve more comment than they have received from the archaeologist.

Quite so. The *meaning* behind culture needs to be more fully integrated within the realm of archaeological theory concerned with sociocultural change. We can regard culture as a mediating bridge between man and his environment. This does not mean that it has a separate reality, or that it may not be constrained by that environment. Culture is carried in the conscious and unconscious thoughts and actions of individuals. It is subject to symbolic transmission and storage and as such forms a field of interaction between men's social relationships and norms of conduct. Culture is available to man as a means of focussing on and coordinating experience, their systems of values, actions and beliefs:

> Physical reality seems to recede in proportion as man's symbolic activity advanced. Instead of dealing with the things themselves, man is in a sense constantly conversing with himself. He has so enveloped himself in linguistic forms, artistic images, mythical symbols or religious rites that he cannot see or know anything except by the interposition of this artificial medium.   (Cassirer 1944, p. 25)

A STRUCTURAL-MARXIST FRAMEWORK FOR THE EXPLANATION AND UNDERSTANDING OF SOCIOCULTURAL CHANGE

A structural-Marxist approach to sociocultural change offers a critique and an alternative explanatory framework to functionalist empiricism, cybernetics and the static synchronic limitations of structuralism. Marxist theory has received scant attention from archaeologists, a situation contrasting with contemporary geography and anthropology. Recent work within the spheres of sociology and anthropology has attempted to build upon and extend basic Marxian concepts (Althusser and Balibar 1970), elucidate Marx's conception of social structure in the terms of contemporary structuralist thought (Godelier 1977a), and extend the analysis to pre-capitalist formations (Hindess and Hirst 1975; 1977; Meillassoux 1973). Analysis has suffered, in the past, from too much concern with 'what Marx really meant', and by confounding the hypothetical structure of Marxism with an all-embracing philosophy of history (Popper 1957).

We may make a basic distinction between 'pure' Marxism and 'pure' structuralism. Lévi-Strauss views the dialectic of history as realising itself harmoniously in the movement of logical oppositions. This leads to a static conception of historical change in which 'through succeeding millennia man has only managed to repeat himself' (Lévi-Strauss 1955, p. 424, quoted in Gregory 1978, p. 97). Human actions are determined by models of intelligibility projected onto the world in an endless series of combinations and recombinations. Individual changes in the way man organises his existence are not really important because they will only reveal the same underlying logic. Marxism, on the other hand, maintains that there is irreversible dialectical movement, qualitative change, abrupt developments and a discontinuous movement of cultural trajectories often marked by a revolutionary transition from one mode of material production and social reproduction to another. There can be no play of universal structural oppositions because of the immanent tendency of material structures to come into contradiction and opposition with their environments, resulting in a new social formation.

Lévi-Strauss, in some of his writings, accepts the Marxian notion of the primacy of the infrastructure as a social determinant: 'I do not at all mean to suggest that ideological transformations give rise to social ones. Only the reverse is in fact true. Men's conceptions of the relations between nature and culture is a function of the modification of their own social relations. We are merely studying the shadows on the walls of the cave' (1966, p. 117). Despite this statement the thought of Lévi-Strauss is inherently anti-Marxist and anti-materialist. The autonomy of the superstructure in his scheme, the discernment and demonstration of an all-embracing psychology to postulate the power over physical reality of the symbolic property of mind, is so great that there appears to be little need for an investigation of any relationship between cultural expression, the social superstructure and the social infrastructure. Lévi-Strauss' conception of social structure is also incompatible with the phenomenological conception of the consciousness of human action. It denies that social reality is managed, negotiated and given meaning by conscious interaction with the environment. For these reasons this type of structuralism would seem to have little utility in an investigation of sociocultural change.

Marxist theory is important for the emphasis it places upon internal rather than exogenous factors in the promotion of social change. The locus of change is found within the emergence of tensions and contradictions within and between the material and social structures that go to make up the totality of the social formation or society.

A mode of production such as 'capitalism', 'feudalism', or 'slavery' is, for Marx, only a particularised historical state which determines, but not necessarily dominates, the entire social formation. Its elements are not linked by any simple cause and effect notion but by the complex relationships existing between variables operating within and between the internal structures making up the social formation. Contradictions are immanent properties entailed by the very notion of relatively autonomous structures. Intra-systemic contradictions may occur within a structure, such as class conflict within the capitalist mode of production. Inter-systemic contradictions are those occurring between structures or subsystems. Contradictions occur because the dominant structures cause inter-systemic relations to strain to the limits of their functional compatibility. This sets limits to the development and stability of the system as a whole.

In Marx's analysis of capital the effectiveness of change depends upon the development of inter-systemic contradictions. The intra-systemic contradiction (class struggle) is insufficient to create a breakdown in the system itself. Friedman (1974) dismisses any hypothesis that purports to explain the development of specific relations of production in terms of underlying forces of production as 'vulgar materialism', possessing negligible explanatory power. Change, in fact, takes place because societies

come into contradiction with their environment, a situation conceivable only in the framework of relative autonomy. An ecosystem is not organized as such...it is the fact that the world is made up of relatively independent structures which must necessarily relate to one another in larger systems of reproduction (where the reproduction of one depends, in the last analysis, on the reproduction of all) which is the root of variability, mutual limitation and ultimately history.

(Friedman 1974, p. 460)

Because people are socially interdependent in production, societies can reproduce themselves despite internal conflicts and contradictions unless these reach unacceptable levels and ultimately, as Marx states in the introduction to his *Contribution to the Critique of Political Economy* (1859), 'it is not the consciousness of men which determines their existence, but their social existence which determines their consciousness'.

Permeating the thought of structural-Marxism is an overall emphasis on unity and opposition. In production, people oppose themselves to nature in order to extract from it. At the same time man becomes one with nature because, in the process of manipulating the natural and social environment, he himself changes. The immanent contradictions that exist within society may be latent for long periods until reaching a point of antagonism activated by a shift of the balance of productive forces or by the technological development of the production process. This is likely to place strain upon the existing social relations of production leading to crisis and qualitative change. Population pressure may lead to soil erosion and ecological degradation in a simple swiddening system, forcing a shortening of the fallowing cycle. This may overload the social mechanisms regulating the use of land, encouraging the development of new strategies. However, ecological degradation and technological development do not themselves cause change in the society but are the outcomes of a particular set of social relations organising reproduction and production. In due course the forces of production may produce a situation where the transformation of the social relations organising production becomes inevitable. The causality is essentially reciprocal. In these respects elements of a structural-Marxist explanation of change resemble those employed in a systemic approach.

In structural-Marxist theory the social structure not only permits or gives rise to social change, but more importantly the process of social change actually determines the social structure at any point in time. As Godelier puts it: 'In short whatever the internal or external causes or circumstances which bring about contradictions and structural changes within a determined mode of production and society, these contradictions and changes always have their basis in internal properties immanent in social structures, and they express unintentional requirements, the reasons and laws for which remain to be discovered' (Godelier 1977a, p. 6). For a complete analysis it is necessary to account for the form, function, mode of articulation and conditions of transformation of the social structures which go to make up society.

Leach (1954, p. 4) considers social structures as ideal orders. For Marx and Lévi-Strauss structures are part of reality. Even though their conception of structure is not directly visible, this does not make them any less real than the tangible and observable. Structure resides in the principles of operation underlying observed entities and governs the relationships which may be perceived to operate amongst these entities. Both Lévi-Strauss and Marx are aware of the possible disparity between an actor's conscious model of the workings of society and the 'reality' of which he may not be aware. A structure might be defined as a group of entities interlinked by certain regularities or laws. Interlinked structures form the wider social system. As any structure combines specific elements which are its proper components, one structure cannot be reduced or deduced from another. Attempts to do so result in the obscuration or fetishisation of relationships. Marx used the term 'fetishisation of commodities' to refer to the fact that the value of commodities is actually made up from the social labour that goes into their production. What is actually a relationship between people is spontaneously represented in the human consciousness as a property of the objects themselves. The internal hidden structure of social relations, the mechanisms by which surplus and value are formed and the fact that profit is unpaid labour are all mystified and hidden by the consciousness of the individual actors involved in the capitalist mode of production. Relations of production become reified and objects personified. Value, actually a social relation, becomes a property of things.

Marx's historical materialism is, primarily, a theory of society incorporating hypotheses about the articulation of its internal structures and the hierarchical causality of various structural levels. The essential task is to discover the types and mechanisms of causality and articulation. Analysis should not start with superficial appearances but must penetrate to a deeper and much more basic level of reality which governs and controls the flux we perceive on the surface of things. For Marx the structural regularities of the world are material. They are also dialectical and therefore constantly evolving. Social structures are dynamic, always relational between the states of being and becoming and therefore cannot be known through their surface form (O'Laughlin 1975). We need to look beyond the apparent visible logic to the underlying invisible logic. Material constraints only provide a partial perspective when considering human society, as a structural order may be cognitively constrained also. These material and cognitive constraints will manifest themselves in the patterning of material culture and may be inferred from 'style' in lithic assemblages, ceramic design, burial patterning, the disposal of rubbish and settlement form (Hodder n.d.).

Marx and Engels advanced the hypothesis, influenced by Morgan's evolutionary theory (Marx 1930; Engels 1972), that the history of humanity was that of the transition from classless forms of social organisation to class societies. They searched for causal mechanisms in terms of the transition from the development of one structural set of the social relations of production and productive forces to another. A fundamental contention is that knowledge of the fundamental structural properties of social reproduction will enable us to predict or 'retrodict' the way in which a society will change over time. The object of analysis is the social formation consisting of a juridico-political and ideological superstructure and an infrastructure made up by the forces of production and the social relations of production. These are *functional* distinctions which go to make up the hierarchy, not institutional distinctions. In small-scale societies institutions are usually embedded within the social formation, forming part of the infrastructure and part of the superstructure. For some anthropologists this fact is sufficient to dismiss Marx's hypothesis of the dominance of the economy. The problem for anthropologists and archaeologists, using a structural-Marxist approach, is how this hypothesis may be retained. The usual standpoint is that the economy in some way 'selects' from alternative social patterns and structural hierarchies the one that will play the determining role in any particular social formation. This is the 'hypothesis that a social structure dominates the functioning of society as a whole and organises its reproduction over time, if and only if, it simultaneously acts as the social relations of production; if it constitutes the social matrix of this society's infrastructure' (Godelier 1977b, p. 15).

The social formation is constrained by intra- and inter-systemic forces. The level of the development of the forces of production are determinant 'in the last instance' because they set the outer limit on the possible variations that may take place among the social relations and forces of production. As Friedman (1974) comments, if this is causality it is negative causality, since it determines what cannot happen rather than the specifics of what takes place and permits a diverse range of possible social relations of production which remain less compatible with the techno-environmental constraints of the forces of production. Determination and domination remain autonomous. The manner in which a social system uses its techno-environment profoundly alters its own conditions of reproduction by causing the emergence of a new set of constraints which eventually become incompatible with the dominant social relations of production and which imply a transformation of the mode of production. Technical activities are organised socially, rather than the social structures being determined by these activities. The internal dynamics of social structure may lead to the evolution of a new mode of production without any change in the technological base, or such change may result from the reorganisation and the intensification of the existing productive forces, directed by changing social relations of production.

Friedman and Rowlands (1977) produce an epigenetic model for the evolution of social systems, attempting to demonstrate the complex interplay of internal variation, structural dominance and inter- and intra-systemic contradictions which may generate multiple directions for the evolution of the overall social formation. As structures are processual entities and not institutional arrangements, it follows that we are constantly dealing with trajectories in which the constitutive structural elements are internally transformed so as to adopt new roles in a larger system of material reproduction. Socioeconomic reproduction is essentially directional and transformational. Evolution might be conceived as a single set of 'homeorhetic' processes in which there is a certain structurally determined order, dependent upon the social relations of production extant at any particular point in time (Friedman and Rowlands 1977, p. 269). A stadial view of evolution becomes no more than a cross-section of a continuously operating complex of processes. The new order emerges from the old and is already changing to a future state.

Social production of the means of subsistence permitting societal repro-duction is a basic element in all societies. Friedman (1975) develops a general model of social reproduction. The determinant aspects of the social formation are the social relations of production. These determine the use to be made of the environment within the limits of the available technology, the division of productive labour and the form of appropriation and distribution of the social product of labour. In short, the social relations of production define the rationality of the economic system. The forces of production form the basic techno-ecological conditions of production. These are the objective energy costs of reproduction and the rate of potential surplus. The manner in which the social relations of production relate to the objective conditions of the forces of production determines the long-term behaviour of the system and limits the conditions of its existence. The forces of production include the organisation of labour on the ground and the means by which that labour produces from the environment – the object of labour. The relationships analysed are both social and material and their integrity depends upon this interdependence. If we are to make use of a structural-Marxist model in an analysis of prehistoric change, attention must be paid to delineating the concepts clearly and operationalising them in terms of archaeological data. We might conceivably arrive at a fairly adequate analysis of the forces of production from the archaeological data but the probable relations of production will have to be hypothesised using anthropological data, adopting the uniformitarian assumption discussed and expanded by George Dalton in chapter 1 above that the social formations existing in the past do not radically differ from those documented in the ethnological record. These hypotheses can be tested against the substantive data. We may then be able to produce models of change resulting from both internal contradictions operating within society and those existing between the forces and relations of production and draw out test implications which may be analysed in terms of their validity for an adequate explanation and understanding of the changing configuration of our archaeological entities.

THE TRANSITION FROM HUNTING AND GATHERING TO AGRICULTURAL COMMUNITIES

A major problem confronting archaeologists is why agricultural societies should develop at all, given that this means of subsistence would seem to require a great deal more energy expenditure than is usual amongst hunting and gathering communities. This is especially so in the context of the profuse range of resources which must have been available in Europe during the post-glacial period, contrasting with the rather marginal environments in which many present-day hunter–gatherers live, from which the notion of a relatively 'affluent' lifestyle has been derived.

Meillassoux (1960; 1973) has contrasted the way in which social structure and territorial organisation are linked amongst hunter–gatherers and subsistence agriculturalists, providing some quite specific models which archaeologists may be able to operationalise. To hunters and gatherers, land is merely the subject of labour. There is little or no investment designed to increase the potential productivity of the resource base. The comparatively low productivity of the land is combined with the high productivity of labour. Labour is applied to the land and yields an instantaneous return rather than a deferred one. The relations of production do not result in any long-lasting social cohesion. Reciprocity is instantaneous and immediate and, therefore, there is no need for the redistribution of the social product of labour. Hunters and gatherers typically have a present orientation and are preoccupied with day to day material production rather than the reproduction of a specific social group. All men are independent in terms of the means of production and in their relationship to the material resource base. Factors promoting band cohesion are more a result of economic contingencies than kinship bonds. The variability in the internal composition of bands is a major factor in relieving internal stress. What is invariable is not the internal composition of bands, but stable relationships between bands in a delimited spatial area which ultimately permits the reproduction of all bands. There is no requirement for the continual membership of any one social group by an individual as mutual interdependence between members of a group operates only in the short term. The social relations of production do not require any long period of social cohesion in order to permit reproduction. Consequently, leadership and authority structures are weak and usually last for no longer than the duration of a particular productive enterprise. Because of a constant state of flux, the geneological memory of hunting and gathering groups is short. Children are not a future labour investment crucial for the reproduction of a particular social group. Therefore, the control of procreative women is not important. Hunters and gatherers, more than any other type of society, are part of nature rather than opposed to it. This feature is clearly demonstrated in Godelier's (1977a, pp. 58–61) analysis of the molimo rites of the Mbuti pygmies. A corollary to this is the lack of ideological or social representation symbolically opposing man to his natural or social environment.

It is important to understand that in the process of social production people not only produce, but also reproduce the conditions of their own existence. This involves the reproduction of labour, the reproduction of the means of production, and the reproduction of the social relations of production. In order to explain why agriculture might develop in any area of Europe a first stage of the analysis would be to single out the contradictions inherent between the social relations and forces of production, operating within local communities, and the particular conditions under which we might expect these contradictions to become antagonistic, leading to the development of a new social formation.

We might postulate that within all hunter–gatherer groups there is a contradiction between the outright exploitation of resources on a largely uncontrolled basis and the conservation and control over the utilisation of resources in a form of investment activity. Indeed agriculture might be characterised, within the terms of an epigenetic model, as an energy cost threshold point when the degree of control (deer herding, fire setting to promote an increase in available animal browse, or the growth of plants such as hazel) exceeds parameter levels and begins to dominate the structure of the economy, resulting, at a certain point, in antagonistic contradictions between the forces and relations of production so that a new social formation results. A new set of social relations of production may then actively promote a further transformation in the mode of production. (This is a specific, not a general term. Neither hunting and gathering nor agriculture themselves constitute a 'mode of production' as structural-Marxists conceive this term.) Increasing sedentism amongst hunter–gatherers might also intensify the development of contradictions between structures. An egalitarian lifestyle, the free movements of individuals and utilisation of resources will come into contradiction with the need, now that a much smaller spatial area is being exploited, to control the access of individuals to resources. In areas with relatively dense populations, as we might expect on ecological grounds in peripheral coastal and fen areas of Europe (*c.* 5000–3000 b.c.) (Clarke 1976), local Mesolithic populations may have become more socially bounded, with the result that the normal flux mechanisms for relieving tensions would not operate so effectively. The corollary of this might be the development of some form of hierarchy to act as a mechanism of social control. Such a transformation in the social relations of production is likely to promote technological change and innovations such as the production of pottery and the selection of genetically responsive plants and animals in order to increase the productive potential of the land. Once sedentism is firmly established the position may become irreversible, as population growth would seem to be inevitable, following the breakdown of physiological and social mechanisms for its control (Binford and Chasko 1976).

Subsistence agricultural systems and the problems of the European megalithic tombs

In simple subsistence agricultural systems such as swiddening, land becomes an object of labour; a means for producing wealth and achieving the reproduction of the social group. Labour is actively invested in the land and output is delayed for a period of time not directly under the control of the producer. Agricultural activity results in the formation of relatively permanent social units as people gather around the social product of their collective labour investment. Productive land is in limited supply and therefore the determination of rights of transmission becomes very important (Meillassoux 1960).

Agricultural activities are more diverse and require more kinds of interaction than amongst hunter–gatherers. There are increased amounts of energy in the system, but slower turnover rates with successive productive and unproductive cycles. Consequently more energy is tied up in organisational and information structures in order to regulate the system. The spatial range of the local group is reduced. The local ecosystem is simplified in order to achieve high energy turnover rates and so populations become more susceptible to local environmental perturbations. This in turn requires increased organisational complexity in the form of buffering mechanisms such as the storage, management and redistribution of the social product of labour. Nature is not seen, ideologically, as a directly productive and benevolent force, but as something opposed to man. Time becomes a paramount concern and land is seen as the property of the dead, the living and the unborn. As a result of investment and delayed pay-off, cooperation becomes lasting and permanent. Meillassoux (1972) points out that the agricultural cycle, in diachronic perspective, is a continually renewed sequence of advance and restitution of food between the producers of each successive season. In effect each seasonal team advanced food and the investment of their labour in land to the next generation. In a system of social control by senior members of the community over juniors the relations of production become hierarchical and may be based on age sets. The fundamental problem for the seniors is the maintenance of this hierarchical distinction and the reproduction of the social unit. Kinship links become a direct expression of the relations of production and reproduction. The actual means of production are so simple and accessible that they provide no basis for control by the seniors. The product of labour can only be controlled by control over the producers and more fundamentally the producers of the producers – procreative women. The authority of the seniors rests on their ability to control the exchange of women with external groups, regulated by a dowry system and also by control over access to ritual information regarded as being essential for the group's survival. The projection of the authority of the seniors into the past justifies their position as they owe nothing except to the ancestors who mediate between them and the gods.

Bloch (1974; 1975; 1977a; 1977b) contrasts ritual communication with other ways of conversing. In mundane contexts notions of time, space and order may be fundamentally different from those portrayed in ritual where there may be no direct link with empirical experiences. The world of ritual is a world peopled by invisible entities. On the one hand there is the real world situation of social control and corporate groups and on the other the gods and the ancestors. The two main characteristics of ritual, according to Bloch, are the dissolution of time and the depersonalisation of the individual. Ritual communication is effected by special types of communication such as formalised speech, song and dance and material symbols. Using a semantic analogy, ritual communication is fossilised and has only limited potential for any adjustments or in its ability to be extended or developed. In ordinary language, rules of syntax govern the linking of statements and there is considerable flexibility in the order of the relationships between statements within a piece of conversation. In ritual communication the syntactic links cannot be reformulated at will, but follow from each other unquestioned as an integral part of a structural unit. Contradiction, requiring subtle reasoning or logic, is ruled out as a result of the specialised premises of ritual communication. As a result of this, the communication of ritual is protected by its form from direct evaluation against empirical data or contradictory statements. As such, ritual cannot serve as an information exchange device regulating the world of the profane, as Rappaport (1971a; 1971b) suggests. As Bloch (1977a, p. 289) succinctly puts it: 'there are systems by which we know the world and those by which we hide it'. Ritual communication makes the social world appear to be organised in a fixed order which recurs without beginning and without end. It projects the social, the political, the discontinuous, the cultural and the arbitrary into the image and the realm of the repetitive and cyclical processes of nature such as the progression of the seasons. Bloch (1977b) persuasively demonstrates that this is why ritual is an important part of the process of leadership in small-scale societies. Those who acquire power institutionalise it in the form of ritual, making it a part of the natural order of things and consequently less vulnerable from attack.

In Europe, megalithic tombs have a predominantly western and coastal distribution. The explanation of this distributional pattern and the precise function of these tombs has been the subject of considerable controversy. Typical explanations have been couched in terms of religion or the movements of peoples. Such tombs were extremely costly to erect, Ashbee (1966) estimating that the construction of the Fussell's Lodge long-barrow, Wiltshire would take about 5000 man days of labour for the mound itself. The excavation of many of these tombs has provided evidence of complex and repeated ritual activities associated both with their construction and later use (Kaelas 1966; Strömberg 1968; 1971; Burenhult 1973; Chapman 1975). In many areas there appears to be a marked correlation between the distribution of these tombs and rich soils (Randsborg 1975; Clark 1977).

In central Europe the Early Neolithic Linearbandkeramik agricultural populations seem to have spread fairly rapidly around 4700–3800 b.c. As Fred Hamond demonstrates in chapter 8 above, the most reasonable hypothesis is some form of demic diffusion (Ammerman and Cavalli-Sforza 1973). The distribution of the LBK sites has a marked correlation with areas of rich loess soils. In a pioneering and land-taking situation it is perfectly possible for the dominant social relations of production to stress an us–them dichotomy. An indication of this type of situation is provided by the burial evidence. Burials are either found in the settlement area or in cemeteries closely associated with settlements (Tringham 1971, p. 124; Modderman 1970; 1975). Another possible indication of the emphasis put on the exclusiveness of the local social group is the construction of massive timber longhouses, often aligned in regular groups (Soudsky and Pavlů 1972). As population densities will have been relatively low it would be possible to continue to emphasise, over a long time period, the social exclusiveness of the local lineage, which can always remain together in a situation characterised by gradual expansion. In the LBK there would probably be no contradiction between the social relations of production stressing exclusiveness and the means and forces of production.

Horton's (1971) study of the Tiv, discussed by Richards (1978, pp. 276–8), clearly demonstrates the way in which an ideological representation of such a social universe may be related to settlement and territorial concepts. The Tiv have been able to expand in a regular accretionary manner into relatively empty peripheral lands, in a similar manner to the spread of LBK populations in prehistoric Europe. This type of contagious spread, as opposed to disjunctive movement, has enabled the Tiv to maintain kinship systems which stress exclusiveness in relation to outsiders.

Agricultural communities in northern and western Europe seem to have been derived, on a broad front, from LBK traditions. In northwest Europe good soils are less plentiful. It is possible that in such areas, after an initial colonisation period, economic stress might arise. There would be more need for the fissioning of lineage groups and a more flexible realignment of social relationships. The social system derived from LBK traditions might not be able to cope, ideologically, with such fissioning. A situation would eventually arise when the contradiction between the social relations and forces and means of production would become antagonistic. The social relations of production stressing boundedness and exclusiveness become logically incompatible with the means or forces of production involving disjunctive movement, fissioning and fragmentation. The construction of megalithic tombs may represent an attempt to re-establish order, acting as an ideological means of denying the inherent contradictions existing between the forces and relations of production. In such a situation we might expect an emphasis upon the identity of the local lineage group to be overtly symbolised, acting as a means of demonstrating its particular relationship to land – a scarce and finite resource. Social control by the seniors, and the maintenance of this control by control over the access to ritual information, would become an important part of the system because ritual establishes an ordered view of the world and is a powerful ideological denial of flux. The purpose of the megaliths may be far more fundamental than acting as territorial markers as Renfrew (1973; 1975) suggests. They may be the material manifestations of a system of social control, attempting to establish the permanence of a set of social relations of production and reproduction, which are in the process of breaking down as a result of the contradiction of these structures with the forces of production. Saxe (1970, p. 119) has hypothesised that 'to the degree that corporate rights to use and/or control crucial, but limited resources are attained and/or legitimised by means of lineal descent from the dead such groups will maintain formal disposal areas for the exclusive disposal of their dead'. It has long been recognised that the megaliths in many areas contain relatively few burials, and so may not be considered places of collective burial for the entire local population. However, the tombs would, in effect, become symbols of the continuity of the local lineage and its relationship to land. In many cases they may have been considered to be the containers of the ancestors and also containers fixed and rooted in a particular place, designed to bolster and represent as pre-ordained a hierarchical system of social control and established social order. Their very monumental size would be a testimony to the authority and power of the elders, direct descendents of the ancestors mediating between them and the gods.

Recent excavations in Scania, southern Sweden, have produced finds of large quantities of richly decorated pottery around and especially at the entrances of the tombs (Strömberg 1968; 1971). Both the frequency of the decorative elements and the shapes of the pottery differ from those found on contemporary settlements (Hulthén 1977, p. 102). In some cases the distribution of sherds from the same vessel may indicate pot smashing at the grave entrance (Hulthén 1977, p. 96). Such frequent ritual activity, focussed at the tombs, would act as an important element in the continual reaffirmation of a stable order in the face of change. Such a hypothesis is amenable to empirical testing, falsification or modification against the substantive data.

CONCLUSIONS

In terms of their emphasis upon the overall unity of the different components going to make up social systems, systems models and structural-Marxist models are very similar. Causality is always multivariate and reciprocal. However, they differ in some quite significant ways. Structural-Marxist analysis proceeds at a deeper level than systemic approaches. The latter tends to put more emphasis upon the immediate, the conscious and the tangible. The notion of structural contradictions resulting in societal change relates to the operation of causative variables at a different epistemological level from that assumed in analysis of interlinked variables and entities resulting in morphogenic feedback processes. Systems models, on the whole, place less emphasis upon the relative autonomy of human culture from its environmental milieu. This is an essential assumption in any structural-Marxist explanation of change.

Gouldner's (1975) notion of the relative autonomy of subsystems within a system is akin to the structural-Marxist notion of the relative autonomy of the functional levels that go to make up a social formation. Both models are genuine attempts to approximate the complexity of the real world, but at different levels. It is not the intention here to suggest that we should replace systems theory with structural-Marxism. The use of different explanatory frameworks, with a clear conception of their strengths and inadequacies, will enable us to gain more insight into the dynamics of change. As Chapman (1977) and Bennett and Chorley (1978) have demonstrated, the concept of 'systemness' is potentially of great explanatory power. In common with any model it can only adequately deal with certain aspects of human experience and sociocultural change. This potential is as yet largely unrealised in the archaeological literature as a result of the stress upon exogenous causality, homeostasis and an inappropriate use of concepts such as adaptation, selection, variety, differentiation and integration. As a whole, systems theory has largely neglected the realm of the social and the symbolic in relation to the vital human characteristics of mind, meaning, intention, motivation and choice. Structural-Marxist theory attempts to integrate these characteristics within the broad constraints of environmental and cognitive parameters. The essential internal characteristics of human systems such as conflict, contradiction, incompatibility and tension are elevated to a far more important causative role in the explanation of societal change.

The process of historical change is far more fundamental than a vehicle which 'proves indispensable for cataloguing the elements of any structure' (Lévi-Strauss 1966, p. 262). A first step in an understanding of human action is neither to postulate an ultimate determination from the physical environment in which man lives nor from the unconscious mind, but to interpret the subjective meanings of individuals and the societies which they form, from the patterned remains of their behaviour. Constraints permit the discernment of regularity and permit generalisation. Men act upon nature in the terms of a cognised model of their world, but it is upon the objective environment that men do act and are acted upon and constrained. Change involves choice, not adaptive responses. Perhaps men are players in an existential game where the only purpose of the game is to remain in it (Vayda and McCay 1975, p. 293). The rules of the game, i.e. the constraints upon behaviour, are always laid out in advance. The particular game that is played out within these constraints may take many directions and be played with a greater or a lesser degree of security and satisfaction. It is the features of any particular game that may generate 'surprise' and hence demand an explanation of sociocultural change.

ACKNOWLEDGEMENTS

I would like to express my thanks to Ian Hodder for the help and encouragement I have received in writing this paper. All errors and inaccuracies are my own. I would also like, especially within the context of this volume, to acknowledge the intellectual debt I owe to David Clarke, whose infectious enthusiasm and outstanding thought was my first introduction to archaeology as an undergraduate.

REFERENCES

Althusser, L. and Balibar, E. (1970). *Reading Capital*, New Left Books
Ammerman, A. J. and Cavalli-Sforza, L. L. (1973). 'A population model for the diffusion of early farming in Europe' in C. Renfrew (ed.) *The Explanation of Culture Change*, Duckworth
Ashbee, P. (1966). 'The Fussell's Lodge long barrow excavations 1957', *Archaeologia* C: 1–80
Bateson, G. (1972). *Steps to an Ecology of Mind*, Ballantine
Bennett, R. J. and Chorley, R. J. (1978). *Environmental Systems*, Methuen
Belrinski, D. (1976). *On Systems Analysis*, M.I.T. Press
Binford, L. R. (1962). 'Archaeology as anthropology', *American Antiquity* 28 (2): 217–25
    (1964). 'A consideration of archaeological research design', *American Antiquity* 29: 425–41
    (1972). 'Post-Pleistocene adaptations' in L. R. Binford *An Archaeological Perspective*, Seminar Press
Binford, L. R. and Chasko, W. J. (1976). 'Nunamiut demographic history: a provocative case' in E. B. W. Zubrow (ed.) *Demographic Anthropology*, University of New Mexico Press
Bloch, M. (1971). *Placing the Dead*, Seminar Press
    (1974). 'Symbol, song and dance or is religion an extreme form of political authority?', *European Journal of Sociology* 55–81

(1975). 'Property and the end of affinity' in M. Bloch (ed.) *Marxist Analyses and Social Anthropology*, A.S.A.

(1977a). 'The past and the present in the past', *Man*, New Series, 12 (2): 278–92

(1977b). 'The disconnection between power and rank as a process' in J. Friedman and M. J. Rowlands (eds.) *The Evolution of Social Systems*, Duckworth

Buckley, W. (1967). *Sociology and Modern Systems Theory*, Prentice Hall

Burenhult, G. (1973). 'Matrix analysis and Scanian megalithic pottery', *Meddelanden från Lunds Universitets Historiska Museum* 29–53

Burnham, P. (1973). 'The explanatory value of the concept of adaptation in studies of culture change' in C. Renfrew (ed.) *The Explanation of Culture Change*, Duckworth

Cassirer, E. (1944). *An Essay on Man*, Yale University Press

Chapman, G. P. (1977). *Human and Environmental Systems : a geographer's appraisal*, Academic Press

Chapman, R. W. (1975). 'Economy and society within later prehistoric Iberia: a new framework', unpublished Ph.D. thesis, Cambridge University

Clark, J. G. D. (1977). 'The economic context of dolmens and passage graves in Sweden' in V. Markotic (ed.) *Ancient Europe and the Mediterranean*, Aris and Phillips

Clarke, D. L. (1968). *Analytical Archaeology*, Methuen

(1976). 'Mesolithic Europe, the economic basis' in G. de G. Sieveking, I. H. Longworth and K. E. Wilson (eds.) *Problems in Economic and Social Archaeology*, Duckworth

Cohen, M. N. (1977). *The Food Crisis in Prehistory*, Yale University Press

Curry, L. (1964). 'The random spatial economy: an exploration in settlement theory', *Annals of the Association of American Geographers* 54: 138–46

(1967). 'Central places in the random spatial economy', *Journal of Regional Science* 7 (supplement): 217–38

Dunnell, R. C. (1978). 'Style and function: a fundamental dichotomy', *American Antiquity* 43 (2): 192–202

Engels, F. (1972). *The Origin of the Family, Private Property and the State*, edited by E. B. Leacock, International Publishers

Flannery, K. and Marcus, J. (1976). 'Formative Oaxaca and the Zapotec cosmos', *American Scientist* 64 (4): 374–83

Friedman, J. (1974). 'Marxism, Structuralism and vulgar materialism', *Man*, New Series, 9: 444–69

(1975). 'Tribes, states and transformations' in M. Bloch (ed.) *Marxist Analyses and Social Anthropology*, A.S.A.

Friedman, J. and Rowlands, M. J. (1977). 'Notes towards an epigenetic model of the evolution of civilization' in J. Friedman and M. J. Rowlands (eds.) *The Evolution of Social Systems*, Duckworth

Godelier, M. (1977a). *Perspectives in Marxist Anthropology*, Cambridge University Press

(1977b). 'Politics as infrastructure: an anthropologist's thoughts on the example of classical Greece' in J. Friedman and M. J. Rowlands (eds.) *The Evolution of Social Systems*, Duckworth

Gouldner, A. W. (1959). 'Reciprocity and autonomy in functional theory' in L. Gross (ed.) *Symposium on Sociological Theory*, Row, Peterson

(1975). *For Sociology*, Penguin

Gregory, D. (1978). *Ideology, Science and Human Geography*, Hutchinson

Harris, M. (1976). 'History and the significance of the emic/etic distinction', *Annual Review of Anthropology* 5: 329–50

Harvey, D. (1969). *Explanation in Geography*, Arnold

Hempel, C. G. (1959). 'The logic of functional analysis' in L. Gross (ed.) *Symposium on Sociological Theory*, Row, Peterson

Higgs, E. S. (ed.) (1972). *Papers in Economic Prehistory*, Cambridge University Press

(ed.) (1975). *Palaeoeconomy*, Cambridge University Press

Hill, J. N. (ed.) (1977). *Explanation of Prehistoric Change*, University of New Mexico Press

Hindess, B. and Hirst, P. (1975). *Pre-Capitalist Modes of Production*, Routledge and Kegan Paul

(1977). *Mode of Production and Social Formation: auto-critique of pre-capitalist modes of production*, Macmillan

Hodder, I. R. (n.d.). 'Material symbols', unpublished manuscript

Horton, R. (1971). 'Stateless societies in the history of West Africa' in J. F. A. Ajayi and M. Crowder (eds.) *History of West Africa*, vol. 1, Longman

Hulthén, B. (1977). 'On ceramic technology during the Neolithic and Bronze Age', *Theses and Papers in North European Archaeology* (Stockholm) 6

Ingold, T. (1979). 'The hunter and his spear', Paper presented at a conference on economic archaeology, Cambridge, January 1979

Jochim, M. A. (1976). *Hunter Gatherer Subsistence and Settlement: a predictive model*, Academic Press

Kaelas, L. (1966). 'The megalithic tombs in Southern Scandinavia: migration or cultural influence?', *Palaeohistoria* 12: 287–321

Leach, E. R. (1954). *Political Systems of Highland Burma*, Athlone

(1976). *Communication and Culture*, Cambridge University Press

(1977). 'A view from the bridge' in M. Spriggs (ed.) *Archaeology and Anthropology: areas of mutual interest* (British Archaeological Reports, S.19), B.A.R. Publications

Lévi-Strauss, C. (1955). *Tristes Tropiques*, Plon

(1966). *The Savage Mind*, Weidenfeld and Nicholson

Marx, K. (1930). *Capital*, Dent

Meillassoux, C. (1960). 'Essai d'intérpretation du phénomène économique dans les sociétés traditionelles d'autosubsistence', *Cahiers d'Etudes Africaines* 4: 38–67. Reprinted in D. Seddon (ed.) *Relations of Production*, Frank Cass, 1978

(1972). 'From reproduction to production', *Economy and Society* 1: 93–105

(1973). 'On the mode of production of the hunting band' in P. Alexandre (ed.) *French Perspectives in African Studies*, Oxford University Press

Modderman, P. J. R. (1970). 'Linearbandkeramik aus Elsloo und Stein', *Analecta Praehistoria Leidensia* 3

(1975). 'Elsloo, a neolithic farming community in the Netherlands' in R. Bruce-Mitford (ed.) *Recent Archaeological Excavations in Europe*, Routledge and Kegan Paul

O'Laughlin, B. (1975). 'Marxist approaches in anthropology', *Annual Review of Anthropology* 4: 341–70

Plog, F. (1974). *The Study of Prehistoric Change*, Academic Press

(1977). 'Explaining change' in J. N. Hill (ed.) *The Explanation of Prehistoric Change*, University of New Mexico Press

Popper, K. R. (1957). *The Poverty of Historicism*, Routledge and Kegan Paul

Randsborg, K. (1975). 'Social dimensions of early neolithic Denmark', *Proceedings of the Prehistoric Society* 41: 105–18

Rappoport, R. A. (1967). *Pigs for the Ancestors*, Yale University Press

(1971a). 'The sacred in human evolution', *Annual Review of Ecology and Systematics* 2: 23–44

(1971b). 'Ritual, sanctity and cybernetics', *American Anthropologist* 73: 59–76

Renfrew, C. (1969). 'Trade and culture process in European prehistory', *Current Anthropology* 10: 151–69

(1972). *The Emergence of Civilisation*, Methuen

(1973). 'Monuments, mobilization and social organization in neolithic Wessex' in C. Renfrew (ed.) *The Explanation of Culture Change*, Duckworth

(1975). 'Megaliths, territories and populations' in S. J. de Laet (ed.) *Acculturation and Continuity in Atlantic Europe*, Dissertationes Archaeologicae Gandenses

Richards, P. (1978). 'Spatial organisation and social change in West Africa: notes for historians and archaeologists' in I. R. Hodder (ed.) *The Spatial Organisation of Culture*, Duckworth

Sahlins, M. (1972). *Stone Age Economics*, Aldine

(1976). *Culture and Practical Reason*, University of Chicago Press

Salmon, M. H. (1978). 'What can systems theory do for archaeology?' *American Antiquity* 43: 174–83

Saxe, A. A. (1970). 'Social Dimensions of Mortuary Practices', unpublished doctoral dissertation, University of Michigan

Soudsky, B. and Pavlů, I. (1972). 'The linear pottery culture settlemente patterns of Central Europe' in P. J. Ucko, R. Tringham and G. W. Dimbleby (eds.) *Man, Settlement and Urbanism*, Duckworth

Strömberg, M. (1968). 'Der dolmen Trollasten in St. Köpinge, Schonen', *Acta Archaeologica Lundensia* 7

(1971). 'Die megalithgräber von Hagestad', *Acta Archaeologica Lundensia* 9

Thomas, D. H. (1972). 'Western Shoshone ecology: settlement patterns and beyond' in D. D. Fowler (ed.) 'Great basin cultural ecology: a symposium', *Desert Research Publications in the Social Sciences* 8: 135–53

Tringham, R. (1971). *Hunters, Fishers and Farmers of Eastern Europe 6,000–3,000 B.C.*, Hutchinson

Vayda, A. P. and McCay, B. J. (1975). 'New directions in ecology and ecological anthropology', *Annual Review of Anthropology* 4: 293–306

14

Archaeological theory and communal burial in prehistoric Europe

ROBERT CHAPMAN

In his article 'Archaeology: the loss of innocence', David Clarke defined archaeology as 'the discipline with the theory and practice for the recovery of unobservable hominid behaviour patterns from indirect traces in bad samples' (1973, p. 17). The nature of these samples has become a focus of attention as archaeologists have formulated models of the processes by which the archaeological record was formed (Schiffer 1976) and have devised methods of obtaining representative data through fieldwork and excavation (e.g., Mueller 1975). But while contemporary research proceeds by the analysis of such samples from well-defined contexts in both settlements and cemeteries, there exist the results of literally thousands of earlier studies based upon less rigorous methods of data collection and analysis. In many cases such studies were undertaken in the formative periods of archaeology's emergence as a discipline. Given the dramatic changes in archaeological perspectives during the last two decades, it must be asked whether earlier excavations are still capable of yielding significant patterning or whether the data samples available are too bad to be of any use. This was a problem which David Clarke (1972) approached in his study of the Iron Age settlement at Glastonbury in southwest England, and which is currently being pursued for the Early Iron Age cemetery at Hallstatt in Austria (Barth and Hodson 1976; Hodson 1977). In both cases analysis produced patterns in the data and at the very least suggested hypotheses which can be tested upon more rigorously collected samples. This is also the aim of the work presented in this paper, which is part of a wider attempt to rethink our approach to the study of prehistoric communal tombs in western Europe.

As with individual burial there has been a strong belief among archaeologists that communal burial should be analysed within the context of religious beliefs (e.g., Daniel 1963; Piggott 1965). Thus the supposed spread of communal tombs in western Europe from c. 3800–1800 b.c. was associated with the dissemination of a belief in an all-powerful divinity, the 'Mother Goddess'. The application of radiocarbon dating has led to a more complex picture of the appearance of these tombs, with several traditions developing in different parts of western Europe and not spreading as part of a single missionary movement of ultimately Mediterranean origin (Renfrew 1973a).

Furthermore, studies in comparative anthropology strongly support a relationship between social organisation and the disposal of the dead (e.g., Saxe 1970; Binford 1971). This has provided the impetus for a number of analyses of the specific and contextual attributes of mainly individual burials in cemeteries (e.g., Brown 1971; Shennan 1975; Tainter 1976; 1977). But European prehistorians have yet to use cemeteries of *communal* tombs as basic units of analysis in studies of social organisation. Indeed there has been little discussion of the social, economic, religious and technological factors whose interaction must be behind the patterning visible, or potentially visible, in the location and organisation of such cemeteries (Chapman 1977).

During the course of research into the southeast Spanish Copper Age attention was directed towards various reconstructions of social organisation in that area during the third millennium b.c. (Chapman 1975). The cultural superiority of supposed 'colonists' of east Mediterranean origin over the indigenous population has been a predominant theme in these reconstructions. There are references to the existence of 'townships' (Childe 1947, p. 267; cf. Bosch-Gimpera 1969, p. 60) and urban (Almagro and Arribas 1963, p. 45) or semi-urban (Savory 1968, p. 146) settlements inhabited by these 'colonists'. Santa Olalla (1946, p. 61) refers to a ruling, warlike aristocracy and Savory (1968, p. 166) to 'overlords' who exerted religious and military power over the indigenous population. Tarradell (1969, pp. 223–4) reconstructs a stratified social organisation which was based upon a developed agricultural subsistence and metallurgy and which was behind the construction of impressive communal tombs in southern Spain. As for the social organisation of the 'colonists', Almagro and Arribas (1963, pp. 45–6) claimed that there was no evidence from either the settlement or the cemetery at the important site of Los Millares which suggested the existence of anything more than an egalitarian social structure. Arguments against the existence of 'colonists' and in favour of a local development for the southeast Spanish Copper Age have been presented elsewhere (Chapman 1975; Gilman 1976). My purpose in undertaking analyses of the Los Millares cemetery was to search for patterns which might provide a preliminary test of the social reconstructions presented above. It was hypothesised that differential disposal of the dead would reflect the existence of social differences within the community. Evidence for the concentration of 'prestige' grave goods within particular tombs or areas of the cemetery might reflect the existence of a ranked society in which there was differential access to wealth and status (Fried 1967, p. 109).

In approaching the Los Millares cemetery my concern has been to check its documentation as a prelude to the search for internal patterning and structure which can be interpreted in terms of social organisation. In David Clarke's terms (1963, p. 16) I have been mainly concerned with the post-depositional, retrieval, analytical and interpretive subtheories of archaeology, and these form the substance of what follows in this paper.

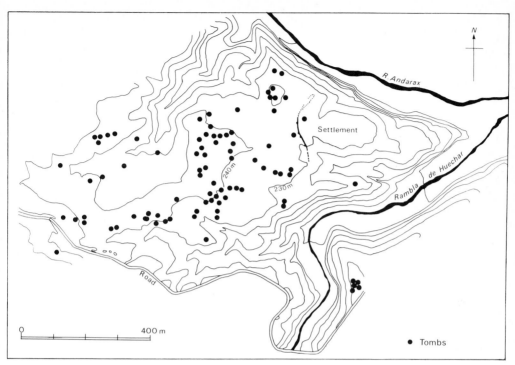

14.1. Los Millares cemetery and settlement. Contours at 10 m intervals.

LOS MILLARES – POST-DEPOSITIONAL AND RETRIEVAL THEORY

The Los Millares settlement with its 'bastioned' wall and cemetery is located in the middle reaches of the Andarax river valley at an altitude of *c.* 230 m and about 2 km from the modern village of Gádor in Almería province. We know that at least twenty-four of the tombs were excavated during 1892 by Pedro Flores, who acted as foreman for Louis Siret, whose fieldwork in the 1880s and 1890s still provides us with the substance of our information about the later prehistoric period in southeast Spain (e.g., Siret and Siret 1887). Although Siret collated the results of Flores' excavations, published a small plan of the site and gave some details of the tombs and their contents (Siret 1893; 1913), he never published a full account. Seventy-five tombs and their grave goods were published by Georg and Vera Leisner in 1943: these comprised two single round chambers, two 'caves', two stone cists (one referred to as 'barranco del Viaducto'), six orthostatic chamber-and-passage tombs with capstone roofs (again one from the 'barranco del Viaducto') and thirty-three dry-stone chamber-and-passage tombs with corbelling and a false vault in the chamber (*Felskuppelgräber* – other terminology after Daniel 1970). From 1953–7 Almagro and Arribas exposed the settlement wall and areas within it, fully re-excavated twenty-one tombs, attempted to identify these and others with those published by the Leisners and prepared a detailed

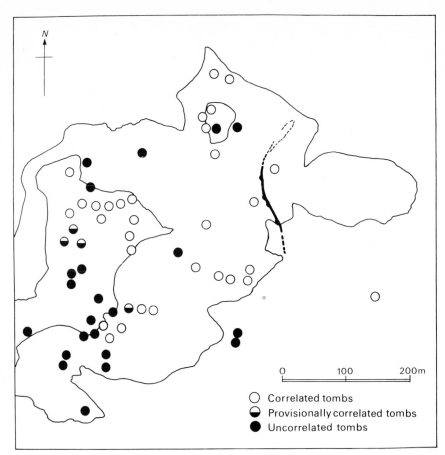

14.2.   Los Millares: inner half of cemetery.

map of the site (1963). There are at least eighty-five tombs visible today (Fig. 14.1), extending from the settlement in a westerly and south-westerly direction on top of the terrace between the River Andarax and the Rambla de Huéchar. In all, the cemetery comprises an area of *c.* 1000 by 400 m. In addition there are five tombs on the opposite side of the Rambla de Huéchar (Fig. 14.1), which may have been included by Siret within the Millares cemetery or which more likely include the three tombs grouped together by the Leisners (1943, pp. 54–5) under the name of 'Rambla de Huéchar'. They are not included in this analysis.

The work of Almagro and Arribas was concentrated on the fifty-seven tombs within the inner half of the cemetery (Fig. 14.2). Before this work was undertaken, only two of the tombs excavated by Flores and published by the Leisners could actually be located on the ground (numbers 17 and 40) and almost nothing could be observed about the distribution of tombs within the cemetery. Almagro and Arribas used three main methods to correlate the

TABLE 14.1. *Correlation of tombs re-excavated by Almagro and Arribas with those published by the Leisners*

Almagro and Arribas number	Leisners' number	Almagro and Arribas number	Leisners' number
I	17	VIII	16
II	47	IX	5
III	63	XII	9
IV	8	XIII	74
V	37	XV	10
VI	6	XVI	21
VII	7	XVII	72

tombs visible on the ground today (their numbers I–LVI) with those published by the Leisners (nos. 1–75):

(1) Siret's unpublished sketch map (Almagro and Arribas 1963, Fig. 3) which marks sixty-four tombs and gives numbers to twenty-three within the inner half of the cemetery;

(2) the inter-tomb distances recorded for forty-two tombs in Flores' diary (Almagro and Arribas 1963, pp. 52–3);

(3) the comparison of the morphology, size and grave goods of the tombs published by the Leisners with those examined by Almagro and Arribas.

As a result of their work, Almagro and Arribas were able to correlate thirty-one tombs with those published by the Leisners (Fig. 14.2). With the provisional correlation claimed for a further four tombs, this gives a maximum of thirty-five tombs which can be identified from the fifty-seven in the inner half of the cemetery (61.4 per cent), the seventy-five published by the Leisners (46.6 per cent), and the possible one hundred which Siret thought were present on the site in the 1890s (*c.* 35 per cent). Thus we can now look with some confidence at the plan of at least the inner half of the cemetery and for the first time we are able to locate many of the tombs and grave goods which Flores excavated over eighty years ago. The implications for the internal organisation of the cemetery were not considered by Almagro and Arribas but will be analysed below.

The work of Almagro and Arribas also gives us a means of evaluating the excavation techniques employed by Pedro Flores. This is important, since we wish to know how far the material he recovered, which was published by the Leisners (1943), was representative of the grave goods present within the tombs. Of the twenty-one tombs re-excavated from 1953–7, fourteen can be correlated with those published by the Leisners and thus enable comparisons of the grave goods found in them (Table 14.1). The results of these comparisons can be summarised in terms of their different raw material and functional categories.

Copper. Objects such as awls, flat axes and dagger blades were found by Flores in ten tombs. In contrast only tomb XIII yielded any copper finds (a tanged dagger and an awl) to Almagro and Arribas (1963, p. 151), but they both came from the passage which Flores had not excavated (cf. two awl fragments from the mainly unexcavated tomb XXI).

Phalange/cylinder idols. Although found in ten tombs by Flores, no further examples were found during re-excavation.

Stone baetyls. The discovery of two new stone enclosures containing stone 'baetyls' outside the passage entrances to tombs VII and IX raises the possibility that further examples may be hidden beneath the mound material which has spilled over the retaining walls of other tombs.

Ornaments/exotic raw materials. Re-excavation led to no new finds of ivory combs, ivory vessels with cross-hatched decoration, bone 'daggers', lunate shaped bone objects, bone buttons, bone tubes, ivory beads or ostrich egg shell beads. Of other materials of non-local origin, two callaïs beads were found in tomb II and a small amorphous amber fragment in tomb IV. On the other hand the numbers of sea shells increased by over 33 per cent and perforated beads (especially of limestone and dentalium shell) by over 25 per cent. This would seem to be evidence of a conscious recovery procedure employed by Flores, concentrating on the 'exotic' raw materials and objects (see below).

Flint arrowheads. The finds of flint arrowheads from the fourteen tombs are listed in Table 14.2. Six tombs yielded no new finds and in each of another three tombs there was only one additional find. If one excludes surface finds, there were four tombs with one new type and one tomb with two new types. It is noticeable that the three tombs with the highest number of finds from the 1953–7 excavations (i.e. nos. III, VII and IX) also yielded the largest numbers from the Flores excavations. On the other hand there are also tombs which originally produced quite large numbers of finds (e.g., VIII, XII) but more recently yielded few or no new examples. The size of the arrowheads, especially when compared with other objects such as beads and ivory containers, does not indicate that excavation technique was at fault. In the cases of tombs III, VII and IX can we suggest that sufficient arrowheads were collected by Flores to indicate their general high frequency and that the rest were left behind?

Pottery. The finds of pottery have been listed for the fourteen tombs in Table 14.3. The figures for the Flores excavations have been taken from Almagro and Arribas (1963) and the number of pots mentioned by the Leisners for each tomb has been added at the bottom of the columns. In many cases it is not clear how the Leisners' figures were derived (e.g., from complete or

TABLE 14.2. *The main types of flint arrowheads found in a sample of fourteen tombs excavated by Flores and Almagro and Arribas at Los Millares*

	I	II	III	IV	V	VI	VII	VIII	IX	XII	XIII	XV	XVI	XVII
	17	47	63	8	37	6	7	16	5	9	74	10	21	72
Tanged	—	—	—	1	—	—	6	1S	1	1	—	3	—	1
Barbed and tanged	1	—	2S / 1	2	—	—	3S / 1	4	9	4	2	3	—	—
Hollow-based	2	1	7S 60/44 / 7	1	1	2	2S 24 / 7	3S 19 / 1	6 48	22	2	11/5	1	1	—
Triangular	—	—	5/13	1 ?1	—	—	7	1	—	—	—	—	—	—
Leaf-shaped	—	—	—	—	—	—	2 / 3	—	1	1	—	1 / 3	—	—
Lozenge	—	—	—	—	1	—	—	1	—	—	—	—	—	—
Lanceolate	—	—	—	—	—	—	1S	1S	4	—	—	—	—	—
Trapeze	—	—	8/5	2	1	2	5S	6S	—	—	—	—	—	—
TOTAL	3	1	95 73/62 (14)	7 3	1	2	5S 34 (10)	6S 24 (3)	8 67	28	4	21/15	1	1

Notes

(i) Finds from the Almagro and Arribas excavations are placed in the left-hand side of each column and those from the Flores excavations are in the right-hand side. Where the figures published by the Leisners (1943) for the Flores excavations differ from those given by Almagro and Arribas (1963) for the material preserved in the National Museum in Madrid, *both* figures are given in the right-hand side of the column (Leisner figure/Almagro and Arribas figure).

(ii) S = surface find.

(iii) In three cases the figure for the *total* number of arrowheads from a tomb given by the Leisners is in error. Tomb 63 should contain 73 rather than 72 arrowheads, tomb 7 should contain 34 rather than 33 and tomb 5 should contain 67 rather than 68 arrowheads.

TABLE 14.3. *Pottery found in the grave goods of a sample of fourteen tombs excavated by Flores and Almagro and Arribas at Los Millares*

	I	17	II	47	IV	8	V	37	VI	6	VII	7	VIII	16	IX	5	XII	9	XIII	74	XVI	21	XVII	72
Beaker	1f	—	—	—	—	—	1f	—	—	—	—	—	—	—	—	—	1f	—	7f	—	1f	—	—	—
Painted	—	—	1f	—	—	—	—	—	—	1f	—	1f	—	—	—	—	—	1c	—	—	—	1c	—	—
Symbol-keramik	1c	1f	—	—	2f	—	1c	1c	—	—	—	1c 2f	—	1c	—	—	—	1c	—	—	3f	—	3f	—
Incised	2f	8f	—	2c	2f	2c	1f	1f	—	3f	—	4f 6f	2f	1c	—	4c	—	1c	—	2c	4f	nf	—	5c
Undecorated (fine)	2c 20+f	1c 6+f	176f	2c 27f	—	4c	3f 26f	3f 17f	118f	—	11+f	—	35f	1f	64f	—	16+f	4c 69f	1c 69f	1c	188f	—	20f	2f
Undecorated (coarse)	1c 85+f	3c 220f	—	2c 5f	—	—	75f	—	29f	—	40f	—	37f	—	56f	1c	51+f	3c	153f	—	32f	—	19f	—
No. of pots given by the Leisners	2	—	2	—	38	—	22	—	—	—	94	—	13	—	70	—	36	—	—	—	12	—	—	—

Notes

(i) The layout of the tombs and columns is the same as in Table 14.2.

(ii) f = fragmentary; nf = unspecified number of fragments; c = complete/restorable vessel; + = minimum number of sherds given.

(iii) The two beaker sherds from tomb 6/VI are not included here as they were excavated from the mound.

fragmentary vessels) and illustrations of them were never fully published. Tombs III and XV are not included as the context of their finds (i.e. chamber/passage/mound) is not made clear by Almagro and Arribas. The clearest observations concern the undecorated pottery, which was clearly not collected systematically by Flores: re-excavation yielded 396 sherds in tomb II, 222 in XIII and 220 in XVI. More surprising are the examples of decorated sherds found from 1953–7: single beaker sherds from tombs I, V, XII and XVI, *symbolkeramik* from tombs I and II and incised sherds in tombs I, II and XVI. No examples were recovered by Flores from these tombs. Other tombs contained examples of these wares which were already known to be present among the grave goods, while the beaker sherds from tomb XIII were from a previously unexcavated part of the tomb.

This investigation of Flores' retrieval methods is based upon fourteen tombs, comprising 18 per cent of the seventy-five tombs published by the Leisners. However, it has been demonstrated that some grave goods are consistently well represented in the Flores' collection (i.e. copper, phalange and cylinder idols, types of non-local material such as ivory, amber and ostrich egg shell and examples of rare types such as the bone daggers and lunate-shaped objects). Others are under-represented (i.e. undecorated pottery, baetyls, limestone and dentalium beads, flint arrowheads and to a certain extent decorated pottery), although in some cases the pattern is not so consistent. This is not simply the result of the size of the different types of grave goods nor, it appears, of differential excavation by Flores. There were two tombs (XIII, XXI) which had their passages completely untouched and there were unexcavated small side-chambers in three tombs (XI, XIII, XVIII), but the plans published by the Leisners suggest that Flores usually undertook a thorough investigation of the tombs' interiors.

An alternative explanation lies in the differential retrieval of grave goods. Although Flores was not an educated man, nor an archaeologist by training or vocation, he must have been guided very strongly in his fieldwork by Siret. The latter was aware of the wider context of the material which was being excavated and probably gave clear instructions to Flores as to the most important grave goods. This would explain the careful attention given to the bone objects, the ivory, amber, ostrich egg shell and callaïs beads, the copper finds and the more *complete* decorated pottery. Other grave goods were accorded less importance in the process of erecting a cultural sequence for southeast Spain in its wider Mediterranean context (Chapman 1975) and were not collected with the same care.

Two final points should be made here. First, the finds of decorated pottery from the 1953–7 excavations remain a problem and we must approach similar finds recovered by Flores with a certain degree of caution when looking at the presence of 'prestige' grave goods in different tombs. Most of the other grave goods which can be interpreted as indicators of social status appear to be well represented in the published records and therefore can be used in an analysis of the cemetery's internal organisation. Second, it could be suggested that many such objects had been removed by clandestine excavation ('buscadores') between the 1890s and the 1950s. Against this we can refer to the finds of fine bifacial flint arrowheads and decorated pottery and to the presence of still unexcavated parts of some tombs when Almagro and Arribas returned to the site in the 1950s. The approach followed in this paper is to accept the grave goods as given at present and see what patterns can be revealed within the inner half of the cemetery. The analysis stands or falls on that assumption.

LOS MILLARES – ANALYTICAL THEORY

In the light of this discussion of the retrieval methods employed in the excavation of the Los Millares cemetery we can now move forward to search for organisational and structural patterns within it. The main effort made in this direction was by the Leisners (1943, especially pp. 566–9) who defined two chronological periods, I(a–d) and II, based upon a study of tomb typology and grave goods. Among the period I tombs were those with corbelled and false vaulted roofs, entrance passages divided into two or more rarely three segments and forecourts, but *without* side-chambers. Their grave goods included copper axes, chisels and awls, stone and bone vessels, objects made of ivory, bifacial flint daggers and arrowheads, *symbolkeramik* and beads of non-local materials. Tombs of period II were often of more complex plans (e.g. including side-chambers) and among their grave goods were copper tanged daggers and saws. bone phalange idols and beaker pottery. The three main reasons for dating the tombs of period II later than period I were the locations of period I tombs nearer the settlement (implying a horizontal stratigraphy), the greater association of beakers with period II tombs and the increase in the complexity of tomb plans from periods I to II. Thus the general interpretation was of an *increase* in the complexity of tomb types and a *decrease* in the 'richness' of the grave goods.

However, it can be demonstrated that the Leisners' periodisation, in the form in which they presented it, is both inconsistent and illusory. A detailed criticism will be presented elsewhere (Chapman, forthcoming) but three main lines of reasoning have been followed. First, the work published by Almagro and Arribas and summarised above enables us to test the assumption that period I tombs were located nearer the settlement. Within the inner half of the cemetery, twenty-six tombs can now be identified according to the Leisners' periodisation (Fig. 14.3). It can be seen that several period II tombs are situated as close to the settlement as those identified as belonging to period I. Furthermore, of the remaining twenty-eight tombs in this area, a *maximum* of twenty could belong to period I (i.e. only fourteen out of the thirty-four period I tombs defined by the Leisners have been identified on the ground), so there *must* be more tombs of period II within this inner part of the cemetery. Second, of the thirteen tombs that have yielded beaker material, no fewer than

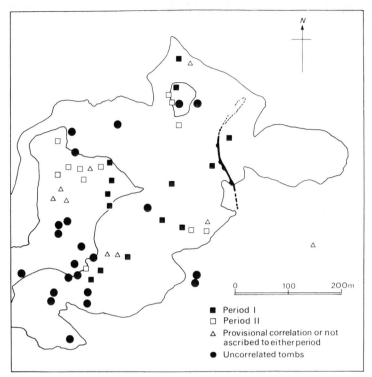

Los Millares: the Leisners' (1943) periodisation in the inner half of cemetery.

ten can be located within the area studied by Almagro and Arribas. In addition to a few later Bronze Age objects, the beaker sherds represent the last phases of the cemetery's use, but the tombs in which they were deposited are not located as predicted by the Leisners. Third, a clear typological sequence for the tombs from periods I to II does not seem to exist and the subdivisions into periods Ia–d are inconsistent.

There are two radiocarbon dates for Los Millares: 2340±85 b.c. (H204/247) from a charcoal sample lying on bedrock beneath a tumble of stones at the inner foot of the settlement wall and 2430 ± 120 b.c. (KN-72) for wood charcoal from tomb 19. Comparable dates have been obtained for tomb 7 at the cemetery of El Barranquete (Almagro Gorbea 1973) and from the settlement at Tabernas. Dates for beaker occupation phases at Cerro de la Virgen (Schüle and Pellicer 1966) span the period *c.* 2000–1800 b.c. Thus a conservative estimate of the period during which tombs were constructed and used at Los Millares would be *c.* 2500–1800 b.c., while the publication of a stratified series of dates from Tabernas may help us to extend the initial date back to *c.* 3000 b.c. Calibration of these dates using Clark's (1975) tables suggests a period of at least one thousand and possibly even fifteen hundred calendar years for the cemetery's usage. Present evidence supports a general evolutionary typology for the tombs during this period of time: in particular it can be argued that the increased segmentation of the passages may be part of a process by which communal burial is being broken down and gradually giving way to the norm of individual burial seen in the succeeding Bronze Age (Chapman 1975).

If we accept this general evolutionary typology and the timespan involved, and reject the detailed periodisation proposed by the Leisners, then we can attempt to view the variation in burial practices within the cemetery in terms of social distinctions. I assume that there is an observable relationship between social organisation and material culture (pre-depositional theory) and that at least a part of the patterning visible in cemeteries of communal as well as individual burials is a reflection of this social organisation (interpretative theory – see Chapman 1977). Communal tombs present particular problems for depositional and post-depositional theory. As excavated they represent a palimpsest of activities, often spanning several centuries, and in favourable circumstances the archaeologist can expect to discern general patterns rather than individual acts of deposition (Chapman 1977, p. 26). This necessitates the development of somewhat different assumptions and procedures to those employed in the analysis of single burials.

Owing to the methods of excavation and recording employed by Flores at Los Millares, there are few reliable conclusions which can be drawn from analysis of structural divisions and the location of burials and grave goods within the tombs (Chapman 1975, pp. 218–20, 333–41 and Fig. 37). However, consideration of the numbers of burials and of the dispersion of prestige grave goods in the cemetery is more profitable. The Leisners gave the numbers of burials present for fifty-eight out of the seventy-five tombs they published. In all there are 1140 individuals represented, ranging from 2–100, with a mean value of just under 20, per tomb. If Siret was correct in his estimate that there were originally one hundred tombs in the cemetery, then we can add the mean value of 20 burials per tomb for each of the forty-two tombs for which we have no details of burial numbers (i.e. not published/excavated) to the 1140 mentioned above, giving a total of 1980. This would give 2 burials per year for one thousand years and 1.5 burials per year for fifteen hundred years of occupation (see above).

It can be objected that the figures given by the Leisners are for the *minimum* number of burials per tomb. The excavation of tomb XXI (Almagro and Arribas 1963) emphasised the difficulty of calculating the number of interments within a single tomb: there was a minimal degree of articulation extant (e.g., crania and cervical vertebrae) and only careful examination could determine whether the numbers present were accurately reflected by a simple count of crania. But even if we double the total number of burials (i.e. 3960), this would still give a frequency of 4 burials per year for one thousand years and 3.6 burials per year for fifteen hundred years.

These figures are well below what might be expected for a pre-industrial population with an agricultural subsistence base. Calculations of the population present within Los Millares also support this line of argument. Siret (1893) estimated that only 2 of the 5 hectares within the settlement wall were actually occupied. If we adopt Renfrew's (1972, p. 251) figure of 300 persons per hectare, which was adapted from Frankfort's estimate for Mesopotamian urban sites and applied to Aegean Bronze Age settlements, then this would give a population of *c.* 600 for the site. Allowing for the range of variation in usage of space by different human groups and the probability that not all of the 2 hectares estimated by Siret was occupied at the same time, it might be wise to allow a range of *c.* 300–600 people. Even if the site's population were as low as 100, the number of dead within the one thousand or fifteen hundred years of the site's occupation would still exceed the maximum number of burials projected above. It has been calculated that a family of only six individuals with a life expectancy of twenty-five years and in the absence of population growth would produce nearly four thousand dead after a thousand years (Renfrew 1973b, p. 545).

The evidence of the burials can be taken as support for the practice of differential burial on the site: clearly many individuals were excluded from interment within the tombs and their bodies disposed of in ways which make them archaeologically invisible. Among these appear to be the bodies of children, who were only found in the side-chambers of two tombs: in tomb 20 there were the remains of eleven children and in tomb XXI five children. Either children were not normally present in the tombs or Flores and Siret did not distinguish them from the adults. No analyses of the age or sex composition of the burials have ever been published.

It is the distribution of 'prestige' grave goods between tombs in the cemetery which produces the most interesting evidence for social distinctions. In many small-scale societies the exchange of (socially or economically) valued goods served as a mechanism by which status or prestige might be acquired, enhanced and symbolised (Sahlins 1972). A number of studies of burial practices have used the distribution of grave goods of non-local materials as indicators of the status of the individuals with which they were associated (e.g. Brown 1971). This approach will be followed here, although it must be remembered that we are concerned more with social *groups* rather than individuals in these communal tombs.

In spite of the lack of characterisation studies on material of this period in southeast Spain, it is possible to separate raw materials which are of external origin or which were circulating within exchange cycles. Both ivory and ostrich egg shell are of north African origin: elephants were present in Morocco until the Roman period (Schüle 1969, p. 20) and ostrich egg shells were used as containers in the Neolithic of Capsian tradition (Gilman 1974). Objects of jet have no local source in Almería and were thought by Siret (1913) to have come from Britain, but there appear to be much nearer sources in southern Spain (e.g. the Sierra Morena). The source of amber finds is more problematical and these need not automatically be assumed to be of Baltic derivation. Indeed there is a source at Agost (Murcia), from which sometimes fist-sized nodules were obtained in the 1930s (Jiménez de Cisneros 1936). Callaïs belongs to the same stone family as lazulite, turquoise and serpentine and has frequently been identified only on the basis of visual examination. Analysis of a bead from one of the Catalan fosa graves (Muñoz 1965, p. 249) showed that it was of variscite, which has an important source at Adra (Almería). Sea shells occur in most settlements and tombs of this and earlier periods in southern and eastern Spain and extend over 100 km inland (e.g., the necklace containing 367 cowrie shells from the Cueva Amador in Murcia – Walker 1973, p. 294). The Sirets (1887, pp. 17–20) found, in the coastal Cueva de los Toyos (Mazarrón, Murcia), a pot containing sea shells in various stages of working, from untouched shells to perforated roundels. This suggests a pattern of coastal production and inland circulation through the later prehistoric period.

The interpretation of the distribution of fine pottery wares in terms of exchange and prestige can also be proposed. David Clarke (1976) emphasised the variable and restricted distribution of the best clays for pottery production and the consequent in-built tendency for the exchange of pottery between sedentary communities. He argued that fine beakers were 'major vehicles of rank, prestige and status display, very expensive to produce both in man hours and in contemporary value terms, and therefore exchanged for these reasons over considerable distances, between various communities, in a context where their utilitarian and functional values were secondary' (1976, p. 462). Following this line of argument it can be suggested that painted pottery and the *symbolkeramik* may also have been exchangeable fine wares and symbols of prestige. That other wares were probably exchanged is suggested by the X-ray fluorescence analyses on surface material reported by Walker (1973, pp. 378–87): one of the clay types distinguished at Los Millares also occurred at the contemporary site of Almizarque, *c.* 75 km away.

With the addition of copper objects, whose position as symbols of wealth and prestige has been argued by Renfrew (1972), grave goods of the above raw materials (with the exception of sea shells) will be analysed for their occurrence in tombs at Los Millares. The scrutiny of Flores' retrieval methods (see above) suggested strongly that these prestige items were carefully collected and are reliably represented in the Leisners' (1943) publication. The exceptions to this are the decorated pottery and the sea shells. The latter were under-represented by as much as 33 per cent in the tombs which could be identified, and in any case are more widely distributed among the tombs. They are excluded from this analysis.

Objects made of ivory, jet, amber, callaïs and ostrich egg shell occurred in seventeen tombs, while copper grave goods (excluding those of Bronze Age date) occur in thirty-two tombs (Table 14.4). We would not expect fresh excavation to increase the frequency of these grave goods to any significant extent. The same may not necessarily be true of the three fine pottery wares.

TABLE 14.4. *The occurrence of prestige grave goods in tombs at Los Millares*

	1	2	3	4	5	6	7	8	9	10	11	12	13	14	15	16	17	18	19	20	21	22	23	24	25	26	27	28	29	30	31	32	33	34	35	36	37	38	39	40
Ivory		×			×		×	×				×								×																				×
Ostrich egg shell												×																												
Amber							×	×				×						×		×																				
Jet							×	×	×			×						×							×															
Callaïs				×	×	×	×	×	×			×		×	×					×		×	×	×	×					×	×	×		×			×			×
Copper	×	×					×		×												×																			×
Painted pottery			×														×	×				×														×	×	×		
Beaker pottery				×			×		×			×			×	×	×			×																	×		×	×
Symbol-keramik																																								

	41	42	43	44	45	46	47	48	49	50	51	52	53	54	55	56	57	58	59	60	61	62	63	64	65	66	67	68	69	70	71	72	73	74	75	XI	XII
Ivory																			×												×						
Ostrich egg shell																																					×
Amber																							×												×		
Jet																																					
Callaïs			×	×			×		×			×		×			×										×							×			
Copper			×				×		×			×		×			×										×										×
Painted pottery																																					
Beaker pottery																																		×		×	
Symbol-keramik							×										×																				

Notes
(i) × = present.
(ii) Tomb numbers are those of Flores published by Leisner and Leisner (1943), with the exception of XI and XXI which were excavated by Almagro and Arribas (1963) and cannot be correlated with the tombs published by the Leisners.

In all there are forty-three tombs containing prestige grave goods, almost exactly half of those visible on the surface today. The different raw materials and other objects are represented in different numbers of tombs (Table 14.4) and in differing total frequencies: the latter range from 821 ostrict egg shell beads to over sixty copper objects, around forty of ivory (allowing for fragments and a few dubious identifications), over twenty of jet and down to less than a dozen each of amber and callaïs.

The most important observation which can be made is that a number of tombs contain a greater range and frequency of prestige grave goods than do other tombs. Tomb 40 is the clearest example as it contains the highest numbers of ivory (over a dozen) and copper (ten) objects of any tomb, as well as one example each of painted pottery and *symbolkeramik*. Although lacking fine wares and containing only one copper object, tomb 12 can also be distinguished in three ways: it has the second largest number of ivory grave goods (eleven), 800 ostrich egg shell beads (one of only two tombs in which they occur) and the highest numbers of jet (fifteen) and amber (five) beads. Tomb 7 contains four copper objects, painted pottery, *symbolkeramik* and a small number of jet, amber and ivory objects. Tomb 8 also contains grave goods of jet, amber, ivory and copper, but lacks all three decorated fine wares. In addition, we should also consider tombs 5 (three copper objects and a possible six ivory objects, 9 (three callaïs beads, two copper objects and one example each of the three fine wares), 16 (three copper awls and one example of *symbolkeramik*) and 63 (twenty-one ostrich egg shell beads and a possible ivory point/awl).

The other grave goods present in these tombs also reveal some interesting information. By far the highest numbers of flint arrowheads came from tombs 40, 63, 5, 57, 7, 9 and 16 (Table 14.2). Apart from two other tombs, the frequency of the arrowheads published by the Leisners does not rise above five per tomb. Four of the eight stone vessels from the cemetery occur in tombs 7, 19, 16 and 40 (the only decorated example). Of the ten tombs which contained stone (e.g., alabaster) idols (nos. 5, 7, 8, 9, 12, 16, 40, 57), all but two have been distinguished by their prestigious grave goods. Half the number of phalange idols from the tombs were present in nos. 5, 7, 8, 12, 16, 40 and 57. Lastly it is also worth noting that in tomb 12, along with the 800 ostrich egg shell beads, were another 1200 each of limestone and shell.

In addition to these grave goods is there any morphological evidence from these tombs which would distinguish them from other tombs and indicate the greater energy expenditure involved in their construction? There is no identity in the basic tomb plan: two of the tombs are of true 'megalithic' type (nos. 8, 63), five have chambers with passages divided into two segments (nos. 7, 9, 12, 16, 57) and two have chambers with passages divided into three segments (nos. 5, 40). As regards chamber size, only tomb 40 with its *c.* 6 m diameter can be clearly distinguished on present evidence; a possible error of ±0.5 m in the measurements of chamber diameter published by the

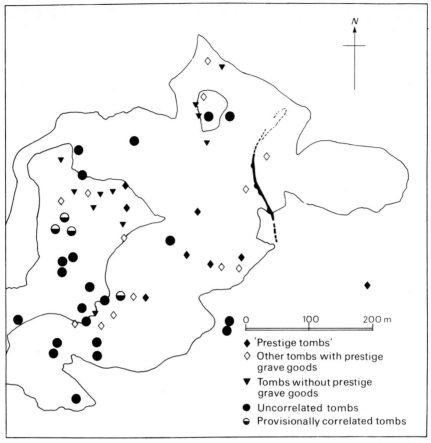

Los Millares: distribution of prestige grave goods and tombs within the inner half of the cemetery.

Leisners makes it impractical to make any other divisions. Evidence for structural divisions within the chambers occurs in five tombs but only in one case (no. 63) in one of the prestige tombs distinguished above. Extra-tomb structures offer more promising lines of inquiry. Baetyl enclosures were found in association with tombs 5, 7, 16, 15, 23, 25 and 68. Tomb 5 was located close to two lines of stones which ran in a southwest direction for at least 40 m, tomb 7 seems to have had a stone enclosure to the right of its entrance and tomb 16 had two concentric stone circles outside the mound. Tomb 9 was joined to tomb 74 by a 4 m long wall and there were two standing stones some 6 m apart on either side of the entrance to tomb 40. Individual or pairs of standing stones were also noted outside tombs 17, 18, 20, 37 and 43 (for details of all these tombs see Leisner and Leisner 1943; Almagro and Arribas 1963). This evidence for tomb morphology and extra-tomb structures shows no pattern of exclusive association with the tombs distinguished by their prestige goods. Re-excavation of further tombs might yield more evidence for internal

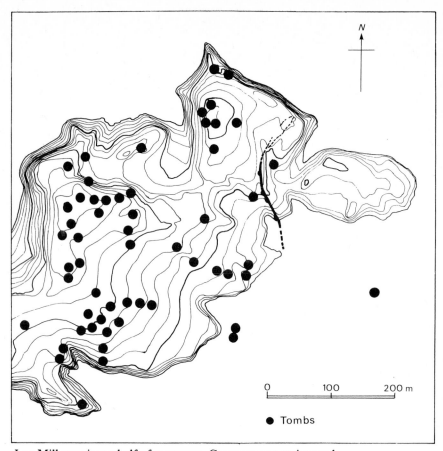

14.5.   Los Millares: inner half of cemetery. Contours at 1 m intervals.

structural differences as well as baetyl enclosures covered by slippage of the
tomb mounds, but all traces of stone circles, alignments and standing stones
have now vanished from the site.

More positive results are obtained from consideration of the location of the
'prestige' tombs within the cemetery. All but one of these tombs (no. 57)
can be located within the inner half of the cemetery (Fig. 14.4). Furthermore
with the exception of tomb 63 they are situated within 150 m of the settlement
wall and can be found within a radius of the same distance from tomb 5. This
is clearly a highly concentrated distribution, although the individual tombs
belong to more than one of the clusters which can be observed in this part
of the cemetery. Those tombs with a lesser range and frequency of prestige
grave goods, as well as those which do not have any at all, are both distributed
around the general concentration of tombs distinguished above, but in the
same tomb clusters (Fig. 14.4). Indeed it may be possible to isolate at least
four burial areas, of which two are centred on the highest points in the
cemetery. There is also a preference for individual tomb locations on small

spurs of slightly higher ground in the centre or on the edge of the plateau. This point is illustrated in Fig. 14.5, in which the contours are plotted at one metre intervals. Clearly the application of more sophisticated quantitative analyses may help to isolate the complex of clustered and linearly arranged tombs that comprise this cemetery (cf. Fig. 14.1).

INTERPRETIVE THEORY

The analysis of the Los Millares cemetery is based upon three explicit assumptions:

(1) that there is an observable relationship between social organisation and material culture (pre-depositional theory);

(2) that the finds of prestigious grave goods from the cemetery were recovered in a systematic way by the excavator in the 1890s (post-depositional and retrieval theory – see above);

(3) that patterning detectable in the dispersion of tombs and grave goods within the cemetery would be at least in part a reflection of the community's social organisation (interpretive theory).

The nature of the data limited the analysis outlined above to an essentially simple manipulative exercise. In spite of these restrictions it can be argued that there is patterning in the distribution of prestige grave goods within the cemetery. The clustering of the 'prestige' tombs within the inner half of the cemetery may seem to take us back to the Leisners' periods I and II, since all the 'prestige' tombs (except nos. 8 and 63) were placed with Los Millares I. However, in addition to the criticisms of the Leisners' chronology summarised above, it should be noted that these tombs include both earlier (e.g., painted ware) and later (e.g., beaker ware) materials, that there is no evidence on the basis of tomb typology for later tombs being situated further away from the settlement and that the linear and clustered patterning of all the tombs must be in some way a reflection of social behaviour.

The patterning of the grave goods seems more indicative of a ranked rather than the egalitarian society proposed by Almagro and Arribas (1963, pp. 45–6). Fried (1967, p. 109) defines a ranked society as 'one in which positions of valued status are somehow limited so that not all those of sufficient talent to occupy such statuses actually achieve them'. Such societies, often referred to as chiefdoms, show an increase in the complexity of their social organisation, with institutionalised leadership presiding over denser populations. Among other things, part-time craft specialisation appears. Redistribution is no longer thought to be a major factor in the appearance of such chiefdoms (Peebles and Kus 1977). Although the use of such evolutionary typologies of social organisation (e.g., bands, tribes, chiefdoms) has been criticised as being of little explanatory value and sometimes anthropologically naive, it has been argued recently that there are important differences (e.g. levels of social regulation and control) which make their use a productive exercise (Peebles and Kus 1977). Peebles and Kus have listed five ways in which a ranked or chiefdom society can be recognised in archaeological contexts (1977, pp. 431–3; see also Ellison, ch. 15 below). As far as the use of burial data is concerned, the evidence from Los Millares allows us to approach an interpretation of social ranking based upon group affiliation, but the nature of communal interment as well as the absence of data on the age and sex of the buried individuals prevents us from reconstructing 'social pyramids'. The occurrence of a settlement hierarchy and of 'subsistence autonomy' (the second and third characteristics of ranked societies suggested by Peebles and Kus) is difficult to document at present, owing to our small and fragmentary knowledge of Copper Age settlements in southeast Spain. Tombs are much better known and an indication of the existence of a settlement hierarchy is revealed in the distribution of prestige grave goods. In the best surveyed area for communal tombs, the Almanzora valley, there is a notable concentration of copper objects, *symbolkeramik*, callaïs beads, beakers and ivory in the nearly coastal settlement of Almizaraque and its associated tombs (Leisner and Leisner 1943; Almagro Gorbea 1965). Grave goods such as these are not evenly distributed among the tombs of this valley and the only significant concentrations occur in three tombs (Loma de la Atalaya 3, Llano de la Atalaya 6 and El Jauton 5) near Purchena, some 50 km from the coast. This pattern may give some support to the reconstruction of a small number of higher-order settlements within each river valley.

Peebles and Kus' fourth characteristic is 'evidence of organised productive activities which transcend the basic household group' (1977, p. 432), such as large monuments erected by communal labour, part-time craft specialisation and intersocietal trade. The size of the tombs in southeast Spain is self-evident with regard to communal labour, and evidence has been put forward above for the existence of intersocietal trade (ivory, ostrich egg shell etc.). In addition there are sites such as Cerro de la Virgen (Schüle and Pellicer 1966) where copper and gold working was practised, but there were no local sources available for either of these metals. As for craft specialisation we may cite at least metalworking and inquire about the production of some of the decorated pottery, fine bifacial flint arrowheads and idols of stone and bone. At the settlement of Cerro de las Canteras (Vélez Blanco) one structure contained a quantity of flint cores, splinters and fragments of arrowheads, scrapers and blades, while another had abundant bone artifacts (points, spatulae), large bones, deer antlers and possible whetstones – in both cases an interpretation of 'workshops' can be proposed (Motos 1918).

Lastly Peebles and Kus propose that 'there should be a correlation between those elements of the cultural system's environment which are of a frequency, amplitude and duration to be dealt with but which are least predictable and evidence of *society-wide* organisational activity to buffer or otherwise deal with these perturbations' (1977, pp. 432–3). Examples of such unpredictable elements are environmental fluctuations leading to variable food yields, warfare and intersocietal trade. Warfare was certainly widespread in south-eastern America among the Mississippian cultures from *c.* A.D. 700–900 until beyond the European colonisation and the bastioned palisade wall at the Moundville site (*c.* A.D. 1200–1500) can be paralleled with sites in both southeast Spain (e.g., Los Millares) and central Portugal (e.g., Zambujal) where structurally analogous societies seem to have developed. But it can be argued that the unpredictable fluctuations in the arid climate of southeast Spain may have been instrumental in stimulating the nucleation of local populations and the developed social organisation which could 'buffer' the effects of variation in water supply (Chapman 1978). The appearance of prestige burials associated with exchangeable materials and more discrete burial locations within cemeteries, which we have seen at Los Millares, can be compared with similar developments in the southern United States around A.D. 1200 (Brown, quoted in Peebles and Kus 1977, p. 433). Such a model of cultural developments, as with the ranking–chiefdom model of social organisation, is proposed as the basis for future research into the development of the Copper Age in southeast Spain. With the data at our disposal ('the bad samples' mentioned at the beginning of this paper) and the absence of sufficient modern surveys and excavations, the ranked society model defines areas of research as well as offering a sounder theoretical approach to the explanation of cultural change in the third millennium b.c. than notions of 'colonists' or 'influences' deriving from the East Mediterranean.

Given the nature of communal burial in prehistoric Europe it is clear that we cannot normally hope to identify 'social personae' (i.e. the selection of statuses possessed by an individual during life which are reflected in the burial ritual) as has been done by analyses of *single* burials (e.g., Brown 1971; Shennan 1975). The long-term usage and structural remodelling of communal tombs require careful analysis before we can approach the problem of the social composition of local communities. In addition to the excavation programmes required, there would seem to be two promising lines of research here. First, analysis of the skeletal material will give us more insights into the actual burial rites themselves and into the social groups which were buried together. Anthropological excavation of the skeletal material from the Buccino cemetery in southern Italy has shown that three tombs contained a consanguineous group (Holloway 1975), while analyses in southern New York State have been claimed to identify residence patterns (Lane and Sublett 1972). As a complement to the analysis of tombs and their grave goods, it has been suggested that the strontium content of human bones may reveal evidence for dietary differences which could be related to hereditary rank within a local society (Pires-Ferreira and Flannery 1976, p. 292). There is much here to be pursued with collections of well-excavated skeletal material.

Second, we have to develop some models for the formation and layout of communal tombs in *cemeteries*. Even the most superficial examination of published tombs reveals a variety of cemetery size and form within prehistoric

Europe. At one extreme we may place a dispersed pattern of often individual tombs with no signs of clustering into a proper cemetery, while at the other are the sometimes densely packed cemeteries such as exist in southeast Spain. Within cemeteries, as I have noted for Los Millares, tomb location may look to be clustered in tight concentrations or there may be linear arrangements. Such patterning clearly requires closer definition, and techniques of point pattern analysis could be useful in this context (Hodder and Orton 1976: Tainter 1976). Once this analysis has been undertaken we can begin to consider the factors which may have been collectively responsible for such patterning: examination of local population densities, economy, social organisation and topography will all offer useful insights (Chapman 1977).

One factor which seems to lie behind the appearance of cemeteries of both communal and individual tombs is the development of corporate descent groups. This has been expressed most comprehensively by Saxe, who writes that 'to the degree that corporate group rights to use and/or control crucial but restricted resources are attained and/or legitimised by means of lineal descent from the dead (i.e. lineal ties to ancestors) such groups will maintain formal disposal areas for the exclusive disposal of their dead' (1970, p. 119). This link between cemeteries, 'lineal ties to ancestors' and pressure on resources was developed by Saxe on the basis of Meggitt's work in New Guinea (1965) and has since received further ethnographic support (Tainter 1976, p. 93 reports the results of Lynne Goldstein's doctoral research on this subject). This raises interesting possibilities for social and economic analyses in prehistoric Europe. If we examine spatial and temporal variation in the appearance of nucleated cemeteries we may be able to identify different rates of social change correlated with population increase and pressure on economic resources. As our knowledge of the settlements which were associated with these tombs is variable and often sketchy for much of prehistoric Europe, the analysis of burial practices assumes greater importance in our attempts to measure and explain cultural change. Where setlements are known, they provide us with an important check on the relationship between the cemetery and the community. In particular, ethnographic studies have revealed the burial of different segments of society not only within distinct burial areas but also in distinct cemeteries (Saxe 1970 on the Ashanti of west Africa and the Kapauku Papuans). An example of the converse situation (a single cemetery serving several settlements) can be seen at Kaloko in prehistoric Hawaii, where *four* discrete residential areas, situated *c.* 300–400 m from each other and comprising a single *community*, all used the same cemetery (Tainter and Cordy 1977, pp. 102–3). One can also imagine that in areas where tombs were located on the boundaries of the contemporary intake such tombs would be the focus for dispersed communities. The association of a single cemetery with a single settlement-locus may be only a restricted example of the spatial relationship between the community of the living and that of the dead.

The general conclusion which we may draw from the ideas presented in this paper is that the development of archaeological theory must be central to our attempts to rethink the role and significance of communal burial in prehistoric Europe. Although the tombs have been the object of public attention, excavation and destruction since before the days of the early antiquaries, there may still be some significant patterning present, especially in their spatial attributes. Of course new excavation and fieldwork will help us to extend our knowledge of the burial practices represented in megalithic tombs, but the 'bad samples' derived from literally thousands of other tombs must be evaluated as well. From both 'good' and 'bad' samples, we can with luck develop and apply the pre-depositional, depositional, post-depositional, analytical and interpretive theories which must underlie any explanations of the development of communal burial in prehistoric Europe. This would be a productive contribution to the discipline of archaeology which David Clarke did so much to proclaim and which is the poorer for his passing.

REFERENCES

Almagro, M. and Arribas, A. (1963). *El poblado y la necrópolis megalíticos de Los Millares* (Bibliotheca Praehistorica Hispana, vol. 3), Instituto Español de Prehistoria del C.S.I.C.

Almagro Gorbea, M. J. (1965). *Las Tres Tumbas Megalíticas de Almizaraque* (Trabajos de Prehistoria, Monografías), Instituto Español de Prehistoria del C.S.I.C.

(1973). *El Poblado y la necropólis de El Barranquete* (*Almería*) (Acta Archaeologica Hispanica 6), Comisaría General de Excavaciones Arqueológicas

Barth, F. E. and Hodson, F. R. (1976). 'The Hallstatt cemetery and its documentation: some new evidence', *Antiquaries Journal* 56: 159–76

Binford, L. R. (1971). 'Mortuary practices: their study and potential' in J. A. Brown (ed.) *Approaches to the Social Dimensions of Mortuary Practices* (Memoirs of the Society for American Archaeology 25)

Bosch-Gimpera, P. (1969). 'La Cultura de Almería', *Pyrenae* 5: 47–93

Brown, J. A. (ed.) (1971). *Approaches to the Social Dimensions of Mortuary Practices* (Memoirs of the Society for American Archaeology 25)

Chapman, R. W. (1975). 'Economy and society within later prehistoric Iberia: a new framework', Ph.D. thesis, University of Cambridge

(1977). 'Burial practices: an area of mutual interest' in M. Spriggs (ed.) *Archaeology and Anthropology : areas of mutual interest* (British Archaeological Reports, Supplementary Series 19)

(1978). 'The evidence for prehistoric water control in south-east Spain', *Journal of Arid Environments* 1: 261–74

(forthcoming). 'Los Millares and the relative chronology of the Copper Age in south-east Spain', *Trabajos de Prehistoria*

Childe, V. G. (1947). *The Dawn of European Civilisation* (4th edn), Routledge and Kegan Paul

Clark, R. M. (1975). 'A calibration curve for radiocarbon dates', *Antiquity* 49: 251–66

Clarke, D. L. (1972). 'A provisional model of an Iron Age Society and its settlement system' in D. L. Clarke (ed.) *Models in Archaeology*, Methuen

(1973). 'Archaeology: the loss of innocence', *Antiquity* 47: 6–18

(1976). 'The Beaker Network – social and economic models' in J. N. Lanting and J. D. van der Waals (eds.) *Glockenbechersymposion Oberried 1974*, Fibula-Van Dishoek

Daniel, G. E. (1963). *The Megalith Builders of Western Europe*, Penguin

(1970). 'Megalithic answers', *Antiquity* 44: 260–9

Fried, M. H. (1967). *The Evolution of Political Society: an essay in political anthropology*, Random House

Gilman, A. (1974). 'Neolithic of Northwest Africa', *Antiquity* 48: 273–82

(1976). 'Bronze Age dynamics in southeast Spain', *Dialectical Anthropology* 1: 307–19

Hodder, I. and Orton, C. (1976). *Spatial analysis in archaeology*, Cambridge University Press

Hodson, F. R. (1977). 'Quantifying Hallstatt; some initial results', *American Antiquity* 42: 394–412

Holloway, R. R. (1975). 'Buccino: the early bronze age village of Tufariello', *Journal of Field Archaeology* 2: 11–81

Jiménez de Cisneros, D. (1936). 'Encuentro del succino o ámbar amarillo en las inmediaciones de Agost', *Boletin de la Sociedad Española de Historia Natural* 26: 365–6

Lane, R. A. and Sublett, A. J. (1972). 'Osteology of social organisation: residence pattern', *American Antiquity* 37: 186–201

Leisner, G. and Leisner, V. (1943). *Die Megalithgräber der Iberischen Halbinsel: Der Süden*, Walter de Gruyter

Meggitt, M. J. (1965). *The Lineage System of the Mae Enga of New Guinea*, Oliver and Boyd

Motos, F. de (1918). *La Edad Neolítica en Vélez Blanco* (Memoria de la Comisión de Investigacion Palaeontologia y Prehistoria)

Mueller, J. W., ed. (1975). *Sampling in Archaeology*, University of Arizona Press

Muñoz, A. M. (1965). *La Cultura Neolítica Catalana de los 'Sepulcros de Fosa'*, Instituto de Arqueología y Prehistoria, Universidad de Barcelona, Publicaciónes Eventuales, No. 9.

Peebles, C. S. and Kus, S. M. (1977). 'Some archaeological correlates of ranked societies', *American Antiquity* 42: 421–48

Piggott, S. (1965). *Ancient Europe*, Edinburgh University Press

Pires-Ferreira, J. W. and Flannery, K. V. (1976). 'Ethnographic models for formative exchange' in K. V. Flannery (ed.) *The Early Mesoamerican Village*, Academic

Renfrew, C. (1972). *The Emergence of Civilisation*, Methuen

(1973a). *Before Civilisation*, Jonathan Cape

(1973b). 'Monuments, mobilization and social organisation in neolithic Wessex' in C. Renfrew (ed.) *The Explanation of Culture Change: Models in Prehistory*, Duckworth

Sahlins, M. D. (1972). *Stone Age Economics*, Tavistock

Santa Olalla, J. M. (1946). *Esquema Paletnológico de la Península Hispánica* (Seminario de Historia Primitiva del Hombre), Madrid

Savory, H. N. (1968). *Spain and Portugal*, Thames and Hudson

Saxe, A. A. (1970). 'Social dimensions of mortuary practices', Ph.D. dissertation, University of Michigan

Schiffer, M. B. (1976). *Behavioural Archaeology*, Academic

Schüle, W. (1969). 'Tartessos y El Hinterland (Excavaciones de Orce y Galera)' in *Tartessos y Sus Problemas*, V Symposium Internacional de Prehistoria Peninsular: 15–32

Schüle, W. and Pellicer, M. (1966). *El Cerro de la Virgen, Orce (Granada) I* (Excavaciones Arqueológicas en España, 46), Comisaría General de Excavaciones Arqueológicas

Shennan, S. (1975). 'The social organisation at Brańč', *Antiquity* 49: 279–88

Siret, L. (1893). 'L.'Espagne préhistorique', *Revue des Questions Scientifiques* (1913). *Questions de Chronologie et D'Ethnographie Ibériques I*, P. Geuthner

Siret, H. and Siret, L. (1887). *Les Premiers Âges du Métal dans le Sud-Est de l'Espagne*, Anvers

Tainter, J. A. (1976). 'Social organisation and social patterning in the Kaloko Cemetery, North Kona, Hawaii', *Archaeology and Physical Anthropology in Oceania* 11: 91–105

(1977). 'Woodland social change in west-central Illinois', *Mid-Continental Journal of Archaeology* 2: 67–98

Tainter, J. A. and Cordy, R. H. (1977). 'An archaeological analysis of social ranking and residence groups in prehistoric Hawaii', *World Archaeology* 9: 95–112

Tarradell, M. (1969). 'El Problema de Tartessos Visto Desde el Lado Meridional del Estrecho de Gibraltar' in *Tartessos y Sus Problemas*, V Symposium Internacional de Prehistoria Peninsular: 221–32

Walker, M. J. (1973). 'Aspects of the Neolithic and Copper Ages in the basins of the Rivers Segura and Vinalopó, South-East Spain', D.Phil. thesis, Oxford University

15

Towards a socioeconomic model for the Middle Bronze Age in southern England

ANN ELLISON

The Bronze Age of southern England is probably one of the most intensively studied periods in the realm of world prehistory. The activities of antiquarians over two centuries in the contrasting spheres of barrow excavation and the collection of aesthetically pleasing metalwork have provided a vast corpus of material and observations although their published works vary in quality through time and space. In particular, the activities of the nineteenth-century Dorset antiquaries Warne, Durden, Shipp, Hutchins and Smart are poorly served by the published accounts in comparison with the lavishly illustrated and more objective descriptions of the parallel discoveries in Wiltshire. However, this disparity is partially alleviated by the remarkable survival of the grave goods themselves, often along with their original nineteenth-century labels, in the basements and storerooms of museums holding carefully curated collections throughout southern England. In many cases the artifacts are accompanied by unpublished manuscripts, catalogues and collections of watercolours which provide a further source of valuable information. From the end of the nineteenth century onwards, investigation by excavation was extended to sites of a more domestic nature. The pioneering work of Pitt-Rivers in his large-scale excavation of the Bronze Age enclosures of Cranborne Chase was followed in the earlier part of the twentieth century by many settlement excavations both in Sussex, where they were implemented or inspired by the Curwens, and in Wessex mainly due to the impeccable researches of J. F. S. Stone and C. M. Piggott. Alongside this interest in settlement excavation the British tradition for landscape-oriented fieldwork was at its height and for Bronze Age studies the key projects were the Curwens' studies of fields, lynchet trackways and linear earthworks on the South Downs, Grinsell's exhaustive county-by-county inventories and surveys of all the known and surviving round-barrows, and two fundamental discussions concerning the relationships between settlements and linear ditches in Wessex (Piggott 1944; Hawkes 1939). Meanwhile, the growing expansion of gravel extraction in the main river basins of southern England led to the discovery of many pottery assemblages, both domestic and sepulchral. These lie virtually unstudied in museum basements, often untouched since the date of their discovery.

Settlement excavations have continued but all too often on a small scale or hastily in advance of imminent destruction. The last decade has also seen a revival of Bronze Age landscape studies exemplified by the work of Bowen (1975) in central Wessex and by Bradley on the Berkshire Downs (in Bradley and Ellison 1975, ch. 5). Meanwhile, full-time research has concentrated on the compilation of detailed corpora of the different classes of artifacts linked to detailed considerations of typology, chronology, and origins. The culmination of this trend in research was the publication of 'British Prehistory: a new outline' (Renfrew 1974) in which the latest typological schemes for the Bronze Age were discussed and related to the absolute chronology supplied by the available carbon-fourteen dates. Research of this nature is fundamental to any future analysis. However, the total lack of rigorous analysis of assemblage composition and of examination of spatial patterning within artifact distributions, settlement and burial sites is noteworthy. It is only for the Early Bronze Age 'Wessex Culture' that general socioeconomic models have been erected (Piggott 1938) and subsequently modified as a result of more detailed analysis (Fleming 1971). The aim of the present essay is to analyse as much of the data as is available using as many appropriate techniques as possible in order to outline a tentative socioeconomic model for the late second millennium B.C. (traditionally termed the Middle Bronze Age) in southern England.

The traditional implicit model for the Middle Bronze Age has been derived from partial studies of certain compartments of the available evidence. The period has been seen to be characterised by a predominantly pastoral economy associated with small settled farmsteads. The cultural break with the Early Bronze Age has been stressed in relation to the apparently innovatory pottery styles, an expansion and diversification in metalworking and a change in burial rite from single interments in barrows to collective burial in urnfields, some in or around individual existing barrows, but others existing as flat cemeteries. Although explanations for the apparent change in the pottery styles and burial rite in terms of 'invasion' are now unfashionable, viable alternatives have not been clearly articulated or tested. Burgess has recently laid emphasis on the degree of change that apparently occurred towards the end of the Early Bronze Age. 'All the established pottery types. . .and the whole range of burial and ritual monuments and practices with which they are associated, vanished at this time. Nowhere is there any evidence that the old linear and circular ritual monuments, the cursus, avenues, alignments, henges and circles survived.' He even suggests that the change may have been catastrophic and caused in part by climatic deterioration (Burgess 1974, 194–7).

DEPOSITIONAL AND RETRIEVAL FACTORS

An underlying assumption of this study is that patterns of behaviour may have been reflected in the spatial patterning of structures and artifacts. Thus such patterning of structures and artifacts within a settlement may reflect the economic activities and social organisation of that site just as the patterning of types of burials in an urnfield or of artifact types across space may reflect social or religious activities on the one hand and the nature of communications–exchange systems on the other.

The possibility of recovering data susceptible to such interpretation depends on the extent to which the artifact and site distributions have been disturbed, transformed or destroyed since their deposition (post-depositional theory). In the case of the earthwork settlement sites and round-barrows, the archaeological deposits are, before excavation, well preserved. Some have been partially disturbed by ploughing but even on the river gravels where virtually no sites survive as earthworks the patterns of structural features and artifact concentrations have often survived (e.g., urnfields with evidence of pyres and reasonably well-preserved settlement sites in the Thames valley). The landscape evidence of fields, earthwork boundaries, and undetected settlement enclosures is suffering heavy erosion by ploughing on the chalk.

The retrieval processes which have led to the production of the currently available data pool have been diverse, selective and destructive. The data for southern England (excluding the southwest peninsula) comprises a total of 2383 burial urns which derive from 480 burial sites, about 1500 pieces of metalwork and 82 hoards. There are also seventy-eight settlement sites which have produced evidence of structures and sherd assemblages representing about 800 vessels, food-processing equipment, a very small amount of floral and faunal data and, in addition, the landscape evidence which has hardly yet been studied and may be lost to the plough without record.

The material has been recovered by three main processes: (1) research excavation (both antiquarian and modern), (2) as stray finds during agricultural, building and quarrying operations and (3) by archaeologists working in salvage operations where the site of operation is determined by non-archaeological criteria. The available settlement evidence mainly derives from processes 1 and 3, which means that a fair sample of sites on most subsoils and different geographical zones has been examined. There is a bias, however, towards more extensive excavation of individual sites on the chalk, where the occurrence of upstanding earthworks has in the past attracted research excavations, while more low-lying sites have mainly been discovered and only partially examined in a rescue context. Of the seventy-eight recorded settlements forty are standing earthwork enclosures of which twenty-two have been excavated. Three of these have been almost totally excavated, in a further nine cases 20 to 70 per cent of the area has been excavated, and in the rest 10 per cent or less has been examined. A further ten sites with no evidence of any enclosure have produced evidence of structures on excavation, while the remaining twenty-eight sites are defined only by the presence of pits, pottery, post holes, animal bone and loom weights in the absence of cremated human bone.

Although a few bronze items have been recovered from settlement and burial sites (Rowlands 1976), most of them derive from process 2 and are stray finds with no known archaeological context. However, the very nature of their process of retrieval suggests that the overall distribution of metalwork may more truly reflect the original patterning of activities than does that of settlements or burials. The retrieval pattern of the burial urns themselves is by comparison disastrous. The 480 sites themselves derive mainly from processes 1 and 3, with a few examples of stray finds. As with the settlement sites there has been a slight bias towards the chalk with its upstanding monuments, but gravel extraction and building works in the Thames Valley, Kent, Hampshire basin and the Sussex coastal plain have largely compensated for this. These 480 sites are known to have produced 2383 urns. Of these, the majority derive from central southern England (Wiltshire, Hampshire and Dorset), where out of 1800 recorded urns 1192 (66 per cent) are not available for study. This is partly due to their inherent fragility, many having 'fallen to pieces' on discovery, but also to the nature of their retrieval. Many were found during mineral extraction or building operations and were smashed by the workmen before they could be studied while, owing to their unaesthetic qualities, many have not survived the test of time in private collections or museum storerooms. The picture is not, however, as gloomy as it may seem, as these agencies of destruction have acted selectively. Thus it is mainly entire site assemblages that have failed to survive and not an unknown percentage from all the assemblages. The poor survival rate of vessels therefore reduces the number of assemblages susceptible to analysis but does not invalidate the analysis of all of them.

ANALYSIS

The magnitude of the Middle Bronze Age data pool is such that, as long as the depositional and retrieval factors discussed above are taken into account, it is susceptible to rigorous analysis at most levels. It was suspected that both the recorded settlement and burial sites and the distributions of certain artifact types might display quantitative and spatial information which could be used to define some characteristics of the social and economic subsystems current in the Middle Bronze Age. The following series of analyses were designed with a view to extracting this latent information. Spatial archaeology has been defined as 'the retrieval of information from archaeological spatial relationships and the study of the spatial consequences of former hominid activity patterns within and between features and structures and their articulation within sites, site systems and their environments: the study of the flow and integration of activities within and between structures, sites and resource spaces from the micro to the semi-micro and macro scales of aggregation' (Clarke 1977, p. 9). At the micro level it is possible to study the location of artifacts within features on settlement sites, the resolution of features into a variety of structures connected with different activities and the spatial relationships between structures on particular sites. The distribution of artifacts and spatial patterning of burials within the cemetery sites can also be investigated. At the macro scale studies of the relationships between sites and sites (patterns of rank and size), sites and resource spaces (site catchment analysis) and artifacts across the landscape are possible. Finally, the results of each inquiry can be compared one with another: patterning within settlements and cemetery sites, artifact distributions against the different classes of settlement site and site catchment data against the size of settlement.

Spatial analysis on the micro scale

Settlement sites. Excavated later Bronze Age settlement sites are characterised by a fairly limited repertoire of archaeological data: banks and ditches, pits, post holes, potsherds, flint and stone artifacts, weaving equipment, faunal and floral remains and a few bronze items. The establishment of the Bronze Age dating of large regular blocks of Celtic fields, alongside extensive systems of linear earthworks which provided territorial boundaries and in some cases divided arable land from permanent pasture, indicates the development of a balanced mixed subsistence strategy through the second millennium B.C. (Bradley and Ellison 1975, ch. 5; Bowen 1975). Faunal assemblages from sixteen sites demonstrate that cattle and sheep were most important as stock, followed by pig, deer and horse. Ovicaprids outnumber cattle in terms of minimum numbers of individuals but a consideration of relative meat weights would reverse their apparent importance. Floral data from three sites and grain impressions on Later Bronze Age pottery indicate that hulled barley, emmer and einkorn were cultivated. The crops contained many weed species which may have been exploited along with the cultivated grain. The importance of plant exploitation is confirmed by the presence of complete or fragmentary stone saddle querns on all sites where a reasonably large area has been excavated, and by the occurrence of flint sickles on a few sites. In contrast the large numbers of flint scrapers which were probably associated with leatherworking and the frequent recovery of equipment associated with weaving emphasise the importance of animal products within the economy.

Small circular or oblong pits occur on most excavated settlement sites. On average they are less than one metre in diameter and 40 cm deep. Only three examples approached one metre in depth and the group as a whole are very much smaller than the pits found on Iron Age settlement sites. They occur within and outside post hole structures. At Itford Hill one pit contained a deposit of carbonised grain while on the other sites they have produced

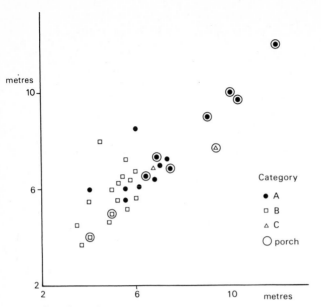

Graph to show the variation in size and shape of huts.

complete pottery vessels, sometimes standing in an upright position. Their main function was probably one of food storage and processing. The post hole evidence presents complex patterns which can be resolved into two main categories of structure: small, rectangular ones and larger circular or oval configurations. The former comprise four- and six-post structures. These are much more common on Iron Age sites than on Bronze Age ones, but definitely occur at Cock Hill, Rams Hill, Park Brow and Thorny Down. They range in size from 1.2 m × 0.8 m to 3 m × 1.5 m (four-posters). Their function is not definitely known but use for the raised storage of foodstuffs and other commodities or the housing of swine seem most likely.

Circular or oval huts can be discerned on fourteen settlement sites. The traditional viewpoint has been that Bronze Age huts were small simple post-ring structures, sometimes with a central post, but not exhibiting the more elaborate features such as the porches, double post-rings and ring gullies which typify many of the huts known from early Iron Age contexts. However, the existence of various types of double-ring house has recently been established by several authorities. Musson (1970) has recognised the presence of larger hut floor areas defined by a scarp outside the inner post-ring of structures at both Itford Hill and Amberley Mount, while Avery and Close-Brooks (1969) have suggested that House A at Shearplace Hill was also of double-ring type and they note that this type of construction is also detectable at Thorny Down. Their arguments concerning House A at Shearplace Hill are, however, not supported by the excavated evidence (P. A. Rahtz pers. comm.). Further examples can be inferred at Chalton, the

Woodhenge 'Egg' enclosure, Plumpton Plain A and Chale. The dimensions of all hut structures with complete recorded plans are summarised in Fig. 15.1 where length is plotted against breadth and the occurrence of porches is indicated.

Study of the features and artifact types found within each recorded hut has allowed the definition of three main classes of structure:

A. *Major residential structure*. These huts are characterised by high concentrations of potsherds which include a relatively high proportion of fine ware vessels which were most probably used for eating and drinking. Quern fragments are sometimes present but the stone assemblages are dominated by the sole occurrence on these sites of items connected with the production and maintenance of tools (e.g., flint flakes, hammerstones and whetstones). Over half of them contain evidence for textile production in the form of clay loom weights, spindle whorls and, in two cases, the remains of upright looms. Fig. 15.1 shows that these major residential units are usually circular in shape, larger in size than the other categories and more often possess porches. Where items of bronze have been recovered from settlement sites they repeatedly occur in category A huts, and other possible status indicators (e.g., a chalk phallus and a shale bracelet fragment) occur in major residential units at Itford Hill.

(Examples: Chalton 1, Weston Wood 1, Trevisker A, Shearplace Hill A, New Barn Down VIII, Plumpton Plain A III: 11, Rams Hill B, Cock Hill 1, Thorny Down I and IV, Itford Hill B, D, K, L, N.)

B. *Ancillary structure*. These huts are characterised by a high proportion of features and artifacts associated with food storage and preparation. The sherd assemblages are relatively smaller than those from category A units and display a higher proportion of coarse vessels relative to fine wares. They often have internal pits for storage, querns and scrapers for food preparation and, in some cases, concentrations of animal bones. It can be seen from Fig. 15.1 that category B huts tend to be smaller and more oval in shape than those of category A and porches were added in only two cases.

(Examples: Chalton 2, Weston Wood 2, Plumpton Plain A II: 1 and IV: 1, Rams Hill C, Cock Hill II, III, AIII, Thorny Down III, V, Itford Hill A, G, E, F, M.)

C. *Animal shelters*. The absence of domestic finds and observations of extensive floor wear have suggested the use of huts for sheltering stock in two instances. They are of medium size (Fig. 15.1). The relative paucity of this structural category may be explained by the segregation of the human and animal populations. Certainly there is earthwork evidence for probable animal pens at two sites. On the other hand possible lean-to annexes to main residential and ancillary huts can be reconstructed at Cock Hill, Thorny Down and Itford Hill.

(Examples: Trevisker B/D, Shearplace Hill B.)

D. *Weaving huts*. On one site there is evidence that small-sized huts were specifically designated for textile production. They possess weaving equipment in primary contexts but no evidence for food storage, preparation or consumption.

(Examples: Itford Hill C and H.)

The main result of the analysis so far has been to demonstrate the existence of two main categories of circular structure which can be differentiated on the grounds of size, shape and function. The larger and more substantial category A huts seem to have been the major residential units where food consumption and productive activities were practised. These activities included predominantly male tasks (manufacture and maintenance of tools in stone, bone and metal; leatherworking) alongside those more often associated with females (notably weaving). In contrast the smaller category B huts seem to have been primarily designed for the storage and preparation of foodstuffs which were probably major tasks for the females. There are hints that certain structures and annexes were provided as byres and pigsties while in one case specialised weaving huts have also been identified.

Study of the spatial relationships between these various categories of structure within individual settlement sites has led to the isolation of significant groupings at the semi-micro level. The incidence of pairs of huts on some Middle Bronze Age sites has already been noted (in Bradley and Ellison 1975, pp. 164, 212). They occur at Trevisker (major residential unit and animal shelter), Rams Hill (major residential unit and ancillary unit), Weston Wood (major residential unit, ancillary unit, working area and pits), Chalton (major residential unit, ancillary unit and pits) and at Shearplace Hill (major residential unit, animal shelter, working area and possible storage structures). At Shearplace Hill Avery and Close-Books (1969) have suggested an alternative phasing of the site which involves the use of one building only at any one time. Their stratigraphic arguments are not conclusive: the outer wall line of House A (F1) is not sealed by the material of the West Bank but by the later F2 deposit which is slip from that bank (Rahtz and ApSimon 1962, p. 303) and there is therefore no reason to suggest that Huts A and B were not contemporary.

Similar pairs of structures can be isolated in the site plans at Cock Hill and Thorny Down where units consisting of major, ancillary and storage structures are sometimes defined by fence lines. A recurring settlement module which includes a major residential unit, an ancillary structure, storage facilities and areas for open air activities can therefore be isolated. The Itford Hill settlement can be resolved into four such modules, each defined by a bank or palisade. They may have been successive. A detailed illustrated analysis of this site has been presented elsewhere (Ellison 1978). In brief, the four units contain the following combinations of structures:

  (i)   major residential structure, ancillary structure;
  (ii) major residential structure, two ancillary structures, weaving hut;
  (iii) two major residential structures, ancillary structure, weaving hut;
  (iv) major residential structure, ancillary structure.

Burial rite

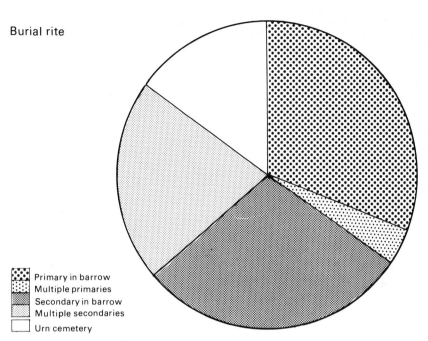

Primary in barrow
Multiple primaries
Secondary in barrow
Multiple secondaries
Urn cemetery

15.2.   The relative incidence of burial rites in the Middle Bronze Age.

The weaving huts in units (ii) and (iii) were located near to major residential structures and may have been functionally related to them, especially as elsewhere weaving is known to have been carried out within the major structure.

The Middle Bronze Age settlement modules described here can usefully be compared with the Glastonbury modular unit isolated by Clarke (1972, Fig. 21.1). Although structures were much better preserved in this waterlogged Iron Age site, the main features are replicated by the Middle Bronze Age modules. Even the division between a major familial, multi-role and activity area on the one hand and a minor largely female and domestic area can be detected in the Bronze Age artifact distributions.

Burial sites. Analysis of the finds from cemetery sites and of the spatial organisation of burials within them has led to some interesting conclusions. The incidence of the urnfield ritual which has often been cited as a defining characteristic of the Middle Bronze Age in southern England is in fact of relatively minor importance. The pie chart (Fig. 15.2) demonstrates that the interment of burials within round-barrows was by far the most common practice. These burials were often inserted into existing barrows of Early Bronze Age type although some were interred as primary deposits, either singly or in a group, under a newly constructed mound. Middle Bronze Age secondary burials have very rarely been discovered in Early Bronze Age 'fancy' barrows, simple bowl-barrows being the preferred focus for continued sepulchral use. Further, it can be noted that the major Early Bronze Age barrow cemeteries on Salisbury Plain and in Dorset were avoided in the subsequent period (Piggott 1938, Fig. 10 for Salisbury Plain; in Dorset the main concentrations of Middle Bronze Age burials lie between or downhill from the two Early Bronze Age barrow concentrations along the Dorset Ridgeway and in Cranborne Chase). The variety of grave goods found in association with Early Bronze Age inhumation and cremation burials which includes weapons, tools, ornaments, many ceramic types and the whole panoply of 'Wessex Culture' prestige items cannot be matched in the succeeding period. A probable change in religious or other attitudes led to the exclusion of metal items from graves but differentiation amongst the individual burials may provide evidence for the continued recognition of rank as a positive parameter within the burial ritual. Within a single cemetery, there are unaccompanied cremations and cremations contained in fine ware, everyday and heavy duty vessels. Some vessels were deposited upright and others inverted, some were sealed with stone slabs or marked with a post and some were associated with accessory vessels or token deposits of sherds. Cremation in the Middle Bronze Age appears to have been an exceptionally efficient process. The cremated remains are usually very fragmentary and anatomical analysis is difficult and sometimes impossible. Few groups of cremations have therefore been aged or sexed and it is not usually possible to test the correlation between age or sex groups and the variations in burial rite noted above.

Consideration of the sizes of the different cemetery sites is, however, of some interest. Many of the cremations seem to have been interred singly (see Fig. 15.2) but of forty-eight sites which have provided known multiple totals of cremations, 78 per cent contained under forty burials, and 52 per cent less than twelve burials. In the larger cemeteries and urnfields where sufficient data have survived the total pattern of burials can usually be broken down into a series of discrete units or clusters each of which includes from ten to thirty burials. A modular unit thus seems to have been a recurring characteristic of the burial practices. If the incidences of less than four associated interments are excluded from analysis the remaining values take the form of a normal distribution around a central value of twenty-four.

At Itford Hill, one such unit has been analysed in detail (Holden 1972). Of the twelve individuals cremated, five were adults, four were children and three gave no indication of their age at death. Of the adults, two were probably male and three female. The primary burial was an elderly male but there was no obvious correlation between age or sex and the variability of the vessels within which the cremations were contained. The presence of adult males and females in association with infants and juveniles suggests that the barrow may

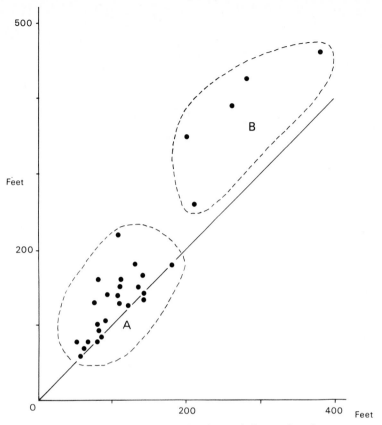

15.3.   Graph to show the variation in size and shape of enclosures.

have been the burial place for a single small kinship group over a short period of time. The finding of parts of the same single vessel within the cemetery and one of the units of the adjacent Itford Hill settlement strongly suggests that the barrow was the cemetery for the inhabitants of that unit.

The distribution of fine wares and other diagnostic ritual aspects amongst the different clusters within some of the larger cemeteries studied suggests that clusters were roughly equal in status. It can therefore be postulated that the burial clusters represent the foci of burial for the members of separate kinship groups of roughly equal size. The validity of this hypothesis and the evidence for ranking within or between modules must, however, be tested by further excavation and anatomical analysis of cremated remains.

Spatial analysis on the macro scale

The settlement hierarchy. The dimensions of all the known complete enclosures were taken and in Fig. 15.3 length has been plotted against breadth in order to investigate the range in settlement size. Two distinct size and shape groupings are apparent. Group A comprises small enclosures which may be square, circular or sub-rectangular in shape, while the Group B sites are much larger and markedly rectangular in form. There are far fewer sites in Group B. The two groups can best be explained in terms of relative rank and function. Group A includes the numerous standard homestead sites with the Group B sites forming a higher rank group. The proposed ranking of the enclosures according to size is supported by a consideration of their metalwork associations. Four out of the five Group B sites have produced Middle Bronze Age metalwork, including an ornament hoard from Norton Fitzwarren and goldwork from Highdown Hill. Only five Group A settlements have bronze items. They tend to be tools rather than ornaments or weapons and the maximum number of items from any one site is three. The five Group A sites which have associated bronzes all lie towards the upper end of the size distribution displayed by the group as a whole.

Limited excavations at Rams Hill and Highdown Hill have shown that the Group B enclosures contain settlement evidence and, at Rams Hill, the presence of a large number of four-post storage structures could indicate the provision of centralised food storage. Only further excavation will elucidate the exact social, economic and possibly ritual functions of these large enclosures, but their spatial distribution may provide some evidence at this stage. The Group B enclosures tend to be located at or near the junction of one or more of the localised pottery distributions to be described below and two of these sites have been indicated in Fig. 15.4 in order to illustrate this apparent spatial relationship. It follows that the function of the large enclosures may have been closely related to the economic exchange networks, not as foci for production but as centres involved in the control of movement of goods between adjacent distribution areas contained within the overall exchange network.

Site catchment analysis. The justification for the use of the site catchment model in southern England and an appropriate methodology have been outlined by Ellison and Harriss (1972). For each settlement the land use potential zones available within a two kilometre radius of the site were plotted as accurately as possible and percentages of each land use potential zone within the catchment area were calculated. The sites considered were spread fairly evenly over southern England and included upland and lowland sites. Of these sixty-five sites, 92 per cent have significant areas of high quality arable land within their catchment areas and in forty-three cases (66 per cent) the percentage of such land exceeds 50 per cent. Only 41 per cent of the settlements possess downland within their catchment areas. In these downland areas relief and land use potential are locally more varied and a second trend in site location has been observed. This is the tendency for the settlement to be located near to the junction of two or more of the land use zones which occupy its site catchment area. Such locations may have been chosen in order to maximise the possible exploitation of the various resource areas contained within the catchment.

The relationship between the results of site catchment analysis and settlement size is also of great potential interest. All except one of the Group B sites have catchments containing 100 per cent high quality land use potential zones The larger Group A settlements mainly control 40 to 80 per cent of high quality zones while the smaller ones are associated with catchment areas containing from 5 to 40 per cent high quality arable land. For the thirty-one sites whose exact size and site catchment components could be accurately measured the relationship between the logarithm ($\log_{10}$) of the site area and percentage of high quality arable within the site catchment was shown to be statistically significant ($N = 31$, $r = 0.739$) and it can therefore be concluded that there seems to be a direct relationship between the size of the enclosure and the potential productivity of the land contained within its site catchment area. Peebles and Kus (1977, pp. 441–42) have recently suggested that such a relationship is indicative of a high degree of local subsistence sufficiency which in turn may be taken as one defining characteristic of a ranked society, while Brumfiel (1976) has further argued that similar relationships for some Late Formative and Terminal Formative sites in the eastern Valley of Mexico provide evidence for a gradual increase in population pressure. In our case the relationship can be shown to be uniform for all ranges of site size and this indicates a general pattern of pressure on the best available arable land during the Middle Bronze Age.

The distribution of pottery types. In a recent critique of Iron Age pottery studies, Collis has argued that analysis should proceed at a series of levels. Careful assessment of closed groups and site assemblages should lead to the definition of regional assemblages while further analysis should lead to the recognition of industrial groupings either within or cutting across the regional assemblages (Collis 1977). This approach formed the basis of a recent study of all the published and unpublished Middle Bronze Age pottery from southern England (Ellison 1975). Detailed analysis of vessel size, shape and fabric (which was assessed using macroscopic techniques) were undertaken in relation to decorative motifs and the positioning of decoration. Typologically the vessel types can all be derived from the diverse ceramic groups which coexisted in the British Early Bronze Age, and consideration of the few available radiocarbon dates indicates that the Middle Bronze Age traditions were firmly rooted in that period (Barrett 1976). Two distinct classes of relief-decorated urns known as Wessex Biconical Urns and Barrel Urns of South Lodge Type can be shown on the grounds of decoration, associations and distribution to have been current by the later Early Bronze Age, but the main series of Deverel–Rimbury ceramics forms an integrated body of evidence which occurs on settlements and burial sites demonstrably later than the Early Bronze Age.

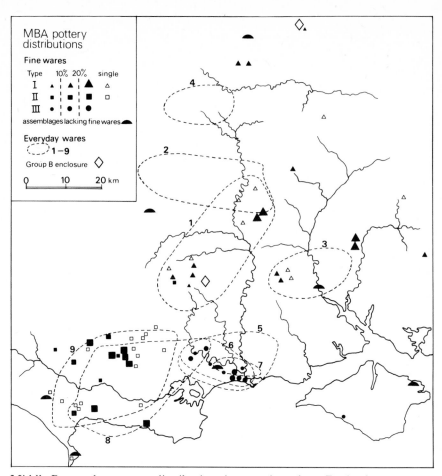

15.4. Middle Bronze Age pottery distributions in central southern England.

Six major regional assemblages have been defined in the following geographical zones: the South Downs and Sussex coastal plain, the lower Thames
valley, the upper Thames valley, central Wessex, the Avon–Stour valleys in
south Hampshire and east Dorset and the Dorset downs. The regional
assemblages contain from seven to twelve distinct ceramic types which,
following Clarke's Model 1 for Beaker assemblages (Clarke 1976, p. 464) can
be divided into three functional groups, namely fine wares, everyday wares
and heavy duty wares. When analysis proceeded to the detection of possible
industrial groupings within and across the regional assemblage zones it was
found that the pottery types belonging to each of Clarke's functional groups
were characterised by distribution areas of different sizes and this in turn
indicated the operation of production on three distinct levels. This pattern
was shown to exist throughout the area studied but will here be demonstrated
in relation to three of the regions originally defined: central Wessex, the
Dorset downs and the Avon–Stour valleys (Fig. 15.4).

Heavy duty wares comprise the extremely large, thick-walled storage vessels and burial urns which were tempered with large quantities of calcined flint and strengthened with applied or raised cordons bearing finger-impressed decoration. It is their lack of aesthetic appeal and their tendency to fall to pieces on discovery or in handling that has delayed the study of Middle Bronze Age ceramics for so long. They form a background noise of low level information which has masked the variability of the other types. Although the same form of heavy duty vessel is found throughout southern England, regional variations in fabric are apparent. Bearing in mind their great size, weight and fragility it might seem likely that such vessels were made on or very near the sites where they were to be used. However, evidence for the repairing of such vessels might suggest that some small-scale local or, more likely, seasonal mode of production was involved.

Everyday wares. Amongst all the regional assemblages studied several types of medium-sized vessels were defined, sometimes characterised by diagnostic fabrics. They comprise small versions of bucket urns displaying a tendency towards a slightly biconical or ovoid profile and decorated with a variety of plain and impressed cordons, perforated and plain lugs of varying shape, horizontal grooves and rows of finger-impressed decoration. These everyday wares have distribution areas ranging from 10 to 20 km in radius which may be contained within or cut across the distribution areas of the regional assemblages. The everyday type distributions have been outlined on Fig. 15.4 where the individual types represented are:

1. Central Wessex type 2: tall, straight-sided urn with slightly concave neck, expanded rim and rows of finger-impressions at the shoulder and just below the rim;

2. Central Wessex type 4: slightly biconical plain urn with a concave neck but no internal rim bevel;

3. Central Wessex type 5: straight-sided urn with slightly flaring rim and a horizontal cordon (sometimes finger-impressed) just above mid-height;

4. Central Wessex type 6: plain straight-sided urn with no decoration (this form is extremely rare elsewhere);

5. Avon–Stour type 5: plain urn with slightly ovoid profile and plain lugs at the point of maximum diameter;

6. Avon–Stour type 7: slightly biconical urn with a plain horizontal cordon at the shoulder;

7. Avon–Stour type 11: urn with marked concave neck and plain horizontal cordons at the rim and shoulder;

8. Avon–Stour type 6/Dorset downs type (c): plain straight-sided urn with lugs linked by a horizontal finger-groove;

9. Dorset downs type (a): plain urn with non-perforated lugs, either circular or horizontally elongated, near the rim of the vessel.

The low totals of vessels within each distribution means that a quantitative spatial analysis of the industries cannot be attempted at this stage.

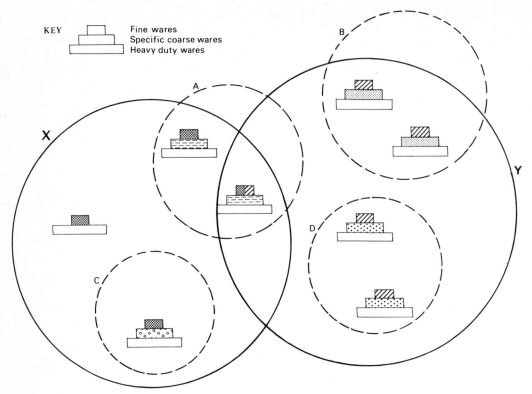

KEY — Fine wares / Specific coarse wares / Heavy duty wares

15.5.   A model for the pattern of pottery distribution in the Middle Bronze Age.

Fine wares comprise the decorated globular urns which have received most attention in previous studies of Deverel-Rimbury ceramics. Calkin (1964) divided them into two main typological groups which were shown to have almost complementary distributions. These distributions have since been variously interpreted as representing cultural divisions (ApSimon in Rahtz and ApSimon 1962) and as the evidence for competitive trade (Bradley 1971). A detailed analysis of shape, size, fabric and motif repertoires has confirmed Calkin's division between Type I in central Wessex and Types IIa and IIb in Dorset. In addition, various subtypes of Type IIb have been distinguished as well as a third major typological group, designated Type III, which occurs in the Avon–Stour valleys region (Ellison 1975, ch. 6).

The distributions of vessels of Types I, II and III are plotted in Fig. 15.4 where it can readily be seen that the Types I and III fine ware distributions are larger than those of the everyday wares considered above. The percentage occurrence of fine wares in each assemblage has also been indicated. The calculation of the percentages presented difficulties owing to the comparison of assemblages containing whole vessels (burial sites) and sherd assemblages from the settlement sites. The sherd assemblages have therefore been analysed on the basis of minimum numbers of vessels represented. As there is some indication that in central Wessex fine wares are more commonly found on settlements than in the cemeteries, percentages above 20 per cent have not been further subdivided. It is apparent that the fine wares are better represented near the centres of their respective distribution areas and that the percentages fall off with distance from that centre. Fine wares of two different types occur on one site only, suggesting that the patterns of production were mutually adjusted. In the absence of kiln sites for this early period centralised specialised production cannot firmly be demonstrated, but a possibly seasonal industry executed by part-time specialists working over carefully defined territories may have been in operation.

The pattern of pottery distribution in the Middle Bronze Age is simply illustrated by the model (Fig. 15.5) within which each set of blocks represents a single site assemblage, A to D represent the distribution areas of specific everyday wares and X and Y denote two fine ware distribution areas.

The distribution of metalwork. The organisation of Middle Bronze Age metal-working in southern England has been exhaustively studied by Rowlands (1976). A detailed typological and chronological study led to the definition of a series of industries which can be divided into three main groups. These groups relate to the three main functional classes of the metalwork: weapons, ornaments and tools. Tools are by far the most common items (68 per cent in the area covered by Fig. 15.4) followed by ornaments (21 per cent) and weapons (11 per cent). Tools occur most commonly in hoards while ornaments and especially the weapons mainly occur as single finds. The tools (mainly palstaves) can be broken down into a large number of small typological groups which have tight distribution areas on average 15 to 25 km in radius (Rowlands 1976, p. 164). The validity of these typological groupings has been tested by regression analysis (Hodder and Orton 1976, pp. 119–25). The ornaments occur roughly equally in small hoards and as single finds. Distinct stylistic groupings have been distinguished and some of these display marked regional patterning (e.g. Rowlands 1976, Maps 22, 23 and 24). Their distribution areas vary from 25 to 80 km in radius. The spatial patterning of the weapons (spearheads and rapiers) which mainly occur as single finds is quite different from that of the tools or ornaments. Localised groupings cannot be distinguished and the typological differences noted have no apparent spatial significance, each weapon type occurring widely across southern England. Thus three distinct levels of distribution seem to have been in operation: local production of tools and ornaments on two separate scales contrasting with the widespread distribution of generalised weapon types. Consideration of available ethnographic data indicates that the production of everyday bronze items was probably undertaken by part-time specialists on a seasonal basis (Rowlands 1971).

The limited spatial distribution of recurring assemblages of metalwork suggests a fairly static pattern of metalworking, implying that the craft was a dispersed occupation serving small settlement units, and predicts a dispersed lineage structure as a mode of organisation. At the same time there is some evidence of specialisation in production and more full-time working, particularly for the production of weapons, linked with the possession of particular skills in complex casting. Such specialist pieces are also found over a much wider area than more mundane metal types and it is possible to postulate a significant correlation between degree of specialisation, the technical skill required to produce an object, and the distance travelled in trade by the finished metalwork product.   (Rowlands 1973, p. 596)

INTERPRETATION

The results of the various analyses summarised above may now be combined in order to propose a general social and economic model for the Middle Bronze Age period in southern England.

Subsistence economy

Consideration of faunal and floral remains and the distribution of features and artifacts within excavated settlements, linked with the recognition of an organised landscape incorporating regular systems of Celtic field blocks and linear earthworks, have indicated that the subsistence economy can be defined as a balanced sedentary mixed farming strategy. Thus the traditional pastoralist hypothesis may be discarded. The relatively high proportions of good quality soils contained within the catchments of the settlement sites confirm the potential importance of arable cultivation and also indicate that the settlements were located in areas which could have ensured a high degree of local subsistence efficiency. This hypothesis is further supported by the apparent preference for ecotone settlement locations which would have maximised the potential exploitation of a variety of resources from any one settlement base. The positive relationship between the percentage of high quality land within the site catchment, which can be taken as a rough measure of potential productivity, and the size of the settlement can also be employed as evidence for local subsistence efficiency (cf. Peebles and Kus 1977, pp. 444–2 and Fig. 4). However, until the relationship between field systems, linear earthworks and their related settlement sites has been further investigated by fieldwork and excavation it is difficult to propose any general land use models at the micro scale.

Systems of exchange

Analyses of the distributions of pottery and metalwork have demonstrated that both artifact categories were produced or distributed on at least three levels. Heavy duty vessels are evenly distributed and probably represent very local, if not on-site, production. Everyday wares have discrete distributions of 10 to 20 km average radius while the fine wares display mutually adjusted distributions with radii ranging from 25 to 40 km. The metalwork distributions can also be broken down into three distinct modes represented in the archaeological record of tool type areas (average radius 15 to 25 km), ornament distributions (with radii ranging from 25 to 80 km) and an overall general distribution of weapon types. It is instructive to compare these scales of production and distribution with those identified in both the earlier and later prehistoric periods within southern Britain.

The Neolithic and Early Bronze Age periods in southern England are characterised by a great variety of ceramic styles which have very large distribution areas. It should also be noted that, in any one phase, these distribution areas overlap to a great extent. The existence of wide-ranging trade or exchange systems has been confirmed (Peacock 1969 for Hembury ware in the early Neolithic) or implied (Clarke 1970 for Beakers) and has been accepted as a general model for pottery production, at least in the Neolithic (Smith 1974, p. 111). An important aspect of ceramic evidence in these periods which has not previously been emphasised is the regular recurrence of vessels belonging to several diverse styles on any one individual site. This applies to enclosures and burial sites alike ranging from Neolithic causewayed enclosures and late Neolithic henges to Neolithic long-barrows and Early Bronze Age round-barrows (for a recent discussion of the latter see Burgess in Burgess and Shennan 1976). The large-scale geographical ceramic styles have all been closely studied in recent years: Early and Middle Neolithic bowl categories by Smith (1974, Figs 14 and 15), the substyles of Late Neolithic Grooved Ware (Wainwright and Longworth 1971), styles of secondary series Collared Urns (Longworth 1970) and Food Vessels by Simpson (1968) and Burgess (1974). However, the complex overlapping character of such distributions has most clearly been exemplified by Clarke's rigorous study of the chronological and typological groups of Beakers (Clarke 1970). The pottery distributions display many of the spatial characteristics of the contemporary stone axe distributions and both may represent wide-ranging exchange networks of a type recently proposed for Late Neolithic and Early Bronze Age Europe as a whole (Sherratt 1976). The contrast between these distributions and the small-sized discrete distributions now seen to be typical of the Middle Bronze Age is considerable and denotes a radical change in both the level and internal diversity of the exchange or trade networks involved. The possible relationship between this development and the change from a predominantly pastoral economy in the Early Bronze Age (as postulated by Fleming 1971) to the balanced mixed subsistence strategy of the Middle Bronze Age could be the subject of an interesting inquiry.

The changes in the patterning and scale of the regional production of pottery which occur in the Middle Bronze Age are potentially of great socioeconomic significance. In part the pattern established in the Middle

Bronze Age foreshadows the fine ware distributions of the southern British Iron Age (Cunliffe 1974; Hodder 1977). The ceramic 'style zones' defined by Cunliffe represent the distribution of the fine ware element of the three-tier model for pottery production outlined above (i.e. X and Y in Fig. 15.5). Detailed quantitative analysis of Iron Age sherd assemblages across space would doubtless lead to the definition of one or more lower tiers of locally distributed regional coarse wares.

Early Bronze Age metalwork includes many artifact types, but, as in the case of the contemporary pottery groups, no small-scale discrete distribution areas can be defined. Detailed recent research has tended to emphasise the generalised nature of much of the material which occurs over wide areas and typological differences display no apparent spatial significance. This pattern contrasts strongly with the complex network of local production at different levels which has been established for the Middle Bronze Age and which can be seen to develop further through the Late Bronze Age and Iron Age Periods (e.g., Hodder 1977 for the Late Iron Age). Reconstruction of the various mechanisms involved is, however, more problematical. Even when a distribution pattern exhibiting a gradual fall-off with distance can be demonstrated this may not reflect an organised exchange network as local styles often display similar spatial characteristics (Hodder 1977, p. 286). Thus the development of tighter artifact distributions may reflect social and political change rather than a development of economic organisation. Such distributions may represent the activities of more closely defined social groups whose identity is reinforced by the use of group-specific artifacts of standard design.

Social structure

The recognition of recurring modular units with Middle Bronze Age settlement and burial sites leads to the suggestion that the standard social unit was one of between ten and twenty individuals. The available anatomical data indicate that each group contained men, women, juveniles and children, and male and female activities are represented within each settlement unit. Sociological reconstruction would therefore suggest that each module was occupied by an extended familial unit. The existence of major residential units and ancillary structures where food preparation was probably undertaken by the females further suggests that, according to the Glastonbury model, the kinship system may have been patrilineal and patrilocal. In the Glastonbury study this model was tested against the sociological information concerning Celtic society preserved in the records of the classical authors and in the Irish vernacular tradition (Clarke 1972, pp. 843–8). However, it must be noted that although the co-residential units postulated seem to indicate virilocal residence, the activity patterns involving common cooking and storage facilities could also have resulted from the practice of uxorilocal residence associated with a patrilineal or a matrilineal society. Further difficulties in the interpretation of residence rules are discussed by Longacre (ch. 2 above). The classical and Irish vernacular accounts show that Celtic society was characterised by a closely defined system of social stratification. It has been noted that the burial customs in the Middle Bronze Age display differentiation although in the absence of diagnostic grave goods and anatomical analyses this cannot yet be taken as evidence for social ranking. However, Coombes has recently argued that the weapon hoards of the Middle Bronze Age show a continuation of the ranked society represented in the Wessex graves, with the gold replaced by other objects of rank and status (Coombes 1975). The identification of weapons as high-value prestige items is further confirmed by evidence that, unlike tools and ornaments, they were probably produced by full-time specialist smiths and distributed over very wide areas.

CONCLUSION

Peebles and Kus (1977) have recently reconsidered the archaeological corre-lates of ranked societies. They have identified at least five major areas of variability distinctive of such societies which can be investigated in relation to data which might survive in the archaeological record (see also Chapman, this volume). The four characteristics which can most easily be tested are clear evidence of ascribed ranking of persons, the existence of a hierarchy of settlement types and sizes, the location of settlements in areas which assure a high degree of local subsistence sufficiency and evidence of organised productive activities which transcend the basic household group (Peebles and Kus 1977, pp. 431–3). Although clear evidence of ascribed ranking cannot yet be recovered from the Middle Bronze Age burial data, the existence of prestige items which were produced by full-time specialists and distributed across the exchange networks of other classes of metal and ceramics strongly suggests the existence of high-ranking individuals. A hierarchy of settlement types and sizes has been established and the correlation between potential site catchment productivity and settlement size suggests a high level of local subsistence sufficiency. The analysis of pottery and metalwork distributions has provided evidence for a complex network of productive activities above the level of the basic household group.

Renfrew has suggested that archaeological evidence from Neolithic and Early Bronze Age Wessex can be used to postulate the rise of a series of chiefdoms during the Late Neolithic culminating in the development of a single inclusive chiefdom in the Early Bronze Age (Renfrew 1973b). Although the details of these processes still need to be tested by a series of carefully designed analyses, a useful working hypothesis has been formulated. The subsequent abandonment of the henge structures and the major barrow cemeteries may indicate the fall of such a chiefdom but it has been demonstrated above that the burial mound rite, a ranking of enclosures and hints of social stratification can all be identified in the Middle Bronze Age period. The main innovation seems to have been the establishment of a complex network of interlocking productive activities on a local level and it is suggested that this may have been linked to the development of a balanced sedentary mixed farming strategy within a highly organised landscape.

Social and economic developments in the Late Bronze Age and Early Iron Age periods include the diversification of ceramic and metal types linked with the development of a more complex system of social ranking, a more varied hierarchy of settlement sites and the growing incidence of warfare which is evidenced by the occurrence of large weapon hoards and the rise of hillforts. The general socioeconomic system prevailing in the Iron Age can, however, be traced directly from that which developed during the Middle Bronze Age.

The main aim of this study has been to combine the results of exhaustive studies of individual groups of evidence such as artifact types, artifact distributions and the morphology and distribution of settlement and burial sites in order to investigate spatial relationships at several different levels. Analysis on the micro scale has been undertaken in relation to both settlement and burial sites. Consideration of faunal and floral remains, the functional aspects of artifact types and the results of recent landscape analysis confirmed that a balanced mixed farming strategy formed the basis of the economy while the analysis of finds and features within structures on settlement sites led to the definition of a series of building types which could be related to specific activities. The analysis then proceeded to isolate a recurring modular unit comprising a group of structures designed to provide facilities for communal living, eating, storage, cooking and manufacture of artifacts. It was proposed that each module represented a single co-residential unit similar to those recognised in Iron Age Britain but on a smaller scale. Analysis of the evidence from burial sites showed that the burial rite displayed distinct differentiation indicative of social ranking and that the larger cremation cemeteries contain modular clusters of burials. The size of these clusters further indicates that they probably represent the burials of the inhabitants of single settlement modules.

On the macro scale, analysis of settlement size has revealed the existence of a simple but distinct site hierarchy although the exact function of the larger (Group B) sites has yet to be demonstrated. Site catchment analysis has provided evidence that settlement sites had access to good arable soils and to a wide range of land potential zones and this would have facilitated the successful execution of a balanced mixed subsistence strategy. The direct relationship between site size and potential land productivity may be indicative of the existence of both social ranking and population pressure.

The study of artifact distributions has led to the definition of a series of types of distribution which can be explained in terms of differential function, levels of production and, possibly, the social significance of particular artifact types. These distributions represent a complex system of small-scale inter-locking exchange networks which cannot be matched in the preceding periods. Their origins seem to be linked to the development of a settled mixed farming strategy in a well-exploited and ordered landscape. Some of the small-scale distributions involve artifacts of very specific type which may have served as symbols and thus aided the social cohesion of local population groups while the frequent overlapping and interlocking of artifact distributions may represent the complexity of exchange networks which served to minimise friction between adjacent competing groups.

It can be concluded that four major socioeconomic processes were current in the Middle Bronze Age period in southern England: the establishment of a balanced and settled mixed farming strategy, population pressure, the consolidation of co-residential units within small local population groups and the development of small-scale interlocking exchange networks. Further research may clarify the nature of the close relationships that link these four developments but the search for the reasons underlying their linked development cannot immediately be attempted. Possible factors to be considered are general population growth, decrease in subsistence productivity due to climatic deterioration or degradation of soils and changes within the subsistence or sociopolitical subsystems.

Further research will concentrate on the detailed statistical comparisons of artifact distributions in relation to resource areas and land use zones and on the further investigation of settlement sizes and distribution in relation to productivity. The Middle Bronze Age data could then be compared with the results of similar analyses for site and artifact distributions from the Neolithic, Early Bronze Age and Iron Age periods in order that long-term changes in the social and economic systems can be investigated in a rigorous manner.

ACKNOWLEDGEMENTS

This paper, although based on data contained in my Ph.D. thesis, was mainly inspired by discussions with David Clarke in 1975. I am grateful to Andy Tubb for numerical help and to the following friends and colleagues who commented on a draft of the paper: John Barrett, Richard Bradley, Bob Chapman, Philip Rahtz, Mike Rowlands and Steven Shennan.

APPENDIX: SETTLEMENTS MENTIONED IN THE TEXT

Amberley Mount. Ratcliffe-Densham, H. B. A. and M. M. (1966). 'Amberley Mount: its Agricultural Story from the Late Bronze Age', *Sussex Archaeological Collections* 104: 6–25

Chale. Dunning, G. C. (1931). 'Late Bronze Age in the Isle of Wight', *Proceedings of the Isle of Wight Natural History and Archaeological Society* 108–17

Chalton. Cunliffe, B. (1970). 'A Bronze Age settlement at Chalton, Hants,', *Antiquaries Journal* 50: 1–13

Cock Hill. Ratcliffe-Densham, H. B. A. and M. M. (1961). 'An Anomalous Earthwork of the Late Bronze Age, on Cock Hill, Sussex', *Sussex Archaeological Collections* 99: 78–101

Highdown Hill. Bradley, R. J. (1971). 'Stock raising and the origins of the hill fort on the South Downs', *Antiquaries Journal* 51: 8–27 and references there cited

Itford Hill. Burstow, G. P. and Holleyman, G. A. (1957). 'Late Bronze Age settlement on Itford Hill, Sussex', *Proceedings of the Prehistoric Society* 23: 167–212

New Barn Down. Curwen, E. C. (1934). 'A Late Bronze Age farm and a Neolithic pit dwelling on New Barn Down, near Worthing', *Sussex Archaeological Collections* 75: 137–70

Norton Fitzwarren. Langmaid, N. (1971). 'Norton Fitzwarren', *Current Archaeology* 28: 116–20

Park Brow. Wolseley, G. R., Smith, R. A. and Hawley, W. (1927). 'Prehistoric and Roman settlements on Park Brow', *Archaeologia* 76: 1–40

Plumpton Plain A. Holleyman, G. A. and Curwen, E. C. (1935). 'Late Bronze Age lynchet-settlements on Plumpton Plain, Sussex', *Proceedings of the Prehistoric Society* 1: 16–38

Rams Hill. Bradley and Ellison (1975)

Shearplace Hill. Rahtz and ApSimon (1962)

Trevisker. ApSimon, A. M. and Greenfield, E. (1972). 'The excavation of the Bronze Age and Iron Age settlement at Trevisker Round, St. Eval, Cornwall', *Proceedings of the Prehistoric Society* 38: 302–81

Thorny Down. Stone, J. F. S. (1935). 'The Deveral-Rimbury settlement on Thorny Down, Winterbourne Gunner, S. Wilts.', *Proceedings of the Prehistoric Society* 7: 114–33

Weston Wood. Harding, J. M. (1964). 'Interim report on the excavation of a Late Bronze Age homestead in Weston Wood, Albury, Surrey', *Surrey Archaeological Collections* 61: 10–17

Woodhenge 'Egg'. Cunnington, M. (1929). *Woodhenge*, George Simpson

REFERENCES

Avery, M. and Close-Brooks, J. (1969). 'Shearplace Hill, Sydling St. Nicholas, Dorset, House A: a suggested re-interpretation', *Proceedings of the Prehistoric Society* 35: 345–5

Barrett, J. (1976). 'Deverel-Rimbury: problems of chronology and interpretation' in C. B. Burgess and R. Miket (eds.) *Settlement and Economy in the Third and Second Millennia B.C.* (British Archaeological Reports No. 33)

Bowen, C. (1975). 'Pattern and Interpretation: a view of the Wessex landscape' in P. J. Fowler (ed.) *Recent Work in Rural Archaeology*, Moonraker Press

Bradley, R. J. (1971). 'Trade competition and artefact distribution', *World Archaeology* 2 (3): 347–52

Bradley, R. J. and Ellison, A. B. (1975). *Rams Hill: A Bronze Age Defended Enclosure and its Landscape* (British Archaeological Reports No. 19)

Brumfiel, E. (1976). 'Regional growth in the Eastern Valley of Mexico: a test of the "population pressure" hypothesis' in K. V. Flannery (ed.) *The Early Mesoamerican Village*, Academic Press

Burgess, C. B. (1974). 'The Bronze Age' in C. Renfrew (ed.) *British Prehistory. A new outline*, Duckworth

Burgess, C. B. and Miket, R. (1976). *Settlement and Economy in the Third and Second Millennia B.C.* (British Archaeological Reports No. 33)

Burgess, C. B. and Shennan, S. (1976). 'The Beaker phenomenon: some suggestions' in C. B. Burgess and R. Miket (eds.) *Settlement and Economy in the Third and Second Millennia B.C.* (British Archaeological Reports No. 33)

Calkin, J. B. (1964). 'The Bournemouth area in the Middle and Late Bronze Age with the "Deverel-Rimbury" problem reconsidered', *Archaeological Journal* 119: 1–65

Clarke, D. L. (1970). *Beaker Pottery of Great Britain and Ireland*, Cambridge University Press

(1972a). 'A provisional model of an Iron Age society and its settlement system' in D. L. Clarke (ed.) *Models in Archaeology*, Methuen

(1972b). *Models in Archaeology*, Methuen

(1976). 'The Beaker network – social and economic models' in J. N. Lanting and J. D. van der Waals (eds.) *Glockenbecher symposium Oberreid 1974*, Fibula-Van Dishoek

(1977). *Spatial Archaeology*, Cambridge University Press

Collis, J. (1977). 'The proper study of mankind is pots' in *The Iron Age in Britain – A Review*, Sheffield University Press

Coombes, D. (1975). 'Bronze Age weapon hoards in Britain', *Archaeologica Atlantica* 1 (1): 49–81

Cunliffe, B. (1974). *Iron Age Communities in Britain*, R.K.P.

Ellison, A. (1975). 'Pottery and settlements of the later Bronze Age in southern England', Ph.D. thesis, University of Cambridge

(1978). 'The Bronze Age' in P. L. Drewett (ed.) *The Archaeology of Sussex to 1500 AD* (CBA Research Report No. 29), Council for British Archaeology

Ellison, A. and Harriss, J. (1972). 'Settlement and land use in the prehistory and early history of southern England: a study based on locational models' in D. L. Clarke (ed.) *Models in Archaeology*, Methuen

Fleming, A. (1971). 'Territorial patterns in Bronze Age Wessex', *Proceedings of the Prehistoric Society* 37: 138–66

Hawkes, C. F. C. (1939). 'The excavations at Quarley Hill, 1938', *Proceedings of the Hampshire Field Club and Archaeological Society* 14 (2): 136

Hodder, I. (1977). 'Some new directions in spatial analysis' in D. L. Clarke (ed.) *Spatial Archaeology*, Cambridge University Press

Hodder, I. and Orton, C. (1976). *Spatial Analysis in Archaeology*, Cambridge University Press

Holden, E. W. (1972). 'A Bronze Age cemetery-barrow on Itford Hill, Beddingham, Sussex', *Sussex Archaeological Collections* 110: 70–117

Longworth, I. H. (1970). 'The secondary series in the Collared Urn tradition in England and Wales', in J. Filip (ed.) *Actes du VIIe Congrès international des sciences préhistoriques et protohistoriques : Prague, 1966*

Musson, C. (1970). 'House-plans and prehistory', *Current Archaeology* 21: 267–75

Peacock, D. P. S. (1969). 'Neolithic pottery production in Cornwall', *Antiquity* 43: 145–9

Peebles, C. S. and Kus, S. M. (1977). 'Some archaeological correlates of ranked societies', *American Antiquity* 42: 421–48

Piggott, C. M. (1944). 'The Grim's Ditch complex in Cranborne Chase', *Antiquity* 18: 65–71

Piggott, S. (1938). 'The Early Bronze Age in Wessex', *Proceedings of the Prehistoric Society* 4: 52–106

Rahtz, P. and ApSimon, A. M. (1962). 'Excavations at Shearplace Hill, Sydling St Nicholas, Dorset, England', *Proceedings of the Prehistoric Society* 28: 289–328

Renfrew, C., ed. (1973a). *The Explanation of Culture Change : models in prehistory*, Duckworth

(1973b). 'Monoments, mobilization and social organizations in neolithic Wessex' in C. Renfrew (ed.) *The Explanation of Culture Change*, Duckworth

(1974). *British Prehistory. A new outline*, Duckworth

Rowlands, M. J. (1971). 'The archaeological interpretation of prehistoric metal-working', *World Archaeology* 3 (2): 210–24

(1973). 'Modes of exchange and the incentives for trade, with reference to later European prehistory' in C.Renfrew (ed.) *The Explanation of Culture Change*, Duckworth

(1976). *The Organisation of Middle Bronze Age Metalworking in Southern Britain* (British Archaeological Reports, No. 31), B.A.R. Publications

Sherratt, A. (1976). 'Resources, technology and trade: an essay in early European metallurgy' in G. de G. Sieveking, I. H. Longworth and K. B. Wilson (eds.) *Problems in Economic and Social Archaeology*, Duckworth

Simpson, D. D. A. (1968). 'Food vessels: associations and chronology' in D. D. A. Simpson and J. M. Coles (eds.) *Studies in Ancient Europe*, Leicester University Press

Smith, I. F. (1974). 'The neolithic' in C. Renfrew (ed.) *British Prehistory. A new outline*, Duckworth

Wainwright, G. J. and Longworth, I. H. (1971). *Durrington Walls* (Soc. Ant. Research Report No. 29), London

Index